HEALTH PROMOTION OF THE CHILD WITH LONG-TERM ILLNESS

Third Edition

HEALTH PROMOTION
OF THE CHILD
WITH LONG-TERM ILLNESS

Third Edition

Shirley Steele, R.N., M.A., Ph.D.

Professor, University of Texas
Clinical Director, Child Health Center
Medical Branch Hospital
Galveston, Texas

10713

Appleton-Century-Crofts/Norwalk, Connecticut

0-8385-3667-0

83 84 85 86 87 88 / 10 9 8 7 6 5 4 3 2 1

Prentice-Hall International, Inc., London
Prentice-Hall of Australia, Pty. Ltd., Sydney
Prentice-Hall Canada, Inc.
Prentice-Hall of India Private Limited, New Delhi
Prentice-Hall of Japan, Inc., Tokyo
Prentice-Hall of Southeast Asia (Pte.) Ltd., Singapore
Whitehall Books Ltd., Wellington, New Zealand
Editora Prentice-Hall do Brasil Ltda., Rio de Janeiro

Library of Congress Cataloging in Publication Data
Main entry under title:

Health promotion of the child with long-term illness.

    Includes bibliographies and index.
    1. Chronic diseases in children—Nursing.   2. Long-term care of the sick.   I. Steele, Shirley.   II. Drapo, Peggy.
RJ245.H37   1983   610.73′62   82-18504
ISBN 0-8385-3667-0

Cover Photo: Douglas E. Haskin
Design: Lynn M. Luchetti

PRINTED IN THE UNITED STATES OF AMERICA

Contributors

Peggy Drapo, R.N., M.S., Doctoral Candidate, Assistant Professor, Texas Woman's University, Denton, Texas

Victoria Erickson, R.N., P.N.P., M.S., Doctoral Student, University of Texas at Austin

Katherine Nugent, R.N., M.S., Assistant Professor, University of Texas, Galveston, Texas

Nancy Quay, R.N., M.S., Clinical Nurse Specialist, Child Health Center, Medical Branch. Formerly Clinical Nurse Specialist, Shriner's Hospital for Crippled Children, Burns Institute, Galveston, Texas

Contents

Preface

This new edition of *Nursing Care of the Child with Long-term Illness* has been given a new title that better fits contemporary health care. The revised title, *Health Promotion of the Child with Long-term Illness*, reflects the advances that are being made in the fields of pediatrics and child health nursing. The prolongation of the lives of seriously ill children requires that attention be focused on creating a life of quality for these children. A major emphasis needs to be placed on health promotion in order to compensate for deficits that are already present and to keep further deficits from occurring. This focusing on health promotion rather than on the illness makes the field of long-term illness management more optimistic and rewarding for health care practitioners as well as for the afflicted children.

Nursing practitioners continue to make important contributions to the care of children with long-term illness. However, there is still a great need for nurses to become better prepared in this area and to lead the way in promoting healthy behaviors that can result in an improved health status for these children. This revised edition provides the reader with many suggestions for guiding the management of these children and their families.

As with any book, there are many people who facilitated this edition's successful completion. Several friends and colleagues—Kathy Nugent, Nancy Quay, Peggy Drapo, and Vicki Erickson—contributed chapters and I thank them for their thoughtful work. These make me extremely proud, as each of the contributors are former students who are making significant contributions to the care of children with long-term illnesses. Several talented persons contributed photographs or illustrations, which help to make the book more interesting to read—I thank Harriet Riggs, Helen Ptak, Ralph Nugent, Doug Haskin, and Martha McGinnis for their contributions. The majority of the typing of the manuscript was done by a special friend, Joan Drachenberg, without whom I would not have met the deadlines for submission of this book. Many clients and their families willingly shared of themselves with the authors and taught us the true value of each life; while it is impossible to name each of them, I wish to thank them for their willingness to participate in the education of nurses.

Several passages in the book were paraphrased or borrowed from other works. The utilization of this knowledge in this volume is acknowledged throughout the text. This material adds substantially to the quality of this volume. And, I am fortunate to have the vast library resources of the University of Texas at my disposal. Although the material in this volume is not an indication of the official stance of the University Hospital, I am indebted to the University of Texas at Galveston for its rich clinical resources that provide ideas for nursing management.

Finally, I would like to thank Charles Bollinger of Appleton-Century-Crofts for guiding this edition of the book as he has each of the two previous editions. As a result of the collective efforts of the foregoing people and institutions, I present this edition to the nursing community, hoping that the ideas that are presented will contribute to creative nursing management of children with long-term illnesses and their families.

S.S.

Part I

Background Information

1

The Scope of the Problem

Shirley Steele

The extent of long-term illness in childhood is not accurately documented. The exact number of children and families that are confronted with this problem is therefore unknown. Many long-term illnesses are not reportable, so it is impossible to give definitive numbers to explain the extent of the problem. According to *The Report of the Select Panel for the Promotion of Child Health* (1981), the overall health of children and youths in the United States is at the present time good in comparison to past figures for children and current figures for adults (U.S. Office of Education, 1981). According to this report, "Relatively few children suffer from chronic conditions or from long-term limitation of activity" and death rates for children are low. These statements suggest that the United States has made significant strides in improving the health status of its children.

MORTALITY RATES

The improvements in the mortality rates for children 1 to 4 years old are dramatic.

DEATHS PER 100,000 CHILDREN 1 TO 4 YEARS OLD*

Year	Number	Year	Number
1930	564	1960	109
1940	290	1970	84
1950	139	1978	69

*From U.S. Office of Education: *Better Health for Our Children: A National Survey.* Washington, D. C., U.S. Department of Health and Human Services, 1981, vol 3, p. 41.

The mortality rates for late childhood (5 to 14 years of age) are lower than for earlier childhood. The number of deaths in 1978 of children in this age range was one-third the number reported in 1940. In 1940, there were 104 deaths per 100,000 children, while in 1978 there were 34 deaths per 100,000 children (U.S. Office of Education, 1981, vol. 2, p. 41).

There are differences in the respective mortality rates of the two sexes. In all age ranges, there are more male deaths than female deaths. These rates reflect a higher incidence of death due to disease as well as death due to external causes. Of special note is the fact that males under age 6 were 41 percent more likely to die of poisonings, accidents, or violence than their female counterparts in 1978. Consistent with these figures, males 16 to 17 years of age were 200 percent more likely to die of accidents of violence than females of the same age (U.S. Office of Education, 1981, vol. 2, p. 42).

Race is also a factor that influences mortality figures. Overall mortality rates are higher for black children than they are for white children. These figures are influenced by a higher infant mortality among blacks. More young black children are dying of poisonings, accidents, and violence than their white counterparts. The annual death rate is 2.9 per 10,000 for whites and 5.4 per 10,000 for blacks. There is a slight decrease in the number of deaths of black adolescents as compared to the number of deaths of white adolescents. This decrease is attributed to fewer black youths having cars, which are involved in the majority of deaths of white adolescents.

Socioeconomic status also plays a role in mortality rates. It is assumed that mortality rates are influenced by socioeconomic status, but accurate statistics are not available to support this assumption.

LIVING CONDITIONS

The living arrangements of families in the United States are in transition. There are aspects of this transition that can potentially influence the health status of children. The number of children under 14 years of age in white families with two parents is greater than the numbers of black children that live in two-parent families (Fig. 1-1).

The number of children under 18 years of age that live below the poverty level is influenced by the family structure. Families that are headed by a female are more prone to poverty than families headed by a male. There is an increasing number of families headed by females. The increase is graphically illustrated in Figure 1-2. Black families remain more commonly below the poverty level than white families. The influence of race and head of household on poverty level is reflected in Table 1-1.

There are also problems relating to housing that have the potential to contribute to a decreased health status. Such defects as basement leaks, roof leaks, cracked walls and ceilings, peeling paint and plaster, and holes in the floors are found in many homes. In addition, plumbing, sewage disposal, and water quality are still substandard in many locations. These problems make it difficult

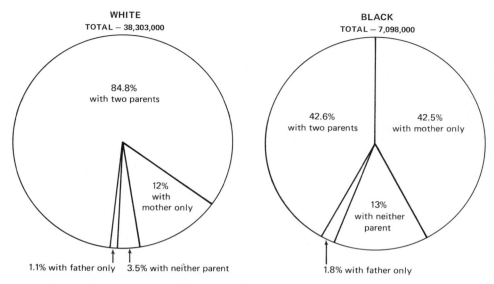

Figure 1-1. Living arrangements of children under 14 years of age by race, March 1978. *(From U.S. Bureau of the Census. Current Population Reports. Series P-20, No. 338, May 1979)*

to control factors that contribute to ill health. These problems are more common in families of lower socioeconomic status and in larger families.

DISABILITY: CHILDREN AND YOUTHS

The terms *disease, illness,* and *impairment* are often used interchangeably when discussing health problems of children. It is helpful to be clear about the differences and relationships between impairment, disability, and handicap (Table 1-2).

The figures for disability are classified into categories of restricted activity, bed, and school loss. These figures based on selected characteristics are found in Table 1-3.

Statistics that identify conditions that are classified as chronic in nature are found in Table 1-4 and Figure 1-3.

The number of children served by programs is an indication of the extent of handicapping conditions in the child population. Figure 1-4 gives these statistics for the school year 1977−1978.

Table 1-5 shows a comparison of the use of school resources by specific handicap from 1963 through 1976.

The government also provides statistics that show the needs of children with handicaps, ages 5 to 17 years, with the numbers served and potentially unserved. These figures are found in Table 1-6.

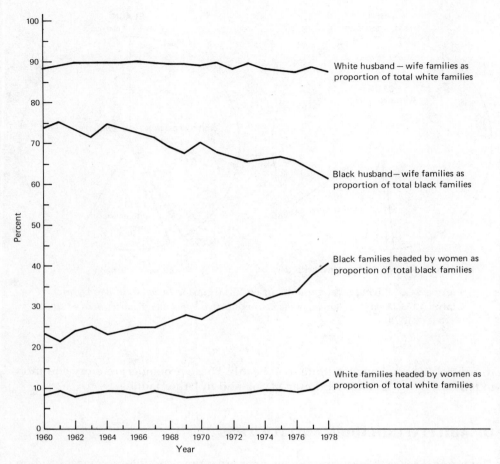

Figure 1-2.   Husband—wife families and families headed by a woman as a
proportion of total families by race, 1960—1978. Data obtained for 1960 through
1967 were for whites and nonwhites rather than for whites and blacks. *(From
U.S. Bureau of the Census. Census Bureau conference on issues in federal statistical needs
relating to women. Current Population Reports, Special Studies, Series P-23, No. 83, 1978)*

REDUCING ENVIRONMENTAL RISKS

Increasing attention is being given to decreasing the environmental risks to
health. However, many of these environmental factors are not easy to control.
There are many potential hazards to health in the physical environment, such as
air quality, diet, technology used, objects in homes, structure of homes, products
that are used, specific factors in the community, byproducts of industry, and
household cleaners, to name a few. It is assumed that 20 percent of all mortality
in the United States is due to environmental factors.

Risks in the environment are especially important when discussing the child

TABLE 1-1.
Children in Families below the Poverty Level by Head of
Household, and Race or Spanish Origins, 1977

	Number of children under 18 years old living below the poverty level (thousands)	Percentage of children under 18 years old living below the poverty level
All types of families		
All children	10,028	16.0
White	5943	11.4
Black	3850	41.6
Spanish origin	1402	28.6
Children in families with male head		
All children	4371	8.5
White	3250	7.1
Black	965	19.3
Spanish origin	716	17.9
Children in families with female head		
All children	5658	50.3
White	2693	40.3
Black	2885	65.7
Spanish origin	686	68.6

From U.S. Bureau of the Census. *Characteristics of the population below the poverty level, 1977.* Series P-60, No. 119, March 1979.

TABLE 1-2.
Relationships Between Impairment, Disability, and Handicap

Biological	Behavioral	
Impairment	Personal disability	Social handicap
Synonyms		
(Disease)	Direct behavioral manifestation of impairment	Effect of disability in performance of specific activities
Illness		
Defect		
Disorder		
(Condition)		

From Pless, I.B., & Pinkerton, P. *Chronic childhood disorder: Promoting patterns of adjustment.* London: Henry Kimpton, 1975.

TABLE 1-3.
Disability Days among Children and Youths under 18 Years Old According to Type of Disability Day and Selected Characteristics, United States, 1975–76, Annual Average

Characteristic	Population (Thousands)	Population 6–16 Years Old (Thousands)	Type of Disability Day (Days per Person per Year)		
			Restricted Activity	Bed	School Loss
Total under 18 years old	65,722	42,201	11.0	4.8	5.2
Age					
Under 6 years	19,217	—	12.3	5.0	—
6–11 years	21,471	21,471	10.6	4.8	5.5
12–17 years	25,034	20,729	10.3	4.5	4.8
Sex					
Male	33,436	21,469	10.8	4.5	4.8
Female	32,286	20,732	11.2	5.1	5.5
Race					
White	54,967	35,419	11.4	4.9	5.3
Black	9831	6272	8.7	4.2	4.1
Other	924	509	9.7	5.4	6.0
Family income					
Under $5000	7707	4483	13.2	6.0	6.6
$5000–$9999	13,634	8304	11.3	5.0	5.8
$10,000–$14,999	15,647	9653	10.9	4.3	4.9
$15,000 or more	23,776	16,457	10.3	4.5	4.7

Parental presence				
Both parents present	52,732	10.7	4.5	5.0
Mother only present	10,126	12.6	5.9	6.2
Neither parent present	2204	12.7	5.8	5.9
Education of family head				
8 years or less	10,945	10.6	4.7	5.8
9–11 years	11,552	11.5	5.0	5.3
12 years	23,053	10.7	4.8	5.0
13–15 years	8946	11.0	4.8	4.7
16 years or more	10,578	11.1	4.5	4.9
Family size				
3 persons or fewer	11,593	13.2	5.6	6.0
4 persons	18,842	12.1	5.0	5.6
5 persons	15,228	10.9	4.5	5.2
6 or more persons	20,059	8.8	4.3	4.5
Residence				
Within SMSA	47,907	11.4	5.0	5.4
Large SMSA	20,192	11.2	4.8	5.3
Core counties	17,203	11.5	5.1	5.5
Fringe counties	8989	10.7	4.2	5.0
Medium SMSA	15,196	11.3	4.9	5.4
Other SMSA	6519	12.0	5.8	6.0
Outside SMSA	17,815	10.0	4.2	4.5
Adjacent to SMSA	11,795	10.5	4.4	4.5
Not adjacent to SMSA	6020	9.0	4.0	4.4

From U.S. Office of Education. *Better health for our children: A national survey.* Vol. 3, 193. Washington, D.C.: Department of Health and Human Services, 1981.

TABLE 1-4.
Selected Chronic Conditions Causing Limitation of Activity in
Children and Youths under 17 Years of Age, According to Degree
of Limitation, United States, 1976

Chronic Condition	Total Limitation	Limited, but Not in Major Activities	Limited in Amount or Kind of Major Activities	Unable to Carry on Major Activities
	Degree of Activity Limitation			
	Number of persons			
Total under 17 years old limited in activity	2,266,695	1,087,587	1,058,928	120,180
	Percent of population in limitation category			
Arthritis and rheumatism	1.0*	1.3*	0.7*	1.7*
Heart conditions	2.4	3.0*	1.9*	1.4*
Hypertension without heart involvement	0.3*	0.5*	0.2*	—*
Diabetes	1.0*	1.4*	0.7*	—*
Mental and nervous conditions	6.7	6.1	7.5	5.7*
Asthma	20.1	19.1	22.6	7.1*
Impairments of back or spine	3.2	5.4	0.7*	4.2*
Impairments of lower extremities and hips	6.9	9.3	4.2	9.0*
Visual impairments	3.7	4.3	1.7*	15.1*
Hearing impairments	5.2	5.6	4.9	3.2*

*Data are based on household interviews of a sample of the civilian noninstitutionalized population.

After National Center for Health Statistics. *Health United States, 1978.* DHEW pub. no. (PHS) 78-1232. Washington, D.C., Government Printing Office, Dec. 1978.

population, as infants and young children are especially vulnerable. Children are more susceptible to harm, as they have an increased sensitivity to certain substances, their bodies are still developing, and they will probably be exposed to environmental risks over a span of many decades.

Attention to environmental risks has improved the health status of children. Improvements in sanitation, housing, and water supplies are credited with reducing mortality rates in the child population. However, many hazards remain that need special attention. The Report of the Select Panel for the Promotion of

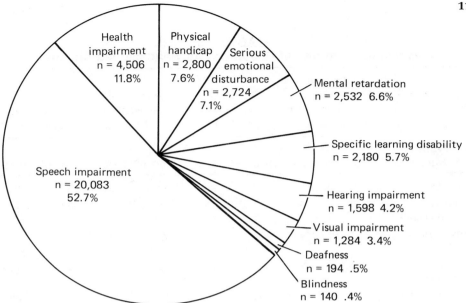

Figure 1-3. Primary or most disabling handicapping conditions of hand-icapped children enrolled in full-year Head Start programs, April–May 1978. *(From U.S. Department of Health, Education, and Welfare. The status of handicapped children in Head Start programs. Washington, D.C.: Government Printing Office, 1979)*

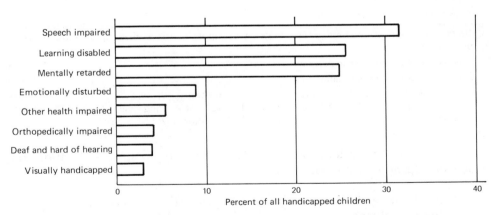

Figure 1-4. Distribution of children served, by handicapping condition, school year 1977–1978. The data displayed include handicapped children counted under Public Laws 89-313 and 94-142. *(From U.S. Office of Education. Progress toward a free appropriate public education. DHEW publication no. (OE) 79-05003. Washington, D.C.: U.S. Department of Health Education, and Welfare, January 1979)*

TABLE 1-5.
Availability and Use of Resources for Handicapped Children*

Types of Handicap	Children for Whom Resource Was Recommended†		Resources Available and Used‡		Resources Available, Not Used‡		Resources Not Available‡	
	1963–65	1976	1963–65	1976	1963–65	1976	1963–65	1976
Slow learners	13	13	29	60	14	13	57	27
Speech impairments	6	6	47	75	19	13	33	12
Emotionally disturbed	3	4	22	26	23	26	55	48
Mentally retarded	1	2	65	78	16	10	19	12
Hearing handicaps	1	1	34	53	14	21	52	26
Visual handicaps	1	1	35	52	14	—	50	48
Orthopedic handicaps	0	1	44	35	23	15	33	50
Total identified as needing one or more special resources	21.4	20.6	—	—	—	—	—	—

*Data are based on teachers' assessments of a sample of the civilian noninstitutionalized population.

†Percent of children in each category.

‡Percent of children recommended.

From National Center of Health Statistics. *Data from the National Health Survey.* Series 11, No. 113. DHEW pub. no. (HSM) 72-1040. Hyattsville, Md., Government Printing Office, Feb. 1972; The 1976 National Survey of Children, Washington, D.C., Child Trends, 1976.

Child Health identifies four domains of risk that require special attention (U.S. Office of Education, 1981, vol. 1):

1. Accidents of all kinds, with special emphasis on motor vehicle and home accidents.
2. Chemical and radiation risks to the fetus, infant, and child, with attention to the dangers of toxic wastes, pesticides, lead, other pollutants, and x-rays.
3. Drugs and foods, with particular focus on nonprescription drugs, food additives, and substances that cause special risks during pregnancy.

4. Problems caused by inadequate or unhealthful water supplies, with attention to fluoridation, potable water in homes, and adequate sanitation (U.S. Office of Education, 1981, vol. 1, p. 75).

Consideration of these domains of risk can contribute to a further increase in the health status of children in the United States and to a decrease in chronic or long-term illness.

HEALTH CARE COVERAGE

The improvement of health care is partially dependent on the financial resources of the family. The preventative aspects of health care services are often omitted from health insurance policies. In actuality, health insurance can be more accurately described as illness insurance. Coverage in many plans is limited to the health care services available in inpatient care facilities. Ambulatory care services are often not reimbursed by insurance companies, and such insurance coverage encourages admission to the hospital.

FEDERAL PROGRAMS

President Reagan's State of the Union address in 1982 proposed sweeping changes in the way that social programs will be administered. Therefore, the following social programs may eventually be changed significantly or turned over to the states. Two major programs that the president proposed to be turned back to the states are the $11.3 billion food stamp program and the largest welfare program, the $15 billion Aid to Families with Dependent Children (AFDC) program. Both of these programs make significant contributions to the quality of life of many families that have children with disabilities. There are wide variances

TABLE 1-6.
Service of Handicapped Children and Youths 5 to 17 Years Old by Educational Facilities, United States, 1977–78

Handicapping Condition	Number in Need of Service	Number Served	Number Potentially Unserved
All conditions	6,060,000	3,766,000	2,293,000
Learning-disabled	1,513,000	967,000	547,000
Speech-impaired	1,764,000	1,224,000	540,000
Emotionally disturbed	1,013,000	288,000	725,000
Mentally retarded	1,168,000	943,000	225,000
Other	607,000	346,000	261,000

From U.S. Office of Education. *Better health for our children: A national survey.* Vol. 3, p. 205. Washington, D.C.: U.S. Department of Health and Human Services, 1981.

in the ways that different states currently contribute to the financial needs of families. For example, the maximum amount of AFDC money received by families in Mississippi is $120/month, while in Texas it is $141/month, in California it is $601/month, and in Alaska it is $634/month. The changes in federal allocations to those who qualify for benefits will influence the clients that we serve (Connell, 1982).

There have been many programs that have contributed significantly to the health status and quality of life of children. The 1975 public law that changed the destiny of many handicapped children is PL 94-142: The Education for All Handicapped Children Act. This law opened the door for many educational opportunities for children with handicapping conditions and pointed the way for a change in the way that children with these problems are treated by communities. The law requires that a free appropriate public education must be provided for these children from the age of 3 years through the age of 18 years. The law applies to all children irrespective of the severity of their disability or handicaps and without consideration of the families' ability to pay for the services.

The ramifications of this act are staggering. The cost of services for handicapped children has increased state education expenses greatly. There is already a growing concern that the law may need to be amended to lower the cost of educating children under the condition that states must provide individualized instruction designed to meet each child's special needs as well as related supportive services that are necessary for the child to benefit from the individualized program. The related services include school health services, speech therapy, psychological services, physical and occupational therapy, counseling services, medical services for diagnostic and evaluative purposes, and parent training and counseling services.

An example of the way that PL 94-142 has changed the care of handicapped children is found in the fact that local schools have increased by 40 percent the number of children who are now served in their classrooms rather than being placed in institutions. Testimony documents that the law has improved the lives of many disabled children and their families. Perhaps the greatest accomplishment of PL 94-142 to date is the change in attitude towards disabled persons that resulted from the bill. Society is now beginning to accept the responsibility of making resources available to these children.

It is impossible for a law to completely eradicate inequities. However, there are some problems that still need to be addressed if the inequities in services to disabled children are to be decreased:

1. A mutually agreed-upon set of terms needs to be developed so that everyone understands the intent of the law and what services are required.
2. Cooperation needs to be established between agencies that provide services to disabled children.
3. Services need to be clustered in order to cut down on the numbers of agencies the families must visit to receive services.
4. Schools must consider the health needs of their students.

5. Health care providers must consider the educational needs of their clients.
6. Extensive and exhaustive probes of the families' financial and social status must be kept at a minimum.
7. Interagency cooperation must be strengthened.
8. Improved training of teachers and school nurses is required to prepare them to meet the special problems of these children.
9. Improved monitoring is needed to make certain that schools are in compliance with the law.
10. Financial support of the program should be assured by ongoing efforts to improve health insurance coverage and state and federal funding for the program.

There are several programs that contribute to the health care of disabled children. At the present time, however, there are several changes being proposed in the way the federal government plans to allocate financial resources, so these programs will probably be changed dramatically in 1982.

Title XX, enacted in 1965 as part of the Social Security Act, provides grants to the states for provision of social and support services to low and moderate income families. Included in the services that states can provide through this funding are support services for the developmentally disabled, blind, and physically handicapped. Also included in these services are funds for early and periodic health screening. The federal funding for Title XX was $2.7 billion in fiscal year (FY) 1980, and 62 percent of the money was used for services to children. Child day care services also receive funds through Title XX. Some 18,300 centers served 870,000 children a year with these funds. If a center receives these funds, children must receive comprehensive health assessments, have appropriate immunizations, and be provided transportation to continuing health services.

Family planning services are funded by Title X of the Public Health Services Act. These services indirectly influence the care of long-term illness in children. This bill was enacted in 1970 in response to the high number of unintended pregnancies in women of low socioeconomic status. The bill provided these women with comprehensive voluntary family planning services. In FY 1980, funding was $162 million and the services were obtained by 2.8 million adults and 1.6 million adolescents. These programs are credited with decreasing the numbers of unwanted pregnancies in minority groups and among the poor and the undereducated. The reduction of pregnancies in these groups contributes to the decrease in the nation's infant mortality rates.

The National Genetic Diseases Act, Title IX of the Public Health Services Act, provides funds to states for genetic screening, counseling, and referrals for treatment. Funds are also allocated for laboratory testing, diagnosis, and educational services. In FY 1980, $11.5 million were allocated to this program. It is estimated that 30 percent of all hospitalized children have diseases that are at least partially genetic in nature.

The Developmental Disabilities Service Act provides for the coordination of services for people with chronic disabilities. Funds are allocated for alternate community living arrangements, nonvocational social development, case management, and child development. States that receive the funds are required to spend a percentage of the money on deinstitutionalization. Funding for FY 1980 was $62.4 million, providing assistance to 300,000 persons.

The Supplementary Security Income Disabled Children's Program provides referral and direct services for blind and disabled children. The requirements include case management, a written Individualized Service Plan for each child, and supportive services. The funding for FY 1980 was $19.8 million and benefitted 209,000 children.

Through the Special Supplemental Food Program for Women, Infants, and Children (WIC), nutritious food and food education are provided to persons who meet the criteria or qualify for the program with a focus on good health care during critical times of growth and development. The FY 1980 budget was $758 million, and annual budget increases are provided.

The Medicaid program, Social Security Act XIX, has provided health care for the poor. Coverage includes families receiving Aid to Families with Dependent Children (AFDC) and most families who receive Supplemental Security Income (SSI), which is for financially eligible pregnant women and families with blind or disabled members. Medicaid is financed jointly by state and federal governments. In FY 1979, the expenditures were approximately $21.4 billion. Included under this source of funding are early and periodic screening, diagnosis, and treatment (EPSDT) programs for children. In 1979, 2.14 million children benefitted from these services.

Title V of the Social Security Act provides money for use by mothers and children. It provides money to promote, improve, and deliver maternal and child health (MCH) care and crippled children (CC) services. Included among the programs funded are the maternal and infant care (MIC) programs that provide prenatal, perinatal, and postpartum care and family planning services to low income clients. The comprehensive health services to children and youths (C and Y) projects are also funded through this act, as are dental services for children. Since 1979, Congress has appropriated $400 million annually for all of the Title V activities.

Appropriations of these funds are also provided for training health care personnel for MCH services and to support research in MCH (U.S. Office of Education, 1981, vol. 2).

Some of the funds allocated for these programs are now being given to the states in the form of block grants. It is up to the states to determine the distribution of funds among particular programs. The funding of these programs has contributed to the improved health status of children and pregnant women. It is hoped that the states will distribute the funds in such a way that the vulnerable populations that have been receiving these resources will continue to receive them.

HEALTH BEHAVIOR

The health or wellness behavior of children is influenced by many things. Health behavior is learned. A major influence on the child is the family. As the child grows, institutions play an increasing and major role in his or her health behavior. The five major institutions that influence the child's health behavior include:

1. Schools.
2. The media.
3. Health care settings.
4. The community.
5. The workplace.

These institutions influence the child's health behavior through education, counseling, and guidance (U.S. Office of Education, 1981). In addition, the child's behavior is influenced by family members, and peers eventually also play a role in the child's selection of health behaviors.

Wellness behavior is the development of behaviors that increase the child's ability to actively seek changes in his or her life situation so that it is possible to function at his or her perceived capacity to achieve satisfaction. The criteria used to determine capacity and satisfaction are established by the individual on the basis of established levels of wellness (Bruhn and Cordova, 1977).

The amount of control that children have over their health-related behaviors varies greatly. Some children have a great deal of control, while others have minimal control. Health behaviors involve value judgments and moral questions that are implicit in behavioral decisions. Health behaviors that are considered to be positive by health care providers may be considered negative by the child. When this is the case, the child oftens exhibits health behaviors that are inconsistent with ones selected by health care providers. In order to decrease conflict, it is wise to offer the child choices and to provide the child with information that allows him or her to make an informed choice and to promote informed decision-making. The education, counseling, and guidance offered to the child should be used to restructure the environment to support the child in making healthful choices (U.S. Office of Education, 1981).

In the effort to enhance health-related behavior, the child's developmental stage, profile of behavioral risks, socializing factors, and opportunities to learn are examined. The interaction of all of these factors has a bearing on how the child expresses himself or herself in life.

Bruhn and Cordova (1977) emphasize the following points concerning wellness:

1. It is a continuously evolving process related to the attainment of specific developmental tasks.
2. The child actively participates in the process to increase wellness.
3. Each child has the potential to achieve wellness.
4. Wellness is evident in all cultures in varying degrees, depending on the value described to it and to life in general.

VALUES

Values exert a major force on health or wellness behavior. The value placed on health and the level of knowledge about healthy behaviors play important roles.

Family values are usually influenced by cultural values. Values are arranged in hierarchies of priority. Unfortunately, health is not often placed at the top of a family's hierarchy of values.

The value placed on wellness is influenced by society. In our society, there have been more rewards for recovering from sickness than for staying well. The health care system has promoted an illness model rather than a wellness model and this has influenced the apparent "disvalue" placed on preserving health. In order to value health, persons frequently have to go through a period of ill health. This societal trend needs to be changed for a greater value to be placed on wellness.

The child's value system reflects the values of the family. However, the mass media are responsible for influencing the child's value system, as well. Children are exposed to values via the media that can run counter to the family values. The child's evolving value system and the place of health in that system reflect the influence of these various persons and institutions. The value that children ascribe to health can be positively influenced if they receive health information that they perceive to be credible and worthy of absorbing. Part of the role of the family and of health care providers is to help children to clarify conflicting values about health and health care practices. In this way, children can choose to value health and to adopt behaviors that support wellness.

ROLE MODELS

The child learns wellness behaviors from role models. The role models are usually adults who place a high priority on the maintenance of health. The child learns about wellness behaviors through observing role models. These role models practice wellness behavior and share information about wellness with the child. The role model discusses with the child the choices that are available. He or she shares the reasons that one action is chosen over another action and discusses the potential outcomes of the selected actions. In this way, people who model positive health behaviors play an important role in increasing the child's ability to exhibit healthy behaviors.

HYGIENE

Cleanliness of the body and neatness of clothing both contribute to social acceptance of disabled children. Traditionally, these subjects were given special attention in hygiene courses during the school year. More recently, variations in dress and cleanliness standards have been expressed in society, resulting in varying levels of acceptance by others. For example, long hair and sideburns on males are more readily accepted when the hair and sideburns are meticulously groomed than when they appear dirty or unkempt.

GROOMING

Hygiene takes on special significance when a child is disabled. Generally, the more severely disabled the child, the more necessary it becomes to give special attention to the child's hygiene and grooming. The appearance of the child is one of the factors that influences whether or not he or she can successfully socialize with other children, most of whom are able-bodied. The physical characteristics of the child often put him or her at a disadvantage, and good grooming helps to diminish this disadvantage. An attractive outfit of clothing and meticulous body hygiene can help achieve acceptance by others.

It is not uncommon for children with disabilities to be dependent on others in achieving cleanliness. Oftentimes, in an attempt to encourage self-help, the child is allowed to develop body odor or to go to a social function with clothes or hair in disarray. An adult needs to offer assistance to the child in overcoming inadequacies in grooming so that such instances are kept to a minimum. Discussion of grooming concerns should involve both the child and his or her caretakers. This discussion should be held in private and should focus on an honest approach to any problem areas in an effort to encourage the family to participate in problem resolution. The care of the child's hair needs special consideration. It is not uncommon for children with disabilities to have unattractive hair. In order to maximize the potential beauty of the hair, it should be shampooed regularly, styled effectively, and combed periodically during the day. In this way, even stringy, lifeless hair can be less damaging to the child's appearance. Reinforcement for keeping the hair in optimum condition can be achieved by taking pictures of the child at optimum moments, using a mirror and demonstrating improvements to the child, and giving praise when it is deserved. As the child matures, participation in good grooming sessions with other children increases enthusiasm for self-grooming.

When the child reaches adolescence, proper use of cosmetics is taught. The effective application of cosmetics can improve the adolescents's appearance. Overuse of cosmetics or improper application can decrease the child's attractiveness.

DENTAL CARE

Body odors of any type are disliked in our culture. One source of body odor that is common in disabled children is the mouth (halitosis). Specific instructions on orai hygiene are given to the child and the caretaker. Children with disabilities need added assistance in maintaining adequate oral hygiene. Frequently, children with physical disabilities have deficits in the oral apparatus. In order to guarantee oral hygiene, it is necessary to focus special attention on high-risk areas, such as high palates, malaligned teeth, and the gums. The child should be allowed to brush his or her own teeth and then an adult should carefully complete the process, paying special attention to functions that are difficult for the child. Flossing should be done by an adult, using unwaxed dental floss. With younger children, the adult should sit on the floor and hold the child's head in his or her lap. In this way, the oral cavity can be easily visualized. Older children can sit in a chair. After the teeth, tongue, and gums are brushed, the child should use a mouthwash to rinse his or her mouth. Emphasis should be placed on consistent mouth care following meals. Routine visits to the dentist should be encouraged. If the resources in the child's local area are not sufficient to meet the child's needs, additional information can be obtained from the National Foundation on Dentistry for the Handicapped, 1726 Champa St., Suite 422, Denver, Colo. 80202.

SPECIAL NEEDS FOR HYGIENE

The special needs of a given child are related to specific needs generated by the child's health problem or age-specific considerations. For example, a child with incontinence needs to know how to protect his or her clothing, how to control odors, where to purchase special supplies, and ways of storing special supplies. A preadolescent female needs to be taught how to manage menstruation in the event that it takes place. Consideration of these special aspects of hygiene are conducted as part of anticipatory guidance so that the child or caretaker is adequately prepared to manage the situation effectively.

In addition to counseling, it is helpful to supply pertinent literature to the family. The family can also be referred to local book stores or the library to seek additional sources of information. It is also helpful to introduce the child and caretaker to other families that have the same problems. The resultant sharing of information can increase the family's ability to cope with the special needs of the child. It is also possible to provide the family with the opportunity to join a group session that is geared to children with a particular problem. When a group is available, the family should be told the goals of the organization, the time and place of meetings, and other information that they desire in order to determine whether they care to participate. Groups are effective vehicles for helping some persons to adjust to a disability. The way that families cope with activities of daily living can be shared in these groups and can result in the child's improved appearance.

SUMMARY

One goal of health care providers is to render services that have the potential to enable the child and his or her caretakers to promote high-level wellness. Therefore, goals should be established that ensure the child's capacity to perform the activities necessary to promoting wellness. Teaching the child and his or her caretakers to perform activities results in increasing the options that are available to them. In the case of the child with a long-term illness, the capacity of the child to perform these activities is of upmost concern, as he or she may temporarily or permanently lack the capacity to achieve a high level of wellness. Therefore, the involvement of caretakers in the child's health care management is an essential part of health promotion for these children.

Baranowski (1981) cautions that due to the large numbers of roles that a person can hold throughout the life continuum, it may be unrealistic to support the notion that each role will be performed at a maximum level. This notion is essential to the health promotion of children with long-term illnesses, as they may during their lifetimes take on roles that they are incapable of fulfilling as efficiently as able-bodied persons. However, this lack of capacity for ultimate fulfillment does not have to interfere with the child's health promotion strategies; the outcomes of these strategies merely have to be adjusted to fit the limitations imposed by the disability. The child should be assured that just because he or she is unable to perform all of the tasks inherent in a social role, he or she not be considered "ill" or as having "illness" rather than "wellness." In fostering a healthy orientation towards these children, the term *illness* should be reserved for conditions that result in acute care management rather than conditions requiring long-term management. For example, the child with diabetes who takes insulin should be considered well, while the diabetic child who has problems related to insulin management and is hospitalized should be considered ill.

The idea that "wellness" actually depends on a person's capacity to perform social role tasks makes it necessary for the health care provider to be aware of the age-related, sex-related, social, and geographic components of roles (Baranowski, 1981). As roles change over the disabled person's life span, it is essential to determine what roles are dominant at a particular age and to determine the importance of each of the potential roles to the person and his or her caretakers. The major tasks that pertain to each role should be determined and the person's capacity to perform these tasks should be identified. In this way, attention can be focused on roles, tasks, and capacities that are *important* to the child rather than on the roles and corresponding tasks that are *possible*.

REFERENCES

Baranowski, T. Toward the definition of concepts of health and disease, wellness and illness. *Health Values: Achieving High-level Wellness* 5:246, 1981.

Bruhn, J.G., & Cordova, F.D. A developmental approach to learning wellness behavior, part I: Infancy to early adolescence. *Health Values: Achieving High-level Wellness* 1:246, 1977.

Connell, C. "New federalism" will end traditional reliance on Uncle Sam. Galveston Daily News, February 3, 1982, p 2a.

U.S. Office of Education. *Better health for our children: A national survey.* Vols. 1, 2, 3. Washington, D.C.: U.S. Department of Health and Human Services, 1981.

2

Health Promotion

Shirley Steele

The emphasis on self-help for health promotion in today's society is not restricted to able-bodied individuals. Self-help is an important part of the health maintenance of persons with long-term illness, as well. For example, a child with a disabling heart condition can be taught to monitor his or her blood pressure using an inexpensive blood pressure kit purchased from a local pharmacy or discount department store. Likewise, the female client can be taught to do monthly self-examinations of the breast despite the presence of disabling and/or long-term conditions. A goal of health maintenance is to assure the child that whenever possible, he or she will be taught the self-help skills that are needed to develop a well-integrated self-concept.

Self-understanding and self-actualization, nutrition, exercise, sleep, relaxation, and stress control are prime components of health maintenance routines. In addition, for children with disabled bodies, special emphasis is focused on personal hygiene and grooming. The concepts that relate to each of these areas for disabled children are similar to the concepts that guide able-bodied individuals in their self-help routines. However, the disabled child or the child with a long-term illness needs to adapt the self-help routine to the specific limitations posed by his or her health problem.

Figure 2-1 is a model that emphasizes high-level wellness. This model is helpful for assessing the self-help potential of the client.

It is necessary to examine the following in order to enhance the health-related behavior of children:

1. Developmental level.
2. Profiles of behavioral risks.
3. Socializing factors.
4. Opportunities and capacities for learning.

Education, counseling, and other efforts are focused on ways to restructure the environment to encourage the child to make healthful choices. To enable the

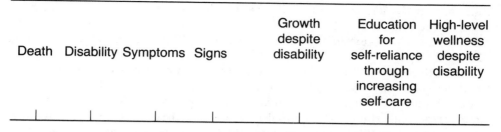

Death	Disability	Symptoms	Signs	Growth despite disability	Education for self-reliance through increasing self-care	High-level wellness despite disability

Figure 2-1. Illness—wellness continuum. *(Adapted from Ryan, R.S., & Travis, J. The wellness workbook. Berkeley, Calif.: Ten Speed Press, 1981)*

child with a long-term illness to change or develop healthy behaviors, an underlying assumption is made that it is possible for the child to use self-help strategies to improve his or her health status and to move in the direction of growth and self-actualization (Fig. 2-2).

The success or failure to enact a self-help model of care is influenced by many factors. Some of these are:

1. The child's or family's interest or disinterest in self-help strategies.
2. The health care provider's ability or inability to emphasize self-help strategies.
3. The child's desire to be independent or dependent.
4. The family's ability to resolve feelings that keep the child in a dependent role.
5. Premature frustration or discouragement that can be associated with learning self-help strategies.
6. The acuteness of the health problem.
7. The severity of the health problem.
8. The duration of the health problem.

A model that emphasizes wellness and self-help strategies takes into consideration the fact that the child is a whole person. The concept of wholeness

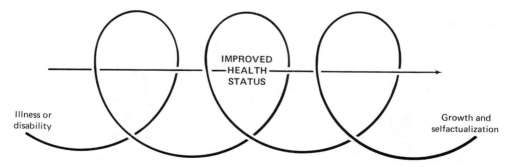

Figure 2-2. Creative use of illness or disability.

assumes that elements of mind, body, feelings, and spirit are integrated (Fig. 2-3). This interaction influences the child's state of wellness or illness. It is thus difficult to pay attention to any one part of the child's being without considering all the other parts.

Sometimes the child and family are able to assume most of the responsibility for their own care, while at other times, they may be unable to assume responsibility for the health care that is needed. Therefore, self-help strategies are interspersed with the child's normal care at appropriate intervals. An ongoing assessment of the child's and the family's needs is required to be certain that independent care and dependent care are available as indicated.

A child with a long-term illness may be minimally or extremely handicapped by the problem. An assessment of the child and the health problem helps to establish a realistic estimate for incorporating self-help strategies into the child's management regime. Depending on the severity of the handicap, it may be difficult to teach the child self-help skills and to encourage the child to use these skills consistently in his or her activities of daily living. It is important to give reasonable attention to teaching the child to assume responsibility for himself or herself so that with increasing age the child will be prepared to be as independent as possible.

SELF-UNDERSTANDING AND SELF-ACTUALIZATION

Buscaglia (1978) notes that persons are of value to the degree to which they are constantly actualizing as unique persons. Focusing on actualization involves an illusion. The illusion is a visionary look at a future self. As such, persons are involved in dealing with something that is imperceptible. Even though this is the case, the challenge in life is to make as much of the illusion become reality as possible. Each stage of development involves an active state of being and a changing state of becoming. Through this combination of states, the person is prepared for the present and conditioned for the future. The role of the environment in the process is to help the person to actualize his or her own potential.

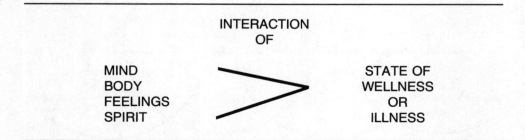

Figure 2-3. Holistic being.

Infants and young children are comparatively helpless human beings. They depend strongly on others in their environment to provide them with the essentials needed to develop. The food, warmth, love, and consideration that they receive influence their ability to become actualized human beings. A consistent and caring caretaker is essential if these dependent human beings are to receive consideration for their physical needs and provision of emotional and cognitive stimulation. Children need someone who is responsible and who assumes that the child deserves respect, has worth, and has an emerging self that has value. The interaction of a caretaker with the child prepares the child to gain control over his or her environment. Therefore, to be actualized, young children need a responsible caretaker.

During adolescence, the child's dependence is decreased. In the struggle towards autonomy, the adolescent can feel abandoned or estranged from others, especially family members. The adolescent who feels dissociated from others and unsure of his or her own identity can become isolated from significant others. In his or her attempt to become a separate person, the adolescent becomes closer to peers who are going through similar experiences. A major part of the adolescent's time is spent in introspection in order to determine his or her first concept of himself or herself as a unique, autonomous human being.

Self-awareness involves a consideration of the mind, body, spirit, and environment. The adolescent gradually learns to understand aspects of each of these areas. As a greater understanding develops, the adolescent progresses towards self-actualization. However, this process is not always a continuous forward movement. It is common for the adolescent to experience trauma and setbacks on the way to self-actualization. These discontinuities often seem more dramatic than the ones that children of younger ages endure. In fact, they often seem more dramatic than problems faced by adults. The passage through adolescence seems to prepare children for expressing self-identity through intimacy with another in adulthood.

Buscaglia (1978) suggests that each stage of life leading to maturity is complete in and of itself and that within each stage, the person is actualized in a manner independent of every other stage. In a way that allows the child to meet the demands of the present and still be ready for the future, life is a continuing process of being and becoming.

The real challenge is to have the child live his or her life as fully as possible, realizing that each moment contributes to self-actualization and that this will be expressed differently by different individuals. At each stage, the child has unique opportunities that can be used effectively to live an actualized life that is different from that of another child but is meaningful to oneself. The need for an understanding of oneself as an important and significant being who contributes positively to society is a key concern when working with children with long-term illness or disabilities. Diminishing noxious stimuli that give the child signals of lack of self-worth is part of the protocol for helping the child to understand himself or herself and become self-actualized.

The child with a long-term illness or disability may have a preoccupation with himself or herself based on past experiences related to his or her illness and the realities of the present. If the child is to adjust to the world, some of the preoccupation with the health problem and the strong focus on oneself as a handicapped person must be relinquished. The child learns to acknowledge what is right about himself or herself without always comparing himself or herself to the desired self or to others that are able-bodied. In actuality, the child learns to value oneself, to forget the past, and to be satisfied with the present. When these goals are achieved, the child is able to relate more freely with others and to enjoy living.

Depending on the illness or disability, the child may have to face setbacks or decreasing ability. These occurrences may cause the child to fear death. In the face of such fears, it is not uncommon for the child to lose a sense of self and to lose enthusiasm for living. Under these conditions, it takes creativity to engage the child in meaningful interactions. If he or she withdraws from social interactions, the resultant inactivity can lead to further feelings of lack of self-worth. Dealing with the child's fears can help to lessen the possibility of withdrawal.

Cox-Gedmark (1980) suggests that as new possibilities are discovered, a person is able to know himself or herself better. In discovering new possibilities, it is possible for the person to actualize some of his or her cherished values in other ways, which suggests that as values shift, new aspects of life become important. In fact, some persons live life with renewed vigor after having a life-threatening disease that causes a reassessment of values and life.

NUTRITION

In determining the nutritional needs of the child with a long-term illness, one must take into consideration the normal nutritional needs of children in general and the special considerations associated with the specific health problem. Age-specific requirements for growth are an important part of the nutrition considerations, and these requirements are adjusted to take into consideration any variations due to the health problem.

A basic assumption is made that children must consume a sufficient amount of energy-producing nutrients and proteins in order for growth to take place. As the child metabolizes fats, carbohydrates, and proteins, energy is generated. This energy is used to maintain the child's body functions and allows for expenditures for activity and growth. Proteins that are consumed by the child provide amino acids that are used for the synthesis of new tissue and nitrogen that is used to provide for maturation of existing tissue.

The child expends energy every day. This energy expenditure is influenced by the child's body size and composition, by the sex of the child, by the amount of physical activity the child engages in, and by the child's rate of growth. Males expend more energy than females and infants expend more than older children (per kilogram of weight), and any child's energy expenditure is increased during growth spurts. This means that as the child gets older, more calories are needed for the increased body size, although at the same time, the energy needed per unit of size is decreased (Pipes, 1977).

The recommended energy intakes of children at various ages are described in Table 2-1. Selected foods that provide sources of energy are found in Table 2-2. The recommended daily intake of protein for children according to age is found in Table 2-3. Selected food sources of protein are found in Table 2-4. Table 2-5 gives food sources of fats, and Table 2-6 gives food sources of carbohydrates. There are no recommended daily intakes of fat. It is suggested, however, that the child's diet should not contain less than 30 percent or more than 50 percent of the total caloric intake as fat (Pipes, 1977). The daily intake of carbohydrate is influenced by protein and fat consumption, as carbohydrate is synthesized through them. It is suggested that an intake of 50 to 100 gm of carbohydrate per day of various sources is adequate.

Another important part of nutrition is the inclusion of adequate amounts of vitamins and minerals in the child's diet. Table 2-7 indicates the recommended daily intake of fat-soluble vitamins A, D, and E. The recommended daily intake of water-soluble vitamins is found in Table 2-8. The recommended daily allowances of calcium, phosphorus, iodine, iron, magnesium, and zinc appear in Table 2-9.

In order to determine whether the child is receiving a diet that is adequate in protein, fat, and carbohydrates, the child and/or the caretakers can be assessed using a questionnaire developed for this purpose (samples of such questionnaires can be found in Appendices A and B).

In addition to the questionnaire, nutritional screening includes the physical examination, anthropometry, and sometimes laboratory determinations, such as hemoglobin or hematocrit and serum cholesterol levels. From these screening procedures it is possible to determine whether the child needs further evaluation and/or treatment for nutritional disorders. During the interview, it is possible to detect that a child's dietary intake is inadequate in content, deviates significantly

TABLE 2-1.
Recommended Energy Intakes For Children of Various Ages

Age (yr)	Energy (kcal/kg)
0–0.5	117
0.5–1	108
1–3	100
4–6	90
7–10	80
11–14	
Males	64
Females	55
15–18	
Males	49
Females	39

After Food and Nutrition Board. *Recommended daily dietary allowances* (8th ed.). Washington, D.C.: National Academy of Sciences, National Research Center, 1974.

TABLE 2-2.
Selected Foods as Sources of Energy

Food	Portion size	Average kcal
2% milk with 2% nonfat milk solids	½ cup	72
Meat, poultry, or fish	1 oz	80
Egg	1 medium	80
Peanut butter	1 tbsp	94
Cheese	½ oz	57
Legumes, cooked	¼ cup	90
Enriched bread	½ slice	35
Ready-to-eat cereals (not sugar coated)	¾ cup	70
Cooked cereal	½ cup	55
Saltine crackers	Each	12
Rice, macaroni, spaghetti, cooked	¼ cup	50
Potato (boiled)	½ medium	45
Potato chips	5	55
Green beans	¼ cup	6
Carrots		
Cooked	¼ cup	15
Raw	2 medium sticks	14
Apple	1 small (approximately 3/lb)	80
Banana	1 small	80
Orange	1 small	50
Orange juice	½ cup	60
Sugar	1 tsp	16
Jam or jelly	1 tsp	20
Butter, margarine, oil, mayonnaise	1 tsp	35
Cookies, assorted	1 each	40–50
Ice cream	¼ cup	70

Adapted from Adams, C.F. *Nutritive value of American foods in common units*, Agriculture handbook no. 456, Washington, D.C.: U.S. Department of Agriculture, 1975.

from suggested intake, or follows fads that are insufficient to support the child's healthy development. The physical examination can detect signs of inadequate nutrition, such as stringy, dull hair; brittle, paper-thin fingernails; dark circles under the eyes; and dull eyes. The anthropometry detects being underweight or obese, which are the result of inadequate nutrition. Laboratory studies are used when there is suspicion of anemia or increased cholesterol intake.

Dietary Patterns
Alterations in dietary patterns of children are difficult to achieve. The child's dietary intake is a direct reflection of the dietary intake of the entire family. Dietary intake is influenced strongly by cultural orientation, social class, lifestyle,

TABLE 2-3.
Recommended Daily Intake of Protein for Children

Age (yr)	Protein (gm/kg)
0−0.5	2.2
0.5−1	2.0
1−3	1.8
4−6	1.5
7−10	1.2
11−14	
Male	1.0
Female	1.0
15−18	
Male	0.9
Female	0.9

After Food and Nutrition Board. *Recommended daily dietary allowances* (8th ed.). Washington, D.C.: National Academy of Sciences, National Research Council, 1974.

economic status, and tradition. In order to successfully change a child's dietary patterns, it is necessary to involve the entire family in the process. As children are frequently dependent on adults in the family to supply, cook, and serve meals, it is the adults that serve as role models for the child. When the child sees the adults eating erratic, nonnutritious meals, it is common for the child to model this behavior. In addition, if the adults do not understand proper nutrition and its

TABLE 2-4.
Selected Foods as Sources of Protein for Preschool Children

Food	Portion size	Protein (gm)
Yogurt, made from whole milk	½ cup	3.7
Cheddar cheese	1 oz	7.1
Hamburger patty	2 oz	15.4
Chicken drumstick	1	12.2
Peanut butter	1 tbsp	4.0
Egg	1 medium	5.7
Liverwurst	1 oz	4.6
Tuna fish	¼ cup	11.5
Frankfurter, 5″ × ¼″	1	5.6
Nonfat milk solids, dry	1 tbsp	1.52

From Adams, C.F. *Nutritive value of American foods in common units.* Agricultural handbook no. 456. Washington, D.C.: U.S. Department of Agriculture, 1975.

TABLE 2-5.
Foods as Sources of Fat for Preschool Children

Food	Portion size	Fat (gm)
Cooking fat	1 tbsp	12.5
Mayonnaise	1 tbsp	11.2
Butter	1 tsp	3.8
Cheddar cheese	1 oz	7.1
Peanut butter	1 tbsp	8.1
Frankfurter	$5'' \times 3\frac{3}{4}''$	11.5
Broiled hamburger patty	2 oz	15.4
Chicken drumstick	1	12.2
Egg	1 medium	5.1
Tuna, drained	$\frac{1}{4}$ cup	3.3
Ice cream	$\frac{1}{4}$ cup	3.5
Potato chips	10	8.0

From Adams, C.F. *Nutritive value of American foods in common units.* Agriculture handbook. Washington D.C.: U.S. Department of Agriculture, 1975.

importance to growth and health, it is unlikely that they will value nutritious dietary plans. Therefore, education is geared to the level of understanding of the family members. An attempt is made to modify family member's behavior so that they will be eager to select a diet that is nutritious and to include all family members in this dietary pattern.

The best way to establish sound food preferences that will assure adequate nutrition is by preventing establishment of faulty patterns of food consumption. It is thought that the child's pattern of food intake is formed before school age. During the preschool years, the child's food likes and dislikes are established. If the child has not enjoyed mealtime at home with the family, enjoying a nutritious meal, it is unlikely that he or she will choose this pattern of eating. Therefore, it is essential that families attempt to establish healthy eating habits early in the child's development.

Generally speaking, the following guidelines can be followed to help the preschool child develop food patterns that lead to a sound nutritional status:

1. Mealtime is scheduled at a predictable time, but flexibility of timing is maintained.
2. Family members are encouraged to be present for meals.
3. Meals take place at a table where distractions are kept at a minimum.
4. Discussion of conflict situations is avoided at mealtime.
5. Mealtime is used to share experiences, although preschoolers can be distracted from eating if the conversation is too involved at the beginning of the meal.

TABLE 2-6.
Carbohydrates in Foods Commonly Consumed by Preschool Children

Food	Portion size	Carbohydrate (gm)
Bread, whole wheat	1 slice	13.0
Corn flakes	½ cup	10.7
Sugar-coated corn flakes	½ cup	18.3
Oatmeal	½ cup	11.7
Potato, diced	¼ cup	6.6
Potato chips	10	10.0
Noodles	¼ cup	9.3
Spaghetti	¼ cup	8.0
Rice	¼ cup	10.0
Corn, whole kernel	¼ cup	7.8
Navy beans, cooked	¼ cup	10.1
Saltine cracker	1	2.0
Graham cracker	2 squares	10.4
Cookie, oatmeal	1	9.5
Apple, 3/lb	1	20.0
Applesauce, sweetened	½ cup	15.0
Banana	1 small	21.1
Orange	1 medium	15.0
Sugar	1 tsp	4.0
Carbonated beverages, cola	3 oz	9.3
Jelly beans	1 oz (10)	26.4

Adapted from Adams, C.F. *Nutritive value of American foods in common units.* Agriculture handbook no. 456. Washington, D.C.: U.S. Department of Agriculture, 1975.

6. Mealtime is not scheduled for times when the preschooler is too tired.
7. Mealtime does not directly follow a period of excessive physical activity.
8. Children are served portions of food that are reasonable for their ages.
9. "Nagging" is discouraged as a way to encourage the child to eat more.
10. New foods are introduced in small amounts and one at a time.
11. The child is allowed to eat independently as soon as possible.
12. A reasonable time is established for the child to complete eating and then either the food is removed or the child is excused from the table.
13. Reinforcement is given to the child when he or she eats a new or a disliked food.

TABLE 2-7.
Recommended Daily Dietary Allowances of Fat-soluble Vitamins

	Age (yr)	Vitamin A		Vitamin D (IU)	Vitamin E (IU)
		RE*	IU		
Infants	0.0-0.5	420	1400	400	4
	0.5-1.0	400	2000	400	5
Children	1-3	400	2000	400	7
	4-6	500	2500	400	9
	7-10	700	3300	400	10
Males	11-14	1000	5000	400	12
	15-18	1000	5000	400	15
Females	11-14	800	4000	400	12
	15-18	800	4000	400	12

From Food and Nutrition Board. *Recommended dietary allowances, 1974* (8th ed.). Washington, D.C.: National Academy of Sciences, National Research, Council, 1974.
*Retinol equivalent.

14. Choices are periodically provided by giving the child two or more nutritious foods to select from.
15. Nutritious foods, such as raw fruits and vegetables, are given as snacks.
16. Rewarding behavior with foods high in carbohydrates or that lack nutrition value is discouraged.
17. Model behaviors are exhibited that the child can simulate.

Another part of establishing sound nutritious practices is dependent on the adult members of the family. The preparation of food influences the child's likes and dislikes of food. Many nutritious foods are decreased in quality by preparation. For example, a raw vegetable is more appropriate for a child than the same vegetable that is fried during preparation. Cultural patterns are very often responsible for the way that foods are prepared. For many families, tradition is the primary influence in food preparation. Under these circumstances, some families eat excessive amounts of carbohydrates or have diets low in cholesterol or high in fruits and vegetables. Tradition may support the use of fried foods, overcooking, or covering foods with heavy gravies. Some foods can be overused in the family's diet while other foods are rarely or never tried due to tradition. When cultural traditions are strong, it is necessary to assess the diet to be certain that adequate nutrition is maintained while not discrediting cherished values.

Hunger Pains
The young child is prone to periods of hunger. It is difficult for young families that have limited experience with children to understand that infants and young children have a need to eat more frequently. Hunger pains cause the child to be restless and weak and to have abdominal pain. If the child does not receive a small amount of food, the pain is not eased. Providing a snack of a raw vegetable is

TABLE 2-8.
Recommended Daily Dietary Allowances of Water-soluble Vitamins

Age (yr)	Thiamine (mg)	Riboflavin (mg)	Niacin (mg)	Vitamin B₆ (mg)	Folacin (μg)	Vitamin B₁₂ (μg)	Ascorbic acid (mg)
0−0.5	0.3	0.4	5.0	0.3	50	0.3	35
0.5−1.0	0.5	0.6	8.0	0.4	50	0.3	35
1−3	0.7	0.8	9.0	0.6	100	1.0	40
4−6	0.9	1.1	12.0	0.9	200	1.5	40
7−10	1.2	1.2	16.0	1.2	300	2.0	40
Males							
11−14	1.4	1.5	18.0	1.6	400	3.0	40
15−18	1.5	1.8	20.0	2.0	400	3.0	45
Females							
11−14	1.2	1.3	16.0	1.6	400	3.0	45
15−18	1.1	1.4	14.0	2.0	400	3.0	45

From Food and Nutrition Board. *Recommended daily dietary allowances, 1974* (8th ed.). Washington, D.C.: National Academy of Sciences, National Research Council, 1974.

an excellent pattern to establish for easing the child's pain without interfering with the next scheduled meal. The easing of hunger pains provides the child pleasure, which is then associated with a nutritious food.

In addition, it is easier to introduce new foods when the child is hungry. The foods are introduced in small amounts when the child is eager to eat. Although the child may not take an instant liking to the food, it is possible that over a period of time the child will develop a liking for the food. Taking advantage of the child's frequent hunger pains is an excellent way to establish a broader, more nutritious diet.

TABLE 2-9.
Recommended Daily Dietary Allowances of Minerals

	Age (yr)	Calcium (mg)	Phosphorus (mg)	Iodine (mcg)	Iron (mg)	Magnesium (mg)	Zinc (mg)
Infants	0.0−0.5	360	240	35	10	60	3
	0.5−1.0	540	400	45	15	70	5
Children	1−3	800	800	60	15	150	10
	4−6	800	800	80	10	200	10
	7−10	800	800	110	10	250	10
Males	11−14	1200	1200	130	18	350	15
	15−18	1200	1200	150	18	400	15
Females	11−14	1200	1200	115	18	300	15
	15−18	1200	1200	115	18	300	15

From Food and Nutrition Board. *Recommended daily allowances, 1974* (8th ed.). Washington, D.C.: National Academy of Sciences, National Research Council, 1974.

A Supportive Environment for Desirable Eating Patterns

Environment is important in establishing desirable eating patterns. Some consideration of environment was included in the guidelines for establishing food patterns. However, there are other aspects of environment that need to be considered. First, it is necessary for the young child to feel secure during feeding times. For the infant, this means being held securely in the arms of an adult and maintaining eye-to-eye contact during the feeding. For the child who can only maintain sitting balance for a short period of time, adequate support is provided. For the child who can maintain sitting balance, a sturdy chair that allows him or her to sit securely with his or her feet on the floor is appropriate. The food is placed so that it is easily accessible. Utensils are used that will allow easy accessibility and enjoyment of the food. Aesthetically pleasing utensils increase the child's appetite and interest in eating. Young children are prone to spill foods and liquids, so unbreakable utensils are desirable. In addition, suction cups on the bottom of bowls or dishes help to stabilize dishes and to decrease accidents. Knowing that spills are common, bibs or other protective coverings for clothing and newspapers for covering the floor are suggested.

The natural progression towards self-feeding follows a predictable pattern, from eating with fingers, to spoon feeding to fork feeding. The child is rewarded for achieving each stage of development, and errors or clumsiness are ignored rather than acknowledged or ridiculed. The child's ability to achieve these developmental tasks is dependent on his or her muscular development. At an early stage, the child uses the muscles of the hand as a whole. It is not until the age of 5 or 6 years that the child develops the fine motor ability to use the fingers to effectively manipulate utensils. In addition, self-feeding is influenced by the child's eye–hand coordination, which is poorly developed when the child begins finger feeding. Based on this information, it is suggested that handles of utensils are short and blunt and of large enough diameter to be easily grasped. In addition, the use of sharp objects, such as a fork or knife, should be delayed until the child's muscles mature. The child's place at the table should be attractively set so that he or she can recognize his or her own place and enjoy the environment. Young children like repetition and familiar objects, so they enjoy having their own plates, cups, and utensils. In addition, the child's enjoyment is increased if some surprises are introduced along with the familiar mealtime offerings. Inexpensive table decorations can be used to add variety to an eating experience. The incorporation of favorite comic or television characters in the decor is a way to make the environment conducive to the eating needs of the child.

Dietary Offerings

The child's food likes are an important consideration in meal planning. Food likes and nutrition requirements should be combined to make the child's menu. Young children seem to prefer simple foods. However, there needs to be enough variety provided to introduce them to new foods. In addition, the smell, texture, and appearance of food influences the child's response to it. Sometimes young children refuse food before it is tasted. This response is not uncommon when foods have a disagreeable odor, are an odd color, or are too hot or too cold. Young children seem to prefer lukewarm foods, and often they will not eat until the desired temperature of the food is reached.

Children prefer foods that are easy to eat. Therefore, pieces are cut small so that the child can easily put them into his or her mouth and chew them. At the same time, it is possible for foods to be so small that they are difficult for the child to get on the spoon. An example of a food that is difficult for the child to spoon up is the pea. Combining peas on a plate with a backdrop of mashed potatoes or using a dish with an outer ridge are ways to help the child to manipulate the peas effectively. Whenever possible, the foods that are served should be ready for the child to eat without undue frustration. If the child experiences high levels of frustration from trying to eat, it is possible that he or she will decide to stop eating prematurely. If this occurs, it is not unusual for hunger pains to reoccur at an early time.

The menu of the young child reflects the child's predisposition to hunger pains. It is planned to include three child-size meals and a morning, afternoon, and bedtime snack. Snacks are planned so that they do not interfere with regular meals. Appropriate snacks include fruit juices, slices of fruit, milk, a cracker, pieces of cheese, and raw vegetables. Keep in mind that one cracker and 4 oz of fruit juice are enough to relieve the hunger pains, and larger amounts can interfere with the child's desire to eat the next meal.

The texture of the food is considered in menu planning. Generally, a combination of textures is desirable. Foods that allow crunching are provided, such as raw carrots or celery. Soft foods are easy to eat and are usually combined with crispy foods. Mashed potatoes and cooked vegetables are examples of soft foods. A chewy food is also included in the menu. Chewy foods increase the child's ability to eat more complex foods. Meats are examples of chewy foods, but care is taken to offer pieces that can be chewed by deciduous teeth, which are not as effective as permanent teeth for chewing. Oftentimes the young child prefers hamburger to steak, as it is easier to chew. Combining a variety of textures in the meal helps the child to accept and prefer foods of various kinds.

The child's menu is influenced by the economic status of the family. While a well-planned nutritious menu may not cost more than other, less nutritious foods, families with limited income may have less enthusiasm for shopping for foods that are essential to healthy living. In addition, it is not uncommon for these families to act spontaneously rather than to plan. Therefore, foods which are convenient for the moment are usually offered to the child. These "fast foods" are often categorized as "junk food" rather than nutritious food. A menu of junk foods can be appealing to the child, but it will not effectively support the child's growth and development. Therefore, junk foods result in ineffective use of the monies available to support the family.

Meal planning also takes into consideration the fact that the child can have a strong dislike for certain foods that is not easily resolved. In this situation, the child's preferences are respected and attempts are made to provide adequate nutritional intake while avoiding the disliked foods. It is not unusual, however, for the child's likes and dislikes to change frequently. In such a case, opportunities are provided for the child to select the disliked foods as an option to other alternatives. As children mature, they are often introduced to foods outside their own homes that they refused to eat at home. Under these conditions, the child can learn to eat foods that are new or that were refused at an earlier time. Food preferences also change due to many other conditions, such as the season of the year, the freshness of the foods, the availability of alternate foods, and the preferences of peers.

DIETARY CONSIDERATIONS RELATED TO LONG-TERM HEALTH CONDITIONS

Specific consideration of nutrition and feeding for specific conditions is covered in another portion of this text. However, in this section some general considerations are offered as guidelines in assessing the child's nutrition requirements and in menu planning:

1. A child with a long-term illness may not be the appropriate size for his or her chronological age. Therefore, the child's dietary requirements will probably be less.
2. The child may be less active than able-bodied peers and will probably need fewer nutrients to support his or her activity.
3. As an infant, the child might have developed poor eating habits due to weakened musculature. These poor habits need to be changed to support proper eating.
4. The dental development of children with long-term illness is often a problem. Special attention needs to be focused on dental health.
5. Dietary restrictions may make the child's menu boring, tasteless, or generally unappealing. Efforts are made to compensate for these distractions.
6. Some children with long-term illnesses tire easily while eating. Adjustments are made in the meals to compensate for this problem.
7. Inability to maintain trunk balance or to control other muscular movements can interfere with feeding. Special adaptation of furniture and utensils is needed to make the child independent.
8. Many prepared foods have large quantities of preservatives or additives that are contraindicated in children's diets. Reading the labels to determine if this is the case is an important part of menu planning for these children.
9. When a child has difficulty eating certain foods, it is not uncommon for these foods to be permanently removed from the child's diet. Periodic dietary discussions with the family and child help to discover such practices, and remedies can be suggested, when appropriate.

10. During periods of illness, anorexia is common. During these periods, adjustments in the diet are made to encourage the child to eat small amounts on a consistent basis. Food preferences are used to encourage the child's interest in foods.

11. Foods are frequently offered as rewards to children. Caution must be exercised not to use high-carbohydrate and high-fat foods for this purpose. An adult's concern for a child's health problem can be incorrectly expressed by giving the child foods that are not conducive to proper growth and development.

12. Children with health problems are often maintained on liquid or puréed foods longer than is indicated. Changing the child's diet to a more adult-like diet is encouraged as soon as possible.

13. As children with long-term illnesses often watch long hours of television, their dietary habits are strongly influenced by this medium. Caretakers need to use discretion and should not respond to all the child's requests for advertised foods, many of which are sugared, chocolate-flavored, or otherwise altered, decreasing their ultimate nutritional value.

14. It is not unusual for families to lack adequate knowledge about nutrition. Thus, it is necessary to discuss nutrition in simple, clear terms so that the caretaker is able to prepare prescribed meals.

15. When variations in diet are prescribed for only one member of the family, it is not unusual for the diet to be ignored. When it is possible to have everyone in the family on the same diet, success is more likely.

16. Short-term dietary restrictions are tolerated more easily than long-term ones. However, when diets are prescribed for long periods of time, there may be periods when the child rebels more strongly than at other times.

Nutrition is one of the major factors contributing to wellness. Therefore, increased emphasis should be placed on nutrition so that the child receives nutritious meals that contribute to his or her well-being.

Obesity

The terms *obesity* and *overweight* are not synonymous. A child is generally considered to be obese when his or her body fat is at least 15 percent greater than normal, while the term overweight refers to a child who has excess weight when compared to average values for sex, height, and body frame. Therefore, the term obesity is usually reserved to describe body fat, the tissue that is directly influenced by an excess of caloric intake, while the term overweight refers to total weight.

The child's self-concept is intimately linked to the health problem of obesity. The perceptual part of the self-concept is influenced by obesity, and this part of the self-concept is subjective in nature. For instance, it is hypothesized that obese persons frequently see themselves as thinner than other persons perceive them to be. Therefore, it is essential to consider the child's self-concept when providing management for this health problem.

The need to lose weight to help bring about physical fitness is a problem faced by children who are overweight. Body weight will decrease when one or more of the body's essential substances is significantly decreased. A decrease in essential substances results in a reduction in the body's total mass. It is noted that a short-term weight loss can be achieved through the loss of body water, fat, protein, or glycogen. The loss of these substances is common during periods of strenuous exercise. However, children who are overweight do not tend to participate in exercise of any type. Therefore, it is often difficult for overweight children to decrease their weight, as the body's loss of mass is proportional to its energy deficit, and such a deficit can be accomplished most efficiently through strenuous and sustained exercise.

For the child to lose weight, it is necessary to decrease caloric intake. The most effective way to accomplish this is by drastically reducing the amounts of refined sugars and starches that the child consumes. In addition, the child is provided a nutritious diet of smaller proportions than are needed to sustain weight. Until the desired weight is achieved, it is necessary for the body to have a decreased daily caloric intake and to have an increased expenditure of calories. Under these conditions, the body will burn fat to compensate for the caloric decreases.

To sustain weight loss, it is important to have the child modify the behavior that contributed to the weight gain. In addition, improved dietary habits lead to success in long-term management of weight. Fad diets may decrease weight more rapidly, but it is not healthy to maintain these dietary patterns for extended periods of time. A smaller, but still nutritious diet leads to changes in dietary behavior that have the potential to encourage the child to eat sensibly on an ongoing basis. In addition, changes are made in the environment that contributed to the weight gain. Oftentimes it is possible to determine stimulators to eating. For example, commercials that advertise food can stimulate the child's desire to eat, or sitting in a particular area may stimulate the same desire. These high-stimulator situations need to be avoided to decrease the child's desire for food. Factors to consider when counseling children who are obese include the following:

1. A place to eat should be selected, and food should be consumed only in this spot.
2. The child should avoid situations where high caloric food is consumed in large amounts, such as parties and picnics.
3. Snacks of raw fruits and vegetables should be readily available.
4. Slow eating with excessive chewing of each mouthful of food should be encouraged.
5. High-roughage foods should be included in the diet to increase the feeling of fullness.
6. The child should put down the utensil between mouthfuls.

7. Low-calorie fluids should be substituted for fluids with high caloric content.

8. Regularly scheduled meal times should be established and maintained.

One of the best ways to achieve weight loss is to have the child set the goals that he or she wants to meet and to have the child monitor his or her own weight reduction program. Limited emphasis is placed on weighing the child, and rewards for success must be rewards that do not include food.

Many children with long-term problems have a predisposition to obesity. This additional weight can interfere with their rehabilitation plans, so it is essential to manage the obesity effectively so that other aspects of their care can be maximized.

EXERCISE

Exercise is a way of developing body awareness. Body awareness leads to a consideration of dietary patterns. The interaction process between exercise and eating is intimately connected to body size and awareness. Determining the amount of exercise that is beneficial for an individual child is part of the assessment process.

The child that has not or is not currently exercising, requires a physical examination prior to beginning an exercise program. A daily exercise program is started with physical conditioning. The physical conditioning is based on the child's physical state and health problem. Many children with long-term illnesses are relatively inactive on a daily basis. This inactivity is a major factor in planning the child's exercise program. In order to develop a sound daily plan of exercise, the child is gently introduced to exercise and the exercise is increased gradually in accordance with the child's tolerance.

Exercise contributes to the child's plysical fitness. Enjoying exercise helps the child to be eager to participate in it on an ongoing basis despite the frustrations that may be connected with it. However, some exercises are more conducive to physical fitness, so it is necessary to include some of these in the child's repertoire as well.

Factors that contribute to the beneficial aspects of exercise include the following:

1. Exercise needs to be sustained—rest periods are kept at a minimum.
2. The chosen activity should increase the pulse rate to approximately 75 to 80 percent of its maximum potential.
3. Exercise that is rhythmical is beneficial, as the muscles alternately relax and contract.
4. Activity should be made progressively more difficult to maintain an increase in pulse rate.

5. As the exercise program is established, it is necessary to increase endurance and to have the child engage in exercise at least three times a week.

A key concept is that a strenuous exercise program creates special dietary and nutritional requirements. Strenuous exercise influences the body's reserves of fluids and energy. In order for the exercise to be most beneficial to the child, the ordinary diet is adjusted and supplemented to meet the energy and fluid requirements.

Generally, the American diet contains extra salt, sugar, saturated fat, and cholesterol and contains too little fresh fruits, vegetables, unsaturated fats, and grains. In order to attain physical fitness, the child's diet needs to be adjusted. The fluid intake is increased throughout the day to replace fluids lost during the exercise program. A combination of proper exercise and diet is essential to healthy living.

The key to success at an exercise program is to have the child feel an addiction for the healthy activities and diet that are instituted. The selected exercises must be such that the child desires or even craves them. In addition, a diet that is appealing as well as nutritious becomes addictive. The goal is to have the child develop the attitude that the exercise and nutritious diet have some mental or physical value that is worth the effort to maintain them on a daily basis.

Preactivity Stretching or Warm-up Exercises

An important part of any exercise program is the preparation of cold muscles for exercise. Muscles are stretched prior to exercising to prevent strains, pulls, or other injuries to the muscles, ligaments, and tendons. Muscles and tendons are tightened by inactivity, so it is necessary to loosen them with warm-up exercises before going on to active exercise. The preactivity stretching tends to relax tight muscles, reduce the stress of exercise on the supporting ligaments and tendons, and increase blood supply to these areas.

The selected exercise influences the type of warm-up exercises that are necessary to obtain an optimum exercise program. For example, tennis requires stretching of the muscles of the upper back, shoulders, and neck as well as the leg muscles used in running, and runners need to stretch the muscles of lower back as well as the muscles of the back of the thighs and calves and the muscles of the inner thighs.

Preactivity stretching should not involve bouncing or overstretching the muscle. Overstretching results in muscle contraction or spasm, while bouncing can cause injury. Proper stretching decreases soreness and/or stiffness of the muscles; however, at the beginning of the exercise program, some soreness or stiffness is common until muscles get used to the activity. Proper stretching entails a static smooth stretch of a muscle for a minimum of 10 seconds. Three goals of the warm-up exercises are:

1. To prevent joint and muscle problems.
2. To prevent cardiovascular problems.
3. To improve exercise performance.

Postactivity Stretching or Cooling-down Exercises

The exercise program is not complete until postactivity stretching is done. Postactivity stretching, like preactivity stretching, is done to decrease the possibility of soreness or injury. However, the merit of postactivity stretching is not always recognized by exercise enthusiasts.

Athletics

A special subset of exercise is athletics, including competitive sports. Athletic activities serve an excellent role in providing children with opportunities to learn cooperation through team efforts. With competitive sports, the child is able to excel in a sport by making a committed effort to become outstanding in the chosen sport. The child's self-confidence can be enhanced by becoming talented in a particular sport. However, the child's self-image can be diminished by consistent failures due to limitations in strength, endurance, range of motion, coordination, and so forth (Diamond et al., 1973). The immature bodies of developing children need special consideration.

1. Children's strength is not proportional to their size, resulting in wide variations in endurance and physical performance.
2. Children do not tolerate rejection from sports and they are impatient with the healing process.
3. Children have flexible ligamentor structures and open epiphyses, which makes them vulnerable to musculoskeletal injuries.
4. Body conditioning is essential before engaging in athletics, and children often lack the motivation to build up their bodies for endurance, strength, and acclimatization to heat or other environmental conditions.
5. Athletic equipment must be protective (Flynn et al., 1980).

Sports activities can provide an opportunity for the child and his or her family to spend time together. The child's relationship with the family can be improved by providing the family with pride in the child's accomplishments in sports. Sports can be a way for the child to bring satisfaction to family members who share in the child's accomplishments by attending sports events and practice sessions. During sports activities, the family is able to encourage the child to do his or her very best in competition. In addition, the family's involvement in the activities tells the child that he or she is special and important, as the family takes time to support the child during activities. The time shared by the child and family offers a way to maintain a family feeling of comraderie.

The value of sports in teaching the child to be part of a team can be lost or diminished if too much emphasis is placed on winning. In every competition, there is a winner and a loser. The child is taught not to take losses as personal failures. It is important for the family to praise the child for his or her efforts rather than merely praising him or her for winning. The family has a major role to play in helping the child to understand that winning is not the only function of sports. When the child tries his or her best, the rewards for the child's efforts are extremely important. It is difficult to remember to praise the child for being a good sport and a good loser despite the desire to win. It is easy to love a winner. It is more difficult to find a way to encourage a loser of a competition to continue to practice after a loss in order to improve performance. The child needs both praise for winning and encouragement to continue despite losses. Sometimes it is necessary to limit the child to athletic activities that are not competitive if failures are persistent or to encourage the child to compete against his or her own performance rather than competing against others.

Limiting Children in Sports.   The trend is to encourage more children with long-term illness to participate actively in athletics. This is definitely a change in philosophy of care. Traditionally, some illnesses have been associated with exclusion from competitive sports. This is now being reconsidered, and more and more children with long-term illnesses are participating in formal and informal athletics according to abilities and interests. When the family is in doubt as to whether the child should participate, the advice of a physician who specializes in sports medicine or exercise physiology should be obtained.

Competitive Sports.   There are as yet no clear research data to prove or disprove the value of competitive sports to the social competence of school-age children. Evidence to date leaves gaps in the understanding of the social outcomes of participating in organized competitive sports activities. Burchard (1979), reviewing available research data, noted that some of the grave disadvantages of competitive sports expressed by educators are not verified, while inconsistencies in conclusions of the available research make it impossible to be clear in making recommendations about the value or lack of value of this type of childhood exercise. There is some evidence to suggest that children who participate in competitive sports to have fun rather than to win seem to benefit more positively from their organized sports participation than do children whose sole goal is to win at all costs.

None of the studies reviewed by Burchard (1979) involved disabled children's participation in organized sports. However, Pepitone and Kleiner (1957) found that low-status teams (chronic losers) showed fewer negative responses to losing than did children who expected to win and lost. Although it is not possible to generalize these findings to disabled children, it is reasonable to hypothesize that because disabled children are expected to lose, their responses to loss might be similar to those of able-bodied children who often lose in competition.

While the social outcomes of competitive sports still remain unclear, it seems reasonable to suggest that when children engage in these activities, the environment is improved if the following conditions are met:

1. Children of both sexes are provided equal opportunities to participate.
2. Value is placed on participation rather than on winning.
3. Participation time is equalized for all children.
4. Adults praise the children for their positive participation regardless of whether the outcome is a win or a loss.

5. Adults role-model a sensitivity towards all the children who participate.

Categories of Competitive Sports.   The various types of competitive sports can
be classified as mild, moderate or vigorous to give direction to parents regarding
the degree of exertion associated with particular sports. The following categories
are suggested:

- Mild: walking, bicycle riding, jogging.
- Moderate: tennis, roller skating, ice skating, baseball, volleyball,
  swimming.
- Vigorous: football, skiing, soccer (Galton, 1980).

Obviously, some persons may take exception to the categories; they are
suggested as guidelines rather than as absolute examples of the sports in which a
given child should be encouraged to participate. A careful assessment of the
child's condition can result in the child being encouraged to participate in a less
strenuous sport rather than being excluded temporarily or permanently from all
sports.

CONSIDERATION OF SPECIFIC ILLNESS CONDITIONS

Heart

Conditions related to the heart have traditionally been associated with exclusion
from sports. However, today there is a remarkable change in attitude about these
conditions and the best prescription for exercise. Children with murmurs are
usually evaluated for cardiovascular defects; if they do not exist, the child is not
excluded from participating in competitive sports.

Children with congenital and rheumatic heart defects that do not result in
hemodynamic blood flow are often capable of participating fully in active,
competitive sports. Again, this represents a change in advice physicians have
given families, so it may take a great deal of re-education to encourage families to
see sports as a way for the child to get exercise without being subjected to undue
risk.

The degree to which the child with hypertension is allowed to engage in
sports is dependent on the child's degree of hypertension. A child with mild to
moderate hypertension is discouraged from participating in isometric activities,
such as weight lifting, since these activities are associated with a rise in the blood
pressure. A child with mild hypertension is encouraged to actively participate in
sports activities. The assumption is made that the exercise may be able to lower
the child's blood pressure in the same way that it does in adults with the same
problem.

Children with abnormal heart rhythm are usually encouraged to participate
in maximum exertion whenever possible. This suggestion is based on the fact that
many abnormal rhythms in children are benign. Again, many of the rhythm

abnormalities disappear with mild exercise, and others disappear with more intense exercise. Before a child is excluded from sports, a cardiologist with experience in children's sports activities should be consulted. A comprehensive cardiovascular examination may be indicated, including a history of response to physical activity, vital signs, and cardiovascular inspection, palpation, and auscultation. A suggestion of abnormalities in the foregoing findings indicates a chest roentgenogram and electrocardiogram (Thornton et al., 1977).

It is obvious from this list that most children with long-term cardiac problems are candidates for participation in sports. The psychological reactions of both the child and the family are taken into account when giving advice on sports participation. Families that fear that the child may be engaged in levels of activity that are inconsistent with the child's cardiac output need considerable encouragement to allow the child to be included in competitive sports. Likewise, a child who has been restricted in activities may be uncomfortable in facing the possibility of participating in active sports. The child is the best judge of his or her tolerance to the sport activity. However, the child is encouraged to increase his or her participation rather than being satisfied with early sports output. In addition, the attitudes of adults in the community can influence the way the child responds to opportunities to participate in sports competition. The traditional sedentary approach to heart problems is well known to many adults. The more contemporary treatment of heart problems is less well known. Based on outdated information, many adults who interact with the child may try to discourage the child from active participation in sports. Key persons, such as teachers, coaches, and scout leaders, need to be re-educated so that they do not interfere with the child being actively involved to the extent that he or she feels capable.

Another parameter to consider is that the child who is kept from participating in sports can have a negative emotional reaction when prohibited from participating in activities that peers are encouraged to be involved in. In order to decrease this possibility, the child is encouraged to participate in sports to the extent that he or she feels comfortable with and to ask to be relieved from participation when tiredness ensues. In addition, the child is cautioned to omit sports activity when an acute illness, such as a cold, is present.

Asthma

Children with asthma have also been discouraged unnecessarily from active participation in sports. This practice has recently changed, and children with asthma are making great gains in respiratory function from participating actively in sports. In addition, the emotional development of these children is enhanced by sports participation. In order to gain the most benefit from participating in sports, the child needs to have proper medical management of his or her asthma. A warm-up period is suggested prior to participation in vigorous sports to decrease the possibility of an asthmatic attack being triggered by the vigorous exercise. In the event that the child is prone to exercise-induced asthma despite proper medical management and warm-ups, the child is encouraged to participate in a less vigorous sport, such as swimming, which produces fewer asthma attacks than comparable exertion in running or cycling (Galton, 1980). Other competitive sports that are appropriate for children with asthma include basketball, track, and soccer.

Sports that take place outside may prove to be better for the child than ones that take place in a gym that has mats (which can contain mold) or dusty floors (which contribute to the induction of asthma in some children).

Children who are exposed at an early age to exercise are usually more eager than other children to continue with their participation as they get older. Therefore, the child with asthma is given an active exercise program at an early age and encouraged to take responsibility for doing the exercises on a daily basis. During the school-age period, the exercise program is expanded to include participation in competitive sports.

The responses of adults to participation of children with asthma in strenuous exercise are similar to the responses of adults to exercises for children with cardiac problems. In addition, if the sports activities result in visible signs of distress, adults can actively discourage the child from trying to compete. Successful inclusion of the child in sports activities is the best way to change attitudes that have prevailed for a long time.

Skeletal Abnormalities

The child with skeletal problems is encouraged to participate in sports that are of interest to him or her. Galton (1980) identifies some specific skeletal abnormalities and the degree of participation in sports that is supported by experts in orthopedic medicine. Children with Osgood—Schlatter's disease are all allowed to participate in active sports until they feel pain that interferes with further participation. When the disease is in its acute phase, the child is either excluded from competition or allowed to engage in mild competition, while the child with chronic disease is able to participate in mild to moderate activity.

A child with spondylolisthesis can participate in moderate to vigorous activity if no symptoms are present. If symptoms are present, the child is required to wear a back brace and complete exercises. If the treatment corrects the symptoms, the child can participate in sports while wearing the brace for support.

The conditions of congenital subluxation of the hip, Legg—Perthes disease, and slipped femoral epiphysis are treated in a manner similar to that used for spondylolisthesis. A child with mild deformity is allowed participation in moderate to vigorous noncontact sports, while with a moderate deformity, mild to moderate activities are allowed. When the child has a severe deformity, it may be necessary to limit exercise to mild activities or to exclude the child temporarily from contact sports.

Rheumatic arthritis interferes with the child's ability to participate in sports while the disease is in its acute stage. When the disease is quiescent and the child is left with a complete recovery of function, moderate to vigorous activity is allowed. If the disease is quiescent and the child has minimal to moderate dysfunction, only mild to moderate activity is encouraged. When functional recovery is complete but the child is still maintained on aspirin or similar treatment, mild to moderate activity is possible.

When there are indications for children to be excluded from sports during intervals of their diseases, it is essential to keep the children well informed of the reasons that a particular course of action is being suggested. A child who is gaining satisfaction from competitive sports can be very disappointed when it is necessary to interfere with practice or participation in competition. It is imperative that the child receive an adequate explanation of the reasons for limitations and the expected period of exclusion or reduction in activity. The child also needs encouragment to regain losses in potential output caused by the interference with active, ongoing participation in the sports competition.

Developmental Delays

Exclusion of children with developmental delays from competitive sports is often advised on the basis that the child cannot learn the rules of competitive sports. Actually, the child needs to participate in sports in order to counteract some of the outcomes of sedentary living that can result from lack of involvement in exercise appropriate to the child's age.

An important part of care of the child with limited intellectual competence is to provide supervision that guarantees safety for the child while he or she is involved in competitive sports. Some retardation may result in the child being encouraged to participate in individual or dual sports activities rather than in team sports. However, each child's capabilities need to be assessed individually so that he or she is not excluded from participation that is appropriate to his or her ability.

Considerations that are essential include an assessment of when the child can benefit from participating in competition with able-bodied children. Competition with children with similar health problems is also suggested. The continual competition with able-bodied children can result in persistent failure for the child with a developmental delay. If the child is mildly to moderately impaired, successfully competing in sports with able-bodied children can be uplifting. It is also essential to realize that competition can be a motivating factor for the child. However, underdeveloped muscles may interfere initially with the child's successful competition in sports activities. A gradual increase in the child's competitive sports activities can increase his or her ability to win against children with greater intellectual capacities. Despite underdeveloped muscles, the child is engaged in regular exercises and conditioning that will contribute to his or her ability to engage in competitive sports at a later date. It may be wise to engage the child in competitive activities that can guarantee some success during the time that the child is preparing to compete with able-bodied children. The sports ability of the child can be a powerful force in improving the child's self-concept if the child's success—failure rate is closely monitored.

Conditions that Disqualify Children from Sports

The guidelines of the American Medical Association (AMA) Committee on Medical Aspects of Sports are useful in determining the amount of participation that is suggested for particular illnesses of childhood. The categories of sports and examples of activities established by the AMA are:

- Collision: football, rugby, hockey, lacrosse, etc.
- Contact: baseball, soccer, basketball, wrestling, etc.
- Noncontact: cross-country track, tennis, crew, swimming, etc.
- Other: bowling, golf, archery, field events, etc. (Galton, 1980).

The Committee suggested that no sport is barred based on the disease condition itself—other parameters influence whether or not a sport is allowed at a particular time. For example, a child may have controlled diabetes and be allowed a wider range of sports activities than a child whose diabetes is poorly controlled. The category of "other" sports is the only category suggested for children with bleeding tendencies, such as hemophilia and purpura. The combined categories of "other" and "noncontact" are suggested for children with one eye, an enlarged liver, skin problems and an enlarged spleen, absence of a kidney, or previous head surgery. Collision sports are inappropriate for children with a previous head injury or concussions (Galton, 1980).

The preceding guidelines are only suggestions for guiding the decisions of adults. To be relevant to a particular child and his or her management, the guidelines may be assessed critically and utilized to try to help the child want to be able to engage vigorously in sports that are conducive to his or her well-being despite the history of chronic illness. As research findings evolve, it may be necessary to rethink the part of competitive sports in the daily activities of these children. It seems obvious that the changes that are likely to emerge are going to increase rather than decrease the children's active participation in these activities.

SLEEP MANAGEMENT

Sleep difficulties are common management complaints of caretakers of children with long-term illness. The use of relaxation techniques can contribute to the successful management of this problem. The range of reasons for sleep disturbances are varied and include:

1. Inability to get to sleep.
2. Sleeping in short, interrupted periods.
3. Restless sleep throughout sleep periods.
4. Wanting to sleep with caretakers.
5. Fear of being alone or in the dark.
6. Having tantrums at bedtime.
7. Disturbance of sleep due to dreaming.
8. Wandering around the house during the night.
9. Fear of scary objects in the bed.

10. Fear of going to sleep or of waking up.
11. Fear of incontinence during the night.
12. Fear of falling out of bed.
13. Disruption of usual routine.
14. Recent painful experience and/or hospitalization.
15. Unfamiliar surroundings, such as a relative's home or the hospital.
16. Stimulating play experiences just prior to bedtime.
17. Excessive food intake just prior to bedtime.
18. An upcoming event, such as a test in school.
19. A predictable event for which the child is not prepared fully.
20. Changes in family structure, such as a new sibling or a divorce.
21. Discomfort, such as that caused by sleeping in a brace.

Success with relaxation as a management technique to improve sleep behaviors can be enhanced if the caretakers show a positive attitude toward the process. If the caretakers seem ambivalent about the use of the technique, their attitudes are transmitted to the child. Therefore, the caretakers are thoroughly introduced to the process prior to its institution. They are given adequate time to ask questions and to raise concerns about its utility. If the caretakers have been inconsistent in their management of previous behavioral problems, they are encouraged to be consistent with this technique. The ways that the caretakers contend with behavioral problems are explored by asking open-ended questions, such as:

1. "Tell me how you manage John's problem with _____."
2. "Give me examples of the way you discipline Jane."
3. "Paint me a verbal picture of the problem as you see it."

It is helpful to have a picture of the child's sleep behavior before beginning the relaxation techniques. Try to establish clearly and accurately what a sleep scenario is at both naptime and bedtime. Establish who is involved in the scenario and the roles of each person. Also try to establish what is done when the child cannot sleep, how this is handled, and who is involved. Getting a realistic picture helps to identify areas that need to be improved as well as areas that are satisfactory and need reinforcement. The length of time that the problem has existed is also important, as well-established behavioral problems are often more difficult to manage than newly acquired ones.

The preparation of the child for sleep is an important part of management. The preparation begins by slowing down the child's activities in advance of bedtime or naptime. Active physical activities are changed to passive, quieting activities, such as listening to a story, reading a calming book, or listening to quiet music. The child may enjoy having a warm glass of milk or quieting fluid (the fluid must not contain caffeine). The child is encouraged to go to the bathroom to empty the bladder. A warm bath can be used to begin the relaxation process. The child's room is kept quiet and free from distracting stimuli and soft music can be played. Next, the child is placed in bed, following the traditional practice for that child. For example, the child may need to take a favorite cuddly toy to bed and use a particular blanket in order to feel secure. Consistency is the key factor in management of this problem. After the child is settled in bed, the relaxation program is started. Two alternative methods are provided.

1. Have the child lie on his or her back and in a monotone quiet voice begin to have the child relax each body part, from the toes to the head: "Your toes are feeling heavy; relax your toes. Your toes are feeling heavy; relax your toes." The part that is being relaxed is gently rubbed or touched during the process.
2. Use a relaxation tape that the child can play in his or her tape recorder. Sit by the child's bedside and encourage the child to concentrate on the tape.

The goal of management is to have the relaxation technique bring the child to a sleep state. It is necessary to guide the child through the various stages of the sleep cycle, which are:

- *Stage 0:* drowsiness; body temperature declines; eyes are closed; rapid, irregular brain waves; images may float in, dreamlike thoughts; time perception deteriorates.
- *Stage 1:* floating sensation; idle images; easily awakened by spoken word or noise; respiration gets even; heart rate becomes slower; lasts only a few minutes.
- *Stage 2:* eyes may appear to be slowly rolling; sound asleep, but easily awakened; usually not awakened by light.
- *Stage 3:* takes louder noise to disturb; muscles very relaxed; breathes evenly; heart rate continues to slow down; blood pressure falling; temperature declines.
- *Stage 4:* muscles very relaxed; little movement; hard to awaken with low noise; heart rate and temperature still falling; respiration slow and even; common time for incontinence; sleeps considerable portion of night in this stage (National Institute of Mental Health, 1976).

An understanding of the various stages of sleep helps to determine additional management considerations, including the following:

1. Evaluate the child's need for sleep realistically before beginning relaxation.
2. It is necessary to continue to promote relaxation until the child reaches stage 3; otherwise he or she can be easily aroused from sleep.
3. Reassure the child that his or her bed is a friendly place to be.

4. Gently soothe the child who awakens from a nightmare and return him or her to bed quietly. Sit by the child's bed and quietly encourage him or her to return to sleep.
5. Apply additional coverings after sleep is established to counteract declining body temperature.
6. Fasten coverings in some manner to keep them secure if the child is restless during sleep.
7. If incontinence occurs and wakens the child, quickly change the child's clothing and return him or her to bed to re-establish sleep.
8. Practice relaxation at other than sleep times to acquaint the child with the use of the technique.
9. Discourage the use of an adult's bed as an alternative to sleeping in the child's own bed.
10. Encourage the caretakers to be patient and not to expect miracles from the relaxation technique.
11. Encourage the caretakers to give the child positive reinforcement when sleep habits are improving.
12. Use the relaxation technique prior to any scheduled stressful events to decrease the child's stress level—e.g., when an EEG is scheduled or a bone marrow aspiration is due.
13. Help the caretakers to be aware that sleep disturbances are usually connected to other stressful events in the child's life and that all stressful situations need attention.
14. Help the caretakers to understand that children tend to respond to the cues of adults and that adults' behavior can thus influence the child.

In order to be successful at managing sleep disturbances, the caretakers need ongoing support. A child who does not sleep and disturbs the rest of the members of the family can be a source of irritation and frustration. The caretakers, deprived of sufficient sleep, can use punishment that is not helpful in resolving the problem. Adults' tempers can flare when they are tired and half-awakened from sleep. Preparation for wakeful periods can deter abusive behaviors. The caretakers need to practice their responses to sleep disruptions so that the behavior they exhibit contributes to the child's ability to settle down once more and return to sleep. While a spanking may help the caretakers to express their frustration, it does not contribute to the relaxation of the child, so wakeful behavior is likely to persist. If the caretakers can engage the child in the relaxation session, the chances of restoring sleep can be improved.

Although it is difficult not to focus attention on the sleep disturbances, the caretakers are encouraged:

1. Not to remind the child of his or her behavior the night before.
2. Not to threaten the child as he or she is trying to go to sleep.
3. Not to embarrass the child in front of others by discussing his or her sleep problem with others.

4. To try to give the child additional positive affirmation during the time the behavior is being treated.
5. To try to get additional rest during the day so that the caretaker does not become overly tired due to sleep interruptions.
6. To keep an accurate record of the child's sleep habits. At times, the caretakers are not able to appreciate or recognize small improvements, so documentation can be helpful.

The goal of the management of sleep disturbances is to have a successful resolution without the use of drugs by the child or caretakers. Therefore, a discussion of drug therapy is deliberately omitted from the potential management plan. In extreme cases, the physician may feel that the child and/or caretakers are nearing exhaustion, and drug therapy may be prescribed for a limited time. However, drugs cannot relieve the ongoing sleep problems, so their use only results in prolongation of the resolution of the problem.

STRESS CONTROL

Swami Rama (1981) suggests that human beings are responsible for their own destinies, but fear, loneliness, and despair tend to interfere with well-being. Inherent in these remarks is a concern that human beings are prone to anxiety that is caused by a lack of control over the environment. This lack of environmental control leads to the creation of stress.

Stress is a condition of the mind as as well as of the body. Stress is often unconsciously created and sustained. It is postulated that some personality traits are destructive to health, as they tend to increase stress levels (Pelletier, 1979). However, it is not clearly determined that personality traits are directly responsible for stress-related illnesses. Nutrition is also thought to play a part in stress. Williams (1973) has prescribed nutritional elements to decrease stress levels. Stress as a purely physiologic response is reported by Selye (1976) and Kobasa (1979), who identified stressful life events that may lead to illness. Habits are also linked to stress. Davidson and Schwartz (1976) identify three components of stress reactions: somatic, cognitive, and attentional, or, stated another way, physical, mental, and emotional. If only external causes of stress are considered, it is possible to ignore the source of stress, which is the way that the individual thinks, acts, and feels in relation to events that are faced on a daily basis.

The concept of stress and stress management is extremely important when families are faced with chronic illness and its management, as creative problem-solving ability is decreased when stress is present. Creative problem solving helps the family to be able to adapt to the chronic illness and to make changes that are required to cope with the problems that arise from the management of chronic illness. Creative thinking is enhanced when the mind is in a state of inner calm. Therefore, creative expression is inconsistent with stress. High levels of stress are correlated with a closed mind, whereas lack of stress is correlated with an open mind. Dealing with chronic illness is facilitated by an open mind that is ready and willing to solve problems, leading to a resolution or dissolution of an existing problem.

There are many indicators of stress. A variety of instruments are available to measure stress. A partial list of indicators or symptoms of stress follows:

1. Irritability.
2. An "uneasy feeling."
3. Forgetfulness.
4. Lack of organizational skills.
5. Inability to keep appointments.
6. Loss of appetite.
7. Loss of energy.
8. Difficulty breathing.
9. Inability to sleep.
10. Palpitations or irregularity of heart rate.
11. Increased perspiration.
12. Accident proneness.
13. Lack of enthusiasm.
14. Localized pain (i.e., headache, backache).
15. Drug and alcohol abuse.
16. Decreased sexual enjoyment.

Identifying indicators or symptoms of stress is essential if the family is to be helped to deal with stress. As many of these symptoms are vague, they can go unrecognized. The first step in stress management is to clearly identify factors that indicate that stress is present and to develop a mechanism for resolving the stress so that it is not taken for granted. It is difficult to change social structures that contribute to family stress caused by the chronic illness, but it is possible to help the family to change their internal responses to pressures that originate from these social structures so that other family members do not become prone to illness.

The knowledge that stress is the result of an imbalance between sympathetic and parasympathetic activity is essential to stress control. Nurenberger (1981) proposes that by maintaining neurologic balance between the sympathetic (arousal) and parasympathetic (inhibition) systems, it is possible to remain free of stress. This balance is essential, for when it is not maintained, anything that a family member does can be stressful. The imbalance principle helps in the understanding that things or events that are stressful one day may not be stressful on another day. For example, if the parent is out of balance and the nurse reports that the child did not eat, the parent may respond with a variety of symptoms of stress, such as increased perspiration, irritability with the child, or a seeming lack of concern. The same announcement by the nurse when the parent is in balance can result in the parent coming up with ideas for making food more attractive to the child.

Nurenberger (1981) identifies a possum response to stress. He suggests that an alternate to the fight or flight response to stress identified by Selye (1976) is, in persons without hope, to adopt a possum-like response and become passive and depressed. Both the fight or flight response and the possum response are attempts at self-protection. According to Nurenberger, "Both responses involve integrated cortical, hypothalamic, autonomic, neuromuscular and hormonal activity." The occurrence of stress is related to the individual's lack of understanding of the dynamics of the responses and a lack of awareness that things are happening that are potential contributors to illness. Either the fight or flight response or the possum response can lead to imbalance if it is not moderated and controlled. Imbalance increases susceptibility to illness and a decreased capacity to function effectively.

The primary source of stress is not the external environment. The primary sources of stress are the emotional and perceptual factors which form the basic personality (Nurenberger, 1981). Arousal of the hypothalamus is directed by the cerebral cortex in response to repetitive thought patterns, constant anxiety, and fear about past, present, or future events that are associated with potentially painful or negative consequences. Chronic illness is a mental image that can cause hypothalamic arousal. As such, the way that the family feels about the chronic illness can result in increased stress. The way the family perceives the chronic illness determines whether or not stress will occur. Because stress is internally produced, it is a conditioned state that can be altered.

It is possible for the impact of a threat situation to continue long after the actual threat has passed. The family can continue to focus on the threat and maintain constant levels of stress long after it seems that the threat is passed. Therefore, the mother of a child with diabetes can be under a great deal of stress even if the child is satisfactorily regulated on insulin and a diabetic diet. She may have a constant need to relate all the details that surrounded the diagnosis and treatment of the disease and to go over and over the family tree trying to identify other members of the family that might have had the disease. In this situation, the mother is probably viewing the disease of her child as a direct threat to herself due to her attachment to the child. The child's disease results in a threat to herself because it is a threat to her child.

Emotional stress, as described by Nurenberger (1981), p. 86 is:

> "... the result of a mental process: it is a state of autonomic imbalance generated as a reaction to perception of some kind of threat, pain or discomfort. This perception involves an interpretation of selected sensory stimuli, which is colored, or structured, by memories of past pain. It is also involved with the anticipation that this pain will occur in the future as a consequence of present sensory stimuli and environmental conditions. It is sustained by indecisiveness, the inability to resolve the threat."

Repeating negative thoughts and images results in a state of continuing arousal and triggers the involvement of the endocrine system; this results in a prolonged stress response or a state of sustained imbalance. Continual preoccupation with the chronic illness and its associated problems can result in an inability to discriminate, select alternatives, and/or follow through with decisions.

An image such as a child with a chronic illness elicits strong arousal responses because it has a high emotional content. The flow of images and feelings associated with the child results in a strong need for the person to act, but the corresponding action does not occur. For example, the mother of the child with diabetes may be angry at her father, who has the disease and whom she believes transmitted it through her to the child. If the father is not available to blame for the situation, the mother is unable to respond adequately to the mental image. The inability to express the anger leads to increasing tension and resulting stress. Fatigue results from an inability to free the mind from thinking about the image.

The family is encouraged to take each day at a time. In this way, the focus of their attention is on the present. Focusing on the present can limit the painful feelings associated with the past or the anticipated future. By focusing attention on the task at hand, the autonomic nervous system is not kept in a state of imbalance. Completing the task results in expression of energy and a balance between mind, body, and action. Being able to take action results in a coordination between the sympathetic and parasympathetic systems and uses the arousal and inhibition responses constructively.

The Child's Response to Stress

Life stress and its effects on the child are influenced by the child's self-concept. The child's ability to cope with stress is dependent on the child's self-concept. The child who has a positive self-concept and who views himself or herself as valuable and worthy is better able to use inner resources to cope with emotional stresses and strains, while a child who views oneself negatively and as worthless is frustrated by stressful situations, as he or she lacks the inner resources to cope with additional emotional strain.

Knowledge of environmental stressors is increasing. Air and noise pollution, chemical additives in food, job-related stresses, and so forth are all implicated as contributing to stress reactions in individuals. There appears to be an increase in the amount of stressful situations that confront individuals in today's society. Efforts to decrease, eliminate, manage, or control stress are suggested to improve the overall well-being of individuals.

The child's perceptions influence the way that he or she responds to internal or external stressors. For example, an internal stressor, such as chemicals in food, can be perceived as normal by the child even though his or her physiologic reaction to the stressor results in hyperactivity. The child's ability to respond in socially responsible ways is evidence of a successful coping mechanism, which prevents stress. If, however, the child cannot behave in socially acceptable ways, then stress is experienced as a result of unsuccessful coping (Fig. 2-4)

Relaxation and Stress Control

The use of relaxation as part of a program for healthy living is well accepted. There are a variety of ways to include a relaxation program in a daily lifestyle. In order to gain the greatest benefit from the relaxation, techniques are learned and internalized so that they can be easily implemented. Relaxation can be used on an ongoing preventative basis or during periods of minor or acute stress to reduce the ill effects of the situation.

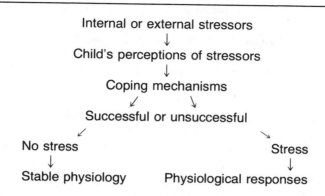

Internal or external stressors
↓
Child's perceptions of stressors
↓
Coping mechanisms
↙   ↘
Successful or unsuccessful
↙   ↘
No stress   Stress
↓   ↓
Stable physiology   Physiological responses

Figure 2-4. Diagram of the influences of internal and external stressors on the potential for stress.

It is wise to establish a time, place, and program for relaxation. The relaxation schedule should be conducive to the client's lifestyle, so the time of relaxation is based on the client's daily schedule. While it is not essential to establish a definite schedule, twice daily is often suggested as a good basis for a preventative program. The time set aside for relaxation should be free from disruptions and distractions to be most beneficial. Having a specific space to relax in is conducive to the goals of relaxation; however, it is not essential to set aside a specific area.

The use of relaxation techniques to relieve stress is strongly suggested. An ability to use relaxation techniques during periods of stress helps the child to feel more comfortable and reduces the possibility of his or her getting stress-related diseases.

Relaxation techniques can be established using audiotapes that guide relaxation. A variety of tapes are available for this purpose. Tapes can also be made to specifically meet the needs of a particular client. Audiotapes can contain instructions or music which facilitates relaxation, or they can combine the two strategies. Some relaxation techniques are combined with imagery.

Relaxation Instructions.

Technique One. Assume a comfortable position. Sit in a chair or lie on a comfortable surface. Loosen any restricting clothing. Pay attention to your body. Is there any part that is uncomfortable? If so, make any minor adjustments that are necessary to relieve this discomfort.

Now start to relax the body by moving your attention from head to foot, or vice versa, focusing attention on each body part. Deliberately relax each part; feel the heaviness and then the relaxation. As the body relaxes, be certain not to fall asleep. An example of this technique follows.

1. Relax the muscles of the forehead. Stretch out the muscles, soothe out each wrinkle.

2. Relax the muscles of the jaws. Pay special attention to each side of the face. Let the jaw drop slightly.
3. Relax the lips. Let them lie freely open.
4. Relax the muscles of the neck, releasing all the tension.
5. Relax the muscles of the shoulders. Move the shoulders slightly and then let them relax. Feel the relaxation spread from shoulder to shoulder.
6. Relax the muscles of the upper chest. Breathe rhythmically and evenly. Just let the breath flow slowly through the nose.
7. Let the muscles of the upper arms relax. Move your attention down the arms and through the fingers.
8. Let the muscles of the abdomen relax.
9. Let the muscles of the pelvis relax.
10. Let the muscles of the upper thighs relax.
11. Let the muscles of the calves relax.
12. Let the muscles of the feet relax and move your attention to the ends of the toes.
13. Lie quietly and feel the relaxed state of the body. After 10 or 15 minutes, gently reverse the process and discontinue the relaxation.

Technique Two. Assume a comfortable position, as in relaxation technique one. Gently contract and relax each muscle group, focusing attention on the stress caused when muscles are contracted and contrasting this feeling with the sensation felt during relaxation. An example of this technique follows:

1. Contract the muscles of the forehead and hold the contraction for 2 seconds. Feel the tension. Relax the muscle. Feel the heavy, warm sensation.
2. Contract the muscles of the jaws. Hold the contraction for 2 seconds. Feel the tension. Relax the jaws. Feel the sensation.
3. Push the tongue against the roof of the mouth. Hold it there for 2 seconds. Feel the pressure. Relax the tongue and let it lie gently on the floor of the mouth.
4. Contract the muscles of the neck. Feel the tension in the neck. Hold the contraction for 2 seconds. Relax the muscles of the neck.
5. Contract the muscles of the shoulders. Hold the tension for 2 seconds. Relieve the strain and let the shoulders fully relax.
6. Take in a deep breath and hold it for 10 seconds, then slowly exhale through the nose, relaxing the chest.
7. Contract the muscles of the arms and clench the fists tightly. Hold this tension 2 seconds and then release it. Let the arms and hands relax and rest comfortably in the lap.
8. Tighten the muscles of the abdomen and buttocks. Hold the tension for 2 seconds. Relax the muscles and feel the heavy, relaxed sensation.
9. Contract the muscles of the legs, feet, and toes. Hold the contracted feeling for 2 seconds. Relax the muscles.

10. Sit or lie quietly and enjoy the sensation. Pay attention to each muscle group. If any tension remains, try to release it. Get rid of all the tension in the body and enjoy 10 minutes of undisturbed relaxation.

Technique Three. Assume a relaxed position, as in relaxation technique one. Turn on soothing music. Take in the music while relaxing each of the muscle groups described in the relaxation technique.

Technique Four: Relaxation and Imagery. Dim the lights in the room. Assume a comfortable position, preferably lying down on a comfortable surface. Loosen constricting clothing. Pay attention to the body. If anything is uncomfortable, make the adjustments that are necessary to relieve discomfort.

Close the eyes but do not fall asleep. Relax the body as described in the first relaxation technique. After the entire body is relaxed, imagine an experience that was very rewarding. Capture the experience and visualize the experience. Imagine that you are part of that experience. Bring back the memories of that experience and feel the warm sensations that accompany that experience. Go with the experience, feel yourself fully involved in the episode, enjoy the experience, make it come alive, fully immerse yourself in the imagery and hold on to it as long as it seems real. Pay attention to your feelings, recall why you enjoyed the experience, let the feelings enfold your whole body and hold the feeling. When the image begins to fade, remain relaxed with the eyes closed for 10 minutes and then gently open your eyes.

Technique Five. Dim the lights in the room. Assume a comfortable position, preferably lying down on a comfortable surface. Loosen any constricting clothing. Make adjustments needed to feel reasonably relaxed. Close the eyes lightly and follow the imagery.

Imagine yourself on a sandy beach. The sky is a crystal blue. The sun is sending gentle, warm rays to the sand and they warm your body on the way. Feel the warm sensation from the sun's rays as they dance across your body and make shadows in the sand. See the blue-green water as the waves gently flow towards the shore. Hear the sounds of the water and relax to the gentle splash as the waves break on the shore and go back to the sea. See the damp sand where the waves depart and touch the cooled sand. Feel the coolness on your warm body and enjoy the contrast.

Smell the salt air as the gentle breeze passes over your face. Breathe in a deep breath captured from the breeze and hold the breeze—feel it capture your body and flow down and out your toes. As the breeze leaves the body, let it take all the impurities out of your body. Lie quietly and feel the refreshed feeling as you combine the sun's rays, the salt-air breeze, and the sounds of the water splashing on the shore. Now let yourself play freely in that scene. Do whatever you like but frolic freely and playfully unfold. Stay with the image as long as you like and then slowly come back to reality.

Technique Six.   Relax as in relaxation technique one. Close the eyes lightly and listen to the following:

The fairy godmother takes her magic wand and gently taps your head. As the wand taps, all the impurities of the body are released up the wand and leave the body.

With all the impurities out, feel the freedom of the body. Imagine that the body is like that of a healthy newborn baby. Feel the softness of the baby's skin, feel the freedom of the body as the body moves freely in space. Take on the carefree nature of the baby. Move your arms and legs freely in space. Imagine that you have just finished eating and are being held warmly in the arms of your mother, feeling the warm sensation that passes over your body as the milk reaches your stomach. Enjoy your mother's smile of approval and her warm cooing to get your attention. Become completely engrossed in the interaction with your mother as she meets all your needs and you fall gently asleep, fulfilled and relaxed.

Hold this image as long as you like and then gently return to reality.

Special Considerations for Children with Long-term Illness.   The child with long-term illness can be successfully taught to use relaxation techniques. However, some children do not have control of their muscles, so deliberately trying to relax the individual muscle groups is difficult or impossible. In this case, the child is still encouraged to relax the muscles, but specific muscle groups are not identified in the process. Music provides a means for the child to feel the benefits of relaxation. Relaxation can also be achieved through water therapy. A child with extensive muscle involvement can feel relaxed by the buoyancy of the water.

Enthusiasm is contagious. Therefore, a role model who has enthusiasm for the technique encourages the child to try relaxation techniques as part of his or her daily routine. Modeling relaxation techniques aids the child in developing the skills.

When there are muscle groups that are causing pain, these muscles are omitted from attention during the relaxation process. The painful muscle may feel improved by relaxation of other muscles, but trying to deliberately relax a painful muscle is not encouraged.

Stressful situations are more common to children with long-term illnesses than to children who are healthy. These stressful situations can be caused by diagnostic procedures, evaluative methods, prescribed therapies, separations from family and/or friends, and fear of the unknown. Stress can reduce the child's ability to cope with situations in his or her life. Stress management is facilitated by the use of relaxation techniques. It is advised that the child be introduced to these techniques at an early point in his or her long-term illness. Relaxation can be combined with other techniques, such as therapeutic play and music therapy, to help the child to cope with stress-producing situations.

The position the child assumes during relaxation is influenced by the long-term illness. A child who is wheelchair-bound can do the relaxation while seated in the wheelchair. It is important to have the child feel as unrestricted as possible, but safety should be maintained by keeping the child's seat belt in place. A variation of the technique can be achieved by having the child do the exercises before getting out of bed in the morning or before a rest period.

It may take longer to teach some children with long-term illness how to gain competency in relaxation techniques. Repetition of directions and role modeling help the child with a learning deficit to achieve the goal.

Relaxation techniques can help the child to cope with painful or uncomfortable procedures. The child can prepare for the procedure by listening to the audiotapes and then use the tapes during the procedure. Following the procedure, the tapes can be used to regain relaxation of muscles that contracted during the procedure despite attempts at relaxation.

REFERENCES

Burchard, J.D. Competitive youth sports and social competence. In M.W. Kent & J.E. Rolf (Eds.), *Primary prevention of psychopathology*, vol 3: *Social competence in children.* Hanover, N.H.: University Press of New England, 1979.

Buscaglia, L.F. *Personhood.* Thorofare, N.J.: Charles B. Slack, 1978.

Cox-Gedmark, J. *Coping with physical disability.* Philadelphia: Westminster Press, 1980.

Davidson, R.J. & Schwartz, G.E. The psychology of relaxation and relaxed states: A multi-process theory. In *Behavior control and modification of physiological activity.* Englewood Cliffs, N.J.: Prentice–Hall, 1976.

Diamond, E.F., Heffelfinger, J.C., Kennell, J., et al. Athletic activities by children with skeletal abnormalities. *Pediatrics* 51:949, 1973.

Flynn, T.G., Kennell, J.H., McLeod, R.N., et al., Injuries to young athletes. *Pediatrics* 65:649, 1980.

Galton, L. *Your child in sports.* New York: Franklin Watts, 1980.

Kobasa, S.C. Stressful life events, personality and health: An inquiry into hardiness. *Journal of Personality and Social Psychology* 39:1, 1979.

National Institute of Mental Health. *Research on sleep and dreams.* Washington, D.C.: U.S. Department of Health, Education, and Welfare, 1976.

Nurenberger, P. *Freedom from stress: A holistic approach.* Honesdale, Penn.: Himalayan International Press, 1981.

Pelletier, K.R. *Holistic Medicine.* New York: Delta, 1979.

Pepitone, A., & Kleiner, R. The effect of threat and frustration on group cohesiveness. *Journal of Abnormal and Social Psychology* 54:192, 1957.

Pipes, P.L. *Nutrition in infancy and childhood.* St. Louis: Mosby, 1977.

Selye, H. *The stress of life.* New York: McGraw–Hill, 1976.

Swami Rama. Introduction. In P. Nurenberger P. (Ed.), *Freedom from stress.* Honesdale, Penn: Himalayan International Press, 1981.

Selye, H. *The stress of life.* New York: McGraw–Hill, 1976.

Thornton, M.L., Eng, G.D., Kennell, J.H., et al. Cardiac evaluation for participation in sports. American Academy of Pediatrics Position Statement, 1977.

Williams, R.J. *Nutrition against disease.* New York: Bantam, 1973.

BIBLIOGRAPHY

Bailey, C. *Fit or fat?* Boston: Houghton Mifflin, 1978.

Bauman, E., Brint, A.I., Piper, L. *The holistic health handbook.* Berkeley, Calif.: And/Or Press, 1978.

Bruhn, J., & Cordova, F.D. A developmental approach to learning wellness behavior, Part II: Adolescence to maturity. *Health Values: Achieving High-level Wellness* 2:16, 1978.

Palmer, B.B., & Lewis, C.E. Development of health attitudes and behaviors. *Journal of School Health* 46:7, 1976.

Parcel, G.S., & Meyer, M.P. Development of an instrument to measure children's locus of control. *Health Education Monographs* 6:2, 1978.

Pentecuff, J. Development of the concept of self: Implications for the teacher's role in promotion of mental health. *Educational Horizons* 55:15, 1976.

Pratt, L. Childrearing methods and children's health behavior. *Journal of Health and Social Behavior* 14:61, 1973.

Rose, K.D. Which cardiovascular "problems" should disqualify athletes? *Physician and Sports Medicine* 3:62, 1975.

Rutter, M. Protective factors in children's responses to stress and disadvantage. In M.W. Kent, & J.E. Rolf (Eds.), *Primary prevention of psychopathology*, vol. 3: *Social competence in children.* Hanover, N.H.: University Press of New England, 1979.

Selye, H. (Ed.). *Selye's guide to stress research*, vol. 1. New York: Van Nostrand, 1980.

Sinacore, J.S. Priorities in health education. *Journal of School Health* 48:123, 1978.

Swogger, G. Toward understanding stress: A map of the territory. *Journal of School Health* 51:29, 1981.

Upton, G. *Physical and creative activities for the mentally handicapped.* Cambridge, England: Cambridge University Press, 1979.

U.S. Department of Health and Human Services. *Children and youth in action: physical activities and sports.* DHHS Pub. no. (OHDS) 80-30182. Washington, D.C., 1980.

U.S. Department of Health and Human Services. *Leisure time activities: A resource manual for developmentally disabled individuals and their advocates.* DHHS pub. no. (OHDS) 80-29006. Washington, D.C., 1980.

U.S. Department of Health and Human Services. *Exercise and your heart.* NIH pub. no. 81-1677. Bethesda, Md., 1981.

3

General Ideas in Relation to Long-term Illness in Childhood

Shirley Steele

The increasing incidence of long-term illness (chronic illness) in the child population is partially due to life-saving medical advances, which have offered new opportunities for children who are born with or who develop life-threatening conditions. The increasing incidence of long-term illness makes it imperative for health care professionals to focus special attention on the health needs of the affected children.

Many of the problems associated with children with long-term illlness originate in fragmentation of the health services they receive.

The reasons that children with long-term illness do not receive adequate health care supervision are many and complex.

The financial burden of a long-term illness is often cited as a cause for discontinuity in services. This is certainly a more significant factor for families with limited income than for families with higher incomes and third-party health insurance. State aid programs are continually changing, and it is imperative to keep up to date with current area coverage in order to help families assess their eligibility for financial assistance. Families can often take care of the majority of the expenses they incur, but they may need some assistance with particular needs, such as the need for a new lower-extremity prosthesis.

Another possibility for the lack of consistency in health care services for children with long-term illness may be related to geographic distance. Services are still clustered near large medical centers and tend to be less accessible for persons who have the most difficulty providing their own transportation. The decline in availability of public transportation has added to this problem. In assessing the community, it is possible to find such circumstances as the following: families are not eligible for particular services because they do not live in a prescribed geographic area, they are not in a particular economic category, or their child is mentally retarded as well as physically handicapped. Each community has unique requirements for eligibility for services that may exclude certain children who could potentially benefit from the services that are available.

Pluckham (1972) suggests that the nurse is prohibited from using judgment by specific policies and rules that limit the nurse's ability to deliver expert services. She suggests that other professionals and employing agencies tend to establish practices that underutilize the nurse in general health care delivery. This is also seen in the delivery of services to children with long-term illness. Some agencies that provide services to these children do not employ a nurse and tend to underestimate the services that a nurse could provide to enhance the child's ability to reach his or her maximum potential. When a nurse is employed, she or he is frequently utilized to keep records, check on follow-up appointments, and so forth, rather than in a more contemporary professional nursing capacity. This underutilization of qualified nursing personnel may partially explain why some children and their families do not get adequate assistance in learning skills for daily living or in making use of community agencies and getting proper placement and services in school. In addition, the whole range of nursing functions related to health teaching and counseling is frequently not available to these children and their families on a consistent basis.

Hannam (1975) states that the parents of handicapped children whom he interviewed were relatively self-reliant and competent people. He states that they frequently expressed the opinion that they felt they had to fight for anything they got for their children. This "fight-minded" approach can lead to isolation for some parents, and when such a situation prevails, it is easy to see why some children do not receive adequate services. They become the victims of the resentment built up toward their parents by the health establishment. If services are lacking and the professionals do not institute new ones, it appears that only parents who have enough initiative and insight will eventually stimulate the right people to get the services that they feel they need for their children.

Another salient reason for inadequate health services is that it takes time for parents to absorb the information they are given. If too much responsibility is given to them when they are anxious, they may forget or become confused by the suggestions. Written and verbal directions are helpful in clarifying what is expected of the parent. Opportunities to check back with the parents about progress will also help to facilitate follow-through on plans.

The child with a long-term illness can be a real challenge to nurses, as well as to other medical personnel and to his or her family. The child develops some unique qualities which are formulated as a result of living with an illness. The way the child learns to live with his or her disability will be influenced by the way others respond to him or her.

DELIVERY OF CARE

The care of many children with long-term illness is provided in a rehabilitation center. The rehabilitation center has the advantage of offering the child and family the expert knowledge, skill, and therapy available through an interdisciplinary team approach to client management.

Interdisciplinary Team

The interdisciplinary team offers a convenient and effective way to manage the care of children with long-term illness. The members of the team can vary from one rehabilitation center to another, but most teams are composed of members that can offer the child an opportunity to achieve his or her highest level of achievement. Common members of an interdisciplinary team for rehabilitation of children include the following:

1. Index child and significant others.
2. Primary physician, frequently a pediatrician.
3. Physician specialists (orthopaedist, surgeon, urologist, ophthalmologist, psychiatrist).
4. Clinical nurse specialist.
5. Staff nurses.
6. Occupational therapist.
7. Physical therapist.
8. Speech therapist and/or pathologist.
9. Educational–vocational counselor.
10. Psychologist.
11. Dentist.
12. Nutritionist and/or dietician.
13. Health educator.
14. Special education teachers.
15. Biomedical engineer.
16. Music and art therapist.
17. Social worker.

The central theme of the interdisciplinary team effort is to provide collaboration between the child and his or her caretakers and the health care providers in the rehabilitation center in an effort to successfully integrate the child into the community. With an interdisciplinary approach, each team member is expected to share his or her expertise with other members of the team and to communicate a basic understanding of his or her particular discipline to other team members. The team, in collaboration with the child and significant others, establishes a plan of management that promotes the highest level of independence and self-satisfaction for the child (Fig. 3-1). The adjustment of the child to society is based on the collaboration and support that is offered by the rehabilitation center in conjunction with the services available in the child's home and community.

Rehabilitation programs go beyond offering isolated services to children to offering a coordinated and intensive program that focuses on such areas as:

1. Locomotion and mobility.
2. Communication.
3. Independence in self-care activities.
4. Integration into the family unit.
5. Integration into the local community.

Figure 3-1. The interdisciplinary team, including the child client, discuss the child's progress using the health record.

6. Referral to appropriate agencies.
7. Consideration of biologic, psychologic, sociologic, and cultural components of care.
8. Use of adaptive appliances to encourage self-help.

The rehabilitation center format requires a high ratio of health care providers to clients. While this may not initially seem cost-effective, this intensive therapy is in the long run often less costly than traditional modes of care, because anticipatory guidance is given to decrease secondary costly problems. The integration of persons with disabilities within the family constellation can prevent a long, expensive period of institutionalization. In addition, the psychologic effects gained from an intensive rehabilitation program may not be measurable in dollars and cents, but they are certainly relevant to the child and significant others.

The term *interdisciplinary* is used rather than the term *multidisciplinary* because interdisciplinary suggests that collaboration and negotiation are part of the rehabilitation process. *Transdisciplinary* might even be a more appropriate term, as this term suggests that the care cuts across disciplines. Whatever the nomenclature, the philosophy that permeates a rehabilitation center is that the client is at the core of the activities and is put into action in the rehabilitation process.

In order for an interdisciplinary team to function effectively and efficiently, each health care provider needs to have a great deal of self-confidence in his or her respective role and also in being able to relate to persons in other roles. Many health care providers know their own disciplines and the contributions they can make to the client's care, but are less familiar with other disciplines and their unique roles; thus education is essential in enabling team members to interact effectively with one another.

Coordinated Care

The team approach is based on the assumption that a coordinated team approach can result in a focus on the "whole" child and cut down on the fragmentation of care that the child and family receive. An essential component of the care is collaboration among team members and the coordination of services. Ducanis and Golin (1979) state that the interdisciplinary team is composed of individuals with varied specialized training who coordinate their activities to provide services to a client or a group of clients. In this model, coordination is another key concept that is associated with rehabilitation programs.

Coordination becomes more difficult as the size of the team increases and as the number of disciplines that are represented increases. The delegation of activities among members becomes increasingly complex. The assumption is made, however, that the collective knowledge and skill of team members can result in a greater output than individual efforts produce.

Nurses as Part of an Interdisciplinary Team

The evolving role of the nurse influences the nurse's participation in the rehabilitation program for children. There are many areas of the child's care in which the nurse can make significant contributions. The nurse's role is influenced by the other members of the team as well as by the expertise and preparation of the nurse. Frequently, nursing care management is coordinated by a master's-prepared clinical nurse specialist or a pediatric nurse practitioner. Nurses with these preparations are able to administer primary care to children with long-term illness. Contributions of nurses to the child's care are varied, but they can include any of the following:

1. Comprehensive family history.
2. Health assessment, including physical examination.
3. Health promotion, including planning programs in safety, rest and sleep, exercise, recreation, and nutrition.
4. Health education, both general and specific to the particular health problem.
5. Counseling of the index child and other family members.
6. Interviewing individual family members and significant others.
7. Administering nursing procedures.
8. Writing protocols for care.
9. Making referrals.
10. Collaboration with other team members.

11. Influencing community policies related to the long-term needs of children.
12. Collaborating with school personnel in the community.
13. Providing educational experiences for other nurses.
14. Assisting families to integrate the child and his or her special needs into the family unit.
15. Designing and implementing nursing research studies.
16. Collaborating in research studies of other disciplines.
17. Preparation for procedures and hospitalizations.
18. Evaluating outcomes of care.
19. Genetic counseling and screening.
20. Publishing scholarly papers and presentations at meetings.
21. Interpreting the nursing role to others.

The nurse that coordinates the total contributions of nursing personnel is also responsible for intraprofessional activities. In some rehabilitation programs, there are a variety of health care providers that are involved in nursing services. Such health care providers include nurses' aides, dormitory parents, transport personnel, staff nurses, client care coordinators, and, sometimes, recreational, art, and music therapy personnel. Recreational personnel can be employed by the agency or they can be volunteers from the community. While this intraprofessional subgroup reports directly to a specific nurse, it must be kept in mind that these health care providers are also members of the interdisciplinary team and have responsibility to be a part of the larger team as well as the nursing team.

Creativity is a key concept. A nurse who is able to use imagination and intuition is able to devise ways to improve the management of these children. As nursing is an art and a science, the use of creativity is essential. Creativity strongly supports the art of nursing and is governed by the right hemisphere of the brain. Many of the needs of these children call for using new and innovative approaches that can result from creative problem solving. The utilization of creative problem solving in conjunction with the nursing process can result in greater contributions of nurses to the client's care.

In order for nursing to be a viable and dynamic part of the interdisciplinary team, all the members of the intraprofessional team need to be interested in helping the child in self-management rather than in "doing things for" the child. The nurses' satisfaction has to be derived from seeing the child achieve goals by himself or herself rather than by doing things for the child. The nurse must be astute to know when to motivate the child to do more, when to offer assistance, and when assistance interferes with the child's self-maintenance goals. Observation of the child for signs of readiness to increase self-help functions is inherent in the nursing role. In addition, the family's willingness to allow the child increasing independence is assessed and encouraged concurrently as the child's self-help program progresses. At times, the nurse focuses more attention on the family than on the child as the family's cooperation is essential to the successful rehabilitation of the child.

Effectiveness of Interdisciplinary Teams

The effectiveness of an interdisciplinary team is partially determined by the team members' willingness to alter boundaries of their particular professional roles, when appropriate. There are many areas in health care delivery that can be effectively served by a diversity of health care professionals. Rigid boundaries are therefore inconsistent with effective team cooperation. One outcome of cooperation among members is that the client can benefit by being able to choose particular health care providers to assist in his or her development. If a client is taught physical therapy exercises by a physical therapist but has a better interpersonal relationship with a nurse, the nurse can supervise the ongoing utilization of physical therapy exercises in the overall rehabilitation program. The client and nurse can consult with the physical therapist when needed. In essence, the expertise of both the nurse and the physical therapist includes management of many activities of daily living, so each health care professional is capable of managing this aspect of care in collaboration with the child and family. Permeable boundaries of both professions allow the client to interact with the particular professional worker who best serves as a catalyst, confidant, and motivator in learning self-help activities.

The effectiveness of the team is also influenced by the setting where the care is delivered. Some settings allow health care professionals a great deal of flexibility in delivering services, while others have hierarchic structures that are inconsistent with the concept of flexibility. The rehabilitation program that offers the greatest potential good for the client is one in which flexibility is not only permitted but is encouraged.

Settings also influence the type of clients that can receive services. For example, there may be a policy that only clients in particular disease categories can receive services. In this instance, a child that does not fit into an identified disease category is excluded from service even when the services might be of benefit to him or her. Some policies are established within the setting, while other policies are established by outside forces, such as financial supporters, legal parameters, and societal constraints.

Another factor that influences the effectiveness of the team is the mission of the organization and whether or not this mission is consistent with the needs of society. Some agencies outlive their usefulness, while other agencies change in response to changing needs. For example, if an agency for the care of children with poliomyelitis did not redefine its mission, its team would be obsolete in today's society. Therefore, agencies must continually assess societal needs and prepare the team to effectively change its mission, when appropriate. Organizations that cannot redefine their goals to respond to changing needs and priorities will become obsolete. Team members are responsible for providing data to administrators of agencies that will help the agency to recognize the need for changes to keep the agency vital and to best serve the needs of clients.

The goals of the team members and of the agency need to be reasonably congruent for the mission of the agency to be achievable. When the goals of some members of the team are too divergent from the goals of the organization, they can have a negative impact on the functioning of the team. Similarly, when the whole team questions the goals of the agency without genuine cause, then the team can be ineffective in fulfilling the goals of the organization. When team members separate from the organization goals, the team can either disintegrate or develop its own set of goals. It is questionable whether a team can function effectively without agency support.

Territoriality

One of the major deterrents to learning the roles of other health care providers is the need by some persons to prescribe territorial domains that are specific to and closely guarded by one profession.

Pluckham (1972) describes behavior of health care professionals that illustrates the concept of professional territoriality. She suggests that man's possessive needs probably extend beyond physical territory and include a need to defend institutions, roles, professions, and areas of operation. There have been instances when children with a particular disease would benefit from other local services offered specifically for his or her condition, but the child was not referred because the professional providers did not wish to relinquish their care to others. Another example of such territoriality is when members of one professional discipline will not share the care of a child with another, as when a nurse does not recommend a child for intensive physical therapy even though the child would benefit from this referral.

The territorial concept also partially explains why some outpatient services have been slow to materialize. The hospital, which has traditionally held the most prestigious position in the health care delivery system, houses professionals who strongly support the acute-care setting and tend to impede the progress of outpatient and home care delivery, which is more conducive to the care of children with long-term illness. The hospital setting offers a convenient way to deliver services, as the child is in a sense a "captive audience." When members of particular disciplines, especially medical professionals, want to have laboratory tests done, surgical procedures scheduled, and so forth, it is convenient to have the child hospitalized. This model of care does not take into consideration the best alternatives for promoting family unity during long-term illness, but it does give the medical professionals the upper hand, as they possess the right to admit and discharge clients from the hospital (which other health care providers cannot do, except in a few progressive agencies). Generally speaking, the hospital territory is strongly controlled by the medical profession. The hospital is its territory.

In some hospitals the control of power by physicians is more evident than in other hospitals. Physicians are slowly learning that the client wants services that are focused on his or her well-being rather than services that are regulated by the needs of health care providers. Despite some changes in orientation, it is frequently assumed that the hospital setting is the territorial perspective of the medical profession, and a significant change in this orientation is not likely to occur in the near future.

In outpatient settings or in rehabilitation centers, the territorial rights can be less well-defined. While a physician frequently remains the "leader" of the team, other health care providers have significant roles in the client's care. In fact, it is possible for children to receive care in an outpatient setting without being seen by a physician, and it is possible for the child's care in a rehabilitation center to be coordinated by a health care provider who is not a physician. Even with these differences in delivery, territoriality can still be a factor. All health care providers can be guilty of wanting to "control their own turf." Territoriality can be overt, as in hospital care, or it can be covert. When territoriality is covert, it is more difficult to discover. However, it does become apparent over time. So, in the long-term care of children, territoriality is a significant factor to keep in mind.

Closely related to the concept of territoriality is the idea of health professionals as a work-force group, as described by Longest (1976). He suggests that health professionals have a high need for achievement and self-actualization and a keen interest in their work and in developing new knowledge. He further states that health care professionals generally have a low degree of loyalty to employing organizations, but a high commitment to specialized role skills. This description would favor inpatient services, as the professional in such a situation is able to maintain a greater control over clients and their families. Outpatient care would give greater control to the families. Inpatient care also favors intensive involvement with individual professional roles, with less consideration being given to team concepts.

It can be assumed that territoriality needs to be kept at a minimum in order for the team to function effectively.

Ducanis and Golin (1979) suggest that several areas related to professionalization need attention in order for the team to function effectively. These areas are:

1. Autonomy.
2. Specialization.
3. Division of tasks.
4. Ethics.
5. Delegation of authority.
6. Knowledge base and overlaps.
7. Roles and stereotypes.
8. Legal responsibilities.
9. Status.

It is evident from this list that territoriality can persist if these areas are not seriously considered by members of the team and if the implications of each area are not shared with team members.

Contracting

The self-help health model can be facilitated by using contracts. The goal of the contract is to help the child to achieve a desired end. The contract clearly states what the child wishes to do and sets a timetable for achieving this goal (Fig. 3-2).

The contract is based on the assumption that the child wants to make a change in his or her life that will contribute to healthy living. Because change is involved, it is usually necessary to establish ground rules to help establish the

I, _____contract to make
these changes:

GOAL:

I will, within _____ days, starting on _____,
complete this contract with myself or with   _____.
The following will help me to keep this contract:

In case of need, I will contact _____,
who is a source of support.

I know these things may get in the way of achieving my goal:

I will get the following reward for completing this contract:

Signed:

Date:

Figure 3-2.   Sample contract.

change. The child can be aided in his or her pursuit by consideration being given
to the following:

1. The change should be consistent with the child's self-image.
2. Positive reinforcement is beneficial.
3. Punishment as reinforcement is only suggested when it is self-administered.
4. Unconscious behaviors influence change and must also be considered.
5. Change is facilitated by declaring to others a willingness to change.
6. Having someone to act as a support person during the change is of paramount importance.
7. Time should be provided to regroup, as necessary.
8. Trying to change numerous things at one time is not wise.
9. Change takes place slowly, so discouragement is common.
10. The care giver should try to make the change seem like fun.

The following steps are part of the contract process:

1. Decide on a goal.
2. Examine the goal to see if it is realistic.

3. Write down the goal, forming a contract with yourself or someone else.

In the event that the contract cannot be kept as defined, it can be renegotiated. During renegotiation, the child is asked to go through the entire contracting process again. A new timetable is established and attempts are made to explore areas that interfered with successful completion of the contract.

When the contract is successfully completed, the child's assets are discussed with him or her and the reward is given. The child is encouraged to express his or her feelings about the contracted activity and about the change. In this way, the child learns that it is possible to make changes in his or her personal life through a concerted effort and a definitive plan of action.

Contracting is useful in bringing about improvement in such components of a child's life as diet, exercise programs, relaxation therapy, and sleep patterns. The success or failure of contracting rests with the child, so it is a viable strategy for encouraging healthy self-help practices.

IN THE HOSPITAL

Hospitalization of the child is covered in several other sections of this book. This section focuses on a general discussion of the hospitalization experience and how it facilitates or impedes the care given to a child with a long-term illness.

Profile of the Child. The child with a long-term illness is likely to want to know the nurse's name. He or she very often prefers to call the nurses by their first names. However, the child will abide by the customs of the institution. The child also expects everyone to know his or her name and delights in showing the other children how popular he or she is.

Children are likely to be well aware of rights on the hospital unit. They are often very authoritative when demanding or asking for things. They frequently find a very prominent place, such as the nurses' station, to spend a great deal of the day. Another favorite spot is by the elevator, where they can watch everyone get off and on. If there is an acutely ill child on the unit, they frequently guard that door to learn all they can about what is going on.

Hospital Vocabulary. The child who is hospitalized a great deal develops a hospital vocabulary, although he or she does not always know or comprehend exactly what is being verbalized. The terms may sound very convincing, but when the nurse explores further, the child is frequently found not to really know what he or she is talking about. Children use hospital vocabulary to impress people. They especially like to use it when new personnel arrive, using terms like NPO, OR, and OT as though every child knows them. These terms are less impressive, however, than very scientific-sounding descriptions of medical conditions and their treatment. Despite apparent satisfaction gained from using hospital jargon when it meets needs, children will pretend they do not understand when health care personnel use medical jargon.

Breaking the Rules. Children also know the rules of the institution and frequently learn how to break them. They delight in "outsmarting" the authority figures, such as the nursing supervisors, learning their schedules and planning activities around them. They soon learn that it is possible to be mischievous without there being much chance of being caught. In their planning, they usually use children with less knowledge about hospital routines; they seem to feel that children who are less well-known are less likely to get reprimanded. Their need to be independent and explore is usually met during these escapades.

Hospital Routines. The child also may become very involved with hospital routines and may get quite upset when the routines are not carried out on schedule. Hospitalized children are used to having wishes granted immediately because of the large number of helping adults that are around; when these wishes are not granted they can become quite intolerant.

The child is quite aware of treatments that are scheduled routinely and enjoys directing the nurse with these procedures. As a means of manipulating his or her environment, the child may refuse to have the treatments done by certain individuals. Any deviation from the usual way of performing treatments may result in great anxiety for the child. If the child has had a tracheostomy for a long time, he or she may prefer to suction and clean it himself or herself. If the nurse attempts to do this, his or her actions may result in any number of responses, such as refusal and temper tantrums. The child may also wish to have his or her parent perform the treatments in an effort to simulate home routines as much as possible. The child with a long-term illness frequently is much more dependent on parents than is the well child, and this dependence may be reflected in the child's unwillingness to have anyone other than the parent do particular treatments.

Tattling. The child also has a tendency to "tattle" on professionals. When you are changing the dressing, you may be told, "Miss Jones didn't use the forceps when handling the 4 × 4 dressings." The child will then watch you eagerly to see if you react to this piece of information. If the child gets a response, he or she is likely to continue to tell you such items of interest whenever the opportunity arises.

The child may also spend a great deal of time tattling on other children. This should be discouraged so that the child does not begin to act as the unit "security officer." A certain amount of tattling is normal for children, but it is easier to handle when the child is not hospitalized, with so many people as the recipients of "information." Tattling is probably an attention-seeking phenomenon. It is essential to provide the child with recognition so that he or she does not have to resort to this activity excessively.

Seeking Information. The child with a long-term illness also feels free to question how much is known about a particular problem. He or she has had a great deal of experience with people with varying degrees of competency and has learned to fear those who are least expert in the field. This is especially true in relation to blood work, injections, and other painful procedures. He or she likes and demands the most skillful person. This may present problems to the nursing student who is just learning child health nursing techniques and who may show a degree of hesitancy. The child may have a need to ask many questions that do not seem realistic to the professionals administering his or her care. He or she may show an unusually keen interest in minute details that frustrate busy people. Simple explanations specifically related to the child's questions help to alleviate concern. The child's persistence in seeking information is probably a reflection of insecurity in the situation. If the child is not answered abruptly or sarcastically, he or she will probably be satisfied and reassured by the answers that are given to such questions.

Placement in the Hospital. The child with a long-term illness may also develop a desire to be on a specific unit or in a specific room. He or she may be far less comfortable when put in an area which is not of his or her choosing. As the child gets older, it may be increasingly difficult to make him or her happy with his or her hospital placement. The child may resent being in with toddlers or hearing them cry. The adolescent with long-term illness frequently does not fit in with adult patients, as he or she is often less mature than would be normal for his or her age. An adolescent unit is ideal for meeting the needs of clients in this age group.

Changing Hospitals. The child who has received health supervision from a children's hospital may find it disturbing to be ineligible, by virtue of age, to continue with familiar health care. On the other hand, some children with long-term illness are eager to change their care so they do not have to tell their friends they are going to a "children's hospital." The reputation of the facility in the community also has a bearing on how the child perceives it. This is especially significant to the adolescent. If the hospital has a positive program for adolescents, the child may be more content to continue going to it. If the adolescent is treated as a second-rate citizen, he or she may be eager to change.

As a Family Member. A child who is hospitalized for long periods may have a very superficial idea of what it actually is to be a member of a family. His or her absences from home are frequent or long, which can loosen ties. The family may consider the child as a burden, financially or socially. They may use the periods of separation caused by hospitalization to recuperate from the strain caused by the long-term illness. This separation is often interpreted by the nursing personnel as lack of interest or even neglect. The staff, which can become very attached to the child, may become resentful of the family that does not seem tremendously attached to the child. This can result in a disturbed nurse–family relationship. The child gets in the middle of this and begins to try to get the staff to side more and more with him or her, creating a bigger gap between the staff and his or her parents. The child may decide to ignore his or her parents when they do visit. The child's attitude makes family members further deny their importance to the child, and their visits are made even less frequently.

The separation from siblings can be lessened if visiting restrictions are made more flexible. It is beneficial to have the other siblings visit the hospital and vicariously learn what hospitalization means to their brother or sister. Visiting provides them with an opportunity to witness, first hand, some of the situations that their brother or sister must face. They are better able to appreciate that hospitalization can be stressful as well as beneficial. Visiting also allows for a continuity in the peer relationships of the children.

Privacy.   The child needs an area that he can identify as his or her own. The child with long-term illness does not feel so comfortable if he or she is moved frequently to "make room" for new admissions. There should be an area where he or she can have private belongings and not worry that they will be moved when he or she is not present. He or she should be encouraged to clean his or her own area and to keep personal items put away.

Possessions.   The child's possessions can be very important to him or her, and their true significance is rarely fully appreciated by the nurse. The child's possessions may take on an additional significance if the child is separated by long distances from significant others. The possessions tend to help to decrease the distance between home and hospital. Possessions used in this way are frequently referred to as transitional items. They help in the transition from a home to a hospital environment. They help in the transition from being a free person in the outside world to being a less free person in an institutional setting. They provide visual evidence that the child is still connected with the outside environment.

If any of the child's possessions are taken home by the family, it should be with the child's full knowledge. This will save a great deal of searching for missing objects. Children feel more secure when treasured possessions are kept in the hospital throughout the hospitalization period.

Simple Chores.   The child also benefits by having simple chores that help him or her feel a part of the hospital. He or she may be expected to put the tablecloth on the table, or distribute the mail, or help compile new charts. If he or she has a chore, it is important to insist that it is done. The chores should also be changed periodically so one does not become bored. He or she may ask to do certain tasks but easily tire of them. Competition with other children with long-term illness may be healthy. Children are used to competition and competition can be beneficial if one child is not consistently the loser. All children need to have some positive experiences in order to be willing to become involved in competition.

Handling Money.   The child also needs assistance in learning to manage money. He or she has fewer chances than the "normal" child to spend money. If hospitalized for long periods, he or she should have an allowance, as do his or her peers. This is especially important for the late-school-age child and the adolescent. They can use their money to buy newspapers, magazines, or small items in the gift shop. If they are interested, they may buy supplies and make small articles to sell or give as gifts. The child will not always buy wisely, but this is also part of the learning experience. The child should not be allowed to "solicit" money from visitors. This will establish a pattern that is difficult to break. The child needs to know how to make money "safe," and precautions should be taken to make sure the money is not stolen.

The availability of coins to use in the pay telephone often poses a problem. Many facilities are not equipped with change-makers, and the child may become bothersome if he or she needs change at an inopportune time. Helping the child to make early plans about the day's expenses enable him or her to seek change early in the day so that he or she has it when ready to place calls. This attention to financial matters gives the child responsibility for planning activities; it also fosters better adult–child relationships.

School.   School is an especially important experience for the child with long-term illness. If no formal schooling is provided in the setting, the nurse is responsible for setting aside a time for the child to do schoolwork. If it is not possible to get books from the child's teacher, books with very explicit directions are readily available in stores. The child is encouraged to do an assignment a day. In addition, there may be school activities (such as drawing) that will increase the child's interest (Fig. 3-3). To study, the child needs an area comparatively free from distractions. Study is usually more interesting if two or more children are studying together. This more closely simulates an ordinary class situation.

The key criterion in providing schooling is consistency. Schoolwork must be planned and implemented in a systematic fashion to meet this criterion. The child knows exactly when schooltimes are scheduled and should be ready to participate in school activities. If the schooltimes are not consistent, the child tends to underestimate the importance of schooling and tends to forget to attend to this very vital part of his or her life.

Many child health facilities have school services to meet the needs of children with long-term illness. The school teachers are valuable members of the health care delivery team and offer age-appropriate learning activities for the child throughout the hospitalization period.

Church or Chapel.   Depending on the institution, chapel or church services may or may not be easily accessible. Most institutions have an area provided for quiet meditation. However, many do not actually have church services. If the child is used to attending Sunday school classes, he or she will usually miss them if they are not available. Inexpensive, illustrated books of children's prayers and hymns can provide a substitute. An area supplied with children's hymnals and an altar can also be made available for the children to hold their own church services in. If the nurse feels comfortable participating with the children, she or he should feel free to do so. The children enjoy learning simple hymns and prayers. These can also be said at bedtime, either as a group or individually. In addition, pastoral care in the major faiths is usually available to most institutions. Many church-affiliated hospitals have very active programs in the children's area. The parents

Figure 3-3.   The school-age child continues school work while hospitalized. The school teacher from home sends him audiotapes to supplement the work provided by the hospital school teachers. *(Photo by D. Haskin)*

are usually helpful in contacting the religious advisor of their choice if they prefer additional spiritual guidance for their child.

The adolescent may be able to leave the hospital and attend a local house of worship. This requires a physician's approval.

Many television and radio stations provide services for shut-ins. If these are chosen, every opportunity is made to have the child actively participate in the program. Passively watching the television or listening to the radio is not as beneficial as actively involving the child in the process.

Admissions of Other Children.   Admissions of other children to the unit may pose a threat to the child. He or she may view them as infringing on his or her territory or his or her adopted family. The new child may require extensive care, and this cuts down on the time given the child with less acute problems. The newly admitted child may also receive a great deal of parental attention as well as gifts, and this may make the child with a long-term illness resentful. The child who has been there a long time may greet the new parents and often will request gifts and favors from them. He or she learns that parents easily feel sorry for children who are hospitalized for long periods or children who do not have visitors. Frequently the child is able to manipulate the parents so much that they have difficulty visiting with their own child. The parents may feel obligated to bring gifts of toys and food to the child. This often complicates the nurse's role as she or he tries to discipline the child or maintain a therapeutic diet. The parent who becomes involved with "long-term" children on a unit may need to be consulted and informed about the needs of the child with the long-term illness. This consulting need not be considered as a violation of the child's privacy. It is rather a necessary part of the medical and nursing supervision needed to guarantee the best possible care to the child who is hospitalized for long periods.

It is important to introduce the children to each other. Sometimes children have difficulty introducing themselves. It is wise to add an additional statement, such as, "John has been in the hospital a long time, probably much longer than you will need to be; he can help you find your way around." This statement helps to allay any anxiety the new child might have about an extended hospitalization and also acknowledges the fact that John has something special he can offer to the new child.

Discharge of Other Children.   Discharges can also produce a stress situation for the child. The hospitalized child sees other children admitted and discharged, and he or she wishes to be discharged too. He or she also makes friends within the hospital, and group relationships are broken each time a child is discharged. While he or she may long to go home, the child may also fear losing the security he or she feels in the hospital. The hospital may be a protection against many of the afflictions he or she endures on the outside. This is especially so in relation to children with physical disabilities who are subject to being stared at or made fun of in the outside world. They like the security of being around health care personnel who are not so likely to be "shocked" by their appearance. At the time of a friend's discharge, the child may wish to exchange addresses or telephone numbers in order to maintain the friendship.

Activities of Daily Living.   The child who is hospitalized for long periods may lack many of the outside experiences of daily living. The child who is physically disabled may be more deprived in this area, since even when sent home he or she may not receive enough stimulation and exposure to everyday experiences. Every attempt should be made to take these children out for walks or to give them weekend passes so they do not become completely deprived of normal experiences. Utilization of volunteers to help with such excursions is very effective. The volunteer often enjoys providing the child with special experiences that elicit positive responses from the child.

Volunteers.   The volunteers utilized in the care of children with long-term illness include persons in a variety of age categories. The grandmother or grandfather is as important as the young high school student. The college student serves another function. The roles of the sexes cannot be underestimated. Males with long-term illness need male figures who do not hurt or examine them. They need the attention of healthy males who exhibit male roles after which they can model themselves. They need to see the ordinary street wear of the male. They benefit from hearing male slang. Diversity is extremely important for both the female and the male with long-term illness, and exposure to many nonmedical persons is needed to provide a balanced sense of the outside world.

Street Clothes.   The child with a long-term illness benefits from wearing everyday street clothes, as opposed to hospital garb or pajamas and robe. The more natural attire may make it easier to retain contacts with people on the outside. It also helps the nursing staff and visitors to relate to the child in a more ordinary fashion. Somehow, the child seems "less sick" if he or she is up and dressed (Fig. 3-4).

Wearing his or her own clothes also gives the child a reason to look after his or her own belongings, which situation more closely resembles the situation at home. The child can be responsible for washing out socks or small items. This may serve as a chore that is easily accomplished.

Hobbies.   The child is encouraged to continue with hobbies that provided satisfaction at home. Tropical fish or goldfish can easily be accomodated in the hospital unit. Children frequently respond quickly to new pets that are easily maintained in the hospital, such as turtles or hamsters. These smaller animals

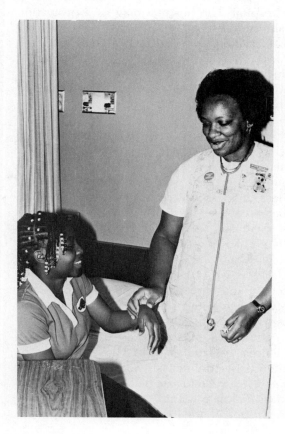

Figure 3-4. The adolescent wears her own clothing while hospitalized.

can sometimes take the place of the bigger, more familiar pets the children have at home.

Another means of supplying pets to children with long-term illness is to have a program similar to that of a lending library. The animal is brought in for a few hours from a veterinarian's office or a zoo to visit in the playroom or hospital lobby. The animal is specifically chosen for its love for children. A responsible adult is present for the entire time the children are visiting with the animal. Children who are used to having pets gain a great deal from this exposure. The period can also be used to introduce children to types of animals they did not previously know about or have close contact with.

Many hobbies can be pursued in the hospital. Examples of easily transported and continued hobbies include stamp collecting, model building, coin collecting, and paper doll collecting.

Trips. The child with a long-term illness can also be taken to the local zoo to see animals. A museum visit may also be beneficial. This trip might stimulate interest in a hobby of collecting pictures of animals, such as butterflies. The trips to these areas can be less expensive in terms of professional time if volunteers are effectively solicited for the project. Volunteers are frequently very knowledgeable about areas that provide good field trip experiences. Any activities planned outside the hospital require the permission of the physician and of the child's parent or guardian.

Limit Setting. The child is exposed to reasonable and realistic limits while hospitalized. This is also carried on after discharge. Limits are very important to the child in that they allow him or her to know his or her boundaries and feel free to function within them. The child should not have free reign, as this does not adequately prepare him or her to live in our society. Limit setting can be very difficult when many persons are involved in the child's management. Consistency is a key concept in making limits reasonable and achievable.

Bathing. The child's care is planned to be as home-like as possible. The normal child is rarely bathed from a basin. He or she is more familiar with the bathtub or shower. If his or her condition warrants it, the home routine is continued. This bath period can be a water-play period for the preschool child who delights in it. For the older child it offers a close association with home.

The bath time is scheduled with the assistance of the child. If he or she prefers to bathe at bedtime, such a routine is established. Special care is taken to be certain that bathing supplies are always replenished. The child is given responsibility for taking his or her own bath if he or she is old enough and capable of assuming responsibility for this aspect of his or her care.

Children with developmental lags will need to have definite programs established to help them achieve the goal of independent functioning in relation to activities of daily living. The plan should be simple. One task is mastered at a time. Repetition and rewards are essential to the program. The child is given adequate time to master the task before the adult providers give assistance.

Recreation and Play.   Play is discussed in detail in another chapter. The nurse utilizes other available team members, such as the play therapist, volunteers, and occupational therapists, to help with the recreational component of the child's care. Recreation is an essential element in the child's life, and other interested citizens can provide movies, slides, or film strips for evening entertainment. More adequately equipped facilities have swings, slides, and monkey bars for the children. Hospital excursions can also be planned. A planned scavenger hunt (collecting inexpensive hospital items such as tongue blades, cotton balls, and soap) can be great fun. With a little preplanning, items can be satisfactorily hidden in the area chosen for conducting the hunt.

Settling In.   The child admitted from a fairly segregated community may experience "culture shock" when first admitted to an integrated hospital setting. The child may quickly be exposed to children of many cultural and ethnic backgrounds. This experience can be very valuable to the child. However, the child may need help in adjusting to the situation. A child who has heard bigoted remarks about another race may begin to incorporate this into his or her own thinking. He or she may find it extremely difficult to be sharing a room with a child of a different race. Fortunately, children seem to accept others for what they really are, and adjustment periods usually evolve into keen friendships. The exposure the child has to other cultural and ethnic groups can prove to be one of the most positive outcomes of long periods of hospitalization. The sharing of experiences during periods of stress with children from all backgrounds may make the child better able to function in the competitive outside world after discharge.

Maturation.   An important factor to keep in mind is that the child will grow socially, mentally, emotionally, spiritually, and physically during hospitalization and illness if an adequate environment is provided. This knowledge makes it necessary to adjust the plan of care to meet the child's changing needs. Each time the child is seen, a new evaluation of progress is made; in this way it is possible to respond appropriately to the maturing child.

Goal Setting.   The short-term and long-term goals of nursing management are spelled out specifically. Some goals can be made independently by the nurse and shared with the child and family for acceptance, others can be made in conjunction with the client and family, and others can be made in collaboration with other members of the health care team. The long-term goals include, in addition to the plans for the hospitalization period, specific discharge planning and follow-up plans.

Preparation for Procedures.

1. Determine what the parents and physician have already told the child about the procedure.

2. Select an appropriate place to hold the discussion, preferably a place that is free from interruptions during the time needed to complete the discussion.

3. Assess the child's level of understanding by talking to the child about a topic that is age-appropriate, such as a game that is currently in vogue.

4. Arrange seating so that eye contact can be maintained with both the child and the adults. If it is a short explanation and seating is not possible, be sure to make eye contact with the child as well as with the adults.

5. Open the discussion by encouraging the child and adults to ask questions freely, and periodically invite questions during the session.

6. Relate facts about the procedure, using examples that include use of the senses. Use terms that are familiar to the child, such as "cool like running cold water" or "like the roar of a car engine." Vividly portray the experience to the child. Provision of empty facts about the procedure is not adequate preparation for most children, as their level of cognition does not prepare them to use the facts to make the upcoming situation understandable. Note: use visual and auditory materials, when available, to assist in the explanation.

7. If choices can be made, offer the child a choice. Often there is no choice about having the procedure, but there are choices about the way the procedure is conducted that allow the child to feel that he or she has some control. For example, if blood is to be drawn from an arm, the child can be asked if he or she prefers that the right or the left arm be used. If the child can either sit or lie down during the procedure, then, he or she can also be given this second choice.

8. Break the explanation of the procedure down into small parts that can be understood by the child. For example, skin preparation can be explained and demonstrated and the child can ask questions and play out this part of the procedure before further information is provided. Note: use terms and words that are age-appropriate. Avoid medical or scientific terminology prior to school age. When using this terminology with school-age or adolescent children, give a lay explanation as well as the scientific terms.

9. If it is a long procedure and the parent will assist in the procedure, have the parent explain how he or she will assist the child during the procedure (the nurse will be certain that the parent has the accurate information to do this).

10. If the procedure is done in stages, prepare the young child prior to each stage, rather than trying to complete the entire preparation at one time. An example of this type of procedure is a glucose tolerance test.

11. Have the child, if age and disability permit, explain or demonstrate what he or she understands from the explanation of the procedure.

In this way, you can determine whether the child has been able to listen to and internalize most of the information that was conveyed in the explanation. It is also possible to correct misinformation with this strategy.

12. Throughout the explanation and during the child's return explanation, make verbal and nonverbal gestures that are appropriate for relaying approval, concern, and empathy. For example, touching the child's hand can convey concern, placing an arm around the child's shoulder can convey empathy, and clapping the hands in approval can signal a child's success.

13. Preparation for painful procedures can also include the use of imagery.

Charting. Modalities for charting information vary from one agency to another. The important point to remember is that the nurse has a responsibility to collect and record information. The way it is collected or recorded is influenced by particular work situations. However, nurses have the responsibility to record observations and to systematically assess the child's progress. Otherwise, only custodial care might be given to the child with a long-term illness. The progress notes should include such items as the child's response to the parents' telephone call or the child's enthusiasm or lack of it for sending postcards. They should also include whether the child reacted positively or negatively to suggestions offered by the parents, as well as include information about whether the parent wanted to talk to the nurse about the child's progress or whether this information had to be given to the parent without a specific request. The progress notes also include new ideas for maintaining a child–parent relationship. An example would be scheduling a visit by the parent and including in this schedule any special services requested by the parent, such as an interview with the physician or a financial counselor. The progress notes include nursing interventions specific to these requests. Children with long-term illness have large charts that are not always utilized effectively by health care providers. Charting that is specific, objective, and timely contributes to the effective care of children with long-term illness.

Parents of Children with Long-term Illness. The parents of the child who is hospitalized frequently are not always well-informed about hospital policies. It is often falsely assumed that repeated exposure to a situation makes one extremely knowledgeable about it. This is not always true, and it is especially important to help the parents receive the information they need or desire. One very important area of concern to parents is the use or misuse of "specialists." Specialists in particular fields of pediatrics are frequently utilized. The parents may not be aware that a new physician is being utilized. They may not realize the need for the physician and, in their ignorance, they may be opposed to having her or him on consultation. The specialist may be known to the parents only by the bill they receive for services rendered. This type of incident rarely occurs with acute illness, but it is quite common with children with long-term illness. It is imperative that parents receive the necessary consideration and information when their child is in continual need of health care supervision.

THE FAMILY OF THE CHILD WITH LONG-TERM ILLNESS

To understand the implications of long-term illness to the family, one must draw upon the work of sociologists and social psychologists. They help to put into perspective the family as it exists in present-day society. We can then more easily understand some of the reasons that families react the way they do to illness.

The individual roles of family members are increasing in variety. Many authors are hesitating to categorize roles of family members, because these roles are undergoing a period of transition. During this transition period, it is difficult to explain role expectations without being open to criticism. Generalizations about families are also difficult to make. Laing (1972, p. 3) states, "We speak of families as though we all knew what families are. We identify, as families, networks of people who live together over periods of time, who have ties of marriage and kinship to one another. The more one studies family dynamics, the more unclear one becomes as to the ways family dynamics compare and contrast with the dynamics of other groups not called families, let alone the ways the families themselves differ." The family as a unit will be discussed first. Knowing perfectly well that it is difficult, if not impossible, to describe the role expectations of families of children with long-term illness, the following broad guidelines are offered as an orientation in beginning to understand this complex social unit.

The unit may be comprised of many small systems, depending on the numbers and types of participants. Within this unit there are a number of interrelationships. Anything that affects one member of the family, directly or indirectly, affects all the other members. The degree to which people are affected varies from member to member. The family is also affected and altered by the environment in which it exists.

These factors are especially important to health care professionals working with children with long-term illness. They are probably even more significant when the long-term illness is acquired rather than congenital. In an acquired illness, the role of the child in the family has already been established and has to be adjusted to the new illness. The interrelationships the child has in the family may be drastically changed due to illness, whereas the child who is born with a long-term illness derives his or her role in the family with the health condition being considered. This does not mean, however, that the child's condition makes the role of the other family members, in relation to his or her illness, any easier.

To understand this more thoroughly, other roles within a family structure, should be examined. Spiegel (1957) has stated that interrelationships of roles are crucial, as no role exists in isolation; it is always patterned to fit the complementary or reciprocal role of a role partner. He states that as long as the role each family member occupies is complementary with and conforms to the role expectations other members have for him or her, the family lives in dynamic equilibrium.

This explains why it is important to understand what the family feels about the child with a long-term illness. If they assume that the child is going to live a long, productive life and this is not the case, the family equilibrium may be shattered when the child does not succeed. If the family has cast the child in the role of a helpless individual and the child assumes an active role, this may shatter the family equilibrium. If another sibling reacts negatively to the role of the child with the long-term illness, this can interrupt the family equilibrium.

Spiegel (1957) states that the family equilibrium brought about by complementary roles is a rewarding state of affairs. He further contends that the disequilibrium serves to motivate family members to attempt some form of resolution of existing role discrepancies. The rewarding nature of equilibrium stems from the fact that when roles are clearly defined and mutually agreed upon, the individual is spared the necessity of almost constantly making decisions about the acts he or she performs.

This can be illustrated by considering the child with a cardiac condition. A mother casts the child in the role of a "cardiac cripple." The child feels well enough to go to school and participate in nonstrenuous sports. The child assumes a role not consistent with the one another vital family member has for him. The mother writes a note to the school forbidding her son to participate in any sports. The school acts as the environmental factor. The principal requests a note from the physician. The mother tries to influence the physician to take her side. The physician intervenes in favor of the son. The son participates in sports. The mother then is faced with a role which is not conducive to the one which she has established for her son. Disequilibrium can result and role expectations must be modified if equilibrium is to be re-established.

The role a parent ascribes to a particular child may also influence the way the other family members accept that child. A child with a cardiac condition is often "coddled" by his or her siblings because they take their cues from their parents. Consequently, the other siblings may wait on the child with the cardiac problem and lessen his or her chances of establishing independence. The child with the cardiac condition may then expect that his or her needs will be consistently met in this way. When the child gets to school, he or she finds it difficult not to have his or her siblings able to continue their indulging role.

Spiegel (1957) states that there are four principal ways in which an individual acquires his or her social role. In each case the individual can accept the role assigned to him or her or he can refuse it, as in the case presented above. Some roles are *ascribed*—that is, universally accepted—such as age and sex roles. Other roles, such as occupation, have to be *achieved*, and others must be *adopted*. The fourth role Spiegel calls *assumption*, which involves roles that have playful qualities. Such assumed roles are taken in make-believe, and it is important that all members concerned realize the playful character of the assumed role. The adoptive roles are informal in character. They are adopted by one member and usually relate to another member. This can be illustrated in the case of a 10-year-old sibling adopting the mother role in relation to the child with a long-term illness rather than the sibling role usually adopted by two children in the same family.

There are two other terms used by Spiegel (1957) which are useful in this discussion. One is the term *allocative discrepancy* and the other *goal discrepancy.* Allocative discrepancy is used when the individual refuses the role allocated to him or her or when others fail to complement his or her role. Goal discrepancy exists when the goal of one family member is to obtain some form of gratification from another, but the other fails to meet the demand because his or her goal is related to withholding or because he or she is unable to gratify the demand, for some reason. Goal discrepancy is especially significant, as long-term illness can cause a family member to be unable to gratify the demands of other family members. A number of examples can be cited. The child born without extremities obviously cannot achieve his father's desire for him to be a football player. The daughter with asthma may not be able to exist comfortably in the frilly bedroom signifying to the mother the height of femininity.

The severity of the discrepancy between what is expected and what is attained can greatly influence the family equilibrium. The severity of the discrepancy may vary from family member to family member. What may be a severe disappointment to the mother may be only a minor disappointment to a brother or sister. However, the degree to which it interrupts the relationships within the family is of major importance.

Current Roles of Family Members

It is useful to examine some of the potential roles that influence the care given the child with a long-term illness.

The Mother Role. The role of the mother has always involved concern for the health of the children. Recently the role has changed, including not only concern for physical health but also concern for the psychologic well-being of the child. This expanded role has put new and greater responsibility on the mother. She is forced to read about new developments in child care and to keep up with advances in medical practices. Formerly, it was sufficient for her to get to a physician when the child was ill. Now she is faced with having to understand preventive health practices and the responsibility to meet the emotional demands of healthy development.

Educationally advantaged women read extensively to improve their parenting skills. In contrast, there are mothers who have little or no education and model their roles after those of a mother or grandmother or learn them by word of mouth from some other educationally disadvantaged mother.

In discussing the mother's role in relation to illness, Bell (1966) states that the middle-class mother usually assumes the role of mediator between the impersonal, rational role decision of the medical expert and the application of those decisions within the highly emotional contexts of her relationships to her husband and children. This mediating role of the mother further extends the impersonal relationship between medical personnel and the clients. This is dynamically illustrated in the case of the adolescent client with a long-term illness. Health care providers usually feel an obligation to talk to the parent before talking to the adolescent. The parent then makes some decision, which is not always consistent with the wishes of the adolescent client. The health care provider then proceeds, incorporating the parent's decision. The relationship between health care personnel and the adolescent may suffer as a result. A decision that directly affects the adolescent has been mediated by an outside source, and the adolescent frequently has to live with this decision. It is probably fortunate that the adolescent has the capacity to rebel, as this rebellion may provide an opportunity for him to be consulted about his own care before decisions are made.

The mother from a disadvantaged family may be so strained by other responsibilities that she has little or no time for illness. According to Rainwater, as cited in Bell (1966), her attitude toward illness even when it becomes chronic is apt to be a tolerant one. People in disadvantaged families learn to live with illness rather than using their small stock of interpersonal and emotional resources to confront the problem.

These attitudes about illness are influenced by the degree to which the family members regard the crisis as a threat to the present or future life of the family. The parent responding to an ill child is responding to both the illness and the dependent status of the child in our society. In other societies, in which the child is less dependent, the parents' need to protect the child may be less than it is in our society.

The mother with a child with long-term nutritional anemia may bring the child to the hospital only when the child is dangerously close to death. The child is treated and responds. The mother is counseled about the dietary requirements of the child and seems to understand. However, the child is readmitted a few months later in the same condition. The mother again is responding only when she considers herself incapable of handling the situation. She is not worrying about the sequela of the frequent brushes with death. Her aim is to keep the child alive, but the overall well-being of the child may be an unknown concept to her. Even if it is known, she may have so many overwhelming crises to handle that she is not physically able to respond to them all and handles each one as she interprets its importance.

Father Role.   The role of the father in relation to child-rearing practices is beginning to be presented as more significant. Fathers are beginning to speak out on their right to influence the nurturing of their children. They are expressing a desire to change their image from one of a financial provider to one of an interacting essential member of the family process. This approach to child rearing influences the way health care providers interact with families. It will not be enough to talk only to the mother about child-rearing practices. Fathers who are integrally involved in the nurturing process will have to be included in the discussions and planning.

Implications of the Effects of Long-term Illness on Parental Roles.   Bell (1966) has stated that some families have the tendency to resist the fact that a problem really exists. However, he has found that the parents of children with long-term illness tend to be less sociable and more withdrawn than parents without such children. He found the mothers less likely to work outside the home than mothers of able-bodied children. He also found that the community of "normal" families was not supportive of the revised norms of child care that must be established by families with severely handicapped children.

In discussing implications for family roles, it is necessary to keep in mind that people raise their children according to their own standards. These standards include definitions of health and illness. Definitions of what is "normal" may be very different from one family to another.

The parents often have difficulty finding baby sitters to accept the responsibility of caring for a child with a disability. This may partially be due to their own fears or lack of knowledge about the special needs of the particular child. There is more emphasis being given to "respite services" through agencies which provide services for children with long-term illness. These respite services include short-term baby sitting and long-term accommodations to allow the family to vacation without the child. Respite services are a welcome addition to the services provided for children with long-term illness.

Hannam (1975) suggests the father is less affected than the mother by the infant with a long-term illness. The situation is explained by the fact that the father can at least get away to work and, by immersing himself in his work, forget the problems at home, while the mother usually stays at home and manages the child's care on a daily basis.

The fathers are probably more affected when the child does not achieve anticipated developmental milestones, such as going to school or being able to secure a vocation. At these times it becomes more obvious to the father that the child is not an average, normal child succeeding in expected developmental tasks.

It is well to remember that all children can "get on their parents' nerves at times. The child with a long-term illness is no exception. He or she is able to cause discomfort and put additional periodic stress on the parents individual roles and their reciprocal roles. The stress can be increased if the parents do not discipline the child consistently. Maddison and Raphael (1971) suggest that mothers caring for a child with a chronic illness should include in the child's care an increased gratification of the child's dependency needs. They suggest that the child needs this attention in order to feel loved and secure. Conversely, they caution that excessive gratification of the dependency needs may impede the child's development and deprive him of the maximum pleasure of passively receiving his or her mother's attention. Maddison and Raphael note that mothers, like their children, are inclined to view the child's condition as punishment for their own wrongdoings or mistakes. They emphasize that material conflict with a particular child may be based on a variety of factors. Included in their list of suggestions are the following: conception coinciding with a personally devaluing experience, attempted abortion, a crisis situation during the pregnancy, or poor family planning. These attitudes may lead to aggressive feelings towards the child that may make the mother feel guilty, and she may then respond by overprotecting the child.

Implications for Sibling Roles.   Child rearing focuses on the individual rights of each child. Young children tend to be egocentric. Their individual demands are frequently granted until a crisis arises. In time of crisis, the individual's rights are relegated to a lower level of priority and the crisis situation emerges with top priority. Let us take, for example, a family with two children. Henry and Mary have been treated with equal concern by their parents. Their needs are individual but easily met with a degree of give and take by the family. Henry has an accident and is severely injured. His developmental level regresses to that of a toddler. The family begins to expend all their energies on behalf of Henry. Mary's normal requests and demands may now seem unreasonable. The parents have no time to spend on the ordinary activities of daily living. They are burdened by going to the hospital, seeing that the best physicians are brought in, getting people to donate blood, checking on health insurance coverage, and so forth. Mary is very much in the background of the medical crisis. Her meals are forgotten or thrown together, her clothing is neglected, no one is available to answer her questions or to ask her about her day. The phone rings frequently but the calls are always about Henry. In her childlike way she tries to adjust her sibling role to meet the crisis, but she becomes more and more painfully aware of her own desires and needs.

This traumatic beginning influences the way Mary is able to handle her new role in relation to Henry with his long-term illness. Her role of equal competitor may change to one of hostility. Her position may be further in jeopardy when Henry returns home in a more dependent role. She may be asked to assume some of the responsibility for his care, casting her in a mother role. She may adopt the role of mother willingly and compete with her mother for this position with Henry. She may assume a role of "cheerful young lady," while in reality she very much resents her new responsibilities. Her exterior facade gives her parents confidence that she is satisfied with her new responsibility. This gives the parents a comfortable feeling and they do not look past it into Mary's true feelings.

The changing role of siblings can be detrimental to the children's normal life pattern. With some degree of predictability, Mary is likely to experience loss of normal activities of her age group. She might resent the premature role of mother and choose never to accept it again. She might become hostile toward her parents and not be able to establish a warm and loving relationship again.

In families that attend clinics for long-term health supervision, it is becoming evident that siblings have an increase in emotional problems. These emotional problems have been manifested in obesity, nail-biting, school failure, etc. The severity of the symptoms is not necessarily correlated with the degree of disturbance.

Data from research studies show differences in the psychologic functioning of siblings or disabled children. A study in Cleveland by Breslau et al. (1981) involving children disabled with cystic fibrosis, cerebral palsy, myelodysplasia, and multiple handicaps and their siblings found that siblings of disabled children did not have higher rates of severe psychologic impairment or greater overall symptomatogy than children who served as controls. However, on two scales measuring interpersonal aggression with peers and within the school, siblings of disabled children had higher levels of pathology. The type or severity of the disability did not correlate with the psychologic functioning of siblings. Birth order had a significant interactive effect with sex; among siblings younger than the disabled child, male siblings had greater impairment, while among siblings older than the disabled child, female siblings had greater pathology.

The data from the Cleveland study were compared to data from a similar study in New York City, with the following findings:

1. The siblings in Cleveland did not differ from those in New York City on conflict with parents and regressive anxiety, but siblings in Cleveland scored lower on isolation.
2. On the fighting and delinquent scales (which include items related to rash behavior, interpersonal relations, and school problems), siblings of disabled children in Cleveland scored significantly higher than did those in New York City.
3. Siblings in Cleveland had significantly higher scores on mentation problems, as well.

The researchers concluded that the higher scores on the fighting and delinquency scales for siblings of disabled children in Cleveland give reason for concern, as these behaviors are correlated with delinquency behavior. They also concluded that the marked excesses in the proportion of seriously impaired younger male siblings and older female siblings requires sensitive screening and intervention for these children (Breslau et al., 1981). The study did not verify the notion that siblings lack parental attention as a result of the parents' involvement with the disabled child. Nor did the mothers think that the attention they gave to the disabled children interfered with their ability to give adequate attention to their other children. However, the aggressive behavior tendencies could be seen as a reflection of the siblings' perception that they did not receive enough attention if one were to accept the notion that inattention gives rise to attention-seeking aggressive acts.

If it is unrealistic to have all the siblings included in the ongoing health care management of the child with long-term illness, it might be wise to at least have a group session in which all family members can get together and ventilate their feelings about their roles and responsibilities periodically. These sessions could be planned in the evening, so they do not interfere with school or employment.

Just as respite care was suggested for the parents, it is also suggested for the siblings. Siblings need a chance to be free from the special considerations given to the child with a long-term illness. This is very important if the affected child has a mental impairment. The siblings may wish to entertain their friends without the potential embarrassment that may arise from the irrational acts of the child with a mental impairment. They may feel that their friends will not come to their homes if they are repelled by their sibling's behavior. Parents need to appreciate the need of siblings for periods of separation and to make sure these are provided. This does not mean that the child with long-term illness is neglected. He or she is merely excluded for certain times in the same way that he or she is included at other times.

Perhaps the best guide for assessing sibling situations is to try to provide respite for all the children. Each has special needs at particular periods and these needs determine when a child's requests are reasonable and when they are unreasonable.

Maddison and Raphael (1971) report that the neglect of siblings results in hostile and aggressive responses to the affected child. They document that the siblings have an increased incidence of school problems and delinquency tendencies, which indicates that the siblings' needs are not being adequately met.

Implications for the Extended Family.   The membership in the extended family has decreased in importance, as today's families are separated by vocational and other interests. Mobility has ranked high on the list of reasons responsible for the decreasing importance and support available from the extended family. Frequently, there are only a few close relatives living nearby and they have families of their own to care for. Therefore, the relatives are able to maintain a psychologic distance which allows them to feel little or no pressure from the effects of the child with the disability.

Implications for Professional Roles

The role of the professional nurse in relation to the child with long-term illness is addressed in each chapter as it becomes appropriate. However, it seems appropriate to include the health care team during hospitalizations, since they periodically become highly significant caretakers for the child. The hospital is geared toward cure of acute episodes of illness. This orientation frequently jeopardizes the care administered to children with long-term illness. In a teaching hospital, the child may not be considered "an appropriate learning experience" by the medical staff for their medical students or residents. Therefore, they may apply pressure to have the child discharged. The social worker or nurse, feeling that the family is not ready for the child to be returned home, may try to delay the discharge. This situation can result in friction between the various members of the health care team. It is during these periods of disagreement that it is extremely evident that the team is not really a team, but rather a group of health care providers all working in the same institution.

Health care providers like to feel that they can cure illness. They may feel frustration that they cannot cure the child's long-term illness. This realization is likely to make the health care providers feel inadequate in their roles. In order to protect themselves against constant reinforcement of their imagined failure, health care providers may tend to avoid the child with long-term illness.

Another point about working with these children is that attention is often focused on the major problem areas and on how the child is responding in relation to them. If the child is making progress in these areas, the health care providers tend to be optimistic, but if the child is not responding in the expected ways then dissatisfaction is apparent. The difficulties which may arise from too narrow a focus on a particular area are many:

1. The child receives impersonal treatment.
2. The professional may be unduly discouraged by lack of progress in the child's particular problem even though the child is making satisfactory progress in other areas.
3. The professional may be focusing on the one area where the child is least likely to show his or her best side. Therefore, the child also appears as uncooperative, moody, and so forth.
4. The child is not rewarded for progressing in the areas that may be most significant to him or her.
5. The child begins to anticipate rejection from professionals and dreads keeping health care appointments.
6. The child and professional tend to miss potential breakthroughs in the delivery of care because the focus is on a particular problem, rather than on how a particular client responded to a particular situation in a given set of circumstances.

In order for health care providers to achieve satisfaction from managing the care of children with long-term problems, educational programs need to focus less on the acute care situation and to provide positive learning experiences with families over long periods of time. This kind of association provides a more realistic picture of the way the family is able to adapt to family stresses.

Implications for Members of the Community

The goal of care of the child with long-term illness is to make the child a productive member of the community. This might be his or her private home or it might be an institution. The child needs to be able to cope with his or her illness and to learn to live with it on a day-to-day basis.

Strauss (1975) emphasized that any given disease has the potentiality of causing many problems in daily living. The day-to-day management of the illness is more complicated than the management during acute care episodes, since the conditions of the daily situation can be so diverse. Clients with long-term illness are beginning to realize the value of sharing their experiences of living with a disability with other individuals with similar problems. Strauss (1975) suggests that the key issues in the management of clients with long-term illness center around the prevention of medical crises, control of symptoms, carrying out prescribed treatments, adjusting to changes in progress, avoiding social isolation, normalizing social interactions, and financial assistance. In order to manage these key issues, a great deal of planning must take place with significant others who will be intimately involved with the child. The special needs of the child change as the child grows and as the significant others change. In order to make the child's adjustments as easy as possible, it is best to anticipate these needs created by maturational crises and to plan for them. A network needs to be established to monitor the child's progress and to establish realistic goals to enhance his or her progress. The child should not miss out on going to school, for instance, because no one anticipated his or her special needs far enough in advance to plan for his or her entry. A child's discharge from the hospital should not have to be delayed because the equipment needs in the home have not been taken care of. Numerous examples of management schemes can be cited to give insight to the special planning that has to be done to facilitate the successful integration of long-term illness with the lifestyle of the child and his or her family or significant others. The special implications of the long-term nature of these conditions makes it difficult to have all the roads paved with a smooth surface. There will always be rocky spots as the child grows in awareness and as he periodically becomes disenchanted with his or her special routines.

A special note needs to be made regarding noncompliance with prescribed regimens. Noncompliance indicates that the child or significant other has not consistently followed through on the routines suggested by health care providers. Noncompliance can imply that there is a lack of cooperation on the part of these people. In long-term care it is necessary to explore the reasons for and the times when noncompliance takes place. Even the slightest request by health care providers may require a significant amount of rearranging of family lifestyles to accommodate the request. For instance, a clinic visit scheduled on a monthly basis during the day may necessitate a parent taking off from work, or arranging for a babysitter or for the car to be at a different place, or changing mealtimes or naptimes, and so forth. In addition, the ongoing attention to regimes sometimes blows them out of proportion.

Long-term management of many childhood conditions requires relatively simple routines that can be learned by the family. Adjusting the routines so that they fit best into their busy lifestyles helps to limit noncompliance. The more complicated, threatening routines demand a great deal of assistance from health care providers. The community health nurse needs to be attuned to the regime and be available to assist in a variety of ways. Frequently, health care providers limit their services to specific times and days. Unfortunately, client needs cannot be limited in this way. Health care delivery must be available around the clock each day if families are to receive the help they need; otherwise, noncompliance might be a term associated with health professionals as well as the clients they serve.

EVALUATION OF THE CHILD'S ASSETS: NURSING HISTORY

The nursing history may be used to collect data in hospital and outpatient settings. Figure 3-5 is a form that has been developed by using formats suggested by other nurses and by adopting this form to get the information needed in a particular setting. This form is just a suggestion and should be tailored to meet the particular agency's needs. The form is merely a guide for collecting data. If it is a deterrent to gathering data, then it should be discarded in favor of another method.

UNIVERSITY HOSPITAL
U.S.A.
Nursing History (In-Patient Pediatrics)

Name: _____

Date: _____

Number of hospital or home care admissions

Duration of hospital admissions

Age(s) during hospital stay(s)

I. Appearance
II. Patient's understanding of illness—preparation for hospitalization
III. Events leading up to present hospital admission
IV. Place in family constellation—identification of family members
V. Significant information relative to:
   a) feeding
   b) toileting
   c) sleep
   d) play
   e) language development
   f) independent and dependent activities of daily living
VI. What is important to this child to make him feel secure in this situation?
VII. What are the policies of this agency which will interfere with or promote the well-being of this child?
VIII. What is the medical plan of care that will influence the nursing plan of care?
IX. What are the short-term goals for this child?
X. What are the long-term goals for this child?
XI. What methods can be identified and tried to meet these goals?
XII. What are the significant principles of growth and development which will be incorporated into the plan of care?
XIII. What community or team resources will be utilized or approached to meet the nursing objectives?
XIV. What nursing intervention needs to be done with the family at this time?

Figure 3-5. Suggested form for the nursing history.

Any child admitted to the hospital feels more secure if he or she realizes that hospital personnel know and understand him or her. One way to get to know the child and his or her parents is to do a nursing intake history. This history helps to identify significant factors in developing realistic nursing managements. The history is taken on admission. However, if the child is admitted in an acute crisis, the information may be more easily obtained a day or two after admission. Figure 3-5 is a guide for obtaining pertinent nursing information. If the information is stored easily, some of it can be saved from admission to admission and just be updated.

Pertinent information obtained from this interview is immediately placed in the child's chart for utilization by the entire health care team. Some of the aspects are gathered specifically for the Kardex. Other information, such as use of community resources, is utilized for instituting proper referrals.

Of the information gathered, some—such as feeding, toileting, and so forth—will need to be further evaluated by direct observation. An example would be: "Mrs. Jones says that 2½-year-old Johnny feeds himself." When you make out his Kardex you include this fact. Johnny experiences regression due to hospitalization and refuses to eat. The Kardex should be revised to read: "Encourage self-feeding; needs assistance."

The question in relation to policies which interfere with meeting certain objectives may lend itself to changes in policy. For instance, you find that Johnny is very attached to his 6-year-old brother. The hospital does not allow children under 14 years of age to visit. If you gather enough information indicating that the child's progress is hindered by being separated from his siblings, a change in policy may be considered.

Nurses should identify their management plan on admission and identify ways to facilitate this care. Nursing progress notes are kept, also.

Needless to say, gathering of information is only one step in the process of improving care. Ways must be devised to disseminate this information to make it readily available and to eliminate some of the duplication that exists. The use of computers to conveniently store and retrieve information will greatly improve our present methods of sharing information. It is imperative to establish how to identify pertinent nursing information, so we can identify what we can contribute to the computer input.

When one studies Figure 3-6, it becomes evident that the role of the nurse is greatly expanded and encompasses a longer time span than it did formerly. The nursing history sets the stage for more dynamic types of nursing management. The information gathered helps the nurse to identify areas of care that uniquely belong to nursing or are shared by nursing. The nurse makes a nursing diagnosis and then formulates the management plan to meet the child's needs. Children with long-term illness may have so many medical diagnoses that nurses hesitate to add a nursing one to the list. However, this nursing diagnosis is somewhat

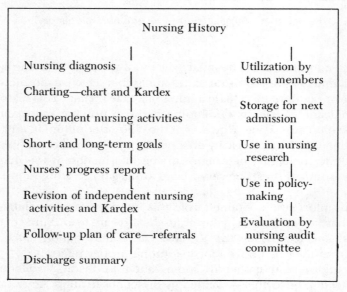

Figure 3-6.   The expanding role of the nurse in history taking.

different. The diagnosis is partially derived from factors relating to growth and development and normal developmental tasks. It is made by considering constraints made by the hospitalization process and by considering the medical diagnosis and the specific limitations imposed by this diagnosis. It is made by considering the child as an integral part of a family unit by considering the social forces that are present. It is made by the types of services available for aiding this child. It is made in consideration of the time element that is available to minister to the child.

Problem-oriented Method

The problem-oriented record keeping introduced by Weed (1971) has been gaining acceptance by all health disciplines for the collection of health data. Therefore, it is one alternative to the nursing history form. Whatever method is used to collect the data, the method must be accurate and complete.

The problem-oriented care process is based on the problem-oriented record. The written material in the chart should form the basis for the care plan. The plan begins with the compilation of an accurate, initial data base. The data base is obtained from a variety of sources: old records and charts, client interviews, physical examinations (including the review of systems), a description of the present illness, and family and social profiles. This initial data base should also include the client profile and the information corresponding to items I through V (in Fig. 3-5) of the nursing history—specifically, the age of the child, school placement, if any; place in the family constellation; and significant information about feeding, toileting, sleeping, play, independent and dependent activities of daily living, and language development. The problem list derives from the data base. Each problem is numbered individually. Next, data are obtained in relation to each of the identified problems. The problems should not be confused with diagnoses. There does not need to be a diagnosis to support the identified problem. However, a client may identify a particular disease as a problem. The list of problems includes social as well as medical concerns. There are columns in which the date of onset and resolution are recorded for each problem. After the problem list is completed, each problem is assessed and evaluated and appropriate plans are made for management. This step is generally referred to as SOAP, or "SOAPing" or "SOAPIE." The four initials stand for Subjective information, Objective information, Assessment, and Plan. Nurses have added two additional areas: Intervention and Evaluation. This information makes up the progress report for the client.

The value of the problem-oriented record over the nursing history is that the problem-oriented method has all health care providers participating in the same format and sharing all information. In the past, much of the information gathered on the nursing history was not adequately shared with the rest of the health care team. Indeed, the name "nursing history" made it seem a tool specific to the needs of one professional team member rather than data that offered challenges to a variety of health care team members. The problem-oriented method is of more value than the nursing history only if all health care providers are included in the formation of the problem list and are encouraged to help resolve the problems that relate to their particular areas of expertise.

The involvement of nurses in recording the initial data base is dependent upon their educational preparation. Many nurses are learning the art of history taking and physical examination. Nurses who are prepared in this way may take on added responsibility for the initial data base. In most cases, the physician assumes this responsibility.

The problem-oriented method of data gathering is a systematic way to gather and analyze data pertinent to client management. The easy accessibility of information related to each problem facilitates the care of and follow-through for the child. Having each problem numbered individually helps to focus attention on all the problem areas. The quick reference to past problems and their resolution aids in the long-term management of children. It should not be necessary to ask the parents many questions about past treatment, since the resolution data are clearly identified.

REFERENCES

Bell, R.R. *The impact of illness on family roles: A sociological framework for patient care.* New York: Wiley, 1966.

Breslau, N., Weitzman, M., & Messenger, K. *Psychologic functioning of siblings of disabled children. Pediatrics,* 67:344, 1981.

Ducanis, A.J., & Golin, A.K. *The interdisciplinary health care team.* Germantown, Md.: Aspens Systems Corp., 1979.

Hannam, C. *Parents and mentally handicapped children.* England: Penguin, 1975.

Laing, R.D. *The politics of the family.* New York: Vintage, 1975.

Longest, B.B. *Management practices for the health professional.* Reston, Va.: Reston, 1976.

Maddison, D., & Raphael, B. Social and psychological consequences of chronic disease in childhood. *Medical Journal of Australia* 2:1265, 1971.

Pluckham, M.L. Professional territoriality: A problem affecting the delivery of health care. *Nursing Forum* 11:300, 1972.

Spiegel, J.P. The resolution of role conflict within the family. *Psychiatry* 20:1, 1957.

Strauss, A.L. *Chronic illness and the quality of life.* St. Louis: Mosby. 1975.

Weed, L.L. *Medical records, medical education and patient care.* (5th ed.) Chicago: Case Western Reserve Press, 1971.

BIBLIOGRAPHY

Beckemeyer, P., & Bahr, J.E. Helping toddlers and preschoolers cope with suturing their minor lacerations. *American Journal of Maternal—Child Nursing* 5:326, 1980.

Bell, R.A. Discontinuity of care in a crippled children program. In *Studies in handicapping conditions.* Rockville, Md.: HEW, 1975.

Bellack, J.P. Helping a child cope with the stress of injury. *American Journal of Nursing* 74:1491, 1974.

Bowlby, J. Grief and mourning in infancy and early childhood. *Psychoanalytic Study of the Child* 15:9, 1960.

Debusky, M. (Ed.). *The chronically ill child and his family.* Springfield, Ill.: Thomas, 1970.

Epstein, C. Breaking the barriers to communications on the health team. *Nursing* 4:65, 1974.

Farber, B. *Family: Organization and interaction.* San Francisco: Chandler, 1964.

Fields, G. Social implications of long-term illness in children. In J.A. Downey & N.L. Low (Eds.), *The child with disabling illness.* Philadelphia: Saunders, 1974.

Freiberg, K.H. How parents react when their child is hospitalized. *American Journal of Nursing,* 72:1270, 1972.

Guerin, L.S. Hospitalization as a positive experience for poverty children. *Clinical Pediatrics* 16:509, 1977.

Hansen, B.D., & Evans, M.L. Preparing a child for procedures. *American Journal of Maternal—Child Nursing* 6:392, 1981.

Jelneck, L.J. The special needs of the adolescent with chronic illness. *American Journal of Maternal—Child Nursing* 2:57, 1977.

Johnson, J.E., Kirchnoff, K.T., Endress, M.P., et al. Easing children's fright during health care procedures. *American Journal of Maternal—Child Nursing* 1:206, 1976.

Kline, J., & Schowalter, J.E. How to care for the "between-ager." *Nursing,* 4:43—51, 1974.

Lawson, B.A. Chronic illness in the school-aged child: Effects on the total family. *American Journal of Maternal—Child Nursing* 2:49, 1977.

Luciano, K. The who, when, where, what and how of preparing children for surgery. *Nursing,* 4:64, 1974.

Mattsson, A. Long-term physical illness in childhood: A challenge to psychosocial adaptation. *Pediatrics* 50:801, 1972.

McLillan, C.L. Hero badges mean more than courage. *Pediatric Nursing* 2:7, 1976.

Petrillo, M., & Sanger, S. *Emotional care of hospitalized children: An environmental approach.* Philadelphia: Lippincott, 1980.

Pidgeon, V.A. Characteristics of children's thinking and implications for health teaching. *Maternal—Child Nursing Journal* 6:1, 1977.

Ramos, S. *Teaching your child to cope with crisis.* New York: McKay, 1975.

Rapoport, L. Working with families in crisis: An exploration in preventive intervention. In H.J. Parad (Ed.), *Crisis intervention.* New York: Family Service Association of America, 1965.

Ross, A.O. *The exceptional child in the family,* New York: Grune & Stratton, 1964.

Smith, D.M. A clinical nursing tool. *American Journal of Nursing* 68:2384, 1968.

Snyder, J.C., & Wilson, M.F. Elements of psychological assessment. *American Journal of Nursing* 77:235, 1977.

Wooley, F.R., Warnick, M.W., Kane, R.L., et al. *Problem-oriented nursing.* New York: Spinger, 1974.

4

Identification of Physical Disabilities

Victoria Erickson

Nurses in private and public hospitals, community health care agencies, and schools have frequent contact with children with a wide variety of disabilities. Nurses have provided and will continue to provide comprehensive care to these children and their families. Nurses with physical assessment and primary care skills have an opportunity to help the family and client with minor childhood health care problems, to teach, and to coordinate services between institutions and the community.

Many excellent physical assessment texts have been written. Most of these texts deal primarily with normal physical assessment reflecting the philosophy that clients with abnormalities are to be referred to others for diagnosis. However, there are many nurses whose entire caseload consists of children who have been previously diagnosed as having long-term disabilities. The nurses who deal with these children need a greater breadth of knowledge of assessment of abnormal health states. This chapter is to be used as a supplement for the nurse practitioner who has basic physical assessment skills.

FOCUS ON ABNORMALITIES

Because this chapter focuses on the abnormal rather than the normal, it is important to emphasize the influence health care providers have on the client's body image. Children are especially susceptible to the development of poor body image because they are still developing their perceptions about themselves. Acceptance of our bodies is a matter of mixed blessings; adults verbalize positive and negative aspects when asked to describe their physical selves to another. During the course of their physical exam, able-bodied children usually hear positive statements made to them or their parents. Unfortunately, children with disabilities usually hear negative statements about their physical appearance that they are ill-prepared to interpret.

Even the most deformed child has some normal, positive physical attributes, and it is important that these aspects be emphasized to the child and his or her parents. Nice, shiny ear drums, good arches, and beautiful hair are some examples of frequent findings that can be acknowledged by health care providers during the physical examination. Of course, many more healthy attributes can be found for any individual, especially when the health care provider is looking for positive aspects that can be praised.

PREVENTION

Often the most important consideration when dealing with disabled children is how the nurse can limit the amount of disability that is incurred as a result of birth injury, trauma, or genetic malfunction. This requires thorough knowledge of the disability and its treatment. For instance, many children, especially those who are institutionalized, do not receive proper dental care. Disabled children frequently are difficult to feed, even as infants. Many times a bottle is used to feed these infants for a longer period of time than it is used to feed able-bodied children, which contributes to an increase in dental pathology in disabled children. The result of extended bottle feeding is early dental decay.

If health care providers are aware of physical disabilities, the effects of the disability may be minimized. Early detection of a hearing disability, for example, may allow alternative communicative techniques and the fostering of normal growth and development. The following text is a guide to some of the more well-known disabilities that occur in the child population. Unfortunately, there is a proliferation of abnormal findings, and thus this chapter is not intended to be all-inclusive of abnormal physical findings or of syndromes and diseases. The reader will be able to cross-reference physical findings with descriptions of syndromes or diseases listed in the text.

A word of caution is needed regarding the interpretation of symptoms. There is individuality in every child; thus a child with a described disability may not have all the associated physical findings. *Mosaicism*, the mixing of normal with abnormal chromosomal cells, has been described in Down's syndrome. This mixing results in a child who may only be mildly affected with the associated physical findings of a syndrome or disorder.

SYNDROMES OR DISEASE CONDITIONS

Waardenburg's Syndrome

This syndrome is an autosomal dominant trait associated with deafness and pigmentary changes (Fig. 4-1). Waardenburg's syndrome appears in all racial groups throughout the world. However, it is not common; it is estimated that 2 percent of congenitally deaf children have this syndrome.

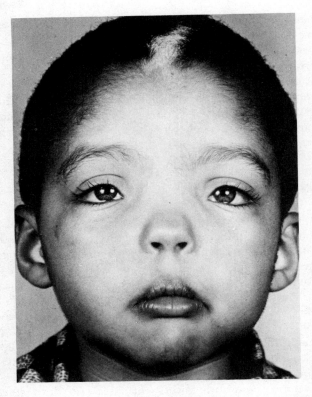

Figure 4-1.   Patient with Waardenburg's syndrome. The patient has bilateral profound neurosensory hearing loss, a white forelock, increased intercanthal distance, abnormal medial canthi, blue eyes, and eyebrows which are beginning to join the midline. The nasal route is also somewhat broader than usual. *(From Ruben, R.J., et al.* Otorhinolaryngology: Medcom Famous Teachings in Modern Medicine. *New York: Medcom, 1971)*

Clinical Features

- Deafness (bilateral or unilateral).
- Hypertelorism—lateral displacement of the inner canthi of the eyes.
- Prominent, broad nasal root.
- Fusion of the eyebrows.
- White forelock (may disappear after the first year).
- Premature graying of the hair (occasional).
- Heterochromia iridum (different-colored irises).

Cornelia De Lange Syndrome

Cornelia de Lange syndrome is thought to be an autosomal recessive trait. This syndrome has occurred in siblings in the same family.

Clinical Features

- Short stature.
- Mental retardation.
- Hirsutism.
- Tapering, short fingers.
- Oligodactylia (subnormal number of fingers or toes).
- Proximally displaced thumbs.
- Abnormal dermatoglyphics.
- Defects of ribs and sternum.
- Hypoplastic nipples and umbilicus.
- Unusual facies, including:
  Brachymicrolephalia (short, small head).
  Bushy eyebrows.
  Long, profuse eyelashes.
  Flat nasal bridge with upturned tip and anteverted nostrils.
  Increased distance from nasal base to lip border.
  Midline notching of upper and lower lips.
  Narrow, high, arched palate.
  Micrognathia (small jaws).
  Low-set ears.

Klinefelter's Syndrome

Klinefelter's syndrome is due to an abnormality in the male sex chromosomes. Most males with Klinefelter's syndrome have an XXY complex, but they may also have XX/YY or XY/XXY sets.

Clinical Features

- Tall stature.
- Small testes.
- Long legs.
- Poorly developed secondary sex characteristics.
- Gynecomastia (enlarged breasts).
- Sterility.
- Normal to mild retardation.
- Abnormal dermatoglyphics—small fingertip patterns with lower ridge count.

Osteogenesis Imperfecta

There are two forms of this disorder. The most severe form is known as osteogenesis imperfecta congenita. Infants appear to inherit a recessive trait that allows multiple fractures to occur during the infant's delivery. Osteogenesis imperfecta tarda occurs late in life and is an inherited dominant trait.

Clinical Features

- Tendency to fracture bones easily.
- Deafness.
- Dental deformities.
- Blueness of sclera.
- Large fontanel (> 5 cm).
- Short stature.

Trisomy 21: Down's Syndrome

Down's syndrome is the most common form of genetic nondisjunction. The actual etiology of the genetic disturbance causing Down's syndrome is unknown. There is an increased occurrence in mothers who are under 18 or over 35.

Clinical Features

Head:	microcephaly, flat occiput, brachycephaly.
Eyes:	inner and outer epicanthal folds slanted upward and outward; bilateral speckling of iris (Brushfield's spots); strabismus; refractive errors; cataracts in early adulthood.
Ears:	simple or aberrant helix formation; low-set.
Nose:	usually small with a flattened bridge.
Mouth:	tongue large and fissured; nasopharynx small (causes mouth breathing); abnormal morphology; frequent absence of teeth.
Neck:	short; occasional webbing.
Hands:	stubby, distal radius; radial loop on fourth finger and ulnar loops on all other digits; in-curved, short fifth fingers (clinodactyly) with single crease; single midpalmar crease (simian line); usually bilateral.
Feet:	short and stubby; wide spread between first and second toes; deep crease leading distally from angle of first and second toes.
Abdomen:	protrudes, umbilical hernia; megacolon, microcolon.
Skin:	dry; decreased elasticity.
Heart:	septal defects; pulmonary stenosis; aortic stenosis.
Genitalia:	male—testes undescended, small penis; female—labia minora underdeveloped, menopause early.
Neurologic:	hypotonia, normoreflexia; poor fine and gross coordination.
Speech:	voice is usually low-pitched and raucous; speech has infantile omissions and substitutions (Rudolph, 1977).

Sickle Cell Anemia

Sickle cell anemia is an inherited homozygous disorder. The incidence among American blacks as 1 in 600. The sickled cells obstruct vessels, causing decreased blood flow to the tissues. Recurrent sickle cell crises damage the liver, kidneys, eyes, heart, brain, and spleen, resulting in the clinical features associated with this disease.

Clinical Features

- Small stature.
- Skin pallor (nailbeds, mucous membranes).
- Jaundice (yellow sclerae).
- Flow murmurs (associated with anemia).
- Hepatosplenomegaly (enlarged spleen and liver).
- Swelling of hands and feet (in infants).
- Small, comma-shaped vessels in the lower bulbar conjunctivae.
- Retinal changes due to infarcts.
- Delayed puberty.
- Skin ulcers on legs (occasional).

Hurler's Syndrome
(Mucopolysaccharidosis Syndrome Type I)

Hurler's syndrome is an autosomal recessive mucopolysaccharide metabolism disorder. It is the most common and most severe of several mucopolysaccharidosis syndromes. Because of the inability to degrade mucopolysaccharides, growth and development are greatly delayed, leading to death in childhood.

Clinical Features

- Gargoyle-like facies with coarse features.
- Hydrocephalus.
- Disorders of bone structures, including:
    Stiff joints.
    Claw-like hands (Fig. 4-2).
    Lumbar gibbus (proturberant or hump-backed).
    Kyphosis and/or scoliosis.
    Dwarfing.
- Excessive body hair.
- Chest deformities.
- Early progressive cornea clouding.
- Progressive mental retardation.
- Progressive hearing loss.
- Hepatosplenomegaly.

Treacher—Collins Syndrome
(Franceschetti's Syndrome or Mandibulofacial Dysotosis)

Treacher-Collins syndrome is inherited as an autosomal dominant trait (Fig. 4-3).

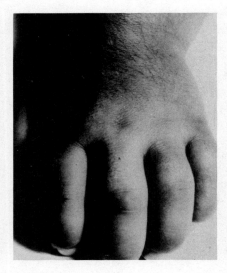

Figure 4-2. Clawhands. *(From Ru-dolph, A.M. (Ed.). Pediatrics (17th ed.). New York: Appleton—Century—Crofts, 1977)*

Clinical Features

- Hearing loss (usually conductive because of external auditory canal and middle ear malformations).
- Hypertelorism.
- Antimongoloid palpebral fissure slant.
- Symmetric colobomas of the lids.
- Abnormalities or absence of the eyelashes.
- Hypoplastic mandible.
- Deformed ears.
- Malocclusion.
- High arched palate.
- Blind fistulae between the corner of the mouth and ears.

Allergies

Allergies are a very common finding in children. Allergic manifestations may be observed in both physical and behavioral characteristics. The clinical features below refer to respiratory allergic manifestations.

Clinical Features

- Mouth breathing and malocclusion of teeth.
- Nasal speech.
- Repetitive sneezing.
- Rubbing of eyes, nose, or ears (allergic salute—the child pushes the nose upward and backward with the palm, which may result in a transverse nasal crease).
- Geographic tongue.

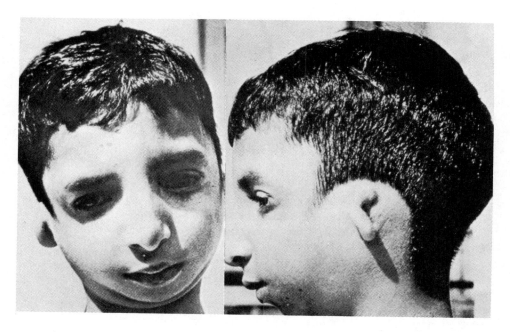

Figure 4-3. Treacher-Collins syndrome (Franceschetti syndrome, mandibulofacial dysostosis): The deformities of the external ears and hypoplastic mandible are clearly shown. The antimongoloid slant of the eyes can be recognized, but the defect of the lower lids (cloboma) is obscured by the heavy shadows. *(From Rudolph, A.M. (Ed.). Pediatrics (17th ed.). New York: Appleton—Century—Crofts, 1977)*

- Edematous and glistening nasal turbinates.
- Allergic shiners (dark circles under eyes).
- Marginal upper eyelid eczema.
- Long, silky eyelashes.
- Occasional nasal polyps (Marks, 1977).

Marfan's Syndrome

Marfan's syndrome is an autosomal dominant disease due to a defect in mucopolysaccharide metabolism.

Clinical Features

- High, narrow palate arch.
- Funnel breast.
- Pigeon chest.
- Long, narrow fingers and toes.
- Long extremities.
- Cataracts.

- Enlarged cornea.
- Strabismus.
- Congenital heart disease.

Cystic Fibrosis

Cystic fibrosis is an inherited disorder that is characterized by a dysfunction of the exocrine glands. The cause of cystic fibrosis is unknown, but treatment and early diagnosis may result in the child surviving longer than was previously thought possible.

Clinical Features

- Salty taste (due to elevated concentration of sodium in sweat).
- Abdominal distention/meconium ileus in newborns.
- Shrunken "hobnail" liver (occurs in less than 5 percent cases).
- Nasal polyps.
- Bronchiolectasis chronic suppurative lung infection.
- Sterility in males.
- Decreased growth.
- Rectal prolapse.
- Enlargement and/or tenderness of the submaxillary and sublingual glands.
- Barrel chest.
- Cough (loose and productive).
- Wide sternum.
- Flattened buttocks.

Hunter's Syndrome
(Mucopolysaccharidosis Syndrome Type II)

Hunter's syndrome is an X-linked recessive mucopolysaccharidosis that is not as severe as Hurler's syndrome (Fig. 4-4). There are severe and mild clinical forms of Hunter syndrome; however, most affected males live to adulthood, dying of cardiopulmonary impairment.

Clinical Features

- Stiff joints.
- Dwarfing.
- Claw-like hands.
- Hepatosplenomegaly.
- Gargoyle-like faces with coarse features.
- Progressive mental retardation.
- Progressive hearing loss.

Turner's Syndrome

Turner's syndrome occurs as the result of a nondisjunction in the sex chromosomes (Fig. 4-5). The child with Turner's syndrome has only one X chromosome

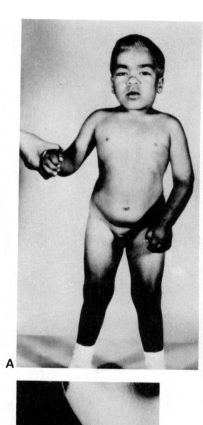

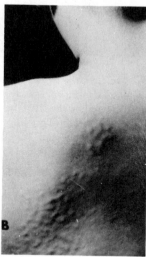

Figure 4-4. Child with mucopoly-saccharidosis type 11 (Hunter syndrome). **A.** General features. **B.** Nodular skin lesions on back thorax. *(From Rudolph, A.M. (Ed.). Pediatrics (17th ed.). New York: Appleton−Century−Crofts, 1977)*

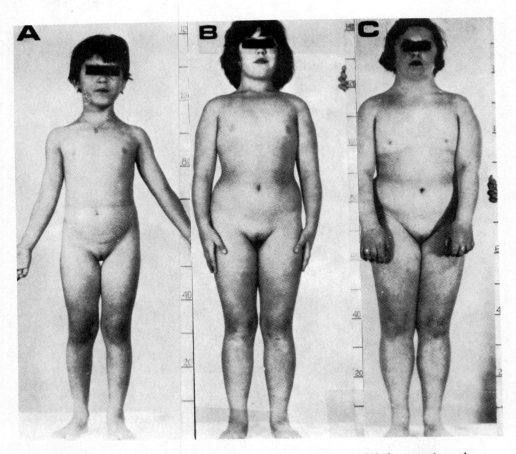

Figure 4-5. Three patients with the syndrome of gonadal dysgenesis and chromatin-negative somatic nuclei. **A.** Age 9 years, 11 months. Short stature was the complaint. **B.** Age 15 years, 4 months. Typical habitus without webbing of the neck. Pubic hair is present, but estrogen-induced gonadotropin excretion was greater than 100 mouse units per day. **C.** Age 15½ years. Classical aspect of Turner's syndrome. *(From Barnett, H.L. (Ed.). Pediatrics (15th ed.). New York: Appleton−Century−Crofts, 1972)*

or has two X chromosomes with one of them defective. The child appears to be female because of the one X chromosome.

Clinical Features

- Lymphedema of hands and feet (found in infancy).
- Coarctation of the aorta.
- Short fourth metacarpal.

- High arched palate.
- Wide-spaced nipples.
- Broad, shield-like chest.
- Low hairline over the nape of the neck.
- Webbed, short neck.
- Hypoplastic nails.
- Renal abnormalities, frequently horseshoe kidney.
- Ear abnormalities, frequent otitis media causing perceptive hearing loss.
- Short stature.
- No secondary sexual characteristics (unless child is taking estrogen).
- Sterile.
- Abnormal dermatoglyphics—large fingertip loops and whorls.

ASSESSMENT

In this section, an *asterisk* after an abnormal feature refers the reader to previously identified conditions or syndromes.

Skin

Normal

Color:	appropriate to genetic heritage, acrocyanosis is normal in newborn infants. Mongolian spots, which are frequently found in dark-skinned infants, are found over the sacrum, buttocks, shoulders, and/or back. Occasional petechiae and transient mottling are normally found when examining newborns.
Consistency and texture:	moist, smooth, not oily or dry, resilient, elastic, good turgor. In newborns, the skin normally appears dry and is peeling at about the third day of life.
Lesions:	newborns may present birth marks, telangiectasis (storkbites), milia, and vernix caseosa.
Dermatolyphics:	whorls on thumbs and ring finger, radial loops and arches on the index fingers, and an ulnar loop on the little finger.
Hair distribution:	lanugo covers the newborn's body and is gradually replaced by the silky, fine hair found in childhood. Sparse, downy pubic hair occurs at 10 to 14 years in males and 8 to 12 years in females. Axillary and facial hair appear at age 12 to 16 in males; axillary hair occurs at age 9 to 14 in females.

Abnormal Features	Possible Cause
Dusky, circumoral cyanosis	Congenital heart disease
Generalized cyanosis	Hypoxia due to respiratory or cardiac disorder
Pallor (nailbeds, mucous membranes)	Circulatory failure, shock, sickle cell anemia*
Salty taste	Cystic fibrosis*
Jaundice	Blood incompatibility, hepatitis, hepatic obstruction, sickle cell anemia*
Poor turgor—nonresilient	Dehydration, poor nutrition, Down's syndrome*
Abnormal dermatoglyphics	Cornelia De Lange syndrome*
Radial loops on fourth or fifth finger	Down's syndrome*
Simian crease, arches, and whorls or ulnar loops on all ten fingers	Down's syndrome*
Small fingertip patterns with lower ridge count	Klinefelter's syndrome*
Large fingertip loops and whorls	Turner's syndrome*
Abnormal hair distribution	
Hirsutism	Adrenocortical problems
Scalp hair on cheeks	Treacher—Collins syndrome*
Excessive body hair	Hurler's syndrome,* hypothyroidism, Dilantin sensitivity
Abnormal hair color	
White forelock	Waardenburg's syndrome*
Premature graying of the hair	Waardenburg's syndrome*

Head and Neck

Normal

Circumference: generally, until the child is 2 years old, the head circumference is the same or slightly larger than that of the chest. The head circumference should be compared with established standards for premature and normal infants. The most important factor in assessing head circumference is repeated measurement over time to find out whether the head is growing in proportion to the body.

Shape/symmetry: vaginally delivered neonates often have a soft swelling of the occipitoparietal region with edema and bruising that resolves within 4 weeks.

Fontanels: At birth, fontanels are open and flat, and light pulsations may occasionally be noted. The average size of the anterior fontanel is 4 to 6 cm (anterior—posterior). The posterior fontanel normally measures 0.5 to 1 cm. The anterior fontanels close by 19 months, and the posterior fontanels close in 4 to 8 weeks.

Scalp: hair is evenly distributed; scalp is smooth, intact, and free from lesions and crusting.

Ears: ears are symmetric, aligned with eyes, with pinna no more than 10° off vertical line. Tympanic membranes are pearly gray, translucent, and mobile and have a light reflex. Hearing is assessed in a newborn by the neuro or blinking reflex reaction to a loud noise. Audiometry may be used in infants and children to assess hearing.

Face: symmetric facial features consistent with genetic heritage.

Eyes: symmetric corneal light reflex; pupils equal in size and reactive to light. Sclera may have a bluish tint in normal newborns. In children, the sclera is white to light brown, varying with genetic heritage. The iris color is symmetric and also consistent with genetic heritage. Red reflex is present; cornea and lens are clear, bright, and shiny. Eyelashes are of medium length and curved upward, and conjunctiva are dark pink and moist.

Nose: located centrally in middle to upper section of the face. The nares are patent, low, and broad in neonates. The septum is straight.

Mouth: symmetric, short, wide, arched palate tonsils, symmetric uvula midline. Deciduous teeth erupt at around 6 months of age, beginning with lower incisors. All 20 teeth are normally present by $2\frac{1}{2}$ years. Until the early teen years, children frequently have enlarged tonsils with an absence of pathology. The mandible should be in proportion to the face.

Tongue: pink, mobile, easily fits into mouth, protrudes in midline, no tremors.

Neck: symmetric, complete range of motion, flexes easily.

Abnormal Features	*Possible Cause*
Increased head circumference	Hydrocephaly, brain tumor, Hurler's syndrome*
Decreased head circumference	Microcephaly, anencephaly, Down's syndrome,* trisomies 13—15, 18
Flat occipit	Down's syndrome*
Brachycephaly (short head)	Down's syndrome,* Cornelia de Lange syndrome*

Large fontanel for age	Hydrocephaly, hypothyroidism, malnourishment, osteogenesis imperfecta,* rubella syndrome
Small or closed fontanel	Cranial synostosis, microcephaly, hyperthyroidism
Depressed fontanel	Dehydration, inanition
Bulging, tense fontanel	Meningitis, encephalitis, lead poisoning, subdural hematoma, brain tumor, cardiac failure
Scalp hair on cheeks	Treacher–Collins syndrome*
Brittle, dry, coarse hair	Hypothyroidism
Low hairline over nape of neck	Turner's syndrome*
Long, profuse eyelashes	Cornelia de Lange syndrome*
Long, silky eyelashes	Allergies*
Marginal upper eyelid eczema	Allergies*
Absence of eyelashes	Treacher–Collins syndrome*
Bushy eyebrows	Cornelia de Lange syndrome*
Fusion of eyebrows	Waardenburg's syndrome*

Ears
    Low-set ears — Cornelia de Lange syndrome,* Down's syndrome,* renal abnormalities,* chromosomal abnormalities

    Deformed ears — Turner's syndrome,* Treacher–Collins syndrome*

    Tympanic membrane red, bulging, short light reflex, perforation, discharge — Otitis media

    Opaque, malpositioned landmarks, perforation — Serous otitis media

    Decreased or absent hearing — Hunter's syndrome,* Turner's syndrome,* Hurler's syndrome,* Treacher–Collins syndrome,* Waardenburg's syndrome,* osteogenesis imperfecta*

    Blind fistula between the corner of the mouth and the ears — Treacher–Collins syndrome*

Face
    Gargoyle-like facies — Hurler's syndrome,* Hunter's syndrome*

    Enlargement and/or tenderness of the submaxillary and sublingual glands — Cystic fibrosis,* mumps

Flat, round or depressed face	Chromosomal abnormalities
Increased distance from nasal base to lip, midline notching of lips	Cornelia de Lange*
Microphthalmia	Chromosomal abnormalies
Cornea clouding	Hurler's syndrome*
Cataracts	Marfan's syndrome,* Down's syndrome,* rubella syndrome, congenital hypoparathyroidism
Enlarged cornea	Marfan's syndrome*
Blue sclera	Osteogenesis imperfecta,* Ehlers−Danlos syndrome
Brushfield spots (specking of the iris)	Down's syndrome*
Heterochromia iridum (different-colored irises)	Waardenburg's syndrome*
Symgtric colobomas of the lids	Treacher−Collins*
Strabismus	Marfan's syndrome,* Down's syndrome,* muscle weakness, unilateral refractive error
Hypertelorism (lateral displacement of the inner canthi of the eyes)	Treacher−Collins,* Waardenburg's syndrome*
Inner and outer epicanthal folds slanted upward and outward	Down's syndrome*
Antimongoloid palpebral fissure slant	Treacher−Collins syndrome*
Unilateral exophthalmos	Cellulitis, orbital abcess, neoplasm, hyperthyroidism
Bilateral exophthalmos	Glaucoma, leukemia, lymphoma, congenital acromegaly, neurofibromatosis
Retinal changes	Diabetes, sickle cell anemia*

Nose

Prominent, broad nasal root	Waardenburg's syndrome,* chromosomal abnormalities
Nasal polyps	Allergies,* cystic fibrosis*
Small nose with flattened bridge	Down's syndrome,* other chromosomal abnormalities
Flat nasal bridge with upturned tip and anteverted nostrils	Cornelia de Lange syndrome*
Edematous turbinates	Allergies*

Mouth
  High-arched palate

Cornelia de Lange syndrome,* Treacher—Collins syndrome,* Turner's syndrome,* Marfan's syndrome,* arachnodactyly

Teeth
  Dental deformities

Osteogenesis imperfecta,* Down's syndrome,* congenital syphilis, acrodynia, cretinism, rickets

  Micrognathia (small mandible)

Cornelia de Lange syndrome,* juvenile rheumatoid arthritis, chromosomal abnormalities

  Large mandible

Crouzon's disease (craniofacial sysostosis), chondrodystrophy

  Large protruding tongue

Down's syndrome,* cretinism, Beckwith's syndrome, lymphangioma, hemangioma

  Malocclusion of teeth

Allergies,* Treacher—Collins syndrome,* thumb sucking after 6 years of age

Neck
  Webbed, short

Turner's syndrome,* Down's syndrome (occasional)*

  Stiff neck

Meningitis, torticollis, pharyngitis, trauma, arthritis

Chest

Normal Findings

Shape and circumference: the circumference of the chest, measured at the nipple line, is about the same or slightly less than the head circumference until the child is 2 years old. After the age of 2, the chest circumference is greater than the head circumference. The chest is round or circular in infancy, expanding in the transversal diameter as the child grows.

Respiration: normally, children are abdominal breathers until 6 or 7 years of age, when the thoracic motion becomes the method of air exchange. Respiration rates are 30 to 50 at birth, 16 to 20 at 6 years, and 14 to 16 at puberty (Barness, 1976).*

Breasts:	a neonate's breasts may be enlarged for one or two months. Between the age of 10 and 14, female breast development begins. Most often one breast develops sooner than the other.
Percussion:	lungs are resonant, with dullness noted over the scapula, diaphragm, and breast.
Auscultation:	bilateral bronchial or bronchovesicular breath sounds.

Heart

Normal Findings

Pulse rate:	normal limits for pulse rates are 70 to 170 at birth, 120 to 140 shortly after birth, 80 to 140 at 1 year, 80 to 130 at 2 years, 80 to 120 at 3 years, and 70 to 115 after 3 years (Barness, 1976).*
Palpation:	in newborns, the PMI is palpated at the fourth intercostal space left of the midclavicular line. By the age of 7 years, the point of maximum impulse (PMI) should be palpated at the fifth intercostal space at the midclavicular line. No thrill should be palpated.
Auscultation:	S_1 is louder than S_2; in about one-third of infants and children an S_3 is present and no pathology is indicated. Sinus arrhythmia is a normal finding in childhood. A venous hum is frequently heard. Many infants and children have low-grade heart murmurs in the absence of cardiac pathology.

Abnormal Findings	Possible Cause
Funnel breast (sternal depression)	Marfan's syndrome,* rickets, adenoid hypertrophy
Pigeon chest (protruding sternum)	Marfan's syndrome,* rickets, osteopetrosis, upper airway obstruction
Abnormal ribs	Hurler's syndrome,* Cornelia de Lange syndrome,* other chromosomal abnormalities
Wide sternum	Cystic fibrosis,* pulmonary hypertension, emphysema, left-to-right shunts
Barrel chest (increased A−P diameter)	Asthma, cystic fibrosis,* emphysema, pulmonary hypertension

Hypoplastic nipples	Cornelia de Lange syndrome*
Gynecomastia (breast development in males)	Klinefelter's syndrome,* side-effect of digitalis administration
Absence of breast development in adolescent females	Turner's syndrome,* anorexia nervosa, adrenal hyperplasia, pituitary failure
Wide-spaced nipples	Turner's syndrome*
Decreased breath sounds	Pneumonia, atelectasis, obstruction
Rales	Cystic fibrosis,* pneumonia, bronchitis, bronchiectasis, pulmonary edema, heart failure, asthma, foreign body aspiration
Wheezes	Foreign body obstruction, asthma, bronchiolitis
Heart Thrill	Aortic stenosis, patent ductus, pulmonary stenosis, coarctation, ventral septal defect
Murmurs	Congenital heart disease, anemia (including sickle cell anemia)

Abdomen

Normal Findings

Flat or slightly prominent, symmetric, and soft; peristalsis noted in all four quadrants; liver 1 to 2 cm below the right costal margin; spleen palpated 1 to 2 cm below the left costal margin (normal until the age of 3 years); femoral pulses equal to brachial pulses; umbilical hernias and diastasis recti are frequent findings in children until school age.

Abnormal Findings	Possible Cause
Distended abdomen	Paralytic ileus, peritonitis, imperforate anus, Hirschsprung's disease, cystic fibrosis*
High-pitched peristaltic sounds	Diarrhea, early peritonitis, gastroenteritis, intestinal obstruction
Enlarged spleen	Sickle cell anemia,* infectious mononucleosis, leukemia, septicemia, hemolytic jaundice, Hunter's syndrome*, Hurler's syndrome*

Enlarged liver

Sickle cell anemia,* hepatitis, leukemia, septicemia, liver tumor, right heart failure, Hunter's syndrome,* Hurler's syndrome*

Absent femoral pulses

Coarctation of the aorta

Genitalia

Normal Findings

Female: prominent labia in the newborn with a bloody or mucoid vaginal discharge. Pubic hair is apparent from age 8 to 13, with menses occurring between the ages of 9 and 17.

Male: at birth, the penis is at least 2.5 cm long and 1 cm wide. Testes are descended. The urinary meatus is at the tip of the penis, centrally located. The foreskin of uncircumcized males may not be retractable under normal conditions until the age of 3 years.

Abnormal Findings

Possible Cause

Small testes

Klinefelter's syndrome,* cryptorchidism, Down's syndrome,* other chromosomal abnormalities, Prader—Willi syndrome

Small penis

Down's syndrome,* hermaphroditism, other chromosomal abnormalities

Sterility

Males—cystic fibrosis,* Klinefelter's syndrome;* females—Turner's syndrome*

Delayed or incomplete secondary sexual characteristics

Constitutional delayed adolescence, hypopituitarism, chronic illness (cystic fibrosis, sickle cell disease, congenital heart disease),* hypothyroidism, congenital sexual anomalies, Turner's syndrome,* Klinefelter's syndrome,* gonadal failure, Prader—Willi syndrome, myotonic dystrophy

Anus and Rectum

Normal Findings
Patent, adequate spincter tone with no fissures or tags.

Abnormal Findings	Possible cause
Rectal prolapse	Cystic fibrosis,* chronic constipation, chronic diarrhea
Flattened buttocks	Cystic fibrosis,* celiac syndrome

Extremities, Spine Joints, and Muscles

Normal Findings
Extremities symmetric with full range of motion and appropriate muscle tone for age. Spine has normal physiologic curves and full range of motion.

Abnormal Findings	Possible cause
Swelling of hands and feet	Sickle cell anemia,* Turner's syndrome,* Milroy's disease
Claw-like hands	Hunter's syndrome,* Hurler's syndrome,* gangliosidoses, Scheie's syndrome
Oligodactyly (subnormal number of fingers or toes)	Cornelia de Lange syndrome*
Polydactyly (more than normal number of digits)	Trisomy 13, Laurence—Moon—Biedli syndrome
Arachnodactyly (abnormally elongated spidery fingers and toes)	Marfan's syndrome,* homocystinuria
Stiffness of joints	Hurler's syndrome,* Hunter's syndrome,* neurologic disorders, rheumatic fever, arthritis, osteochondritis
Increased flexibility of joints	Down's syndrome,* other chromosomal abnormalities
Short fingers	Cornelia de Lange syndrome,* myositis ossificans, Down's syndrome,* achondroplasia, dwarfism
Long, narrow fingernails	Marfan's syndrome,* hypopituitarism

Short stature	Osteogenesis imperfecta,* Hurler's syndrome,* Turner's syndrome,* Cornelia de Lange syndrome,* Hunter's syndrome,* chronic illness (cystic fibrosis,* sickle cell anemia,* congenital heart defects,* kidney disease, malnutrition, food allergies, liver disease, diabetes)
Tall stature	Klinefelter's syndrome,* Marfan's syndrome*
Scoliosis	Structural, idiopathic, rickets, poliomyelitis, muscular dystrophies, neurofibromatosis, other neurologic disturbances, Hurler's syndrome*
Lumbar gibbus (protruberance or humpback)	Hurler's syndrome*

Neurologic

Normal Findings
Orientation, language, and knowledge appropriate for chronologic age; cranial nerves intact, DTR's, brisk and equal; performs appropriate developmental tasks.

Abnormal Findings	Possible Cause
Mental retardation	Down's syndrome,* Cornelia de Lange syndrome,* Klinefelter's syndrome,* Hurler's syndrome,* Hunter's syndrome,* neurologic trauma hypoxia, other chromosomal abnormalities, other mucopolysaccharide abnormalities, rubella syndrome, other maternal infections, central nervous system infection, poliomyelitis, meningitis, encephalitis, Tay—Sach's disease, lead poisoning, cretinism, Rh, ABO incompatibility
Increased muscle tone	Upper motor neuron lesion, central nervous system injury, poliomyelitis, tetanus

| Decreased muscle tone | Down's syndrome,* hypoxia, central nervous system injury, rickets, Prader—Willi syndrome, Werdnig—Hoffmann disease, lower motor neuron lesions, malnutrition, muscular dystrophies, hypothyroidism, hypopituitarism |
| Athetosis (constant gross incoordinated movements that are slow, writhing, and usually associated with increased muscle tone) | Tuberous sclerosis, Tay—Sach's disease |

REFERENCES

Barness, L.A. *Manual of pediatric physical diagnosis* (4th ed.). Chicago: Year Book Medical, 1976.

Marks, M.B. Recognizing the allergic patient. *American Family Physician* 16:72, 1977.

Rudolph, A.M. (Ed.). *Pediatrics* (16th ed.). New York: Appleton—Century—Crofts, 1977.

BIBLIOGRAPHY

Eisenberg, L. The care and treatment of handicapped children. *Dentistry for Children* 43:4, 1976.

Evans, J.C. Newborn assessment. In J.A. Fox (Ed.), *Primary health care of the young.* New York: McGraw-Hill, 1981.

Lober, C.W. Manifestations of cystic fibrosis. *Primary Care* 4:4, 1977.

Meservey, P.M. Congenital musculoskeletal abnormalities. *Comprehensive Pediatric Nursing* 2:14, 1977.

Pillitteri, A. *Child health nursing* (2nd ed.). Boston: Little, Brown, 1981.

5

Communication Through Play

Shirley Steele

Play is the work of children. It is the child's mode of self-employment. The play requirements of childhood vary from age to age. However, the benefits of play activities are apparent throughout childhood. The child receives satisfaction from completing play activities. This sense of satisfaction is self-fulfilling. It seems that the healthy child seldom tires of play because of the rewards it provides him or her.

Many persons have studied the play activities of children (Groos, 1901; Huizinga, 1950; Piaget, 1962). These authorities present definitions and a rationale for play. However, the individual styles of play are influenced by the life experiences of the child.

PLAY AND RIGHT HEMISPHERE ACTIVITY

Play is closely associated with activity of the right hemisphere of the brain. The child's right hemisphere is responsible for intuitive imaginative activity. Play is a natural vehicle for the development of the imagination. Due to the young child's limited past life experiences, the child uses a great deal of imagination to fill in gaps in his or her knowledge base. This active imagination allows the child to act out many experiences about which he or she does not have a good knowledge base. Therefore, a child can be a "space man" or a "fireman" even though he or she has limited first-hand exposure to either of the roles. The vivid imaginations of preschool children draw heavily on right hemisphere activity and compensate for the lack of logical left brain activity. Seldom does a preschooler withdraw from play activities stating, "I don't know how to do it." Rather, the preschooler "makes up" the unknown in a realistic way during play activities. Make-believe is a technique used by the child to decrease limitations posed by the child's time and space, thus allowing the child to experience real-life events in a richer way.

ASSIMILATING REALITY

Play is used by the child to assimilate reality. It is used by the child to strive towards self-realization (Piaget and Inholder, 1969). Following this notion, play can be used as a dress rehearsal for experiences that are likely to occur. This is the rationalization for using play with masks, stethoscopes, hospital garb, and so forth to prepare the child for hospitalization (Fig. 5-1). While the child may not understand the full implication of the play activity, he or she is still able to assimilate it and to become aware that hospitalization is a real possibility.

THE CATHARSIS OF PLAY

Play is also used as a source of catharsis, or as a way to control stress. The child engages in play activities to rid himself or herself of painful thoughts or experiences. By playing out the situation, the child is able to express things that he or she cannot express verbally. This notion supports the practice of using therapeutic play activities after the child undergoes a painful procedure or an uncomfortable activity. In these cases, the child is allowed to play out the same scene that was experienced—e.g., injecting a doll with a syringe, bandaging a doll with ace bandages, or casting a doll with plaster of paris casts. After the child has an opportunity to play, a sense of freedom usually prevails and the child is able to attend to other things. Children who are not provided with therapeutic play activities can store up the hostility and frustrations that can be associated with these experiences rather than relieving themselves of these uncomfortable feelings.

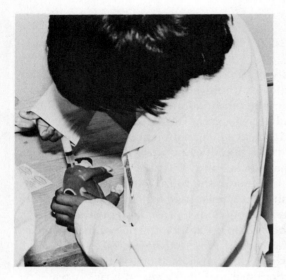

Figure 5-1.   A child dressed in a laboratory coat rehearsing for hospitalization by giving the puppet an injection. *(Photo by D. Haskin)*

MASTERING OF ANXIETY

Another area that is closely associated with the cathartic use of play is the power of play to help children master anxiety. Use of play for this purpose is based on the assumption that play serves a humanitarian function by lessening children's pain as well as a cognitive function by lessening emotional turmoil that interferes with the learning process (Arnaud, 1971). The use of play periods to prepare the child to have a new experience, such as enrollment in school or going to the dentist, is based on this power of play.

PLAY AS ENJOYMENT

Play activities should provide the child with enjoyment. Children are often happy during play periods. Play periods are spontaneous and serve as an energizer and organizer of cognitive learning, although there need be no tangible outcomes of play. The experience itself is enough to provide the child with enjoyment. Adults should avoid asking the child what is being made or being drawn as well as other questions that indicate a need for tangible outcome. The emotional well-being and cognitive development of the child are the most tangible results of play interludes (Fig. 5-2). The rationale behind providing the child with recreational play activities and including free play in schools is based on this notion.

Figure 5-2.   A group of children busily drawing in one area of a play room.
(Photo by D. Haskin)

ADULT INVOLVEMENT IN PLAY

The encouragement or lack thereof of adults influences the play activities of children. Some adults view play as a waste of time, while others thoroughly understand the value of play to the child's emotional, social, cultural, and biologic development. If more adults could internalize the fact that play is valuable to all these parameters of the child's development, more emphasis might be placed on providing children of all ages with play opportunities. The disvalue placed on play is often based on the work ethic of our culture or on our puritan tradition.

The way that adults interact with children during play activities varies greatly. Some adults tend to monopolize children's play, some interact occasionally, some ignore the play, and some provide encouragement for the child to play. Some adults have very little opportunity to play with children and/or are ill-equipped to engage positively in such activity. Other adults enjoy the playful experiences and enjoy opportunities that allow them to engage in play with children (Fig. 5-3). At times, when a child is confronted with an adult who cannot play, the child tries to teach the adult to play. This type of activity can result in an uncomfortable adult trying to participate in an activity that may or may not become comfortable enough to do. Children sense adults' uncomfortable feelings and may end up trying to ease these feelings. This discussion logically leads to the question of whether or not adults should intervene in order to help children to develop their abilities at play. Smilansky (1968; 1971) takes the position that without some adult intervention, dramatic play ability does not develop. She bases her assumption on the realization that dramatic play incorporates the emotional, social, and intellectual development of the child. Therefore, adults play an essential role in the child's ability to play, as adults influence these spheres of the child's development. In addition, children enter preschool programs with a wide range of play abilities that are probably influenced by adult interventions or a lack thereof.

Adult interventions that can facilitate children's play include:

1. Providing raw materials.
2. Teaching the use of raw materials.
3. Providing children with observation and understanding of their experiences.
4. Encouraging the child to use past experiences in his or her play.
5. Exposing the child to uses of make-believe.

These interventions require that the adult be able to diagnose the child's play behavior and to guide the child to develop play behaviors.

It is assumed that there are developmental sequences to play that are probably biologically determined but which need to be nurtured, patterned, and elicited by the child's family and cultural milieu (Curry, 1971).

Generally, children play with peers. Under these conditions, the children are usually on a somewhat equal basis. When adults play with children, the equality

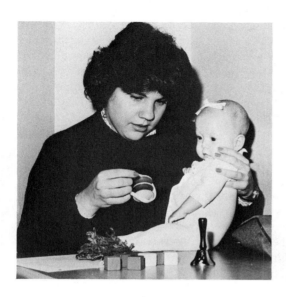

Figure 5-3. This infant seems to enjoy watching the toys from the Denver Developmental kit. *(Photo by D. Haskin)*

factor is often changed significantly. Adults need to be sensitive to the child and to let the child explore through play. Limiting the "I'll show you" statements and corresponding actions will benefit the child. Adults too often want the child to perfect skills rather than to enjoy the activity, and this notion can interfere with the child's use of creativity during play.

ENGAGING IN PLAY

Most children will find a way to play. Expensive and elaborate toys are not necessary for children's play. Old boxes, cartons, pots and pans, and paper bags are all valuable tools of play. Through imagination, these inexpensive items can be transformed into most anything. Again, there does not have to be tangible evidence of the transformation for the child to skillfully play out a theme. The fact that almost anything can be used in play activities makes play possible under all economic situations. In fact, at times it is judicious to suggest that expensive nonimaginative toys not be given to children, as they do not help children to create. In addition, they are an unnecessary expense for the family.

PLAY AS COMMUNICATION

Play is a form of communication for children. It is a way for children to make their feelings known even when they lack the verbal ability to do so. A toddler can bring a block to a nurse and in this way become engaged in a nonverbal interaction with the nurse. This same toddler may not be able to ask a nurse to come to him or her to engage in an interaction. In this case, the block serves as a communication channel for the child. The school-age child may be able to draw a picture that depicts his or her feelings about the hospital experience, but he or she may be reluctant to express these same feelings verbally (Fig. 5-4). The use of a hand puppet to explain procedures to the child helps to make complicated concepts seem more understandable. The child can also use a puppet to communicate with the nurse (Fig. 5-5). To some children, it is safer for the puppet to say things than for the child to say those things himself or herself.

MASTERY OF THE ENVIRONMENT

The child learns to master the environment through play experiences. Even children who live in disadvantageous situations are able to cope through the use of play. Curry (1971) suggests that play facilitates survival during difficult periods and may actually make survival seem worthwhile through the rewards of playfulness, such as imagination, flexibility, joyousness, and competence. The

Figure 5-4. This school-age child is dressed in a laboratory coat and is drawing a picture of the hospital to hang on the peg board for display. A helmet is needed to protect his head, as he has seizures. *(Photo by D. Haskin)*

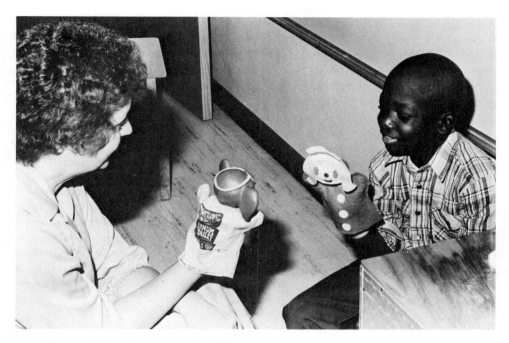

Figure 5-5. The nurse and child use puppets to communicate. *(Photo by D. Haskin)*

mastery of the environment is especially important to consider when a child is hospitalized and is even more significant when a child is hospitalized with a long-term illness. The unfamiliar hospital, the painful and uncomfortable procedures that are done, and the feeling of loneliness that can prevail can discourage the child from wanting to survive. Therefore, play activities in the hospital are considered to be essential to the child's care.

WAYS OF PLAYING

Arnaud (1971) suggests that there are four ways of playing:

1. Exploration.
2. Testing.
3. Imitation.
4. Construction.

She uses this conceptualization to encourage closer and more systematic observations of children's play. Exploration precedes play. In this stage, the child is enticed by a stimulus and rather passively surrenders himself or herself to the stimulus as he or she becomes interested in the stimulus. Imitation is based on notions explored in modeling theory and social learning theory. The child actively engages in activities that model or imitate. Testing is the activity by which the child tries out himself or herself in a variety of ways. The child is asking questions of himself or herself, such as "What can I do?" or "Can this fit in here?" Construction is the child's form of planning. The child is constructing his or her own world by putting new facts together with old facts, making ideas fit together.

Arnaud (1971) presents the position that the uses the child makes of play are significant enough to suggest that the four ways of playing are really modes of knowing. She tries to establish a difference between play and playfulness. In play, the modes of knowing are already established, while playfulness involves something quite different. In play, the child is engaged in a serious task, such as imitating the nurse giving an injection, while in playfulness the child may throw the sponges up in the air and yell, "Bombs away!" During play, the child increases cognitive skills and gains a sense of personal achievement. During playfulness, the child's cognitive skills are not necessarily involved and the emphasis is often on novelty. Playfulness often follows a period of mastery of a task through play, to which the child responds by expressing euphoria. Or, as Arnaud (1971) suggests, the mastery leads to playful diversification.

CONSTRAINTS POSED BY LONG-TERM ILLNESS

The play of children is often forestalled by the consequences of long-term illness. There are many things that can contribute to the child's inability to play. Some of these include:

1. Feeling too tired to play.
2. Lack of enthusiasm for play.
3. Extremely high levels of stress.
4. Restrictions in mobility.
5. Limited interactions with other children.
6. Lack of interest, motivation, or self-confidence.
7. Overprotectiveness of adults.
8. Fear of injury or worsening of a long-term condition.
9. Hesitancy to be involved in new experiences.
10. Limited opportunities.
11. Fear of failure.
12. Previous negative experiences, such as other children's derogatory remarks.
13. Unfamiliar setting.
14. Loneliness of separation.
15. Effects of hospitalization during hospitalization.
16. Regression due to hospitalization after discharge.

During the time that the child is hospitalized for acute episodes during the long-term illness, additional factors influence the child's ability to play. These factors include:

1. Decreased opportunities for socialization.
2. Repeated threats to body integrity.
3. Feelings that caretakers have let him or her down, as the caretakers are unable to protect him or her from pain and other uncomfortable experiences.
4. Availability of play space and materials.
5. Philosophy of the agency and health care providers.
6. Restrictions posed by the illness and its treatment.
7. Reactions of the child and the caretakers to the stress.
8. Physical changes that interfere with play activities.
9. Extended periods of dependency.
10. Isolation from peers who ordinarily engage in play with the child.
11. Limitations imposed on the child's freedom.
12. Feelings of discouragement that result from lack of progress.

The identification of factors that interfere with the successful involvement of a child in play can serve to identify ways that nurses can intervene on behalf of the child.

NURSE'S INVOLVEMENT IN PLAY

Despite the fact that many nurse experts state that play is an essential part of the nursing process, many nurses do not include play in their nursing management of children. This situation contributes to the child's inability to use play to cope with stressful aspects of the long-term illness and especially with the acute care periods of the illness.

The role of the nurse in the play program is often influenced by the other members of the team that contribute to the play aspects of the child's care (Fig. 5-6). Some hospitals have very elaborate structured play programs, while other hospitals leave play to chance. No matter what the play structure is, the nurse has an essential role to play in this important part of the child's care.

The nurse uses play supplies, objects, and concepts to guide interventions. As play is very familiar to children, it offers a way to keep the child feeling some sense of the known even during periods filled with unknowns. The nurse can use a hand puppet to encourage the child to go to sleep in an unfamiliar bed or take the child to the playroom to see familiar toys after admission. A playroom that is filled with familiar toys makes the child feel that the hospital has some friendly places where a child can have fun (Fig. 5-7). It takes a limited amount of time to include play in most of the child's experiences. However, the nurse must feel a commitment to this role or it will not be fulfilled (Fig. 5-8).

The cooperation of the child is gained much more easily when play is used to engage the child in activities. The nurse's realization of the value of play in

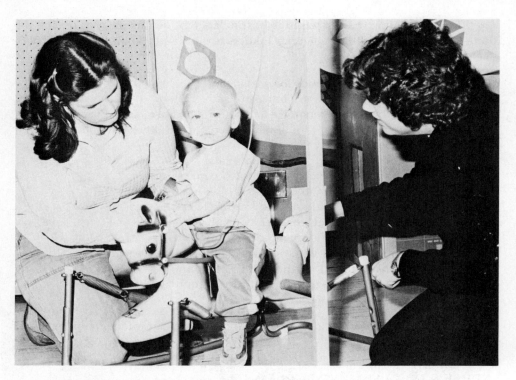

Figure 5-6. This acutely ill child enjoys riding the horse in the playroom. The mother and nurse assist her in this activity despite continuous intravenous therapy. *(Photo by D. Haskin)*

gaining the child's cooperation usually serves as a motivator to use play more readily. A child who needs to learn to zipper his or her clothing is enticed to participate in the activity if the zipper is in an attractive toy, such as a book or an attractive wooden toy. A child who must be placed in oxygen tent can be lured into the tent by a wind-up wooden musical toy that makes the tent seem less frightening. Play opportunities are extensive, so the nurse must be creative in determining how to use play activities effectively in the child's management.

There are variations of play that are associated with the nursing process. *Recreational* play is play that allows the child to play freely in the environment (Fig. 5-9). *Therapeutic* play is comprised of structured play activities that are planned for a specific reason (Fig. 5-10). *Play therapy* is a more involved process that uses information gathered from the child's play in order to draw inferences about things that are happening in the child's life. All nurses engage children in recreational and therapeutic play activities, while play therapy is usually reserved for health care providers specifically prepared to engage in this more intensive use of play.

Recreational play is facilitated by having the child bring toys from home and/or by introducing the child to the playroom. Therapeutic play is designed by

Figure 5-7. Toys for mobility are available in the playroom and help the child to feel that the hospital experience is not "all bad." *(Photo by D. Haskin)*

the nurse to specifically meet the needs of the child. Combinations of recreational and therapeutic play activities result in optimum care. During the recreational play, the child is free to engage in any activities that meet his or her fancy. Therapeutic play activities can be exhausting during the session but can result in a lessening of the child's stress. It will take less encouragement to engage the child in recreational play than in therapeutic play. However, in both instances, children will need assistance from adults to gain the self-confidence that is needed to participate in the play acivities that are provided.

The nurse's role in play is multifaceted. Responsibilities of the nurse include the following:

1. Diagnose the play needs of individual children.
2. Determine the need for individual or group play experiences.
3. Maintain supplies that are essential to the play program.
4. Elicit a play profile on each child.
5. Ask other adults to be involved in play activities.
6. Modify play activities to accommodate the child's disabilities or illness.
7. Introduce the child's significant others to ways to play with the child.

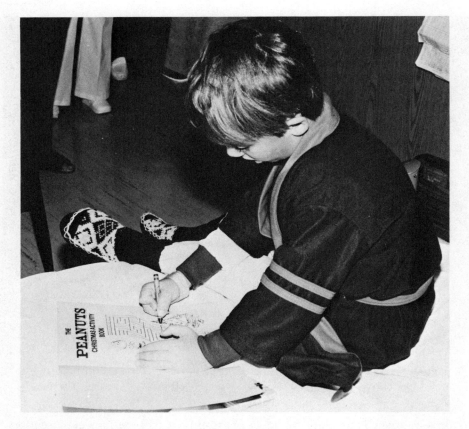

Figure 5-8.   After his bath has been completed, a coloring book and crayons are made available to this school-age child who is confined to his room. *(Photo by D. Haskin)*

8. Encourage caretakers to bring toys to the hospital.
9. Use play as part of the nursing process.
10. Interact and share observations with other persons involved in the play program.
11. Share observations gained through the play activities with other members of the health care team.
12. Actively engage in periodic special play offerings.

Play can be useful in all parts of the nursing process. Examples of uses in each of the parts of the nursing process are as follows:

1. Assessing.
    a. Using play to assess the child's developmental level; the Denver Developmental Screening Test (DDST) is an excellent example.

Figure 5-9. Recreational play using musical instruments. *(Photo by D. Haskin)*

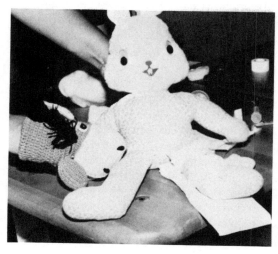

Figure 5-10. A therapeutic play episode—an area is ready for the child to engage in needle play to act out feelings related to her immobilized leg. *(Photo by H. Riggs)*

    b. Using finger paints to see if the child is able to be involved in a messy activity.
2. Planning.
    a. Showing the child slides of an upcoming experience.
    b. Engaging the child in dramatic play to prepare for an anticipated activity.
3. Implementing.
    a. Using animal-shaped sponges in the child's bath water.
    b. Putting plastic toys in the tub during skin debridement.
    c. Pulling a child in a wagon to the treatment room.
4. Evaluating.
    a. Observing the child's affect while engaged in play.
    b. Having the child attempt to dress himself or herself in dress-up clothes after using simulated dressing techniques.

INDIVIDUALIZING PLAY BY AGE

The play activities that are most useful in one age group are not the most appropriate for another age group. Therefore, the nurse individualizes play on the basis of the age of the child and the special considerations connected with the health problem. Juenker (1977) suggested the play profile as a technique for individualizing play activities. Juenker's explanation of the play profile follows:

Use of a Play Profile

    A play profile can be employed as an assessment tool at all stages of the child's illness—at the time of admission to the hospital, periodically throughout the hospital stay, at the time of discharge, and during convalescence (Figs. 5-11, 5-12, and 5-13). The profile obtained at the time of admission resembles a history of information about play behavior at home, as described by parents and the child. It is important to remember that this history provides only baseline data and therefore should not give a sense of finality to expected play behavior. The admission play profile is a guide for initial nursing intervention.

    After the profile is determined, a plan for play is developed jointly by the parents, child, and nurse. The plan is implemented and the child's response to it is recorded. Observation of the child's behavior may validate the nurse's expectations or may indicate that the play program needs modification.

    It is a well-known fact that play behavior will change as the child's condition either improves or deteriorates. Change in play may result from the child's ongoing maturation. This is particularly significant when children are hospitalized for a period of months. Play behavior may reflect everyday experiences as well as special hospital events, such as surgery or transfer to

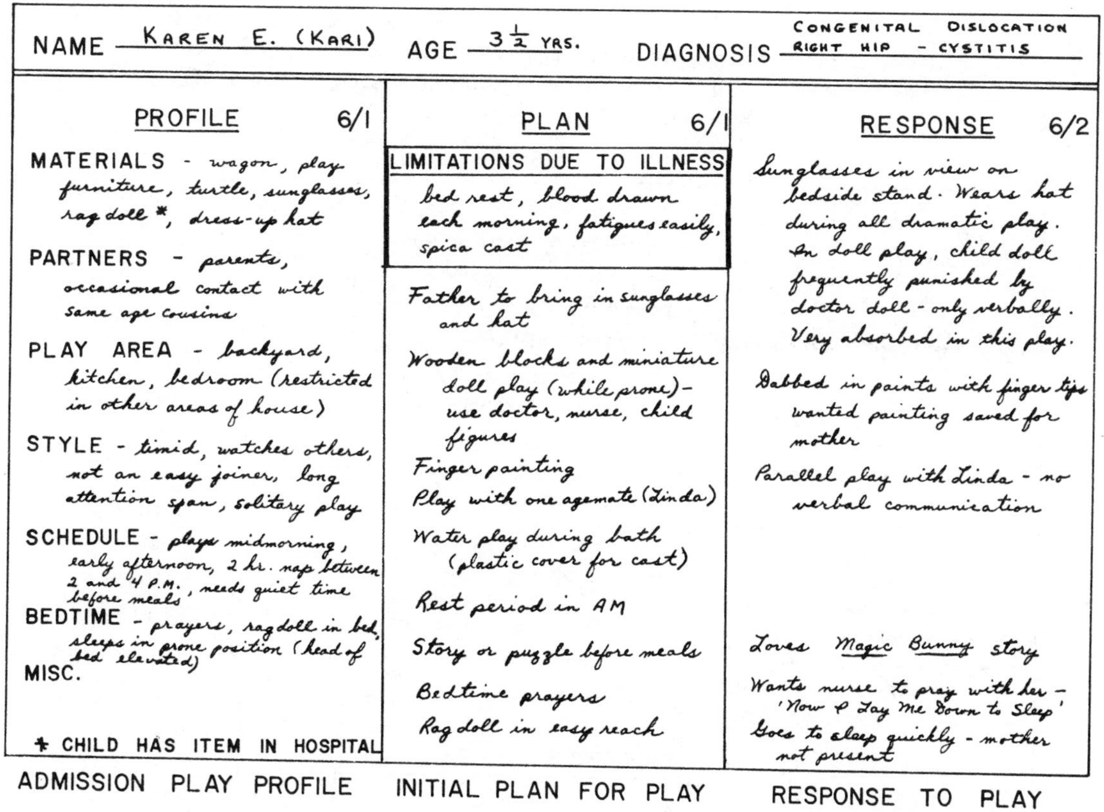

NAME __KAREN E. (KARI)__   AGE __3½ YRS.__   DIAGNOSIS __CONGENITAL DISLOCATION RIGHT HIP – CYSTITIS__

PROFILE 6/1	PLAN 6/1	RESPONSE 6/2
MATERIALS – wagon, play furniture, turtle, sunglasses, rag doll *, dress-up hat	LIMITATIONS DUE TO ILLNESS Bed rest, blood drawn each morning, fatigues easily, spica cast	Sunglasses in view on bedside stand. Wore hat during all dramatic play. In doll play, child doll frequently punished by doctor doll – only verbally. Very absorbed in this play.
PARTNERS – parents, occasional contact with same age cousine	Father to bring in sunglasses and hat	
PLAY AREA – backyard, kitchen, bedroom (restricted in other areas of house)	Wooden blocks and miniature doll play (while prone) – use doctor, nurse, child figures	Dabbled in paints with finger tips. Wanted painting saved for mother.
STYLE – timid, watches others, not an easy joiner, long attention span, solitary play	Finger painting Play with one agemate (Linda)	Parallel play with Linda – no verbal communication
SCHEDULE – plays midmorning, early afternoon, 2 hr. nap between 2 and 4 P.M., needs quiet time before meals	Water play during bath (plastic cover for cast) Rest period in AM	
BEDTIME – prayers, rag doll in bed, sleeps in prone position (head of bed elevated)	Story or puzzle before meals Bedtime prayers	Loves _Magic Bunny_ story Wants nurse to pray with her – "Now I Lay Me Down to Sleep"
MISC.	Rag doll in easy reach	Goes to sleep quickly – mother not present
* CHILD HAS ITEM IN HOSPITAL		

ADMISSION PLAY PROFILE   INITIAL PLAN FOR PLAY   RESPONSE TO PLAY

Figure 5-11. Juenker's play profile. *(From Juenker D., Play as a tool of the nurse. In S. Steele (Ed.), Nursing care of the child with long-term illness (2nd ed.). New York: Appleton–Century–Crofts, 1977)*

135

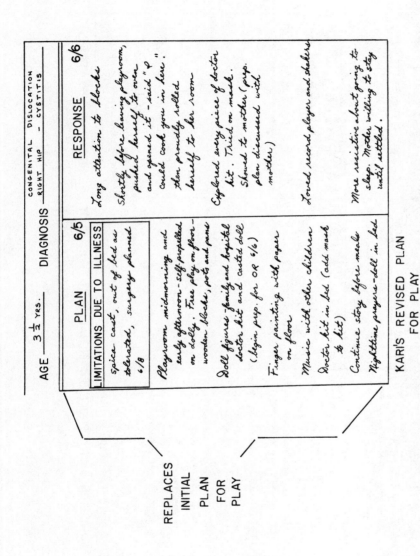

AGE ___3½ YRS.___   DIAGNOSIS   CONGENITAL DISLOCATION RIGHT HIP — CYSTITIS

PLAN 6/5	RESPONSE 6/6
LIMITATIONS DUE TO ILLNESS	Long attention to blocks
spica cast, out of bed as tolerated, surgery planned 6/8	Shortly before leaving playroom, pushed herself to oven and opened it – said " I could cook you in here." then proudly rolled herself to her room
Playroom midmorning and early afternoon – self-propelled on dolly. Free play on floor – wooden blocks, pots and pans	
Doll figures–family and hospital doctor kit and cuddle doll (begin prep. for OR 6/6)	Explored every piece of doctor kit. Tried on mask. Showed it mother (prep. plan discussed with mother.)
Finger painting with paper on floor	
Music with other children	Loved record player and shakers
Doctor kit in bed (add mask to kit)	
Continue story before meals	More resistive about going to sleep. Mother willing to stay until settled.
Nighttime prayers–doll in bed	

REPLACES INITIAL PLAN FOR PLAY

KARI'S REVISED PLAN FOR PLAY

Figure 5-12. Revised play profile. *(From Juenker D., Play as a tool of the nurse. In S. Steele (Ed.), Nursing care of the child with long-term illness (2nd ed.). New York: Appleton–Century–Crofts, 1977)*

another unit. Consequently, the play profile is reassessed periodically during the hospitalization. The revised profile is not derived from a history-taking process, but from the nurse's own observations of the child at play. Others who have participated in the child's play add their contributions, as well. The nurse then compares the new observations with the previous profile. She or he may find that a child who manifested aggressive behavior at the time of admission is now tending to withdraw from social contacts. The circumstances surrounding this behavior will need careful interpretation, and play stimuli may need to be altered to encourage more free expression. A reassessment of an infant's play experience might reveal that an infant hospitalized for 1 month has gained sufficient eye–hand skill to benefit from block play. The profile in such instances can become a tool that draws attention to the subtle clues that indicate learning readiness.

While the child is in the hospital, the profile is available to all persons who care for the child. Persons (including the parents) who have significant information about the child's play are encouraged to make notations. Productive ideas can be lost through ineffective communication. Someone's good idea can generate many new ways of approaching a particular problem. However, to avoid a hodgepodge of information, some one person (such as the team leader) should oversee the plan and coordinate activities. It is her or his special responsibility to see that play becomes a meaningful part of nursing care. Realistically, this nurse cannot note the play behavior of all of his or her young clients. It is not necessary that he or she do so. If members of the nursing team are knowledgeable about how to encourage ordinary play and what to observe about it, the team leader can direct attention to those high-risk children who are more likely to have potential play problems. These children can be categorized into four major groups.

In the first group are those children who have a developmental lag or are mentally superior. The nature and quantity of stimuli will be quite different for these children, since they must keep pace with the child's maturational readiness rather than his or her chronologic age. A second group consists of children who demonstrate psychosocial limitations in the style of their play. These children benefit from carefully selected play materials that specifically encourage energy release as well as interpersonal contacts that reflect awareness of the child's defense mechanisms. Children who have had or who are about to experience stressful situations comprise the third group. Play can serve as an excellent vehicle to prepare a child for an unpleasant event, and, of course, the content of play following the event may reveal feelings about the experience that cannot be expressed in other ways. A fourth high-risk group is comprised of children with kinds of physical disabilities that could be improved through the judicious use of play. For example, the spastic hands of an infant with cerebral palsy might open more easily if the infant could support his or her weight in a prone position. Placing toys within reach or hanging a jingly mobile within his or her view add to enjoyment and encourage him or her to sustain the prone position.

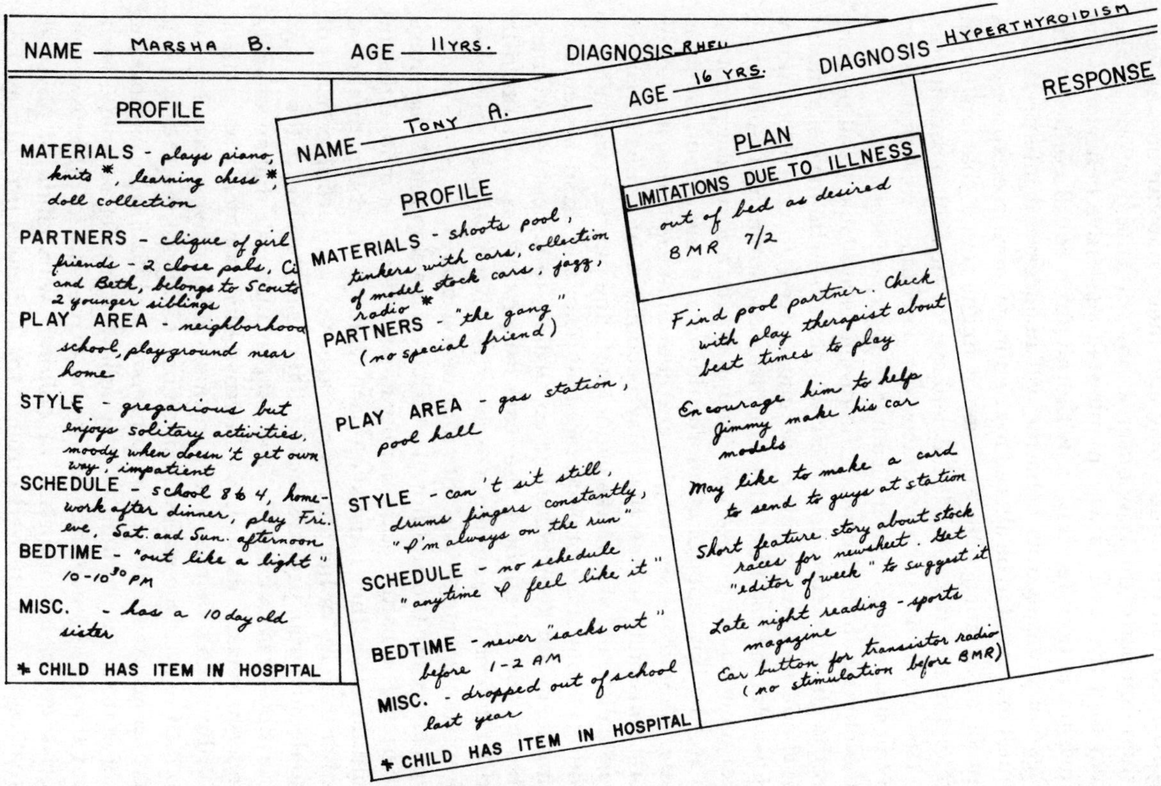

Figure 5-13. Play profiles for children of various ages. *(From Juenker D., Play as a tool of the nurse. In S. Steele (Ed.), Nursing care of the child with long-term illness (2nd ed.). New York: Appleton—Century—Crofts, 1977)*

Since these children have such special play needs, the nurse must rely on other members of the health care team for guidance in selecting effective methods of stimulation. The occupational, physical, and recreational therapists and the child life worker are important consultants. In unusual instances in which the child's behavior reveals a deep-seated conflict, a psychiatric consultant becomes necessary. A reciprocal relationship among the team members is essential if the child is to benefit from these people's individual talents. A meshing of goals will make sure that the child will be looked at as a totality. A consistent approach is used 24 hours a day—not just during the hours that the therapist is present.

When the child is about to leave the hospital, the play profile becomes part of the discharge plan. The content of the profile provides practical guidelines to parents as they anticipate convalescent play. The nurse can use the play profile to illustrate how the child can be expected to behave at home.

The discharge profile is not discarded. It becomes part of the child's record so that it can be used for comparison when the child visits the clinic or is readmitted to the hospital.

Significant information from the play profile is included when referral is made to the community health nurse so that she or he can provide continuity in the constructive use of play for a particular child. The community health nurse is in the enviable position of seeing the child in the home environment, where she or he can assess resources and suggest responsible improvisations. She or he can encourage the parents—and the child, if he or she is old enough—to compile their own profile periodically. If the whole family takes a purposeful look at play activities, their collective creativity will certainly enrich the experiences of the child with the long-term illness. If and when the child returns to the hospital for continued treatment, the community health nurse offers input to the admission profile—in effect, the cycle repeats itself.

The precise format of the assessment tool is not essential to its success. Many different styles can be effectively used. Nurses should develop a tool to suit their own needs, the needs of the specific child population that they are serving, and the needs of their particular agency. However, the format that is devised should reflect consideration of conciseness in recording and an easy way of making changes in plans whenever necessary. If the tool is highly complicated or too time-consuming for practical use, its benefits are not appreciated. And, of course, experience dictates that when an idea fails, it takes doubly long to generate enthusiasm to revive it. Assessment and planning of play experiences can be easily incorporated within the general admission assessment process as well as becoming part of the ongoing revision in the plan for care.

For purposes of illustration, consider the following situation:

Karen K., better known as Kari, was admitted to the pediatric unit for an open reduction of the congenitally dislocated hip that had responded poorly to conservative treatment. This $3\frac{1}{2}$-year-old girl had been in a double-leg cast for 3 months prior to the admission. On the day following her arrival in the hospital, Kari developed symptoms of cystitis. The anticipated surgery was delayed until recovery from the urinary tract infection was complete.

Kari was an only child who lived with her parents in an isolated rural area. Her mother stayed in a nearby motel to be with her during the hospitalization. Her favored play materials at the time of admission were a rag doll that she brought with her and a pair of green sunglasses that her grandmother had given her a week before. Unfortunately, the glasses were forgotten in the excitement of coming to the hospital. Her father brought along the low, wheeled platform that he had constructed so that Kari could scoot easily around the house. Figure 5-11 gives the admission play profile, the initial plan for play, and Kari's response. The revised plan based on the same profile but reflecting her changing needs is illustrated in Figure 5-12. Figure 5-13 shows how the same basic format can be adapted to suit the needs of children of different ages.*

The Neonate

Neonatal intensive care nursing incorporates concepts that relate to play. The neonatal nursery is decorated with pictures that reflect child preferences for art and tend to bind the parents to the reality that they are the parents of a viable child. Isolettes and warmers are gaily decorated with mobiles and toys that counterbalance the evidence of complicated technology that permeates these areas. Parents are encouraged to bring small toys to the neonate to help them to face the reality that they have a child even though the neonate is still dependent on advanced medical technology and skill for survival. In the early days following birth, the toys may be more beneficial to the emotional adjustments of the parents than to the child. However, as the neonate gains strength and awareness, the toys provide diversion from the monotony of the neonatal intensive care nursery. In addition, the toys serve to remind health care providers of the human elements that are essential in care areas connected with high levels of stress. The toys serve as constant reminders of the value of life of each child.

Despite the severity of the neonate's physical condition, it is imperative to pay attention to both the parents' and the neonate's emotional development. Utilizing principles that are used with the birth of a full-term infant will help to decrease the sequelae of the early health problem. Hopefully, the negative aspects of being a high-risk neonate can be decreased by trying to normalize some parts of the child's life.

Infancy

There is a wide range of activities that are appropriate to use during the infancy period. This age period heralds rapid growth for the child; needs and skills

*With permission Juenker, D. Play as a tool of the nurse. In S. Steele (Ed.), Nursing care of the child with long-term illness (2nd ed.). New York: Appleton-Century-Crofts, 1977.

change dramatically during the infancy period. Therefore the play prescriptions for the infant are assessed frequently and caretakers are encouraged to observe the infant closely for signs for readiness to engage in more complicated play interactions.

An infant with an able body progresses easily from one play activity to another as physical development proceeds (Fig. 5-14). The infant who is disabled may have handicaps that interfere with the expected progression, resulting in delayed development and a prolonged time between anticipation and actual achievement of play activities. Even under these conditions, the development of the infant influences the kinds of play activities that will bring satisfaction to the child.

The infancy period is referred to as the sensorimotor period. During this period, stimuli are introduced to heighten the infant's awareness and to involve gradually evolving motor skills. During the early infancy period, an adult must assume responsibility for introducing the stimuli, as the infant lacks the ability to engage himself or herself with stimuli. The presented stimuli cause the infant to react, and early habits of play are established.

Play stimuli are introduced on the basis of the developmental maturation sequence—i.e., cephalocaudal (head to toe) or proximodistal (from the center of the body outward; Fig. 5-15).

Initially, the infant's responses to stimuli may be reflexive in nature, but gradually the infant will develop well-established play behaviors in response to stimuli. For example, an infant may move all four extremities in response to the ringing of a bell—a reflexive response to a noise stimulus. At 3 months of age, the able-bodied infant may reach for the handle of a rattle when the rattle is placed in his or her visual field. Infants with some disabilities retain reflex-like responses longer than their able-bodied peers. The primitive responses sometimes interfere with the infant's ability to assume increasing responsibility to participate in play activities with adults.

Figure 5-14. An infant enjoying play with his father. Note how the child's entire body responds to his father's stimulation. *(Photo by H. Riggs)*

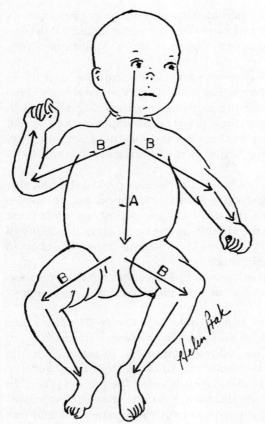

Figure 5-15. Developmental maturation sequences: **(A)** Cephalocaudal and **(B)** Proximodistal.

As play behaviors are established by the infant, they become an important part of the rituals that the infant cherishes. Anything that interferes with the rituals tends to be stressful to the infant. Therefore, consistency in play behaviors is an important part of the nursing management of children with long-term problems. The infant who is accustomed to a particular mobile on his or her crib can benefit by having a similar mobile on the hospital crib (Fig. 5-16). Inclusion of the mobile in the hospital environment helps to bring stability to the infant's psychosocial sphere of development despite interference in other spheres of development.

The selection of which stimuli to present to the infant is based on the infant's assessed level of development, suggestions provided by the caretakers, and the goal of promoting the infant's development to higher levels of mastery. In addition, the limitations imposed by the long-term illness are taken into consideration, and adaptations are made to compensate for deficits.

Stimulation of the infant is achieved through eye contact (Fig. 5-17) and through verbal interactions (Fig. 5-18). These two processes can be incorporated into the infant's play protocol through simple games that involve movements and

Figure 5-16. This 4-month-old infant is excited by the bright mobile. Her animated expression and body movements indicate responsiveness to her environment. *(From Juenker D., Play as a tool of the nurse. In S. Steele (Ed.), Nursing care of the child with long-term illness (2nd ed.). New York: Appleton–Century–Crofts, 1977)*

music. An early game that is loved by infants is "peek-a-boo." In this simple ritual, an adult can cover his or her eyes and make believe the infant disappears. When the eyes are uncovered, the adult expresses glee at seeing the infant once more. The infant soon models this behavior and uses "peek-a-boo" to gain a sense of self-confidence through the apparent fact that people can temporarily disappear and then reappear. This adult–infant interaction provides the infant with an opportunity to act out frightening feelings and then to replace these feelings with the joy that accompanies rediscovery of a loved adult.

As the infant becomes more sensitive to the environment, games like "pat-a-cake" and "bye-bye" are ways to engage the infant in interactions. To encourage body awareness, games like "this little pig" and "how big" are taught. Toys offer additional opportunities to enrich the infant's environment. During

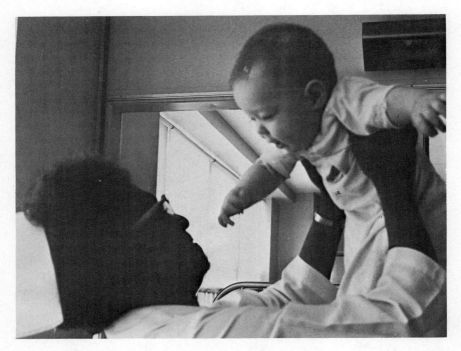

Figure 5-17.   This nurse and infant are enjoying a special kind of play—an infant "game." *(From Juenker D., Play as a tool of the nurse. In S. Steele (Ed.), Nursing care of the child with long-term illness (2nd ed.). New York: Appleton—Century—Crofts, 1977)*

this period, busy boxes are attached to cribs and play pens, and the walls of the infant's room are delightfully lined with pictures of animals, designs, or fairy tale characters. These same play stimuli can be part of the hospital environment for infants.

Play activities for the infant are based on stimulating the visual, auditory, tactile, and kinesthetic senses of the infant. Care is taken not to overstimulate the infant, however. There are particular times when active play activities can be too stimulating. The following are examples:

1. As the infant is nearing a sleep time.
2. Just before or after feedings.
3. When the infant has been quieted after a particularly stressful period.
4. When the infant is scheduled for an energy-absorbing activity in the near future.

Appropriate play activities at these times are focused on passive involvement of the infant, so a soft fuzzy teddy bear can be placed in the infant's crib and soft music can be played on the record player. Play activities of this nature are

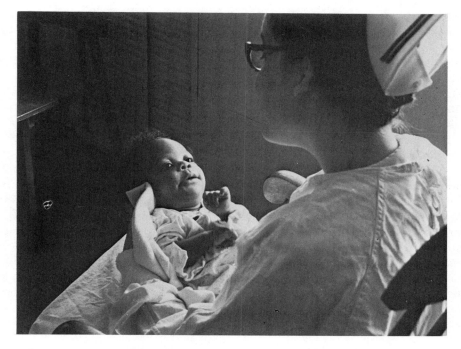

Figure 5-18. This nurse and infant are enjoying an intimate "conversation." *(From Juenker D., Play as a tool of the nurse. In S. Steele (Ed.), Nursing care of the child with long-term illness (2nd ed.). New York: Appleton–Century–Crofts, 1977)*

soothing and do not require energy expenditures by the infant; therefore, they promote relaxation and sleep. Children with long-term illnesses often develop many rituals that are retained for extended periods. During stressful periods, these rituals take on additional importance, and being able to use the rituals to support the child is an essential component of the nursing management of these children.

As the infant develops, enjoyment is derived from random movements of the body. Activities that encourage these random movements are provided, unless the infant is restrained for safety. Many toys will cause the child to use random movements—rattles, bells, or even a feather that can be used to stroke the infant's skin. At times, the infant moves so enthusiastically in response to stimuli that the whole bed shakes. When the child is held in an adult's arms during this activity, it is imperative that the adult have a firm grip on the infant so that he or she does not inadvertently fall. While the infant is seated in a high chair, small toys placed on the food tray are immediately used to express motor activity. In addition, toys are dropped to the floor on endless occasions. The infant enjoys the repetition of dropping the toy and having an adult make it appear. It never occurs to the infant that the adult is not receiving similar pleasure from the experience.

The infant tends to put everything into his or her mouth. Therefore, precautions are taken to have toys be safe for this stage of development. Despite cautious awareness, it is still possible for injuries to occur as the infant crudely places objects into the mouth or as the infant misses putting the object into the mouth and mistakenly hits his or her own eye. Oral gratification can be inhibited when the infant is restrained. Therefore, pacifiers are often substituted and the restraints are released while supervision is possible so that the infant can suck on a thumb or place a favorite object in his or her mouth. When oral gratification is lessened, tactile stimulation can be utilized by softly caressing the infant's skin with a warm hand or by softly moving a soft fluff of wool over the infant's exposed skin surfaces.

Infancy is a rapid period of development, and the nurse engages the caretakers in observations of this development. Through the use of play prescriptions, the caretakers can become active participants in encouraging their infant's play behaviors. In addition, the caretakers facilitate play by their warm, loving, nurturing attitudes. These behaviors indicate to the infant that adults are trustworthy and dependable, and through these behaviors the infant develops a sense of trust. Since long-term illness can negatively impact some spheres of the infant's development, it is essential that special attention be focused on the nurturance of trust, lest mistrust becomes the outcome of the psychosocial development of the child. Figure 5-19 identifies toys appropriate during the infancy period.

Toddlers

The toddler's style of play proceeds beyond the solitary play of infancy to parallel play. Parallel play indicates that the child plays side by side with another child but that usually there is minimal cooperative interaction. When interaction does occur, it is usually a power struggle between toddlers that results from their egocentric orientation.

The toddler period witnesses the child's mastery of mobility. The toddler who masters mobility broadens his or her world, as he or she no longer has to depend on adults to get to another place. The child's increased ability to move around increases his or her sense of autonomy. The toddler thrills in opportunities to use his or her new skills, so play activities that support this newly acquired skill are warranted. Figure 5-20 identifies toys that are appropriate for toddlers.

The toddler also enjoys hearing stories. Simple story books are memorized by the toddler after being repeatedly read by an adult. The toddler points at pictures and soon makes associations with the story. The toddler enjoys repetition and does not tire of hearing the same stories over and over. The toddler's involvement in the story is increased by asking him or her to make the sounds of the pictured animals or to point to a girl character or an adult in an identifiable role. The toddler's vivid imagination makes storytelling a fine way to provide amusement. Fortunately, storytelling lends itself to the special needs of almost all children with long-term illness. The toddler can be restrained and still be engaged in a storytelling session, and a tired toddler can be read a story in preparation for sleep. Reading to a child stimulates his or her cognitive develop-

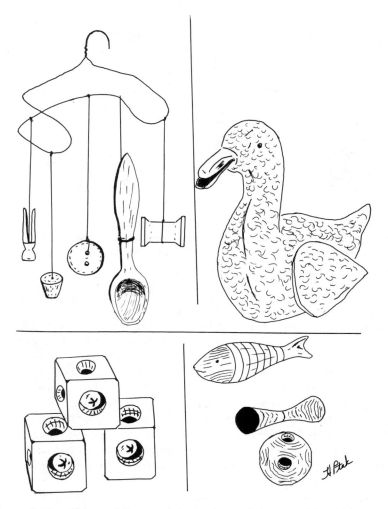

Figure 5-19. This mobile can be constructed from ordinary household materials. An infant unit should have an ample supply of toys like these to provide age-appropriate stimuli. *(From Juenker D., Play as a tool of the nurse. In S. Steele (Ed.), Nursing care of the child with long-term illness (2nd ed.). New York: Appleton—Century—Crofts, 1977)*

ment as well as being recreational. A generous supply of books for children of all ages is a must on a children's unit. In addition, caretakers are encouraged to purchase or borrow books to read to the toddler on an ongoing basis. The toddler with a long-term illness that interferes with his or her intensive exploration of the environment can receive compensation for this handicap by vicariously participating in experiences by reading and storytelling.

The toddler's attention span is limited. Due to this limited attention span, it

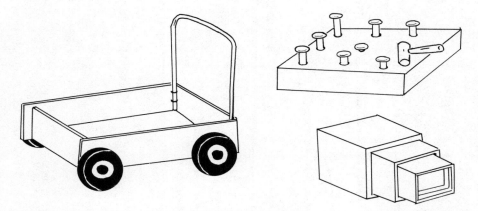

Figure 5-20. These toys will interest the toddler, since they encourage locomotion and hand skills. *(From Juenker D., Play as a tool of the nurse. In S. Steele (Ed.), Nursing care of the child with long-term illness (2nd ed.). New York: Appleton—Century—Crofts, 1977)*

is necessary to have a series of play experiences available for the toddler's involvement. As the toddler does not interact with other children to a significant degree, it is still usually an adult that provides the play opportunities that fill the wakeful hours of the toddler's day. If the toddler's play is not supervised effectively, the toddler is prone to injury during play. It is still necessary to check toys for safety before letting the toddler explore them independently. Removable parts of toys are easily removed and swallowed by toddlers. The toddler's curiosity also leads to an exploration of areas in the home or hospital that harbor potential danger. When supervision cannot be continuous, it is necessary to place the toddler in a playpen temporarily. The playpen is decorated with interesting toys to engage the toddler in interesting activities to compensate for his or her imposed limitations in mobility.

The toddler's language development is slow to emerge during this period when motor development is proceeding steadily. Play activities can still encourage the toddler's vocalizations, however. Vocalization is encouraged by pointing to the toy and stating its name and urging the toddler to repeat it. Likewise, vocalizations that are made spontaneously by the toddler can be repeated by an adult to encourage ongoing vocalization.

Teaching the toddler to play is fostered by getting the child's attention, giving complete and explicit directions, allowing the toddler to complete the task, and verbally rewarding the toddler for trying the task. Often, incomplete teaching by adults interferes with the toddler's potential for mastery. It seems unwarranted to have to stress that it is imperative to get the toddler's attention before proceeding to teach him or her to play. Getting the child's attention influences whether or not the child will be successfully engaged in learning as a result of play sessions. Toddlers with long-term illness can be a special challenge, as their limited attention spans, combined with the other problems, make it possible for them to have frequent periods of frustration. The frequent temper tantrums of toddler-hood are more common in toddlers who have health problems. Involvement in play that tells the toddler that he or she is special helps to cut down on the use of temper tantrums and leads to the toddler's drive toward autonomy rather than shame and doubt.

Major developmental tasks of this age period are toilet training and self-feeding. Both of these tasks can be frustrating for the toddler prior to mastery. Play that helps to relieve the toddler's frustration includes water play and finger painting or painting with pudding or nontoxic shaving cream. These media allow the child to make a mess in an appropriate way.

Preschoolers

The preschool child moves from the parallel play of the toddler to a cooperative play style. The preschooler is striving toward initiative, which makes the preschool time a delightful period in which the child is able to spend longer periods in interaction with other children as well as in play that is self-initiated and self-maintained.

The preschool child learns to have better self-control in a variety of ways. Masters and Santrock (1976) found that children could be encouraged to stay at a task for longer periods of time by having them say things to themselves. For example, when children tell themselves that a task is fun or easy or when they express pride in their work rather than expressing self-criticism, they persevere for longer periods. In addition, when children think of pleasant things that they might earn due to task completion, they persist at the task longer. These techniques can be incorporated to increase the length of time that preschool children engage in a single activity.

The preschooler's ability to get around freely cuts down on the need for adults to plan the preschooler's play, but it is still important for adults to supervise the play and to make suggestions when the preschooler exhausts his or her own ideas.

Activities that involve large muscles are appropriate for the preschooler. Toys that are useful include tricycles, wagons and other push and pull toys, and balls. In addition, the preschooler enjoys a blank sheet of paper to color or finger paint with broad strokes. Water play continues to be a favorite, and swimming pools, especially small plastic ones, allow the preschooler endless hours of enjoyment.

Dramatic play emerges in this age period, and this dramatic play makes it possible for the child with a long-term illness to use this play style to decrease stress, frustrations, and other negative feelings associated with his or her health problems. Figures 5-21 and 5-22 show some of the toys that are useful for this purpose. Figure 5-23 shows a preschool child engaged in dramatic therapeutic play while hospitalized.

Dramatic play potential (or make-believe) is also the basis for providing the preschool child with opportunities to model roles of adults. The child loves to dress up and also loves to enact roles. These loves continue in the hospital setting, so "dress-up" clothes and play room settings that encourage imaginative play are kept easily accessible (Figs. 5-24 and 5-25).

DOLL FIGURES

AGGRESSIVE TOYS

REGRESSIVE TOYS

Figure 5-21.   Preschool children can give expression to their strong feelings in dramatic play. These "props" will encourage them to work out conflicts, allowing for both aggressive and regressive responses. *(From Juenker D., Play as a tool of the nurse. In S. Steele (Ed.), Nursing care of the child with long-term illness (2nd ed.). New York: Appleton–Century–Crofts, 1977)*

The preschooler likes to put large-piece wooden puzzles together. Storytelling and listening to stories continue to be favorite pastimes. Toys that model environmental scenes (such as gas stations, hospitals, and airports) allow the child to learn about the environment as figures associated with the settings are placed into the toy buildings. These play opportunities allow the preschooler to combine reality and imagination. At times, the child uses the toys as expected, while at other times the toys are used in a completely unrelated way.

The preschooler also enjoys group games played to music. Simple tunes are easily recognized by the child, and words are learned through repetition. Through this play, the preschooler learns to take turns and learns important concepts, such as colors and components of health. Children's records offer the preschooler opportunities to develop language, learn songs and dances, and engage in individual or group games. The basic skills fostered by children's records are precursors to more complicated cognitive skills that the child will need during the school-age period.

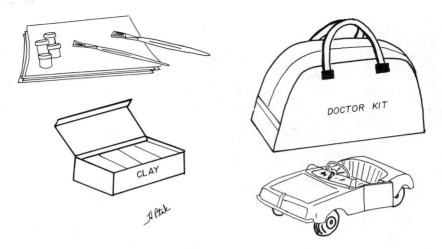

Figure 5-22. Brush painting and modeling with clay provide pleasant sensory experiences. The car and doctor kit are good tools, as they involve the child in identification—imitation processes. *(From Juenker D., Play as a tool of the nurse. In S. Steele (Ed.), Nursing care of the child with long-term illness (2nd ed.). New York: Appleton—Century—Crofts, 1977)*

School-age Children

The school-age period has one central theme: industry. The cooperative play of the preceding stage of development expands into group play in the school years.

The early school-age years increase the child's ability to participate in a wider range of play activities as the child's eye—hand coordination is developed. In addition, fine muscle coordination emerges. Eye—hand coordination and fine motor control allow the play activities to include board games, such as Chinese checkers, Candyland, and Yatsee.

These same physical advances, along with increasing cognitive skills, form the basis for including games of chance and skill in the child's repertoire. Games of this sort include Monopoly, checkers, and electronic games. A large variety of board games are useful for children who are ill as well as for those who are healthy. The school-age child enjoys making choices about the games in which he or she wishes to engage. Peers and adults can serve as partners during the play periods. The school-age child has a strong urge to win. This emotional involvement in games can be energy-consuming, so even fairly passive board games can be very taxing, depending on the amount of emphasis the child places on winning.

The school-age period brings with it the age of hobbies. The child may begin to collect stamps, shells, bottles, baseball cards, marbles, dolls, paper dolls, insects, rocks, or any other thing that takes his or her fancy at the moment. These collections are often shared with peers, and swapping items in the collection is common. Collecting can teach the child many skills that are useful in adulthood. Hobbies can be useful ways to engage a child's time when long-term illness interferes with the ability to participate in more active pursuits.

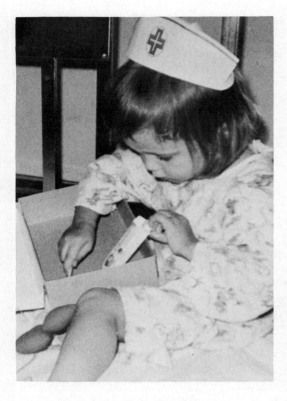

Figure 5-23. This preschool child is learning by doing. Playing out stressful situations relieves anxiety. *(From Juenker D., Play as a tool of the nurse. In S. Steele (Ed.), Nursing care of the child with long-term illness (2nd ed.). New York: Appleton−Century−Crofts, 1977)*

The competitive nature of the school-age child leads to his or her interest in games such as baseball, soccer, and basketball. A wide range of sports is taught to school-age children, taking into consideration that the sports cannot be played as they are by adults due to the child's immature skeletal structure.

Crafts are also a favorite of this age group. Special products emerge from these activities that provide the school-ager to give gifts to loved ones. Artistic abilities are encouraged by providing the child with blank sheets of paper and crayons, magic markers, or paints. In addition, the school-age child is able to concentrate for longer periods and is easily enticed to put puzzles together, to trace pictures, to read books, or to listen to records (Fig. 5-26). This age group still enjoys group games played to music, with parachute play, gymnastics, and others being favorites.

During this period, many children experiment with musical instruments. The child can be serious about learning the instrument or just experimenting. The degree of involvement the child feels with the instrument influences whether or not the child will devote the time needed to practice adequately. Often parents are more eager to have the child play an instrument than the child is. This situation can result in the child's resistance to practicing, and this can result in adult−child dissatisfaction. Participating in the band can be a nice alternative to

Figure 5-24. The 3- to 6-year-old enjoys these materials. House play is readily stimulated by sturdy replicas of household furnishings. The doll house is another favorite, as it helps the child to explore new roles. *(Courtesy of Children's Hospital of Buffalo, New York)*

playing a contact sport when a long-term illness interferes with the child's ability to be involved in contact sports.

The large muscle coordination of the school-age child continues to mature, allowing the child to progress from a tricycle to a bicycle or unicycle. The bicycle allows the child to increase his or her area of exploration, and the family decreases in importance as the center of the child's social environment. The same-sex peer culture becomes more and more significant in the school-age child's life. Large muscle activities such as tag, swimming, hopscotch, and jumprope fill in many free hours. These activities help the child to release excess energy and also to reduce stresses. Long-term illnesses that prolong dependence on parents interfere with the school-age child's development. During hospitalizations, wheelchairs replace bicycles as vehicles for locomotion and seeking peer relationships.

There is also a secretive aspect to the school-age child's play. Clubs are formed and dissolved, rules are made up and discarded, name-calling is common, and language is often invented for a particular purpose. All these characteristics of play allow the school-age child to gain independence from adults, which takes on increasing importance as the child nears early adolescence.

154

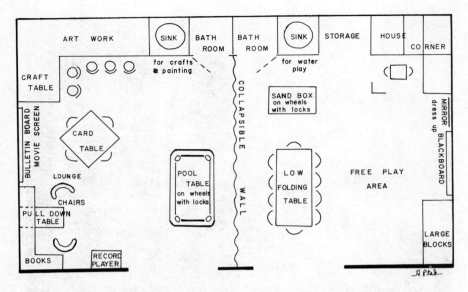

Figure 5-25. A playroom designed for flexibility. *(From Juenker D., Play as a tool of the nurse. In S. Steele (Ed.), Nursing care of the child with long-term illness (2nd ed.). New York: Appleton—Century—Crofts, 1977)*

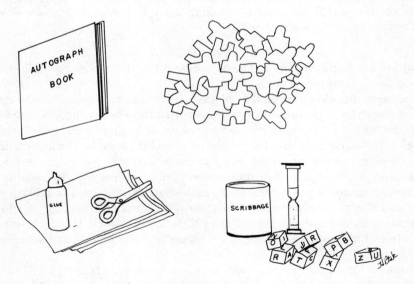

Figure 5-26. These simple materials provide the school-age child with opportunities for creative expression and for development of intellectual and manipulative skills. *(From Juenker D., Play as a tool of the nurse. In S. Steele (Ed.), Nursing care of the child with long-term illness (2nd ed.). New York: Appleton—Century—Crofts, 1977)*

Adolescence

All periods of development are periods of transition from one stage of development to another. But adolescence involves a greater transition, as the child moves from the dependence of childhood to the independence of adulthood. The early adolescent period brings forth many feelings of ambivalence, as the child cherishes independence but still has many moments when dependence is more comfortable.

The adolescent forms gang relationships that revolve around areas of interest, such as religious groups, scouting groups, science clubs, bands, cheer-leading teams, and sports teams. These relationships outside the family are very gratifying to the adolescent. Parties, gatherings, and dances emerge as areas of interest. Early adolescents go to the activities with peers of the same sex, and dating emerges later in the period. There are wide variations in the heterosexual relationships of this age period, varying from abstinence to early marriage or single-parent pregnancies.

Many pressures influence the way the adolescent expresses his or her identity during the adolescent period. Play that provides great satisfaction to one adolescent can seem like "child's play" to another. There is a broad range in the rate of maturation of adolescents that influences their interest in play activities, but play activities in general begin to approach adult interests (Fig. 5-27).

The adolescent is capable of extended periods of concentration. This ability makes games such as chess and backgammon very attractive to some adolescents. Adolescents also spend long periods listening to their favorite music and

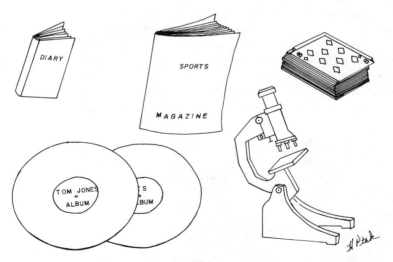

Figure 5-27. The adolescent is approaching adult interests. These common materials serve a wide range of abilities and help to bridge the gap between childhood play and adult recreation. *(From Juenker D., Play as a tool of the nurse. In S. Steele (Ed.), Nursing care of the child with long-term illness (2nd ed.). New York: Appleton—Century—Crofts, 1977)*

enjoy music that is not often pleasant to adults (Fig. 5-28). Dancing is taken more seriously, and both heterosexual and same-sex partnerships are seen on the dance floor.

More serious reading, art work, musical involvement, and sports activities are common. The bicycle continues to be a main mode of locomotion for many adolescents, but many turn in the bicycle for a driver's license. Increasingly, activities take place farther away from home, and the family continues to gradually decrease as the adolescent's center of concern.

Electronic games continue to have a contagious appeal. Adolescents spend many hours testing their skill at machines, on hand computers, and on games attached to the television. Table games such as pool, table tennis, and bumper ball are also enticing. All these activities involve both cognitive skills and muscle coordination.

While a great deal of the adolescent's time is spent with favorite age-mates, there is still a need for the adolescent to spend periods alone searching for identity. The adolescent requires space and time to meet his or her solitary needs. Identity requires time for the adolescent to keep asking the question, "Who am I?" and then time is needed to get affirmation from others.

As the late adolescent period emerges, identity is accomplished and intimacy emerges as a central theme. Favorite games that are precursors to serious relations involve heterosexual interactions, with variations of post office and spin the bottle bringing out affectionate feelings that can be expressed in the safety of the game.

Adolescence is a particularly important period, and children with long-term illnesses can be disadvantaged as they traverse this period. Long-term illness often requires increased periods of dependence and brings forth particularly powerful feelings of protection in parents, especially mothers. These factors interfere with the ability of the adolescent with a health problem to have opportunities to interact with other adolescents of the same age to get affirmation and cues that result in his making adjustments in behaviors. Providing the adolescent with choices about the way he or she uses his or her free time helps to facilitate his or her ability to make decisions. Adolescents with health problems

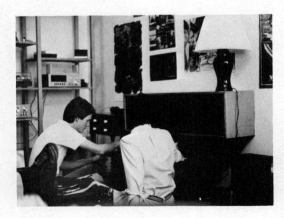

Figure 5-28. These adolescents take their music seriously. In the hospital, a special recreation room makes it possible for them to continue their interest without interference from younger children. *(Photo by H. Riggs)*

are often deprived of opportunities to make choices about matters that directly affect them.

Long-term illnesses that seriously interfere with the dependence of the adolescent are likely to be most stifling during this age period. The sexuality tasks of adolescence are potentially high-risk areas, as attitudes of society strongly influence this area of the adolescent's life. Historically, human sexuality needs were repressed in persons that were different from the norm. Despite a slow change in attitudes, many adolescents with health problems are delayed in achieving intimacy goals.

ENVIRONMENTS THAT SUPPORT PLAY

The goals of play as a source of satisfaction and stress alleviation are advanced when environments are supportive of play strategies.

Components of environment include people, structure, and supplies. Individually as well as in interaction, these parameters influence the potential benefits of play or the lack thereof. It is difficult to assess the absolute potential of any of these parameters to influence the effects of play, but some hypotheses about their impact follow:

1. An environment that provides children with play materials and supplies is more likely to facilitate the child's emotional adjustment than one that is devoid of these materials and supplies.
2. Persons that possess a personal philosophy that play is important to the child's development are more likely to provide children with play opportunities than persons who do not hold this philosophy.
3. Having supplies for play will encourage the child to play actively, whereas a lack of supplies interferes with the child's ability to play.
4. An environment that makes it possible for adults to interact in play with children is more supportive of the psychosocial needs of families than ones that do not provide this opportunity.
5. An environment that provides the child with play opportunities gives the child more of a chance to make choices than one that does not.
6. An environment that has people, space, and supplies for play is more likely to make play opportunities available to children than an environment that does not.

Play in the Home

Homes of well children where families have adequate financial income are usually generously supplied with toys and other play materials. Homes where finances are a problem can be deprived of supplies that support play. In addition, it is not unusual for caretakers to perceive that children with long-term illness do not need or cannot benefit from play materials.

The community health nurse can be very beneficial in helping families to make play materials available to the child. In addition, encouragement is often needed to help caretakers to receive gratification from even small accomplishments of children during play periods. It may be necessary to show caretakers how to make toys or how to improvise to make things available to the child for play when toys are not feasible. Almost every home has a wealth of objects that can be safely used as toys. Children often enjoy the box more than the toy it contained, as the box allows the child to use his or her imagination more freely. The toy may be so specific to one function that it becomes boring to the child very quickly, whereas the box can serve many functions.

Some long-term illnesses require inordinate amounts of the caretaker's time to manage the child's health problem. In these instances, the caretaker may have little time or energy available to provide play experiences. In these cases, other members of the family or a neighbor may be willing to take responsibility for the child's play experiences.

A home environment that concentrates on having play experiences accessible to the child and takes into consideration the child's inability to be completely independent in retrieving these experiences will foster the child's involvement in play. Too often, children with long-term illness are deprived of play experiences because they need adjustments in the usual play routines. For example, a child may require a restraint to be safe on a toy, while a child without the health problem may not require the restraint. The child should not be deprived of the experience because adjustments are necessary. Adults often need assistance to see how adjustments or adaptations can be made to make a variety of play experiences available for the child.

Play in the Outpatient Department

The outpatient department is a fertile area for play. Often there are long waits during which children and caretakers are bored from lack of activity. The hours of boredom can be successfully replaced by periods of play that may be enriching for the child and may teach the caretaker additional play experiences that are appropriate for the child. Even children confined to wheelchairs can be actively engaged in play experiences while they wait for scheduled outpatient appointments (Fig. 5-29).

The use of music to get groups of persons, both children and adults, engaged in joyful experiences is suggested. The music can be a welcome change from the noises of a busy outpatient department.

Play can be incorporated into health teaching that is an integral part of the outpatient services. Film strips and audiotapes of health concepts can be combined, with children enacting their involvement in the expression of the health behavior that is being taught on the instructional media. An outpatient department that provides these components of care helps to promote the development of the child and tends to foster growth as a result of having a long-term illness. Children who do not have illness are not exposed to these same health teaching opportunities, so the child with the long-term illness receives a special bonus from these planned play and health teaching experiences.

Specialty clinics of outpatient facilities often play an essential role in the lifestyles of both the children with long-term illness and their caretakers. As such,

Figure 5-29. Children in the outpatient department watch a puppet show and then play with the puppets while they wait for their check-ups. *(Courtesy C. Cantania)*

these clinics and their health care providers have a unique opportunity to make the environment a positive place for the children and caretakers. Each specialty clinic needs a supply of toys that engage the child in purposeful activities during waiting times and during examinations. In addition, the clinics can make an effort to recognize special days or to mark significant milestones in the child's life. For example, a small gift can be given to the child to mark a birthday or a required loss in weight or to acknowledge the loss of a tooth. As the children return again and again, it is fairly easy to remember favorite toys of the children and to have the toys available for the children to use on the day of their appointment. In this way, the children are made to feel important because the health care providers care enough to personalize care in this way. Ongoing play profiles of the child are part of the child's outpatient record, so this component of the child's management receives the same thoughtful attention as other areas of the child's management.

Play in the Inpatient Acute Care Setting

Many children with long-term illness have periodic admissions to the hospital for evaluation, follow-up surgery, or treatment of acute episodes of illness. Hospitalization often results in disturbances in the child's emotional development. However, some children with long-term illness even seem to enjoy periods of

Figure 5-30. A group of excited children is watching this theater troupe perform. *(Hamburg Children's Theater, Hamburg, N.Y.)*

hospitalization. Attention to the play needs of children helps to decrease the negative effects of hospitalization.

Hospitals that have a separate pediatric unit usually have an area set aside for children's play activities. These playrooms are designed to allow children to engage in a variety of activities. Usually the free play is interspersed with special activities, such as a theatre group presenting a show (Fig. 5-30), a birthday party (Fig. 5-31), or the celebration of a holiday (Fig. 5-32). The playroom is flexible enough that it can be converted to meet the needs of the various age groups at appropriate times. Daytime hours are for younger children, while adolescents can have free access to the area after the younger children retire for the evening.

Children who are unable to engage in the activities in the playroom are engaged in activities in their rooms (Figs. 5-33 and 5-34). Children who cannot join the playroom activities can be visited by other children and thus get the needed social interaction.

One of the major problems that arises during hospitalization is interference with mobility. Children tend to feel stifled by being confined in the hospital. Therefore, opportunities are provided which help children feel as though they are more mobile. Big Wheels, tricycles, and wagons are useful vehicles to help children feel a sense of movement despite the limitations imposed by hospitalization. The stroller is useful for younger children (Fig. 5-35), and the scooter board

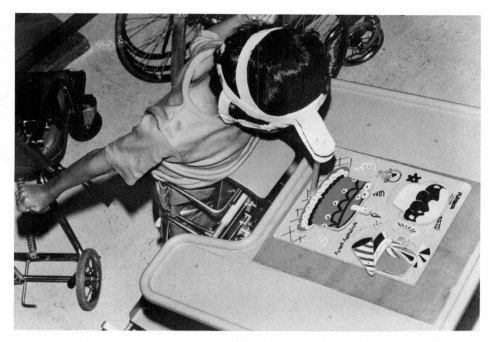

Figure 5-31. This child with cerebral palsy celebrates his birthday by completing a puzzle with his head pointer. *(Photo by N. Patrick)*

and dolly are useful for the child in a spica cast or a child who wears leg braces (Fig. 5-36).

Children who are hospitalized for extended periods of time can be aided by having a volunteer help to individualize their play programs. A volunteer can "adopt" the child for the length of the child's stay and can help to provide special activities that help the child to feel special because extra attention is being given. A non-health care provider, such as a volunteer, can help to bring a semblance of normalcy to the child's life during hospitalization. The volunteer who "adopts" a

Figure 5-32. Children and adults enjoy the celebration of a holiday. *(Photo by M. McGinnis)*

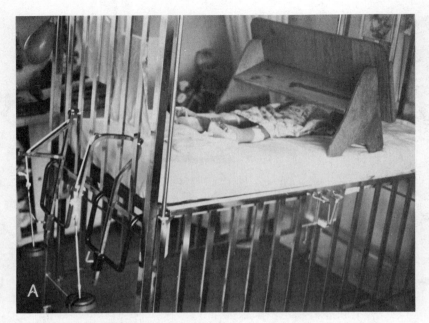

Figure 5-33. **A.** this child is hiding behind a tilted table that provides a convenient play surface for an unmobilized child. **B.** On the other side of this table, an artist is at work. Still clutching her mother's finger with one hand, she is gradually "moving out" to express herself in green paint. *(From Juenker D., Play as a tool of the nurse. In S. Steele (Ed.), Nursing care of the child with long-term illness (2nd ed.). New York: Appleton–Century–Crofts, 1977)*

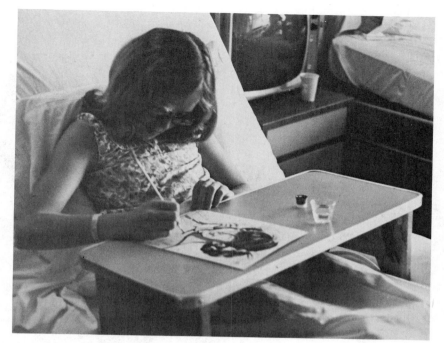

Figure 5-34. The art of concentration. The fine detail of her work is satisfying to this adolescent who places a high premium on the quality of the finished product. *(From Juenker D., Play as a tool of the nurse. In S. Steele (Ed.), Nursing care of the child with long-term illness (2nd ed.). New York: Appleton—Century—Crofts, 1977)*

Figure 5-35. The expression on this toddler's face reveals the excitement that freedom of mobility arouses. *(Courtesy of Children's Hospital of Buffalo, New York)*

A

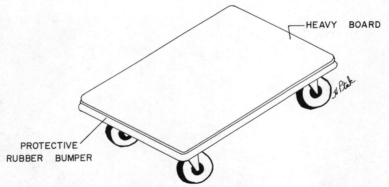

HEAVY BOARD

PROTECTIVE
RUBBER BUMPER

B

Figure 5-36. **A.** This child with cerebral palsy is able to get around despite lack of independent ambulation skills. A dolly like this one permits him to participate actively in his environment. *(Photo by N. Patrick)* **B.** If not available commercially, a dolly can be easily constructed as illustrated. *(From Juenker D., Play as a tool of the nurse. In S. Steele (Ed.), Nursing care of the child with long-term illness (2nd ed.). New York: Appleton–Century–Crofts, 1977)*

child usually feels a special connection to and responsibility for the child. This commitment to the child stimulates the volunteer to invest a great deal of energy on behalf of the child, and novel and creative activities usually emerge. Volunteers come in many varieties, including elementary and high school students, homemakers, retired adults, parents of former clients, representatives of community organizations, and spouses of students and health care providers (Fig. 5-37). The interactions with the volunteer diminish the negative effects of extended periods of hospitalization. Hospitals that have the services of volunteers offer an enriched environment for children with long-term illness.

Play activities during hospitalizations are designed to counteract specific insults that affect the child. For example, play is adopted to limit the effects of restraints, pain and painful procedures, isolation, diet restriction (especially "nothing by mouth"), separation and regression, sleeplessness, changes in body image and appearances, loneliness, family disruption, and school disruption. See Table 5-1 for ideas for combatting each of these problems.

Play in Long-term Institutions

Institutionalization is decreasing in importance as a method of care for children with long-term illness. However, there probably will always be a need for institutions to care for a small percentage of children with long-term illness or disability. Selecting this alternative for care results in long-term or permanent separation from the primary family. This realization results in the need for

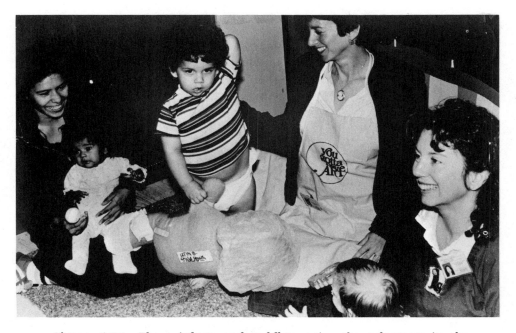

Figure 5-37. These infants and toddlers enjoy the volunteers in the playroom. *(Photo by D. Haskin)*

TABLE 5-1.
Play to Help Cope with Hospitalization

	Types of Play	
Hospital Insults	Preschool Children	School-age Children and Adolescents
Restraints	Mobiles, toys in child's visual field, musical toys—record player	Audiotapes, record players, television
Pain and painful procedures	Relaxation tapes and imagery, therapeutic play simulating procedure	Same
Isolation	Washable toys, musical toys, books, storytelling, television	Washable toys and games, television, audiotapes
Diet Restrictions (NPO)	Diversional activities during mealtime, therapeutic play techniques	Same
Separation, regression	"Adoptive" adult, consistent caretaker for play, use toys for younger children (e.g., bottle play)	Peer partners in games, letter writing to friends, audiotapes from family and friends, keeping a diary, record player, musical instruments
Sleeplessness	Quiet music, relaxation tapes, consistent caretaker, transition toys	Quiet music, relaxation tapes
Body image and appearance	Drawing pictures of self, outlining body on brown paper, polaroid snapshots	Drawing pictures of self, polaroid snapshots, grooming sessions
Loneliness	Play with other children or adults, playroom sessions, imaginary friends	Play with other children or adults, telephoning friends, letter writing, card sending, imaginary friends (10 yr or under)
Family disruption	Therapeutic play with family members and doll house, pounding toys, imaginary friends	Telephone calls, writing letters, sending audiotapes, imaginary friends (10 yr or under)
School disruption	Playroom activities simulating nursery or preschool, pictures from preschool classmates, pictures sent to preschool	Referral to school teachers, school work from home, visits from friends, peer group play

increased emphasis to be placed on the emotional needs of the child. Play is beneficial in helping to meet the increased need for emotional support of the child.

The long-term institutional staff attempts to simulate a family setting. Oftentimes, house parents are responsible for a group of children. The children's day is structured to meet both their therapy needs and their needs for nurturing growth and development. The house parents are generally assisted in meeting the play components of the children's day by recreational, occupational, and physical therapists. A play aid or assistant also assists in individualizing play activities and promoting group sessions. Play is considered to be an essential part of the children's day, and time is made available for both structured and unstructured play activities. Ideas that pertain to play in the inpatient setting also pertain to institutionalized children. In addition, the health problems of the particular child influence specific play interventions that are designed to improve the child's health status. Play activities are also provided to counteract the effects of separation and emotional upheavals that are not uncommon when children are separated from their families and familiar communities. Periods of time are also provided for free play inside and outside the institution (Fig. 5-38).

Swimming is a particularly positive activity for children with most health problems. For example, children with asthma and cerebral palsy can improve their respiratory functions by swimming. Swimming also helps children with cerebral palsy to feel more relaxed, as the water helps to buoy up their bodies.

Bowling is a favorite and beneficial exercise. Children with cerebral palsy can be placed on a scooter board to participate, and children with asthma have bronchospasm only infrequently due to this exercise.

Figure 5-38. These children with disabilities have been taken from the institution and are enjoying interaction with a clown at the local shopping mall. (*Photo by M. McGinnis*)

Children in body casts can play pool or similar games to relieve tension. Children who have elimination problems are engaged in water play, finger painting, and clay play. Children who have suffered severe head trauma are given games that reteach skills that are lost as a result of the injury. Preschool children benefit from play experiences that simulate the home, such as doll play or going to the store. Allowing opportunities to run or to get around on toys with wheels helps to limit the children's feelings of confinement. Swinging can also be useful in helping the child feel free despite institutionalization.

Transition objects play a special role in the child's play program. Favorite transition objects are toys that the child takes to bed. Bedtime rituals are not complete without paying specal attention to these toys.

REFERENCES

Arnaud, S. Introduction: Polish for play's tarnished reputation. In *Play: The child strives toward self-realization*. Washington, D.C.: National Association for the Education of Young Children, 1971.

Curry, N.E. Contribution of current basic issues on play. In *Play: The child strives toward self-realization*. Washington, D.C.: National Association for the Education of Young Children, 1971.

Groos, K. *The play of man*. New York: Appleton, 1901.

Huizinga, J. *Homo ludens: A study of the play-element in culture*. New York: Roy, 1950.

Juenker, D. Play as a tool of the nurse. In S. Steele (Ed.), *Nursing care of the child with long-term illness* (2nd ed.). New York: Appleton—Century—Crofts, 1977.

Masters, J.C. & Santrock, J.W. Studies in self-regulation of behavior: Effects of contingent cognitive and affective events. *Development Psychology* 12:334, 1976.

Piaget, J. *Play, dreams and imitation in childhood*. New York: Norton, 1962.

Piaget, J., & Inholder, B. *The psychology of the child*. New York: Basic Books, 1969.

Smilansky, S. *The effects of sociodramatic play on disadvantaged preschool children*. New York: Wiley and Sons, 1968.

Smilansky, S. Can adults facilitate play in children? Theoretical and practical considerations. In *Play: The child strives toward self-realization*. Washington, D.C.: National Association for the Education of Young Children, 1971.

BIBLIOGRAPHY

Azarnoff, P., & Flegal, S. *A pediatric play program*. Springfield, Ill.: Charles C. Thomas, 1975.

Brooks, M.M. Why play in the hospital? *Nursing Clinics of North America* 5:431, 1970.

Bruner, J. Play is serious business. *Psychology Today* 8:81, 1975.

Burns, S.F. Children's art: vehicle for learning. *Young Children* 30:193, 1975.

Call, J.D. Games babies play. *Psychology Today* 3:34, 1970.

Caplan, F., & Caplan, T. *The power of play*. Garden City, New York: Anchor Books, 1973.

Cramer, P., & Hogan, K.A. Sex differences in verbal and play fantasy. *Developmental Psychology* 11:145, 1975.

Crawford, C.F., & Palm, M.C. Can I take my teddy bear? *American Journal of Nursing* 73:286, 1973.

DiLeo, J.H. *Young children and their drawings*. New York: Brunner/Mazel, 1970.

Eckerman, C.O., Whatley, J.L., Kutz, S.L., et al. Growth of social play with peers during the second year of life. *Developmental Psychology* 11:42, 1975.

Elmassian, B. A practical approach to communicating through play. *American Journal of Maternal—Child Nursing* 4:238, 1979.

Erikson, E. *Toys and reason.* New York: Norton, 1977.

Gerbing, D.D. Putting play to work in pediatrics. *American Journal of Maternal—Child Nursing* 2:387, 1977.

Gibbons, M.B. When parents ask about play. *Pediatric Nursing* 3:19, 1977.

Gnus, M. A therapeutic play session in a health center. *American Journal of Maternal—Child Nursing* 2:193, 1973.

Goodnow, J. *Children's drawings.* Cambridge, Mass.: Harvard University Press, 1977.

Green, C. Larry thought puppet-play "childish". But it helped him face his fears. *Nursing* 5:30, 1975.

Green, C.S. Understanding children's needs through therapeutic play. *Nursing* 10:30, 1974.

Hott, J. Rx: Play PRN in pediatric nursing. *Nursing Forum* 9:288, 1970.

Knudsen, K. Play therapy: Preparing the young child for surgery. *Nursing Clinics of North America* 10:679, 1975.

Lebane, S. *The creative child.* Englewood Cliffs, N.J.: Prentice—Hall, 1979.

Mitchell, S.H. Imaginary companions: Friend or foe? *Pediatric Nursing* 6:29, 1980.

McLeavey, K.A. Children's art as an assessment tool. *Pediatric Nursing* 5:9, 1979.

Murphy, D.C. The therapeutic value of children's literature. *Nursing Forum* 11:141, 1972.

Norbetta, M. Caring for children with the help of puppets. *American Journal of Maternal—Child Nursing* 1:22, 1976.

Olds, A.R. A play center for handicapped infants and toddlers. In M.T. Fields, (Ed.), *Infants born at risk.* New York: SP Medical and Scientific Books, 1979.

Petrillo, M., & Sanger, S. Play in the hospital. In *Emotional care of hospitalized children.* Philadelphia: Lippincott, 1980.

Plank, E. *Working with children in hospitals* (2nd ed.). Cleveland: Case Western Reserve University Press, 1971.

Robertson, J. *Young children in hospitals.* New York: Basic Books, 1958.

Shufer, S. Communicating with young children: Teaching via the play—discussion group. *American Journal of Nursing* 77:1960, 1977.

Smith, L.F. An experiment with play therapy. *American Journal of Nursing* 77:1963, 1977.

Sponseller, D. (Ed.). *Play as a learning medium.* Washington, D.C.: National Association for the Education of Young Children, 1974.

Sutton-Smith, B. The playful modes of knowing. In *Play: The child strives toward self-realization.* Washington, D.C.: National Association for the Education of Young Children, 1971.

Sutton-Smith, B., & Sutton-Smith, S. *How to play with your children.* New York: Hawthorn Books, 1974.

Upton, G. (Ed.). *Physical and creative activities for the mentally handicapped.* Cambridge, England: Cambridge University Press, 1979.

Whitson, B.J. The puppet treatment in pediatrics. *American Journal of Nursing* 72:1612, 1972.

Winnicott, D.W. Transitional objects and transitional phenomena. In *Playing and Reality.* New York: Basic Books, 1971.

6

The Child's Perception of Illness

Shirley Steele

The child's ability to perceive illness changes over his or her life span. The child's perception of illness is influenced by his or her ability to internalize reality. What is real to the child is influenced by cognitive abilities and life experiences. As the child develops, reality is tested and perceptions change on the basis of the reality testing.

The infant's perceptions are very limited. Presenting the infant with objects begins to develop the infant's ability to perceive objects and to respond to them. A mobile placed in the infant's view results in a response. The infant usually responds to the whole rather than the parts. The mobile serves as a stimulus which eventually leads to the infant's perception of a mobile as a stimulus that requires a response. The infant's response to the mobile results despite the fact that the infant does not perceive the characteristics of each part of the mobile.

As the infant develops, meaning is placed on objects. The objects are perceived by the child in relation to what the object can do for the child. Eventually the child perceives that things have different properties—a hat is different from a coat and the letter B is different from the letter D.

The infant's perceptual ability is facilitated by adults who teach the child likenesses and differences between objects, things, and people. With assistance from adults, the child's perceptions become more accurate. This results in the child's increasing ability to respond to stimuli in an appropriate way. Until the child's perceptual skills are developed sufficiently, it is not uncommon for the child to act in unsafe ways. For example, the young child's perception of fire as an attractive object can result in a burn accident if an adult does not intercede to change the child's faulty perception.

The child's perception is influenced by the intensity of the stimulus. A strong stimulus can absorb the child's attention and block out other influences. A young child who is separated from the parent can perceive the situation as completely unacceptable. Under this condition, the young child perceives the loss of the parent as a major stressor, narrowing the child's ability to perceive other stimuli that are introduced to reduce the effects of separation. The child's perceptual field needs to be expanded for him or her to be able to respond to stimuli during periods of stress. Experiences that help the young child to feel comfortable despite separations lead to an ability to perceive stimuli during periods of stress, such as hospitalization or illness.

The developing child has a limited past experience and therefore does not have a ready set of images and coping mechanisms to use in response to illness. The child's perceptions of illness, therefore, are being developed concurrently with the course of the illness. Since the child's perception of illness is not developed, the emerging perceptions are influenced by the parent's reactions, the amount of pain or discomfort associated with the illness, the responses of health care providers, and the limitations caused by the illness. The child's perceptions of the illness influence the way that the child responds to and during illness. Emerging perceptual images can be consistent with others' perceptions or different than others' perceptions, so it is necessary to try to understand the young child's perceptions.

The perceptual powers improve with age and reality testing. However, perceptual distortions can occur throughout life. Observation is a major life activity. Observation is composed of two complex human functions: attention and perception. As such, it is possible for two people to look at exactly the same image and to obtain different meanings from it. The child uses all the senses to decipher images that are observed. Observation is the welcoming of stimuli and perception is the response registered by the child's brain. As the child learns to observe more accurately, perceptions improve. Attention is the time the child spends in observation. Increased attention spans increase the child's ability to observe. In addition, the use of all the senses aids the child's ability to observe with increased awareness. The child's senses send signals to the brain, and the perceptions are translated into meaningful responses. As the child experiences, perceptions are stabilized and the child feels increasing satisfaction from stimuli from the environment.

As the child matures, he or she learns to shut out stimuli. In times of stress, the child can use this mechanism to maintain equilibrium. In an intensive care unit, the distracting environmental stimuli can cause perceptual confusion and disorientation. If the child is not able to cut out the abundance of distracting stimuli, illness can be viewed as a scary experience and health care providers can be perceived in a negative way. Adults can help to cut down the negative stimuli by introducing music, familiar voices, and musical toys to counter the negative stimuli.

Illness brings experiences to the child that are often boring, confusing, and unfamiliar. The child attempts to make some sense out of the illness while responding to stimuli produced by the illness. Pain associated with illness can result in perceptual distortions. The child's ability to withstand pain is associated with many factors. For example, a child who perceives an injection to be painful can choose to withstand the pain of illness rather than receiving a needle. A child who dislikes the taste of oral medications can perceive the treatment for illness as being more punitive than helpful, thereby increasing the pain of illness. A child that perceives the physician to be a distributor of painful acts can intensify the pain that is experienced when the physician enters the room. In order to make an illness experience more tolerable, happy experiences need to be introduced during periods of illness. Including happy experiences along with illness can help to bring the child's perceptions more in concert with reality.

THE CHILD'S INTERPRETATION
OF ILLNESS

The way the child perceives and interprets illness is influenced by many factors: age, past experience with illness, the family's response to illness, the type of onset, the nature and extent of the illness, the degree of limitation caused by the illness, and the treatment and prognosis of the illness. Each child has a unique response to illness. The responses are rarely predictable, although there are some common responses associated with particular diseases, age groups, and family constellations. It is safe to assume that the child's perception of the illness can be aided by strong family support, conscientious health care administered by empathetic health care providers, and speedy resolution of discomforting sensations. In the absence of these factors, the child can easily perceive illness to be a punishment involving unfair intrusion into his or her body.

Young children often interpret illness as punishment. In addition, the child does not understand why the parent did not provide protection from the illness and can place blame on the parent for this lack of protection. Young children also associate illness with "bad thoughts." They may wish for the parent to die when a spanking takes place and harbor the guilt associated with these thoughts. When illness occurs, the child interprets it as punishment for the bad thoughts and the guilt feelings emerge. It is imperative to help these children to understand that they did not cause the illness and that it is not always possible for parents to deter illness.

Even older children have difficulty perceiving illness accurately. The school-age child begins to know more about the causes and effects of some illnesses, but many aspects of the illnesses are poorly understood. For example, the child may perceive and interpret accurately that "a germ" caused the illness. However, the same child may not be able to perceive why isolation is necessary as part of the treatment protocol. Isolation may be so intolerable that the child perceives it as punishment, which, if not explained to the child, can lead to regression as the child perceives that the treatment is not helping to resolve the illness.

The adolescent can perceive illness as a direct insult to body image. At a time when the adolescent is increasing in independence, illness can cause dependence and lack of control of bodily functions. The adolescent is impatient and ill-prepared to cope with illness that separates him or her from peers or interferes with daily routines. Even a simple upper respiratory infection can be perceived as a catastrophe when it interferes with a planned function. Although the adolescent has more past experiences that influence perceptions and interpretation of illness, the turbulence associated with this age group makes it vulnerable to perceptual distortions when illness occurs.

CONSEQUENCES OF ILLNESS

The illness and its management influence the way the child experiences an illness. For example, the infant who is restrained is distressed by the illness, as it interferes with the movement of extremities during periods of restraint. The preschool child that is immobilized when yearning to use new motor skills perceives the illness as unjustly taking away his or her ability to explore. The school-age child that fractures an arm during baseball season perceives the illness as depriving him or her from participating in a favorite activity. The adolescent with acne can blame the condition for a lack of opportunities to date. All of these examples illustrate that the consequences of the illness can be as painful as the illness itself.

Other consequences of illness include absenteeism from school, separation from family and friends, financial strain, change in body integrity, changes in dietary patterns, return to dependency, and loss of cognitive or motor skills. Each child perceives and interprets the consequences of illness on the basis of his or her unique lifestyle. The responses of the child to the consequences of illness are influenced by temperament, attitudes, and values.

PHYSICAL ASPECTS OF ILLNESS

The child responds in a variety of ways to the physical aspects of illness. Infants rarely perceive the significance of altered body function. However, as the young child gains control of bodily functions, changes in this function caused by illness are not tolerated well. The toddler who masters crawling is frustrated by a body cast and the preschooler is intolerant of withheld fluid intake, which ordinarily provides oral gratification. The preschooler fears mutilation, and any changes in the body are perceived in this light. The significance of the involved body part influences the way the child perceives the illness. For example, diseases of the heart, brain, and eyes are connected to higher levels of anxiety due to the significance placed on these organs. In addition, illnesses that involve the genital areas are frequently associated with fears of castration.

The child seems to be able to understand the illness better when there is overt physical evidence of the disease, as with a fractured arm or a lacerated finger. Illnesses with hidden physical problems, such as cardiac defects, are less well understood. The child's immature understanding of the way the body functions can be a partial explanation for this response to particular illnesses.

The degree and intensity of the symptoms of the illness can influence the child's response to illness. When vomiting and diarrhea are present, there is evidence to support the notion that something is wrong with the body. These symptoms confirm illness for the child. Resolution of secondary symptoms can be misconstrued by the child as resolution of the primary illness. The child may need assistance to understand that illness persists even when visual signs of illness are gone. The interpretation of abnormal laboratory findings is an abstract concept that rarely is understood before adolescence. Therefore, treatment for rheumatic heart disease is often disregarded by the school-age child after the joint pain resolves.

THE SIGNIFICANCE OF PAIN

A tangible consequence of physical illness is pain. Pain is a complicated phenomenon that varies with age. It is not clearly understood why infants have limited reactions to painful stimuli, such as circumcision. However, the ability to witness pain develops quickly, and a 4-month-old infant can remember the pain of an injection when returned to the place where the injection was given. The young child's ability to identify where pain originates is limited. The child's expression of pain of the inner ear may be expressed by pulling on the ear lobe and being irritable. The child's inability to verbally explain pain and to identify its location makes it difficult to assess pain and its intensity.

The way persons behave in response to pain is influenced by conditioning. The male child is less likely to express feelings freely, while female children are encouraged to express feelings. Some cultural groups condition their children to respond in particular ways, varying from stoicism to free expression. Children model their responses to pain after those of the adults in their environment. Children are more likely to express their reactions to pain when they see others responding to pain. Intolerance to pain is easily adopted as a response, and children are often impatient to have pain relieved. Therefore, they need support when pain is present to feel secure. If they feel insecure, the pain is usually intensified and it is difficult to differentiate the physical from the emotional causes of the pain.

The child learns that pain can increase attention from adults. Thus the child can use pain to get adults to respond in a particular way. A child who does not want to go to school can "develop" pain in a particular location that the parent finds difficult to assess. Lacking the skill to assess the pain more accurately, the parent allows the child to stay home from school. If the pain was unreal, the child realizes that the parent is unable to judge his or her behavior accurately and the child learns that it is possible to use pain as an excuse to get something that is wanted or to avoid situations that are difficult to face.

Children also learn to disguise pain when they feel it is to their advantage to do so. This can lead to negative consequences that the child cannot predict. Nonverbal clues can be used to assess pain that is present when the child is trying to disguise it. A tense body or facial expression or rubbing a body part are indicators of pain even when the child is not sharing the pain with others. Also, the child who is quiet and inactive or irritable can be experiencing pain.

Children can also exaggerate the pain that is present when it is to their advantage to do so. If a parent is leaving the hospital, an increasing amount of pain often changes his or her mind. Not infrequently, children complain of more serious pain as visiting hours are coming to an end.

Assessment of children's pain is difficult and often requires time to put the child at ease before exploration is attempted. When pain is suspected in a particular area, that area is examined last, as the child's cooperation is lost quickly if painful sensations are produced during the examination. The parents can be helpful during the examination, as they can soothe the child and encourage the child to cooperate with the examiner. Relief of pain is dependent on localizing the pain and diagnosing and treating its cause.

The assessment of pain is based on several assumptions:

1. Pain is an individualized response.
2. Pain is closely associated with emotional responses such as fear, anxiety, anger, loneliness, depression, disappointment, and expectation.
3. As pain is associated with other emotions, it can be intensified as a result of the other emotion(s).
4. The way pain is expressed is subjective.
5. Thresholds for pain vary from one individual to another.
6. Children often express pain through nonverbal messages, such as wriggling, frowning, and tensing of facial muscles.
7. Both verbal and nonverbal communication of pain are valuable in the assessment process.
8. It is possible to assess the pain of children if the adult does not threaten the child.
9. Children are not always able to be fully cooperative when pain is being assessed.

EVALUATION OF SEVERITY OF PAIN

The evaluation of the severity of the child's pain is influenced by the age of the child, the child's past experience with pain, and cultural and ethnic orientation. Since responses to pain vary with age, indications of the intensity of the pain are age-specific. The infant and toddler use crying and body posture as indicators of pain severity. They cry loudly, are extremely irritable, and cannot be easily consoled. Their bodies are tense, they flex their extremities, and they use rolling movements or pull at body parts to try to ease the pain. Extensive pain may result in lethargy and minimal response to environmental stimuli. The preschool child can give limited verbal cues as to the intensity and location of the pain. Preschool children still use some of the nonverbal cues of the earlier age periods, but they are more apt to be able to help with localization of the pain. The preschool child begins to adopt cues that are culturally or ethnically influenced, and these are reflected in his or her response to the pain. Even at this early age, the child is capable of expressing psychosomatic pain in response to environmental stimuli. The preschool child is still impatient with pain experiences and wants pain removed immediately. School-age and adolescent children are able to identify the severity and location of pain. However, they show a wide variability in their response to painful stimuli. They can exaggerate the pain to get personal benefits and they can cover up the pain if they think it is to their advantage. Throughout childhood, therefore, it is imperative to assess the nonverbal as well as the verbal cues that relate to the pain response in order to determine the severity of the pain.

The child can be helped to express pain by asking him or her if the pain is like or unlike another pain that was witnessed. For example, a preschool child that has had an immunization will remember that pain. He or she can be asked if this pain is greater or less than the pain from the needle. Another way to assess the pain is to ask the child to describe a situation that felt the same and give an example, such as, "Does the pain feel like you skinned your knee?"

The assessment of pain and its severity is aided by observation of the child, using verbal and nonverbal cues, noting behavioral changes and physiologic responses, and assessing the child's physical activity or limitations. It is useful to use toys during the process, especially with children younger than school age. Checking a teddy bear or doll for pain helps the child to gain trust in the health care provider and takes some of the tension out of the situation. The severity of the pain can be decreased and the child can cooperate more fully when the experience is less frightening. The assessment of the severity of pain is an important part of the management of pain, and health care providers as well as family members need to develop skills to derive accurate conclusions about the pain.

In some instances, it is necessary to give medication to help to assess the severity of the child's pain. However, even the response to medication can be subjective, as the child's fears can be lessened when he or she feels that something is being done. Therefore, responses to medication must also be assessed on an ongoing basis to be certain that the response is evaluated accurately.

PAIN MANAGEMENT

The management of pain is of major concern to children with long-term problems that cause pain or discomfort. Pain can cause minimal to extreme discomfort. In either case, the child dislikes pain sensations and is usually eager to have the pain resolved. The management of pain is based on the child's perceived pain. The pain threshold of individual children is difficult to assess. However, it is known that the child's ability or willingness to report pain is based on many factors. These factors include:

1. Whether the child feels that reporting the pain will result in an action that he or she does not want taken (i.e., receiving an injection or being admitted to the hospital).
2. Whether the child feels that reporting the pain will cause a financial burden to the family.

3. Whether reporting the pain will result in actions that relieve the pain; these actions are perceived as less threatening than the pain (i.e., receiving a pill or having a hot water bottle applied).
4. The child's belief that reporting the pain to another person will not jeopardize his or her self-concept or self-image (e.g., the other person will not think he or she is a "sissy" or "being a baby").
5. Whether the pain is so intense that the child cannot give an adequate description.
6. The age of the child (e.g., infants and toddlers have limited communication skills and generally report their pain nonverbally).
7. Whether reporting the pain will interfere with an activity that the child cherishes (e.g., interrupting a scheduled special event or interfering with baseball practice).
8. How other people responded when he or she reported pain in the past (were other people empathetic and did they help to relieve the pain?).
9. The place the child is in at the time the pain begins (he or she may not want to report pain to a school teacher but may be willing to report pain to a nurse at the hospital).
10. Past experiences with pain (has the child had success in resolving pain without the help of others?).
11. The way the family members respond to pain (do family members take medication for each pain or do they use a "leave it alone and it will go away" approach?).
12. The severity of the pain.
13. The child's perception of health care providers (does he or she see these persons as being helpful or as adversaries?).

PERCEPTIONS OF TREATMENTS FOR ILLNESS

The child may perceive that treatment of the illness is worse than the illness. Treatments can range from very simple attention paid to superficial lacerations to extensive surgical intervention. The child's perception of the treatment is not always consistent with the intensity of the treatment. A toddler can perceive a laceration of the finger as a way to bleed to death; therefore Band-Aids are welcomed additions to their cut fingers. The Band-Aid is perceived as lifesaving.

Fantasy or magical thinking plays a part in the way the child perceives treatment. Many treatments bring out the child's use of fantasy. A scheduled bone marrow aspiration can be denied through the use of fantasy. Using this notion, imagery and relaxation are sometimes used to decrease the threat associated with painful treatments.

It is often difficult for the child to perceive the need for painful treatments or procedures. Just as some of the discomfort of the illness is subsiding, painful treatments or procedures are done that intensify feelings of discomfort. The child tolerates these intrusions poorly when they are perceived as interfering with

progress. An example is a lumbar puncture done to assess progress of the child
with leukemia.

There are many illnesses that require periodic treatments that interfere with
the child's ability to have a normal lifestyle. Dialysis treatments needed three
times a week for advanced kidney disease can make it difficult for the child to
keep in touch with friends, to keep up in schoolwork, or to have a consistent
relationship with siblings. The perception these children have of their treatment
is influenced by the degree of dissatisfaction that the child feels about the
interference with social relationships.

It is necessary to help the child understand the relationship of treatments to
the course of the illness. The child's cognitive development influences his or her
ability to use information of this nature. Giving explanations that are age-
appropriate helps to achieve this goal. Honesty is an important part of these
explanations, as the child soon perceives adults to be deceptive if they are
untruthful about the treatments.

The threat children feel during illness influences their perceptions of
treatments. If children are not kept informed of scheduled treatments, they often
perceive that their treatment is completed. The threat of treatments usually
persist as long as the child is hospitalized, and the threat is decreased
substantially with discharge even if illness remains.

Threat can be decreased by preparing the child for treatments (see Chapter
3). When the child understands what is going to happen, perceptual accuracy is
increased. By listening to the child explain the treatment, it is possible to
decrease perceptual ambiguity and to make therapy less threatening and easier
to tolerate.

HOSPITALIZATION

The child's perception of illness is influenced by the changes that are necessary
in his or her lifestyle to cope with the illness. Hospitalization is a major change in
the child's life and is perceived as a major threat to the child's integrity. The
hospital is an unfamiliar place even when the child is admitted frequently, as it
separates the child from family, friends, and community.

Separation

Over the years, many researchers have explored the effects of hospitalization or
institutionalization on children (Robertson, 1958; Bowlby, 1960; Spitz, 1965; Fagin,
1966; Branstetter, 1969). These studies strongly support the notion that young
children suffer adverse effects from being separated from the mother.

Robertson's (1958) work is cited when behavioral aspects of separation are
described. He noted three phases of threat the child goes through during periods
of separation: (1) protest, (2) despair, and (3) detachment or denial. Based on
Robertson's work, hospital policies now encourage the mother to actively
participate in the child's hospitalization by being present, nurturing the child,
and enacting supportive measures. When the mother or other caring adult is

close by during hospitalization, it is possible to limit some of the negative influences of hospitalization.

Long-term illness frequently is associated with periods of hospitalization. This pattern can begin at birth when a high-risk neonate enters the world (see Chapter 7). This hospitalization can interfere with the initial bonding of infant and parent unless hospital policies encourage attachment behaviors despite the neonate's precarious physical condition. The perceptions of the family members about the neonate influence the way they respond to the infant and start to establish a pattern for future interactions.

The nature of the illness can have a profound effect on the way the parents respond to the child. Parents perceive illness in particular ways. For example, they may perceive that a cardiac problem is much more serious than an infectious disease or that a childhood disease such as measles is less severe than meningitis. The way they perceive the illness influences the way they respond to it. When an illness requires hospitalization, perceptual awareness is heightened. An acutely ill infant can bring feelings of terror and fear of death to the parents. Even when the infant is acutely ill and in an intensive care unit, the parents are included in the infant's care.

Social Isolation

Long-term illness is associated with feelings of isolation. Hospitalization intensifies these feelings. School-age and adolescent children are more prone to these feelings, as they are separated from their cherished activities and confined in an area where they have little or no control over their bodies and their daily activities. Feelings of isolation from ordinary activities of living are intensified by the hospitalization experience and often cause the child to perceive hospitalization as the reason for all his or her feelings of isolation.

Mutilation

Fears of mutilation and/or castration can accompany the hospitalization experience. The reason for the hospitalization can exaggerate these fears, especially when surgery is anticipated. The child's body image and body concept are threatened by surgical intervention. Despite the reasons for the surgery, children can perceive it to be a direct intrusion on their body's integrity. The slightest changes, such as a scar, removal of a small lesion, or release of a tendon, can be perceived as mutilation, as it changes the child's body image. When surgery is scheduled, the parent is encouraged to be with the child as long as possible.

Loss of Control

The school-age or adolescent child often feels that hospitalization interferes with his or her ability to feel a part of what is happening. Activities that were formerly controlled by the child (such as toileting, eating, bathing, setting a bedtime, and so forth) are now at least partially controlled by others. It is not possible for the child to retreat to the friendly corner of his or her own room and feel free to be himself or herself. The hospital room is "sterile-looking" and affords few opportunities for privacy or contemplation.

Figure 6-1. In the care-by-parent unit the mother and child share a book in a convertable chair-to-bed. *(Photo by H. Riggs)*

Hospital routines are scheduled without the child's input and often interrupt the ordinary sleep–awake cycle. Awakening the child at an early hour for treatments can interfere with the child's feelings of well-being. The loss of control of the environment is one of the reasons that the child objects to hospitalization, so it is necessary to find ways for the child to feel some sense of control during the hospitalization experience.

The Influence of Parental Responses

The parents' responses influence the child's responses to illness and hospitalization. Parents who exhibit anxiety convey this feeling to the child. The child's fears are heightened when he or she sees the parents' responses. When parents discuss the child's illness in front of him or her without explaining it in terms the child can understand, the child's anxiety is increased.

Parents use coping mechanisms to deal with stressful situations. Children model these strategies. Common responses are denial, hostility, repression, anger, and withdrawal. The use of coping mechanisms makes it possible for the parents and child to contend with the increased stress caused by the illness and hospitalization.

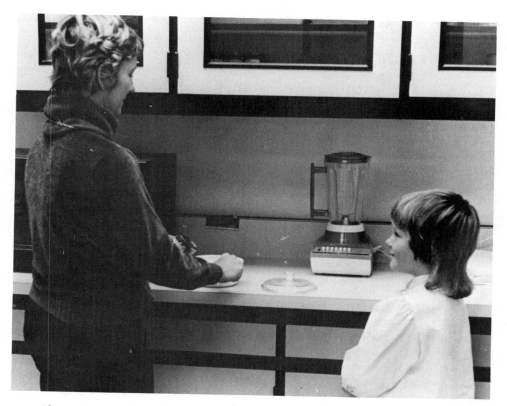

Figure 6-2. The care-by-parent unit is home-like and includes laundry and cooking facilities. *(Photo by H. Riggs)*

Figure 6-3. The living room space in the care-by-parent unit allows the extended family to visit in comfortable surroundings. *(Photo by H. Riggs)*

Decreasing Negative Effects of Hospitalization

There are many ways to decrease the negative effects of hospitalization. Changes in structure such as rooming-in, unlimited visiting hours, and care-by-parent units achieve this goal (Figs. 6-1, 6-2, and 6-3). Involving the grandparents in the child's care helps the extended family members to be attached to the child even during periods of hospitalization (Fig. 6-4). In addition, play areas are an important part of the hospital milieu for children (Fig. 6-5). Involving the parents or other caring adults in the child's stressful treatments and procedures can decrease the stress felt by the child. In addition, health care providers who consider the normal developmental needs of children and communicate with them at age-appropriate levels help the child to understand the unfamiliar and to decrease its threat. Providing opportunities for the child to engage in self-care activities makes the hospital experience less threatening and provides a way for the child to learn new skills during the confinement. Attention is focused on making the hospital environment more similar to the home environment through the use of familiar furniture and transitional objects (such as toys, blankets, and musical instruments) and by allowing children to dress in their own clothes rather than in hospital clothing (Figs. 6-6 and 6-7). In between stressful periods, the child enjoys participating in childlike activities (see Chapter 5). There are many ways to transform the hospital environment to consider the needs of child clients; even the busy operating room can have pictures of favorite characters of children (Figs. 6-8 and 6-9). Adolescents need a room where they can make telephone calls, feel free from the distractions of younger children, and escape from the reality of the busy hospital unit (Figs. 6-10 and 6-11). It is also essential for adults to take the time to prepare the child for new experiences (Figs. 6-12, 6-13, 6-14, and 6-15). Allowing the child to play with toys until treatments or surgery begin is also a strategy to decrease the negative effects of hospitalization (Fig. 6-16; see Chapter 5). Health care personnel who care for children in hospitals need to be creative in figuring out how they can improve their particular setting to make hospitalization less stressful for the child and family.

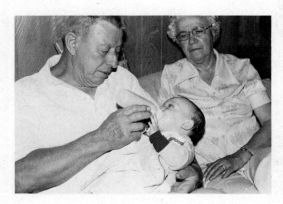

Figure 6-4. Grandparents share their grandchild's day in the care-by-parent unit. *(Photo by H. Riggs)*

Figure 6-5. A hospital outside-play area provides the child with outside activities during periods of long hospitalization. *(Photo by H. Riggs)*

The child's perceptions of illness and the hospital play an important role in the nursing management of children. Perceptions are very important in the care of disabled children. (See Chapter 10 for additional discussion of this important area.)

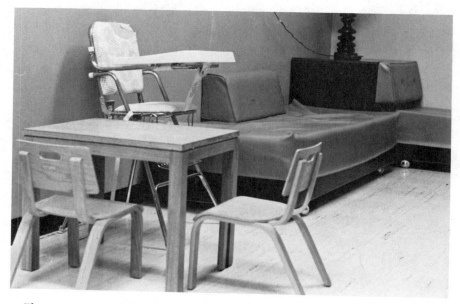

Figure 6-6. Familiar furniture can make the hospital environment seem less frightening. *(Photo by H. Riggs)*

Figure 6-7. These clients are dressed in their own clothing and are enjoying their music. *(From Juenker, D. Play as a tool of the nurse. In S. Steele (Ed.), Nursing care of the child with long-term illness (2nd ed.). New York: Appleton-Century-Crofts, 1977)*

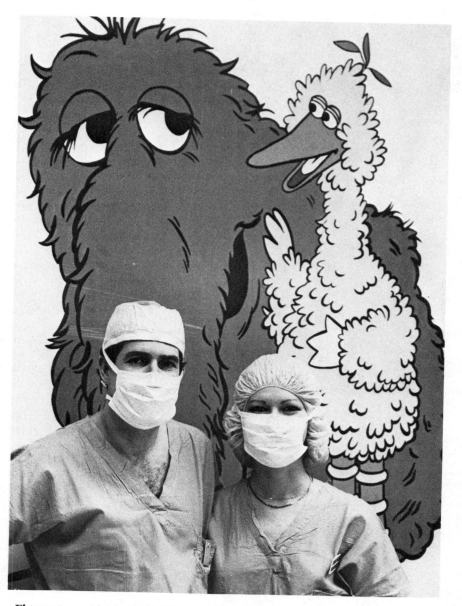

Figure 6-8. The large, familiar animal characters painted on the operating room walls help to decrease the strangeness of nurses and physicians dressed in unfamiliar clothes. *(Courtesy of UTMB hospitals)*

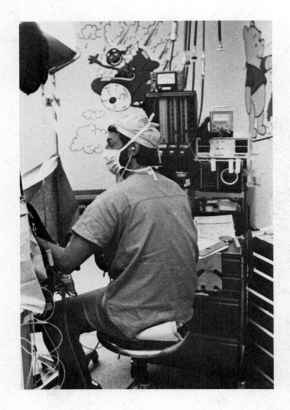

Figure 6-9. Anesthesia is less frightening when the child can focus on familiar scenes on the walls of the operating room. *(Courtesy of UTMB hospitals)*

Figure 6-10. The adolescent recreation area provides the adolescent with privacy while in the hospital. *(Photo by H. Riggs).*

Figure 6-11. The telephone allows the adolescent to keep in touch with peers while in the hospital. *(Photo by H. Riggs)*

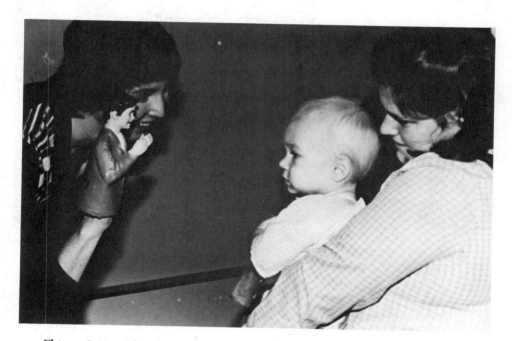

Figure 6-12. The nurse prepares the toddler and mother for a treatment using a hand puppet. *(Photo by D. Haskin)*

188

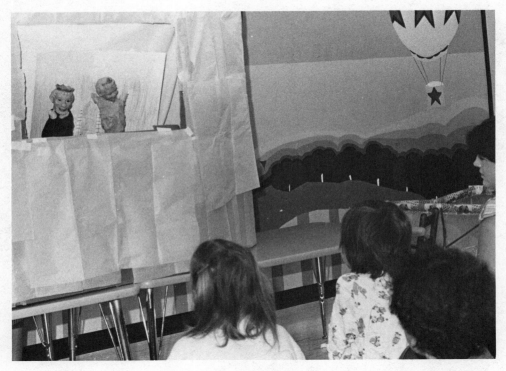

Figure 6-13. A group of children are prepared for surgery through the use of a puppet show. *(Courtesy of UTMB hospitals)*

Figure 6-14. The adult takes time to adequately prepare the child for an x-ray before doing the procedure.

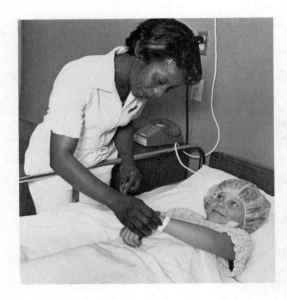

Figure 6-15. This nurse–client interaction demonstrates how the child is able to perceive an experience as positive when the nurse takes time to prepare the child adequately.

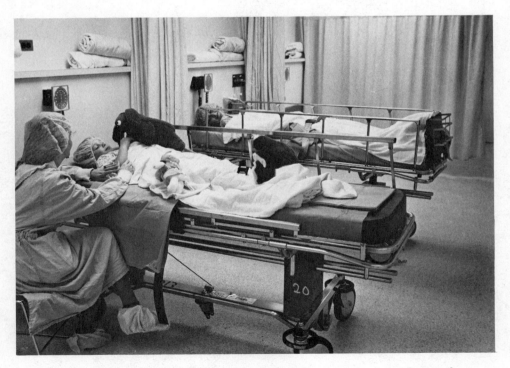

Figure 6-16. A child playing with toys until surgery is begun to lessen the stress of the experience.

REFERENCES

Bowlby, J. Separation anxiety. *International Journal of Psychoanalysis*, 41:89, 1960.

Branstetter, E. The young child's response to hospitalization: Separation anxiety or lack of mothering care? *American Journal of Public Health* 59:92, 1969.

Fagin, C. *The effects of maternal attendance during hospitalization on the post hospital behavior of young children: A comparative survey.* Philadelphia: Davis, 1966.

Robertson, J. *Young children in hospitals.* New York: Basic Books, 1958.

Spitz, R. *The first year of life.* New York: International Universities Press, 1965.

BIBLIOGRAPHY

Anthony, E.J. The child's discovery of his body. *Physical Therapy*, 48:1103, 1968.

Arneson, S.W., & Triplett, J.L. How children cope with disfiguring changes in their appearance. *American Journal of Maternal—Child Nursing* 3:366, 1978.

Bartoleschi, B., & Novelletto, A. Child analysis and paediatrics: The influence of severe bodily illness in early childhood on mental development. *International Journal of Psychoanalysis* 49:294, 1968.

Bell, J.E., & Bell, E.A. Family participation in hospital care for children. *Children* 17:154, 1970.

Bergmann, T. *Children in the hospital.* New York: International Universities Press, 1965.

Berner, C. Assessing the child's ability to cope with stresses of hospitalization. In P.A. Brandt, et al (Eds.), *Current practice in pediatric nursing.* St. Louis: Mosby, 1976.

Bowlby, J. *Maternal care and mental health.* Geneva: World Health Organization, 1952.

Clancy, H., & McBride, G. The isolation syndrome in childhood. *Developmental Medicine and Child Neurology* 17:198—219, 1975.

Coffin, M. *Nursing observations of the young patient.* Dubuque, Iowa: Brown, 1970.

Coshman, B., & Yunck, M. Dealing with the threats of hospitalization. *Pediatric Nursing* 5:32, 1979.

Crawford, C.F., & Palm, M.C. Can I take my teddy bear? *American Journal of Nursing* 73:286, 1973.

Crowley, D. *Pain and its Alleviation.* Sacramento, Calif.: Regents of the University of California, 1962.

Davidson, A., & Fay, J. *Phantasy in childhood.* New York: Philosophical Library, 1953.

Di Leo, J. *Young children and their drawings.* New York: Brunner/Mazel, 1970.

Dzik, H. The use of mobility by a pre-school boy during hospitalization. *Maternal—Child Nursing Journal* 3:169, 1974.

Eichelberger, K.M. Self-care nursing plan: Helping children to help themselves. *Pediatric Nursing* 6:9, 1980.

Fleming, J. Hospitalized physically disabled children focus on things, not people. *Perceptual and Motor Skills* 39:1002, 1974.

Gellert, E. Children's conceptions of the content and functions of the human body. *Genetic Psychology Monographs* 65:293, 1962.

Gildea, J.H., & Quick, T.R. Assessing the pain experience in children. *Nursing Clinics of North America* 12:631, 1977.

Glasser, P., & Glasser, L. (Eds.). *Families in crisis.* New York: Harper and Row, 1970, pp. 290−301.

Hardgrove, C.L., & Dawson, R.B. *Parents and children in the hospital: The family's role in pediatrics.* Boston: Little, Brown, 1972.

Hardgrove, C.L., & Rutledge, A. Parenting during hospitalization. *American Journal of Nursing,* 75:836, 1975.

Hennessey, J.A. Hospitalized toddler's responses to mothers' tape recordings during brief separations. *Maternal Child Nursing* 5:69, 1976.

Hirt, M., & Kurtz, R. A reexamination of the relationship between body boundary and site of disease. *Journal of Abnormal Psychology* 74:67, 1969.

Hodapp, R.M. Effects of hospitalization on young children. *Children's Health Care* 10:83, 1982.

Issner, N. The family of the hospitalized child. *Nursing Clinics of North America* 7:5, 1972.

Johnson, J.E., Kirchhoff, K.T., & Endress, M.P. Easing children's fright during health care procedures. *American Journal of Maternal−Child Nursing* 1:206, 1976.

Johnston, M. Toward a culture of caring: Children, their environment and change. *American Journal of Maternal−Child Nursing* 4:210, 1979.

Juenker, D. Child's perception of his illness. In S. Steele (Ed.), *Nursing care of the child with long-term illness.* New York: Appleton−Century−Crofts, 1977.

Knudsen, K. Play therapy: Preparing the young child for surgery. *Nursing Clinics of North America* 10:679, 1975.

Kunzman, L. Some factors influencing a young child's mastery of hospitalization. *Nursing Clinics of North America* 7:13, 1972.

Linkheim, R., Glaser, H., & Coffin, C. *Changing hospital environments for children.* Cambridge, Mass.: Harvard University Press, 1972.

Lyons, M. What priority do you give preop teaching? *Nursing* 7:12, 1972.

McCaffery, M. *Nursing management of the patient with pain.* Philadelphia: Lippincott, 1972.

McCain, G.C. Parent created recordings for hospitalized children. *Children's Health Care* 10:104, 1982.

Mechanic, D. The influence of mothers on their children's health attitudes and behavior. *Pediatrics* 33:444, 1969.

Mellish, R.W.P. Preparation of a child for hospitalization and surgery. *Pediatric Clinics of North America* 16:543, 1969.

Mennie, A.T. The child in pain. In L. Burton (Ed.), *Care of the child facing death.* London: Routledge and Kegan Paul, 1974.

Milar, I. The hospital and the preschool child. *Children* 17:171, 1970.

Nathan, S. Body image in chronically obese children as reflected in figure drawings. *English Journal of Personal Assessment* 37:456, 1973.

Olshansky, S. Chronic sorrow: A response to having a mentally defective child. *Social Casework* 43:190, 1962.

Oremland, E., & Oremland, J. (Eds.). *The effects of hospitalization on children.* Springfield, Ill.: Thomas, 1973.

Petrillo, M., & Sanger, S. *Emotional care of hospitalized children.* New York: Lippincott, 1972.

Pomarico, E., et al. Hospital orientation for children. *Am J. Oper Nurs* 29:864, 1979.

Poznanski, E.O. Children's reactions to pain: A psychiatrist's perspective. *Clinical Pediatrics* 15:1114, 1976.

Provence, S., & Lipton, R. *Infants in institutions.* New York: International Universities Press, 1962.

Prugh, D., Staub, E., Sands, H.H., et al. A study of the emotional reactions of children and families to hospitalization and illness. *American Journal of Orthopsychiatry* 23:70, 1953.

Scahill, M.P. Preparing children for procedures and operations. *Nursing Outlook* 17:36, 1969.

Schowalter, J., & Lord, R. Utilization of patient meetings on an adolescent ward. *Psychiatric Medicine* 1:197, 1970.

Schultz, N. How children perceive pain. *Nursing Outlook* 19:670, 1971.

Smith, J.C. Spending time with the hospitalized child. *American Journal of Maternal−Child Nursing* 1:164, 1976.

Steinhauer, P., Muskin, D., & Rae-Grant, L. Psychological aspects of chronic illness. *Pediatric Clinics of North America* 21:825, 1974.

Thomas, E. The problems of disability from the perspective of role theory. In P. Glasser, & Glasser, L. (Eds.), *Families in crisis.* New York: Harper & Row, 1970, pp. 250−72.

Vernon, D., Foley, J.M., Sipowiez, R.R., et al. *The psychological responses of children to hospitalization and illness.* Springfield, Ill.: Thomas, 1965.

Vistainer, M.A., & Wolfer, J.A. Psychological preparations for surgical pediatric patients: The effect of children's and parents' stress responses and adjustment. *Pediatrics* 56:187, 1975.

Watson, J. Research and literature on children's responses to injections: Some general nursing implications. *Pediatric Nursing* 2:7, 1976.

Williams, T. Responses of a 12-month-old girl to physical restraint during hospitalization. *Maternal−Child Nursing Journal* 4:109, 1975.

Wu, R. Explaining treatments to young children. *American Journal of Nursing* 65:71, July 1965.

Part II

Specific Conditions and Management

7

Health Promotion of the High-risk Infant

Katherine Nugent

Tremendous advances have been made in the fields of perinatology and neonatology in the last decade. Knowledge has increased dramatically concerning the relationship between maternal complications and fetal and neonatal well-being. Criteria were established to identify at-risk mothers and infants, and protocols were established to reduce morbidity and mortality associated with the identified high-risk conditions. To say that these advances have been successful would be an understatement. Infants who at one time would not have survived the neonatal period are now surviving (Fig. 7-1). Not only are they surviving, they are surviving with decreasing incidences of complications, once thought associated with at-risk birth and extended intensive care. However, in spite of this success story, a major responsibility still exists for health care providers to provide an environment to promote the best quality of life attainable for high-risk infants. Not only is there a responsibility to provide optimal acute care to prevent morbidity and mortality, there is an increasing commitment to promote optimal development in all realms of the infant's life. This is the basis upon which the theoretic concept of health care for the infant requiring prolonged hospitalization has evolved. The theoretic concept has as its central theme the nurse's active involvement in providing an environment throughout neonate's progression to discharge in supporting, facilitating, and promoting optimal total health (Fig. 7-2).

Total health of the infant is conceptually defined as optimal physical, psychosocial, emotional, and cognitive well-being. This concept also incorporates as an interwoven integral quality parenting and family interaction. The nurse has a major role in facilitating attainment of total health from the time the infant is admitted to the intensive care unit to the time of discharge. The facilitation of the attainment of this goal depends upon the basis of nursing care in all realms, from complete physiologic monitoring through transition to recovery; this is promotion of total health.

A major emphasis of the conceptual framework is on the provision of an

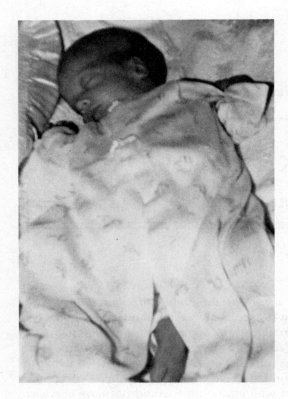

Figure 7-1. Due to advances in perinatology and neonatology, infants who at one time would not have survived the neonatal period are now surviving.

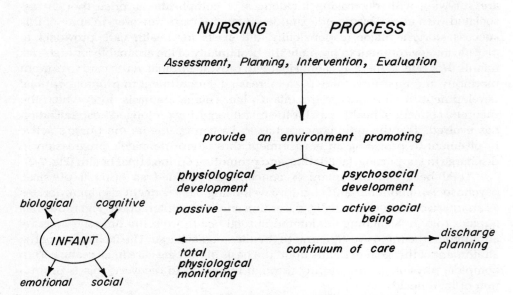

Figure 7-2. Model of conceptual framework.

optimal environment. An optimal environment is defined as the aggregate of conditions or influences that promotes the most favorable potential for attainment of desired outcomes.

OPTIMAL ENVIRONMENT

Implementing the concept of providing an optimal environment requires recognition that the components of the environment change as the infant progresses from a state of illness to a state of wellness. When the neonate is initially admitted to the intensive care unit, the environment and subsequent nursing care are centered on facilitating total physiologic monitoring. Nursing care is focused on preventive nursing management to eliminate physiologic disruptions that can hinder development or life itself, such as respiratory compromise, hypothermia, and hypoglycemia. As the neonate becomes more physiologically stable, the focus of the environment shifts to incorporate the facilitation of other realms of the infant's development into the continuing physiologic management. Preventive nursing management then shifts to incorporate the elimination or disruption of stimuli that hinder psychosocial, emotional, and cognitive development, such as disruption of the family unit, sensory overload, and/or disruption of biorhythmic cycles.

In order to provide the environment necessary for optimal health, it is necessary from the start of the neonate's life to identify vulnerable areas that have the potential for interference with total development of health. These vulnerable areas are assessed in both the physiologic and the psychosocial realms of development. It is only through this comprehensive assessment that nursing management aimed at preventive measures is initiated.

PHYSIOLOGIC ASSESSMENT

Physiologic assessment of vulnerable areas begins at birth, with the use of the Apgar score (Table 7-1). This evaluation tool is used to assess the neonate's physiologic functioning at 1 minute and 5 minutes after birth. The Apgar score evaluates heart rate, respiratory effort, muscle tone, reflex irritability, and color. Although the validity of the Apgar score is sometimes questioned, it establishes a data baseline and can be used to predict vulnerable areas of transition.

The importance of early identification of vulnerable areas is emphasized when considering the magnitude of the birth process, the transition period immediately following birth, and the major physiologic changes that occur as a result of these processes. Both the birth process and the following transition period place enormous demands on the neonate for adaptation. This call for adaptation can be met successfully by the neonate's ability to compensate. However, if the neonate possesses vulnerable physiologic areas related to congenital anomalies, immaturity, or other conditions associated with gestational age and/or the birth process, then the neonate's compensatory mechanism is

TABLE 7-1
APGAR Scoring Chart

Sign	0	1	2
Heart	Absent	Slow (below 100)	Over 100
Respiratory effort	Absent	Slow irregular	Good crying
Muscle tone	Flaccid	Some flexion of extremities	Active motion
Reflex irritability	No response	Grimace	Cry
Color	Blue pale	Body pink, extremities blue	Completely pink

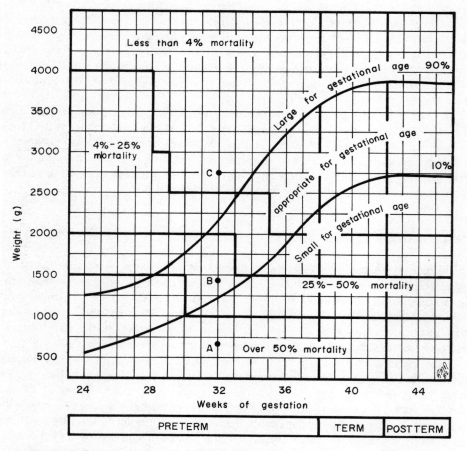

Figure 7-3. Intrauterine growth chart showing the correlation of birthweight with gestational age. *(Adapted from Battaglia, F.C. & Lubchenco, L.O. Intrauterine growth chart showing the correlation of birthweight with gestational age. Journal of Pediatrics 71:59, 1967)*

compromised, placing him or her at risk of developing complications during the progression through the transition period. The importance of early identification of vulnerable areas is magnified further if one adopts the theoretic framework of using assessment as a basis for intervention. A nurse who is knowledgeable in the physiologic demands of transition and who has assessed and identified areas of vulnerability is alerted to potential complications and is able to implement preventive nursing management to eliminate or minimize the potential interference.

ESTIMATION OF GESTATIONAL AGE

The estimation of gestational age is an essential evaluation tool for identifying areas of vulnerability that can have an impact on the total development of the neonate. The maturity of the neonate is an important determinant in identifying areas of vulnerability. The process of evaluating gestational age according to physical and neurologic characteristics provides valid and reliable data about the neonate. These data are used to effectively plan preventive nursing management.

Several tools for estimating gestational age based on physical characteristics and neurologic findings have been developed. It is not the purpose of this text to elaborate on the mechanics of this assessment. For further information, the reader should refer to the reference list, bibliography and Figures B-1 through B-4 and Tables B-1 and B-2 in Appendix B.

Once the gestational age is determined, this age is correlated with the birthweight. On the basis of this correlation, the neonate is classified according to age and weight (Fig. 7-3; Table 7-2). This classification alerts the health care team to potential medical and nursing problems (Table 7-3). Being alert for anticipated

TABLE 7-2
Classification of Neonates According to Estimated Gestational Age and Birthweight

Classification	Age (weeks)	Birthweight (%)
Preterm, small for gestational age (SGA)	Less than 38	Below 10
Preterm, appropriate for gestational age (AGA)	Less than 38	Between 10 and 90
Preterm, large for gestational age (LGA)	Less than 38	Above 90
Term SGA	Between 38 and 42	Below 10
Term AGA	Between 38 and 42	Between 10 and 90
Term LGA	Between 38 and 42	Above 90
Postterm SGA	After 42	Below 10
Postterm AGA	After 42	Between 10 and 90
Postterm LGA	After 42	Above 90

TABLE 7-3
Problems Associated with Classification Based on Estimated Gestational Age and Birth Weight

Small for Gestational Age	Large for Gestational Age	Preterm	Postterm
Hypoglycemia	Trauma related to delivery	Respiratory distress syndrome	Hypoglycemia
Cold Stress	Respiratory distress due to aspiration	Cold Stress	Cold Stress
Polycythemia	Hypoglycemia	Hypoglycemia	Polycythemia
Aspiration syndrome	Hypocalcemia	Jaundice	Aspiration syndrome
Increased risk for congenital abnormalities	Transposition of the aorta	Neonatal necrotizing enterocolitis	
Perinatal asphyxia	Beckwith's syndrome	Hyperbilirubinemia	
Cerebral edema	Polycythemia and hypercoagulability	Anemia	
Interuterine infection		Retrolental fibroplasia	

problems allows for preventive and therapeutic measures to be instituted to alleviate conditions interfering with the neonate's adjustment and attainment of health.

PERIOD OF TRANSITION

One of the most significant times in the neonate's life following birth is the period of transition. Transition places tremendous stress on the neonate as his or her physiologic systems adapt to extrauterine life. Assessment of the neonate's attainment of health is made during this time. To make a valid assessment, the nurse must possess a knowledge of the identified periods of transition and the expected physiologic manifestations of neonates during each stage of transition. The period of transition is divided into two or three stages, depending on how the theory is applied to clinical practice. Regardless, transition is divided into major stages of activity separated by quieter intervals of inactivity characterized by sleep. The physiologic manifestations identified in each stage are based on the work of Arnold et al. (1965). The first period of reactivity occurs after birth and lasts up to approximately 1 hour. During this phase of transition, the neonate displays intense generalized movement throughout the body systems. The neonate appears alert with open eyes and has increased motor activity and reflexes. Tachycardia; tachypnea; irregular, shallow respirations; and transient cyanosis may be present. During this first phase (shortly after birth), retractions and nasal flaring may also be noted. Toward the end of this period of reactivity, the intense motor activity is replaced by quiet, alerting, exploratory behavior which ends in sleep. During this nonresponsive interval, the neonate's body temperature begins to fall. The time that the neonate spends in this stage of transition varies and may last up to 3 to 4 hours.

Following this nonresponsive interval, the neonate once again enters a period of intense activity. This second period of reactivity is characterized by physiologic symptoms similar to those noted in the first period. The difference between these two periods is that in the second period of reactivity, presenting symptoms may be variable, so that increased motor and physiologic activity may be interspersed with normal findings. Increased mucus production is present in both periods of reactivity, and the body temperature begins to return to normal at the beginning of the second period of reactivity (Fig. 7-4).

The nurse caring for the neonate during transition utilizes baseline data identifying areas of vulnerability; these data are gathered from the summary of the birth process, Apgar score, and gestational age assessment. The data, including the nurse's analysis, are applied to the nurse's knowledge of the expected course of transition. Assessment with the intention of intervention is continued as the nurse recognizes variations in the neonate from the expected norms. Throughout this complete process, skilled, competent nursing management is delivered on a basis of valid data that helps to predict the neonate's areas of vulnerability. Through preventive and therapeutic measures, an environment is established that alleviates or eliminates disturbances hindering progression through transition, which in turn can hinder the neonate's attainment of optimal health.

SOCIAL, EMOTIONAL, AND COGNITIVE ASSESSMENT

Assessment to identify vulnerable areas in the social, emotional, and cognitive development of the neonate is important. Two tools that can be used to assess these areas of development are the Brazelton Neonatal Behavioral Assessment Scale and the Neonatal Perception Inventory. These assessment tools are important because the emotional, social, and cognitive development of the neonate is dependent upon a quality interaction with a consistent caregiver.

The Brazelton Neonatal Behavioral Assessment Scale, developed by Brazelton (1973), identifies individual differences in newborns that enable nurses to predict how these differences might influence the neonate's ability to interact with the environment and caregiver. This ability of the neonate to interact influences how the caregiver interacts with the neonate. The Brazelton assessment assesses the newborn's neurologic intactness by assessing reflex reactions. The assessment tool also consists of behavioral items which measure the following capacities of the neonate:

1. The capacity to attend to and process visual and auditory stimuli.
2. The capacity to maintain motor tone and to control his or her motor behavior to perform integrated motor acts.

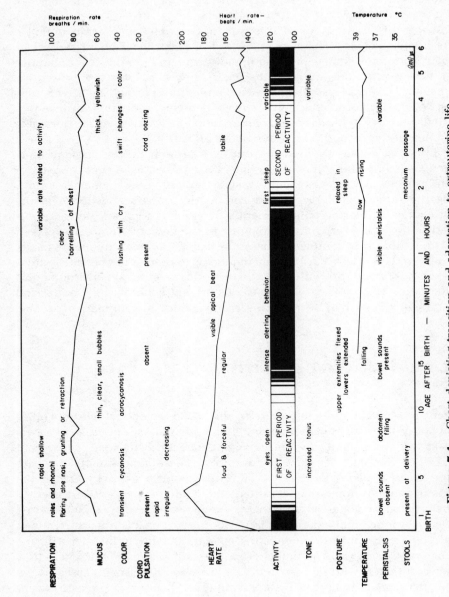

Figure 7-4. Chart depicting transition and adaptation to extrauterine life.
(From Arnold, H., et al. The newborn: Transition to extrauterine life. American Journal of Nursing 65:77, 1965)

3. The capacity to organize and modulate his or her state.
4. Stability in response to stress.

The reader is referred to the reference list and bibliography for more detailed information on the scale.

The nurse can effectively utilize the Brazelton assessment tool as an operative

TABLE 7-4
Neonatal Perception Inventory I: Your Baby*

How much crying do you think your baby will do?

great deal	a good bit	moderate amount	very little	none

How much trouble do you think your baby will have feeding?

great deal	a good bit	moderate amount	very little	none

How much spitting up or vomiting do you think your baby will do?

a great deal	a good bit	moderate amount	very little	none

How much difficulty do you think your baby will have sleeping?

a great deal	a good bit	moderate amount	very little	none

How much difficulty do you expect your baby to have with bowel movements?

a great deal	a good bit	moderate amount	very little	none

How much trouble do you think that your baby will have settling down to a predictable pattern of eating and sleeping?

a great deal	a good bit	moderate amount	very little	none

*The same questions are asked in another form entitled "Average Baby." Courtesy of Hellmuth, J. Exceptional Infant. New York: Brunner/Mazel, 1971, vol. 2.

method of intervention. The assessment tool supplies the nurse with a wealth of information about the neonate's personality, temperament, motor intactness, and ability to react and/or interact with stimuli in the environment. All of these concepts are important in an interaction between neonate and caregiver. The nurse utilizes data from the assessment to teach parents about their neonate's response to stress and to the introduction of new stimuli and about how their neonate exercises control through consolability. Thus, by knowing this important information about their infant, parents will know how to introduce new stimuli and experiences and how to help the neonate to meet his or her needs. This intervention promotes establishment of quality parent–infant interactions, which influence potential for emotional, social, and cognitive development. This same assessment also identifies areas of vulnerability, and the nurse can use this information to help parents to work to resolve vulnerable aspects.

The social, emotional, and cognitive development of the neonate is also dependent upon the mother's/parent's perception of the capabilities of the newborn. Therefore, the nurse assesses the expectations of the mother and/or parents, determining areas of vulnerability early so that intervention can be initiated. The nurse can assess the mother's expectations through the use of the following Neonatal Perception Inventory (Table 7-4). This assessment is based on the concept that in order for emotional and social development to occur, the mother must perceive her infant as better than the average infant. Therefore, the assessment tool is used to obtain data concerning the mother's perception of the capabilities of the average infant. It is also used to obtain data concerning the mother's perception of the capabilities of her own infant. A comparison is made between the two categories of data. These data are further validated by data obtained concerning the amount of bother the mother feels is associated with caring for an infant. The nurse utilizes these data to assess areas of unrealistic expectation and to implement intervention before the potential for emotional and social development of the neonate can be affected.

The attainment of optimal health of the neonate is dependent on the nurses' ability to assess existing or potential areas of vulnerability that can interfere with development. The neonate who is hospitalized for an extended period of time is at risk of developing many vulnerable areas. Thus his or her attainment of optimal health is influenced by the health care providers' ability to assess vulnerability and to intervene effectively.

MANAGEMENT IN THE INTENSIVE CARE UNIT

Nursing management of the neonate in the intensive care unit is based on promoting an environment necessary to maintain physiologic functioning, and preventing further physiologic complications. The first step is to assess the neonate's strengths and areas of vulnerability and then to plan nursing management taking these findings into account. An important concept in preventing further physiologic complications is the maintenance of a neutral thermal environment. A neutral thermal environment is defined as any environment in which the neonate can stabilize his or her body temperature with minimal oxygen consumption and energy expenditure (Dahl and Frazier, 1976). Failure to maintain this environment can worsen any physiologic vulnerability.

In order to understand why maintaining a neutral thermal environment is important to the neonate's attainment of health, it is necessary to understand the concepts associated with heat loss, heat production, and cold stress.

The neonate loses heat in the following ways:

1. Evaporation: heat loss through the utilization of thermal energy that occurs during conversion of liquid to vapor.
2. Conduction: heat loss that occurs when the neonate's skin is in direct contact with a cooler object.
3. Convection: heat loss that occurs when heat flows from the body surface to the cooler surrounding air.
4. Radiation: loss of heat to cooler solid objects in the environment that are not in contact with the neonate.

The main mechanism that neonates use for raising their body temperature or for producing heat is through nonshivering thermogenesis. Nonshivering thermogenesis is defined as the ability to raise body heat through increasing metabolic activity. The main heat-producing process available to the neonate is the metabolism of brown adipose tissue. Brown fat, which is unique to the neonate, is located around the midscapular region, the posterior neck, the thoracic inlet, and behind the sternum. This fat is vascular in nature, with an excellent venous drainage system. When the neonate becomes cold, the brown fat is metabolized and heat is generated and distributed throughout the body by means of the rich vascular system.

In addition to knowing the concepts of heat loss and heat production, it is important for the nurse to understand the adverse physiologic effects of cold stress. When a neonate becomes cold, metabolic changes occur that can be life-threatening, depending on the neonate's areas of vulnerability. The metabolic changes associated with cold stress are increased oxygen consumption, increased utilization of calories and glucose, altered pH (resulting in acidosis), and inhibited surfactant production. By assessing the neonate's areas of vulnerability, it is easy to determine that some neonates cannot afford to become cold, as lowering the body temperature compromises their ability to adapt to intrauterine life, and this compromise can result in altered functioning, which can affect development.

Nursing management concerning thermoregulation is directed at assessing and identifying the neonates who by virtue of physiologic vulnerability are at risk for hypothermia. Some infants' thermoregulatory vulnerability is directly related to their gestational age classification. Small-for-gestational-age infants have reduced skin fat, resulting in decreased insulation and increased risk of hypothermia. Because of compromised intrauterine nutrition, some small-for-gestational-age infants may have a limited supply of glucose, making them at-risk for losing their thermoregulatory response.

Premature infants are at risk for some of the same reasons as the small-for-gestational-age neonates. They are also susceptible for other reasons as well. Premature infants have a diminished supply of brown fat, according to gestational age. In addition, their ability to activate the thermoregulatory response is hindered due to the immaturity of their physiologic systems.

The nurse identifies those neonates who have existing physiologic conditions that tend to interfere with the neonate's ability to activate the nonshivering thermogenesis process or the neonate's ability to maintain the process. Neonates who are in this category include:

1. Neonates who have hypoglycemia are at risk of developing hypoglycemia.
2. Neonates who have respiratory compromise, such as respiratory distress syndrome or aspiration syndrome.
3. Neonates who have neurologic compromise, such as intracranial hemorrhage or defects of the central nervous system.
4. Neonates who have experienced prolonged cold stress.
5. Neonates who are depressed following birth due to maternal drugs.

After identification of those neonates who are at risk for developing hypothermia, nursing management is centered around monitoring the stability of temperatures. The nurse observes the neonate for the following signs: poor feeding, "cold to touch," lethargic behavior, and change in respiratory status (slow, shallow, irregular). The nurse also monitors the servo control and isolette temperature. These are documented and correlations are made between the ambient temperature, the neonate's skin temperature, and the temperature of the servo unit. The nurse is alert for any conflicting data, determines the cause, and initiates corrective actions.

Nursing management is also centered on prevention of cold stress through implementing nursing interventions designed specifically to prevent heat loss through evaporation, conduction, convection, and radiation. The nurse is consciously aware of the environment and removes anything that produces heat loss. Nursing and medical producers are coordinated so that there is minimal opening of isolette tops and portholes. If a neonate needs continuous treatments/procedures, then he or she is placed under a radiant warmer (Figs. 7-5 and 7-6). Oxygen and humidity are warmed, as the face contains receptors which will respond rapidly to a cold stimulus. The bathing procedure takes place in a neutral thermal environment under close observation. If the nurse incorporates his or her knowledge of thermoregulation into specific nursing actions, then exposure of the neonate to cold stress through carelessness or ignorance can be eliminated.

It is recognized that hypoglycemia is a physiologic complication that occurs in neonates and can, if untreated, interfere with attainment of health. Hypoglycemia can lead to brain damage and life-long impairment. The consequences of hypoglycemia are exaggerated by the vulnerability of the neonate's central nervous system; the at-risk neonate is especially vulnerable.

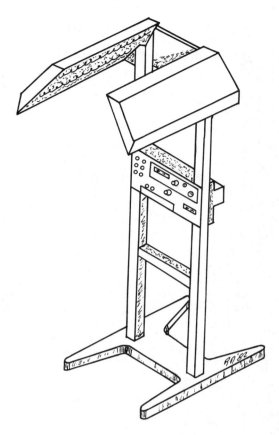

Figure 7-5. Treatments and procedures should be performed under a radiant warmer.

In utero, the fetus receives glucose across the placenta from the mother. This glucose is stored as glycogen during the last 2 to 3 months of gestation. With birth and the separation of the placenta, the neonate no longer has access to the maternal supply of glucose and depends on his or her own stored supply. The birth process and the following period of transition place enormous stress on the neonate, which involves compensatory mechanisms that are dependent on glucose.

At the very time that the neonate is subjected to these increased demands to adapt, he or she is without an external supply of glucose and thus completely dependent upon his or her own supply. This situation is further complicated by the fact that the glucose level in the blood reaches its lowest point 1 to 2 hours after birth. All of these factors combine to establish a potential for hypoglycemia.

The potential for hypoglycemia can be readily actualized when certain neonates who are identified as being at risk of developing hypoglycemia are exposed to these factors. Premature neonates are at risk for hypoglycemia, as their birth may occur before glycogen stores are developed. In addition, the transition of the premature infant may be complicated by physiologic immaturity, creating an even greater demand for glucose. In addition, the premature infant is

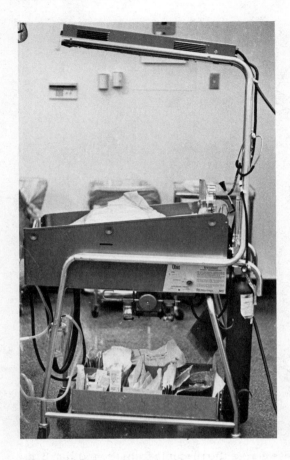

Figure 7-6. A radiant warmer used in labor and delivery.

predisposed to physiologic conditions, such as hypothermia and respiratory distress, that create a demand for the utilization of the limited supply of glucose.

Small-for-gestational-age infants are also at risk for hypoglycemia due to a compromised intrauterine nutritional environment and their potential to have diminished glycogen storage. The postterm neonate may remain in utero past optimal functioning of the placenta, making him or her dependent upon utilization of stored glycogen while in utero and thus causing depletion of the supply before birth.

Regardless of gestational age, there are some conditions that exist before, during, or after birth that can make a neonate at risk of developing hypoglycemia. Neonates of mothers who have diabetes or toxemia are predisposed to hypoglycemia. A prolonged or difficult labor places the fetus in stress, which in turn creates excessive demands for the utilization of glucose. Similarly, any stressful condition after birth (such as cold stress, respiratory distress, sepsis, and /or feeding problems) may cause increased utilization of glucose.

The main goal of nursing management is the identification and the prevention of hypoglycemia, especially in neonates who are at risk. Based on the rationale that hypoglycemia is not always symptomatic, nursing management consists of performing heel-stick screening on all infants who, because of gestational age classification or pre-existing conditions of the birth process, are identified as being predisposed to hypoglycemia. Intervention is usually initiated if the blood glucose level is below 40 mg/100 ml (Dublock, 1976). However, if existing conditions are favorable for early feeding, then early feeding of glucose water is initiated with neonates suspected of having hypoglycemia.

Another aspect of nursing management associated with hypoglycemia is the identification of clinical signs indicative of hypoglycemia. The clinical manifestations of hypoglycemia are often subtle and may be overlooked unless the nurse is alert. One of the first signs that alerts the nurse is a change in the neonate's condition, such as a change in feeding pattern or a refusal to feed. The neonate may have difficulty regulating body temperature or may experience more frequent or more prolonged periods of apnea. Other clinical signs of hypoglycemia are tremors or jitteriness, cyanosis, irregular respirations, lethargy or changes in muscle tone, and convulsions.

In summary, nursing management consists of early identification of neonates' predisposal to hypoglycemia, early recognition of clinical signs of hypoglycemia, initiation of screening procedures to determine glucose level, and implementation of preventive nursing measures.

RESPIRATORY DISTRESS

Another major concept in providing an environment to prevent further physiologic complications lies in the prevention and management of respiratory distress.

Respiratory distress that is present at birth or that develops after respirations are maintained may be due to a variety of causes. A major cause of respiratory distress in the high-risk neonate, respiratory distress syndrome, is discussed later in this text. In this section, the focus is on nursing management of the neonate with respiratory distress regardless of the cause.

The first component of nursing management is to recognize the clinical signs of respiratory distress. It is important to emphasize that regardless of the parameters of the respiratory rate and pattern, the nurse initiates action any time there is a deviation from the baseline data. A neonate who is experiencing respiratory difficulty tries to compensate by increasing respiratory effort. It is for this reason that tachypnea is one of the earliest signs of respiratory distress. The neonate's compensatory mechanism does not result in more effective ventilation.

Along with the increase in respirations, the neonate also tries to compensate by increasing his or her respiratory effort. As the respiratory effort increases, negative pressure increases, which results in a sinking of the neonate's rib cage during inspiration. This phenomenon is termed "retractions." The type of retractions noted is directly related to the amount of respiratory effort being expended and the muscles that are involved in this effort. Retractions are termed subcostal, substernal, intercostal, supraclavicular, or suprasternal on the basis of anatomic locations. Marked retractions associated with severe respiratory distress are termed "see-saw respirations." See-saw respirations are characterized by the abdomen rising and the chest sinking on inspiration, and by the chest expanding and the abdomen sinking on expiration. The accessory muscles that are used for this increased respiratory effort make this respiratory pattern markedly identifiable. It is important for the nurse to document the respiratory rate and the presence of retractions in terms of degree and location. One means of assessing respiration is through use of the Silverman–Anderson Index of Respiratory Distress (Fig. 7-7).

Another sign of respiratory distress is a prolonged expiratory phase of the respiratory cycle. This involves a reflex mechanism that the neonate uses to maintain enough air pressure to enlarge the alveolar openings and thus promote a more effective gaseous exchange. Another reflex mechanism that the neonate employs to prolong end-expiration is the expiratory grunt. The expiratory grunt is a vocal sound that is transmitted when the neonate attempts to approximate the vocal cords, which results in an increased air pressure behind the partially occluded glottis. The expiratory grunt is heard when the expired air passes the vocal cords. The expiratory grunt may be audible to the naked ear or may be audible only with the use of the stethoscope, but in either case it is also indicative of marked respiratory distress.

Other signs associated with respiratory distress are nasal flaring, chin tug, and frequent or prolonged apnea periods. Generalized cyanosis is associated with respiratory distress but is a late clinical sign. It is also important to note that the neonate's muscle tone and reflex ability are related to the degree of respiratory distress. Therefore, an infant who is experiencing respiratory distress will have corresponding limpness, poor reflex responses, and a quiet, feeble cry. Changes in respiratory status are noted and interventions are initiated when the earliest signs of respiratory distress occur.

Another component of nursing management of the neonate in respiratory distress is the administration of oxygen. The administration of oxygen is an early intervention necessary to promote optimal attainment of health and, many times, to save the life of the neonate. Conversely, the administration of oxygen, if not monitored properly, can result in serious complications that can compromise the development and/or the life of the neonate. This concept further emphasizes the necessity of providing an environment that promotes optimal development. Oxygen can be administered to the neonate in a variety of ways: with a mask or oxygen head hood, by direct administration into the isolette, or through respirators. It is not the purpose of this text to discuss each of these methods specifically, but only to cover general principles associated with the nursing management of neonates receiving oxygen. The reader is referred to the bibliography at the end of this chapter for articles that discuss oxygen administration in detail.

The administration of oxygen can result in complications; therefore, one of the components of nursing management is monitoring the oxygen concentration. The nurse is responsible for making sure that the correct concentration of oxygen

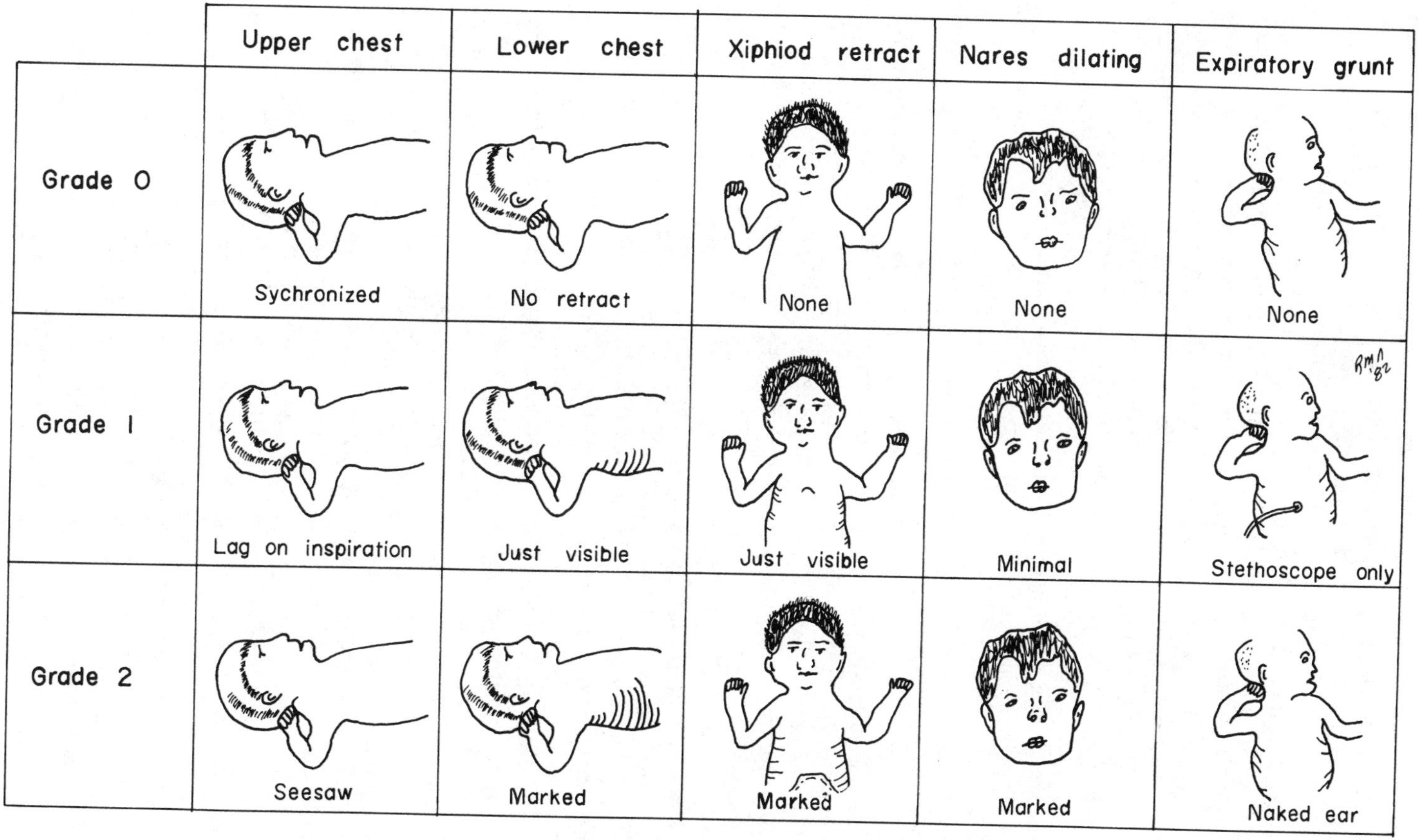

Figure 7-7. Silverman's Index for evaluating respiratory distress. *(From Silverman, W.A., & Anderson, D.H. Index of respiratory stress. Pediatrics 17:1, 1956)*

The table below shows Silverman's Index:

	Upper chest	Lower chest	Xiphiod retract	Nares dilating	Expiratory grunt
Grade 0	Sychronized	No retract	None	None	None
Grade 1	Lag on inspiration	Just visible	Just visible	Minimal	Stethoscope only
Grade 2	Seesaw	Marked	Marked	Marked	Naked ear

is delivered. He or she is also responsible for monitoring via the oxygen analyzer the concentration of oxygen that the neonate is actually receiving. It is the nurse's responsibility to check the calibration of the oxygen analyzer. The calibration of the oxygen analyzer, the concentration being received, and the settings of the oxygen gauge are documented in the chart.

Total monitoring of oxygen administration includes monitoring the neonate's tolerance of oxygen, as tissue damage or oxygen intoxication usually occurs with hyperoxia. The neonate's tolerance of oxygen is monitored through blood gases. Nursing management includes coordinating that blood gases are drawn if the neonate has an umbilical artery, noting changes if the neonate is being monitored transcutaneously, and reporting any significant changes in the level of blood gases. Blood gas results are documented, along with the concentration of oxygen being administered, the gauge readings on the ventilator, the neonate's respiratory rate, and the amount of blood that is withdrawn for the assessment.

Other components of nursing management associated with the neonate in respiratory distress include careful and deliberative suctioning as needed, percussion and vibration, and proper positioning to facilitate maximal lung expansion. The neonate is placed in a supine position with the head and trunk slightly elevated to prevent negative pressure on the thoracic cavity hindering respiratory efforts. The neonate's arms are also flexed and positioned at his or her side to prevent them from crossing over the chest and exerting pressure. The neonate's position is changed frequently to aid in loosening secretions and to promote lung expansion.

An extremely important part of nursing management of the neonate in respiratory distress is the maintenance of a neutral thermal environment. The effects of cold stress are easily recognized, and it is essential to conserve the neonate's energy while maintaining breathing. This principle of conserving energy is stressed during all nursing procedures (including feeding) performed on the neonate with respiratory distress. The main goal when feeding the neonate with respiratory distress is to give the maximum amount of calories in a limited amount of time and with a minimum amount of energy expenditure. The neonate is often fed by alternate feeding methods. Placing the neonate in a semi-Fowler's position and proper suctioning are components of oral feeding of a neonate with respiratory distress.

One of the most common causes of respiratory distress in the high-risk neonate (especially the premature neonate) is respiratory distress syndrome (RDS), also termed hyaline membrane disease. Although advances in neonatal management have benefited neonates with respiratory distress syndrome, the syndrome still carries a high incidence of mortality.

Respiratory distress syndrome has as its basic etiologic manifestation a deficient amount of surfactant in the lungs. Due to the impaired production of surfactant, a series of cyclic events is initiated. Without sufficient surfactant, the aveoli in the lungs remain collapsed instead of reopening on inspiration. With collapsed aveoli, there is ineffective gaseous exchange; due to this ineffective ventilation, a series of metabolic changes takes place. The PO_2 drops because the blood is unable to pick up sufficient oxygen from the collapsed alveoli; as the P_{O_2} drops, the CO_2 level of the blood rises and the pH level is altered, resulting in respiratory acidosis. Hypoxia occurs, resulting in anaerobic metabolism, which produces a byproduct of lactic acid. As the production of lactic acid increases, metabolic acidosis results. Metabolic acidosis further contributes to decreased hypoperfusion of the lungs. Unfortunately, surfactant needs a rich supply of oxygen and glucose to regenerate; therefore, the future production of surfactant is hindered. The management of respiratory distress syndrome centers on intervention in the cycle of events and of supportive management of metabolic changes and the established respiratory pattern. The management of care involves the delivery of oxygen in high concentrations. Since one of the main problems in RDS is the collapse of alveoli, oxygen is usually administered via a nonmechanical ventilatory device termed Continuous Positive Airway Pressure (CPAP). CPAP administers oxygen with continuous positive pressure during both inspiration and expiration, thus promoting expansion of collapsed alveoli.

Supportive management also consists of correcting electrolyte and acid−base imbalances. Recently, clinical research has been done on the use of betamethasone, which is a glucocorticoid thought to decrease the incidence of RDS by stimulating the production of surfactant through acceleration of maturation of the fetal lung. The drug is administered before birth as a preventive measure. As stated before, the giving of betamethasone is still being studied, along with its success and any adverse side-effects.

Nursing management of the neonate with RDS has already been discussed. Nursing management includes general measures of support, such as giving oral or parenteral fluids, monitoring fluids and electrolytes, and nursing care associated with neonates with ventilators and umbilical catheters. The reader is referred to the bibliography for further reading in these areas.

COMPLICATIONS OF OXYGEN ADMINISTRATION

The administration of oxygen, especially in high concentrations and over a prolonged period of time, can cause complications. Two of those complications will be discussed briefly: retrolental fibroplasia and bronchopulmonary dysplasia. Retrolental fibroplasia occurs as a result of several contributing factors. One factor is that, due to prematurity, the neonate has an immature blood supply to the retina, which makes the retina vulnerable to damage from oxygen flow. When oxygen is administered, the vessels in the retina immediately constrict. If the administration of oxygen is prolonged, the vessels dilate and new vessels are formed. Edema and hemorrhage occur and can result in detachment of the retina and potential blindness. It is important to recognize that retrolental fibroplasia occurs when the concentration of oxygen is too high. This usually occurs when there is a sudden change in the arterial oxygen levels in the blood and the neonate no longer needs a high concentration; thus hyperoxemia occurs. Careful monitoring of blood gases can prevent retrolental fibroplasia. The degree and severity of retinal damage is directly proportionate to the degree of immaturity of the retina, the concentration of oxygen, and the length of time the oxygen is administered.

Bronchopulmonary dysplasia (BPD) is a chronic obstructive pulmonary disease that occurs when the following conditions exist: prematurity with RDS, administration of high concentrations of oxygen over a prolonged period of time, and positive pressure ventilation. The symptoms of bronchopulmonary dysplasia may last 1 to 2 years or longer. The main clinical manifestations of BPD are the cystic changes in the lung, resulting in poor ventilation and poor gaseous exchange.

Nursing management associated with BPD is divided into two stages. The first stage of nursing management takes place during the acute phase and is the same as the management of neonates in severe respiratory distress. As the neonate recovers, nursing measures necessary to support respiratory status are retained, and the nurse begins to prepare the family to care for the neonate at home. Some infants are sent home while still dependent on oxygen; therefore, the parents are taught to administer the oxygen, monitor the infant's progress, and care for the equipment. Information and instruction are provided on how to perform suctioning, postural drainage, and percussion and on how often these procedures are needed. Parents are taught how to recognize changes in their neonate's respiratory status and how to know when a respiratory infection is developing. Instructions that relate to home management include information about prescribed medications and their side-effects. The parents also need to know how to recognize signs of fluid retention, such as weight gain, edema, and increased respiratory rate, as well as signs of dehydration, such as depressed fontanel, decreased skin turgor, and decreased voiding, as evidenced by fewer wet diapers. The parents need tremendous support to learn how to adapt routine infant care, such as bathing and feeding, to conserve energy and promote maximum growth. Family members also need counseling on the importance of providing their infant with the opportunity to master the important developmental milestones and how to adapt the infant's environment to facilitate this opportunity. In summary, the nursing management involving the long-term care of the neonate with BPD is extremely important, because it is during this time that the nurse has a major opportunity to influence the level of development and health that the infant will achieve.

HYPERBILIRUBINEMIA

Hyperbilirubinemia is another condition that is associated with physiologic complications during the neonatal period. Hyperbilirubinemia is a common problem in the premature neonate, reflecting the immaturity of the liver and its decreased ability to conjugate bilirubin. The underlying etiologic factor of hyperbilirubinemia in the preterm child is similar to what causes physiologic jaundice in the term newborn. However, there are several factors that make the physiologic process more significant in the preterm infant. One factor is that the premature infant often has less serum albumin to bind the bilirubin; thus indirect bilirubin increases more rapidly. Another contributing factor is due to pre-existing conditions—the neonate may be acidotic, which is thought to enhance the passage of bilirubin in the central nervous system. In addition, the premature neonate is predisposed to easy bruising, thus increasing hemolysis. However, the most significant factor is that the dangers of hyperbilirubinemia are increased because kernicterus occurs at a lower bilirubin level in the premature infant.

Management of care is directed toward lowering the serum bilirubin level to prevent brain damage caused by kernicterus. Bilirubin levels are usually lowered through phototherapy, blood transfusions, and increased fluid intake.

Nursing management of a neonate with hyperbilirubinemia consists of monitoring the degree of jaundice and the bilirubin levels. The nurse also needs to carefully monitor the neonate's body temperature, as the neonate is left undressed in the isolette or the radiant warmer while under the phototherapy lights.

Careful monitoring of fluid administration for signs of overhydration and/or dehydration is required. Dehydration is of greatest concern, as phototherapy causes an increased insensible water loss and overheating. If the neonate is on oral feedings, the nurse has the responsibility of scheduling frequent feedings and making certain the neonate takes the required amount of fluids.

The infant's feeding schedule is individualized according to the infant's tolerance. The aim of the fluid therapy is usually to give the infant breast milk or formula every 4 hours, with 20 to 30 cc of glucose water or sterile water every 2 hours.

The nurse also weighs the neonate twice daily and monitors the number and consistency of stools, as frequent, greenish, fluid stools occur as a result of phototherapy. The following signs are indicative of dehydration:

1. Weight loss; usually, if weight loss is greater than 2 percent, fluid intake is increased.
2. Sunken fontanels.
3. Decreased skin turgor.
4. Oliguria.

Increased weight gain, bulging fontanels, and increased respiratory rate are evidence of fluid overload and indicate a need for adjustments in fluid therapy. Concurrent electrolyte monitoring is also indicated.

Nursing management is also centered around protecting the neonate's eyes from damage by the phototherapy lights. Bilateral eye pads are secured in place while the neonate is under the lights. The nurse needs to schedule times (preferably during feedings) when the eye pads can be removed to allow for alert exploratory behavior.

Other components of nursing management include skin care, cleanliness (especially around the genital area), and frequent changing of positions.

NECROTIZING ENTEROCOLITIS

Nursing observations to detect necrotizing enterocolitis (NEC) are important in providing an environment necessary to prevent complications interfering with attainment of health. Necrotizing enterocolitis is a life-threatening condition that can affect neonates who are predisposed to conditions associated with being in a neonatal intensive care unit, such as sepsis, umbilical catherization, low gestational age, and hyperosmolarity feeding.

Necrotizing enterocolitis results from hypoxia, which causes a compensatory shunting of blood from organs that tolerate ischemia well (such as the intestines) to those areas of the body that need continuous oxygenation (such as the brain). When this shunting occurs, the intestinal cells stop secreting mucus and are invaded by gas-forming bacteria, causing damage to the cells. If not corrected, the end result can be intestinal perforation and death.

Management includes stopping oral feeding, allowing the intestines to rest, and the administration of antibiotics and parenteral fluids. Nursing care is based on recognition of symptoms of NEC. Symptoms include abdominal distention, failure to absorb feedings, shiny abdominal wall, absence of bowel sounds, and presence of blood in the stools. The nurse measures the size of the abdomen at least every four hours, and any significant changes are reported. The neonate is observed for signs of impending shock, such as inability to maintain normal body temperature, decrease in blood pressure, bradycardia, an ashen gray color, and listlessness. The neonate is handled gently to avoid trauma to the abdomen. Nursing management is also centered on the management of the parenteral fluids and administration of antibiotics.

Another component of providing an environment promoting optimal development of the neonate is the recognition and prevention of sepsis. Sepsis can occur for a variety of reasons either before, during, or after birth. Management of sepsis includes early recognition, administration of antibiotics, and isolation as needed. The nurse has an invaluable role in detecting sepsis, as the signs of sepsis are often very subtle and the first clue given by the neonate may be a change in behavior. Signs of sepsis include change in behavior (such as lethargy or irritability), change in feeding behavior (such as poor sucking), poor tolerance of feeding (evidenced by vomiting and diarrhea), poor weight gain, episodes of cyanosis, irregular respirations, and inability to regulate body temperature.

PROMOTION OF HEALTH

Recently there has been a move from concentrating on illness to concentrating on health. This viewpoint is reflected in the neonatal intensive care unit. Just as nursing care focuses on providing an environment designed to maintain physiologic functioning and to prevent further complications, it also focuses on providing an environment designed to facilitate total development of the infant. When the neonate no longer needs total physiologic monitoring, focus is placed on identification of vulnerable areas of future development in all realms of the neonate's life. It is important to emphasize that if optimal development and optimal health are the goals of nursing management, then nursing care does not focus on the neonate alone but also on his or her family unit and environment. This concept is based on the rationale that development of the infant during the first years is dependent on the stimulation received from caregivers and from other sources in the environment. Therefore, it is extremely important to introduce sensory stimulation using a variety of sources.

The neonatal intensive care unit contains a great deal of technologically advanced equipment that can produce disturbing sounds (Fig. 7-8). These sounds, when combined with the adverse stimulation received from multiple procedures performed on the neonate throughout each day, provide an environment capable of producing sensory overload. Sensory overload can be classified as disruptive stimuli and can interfere with development. Infants are very responsive to stimuli, and because of their responsiveness, they are more vulnerable to the adverse effects of overstimulation. Conversely, given an environment containing appropriate stimulation and interactions with a consistent caregiver, development of the neonate can progress effectively even in an intensive care unit—this is the main goal of nursing management.

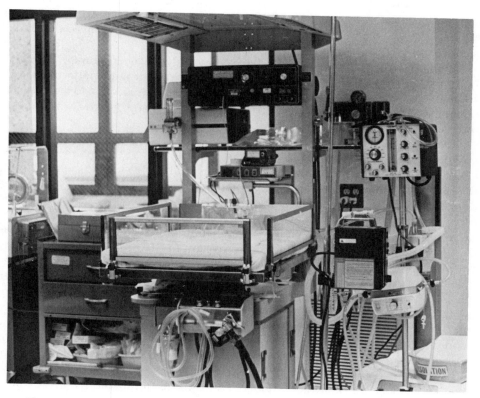

Figure 7-8. Equipment used on neonates requiring extended hospitalization produces adverse sounds that contribute to sensory overload.

Touch has long been identified as a very important source of stimulation for the neonate, as neonates are very sensitive to touch. Appropriate touch has a soothing, relaxing effect on the neonate. Thus the provision of appropriate touch is essential in an environment where painful stimuli are produced. Touch is a form of stimulation that is very easy to introduce into nursing management even while the neonate is still on total monitoring and care. As the neonate's condition improves, additional forms of tactile stimulation can be introduced, e.g., through varying the types of touch, varying the texture of the material the infant lies on, and placing different objects in the infant's hand to stimulate the primitive grasp reflex.

Auditory stimulation is also important to the neonate. One of the most important and easiest forms of auditory stimulation to provide is the human voice. The neonate has an innate ability to react to the human voice, as evidenced by the movement of the neonate's extremities in response to the human voice. It is essential to capitalize on this innate ability by providing a soothing human voice that helps to counteract adverse environmental auditory stimulation. Rhythmic sounds suggestive of a mother's heartbeat can give a sense of security. A tape recording of the mother's voice not only helps to soothe the infant but can help with promoting mother—infant bonding. Music as a form of auditory stimulation is used increasingly with infants who are hospitalized. As neonates are selective and discriminative in choosing which stimuli they will respond to, it is imperative to offer them soothing auditory choices.

Research has shown that newborns not only have an innate ability to recognize the human face but can also discriminate between patterns, colors, and forms (Hack, 1981). Therefore, in order to promote optimal development, visual stimulation is also provided. This can be done easily by providing colorful or black and white mobiles.

The importance of stimulation is further emphasized when considering the mode of cognitive development. Cognitive development of the infant cannot be discussed without considering the importance of the physiologic capabilities of the neonate's neurologic system. Since many high-risk neonates have conditions due either to gestational age or to disease processes in which neurologic functioning can be impaired, the importance of providing an environment that promotes cognitive development must not be underestimated. Past research has demonstrated that early stimulation is important to the future learning capacity of the neonate (Czarniecki, 1978). Much of the cognitive development during the first month of life revolves around those processes that allow the neonate to become attentive to the environment. Piaget's (1952) theory of cognitive development further supports the importance of stimulation in cognitive development. He calls the earliest stage of cognitive development the sensorimotor period. The main characteristic of the sensorimotor period is that cognitive development is derived from sensation and movement and is dependent upon the child's motor and sensory experiences.

Considering the above-mentioned concepts of stimulation and cognitive development principles, providing appropriate sensory stimulation in the nursing management of neonates is essential. This need is emphasized further when considering the length of time that an infant can be hospitalized and the effect it can have on his or her cognitive development if he or she is deprived of the stimulation necessary for learning during periods of long hospitalization. The amount and quality of sensory stimulation are planned in accordance with the neonate's individual needs to nourish his or her increasing interest in exploring the environment. The nurse also monitors the amount of stimulation presented, as too much stimulation can cause the neonate to either tune out stimuli or to become hyperirritable. Therefore, the nurse is aware of individual differences and tolerances of stimuli and gauges the stimuli accordingly. Such awareness is achieved by being alert to the infant's cues.

It is also important to provide an environment that promotes social and emotional development of the high-risk neonate. One of the major attainments of social development of the infant is the attainment of trust, as defined by Erikson (1963). The main way that trust is developed is through consistent meeting of the neonate's needs by a consistent caregiver, usually defined as the mother.

Many questions can be raised about the ability to nurture infants in neonatal intensive care nurseries. Some of these questions follow: Is it possible for trust to be established in an environment filled with negative stimuli derived from total physiologic monitoring, or in an environment filled with frequent interruptions, many of which are painful, or in an environment where the infant is separated the majority of the time from his or her mother? Can these factors that seem to support mistrust be altered to promote the development of trust? Does it really matter whether or not the infant in the hospitalized situation develops trust? If it is the responsibility of health care providers to promote high-level wellness, then the answer to all these questions is obviously "yes." In planning nursing management and implementing care, it is essential to alter the environment so that trust develops rather than mistrust. While the neonate is on total physiologic monitoring, the nursing actions that promote this goal include using the voice effectively, using touch to counteract any painful interruptions, and incorporating a pattern into the neonate's care so that the neonate can predict the periods of interaction that will occur that include such touch strategies as stroking. Some interesting studies have shown that predictability can be promoted by covering the neonate's eyes or simulating in some other manner a day/night cycle in the intensive care nursery, where bright lights interfere with the neonate's ability to sleep soundly (Dryfus-Brisac, 1974; Parmelee and Stern, 1972). Playing of tape recordings of the mother's voice at regular intervals can also promote a sense of trust. In addition, providing a consistent caretaker helps the neonate to develop trust.

As the infant becomes less dependent on total monitoring and is no longer expending all his or her energy on physiologic functioning, he or she is able to begin to spend more time responding to his or her environment and stimuli. At this time, the neonate displays a variety of nonverbal behavior or cues in response to stimulation or interaction. Beebe and Stern (1977, 1979) identify these cues as "coping behavior" and state that it is by the use of these nonverbal cues that infants manage stimulation, avoid overstimulation, and alert caregivers to their needs. Therefore, if nurses are alert to cues the neonate gives during stimulation and interaction, they will be able to assess patterns and then respond consistently to these patterns of cues, giving the neonate the potential for the establishment of trust. (Refer to bibliography for information concerning interpretation of cues).

The incorporation of the mother into these nursing actions is a primary goal. The nurse helps the mother to learn her neonate's clues so that she can learn to meet the child's needs. As the neonate's physical condition continues to improve, verbal cues as well as nonverbal cues are given that can be used by the mother to anticipate the child's needs. In Barnard's *Nursing Assessment Satellite Training Project Learning Resource Manual* (1978), an example is given of how a Sleep/Activity Record is kept by nurses, showing times of feedings, times of interruptions for procedures, and times of sleep (Fig. 7-9). As a result of this information over a specified period of time, the neonate's attempt at establishing a pattern or routine is depicted. These findings are shared with the mother to assist her in anticipating her neonate's needs. In addition, instructing the mother to keep a sleep/activity record assists her in being aware of the changing needs of her neonate as he or she matures and adapts to a changing environment.

It has been documented again and again that the emotional development of the infant is dependent upon the mother—infant relationship and the father—infant relationship. These interaction processes play a significant role in emotional development and contain many identifiable variables that are vulnerable areas for the infant who is hospitalized following birth. It is important to realize that the fostering of emotional development is dependent directly on events and feelings that occurred before, during, and after the birth of the neonate, as these factors affect how the parents perceive their infant and what expectations they have for their infant. Factors to be considered are as follows:

1. How did the parent(s) feel about conception?
2. Was the pregnancy planned or unplanned?
3. Were any other positive and/or negative life events occurring at the time of conception or during pregnancy?
4. What is the relationship of the mother and father to each other?
5. What was the mother's physical and emotional condition during pregnancy?
6. What support systems did the mother and/or father have during pregnancy?
7. What was the mother's perception of her pregnancy? of the birth itself?
8. What was the father's involvement in the pregnancy and birth process?
9. Were the pregnancy, labor, and delivery difficult?
10. Was the birth process a financial burden for the parent(s)?
11. What are the mother's and father's expectations of the infant's capabilities?
12. Are the mother and father in agreement on patterns of childrearing?

CAREGIVER'S USUAL BEDTIME ______
CAREGIVER'S USUAL AWAKENING ______

CHILD'S NAME ______________ (LAST NAME, FIRST NAME)
BIRTH DATE ______________
DATE OF RECORDING ______________

Date	12 Noon	1	2	3	4	5	6	7	8	9	10	11	12 Mid.	1	2	3	4	5	6	7	8	9	10	11	24 HR SUMMARY			
																									Totals				

SYMBOLS

SUMMARY

Figure 7-9. Nursing child assessment sleep activity record. *(Courtesy of Barnard, K, School of Nursing, NCAT Project, University of Washington)*

13. Does the infant have gestational or physical conditions that hinder adaptation to transition, making prolonged hospitalization necessary?
14. What is the mother's ability to cope or adapt to periodic crises?
15. What are the infant's temperament and capabilities for interaction?

This list is not exhaustive, but it is easy to see that a neonate who requires extended hospitalization after birth is at risk for several factors that can potentially influence his or her emotional development. At an early stage in the infant's hospitalization, the parents are informed of the emotional needs of the neonate and are provided assistance in coping so that they can begin to think about ways to promote the emotional development of their infant. It has been documented in studies (Nover et al., 1981) that high-risk newborn infants, even in families that are found to be constitutionally intact at birth, are at risk of moderate to severe development morbidity in the first year of life, particularly concerning social, emotional, and cognitive development, due to the increased stresses that accompany the birth of a neonate needing extended care. It is important to recognize that risk factors can be multiple and can interrelate with and compound each other, making preventive intervention complex but necessary.

MATERNAL–INFANT BONDING

A major portion of nursing management is focused on promoting maternal–infant bonding throughout the extended hospitalization. Klaus and Kennell (1981) note that there is a sensitive period following birth that is extremely important to the establishment of the maternal–infant bond. Clinical practice has also supported the theory of the strengthening of the initial bond through continued interaction between mother and infant in the days following birth. Unfortunately, with the birth of a neonate requiring extended hospitalization, both the sensitive period after birth and the time following birth are plagued by interruptions and separation of mother and infant; this interferes with maternal-–infant bonding. Actions that promote maternal–infant interaction are:

1. Providing the opportunity, no matter how brief, during the sensitive period for the mother to see and touch her infant.
2. Encouraging the mother to touch, talk to, and maintain eye contact with her infant.
3. Keeping open lines of communication between the infant and the mother during separation—e.g., through phone calls, letters written about the infant concerning progress, and tape recordings of the mother's voice.
4. Giving the mother support and assisting her in adjusting to an environment filled with unfamiliar technical equipment.
5. Encouraging visitation and incorporating the mother's assistance, no matter how minimal it is, as soon as possible in the infant's care.

6. Encouraging the mother to recognize the uniqueness of her infant by providing stocking caps, mobiles, musical toys, etc. and by calling the infant by name (Fig. 7-10).

The nurse is also responsible for recognizing signs of negative bonding. These signs are usually expressed through negative behavior or negative verbalization by the mother. Negative clues include infrequent visits from the mother, refusal to touch the infant, and inability to perceive anything but the negative qualities of the infant. The mother's visits, her interactions with the neonate, her progression of ability to care for the infant, and any observations of negative bonding behavior are documented. It is wise to validate findings with the mother and with other health care providers before drawing premature conclusions about the mother's behavior. For example, inconsistent or infrequent visiting can be a clue that the mother is dissatisfied with her infant, but it can also mean that she lacks transportation to the hospital or adult caretakers for her other children. Each clue is carefully assessed so that the proper actions are taken. Any time there is a suspicion that a mother needs additional assistance in bonding, intervention is instituted. Interventions range from positive role modeling to referral to other health care personnel for in-depth counseling and therapeutic intervention.

FAMILY INTEGRATION

Maternal–infant bonding is the first step in promoting family unity. However, interventions go beyond this step to successfully integrate the infant into the family unit. Neonates who require extended hospitalization are separated from the family unit because the child's condition is life-threatening.

All of the quality care extended to prevent physiologic and psychosocial interferences with development is of little value if the neonate is unable to join a nurturing, supporting family capable of expending the energy and time necessary to further the neonate's development and attainment of health. In studies done

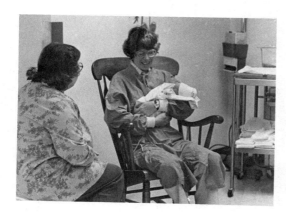

Figure 7-10. Nurses are actively involved in promotion of the maternal–infant bond.

on institutionalized infants and deprivation, and in more recent studies on the relationship between child abuse and premature infants or infants who require extended hospitalization at birth, more emphasis is being placed on maintaining the family unit at all times (Fig. 7-11). When a neonate requires extended hospitalization, stress is placed on the family in terms of grief, anxiety time, energy, and finances. It is a time of crisis, and the family needs support and intervention to prevent these stresses from resulting in family disorganization. Institutions have recognized this factor and have changed their policies to allow for more frequent visitation, more incorporation of parent care, and opportunities for parents to care for the infant with supervision and support before discharge. Health care providers have organized parent support groups so that parents can meet with each other and a supportive member of the health care team to discuss problems and concerns. These parent groups have proven to be very effective, and support and contact has been given after the neonate's discharge, when the most assistance is often needed but the least amount of assistance is available.

Across the country a new concept in the maintenance of the family unit has developed, that of a transitional family care unit. As soon as the neonate is physiologically stable and is no longer totally dependent upon monitoring, he or she is moved into a transitional nursery. This family care nursery is designed to look more home-like and less like a highly advanced technologic world, and families, including siblings, are encouraged to spend as much time as possible with the infants. Parents are encouraged to assume increasing responsibility for the infant's care while still being able to get assistance, if needed. Due to the improved environmental setting, parents are able to relax and become comfortable in caring for their neonate and are usually more ready to learn and practice any required technical care under these calmer conditions.

The nurse is the person who helps the parents to get to know their infant as a

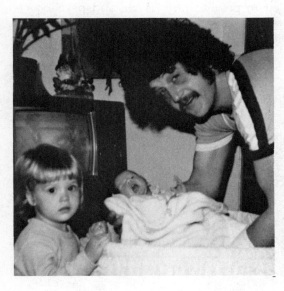

Figure 7-11. Incorporating the infant who has experienced extended hospitalization after birth into the family is a priority of nursing management.

unique person, to know his or her personality characteristics and his or her specific care needs. Gradually, the emphasis of the nursing process changes from the intense concerns for the neonate to the concerns of the family as a unit. Although the family is included from day one in the nursing process, two very important concepts are operationalized. The first concept is that in the beginning, the main emphasis of the nursing process has to be on the neonate and his or her need for total physiologic monitoring. The second concept is that the attachment process between the family and the neonate is a gradual process. This gradual process is similar to the attachment process defined by Rubin (1967). Attachment begins with aspects of the bonding process, such as touch, voice, and eye to eye contact. It begins to evolve as the parents begin to participate more in infant care. The culmination of the bonding process occurs when the family begins to recognize their neonate as a separate identity with his or her uniqueness.

When the nurse shifts the focus of the nursing process onto the family unit, it is important that this process, like any other nursing process, be based on an assessment. Therefore, the nurse does a family assessment which includes the following information:

1. Family identification: members of the family.
2. Family health history: current, past illnesses.
   a. Assessment of current health.
   b. Assessment of current health practices.
3. Assessment of socioeconomic status.
4. Assessment of environmental conditions.
5. Family characteristics.
   a. Roles of each family member.
   b. Perceptions of each family member concerning his or her role, place in the family, and expectations.
6. Communication and interaction.
   a. Between family members and the family.
   b. Members' perceptions of this interaction; discipline patterns.
7. Family views concerning child care.
8. Assessment of family strengths.
9. Assessment of family weaknesses.
10. Assessment of daily routine.
11. Assessment of goals of the family.

After the assessment has been completed, the data are used to plan appropriate interventions that are determined cooperatively by the family and the nurse. Interventions aimed at incorporating the infant into the family unit also include the siblings. The concept of a family-centered birthing experience has gained popularity. This concept has as its components at-home deliveries, the birthing room, and rooming-in after birth. The family-centered concept also incorporates the siblings into the birth experience through such modalities as sibling prenatal classes, inclusion of the siblings in the birthing room, and allowing the siblings to be present during the rooming-in experience. It is necessary to include the siblings in the preparation for discharging the infant from the intensive care unit. Nursing management includes allowing the siblings to touch the infant, including the siblings in some small aspect of care, and helping the siblings to get to know the infant so that they know what to expect of the infant's growth and behavior. Management of care also includes special sessions with just the siblings so that they can express feelings through play or other appropriate modalities about the new family member.

Promotion of optimum health after discharge from the hospital is fostered by assessing the predisposing variables that affect the infant's potential for development. A follow-up program is established based on the family's needs identified in the assessment. Various kinds of follow-up programs are available, from a registry of high-risk neonates to an infant stimulation center attended by infants who require extended hospitalization to programs having the primary nurse or another qualified nurse make home visits to vulnerable infants to assess continued development. Regardless of the type of program, the nurse has a major responsibility in identifying infants and families who are vulnerable and who need follow-up and in promoting implementation of the follow-up plans (Figs. 7-12 and 7-13).

A follow-up program consists of assessment of the infant's total development. Therefore, the infant is screened periodically for physical growth and development, for cognitive development, and for emotional and social development. Parents are counseled and advised concerning any problems and achieve-

Figure 7-12. Promotion of optimum health after discharge from the Neonatal Intensive Care Nursery (NICU) includes a follow-up program consisting of assessment of the child's physical growth and development through early childhood.

Figure 7-13. Parents are counseled concerning the importance of providing the child opportunities to attain developmental milestones.

ment of developmental milestones. They are given anticipatory guidance on how to assist their child through each developmental stage and ways to determine if development is progressing satisfactorily.

Studies have stressed that the potential for development of a vulnerable infant is dependent upon his or her environment (Haynes, 1980). Based upon this concept, Caldwell and Snyder (1978) have developed an assessment tool which evaluates the quality and quantity of factors found in the home environment that support the emotional, cognitive, and social development of the child—Home Observation for Measurement of the Environment Inventory. This includes looking at the following aspects: "emotional and verbal responsibility of the mother, avoidance of restriction and punishment, organization of the physical and temporal environment, provision of appropriate play materials, maternal involvement with the child, and opportunities for variety in daily stimulation." This assessment tool, which requires an interview and observation, can easily be used to assess the home environment.

After discharge from the intensive care unit, the prognosis of the infant's development depends upon multiple variables, including the environment. Another major variable is the continuing caregiver–child interaction. There are various methods for assessing this continuing interaction. One of the most recent advancements in overall assessment of interaction has been developed by the National Center for Clinical Infant Program and is based on adaptive and maladaptive personality organizations in infancy and early childhood (Greenspan, 1981). The observation of these behaviors in turn establishes a basis for anticipatory guidance and intervention before deterioration in the attachment process occurs. This assessment is based on different organizational levels and the different tasks, experiences, and capacities of the infant at each level. Observations are made of such aspects as the infant's internal mechanisms of control, as evidenced by his or her basic patterns, the sensory modalities of the infant and mother, and the ability of the infant and mother to interpret each other's cues. The different organizational levels of this assessment are:

1. Homeostasis (0 to 3 months): infant's capacity for regulation.
2. Attachment (2 to 7 months): ability to form interactions.
3. Somato—psychologic differentiation (3 to 10 months): ability to form internal representations.
4. Behavioral organization, initiative, and internalization (9 to 24 months): centers on complex organized emotional and behavioral patterns.
5. Representational capacity ($1\frac{1}{2}$ to $2\frac{1}{2}$ years).
6. Differentiation and consolidation ($2\frac{1}{2}$ to 4 years).

Refer to the reference list and bibliography for further readings in this area (Greenspan, 1981).

In assessing continued interaction between the mother and infant, Barnard (1978) has identified two important tasks that the mother does routinely that are significant indicators of continued interaction and potential for development. These identified events are the feeding cycle and any teaching of the infant, such as how to perform a new task. Assessment tools have been developed that both look at the interaction between mother and infant during these events and look at the potential for cognitive, social, and emotional development. As with the other child assessment tools mentioned, the feeding scale and the teaching scales are important intervention tools for the nurse, as their use usually promotes supportive anticipatory guidance (see Table B-3 in Appendix B).

In discussing follow-up and other aspects of care of the neonate who required extended hospitalization, it is important to acknowledge the value of research. Research in all aspects of nursing is extremely important, as it is the main mechanism for advancing the management of clients as well as the profession of nursing. Clinical nursing research in the care of high-risk neonates is extremely important, as it is essential to be able to correlate the method and effects of acute care with a longitudinal study concerning the total development of the child. These types of studies will validate the effectiveness and quality of care and provide theories upon which clinical practice can be based and upon which ethical decisions associated with this aspect of health care can be made. Nurses who have a commitment to provide holistic health care for the high-risk neonate should have the same commitment to perform clinical research using valid and reliable tools. Only through clinical research, that refinement of a base of theoretic knowledge, and through the application of theory into a creative, competent nursing practice can the attainment of optimal health for the high-risk neonate become a reality.

REFERENCES

Arnold, H.W., Putman, N.L., Bernard, B.L., et al. The newborn: Transition to extrauterine life. *American Journal of Nursing* 65:77, 1965.

Barnard, K., *Nursing Assessment Satellite Training Project learning resource manual.* Washington, D.C.: Department of Health, Education, and Welfare, no date.

Barnard, K. *Nursing Child Assessment Satellite Training Project: Nursing child assessment feeding scales.* Washington, D.C.: Department of Health, Education and Welfare, 1978.

Barnard, K. *Nursing Child Assessment Satellite Training Project: Nursing child assessment sleep activity record.* Washington, D.C.: Department of Health, Education and Welfare, 1979.

Barnard, K., *Nursing Child Assessment Satellite Training Project: Nursing child assessment teaching scales.* Washington, D.C.: Department of Health, Education and Welfare, 1978.

Beebe, B., & Stern, D. Engagement—disengagement early object experiences. In N. Freeman and S. Grand (Eds.), *Communicative structures and psychic structures.* New York: Plenum, 1977.

Brazelton, T.B., *Neonatal behavior assessment scale.* Philadelphia: Lippincott, 1973.

Broussard, E.R., & Hartner, M. Further considerations regarding maternal perceptions of the first born. In J. Hellmuth (Ed.), *Exceptional infant studies.* New York: Brunner/Mazel, 1971, vol. 2.

Caldwell, B., & Snyder, C. *Nursing child assessment satellite training: Home observation for measurement of the environment.* Washington, D.C.: Department of Health, Education, and Welfare, 1978.

Czarniecki, L. Developmental nursing care, infant stimulation for high-risk children. *Pediatric Nursing* 4:32, 1978.

Dahl, N., & Frazier, S. Neonatal thermoregulation. In M. Duxbury (Ed.), *The first six hours of life.* New York: National Foundation/March of Dimes, 1976.

Dreyfus-Brisac, C. Organization of sleep in prematures: Implications for caregiving. In M. Lewis & L.A. Rosenblum (Eds.), *The effect of the infant on its caregiver.* New York: Wiley, 1974.

Dublock, H. Hypoglycemia in the newborn. In M. Duxbury (Ed.), *The first six hours of life.* New York: National Foundation/March of Dimes, 1976.

Erikson, E.H. *Childhood and society* (2nd ed.). New York: Norton, 1963.

Greenspan, S. Adaptive and psychopathologic patterns in infancy and early childhood. *Children Today* 10:21, 1981.

Hack, M. (Producer). *Amazing newborn* (Film). Boston: Department of Pediatrics, Case Western Reserve University, Polymorph Films, 1975.

Haynes, J. Premature infant development: The relationship of neonatal stimulation, birth condition and home environment. *Pediatric Nursing* 6:33, 1980.

Klaus, M., & Kennell, J. *The impact of early separation or loss on family development: maternal—infant bonding* (2nd ed.). Saint Louis: Mosby, 1981.

Nover, R., Williams, D., & Ward, D. Preventive intervention with infants in multi-risk factor families. *Children Today* 10:27, 1981.

Parmelee, A.H., & Stern, E. Development of states in infants. In C. Clemente, D. Purpura, & F. Mayer (Eds.), *Sleep and the maturing nervous system.* New York: Academic, 1972.

Piaget, J. *The origins of intelligence in children.* New York: International Universities Press, 1952.

Rubin, R. Attainment of the maternal role, part I: Processes. *Nursing Research* 16:240, 1967.

Silverman, W., & Anderson, D. Index of respiratory distress. *Pediatrics* 17:1, 1956.

BIBLIOGRAPHY

Bell, R. Contributions of human infants to caregiving and social interaction. In M. Lewis & L.A. Rosenblum (Eds.), *The effect of the infant on its caregiver.* New York: Wiley, 1974.

Bliss, J.V. Nursing care for infants with neonatal necrolizing enterocolitis. *American Journal of Maternal—Child Nursing* 1:37, 1976.

Booth, C.L. Sleep patterns and behavioral patterns in preterm and fullterm infants. *Neuropediatrics* 11:354, 1980.

Bradley, R. The relation of infants' home environments to mental test performance at 54 months: A follow-up study. *Child Development* 47:1172, 1976.

Bradley, R., & Caldwell, B.M. Early home environment and changes in mental test performance in children 6—36 months. *Developmental Psychology* 12:93, 1976.

Brazelton, T.B. Assessment as a method for enhancing infant development zero to three. *Bulletin of the National Center for Clinical Infant Programs* 2:1, 1981.

Cropley, C. Assessment of mothering. In S. Johnson (Ed.), *Behaviors in high-risk parenting, nursing assessment and strategies for the family at risk.* Philadelphia: Lippincott, 1979.

Curry, M.A. Maternal attachment behavior and the mother's self-concept: The effect of early skin-to-skin contact. *Nursing Research* 31:73, 1982.

Davis, D.P. Growth of small-for-date babies. *Early Human Development* 5:95, 1981.

Desmond, M., Wilson, M., Wilson, G., et al. The very low birth weight infant after discharge from intensive care: Anticipatory health care and development course. *Current Problems in Pediatrics* 10:6, 1980.

Dinger, R.E. Continuous transcutaneous oxygen monitoring of the neonate. *American Journal of Nursing,* 80:890, 1980.

Dubowitz, L.M.S., Dubowitz, V., & Goldberg, C. Clinical assessment of gestational age on the newborn infant. *Journal of Pediatrics* 77:1, 1970.

Duxbury, M.L., Henly, G.A., & Armstrong, G.D. Measurement of the nurse organizational climate of neonatal intensive care units. *Nursing Research* 31:83, 1982.

Eager, M., & Exoo, R. Parents visiting parents for unequaled support. *American Journal of Maternal—Child Nursing* 5:35, 1980.

Ehrlich, C., Shapiro, E., Kimball, B., & Huttner, M. In J. Schwartz & L. Schwartz (Eds.), *Vulnerable infants, a psychosocial dilemma.* New York: McGraw—Hill, 1977.

Ennis, S., & Harris, T.R. Positioning infants with hyaline membrane disease. *American Journal of Nursing* 78:398, 1978.

Erdman, D. Parent-to-parent support: The best for those with sick newborns. *American Journal of Maternal—Child Nursing* 2:291, 1977.

Fanaroff, A.A., and Kennel, J. Follow-up of low birthweight infants: The predictive value of maternal visiting patterns. *Pediatrics* 49:288, 1972.

Field, T., Hallock, H., Ting, G., et al. A first year follow-up of high risk infants: Formulating a cumulative risk index. *Child Development* 49:119, 1978.

Flores, R.N. Necrotizing enterocolitis. *Nursing Clinics of North America* 13:39, 1978.

Garvey, J. Infant respiratory distress syndrome. *American Journal of Nursing* 75:614, 1975.

Glassanos, M. Infants who are oxygen dependent: Sending them home. *American Journal of Maternal—Child Nursing* 5:42, 1980.

Hack, M., De Monterice, D., Merkatz, I., et al. Rehospitalization of the very low-weight infant, a continuum of perinatal and environmental morbidity. *American Journal of Diseases of Children* 135:263, 1981.

Hawkins-Walsh, E. Diminishing anxiety in parents of sick newborns. *American Journal of Maternal—Child Nursing* 5:30, 1980.

Hommers, M., & Kendall, J. The prognosis of the very low-birth weight infant. *Developmental Medicine and Child Neurology* 18:745, 1976.

Iyer, P. My baby was premature. *JOGN Nursing* 10:304, 1981.

Jacobson, J.T. Intensive care nursery noise and its influence on newborn hearing screening. *International Journal of Pediatrics and Otorhinolaryngology* 3:45, 1981.

Jensen, M., Benson, R.C., & Babak, S.M. *Maternity care, the nurse and the family.* St. Louis: Mosby, 1977.

Kelly, D. Managing apnea in infancy. *Perinatology/Neonatology* 3:38, 1979.

Kiely, J.L., and Paneth, N. Follow-up studies of low-birthweight infants: Suggestions for design, analysis, and reporting. *Developmental Medicine and Child Neurology* 23:96, 1981.

Klaus, M.H., & Fanaroff, A.A. *Care of the high-risk neonate.* Philadelphia: Saunders, 1973.

Korones, S. *High-risk newborn infants: The basis for intensive nursing care* (2nd ed.). St. Louis: Mosby, 1976.

Krajecek, M. Nursing assessments: Screening for developmental problems. In A. Tearney (Ed.), *Detection of developmental problems in children.* Baltimore: University Park Press, 1977.

Lates, C.O. Clinical assessment of gestational age in the newborn infant: Comparison of two methods. *Early Human Development* 5:29, 1981.

Lubchenco, L.O. Assessment of gestational age and development at birth. *Pediatric Clinics of North America* 17:125, 1976.

Lubchenco, L.O., Searls, D.T., & Brazie, J.V. Neonatal mortality rate; Its relationship to birth weight and gestational age. *Journal of Pediatrics* 81:814, 1972.

Mangurten, H., Slade, C., & Fitzsimmons, D. Parent–parent support in the care of high-risk newborns. *JOGN Nursing* 8:275, 1979.

Markestad, T., & Shephard, F. Growth and development in children recovering from bronchopulmonary dysplasia. *Journal of Pediatrics* 98:597, 1981.

McCormick, M.C., Shapiro, S., Starfield, B., et al. Rehospitalization in the first year of life for high-risk survivors. *Pediatrics* 66: 991, 1980.

Medoff-Cooper, B., & Schraeder, B.D. Development trends and behavioral styles in very low birth weight infants. *Nursing Research* 31:68, 1982.

Milliones, J. Relationship between perceived child temperament and maternal behavior. *Child Development* 49:255, 1978.

Miner, H. Problems and prognosis for the small for gestational age and the premature infant. *American Journal of Maternal–Child Nursing* 3:221, 1978.

Parkinson, C.E. School achievement and behavior of children who were small-for-dates at birth. *Developmental Medicine and Child Neurology* 23:41, 1981.

Plapp, R.P. Nursing implications in the early recognition of NEC. *Issues in Comprehensive Pediatric Nursing* 4:77, 1980.

Porth, C., & Kayler, L. Temperature regulation in the newborn. *American Journal of Nursing* 78:1692, 1978.

Rubin, R., Rosenblatt M., Balow, B. Psychological and educational sequelae of prematurity. *Pediatrics* 52:352, 1973.

Schraeder, B. Attachment and parenting despite lengthy intensive care. *American Journal of Maternal—Child Nursing* 5:37, 1980.

Steele, S. *Child health and the family: Nursing concepts and management.* New York: Masson, 1981.

Stern, L. The use and misuse of oxygen in the newborn infant. *Pediatric Clinics of North America* 20:447, 1973.

Stewart, A., & Reynolds, E. Improved prognosis for infants of very low birthweight. In J. Schwartz & L. Schwartz (Eds.), *Vulnerable infants, a psychosocial dilemma.* New York, McGraw—Hill, 1977.

Tobiason, S.J. Touching is for everyone. *American Journal of Nursing* 81:728, 1981.

Varner, B., Ossenkop, D., & Lyon, J. Prematures, too, need rooming-in and care-by-parent programs. *American Journal of Maternal—Child Nursing* 5:431, 1980.

Voyles, J.B. Bronchopulmonary dysplasia. *American Journal of Nursing* 81:510, 1981.

Wedmayer, S., & Field, T. Effects of Brazelton demonstration on the development of preterm infants. *Pediatrics* 67:711, 1981.

Whaley, L.F., & Wong, D.L. *Nursing care of infants and children.* St. Louis: Mosby, 1979.

Wingert, W.A., Teberg, A., Bergman, R., et al. PNP's in follow-up care of high-risk infants, comparing two clinics. *American Journal of Nursing* 80:1485, 1980.

8

Health Promotion of the Child with an Acquired Disability: Burns

Nancy Quay and Shirley Steele

According to Parks (1977), an estimated 2,000,000 burn clients seek medical attention in the United States annually, and of those, 70,000 to 100,000 require hospitalization. Twenty percent of those hospitalized are children.

The high incidence of burns in children is due primarily to their innate curiosity and the lack of supervision by adults. Children of all ages have an urge to "know about the unknown." Unfortunately, that need to know sometimes results in injury:

A 2-year-old girl wants to know what is cooking on the stove. She reaches for a pan . . . .

Adults who fail to supervise their children are not always aware of the dangers that are present in the everyday environment.

CHARACTERISTICS OF BURNS

A burn injury is classified according to the agent causing the injury and the depth of injury. Agents are classified into four groups: thermal (flame and scald), electrical, chemical, and radiation. The depth of a burn is classified into three degrees. First degree involves the outermost layer of the skin, the epidermis. The skin appears red and is painful. A first degree burn heals spontaneously. A second-degree burn is classified as either superficial or deep. It involves the dermal layer of the skin. A superficial second-degree burn blisters and heals spontaneously. A deep second-degree burn is sometimes difficult to distinguish from a third-degree burn. It heals spontaneously, but sometimes takes up to 3 weeks to do so. A third-degree burn involves the subcutaneous tissue. The appearance of the skin is either charred or pearly gray. Hair follicles and sweat glands are destroyed. Third-degree burns require a skin graft for healing (Fig. 8-1).

The severity of the injury is dependent upon the intensity of the heat source, the duration of exposure to the heat, the depth of the injury, and the amount or location of the surface areas burned. A second-degree burn involving the face and neck may be more severe than a third-degree burn on the lower leg (Fig. 8-2).

Two priority levels seem to be significant when caring for a child with burns: client needs related to survival and those related to the quality of recovery or the quality of life a child can expect to have following a burn injury. There are certain situations—such as the admission of a child with a massive burn injury or of a child whose injuries are complicated by smoke inhalation or by such acute complications as sepsis—that survival needs are the overwhelming focus of the child's management. In these situations, physiologic care accounts for the major demands on nursing time, skills, and knowledge (Pearson, 1981).

However, once the immediate crisis period is over, survival goals can be balanced with quality of life goals. Rapid healing of the burn wound and early positioning and splinting of the affected areas are extremely important in terms of survival and the quality of rehabilitation that can be achieved (Parks et al., 1978). Care strategies related to the child's psychosocial needs contribute to a more positive response from the child and family to both hospitalization and the traumatic insult caused by the burn injury.

GOAL OF MANAGEMENT

The overall long-term nursing goal for a child who has sustained a major burn is to discharge him or her with his or her family in the most positive physical and emotional condition that can be achieved. In order to do that, the nurse

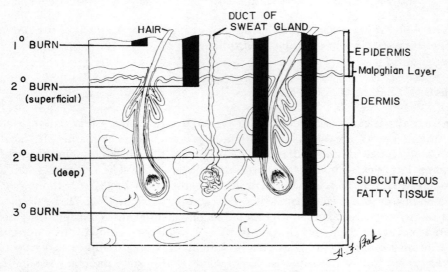

Figure 8-1.   Skin layers involved with first-, second-, and third-degree burns.

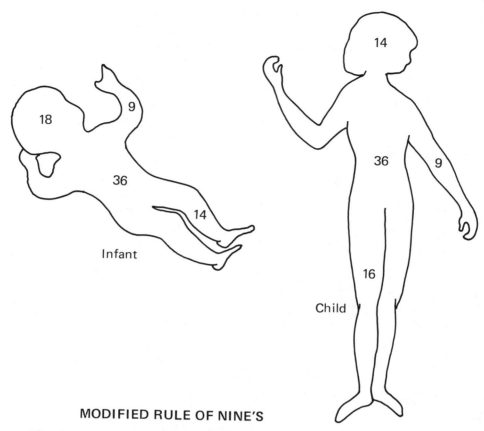

MODIFIED RULE OF NINE'S

Figure 8-2. Modified rule of nines used in determining the extent of burns in children.

incorporates that goal into the daily management of the child. Whether caring for open wounds, caring for grafts, applying splints, or talking with the child's family, that goal is never forgotten. Long-term care includes care related to wound healing, prevention of contractures and scarring, the emotional needs of the child and his or her family, and discharge preparation to help ensure continuity of care even after the child's hospitalization is completed.

Statistics in burn management reflect survival with no indication as to the morbidity related to rehabilitation of the client with burns. Once recovered from the acute injury, the client with burns can face long-term mental and physical problems (Parks et al., 1977). Hypertrophic scarring and scar contracture are the most common late complications of burn injury. Therefore, management protocols aimed at controlling or preventing these complications are most important to a child's physical rehabilitation.

The above complications are associated with injury to the deep reticular dermis layer of the skin, as in deep second- or third-degree burns. Healing of the deep wounds results in the replacement of normal skin with a mass of metabolically highly active tissue that lacks the normal properties of the skin (Parks et al., 1977). Abnormal amounts of collagen, deposited as part of the healing process, continue to be deposited even after the epidermis is restored. This, in combination with the contractibility of the myofibroblasts and the forcing of the collagen tissue outward, results in a hypertrophic scar and scar contracture (Parks et al., 1978). The appearance of the tissue is red, raised, hard, and whorl-like.

CONTRACTURES AND SCARRING

During the immediate postburn period and after the wound is closed and/or healed, the nurse in conjunction with the occupational and physical therapists helps to control the severity of hypertrophic scarring and scar contractures. Contracture formation can be controlled by proper positioning, splinting, and exercise. The neck is positioned in slight extension and use of pillows is avoided. Ankles are flexed to 90°, preferably against a footboard, in order to prevent foot drop. Elbows and knees are maintained in an extended position. Three-point splits or conformers made of thermoplastic material are often used to help maintain that position. For hands that have been burned, the fingers are maintained in extension at the proximal and distal interphalangeal joints with 10° to 15° flexion at the metacarpophalangeal joint. The wrist is placed in slight extension; the thumb is abducted. This position can be maintained with a thermoplastic splint secured by an elastic wrap (Abston, 1976; Parks et al., 1977; Willis et al., 1973; Fig. 8-3).

All splints are removed at least every 4 hours for 10 to 15 minutes and then reapplied. The child is encouraged to exercise the affected parts during the time the splints are removed. Splints are also cleaned at this time. The nurse caring for the child also notes the child's tolerance of the splints and observes for areas of rubbing or skin breakdown.

Hypertrophic scarring and scar contracture can be controlled after grafting by the application of constant, controlled pressure and the continuation of conforming splints to areas where the deep reticular dermis has been damaged. Pressure applied to these areas from 6 months to 1 year (sometimes longer) after grafting induces scar flattening, softening, and decreased redness, all features of a mature scar (Abston, 1976; Baur et al., 1978; Huang et al., 1978; Parks et al., 1977).

If pressure therapy is to be effective, it is essential that the pressure be applied 24 hours a day. Pressure is only removed for bathing. Interruption of pressure for 8 hours may require renewed pressure for days to regain the accomplished effect (Parks et al., 1977).

Pressure can be applied to affected extremities and the trunk by the use of elastic bandages as soon as healing or graft take permits. The bandages are commenced distally and carried proximally in a spiral fashion. In order to provide the proper amount of pressure, the spiral is done in such a way as to ensure a double thickness of bandage. The bandages are crisscrossed over all joints in order to provide even pressure to these areas.

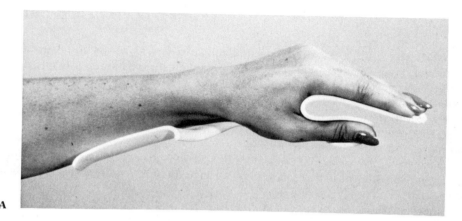

A

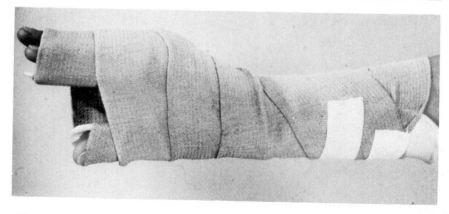

B

C

Figure 8-3. **A.** Thermoplastic splint to position arm. **B.** Proper wrapping with elastic wrap. **C.** Properly positioned and wrapped arm.

Once the child's weight has stabilized and the skin has toughened, the elastic bandages can be replaced by customized elastic garments. Jobst garments provide an easy and more cosmetic method of applying constant, controlled pressure (Fig. 8-4).

In addition to maintaining the child in proper position and applying prescribed splints, promotion of maximum rehabilitation is achieved by encouraging the child to perform range of motion exercises for all joints. These exercises are active or active assistance in nature rather than passive. Forcing a joint to move with passive exercise may damage the joint rather than improve its function.

Exercise routines are simple and include desired movements for strengthening of weak muscles, stretching of contractures, and maintenance of functional mobility. Exercises include play and activities of daily living, such as throwing a ball, grasping a small toy, completing a puzzle, riding a tricycle, or feeding or dressing oneself.

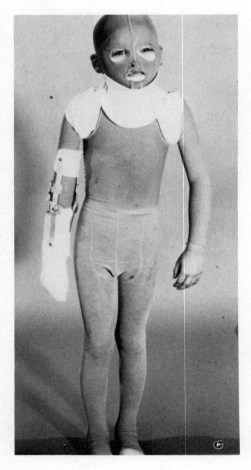

Figure 8-4.   Child with burns in Jobst garment.

EMOTIONAL RESPONSES

The burn injury is an emotionally traumatic experience for both child and family. The child is confronted with physical discomforts and with separation from his or her family, isolation from the world with which he or she is familiar, unknown people, frightening equipment, and the probable disfigurement of his or her body.

The average length of stay for a child hospitalized for a burn injury ranges from two weeks to several months. During that time, the nurse helps the child to adapt to the hospital, cope with the injury and the required treatments, and cope with the probable disfigurement.

On admission, the nurse introduces herself or himself, orients the child and the family to the surroundings, explains the purposes of equipment and the daily routines, and, most important, identifies the times when the family can visit. From the very beginning, the nurse emphasizes that he or she values the family and includes references to the family during interactions with the child. The family is included in decision making and in the child's management as is appropriate. Throughout treatment, the child's psychologic and developmental needs are incorporated into the care plan. It is important to convey a positive and caring attitude toward the child. A trusting relationship is established by helping the child to understand what is happening to him or her. Emphasis is placed on establishing trust, because a child who is burned has reason to distrust the adults in his or her world, as they were unable to provide protection from the burn. In addition, the treatments are often painful and the child associates the pain with the adults who contribute to it. Therefore, trust is difficult for the child to gain during periods of long-term confinement and rehabilitation. Explanations about the care in terms the child can comprehend is important. The nurse also allows the child to participate in the care (e.g., dressing changes) whenever possible. A child has the need to have some control over his or her life and what is happening to him or her and participation in activities provides the child with opportunities to gain control.

For the young child, play offers an excellent opportunity to become comfortable with the hospital experience as well as to promote normal development. It may also be used by the child to express positive and negative feelings. Many times the child has the need to play out the accident as well as conflicts within himself or herself and the family. He or she may also need to express feelings about the resultant scars. Rap sessions with peers may be extremely beneficial in achieving this goal with the older child.

Statistics indicate that chances for survival of the acutely burned child are ever improving. The child who does survive always has some degree of disfigurement due to scarring and/or contractures. This disfigurement requires the child to reassess his or her body image.

BODY IMAGE

Body image is a central part of a person's self-concept. It consists of a person's feeling about his or her body and is significantly affected by interpersonal and intrapersonal experience. For the young child, body image is connected to the reactions of his or her parents. As that child moves into adolescence and adulthood, his or her body image begins to become increasingly affected by the reactions of his or her peers. The development of body image is a continuous process of reassessment of self on the basis of life stages and experience (Knudson-Cooper, 1981; Riddle, 1972).

The nurse is with the child on a daily basis from the time he or she is admitted to the hospital to the time he or she is discharged. The nurse is a key person in helping a burned child positively adjust to the loss of his or her prior body image. By establishing a therapeutic environment in which the child is treated with respect and given the opportunity to develop a trusting relationship with one caring person, the nurse influences the way in which a child perceives himself or herself.

Throughout hospitalization, a positive body image is promoted by teaching the child about the body and the effects of the injury. Physical appearance is not emphasized; however, methods used to control disfigurement and improve appearance are discussed.

The beauty of the inner self is stressed rather than the appearance of the outward self. Positive attributes are emphasized, such as the child's caring attitude toward the other children. Accomplishments of past burn clients are shared with the children in order to give them some hope for the future. Life does not end after a disfiguring burn injury.

The reactions of significant others greatly influence a child's body image. Therefore, it is extremely important to support the family members and help them deal with their reactions to the injury and resultant disfigurement. Support groups designed to help family members are utilized, as well as one-to-one contacts. Problems which may be encountered with peers after the child's discharge are lessened by contacting the child's school, talking to the child's classmates, and showing them a picture of the child and the special clothing he or she is required to wear.

FAMILY-CENTERED CARE

The child hospitalized for burns continues to be a member of a family. The injury not only affects the child, it affects all of the family members as well. Day-to-day life is interrupted as well as the usual parent−child relationships when a child is burned (Talabere and Graves, 1976).

Family reactions to the burn include anxiety, guilt, grief, anger, and depression. These reactions are addressed by the nurse in order to strengthen the family and to keep the reactions from interfering with the child's rehabilitation (Bernstein, 1976; Bowden and Feller, 1973; Campbell, 1976; Martin, 1970). The nurse's initial contact with the family greatly influences the relationship that develops during the child's hospitalization. The nurse projects a caring manner, and information on daily routines, including visiting hours, is shared with the family. Throughout hospitalization, the family's questions are answered honestly and promptly. The nurse shares knowledge about normal reactions to the burn and is available for counseling. An effective means of supporting the family during the child's hospitalization is to organize parental support groups; these get parents in touch with other persons who are going through similar crises, encourage sharing of coping strategies, and allow expression of feelings with no fear of retribution. The times and location of the group meetings are made known to the parents, and the nurse encourages new parents to attend by describing the group's function and introducing the parents to others who attend and find value in the group.

Parents often feel "left out" once their child is hospitalized if most of their care-giving activities are taken away. The nurse can help parents to feel more positive about themselves by involving them in the child's care. This can be done by encouraging them to hold, feed, and play with their child. As their child's condition improves, the parents can be given more responsibility, such as direct care (e.g., a bath). The parent's ability to participate in the child's management is gauged carefully. The reactions of the parents, such as revulsion, can be misconstrued if the nurse does not spend time talking with the parents. Assistance is provided to give the parents encouragement to provide care to the child. The parents need to know that when they assume care for the child, they will not be abandoned by the nursing staff. Cooperation of the family and the nurse results in the best management of the child's care.

DISCHARGE PLANNING

The nurse focuses on continuity of care throughout the child's hospitalization, during discharge planning, and when the child returns home. Discharge planning can be defined as a process and a service, identifying client needs and providing assistance that prepares the child and family to move from one level of care to another (Bristow et al., 1976). Discharge planning ideally begins when the child is admitted to the hospital; assessing and reassessing the child's and family's ability to understand and cope with the injury are essential to a smooth transition from hospital to home. Discharge planning involves interacting with the child and family, listening to them, identifying their needs, matching appropriate resources to those needs, and teaching them about the injury and responses to hospitalization. Without this planning, clients and families may have difficulty adapting therapeutic regimens to their lifestyle. This may result in relapse or loss of rehabilitation gains (Reichelt and Newcomb, 1980).

Discharge planning for a child with burns involves the entire health care team. However, the nurse is a key person in the process because of her or his prolonged contact with the child and family. This role includes consulting other disciplines, teaching the child and his or her family, and coordinating the follow-up care.

The nurse assesses and reassesses the child and family throughout hospitalization. Discharge needs are identified and the appropriate resource people or groups are contacted to meet those needs. The nurse communicates with the family when determining plans for discharge. The family members' strengths and weaknesses are assessed and a determination of their ability or willingness to assist the child after discharge is made. The social worker can assist the nurse when the family is in need of financial assistance or when community referrals are necessary. The nurse can consult the occupational and/or physical therapists when she or he identifies needs related to exercise, positioning, splinting, or scar suppression. The community health nurse can assist the hospital nurse by supporting the family and reinforcing hospital teaching once the child is discharged.

The goal of client education is to improve the child's health and promote self-care. It begins as soon as the child and family are ready and continues until the child is discharged. Teaching plans designed to promote learning by the child and family are formulated. Areas which are addressed include wound care, control of contractures and scarring, nutrition, comfort measures, and psychosocial adjustment after a burn. The plans include assessments of the child and family, objectives, means of implementation, and methods of evaluating whether learning has taken place. Teaching plans take into account levels of learning, ranging from observing and participating with assistance to eventual self-care.

The nurse coordinates the child's follow-up care, making sure the family has a return-to-clinic appointment and has been given a written reminder of that appointment. In addition, service people or groups in the community that the family can utilize are contacted. The family is made aware of those contacts and of times when the services are available. If the family is also in need of transportation assistance, the nurse coordinates it. An example of a discharge plan for a hypothetical client and family follows:

Mark is a 3-year-old who sustained a 93 percent burn as the result of a hot water heater explosion. His 1-month-old sister was also injured in the same accident.

Mark and his sister were transferred to a hospital, 1500 miles from their home three days after the accident. Both parents accompanied the children to the hospital.

Throughout Mark's hospitalization, the nurse and social worker worked closely with Mark and his family. Problems affecting Mark's discharge from the hospital included:

1. Hypertrophic scarring and contractures.
2. Open wounds.
3. Emotional lability of the mother.
4. Need for organized P.T./O.T. postdischarge.
5. Lack of a support system for the family.
6. Presence of a younger sibling also requiring burn care.
7. Distance of the home from our hospital.
8. Poor financial status of the family.

Educating the family began early in Mark's hospitalization. Although his condition was unstable at times, the family was aware of the reasons for the care, the purposes of the different surgeries, and the possible complications. As Mark's condition improved and his parents began asking questions about how to care for him at home, required treatments were demonstrated. The parents gradually assumed responsibility for the treatments (bath, wound care, pressure, and splint application).

The family decided to move closer to the hospital. Finances were tight; the social worker guided the father into areas where employment could probably be obtained. Applications for Supplemental Security Income and Crippled Children Services were filed.

A support system for the family was set up. A home health care nurse was contacted to assist the mother with Mark's treatments three days a week. In addition to the nurse, a physical therapist was contacted to work with Mark at home three times per week. The hospital social worker agreed to keep in close contact with the family and be available to the mother for counseling.

The goal of all nursing care is to promote the child's health and normal growth and development. If this goal is achieved, the child is discharged with his or her family in the most positive physical and emotional condition possible.

FACTORS THAT INFLUENCE LONG-TERM MANAGEMENT

Implications of Isolation

Another area which needs exploring is the use of isolation for children with burns. Isolation has been readily accepted, as it "cuts down on infection." Protective isolation is usually instituted when the child has burns on 40 to 50 percent of the body. In addition, children who have infected wounds or streptococcal throat infections are isolated. It is evident that isolation also cuts down on the child's interest in living. The child is cut off from parents by masks and gowns and frequently by touch. He or she is also cared for by personnel who are silhouetted as gowned bodies, with only their exposed eyes giving the child nonverbal communication. The child is frequently in an area where there are other acutely ill children who need similar demanding care. He or she may be in a sideroom and frequently has a cradle over the bed to keep bed clothes off the skin areas. The child may even be on a Foster frame or Circulo-matic bed. The hospital bed is not like the one he or she is used to at home. It isn't familiar and, for that matter, it may not even be comfortable.

In the isolation procedure, the child is placed in a single room in a bed by himself or herself. These two factors, a single room and a single bed, may be unknown to the child—especially if he or she comes from a large or disadvantaged family. The stimuli in this room are medical in nature and may be more depressing than stimulating.

The child may be interested, at first, in the intravenous bottle or the equipment for checking specific gravity, or in listening to his or her heart beat with a stethoscope. These stimuli quickly change to boring ritualism, and the child can become disinterested in the environment. The room may be air-conditioned, and this provides an auditory stimulus for a short period. This noise quickly becomes agitating and tends to lead to disorientation over a period of time. The disorientation is further enhanced by the lack of clocks, calendars, and other daily reminders of time and place. Reminders such as the school bell's ringing at 9:00 A.M., the factory whistle's blowing at noon, and the mailperson's coming in the morning are all removed and the child's immature sense of time is destroyed completely. There are interruptions to sleep patterns. He or she is used to going to sleep and not being awakened until morning. Now, just as he or she is able to fall asleep, it is time to be disturbed for treatments or other activities that are scheduled during the night. These frequent interruptions during the acute stage establish a pattern of wakefulness that is likely to carry over into the long-term treatment. The child may be given sedatives or tranquilizers, but these do not provide him or her with the same restful sleep that was experienced prior to injury. The periods spent in isolation are likely to be associated with sleep problems due to the unfamiliar and necessary situations that take place during the early stages of the illness.

The isolation may indicate to the child that he or she is being punished. This connotation sets the stage for the child's feelings towards the burns and his or her revised body image. The child who is burned accidentally feels that the burns are punishment for "wrongdoings," and the isolation serves to accentuate this feeling. The child who is burned as a result of playing with matches or fire is especially prone to this reaction. He or she has probably been cautioned many times not to play with fire and has disobeyed this wise counsel. This can lead the child to believe that the burns are a punishment given to children who disobey adults.

Children frequently display regressive behavior during periods of isolation. This may be displayed in many ways, such as an unwillingness to use a bedpan, whining and screaming when asked to participate in activities, or sucking the thumb for extended periods of time. If not treated, the regression may become more serious, with the child completely withdrawing from interest in the surroundings.

The isolation further adds to the separation of child and parent and nurse and parent. It hinders normal communication. Frequent touching is utilized in normal adult–child relationships. The child learns early to cuddle and caress. He or she receives a great deal of gratification from this touch, no matter how frequently or infrequently it is utilized in early childhood. As the child grows older, he or she relies less and less on this touch, but frequently resorts to it in time of illness. Thus isolation, whether complete or partial, decreases the gratification the child receives from touch.

Touch Deprivation.   An effect of isolation can be that the child is deprived of the normal comforting sensation of touch. The touch he or she receives is usually painful if the injury is severe. Even turning can be a painful experience. Because the child learns to associate touch with pain, he or she soon learns to prefer not to be touched. In addition, the skin is often itchy. In an attempt to relieve this discomfort, the child can inadvertently cause further damage to his or her skin. Therefore, restraints, mittens, Ace bandages, or Jobst garments are often used to decrease the child's scratching.

During long-term care, it is necessary to help the child feel good about his or her body and to help the child begin to get some gratification from touch. Taking the severity of the trauma into account, the nurse can begin to reintroduce the child to kinesthetic sensations.

A convenient method of reuniting the child with touch is established when the child is started on tub baths. In the tub it is acceptable to touch the child. As the child is being taken out of the tub, the nurse leans over and makes her or his neck readily accessible for the child to reach for support. This brings the child in close physical contact, which can be satisfying. After the bath, soothing lotion can be gently rubbed on the scar area. The soothing, relaxing motion and the warmth and tenderness of fingertips can bring soothing feelings to the child. At first, tolerance may be extremely low, but it will increase with time. From this begining, the nurse can then proceed to have the child apply the lotion or to have his or her mother apply it.

The younger child may need to start by applying the lotion on the nurse. This gives him or her an excuse to get close. The younger child might also enjoy applying the lotion to a doll.

If the child's body is covered by Jobst garments, they can be removed for bathing, lotion, and touch and reapplied. While the bandage is off, it is important to have the child become readjusted to his or her revised body. Being free to touch the scarred areas helps the child to include the revised skin area into his or her body image. Soothing touch helps to establish more positive feelings.

Auditory and Visual Deprivation.   Sensory confusion can take place during periods of confinement. This sensory confusion is very relevant to young children, because their sensory experiences are already limited by their age. They interpret sensory input on the basis of their limited exposure. This can result in serious misinterpretations. The unfamiliar sounds in the hospital can be very frightening. The familiar sounds of childhood are missing, especially during periods of isolation. In addition, visual perceptions may be distorted. Shadows cast by night lights may cause moments of panic. Health care providers dressed in gowns and masks can be scary, especially when the child is awakening in the night.

The auditory effects of isolation are usually reversed as soon as isolation is discontinued. They can, however, be diminished by providing music, radio, and normal voices during the isolation period. It is possible for young children to forget their parents' normal voices when separated from them for long periods or when the parents' voices are only heard through a mask. Tapes of the family members' normal voices can be made and played on a tape recorder. In addition, tapes of the voices of persons who cannot visit (such as siblings) can be played periodically throughout the day.

If it is not permissible for the parents to enter the child's isolation room, an intercom can be successfully utilized. Many children play with intercoms as toys, and they are well-known items to today's child. Intercoms can be bought very inexpensively if the hospital is not equipped with them. The value of getting a set, especially for the child, is that the parent can stand by a window so the child can see him or her as well as hearing his or her voice. In some of the more progressive hospitals, closed-circuit television is also utilized, and the child can see and hear the parent who is located in another area, such as the lobby. This is also a means for the siblings to communicate with the hospitalized child. The disadvantage is that the child is not able to answer back directly.

Isolation may even occur when the child is simply subjected to long periods of hospitalization. He need not be subject to an "isolation technique" to be isolated. The isolation may be due to a decrease in normal developmental experiences. For instance, the child who is burned may have to be hospitalized during a very important Spring. Spring is essential to introducing a toddler or preschooler to the rebirth of flowers, grass, and trees. It is important to expose the child to them at the time that he or she is developmentally ready for this experience. The nurse must provide substitute ways of providing the child with such an experience. Books with simple stories about Spring are useful. The stories can be read and then the books left with the child for his or her own exploration, if it is possible to do so at the particular stage of the child's illness. A garden can be started in his or her room. He or she can plant seeds to watch the various stages of growth. House plants which flower can be added for variety. In addition, the child can be placed near a window so that he or she can see changes outside. Binoculars may be needed to bring things into better focus. The family can be encouraged to take photographs of their yard and home during the season to keep the child up to date on his or her familiar environment. A bulletin board can be utilized to put up pictures which help to orient the child to time. Very appropriate pictures for display are those drawn by peers or siblings. The bulletin board should be easily movable so the child can change it if he or she is old enough to participate in the activity. If he or she is too young, the parents or health personnel can assume responsiblity for updating it frequently. Other helpful items are pegboards, blackboards, magic slates, and drawing boards. All of these can be utilized to help cut down on the child's isolation and to nurture developmental progress.

Children's Views of Isolation.   In a study by Pidgeon (1967), children were interviewed regarding their understanding of isolation. Pidgeon found that 71 percent of the 3.6- to 6.11-year-olds gave incorrect responses to her questions regarding the cause and effect and rationale for isolation. This high percentage indicates the real need for nurses to work with children to help them understand why they are isolated. The older age groups had a better understanding but still demonstrated the need for factual information regarding isolation. The younger age groups had the idea that the cause of isolation was related to psychologic or moral issues. The school-age children were able to draw upon more experience and could identify physical aspects as the causative agents. In the adolescent age groups, 92 percent of those interviewed gave correct responses regarding their isolation. The findings suggest that a great deal needs to be done to help preschoolers understand isolation, while the school-age child and adolescent seem to need less professional help to supplement their other resources.

Parents and Isolation.   The effects that isolation can have on the parents can be as detrimental as the effects on the child. The parent is placed in an awkward position by virtue of the child's being burned in the first place. Burns are referred to as preventable accidents in childhood. But the prevention is not as easy as prevention provided by periodic immunizations. It is prevention which requires almost constant supervision of the child. Burns may occur despite the most conscientious guidance, or, conversely, they may occur as the result of a battering parent.

Bright (1967) identifies an assessment tool that she used to record, assess, and plan care for the parent. Such a tool can be useful when isolation interferes with a close mother–child relationship. This is especially significant for children with burns, as there is a high incidence of disturbed mother–child relationships in this pediatric population. What can the tool do? It can begin to identify the way the parent reacts and responds when isolation is a major obstacle to effective communication. It can also help to identify areas of concern which cause anxiety in the parent and further add to the communication gap.

Recordings such as the following may help to identify ways the nurse can begin to help the parent and child to understand one another. One mother stated: "Jerry always does the darndest things! He's my trouble maker. He got what he deserves!" This statement, along with the following description of the mother, are recorded on the tool for use by the professional team:

Mrs. M. spoke with real feeling. She emphasized the words "he," "trouble-maker," and "deserves." She maintained eye contact during the conversation and her facial expression was stern and determined.

From first glance, this information reveals a mother and child who may be temporarily helped by the isolation technique. It would not be beneficial to Jerry to hear his mother expressing her hostility. The isolation also provided an opportunity for the mother to release negative feelings.

There is, however, much more to be done for this family. Parod and Caplan (1960) suggest that when families are in crisis, it is possible to help them resolve the acute stress situation and at the same time to help them bring satisfactory solutions to unresolved problems. They found that people can "rise to the occasion" and seem to find new strength to deal with the current crisis, and in the long run resolve other situations which have interfered with healthy family relationships.

The situation quoted would seem to need this type of intervention. How can nurses help the mother to see her responsibility to her child during this acute crisis and perhaps at the same time improve her feelings toward him when he is well? First, we must help the mother understand that her presence is essential despite her present feelings. A statement such as, "I know how frustrated you must feel, but please try to understand that Jerry needs you very much while he is in isolation." Or, "Isolation is only to prevent infection; we do not use it to separate the child and parent. We thoroughly believe that parents are the best therapy for their children."

Isolation is a barrier that interferes with the expression of motherly instincts when they are at their height. For instance, Mrs. M.'s first reaction might be to rush to Jerry and hug him and ask her forgiveness in an effort to release her guilt. Because he is isolated, she is deprived of this experience and must try to relieve her guilt without the help of her son. Despite a strained mother–child relationship prior to the insult, she might have benefited from this experience. Jerry might also have benefited by witnessing his mother being genuinely interested in his welfare and asking for his understanding. Each might have begun to see the other in a different light, but isolation blocked out this opportunity.

We can minimize the effects of isolation by helping the mother to verbally express her feelings to Jerry. The nurse might say, "Don't be afraid to tell Jerry how you feel. Let him know you are sorry he must withstand the pain." When working with Jerry, you can help further by sharing with him his mother's desire to help despite the limitations created by the isolation. For example, you could say, "Your Mom would love to be able to come in the room. As yet, the doctors still feel it is best not to let her come in. Is there anything you want me to tell her?"

The success of intervention will depend on the ability of the nurse to provide opportunities for the parent and child to interact in a meaningful way, despite the isolation, and to draw upon their hidden capacities to resolve conflicts that interfere with coping with acute stress.

Implications of Whirlpool Treatment (Hydrotherapy)

The use of whirlpool treatment during the acute stages is a commonly accepted practice. Whirlpool treatment helps to cut down on infection, removes decaying tissue and old dressings, and cleanses the wounds. Solutions used for this purpose are not toxic if absorbed systemically, are comfortable for the child, and are bacteriostatic or optimally bacteriocidal, with a low incidence of skin irritation and ability to interfere with body fluid and electrolytes. Clorox and water and Betadine are widely used in whirlpool treatment. It can be an extremely soothing procedure. The way it is introduced to the child is most important, especially if the child has been burned by liquid. The whirlpool may bring back uncomfortable memories for the child. If the original introduction to the procedure is handled correctly, the long-term use of the therapy is enhanced. The temperature of the water is usually 35° to 37°C, and the hydrotherapy is usually prescribed for 15 to 30 minute periods. The temperature of the room should be regulated to decrease chilling, to which the child is more prone due to a decreased skin barrier. This factor is most important during the acute stages, but it should also be considered during long-term care.

Children innately enjoy water play, and the whirlpool can be utilized this way. The use of squirt guns, boats, sponges, etc. help to make the therapy a treat instead of a treatment. The whirlpool is also a way to encourage the child to actively exercise. The water makes it possible for the child to do this without excessive pain.

The trips to the whirlpool should not be used as a bribe for good behavior. They should not be withheld for uncooperative behavior. This method of control interferes with the long-range satisfactory use of the whirlpool in the child's care. Withholding whirlpool therapy may meet a short-term goal of care, but it really interferes with the long-term care of the child. As concerns long-term goals, we want the child to appreciate and enjoy the whirlpool as a method of enhancing grafting and promoting a return to health. As a part of the long-term therapy, it is judicious to have the child have only positive associations with the whirlpool (Fig. 8-5).

Vulnerable Areas

Fortunately, in the care of children there are fewer situations in which pressure sores are a problem than in adults. However, children who are immobilized due to burns or grafting are candidates for developing them. The positioning and turning done to prevent contractures also aids in the prevention of pressure sores. If the child is immobilized for very long periods, an alternating-pressure mattress may be helpful. Pressure sores are easily started on already destroyed tissues, such as burns, so close attention is paid to the burned areas. Common sites for decubitus formation are the heels, sacrum, elbows, and, in young children, the back of the head.

The treatment for pressure sores is selected carefully. Routine care, offered in some hospitals, is not instituted without checking with the physician. The application of a heat treatment with use of a light bulb can further aggravate the burn. The application of ointments can interfere with the therapy being given. The best treatment may very well be to keep the area clean and exposed to the air, with additional consideration given to not putting pressure on the already involved area.

Other areas that require meticulous care are the areas around pins used to keep extremities in good alignment after grafting. In order to decrease the potential for infection, the pin sites are cleansed with hydrogen peroxide to

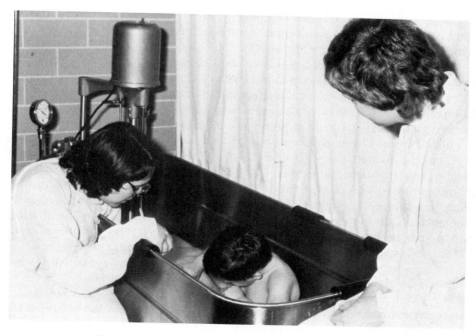

Figure 8-5.   Child receiving hydrotherapy for burns.

remove serous drainage and an antiseptic agent is applied. This procedure is usually done two or three times daily.

Children frequently like to wear jewelry or clothing that may cause constrictions and result in pressure sores. Removal of all constricting bands aids in circulation and helps in prevention of pressure sores. If the constricting band is a "good luck charm," the child can choose another area in the room where it can be kept. He or she may want it taped to the foot of the bed or left hanging on a mobile. Making a game of where the article can be placed is fun and makes the child feel that he or she is in control of the decision to remove the article and to place it in another spot.

DEPENDENCE ON ADJUNCT THERAPY

One of the concerns of long-term care of children who are burned is the dependence they may develop on measures taken to lessen their pain or to help them progress. Although narcotics are used sparingly, they can become a problem. The older child quickly learns that the stick of the needle is worth the relief obtained from the medication. It is necessary to evaluate the child's real need for the narcotic. This can be a real challenge. Each child's pain threshold is different, and no one wants to expose the child to severe pain when it can be alleviated. The greatest adjunct to relief of pain is the alleviation of psychologic components of pain: fear, separation anxiety, and loss of independence and control. The child who is afraid frequently requests pain medication so that he or she can go to sleep and forget everything. More recently, relaxation techniques, including hypnosis, have contributed to the relief of pain and the decreased need for medications during acute illness.

To lessen fear, it is necessary to assess the things children fear and how they can be handled. Many children fear darkness. The use of a light in the room can take care of this to some extent. Close proximity to the nurses' station allows the child to see people when he or she wakes up. Some children fear being left alone. The use of volunteers or other roommates can lessen this fear. Some children fear unfamiliar noises. This is harder to control in a hospital. However, if each time a noise is made, no matter how familiar it is to the nurse, it is explained to the child, it will eventually become familiar and less of a threat. Some children fear unfamiliar voices. This is especially true when positioning keeps the child from seeing the person. The common courtesy of adults identifying themselves by name and function when entering the room can lessen this fear. Some children develop fears because the hospital does not conform to the home routine. If the child is used to sleeping with his or her door open, with a radio playing, or with a favorite toy, the change in routine may cause concern. Any return to normal conditions for the child helps to make the child more comfortable.

The child also fears the extent of the injury. The older child senses the severity of the involvement and knows how others have responded to him or her during and after the acute stages of illness. Now, during long-term interventions, the child begins to perceive that additional therapy is not going to eradicate all the problems.

Separation anxiety can be lessened when the family is included in the child's ongoing care. Every attempt is made to build connections between the child and family when separations are necessary.

The child also feels anxiety when separated from friends, pets, home, school, and church. Making connections with these familiar aspects of his or her life whenever hospitalization is necessary makes separation more tolerable. For example, if reconstructive surgery is necessary, it is scheduled when school is out if this does not interfere with the prognosis. If surgery is done during school, the caretaker is encouraged to tell the school teacher the child's place of hospitalization so that the schoolchildren can be encouraged to send cards or messages to the child. In this way, the child's separation is lessened during stressful periods.

The child's feelings of loss of independence and control need special attention. Whenever choices can be offered, the child is encouraged to make the choice that is most attractive. For example, the child can be asked if he or she wants whirlpool treatments before or after lunch or the child can be offered choices of snacks that are nutritionally sound. There are often occasions to offer the child alternatives when he or she is acutely ill, and as treatment enters the convalescent and long-term phases, these opportunities increase significantly.

One way to determine whether a child really needs a narcotic is to watch closely the times and conditions when the requests are made. The child may request narcotics when he or she wishes to withdraw from a situation—e.g., when exercises are scheduled. He or she may request narcotics when parents visit. This request may be made because the child wants them to know how painful the burns or surgical procedures really are. He or she may request them to make the parents feel guilty for the confinement. He or she may request them so that he or she is conveniently asleep when the parents visit or when meals are served.

These types of clues can help to determine the use or misuse of the narcotic or other medication at a particular time. While it is certainly important to have the child as free from pain as possible, it is not fair to have the child become dependent on drugs. Careful evaluation of the foregoing factors helps in making a more realistic evaluation of the child's need for medication to alleviate physical pain. The emotional pain he or she has is more adequately treated by other methods.

It is also necessary to search for clues which might indicate that the child is having pain but will not request medication because he or she does not want another needle. The child is told that after the "stick" there will be relief of pain. He or she should also know that at this time only a "needle stick" can be used to give the medication. He or she should know that you do not enjoy hurting him or her but you know that children do feel better after they have had the medication.

The parents also need to know that narcotics are not used without jurisdiction. With the current emphasis on narcotic addiction among youths, the parents have real concern about introducing the child to drugs. The parents should also know that occasionally a child may request narcotics when they cannot be given. They need to be assured that the aim is to make the child as comfortable as possible while ensuring safe delivery of medications.

Another adjunct to burn therapy, one that is decreasingly necessary, is the use of tracheostomy when the area around the face and neck are involved or when caustic inhalants are involved. The child can become very dependent on the tracheostomy. The longer it is utilized, the more difficult it usually becomes to close it off and remove it. Partial "corking" can be attempted while the child is sleeping. During sleep, it is easier to evaluate the child's need for continuance of the therapy. If the partial corking is successful, complete corking is tried. When it is quite clear that the child can breathe with the tube corked, he or she can be introduced to the idea. This does not mean that the child will still not become anxious and develop respiratory difficulty, however. Very close supervision is warranted, and removal is done by the physician when the child is calm. Occasionally, repeated attempts at corking fail and removal is still attempted under close supervision. The child is not left alone during this time, and sterile equipment must be close by in readiness for reinsertion.

It is sometimes necessary for the child to be discharged with the tracheostomy. The nurse is responsible for teaching the parents the proper care and danger signals. The child who tends to have difficulty swallowing liquids or foods can be taught to flex his or her head forward. The caretaker is taught that hyperextending the neck narrows the esophagus, allowing food and fluid to easily flow into the trachea. Flexing the head allows the esophagus to open and makes the epiglottis close, facilitating swallowing (Weber, 1974). The child is not discharged until the equipment is in the home and the caretaker is comfortable with caring for the tracheostomy, including suctioning. A referral to the local community health nurse is also indicated. The community health nurse is able to check for outlets for the suction machine, to evaluate home facilities for cleaning equipment, to talk with the caretaker about concerns, to make sure that emergency telephone numbers are available near the telephone, and to elicit the parents' understanding and willingness to assume the responsibility for the child's management. When there is no community health nurse referral, the discharge planning includes a thorough discussion of the home environment and the family's ability to manage the child and to follow through with follow-up care.

Reconstructive Surgery

The need for reconstructive surgery is decreased if proper splinting, exercise, and pressure are used during the acute phase of the illness. Despite the conscientious care, it is still necessary for some children to have reconstructive surgery. Children who are prone to developing this need are:

1. The young child who, as he or she grows, develops scar bands over joints. Bands of this nature are commonly found in the axilla, antecubital fossa, popliteal area, groin, and neck.
2. Any child who has second- or third-degree burns of the scalp, resulting in hair loss. When hair-bearing tissue remains, the child can undergo serial excisions on scalp flaps.
3. The adolescent with burns of the thorax who needs surgery to release the breast at puberty or to reconstruct the nipples of the breast.

4. The child with face scars that can be improved by overgrafting or excision and grafting.

5. The child with tendon, muscle, bone, and/or joint destruction that results in fusion of the joints or amputations.

6. The child with severe damage to the face or ears whose deformed featured can be reconstructed surgically or through the use of prostheses (Pearson, 1981).

REFERENCES

Abston, S. *Burns in children: Clinical symposia*. Summit, New Jersey: CIBA Pharmaceutical Company, 1976.

Baur, P.S., Barratt, G., Linares, H.A., et al. Wound contractions, scar contractures and myofibroblasts: A classical case study. *Journal of Trauma* 18:8, 1978.

Bernstein, N. *Emotional care of the facially burned and disfigured*. Boston: Little, Brown, 1976.

Bowden, M., & Feller, I. Family reaction to a severe burn. *American Journal of Nursing* 73:317, 1973.

Bright, F. Parental anxiety: A barrier to communication. In *ANA Regional Clinical Conferences, 1966*. New York: Appleton–Century–Crofts, 1967.

Bristow, O., Strickney C., & Thompson, S. *Discharge planning for continuity of care*. New York: National League of Nursing, 1976.

Campbell, L. Special behavioral problems of the burned child. *American Journal of Nursing* 76:220, 1976.

Cosman, B. The burned child. In J.A. Downey, & N.L. Low (Eds.), *The child with disabling illness*. Philadelphia: Saunders, 1974.

Huang, T., Blackwell, S., & Lewis, S. Ten years of experience in managing patients with burn contractures of axilla, elbow, wrist, and knee joint. *Plastic and Reconstructive Surgery* 61:70, 1978.

Knudson-Cooper, M. Adjustment to visible stigma: The case of the severely burned. *Social Science and Medicine* 15:31, 1981.

Martin, H.L.. Parents' and children's reactions to burns and scalds in children. *British Journal of Medical Psychology* 43:183, 1970.

Parks, D., Baur, P., & Larson, D. Late problems in burns. *Clinics in Plastic Surgery* 4:547, 1977.

Parks, D., Carvajal, H., & Larson, D. Management of burns. *Surgical Clinics of North America* 57:875, 1977.

Parks, D., de la Houssaye, A.J., & Larson, D. The management of hypertrophic scarring with pressure. (Unpublished.) Surgery Division, Shriners Burns Institute, Galveston, Texas, 1978.

Parod, H.J., & Caplan, J.A. A framework for studying families in crisis. *Social Work Journal* 25:3, 1960.

Pearson, M. Burns. In S. Steele (Ed.), *Child health and the family: Nursing concepts and management*. New York: Masson, 1981.

Pearson, M. Nursing care in treatment of the burned patient. Paper presented in Mexico City, Mexico, May 1–3, 1981.

Pidgeon, V.A. Children's concepts of the rationale of isolation techniques. In *ANA Regional Clinical Conferences, 1966*. New York: Appleton—Century—Crofts, 1967.

Reichelt, P.A., & Newcomb, J. Organizational factors in discharge planning. *Journal of Nursing Administration* 12:36, 1980.

Riddle, I. Nursing intervention to promote body image integrity in children. *Nursing Clinics of North America* 7:651, 1972.

Talabere, L., & Graves, P. A tool for assessing families of burned children. *American Journal of Nursing* 76:225, 1976.

Weber, B. Eating with a trach. *American Journal of Nursing* 74:1439, 1974.

Willis, B., Larson, D., & Abston, S. Positioning and splinting the burned patient. *Heart and Lung* 2:696, 1973.

BIBLIOGRAPHY

Ballack, J.P. Helping a child cope with stress of injury. *American Journal of Nursing* 74:1491, 1974.

Campbell, L. Special behavioral problems of the burned child. *American Journal of Nursing* 76:220, 1976.

Candle, P.R., & Potter, J. Characteristics of burned children and the after effects of the injury. *British Journal of Plastic Surgery* 26:63, 1970.

Einhorn, A.H., & Jacobziner, H. Accidents in childhood. In H.L. Barnett (Ed.), *Pediatrics* (16th ed.). New York: Appleton—Century—Crofts, 1977.

Jacoby, F. *Nursing care of the patient with burns* (2nd ed.). St. Louis: Mosby, 1976.

Krieger, D. Therapeutic touch: The imprimatur of nursing. *American Journal of Nursing* 75:784, 1975.

Keuffner, M. Passage through hospitalization of a severely burned, isolated school-age child. In M.V. Batey (Ed.), *Communicating nursing research*. Boulder, Colorado: WICHE, 1975, pp. 181.

Long, R.T., & Cope, O. Emotional problems of burned children. *New England Journal of Medicine* 264:1121, 1961.

Morse, T. On talking to bereaved burned children. *Journal of Trauma* 11:874, 1971.

Rubin, M. Balm for burned children. *American Journal of Nursing* 66:297, 1966.

Seligman, R., et al. Emotional responses of burned children in a pediatric intensive care unit. *Psychiatric Medicine* 3:59, 1972.

Siligman, B., et al. The burned child: A neglected area of psychiatry. *American Journal of Psychiatry* 128:84, 1971.

Stone, N.H., Rinaldo, L., Humphrey, C.R., et al. Child abuse by burning. *Surgical Clinics of North America* 50:1419, 1970.

9

Health Promotion of the Child with an Invisible Disability: Type I Diabetes Mellitus

Shirley Steele

The importance of diabetes as a long-term illness of childhood cannot be underestimated. The disease can become evident in various age groups, from the newborn period through adolescence. The incidence increases with age, with two peak periods: 5- to 6-year-olds and 11- to 13-year-olds. The onset of diabetes is sudden and the symptoms can mimic other childhood illnesses. Early symptoms can be skin irritation, vomiting or abdominal pain. Advances in treatment have expanded life expectancy for diabetics. Diabetes is a hereditary disease transmitted by a recessive gene. In many cases, there is no family history of the disease. The hereditary factor is responsible for some unique aspects of nursing care of the child and the family. These factors will be described in greater detail later in the chapter. Benoliel (1975) dramatizes the situation by noting that the disease interferes with the lifestyle of the family. She emphasizes that the immediate care of the child is within the domain of the physician. However, the care of the child is abruptly switched from the physician to the family at a given point in time. The family members may not want or be able to provide this specialized care, but they have little or no choice in the matter. She suggests that the management of the child necessitates infringement on two very personal matters: the management of time and the uses of food. Also, the life expectancy of the diabetic is shortened—less than 50 percent of diabetics survive as long as 40 years.

Gorwitz et al. (1976) quote estimates regarding type I diabetes (formerly called juvenile diabetes) in childhood in the United States. It has been estimated that there are 86,000 persons under 17 years of age who have the disease, a rate of

1.3 to 1.6 per 1000 persons. The incidence is about the same in females as in males. The white population has a higher incidence than the nonwhite population—74,000 to 12,000. At least 95 percent of the children who have the disease have the classic insulin-deficiency form.

A brief explanation of the clinical entity is essential to understanding the disease, because nursing care in all of the age groups will be influenced by the pathology and the physiologic response of the body.

PATHOLOGY

Marshall (1982) hypothesizes that the etiology of type I diabetes mellitus is multifactorial, suggesting viral, genetic, and immunologic components. It might emerge as an autoimmune process triggered by a viral infection in a genetically susceptible child.

Diabetes reflects a disturbance in carbohydrate metabolism. It is caused by a deficiency in insulin, with a resulting hyperglycemia and glycosuria. Most children have no detectable endogenous insulin secretion within 3 years of the onset of the illness. The complicated process also results in an abnormal metabolism of proteins and fat. The pathologic process is aggravated by the loss of water, electrolytes, amino acids, base, calcium, phosphate, and other biologic substances by diuresis. When the disease is not under control, urinary losses of glucose may exceed 1000 Calories/day (Drash, 1978). These losses are from both the extracellular and intracellular compartments. Hemoconcentration and dehydration occur as a result. Renal dysfunction occurs as a result of the dehydration and hemoconcentration (Fig. 9-1).

This situation is further complicated by tissue breakdown. The body is unable to utilize glucose, so protein and fat are utilized in an attempt to compensate. The increase in fat breakdown in the liver results in an overproduction of ketones. These ketones are released into the circulatory system and

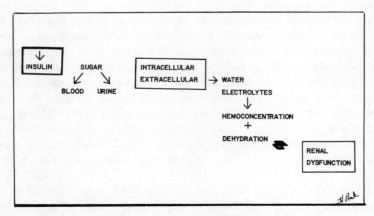

Figure 9-1.   Schema of the pathologic effects of diabetes.

overload the excretory system. The accumulation of ketone bodies is of particular importance when the diabetes is out of control (Fig. 9-2). The above explanation is, of course, a simplification. For a detailed explanation, the reader should consult a text on pathophysiology.

The etiologic process is usually abrupt in type I diabetes. In the obese adolescent, the onset more generally resembles the adult response to the illness. Another variation of onset in children is one described as a latent phase of the disease (Weil, 1968). Weil describes children with hyperglycemia and glucosuria resulting from surgery, acute stress situations, or illness as being in a state of latent diabetes. He states that these children frequently become overtly diabetic in later years. The child is usually underweight, as opposed to the adult patient, who is generally overweight at the onset. The symptoms that are common in type I diabetes include loss of weight, polydipsia, polyphagia, polyuria, visual disturbances, and muscle weakness. The child may be seen in coma or stupor or with central nervous system depression. The symptoms that may precede the coma are flushing, drowsiness, dry skin or skin lesions, abdominal pain, nausea and vomiting, and generalized body pain (Nelson, 1960).

There are stages of the disease: metabolic stabilization, remission, exacerbation, and total diabetes. These stages make it difficult to stabilize the newly diagnosed child. The stages are probably due to the beta-cell function. The total loss of islet cell functioning occurs between 12 and 18 months after the diagnosis is made.

The objectives of treatment of the child include alleviation of polyuria, polydipsia, polyphagia, and weight loss; prevention of ketoacidosis and hypoglycemia; control of glucosuria; and maintenance of normal plasma lipid levels. In addition, the psychosocial parameters of the child's growth are fostered by avoiding obesity, maintaining growth for age, fostering maturity, enhancing physical fitness, supporting a positive outlook, and promoting emotional stability.

The initial disbelief of the parents and the child is very understandable when a disease has such a rapid onset. The child may have a mild skin or throat infection and become acutely ill. He or she is then admitted to the hospital and blood tests reveal type I diabetes. The child is treated vigorously and can have a remarkable response to therapy. The parents are usually very relieved to see the dramatic improvement in their child. Their elation is short-lived, when they begin to realize the implications of the disease for their child and the family.

It is usually easier for the parents to understand the possibility of their child

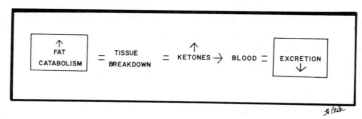

Figure 9-2.　Schema of diabetes resulting in an abundance of ketone bodies.

having diabetes if close relatives in the family have the disease. Even though it is easier for them to understand, this may not be a "plus factor," as they may have some misconceptions and fears because of their previous experiences with the disease. It is especially difficult for parents to understand how their child can be the "first" to have the disease.

According to Hughes (1967), parental acceptance, adjustment, and cooperation are hindered by several factors:

1. The long-term nature of the disease.
2. Dangerous immediate complications, arousing fear.
3. Well-known later complications, causing chronic anxiety.
4. Worries about future vocation.
5. Thoughts of marriage and transmission of disease.
6. Monotonous problem of proper management.

While the list of six items may seem short, the magnitude and scope of the problems can present unlimited problems in gaining parent cooperation. It is easy to see why at certain periods in time, the parents will be able to cope with the disease more readily than at others. For example, when the child is of school age and has been controlled on a constant amount of insulin for a period of time, the parents may be comparatively relaxed. When the child reaches the preadolescent growth spurt and the insulin requirements are radically changed, the child is frequently absent from school because of feelings of discomfort. The mother becomes very anxious because the child is not well; she becomes impatient with the health care providers because they cannot get the insulin adjusted; she worries about the child's falling behind in school work. The constant worry generated by the uncertainty makes the disease seem terrible. Her once relaxed attitude has been disrupted by this new need to focus on the disease. Her ordinary routine is disrupted, and this can cause anyone to be impatient with the causative agent. Her anxiety influences other members of the family, but particularly her child and her husband. The adolescent period is also one of stress. It is not uncommon for the adolescent to rebel against the entire disease management. This rebellion can result in a lack of control of the disease and turmoil in the family.

Benoliel (1975) writes about the fragility of arrangements over time. She starts with the transition in roles of the parents and child with the onset of the disease and emphasizes that there are serious adjustments to be made:

> If tensions within the family are already high, the diabetes can serve as a focal point for the expression of unresolved conflicts and unmet expectations . . . So, the potential for instability is always present in the changing symptomatology and social effects of the disease and treatment, and in the changing nature of the parent–child relationships (Benoliel, 1975, pp. 95–96).

The parents' reactions are of utmost importance because they have such a strong influence on the way the child copes with the disease. The child's emotional adjustment prior to the illness is another important element. If the child has a firm foundation to build on, he or she is in a better position to make the needed adjustments. The basic emotional needs of the child are unchanged by illness. He or she still has a strong desire for parental love and acceptance. If the parents are overwhelmed by the situation, they may be immobolized and unable to provide these basic needs. One of the most common parental reactions to the disease is overprotection. It is hypothesized that this response is based on the parents' feelings of guilt for the child developing the disease.

As with other chronic conditions, the parents' long-term response to the disease is based on several factors: the way the family functions as a unit, cultural background, the education of the family, the support that is provided through the family and by health care providers, the response of the child to the illness, the degree of disruption caused by the illness, and the child's adjustment to the disease. Each family unit will therefore respond in an unique way to the ongoing management of the disease.

The role of the family is to mediate the situation so that the child is successfully maintained as a member of the family. Therefore, after the initial mourning process is completed, the goal of management is to have family stability reinstituted. Despite this goal, it is known that many families are unable to stabilize after the initial stress. The child can spend inordinate amounts of time mourning his or her previous self-image as a healthy individual. This extended mourning of the desired self might be part of the reason that many of these children are prone to depression or other emotional sequelae of the disease. The child's unhappiness probably contributes to the family's inability to stablize. Both the parents and the child may need help to successfully complete the mourning process.

The siblings of the child are also involved in the goals to establish family stability. They cannot be left out of the management, as their feelings about the affected child, themselves, and the parents all influence the family's ability to regain stability. While various members of the family have different responsibilities in relation to the disease, the role renegotiations affect all members of the family.

The long-term management of the disease involves special consideration of the changes that take place during various stressful periods in the child's and family's life cycle. For example, the extra attention needed for the child's management can be viewed by the family as the child requiring a more extended period of dependence. The family members may feel that they cannot progress in their developmental sequence as a family, due to the child's special needs. This attitude can lead to oversolicitousness and overprotection of the affected child and sometimes even of the siblings. In addition, the affected child must reconsider the disease in light of each development stage that is transversed. As the child increases in cognitive ability, the disease and its management are reassessed, causing the child to have to cope with the new understanding of the implications of the disease for himself or herself and significant others.

Basically, the problems of the family fall into the following categories:

1. Attitudes of the parents to the etiology and hereditary factors.
2. Attitudes of the parents to the management routine.

3. Attitudes of the parents to the health care providers.
4. Attitudes of the child to the health care providers.
5. Attitudes of the parents to their child.
6. Attitudes of the parents to each other.
7. Responses of the siblings to the affected child.

FAMILY DYSFUNCTION

There is a higher incidence of family disintegration when the family has a child with a long-term health problem. Therefore, it is necessary to use strategies to help the family to maintain or establish equilibrium and to try to have the family grow as a result of their life challenges. Family members may require family therapy if they are not adapting successfully.

Maluccio (1981) proposes a model whereby the health care provider focuses on helping family members to promote each other's growth by mobilizing their own resources and supporting their selected coping patterns. He suggests that emphasis be placed on life experiences, family tasks and activities, and other opportunities for enhancing the personal autonomy and competence of family members. This approach involves the thoughtful use of activity, which Maluccio suggests is a therapeutic way to help families to master their life circumstances.

The family is uniquely organized to mediate the tasks that are associated with families. Under most life circumstances, the functional family has the potential to use coping mechanisms and to resolve problems that arise. The family is usually able to carry out the integrative and adaptive functions that keep it functional.

When Maluccio's framework is utilized with families, it is essential to explore the task to be accomplished and to be certain that each family member has a clear understanding of the responsibilities involved in achieving the identified task. In accomplishing the task, each family member takes an active part and can visualize a potential benefit. When each family member realizes a potential personal gain, then motivation is higher and there is a greater potential for success.

There are several purposes of tasks identified by Maluccio. These include:

1. Changing a family's dysfunctional interaction patterns.
2. Changing dysfunctional family structure.
3. Improving the family's ability to make decisions.
4. Improving the competence of individual family members.

In order to achieve success with this approach to family therapy, it is necessary for family members to negotiate the task and to show feelings openly. One advantage of this approach is that each family member is clear about the goals that are set and is involved in working towards achieving the goal. When each family member participates in a common goal, it is possible to resolve challenges that were overwhelming the family before an organized attempt was established to meet the challenge.

Maluccio (1981) proposes that when life challenges are expressed as tasks to be accomplished, family members are able to achieve personal satisfaction from achieving the task. In this way, family members can gain self-esteem and increased competence in expressing their roles as family members.

Based on Maluccio's notion that a "task refers to what is to be done by the family or its members in any specific situation so as to meet their needs or enable them to deal successfully with environmental challenges," the following family example is given:

> Mr. and Mrs. Jones were raising two school-age children with minimal effort when James was diagnosed at age 8 as a diabetic. Mrs. Jones immediately took over the management of James's health problem. Initially, she complained openly about the additional responsibilities that the health condition imposed, but eventually she became depressed and silent. She began going to bed with James at 8 P.M., stating that she needed more rest and she wanted to be sure that James was alright during the night. Mr. Jones and the younger sibling became less and less involved with Mrs. Jones and James.
>
> Eventually, the family was involved in family therapy. Mr. Jones was directed to assume responsibility for supervising James's therapy, with James being given responsibility for his own therapy. Mrs. Jones could not sleep in James's room and she was to do at least one activity with the younger sibling each day. She could not ask about James's therapy but was directed to show interest when either her husband or James talked about the therapy. When therapy was discussed, each family member was encouraged to express his or her feelings about the health problem and its impact on the family.

Through family therapy, the family members are rewarded for restructuring the family so that each family member engages in a different interaction pattern that can lead to improved communication.

The family that engages in family therapy has the potential to change so that family disintegration is less likely.

EDUCATION

There are many aids to use in the educational program. Numerous pamphlets and guides are available for use in teaching. An example of this is the book supplied by Eli Lily Drug Company entitled *Tile and Till* (1971). This is geared to the diabetic and offers a relaxed way for the child to learn about the disease. Another aid is *An Instructional Aid on Juvenile Diabetic Mellitus* by Travis (1980). This is a comprehensive popular publication, specifically designed for children with diabetes to learn about their disease and its management.

The child newly diagnosed as having diabetes is usually taught a few simple facts about the disease, depending on his or her age. A toddler may only be told that it is necessary to have needles to help him or her stay well. It is very difficult for a toddler to understand this concept, and he or she may think it is better to be sick than to get stuck every day. The preschooler can understand a little more, but he or she is not any happier to get needles than the toddler. It may be helpful to talk to a school-age child with the disease while observing another child also taking injections. The school-age child is usually the most cooperative in learning and assuming responsibility for the disease. However, even the school-age child will have periods when it becomes a bore and will need assistance to continue with the successful management of the disease. During adolescence, the child's natural tendency is to rebel, and the disease management receives its share of the rebellion. The actual degree to which the adolescent does rebel, however, is not easily predictable. Utilizing factors of normal growth and development, it is assumed that the child will rebel, but, again, this is probably more related to each child's individual emotional make-up than to the adolescent group as a whole.

Urine Testing

After the child has been told about his or her disease in a manner commensurate with his or her age, the next step is to have the child learn to test the urine. The school-age child or adolescent is ready for this task. Generally, children with mental ages of 6 years or over are capable of testing their own urine. The school-age child will need props to help with understanding. In addition, the school-age child uses mental images to help in the learning process. The adolescent can benefit from concrete examples but is not absolutely dependent on them for learning. Therefore, demonstrations accompany the explorations of all learning concepts. Audiovisuals help to add variety to the teaching sessions.

The child becomes quickly aware that urine specimens play a large role in the disease process. It is necessary to prepare a place in the utility room and set up a teaching session. This need not be at a time that the urine should be tested (Fig. 9-3). This session will allow more time for teaching and discussion. The child should be taught to test the urine and record the results. He or she should also be shown how to clean and replace the equipment. There are several methods available to test the urine. Each type of agent used for urine testing will have its own directions on the bottle or the box. Go over them carefully with the child and parent. One of the most popular tests for glucose is the two drop Clinitest method. The parents should also learn the selected procedure, as it will be their responsibility if for any reason the child is unable to assume the task. The toddler is too young to understand how to test urine. The preschooler may be interested in seeing it done, but is too young to do it himself or herself. The parents of these younger children must assume total responsibility for the child's urine testing (Table 9-1).

At first, the child receives real satisfaction from achieving this task, as it is a new skill. It must be remembered, however, that the repetitive nature of the task may convert it to a chore and the child may lose interest. The strict routine of testing is frequently relaxed after the child's condition is stabilized. However, some children are managed on a protocol that requires urine testing four times daily even after stability is achieved.

Whether the child or the nurse assumes the responsibility for the urine

Figure 9-3. A separate area should be set aside in the utility room for the child to test his or her urine. All equipment should be readily available.

testing is not so important as what is done with the results. Talking with the child about the results helps to correlate how the child feels when a urine test result is +4, with how he feels when it is negative. The child begins to see the relationship between what is eaten, the amount of insulin, the amount of activity in which he or she engages, and the urine test results.

Many children are hospitalized during the initial stage of the disease. However, some physicians prefer to regulate the child at home. This allows for more accurate assessment of the child's activity as related to the insulin needs. If the child is not hospitalized at the onset, hospitalization for an acute episode may be the child's first experience with hospitalization.

Periodically, 24 hour urine specimens are collected for analysis. These are more accurate than single specimen checks. According to Drash (1978), if the urinary 24 hour urinary glucose is less than 7 percent of the total amount of carbohydrates ingested, an increase in insulin is required. The family is prepared to collect the specimen by being given an explanation of why it is necessary, providing supplies that are needed, and giving specific instructions on where and how to bring the specimen after it is collected.

TABLE 9-1
Suggested Procedure for Teaching Urine Testing

Select time mutually acceptable to child and nurse
Select place free from distractions
Have equipment ready

    a. test tubes
    b. medicine dropper
    c. water supply
    d. Clinitest and Acetest tables
    e. appropriate color charts
    f. place to record results

Have place to store supplies after use

Insulin Injections

If the child is hospitalized, there is usually sufficient time to space the teaching. It is not necessary to immediately begin to teach the child to give himself or herself his or her own insulin. Timing is important in obtaining the child's cooperation. If he or she is feeling depressed from learning about the disease, there is not enough energy left over to assume new tasks. After he or she has had time to psychologically internalize the disease, the child is in a better position to proceed with learning. A child with a mental age over 9 years can be taught this skill.

There is not total agreement among health care providers as to whether the school-age child should be expected to administer his or her own insulin. Utilizing the developmental factor that the child of this age has good eye-to-hand coordination, it is assumed that he or she is capable of the task. The decision would better be made on an individual basis, taking into consideration the way the child and the parents feel about the procedure.

Assuming that the child is to take the responsibility for the task, a lesson plan is prepared for teaching the procedure. An adequate amount of time is set aside to allow for the child to become comfortable with the teacher and the equipment. The equipment utilized should be equivalent to the equipment that will be used at home. If disposable syringes will be used, then it is realistic to use them in the hospital. If a glass syringe is to be used and boiled each time, then this should be utilized for teaching.

The principle of sterility may be an entirely new concept to the child. The child may need considerable help in understanding it. Proper handling of a syringe is built on knowledge of what is or is not sterile. A safe way to sterilize the syringe is established. The safety factors are of utmost importance with the school-age child, who probably has had limited experience working with a stove.

The community health nurse is contacted to be sure that the home situation can accommodate the procedure. Frequently, parents are too embarrassed to say that they do not have the necessary equipment at home. The parents need to know exactly what they will be given by the hospital and what it is their responsibility to have purchased prior to the discharge. If the child has not been hospitalized, the home will probably be better equipped, as the parents have had to assume the full responsibility from the beginning (Table 9-2).

The child will need time to practice handling the equipment. The child practices giving injections to an orange or similar object that can be easily injected by a needle. He or she needs encouragement to transfer to his or her own person what is learned using the orange or other object. A chart of the sites utilized for injection is made available. The child is taught the necessity of rotating sites and establishes a pattern for himself or herself. Injection sites include the arms, thighs, hips, and abdomen. The injections are spaced an inch apart.

As soon as the insulin requirements are established, the child is given an explanation of the types of insulin and their expected actions. The child needs to know that regular insulin is quick-acting and that results begin in a half hour. Its peak action is in 3 hours and its activity is over in 6 to 12 hours. Regular insulin is

TABLE 9-2
Suggested Procedure for Teaching Insulin Injection

Prepare simple chart of role of insulin in body
Select time acceptable to nurse and child
Select place free from distractions
Assemble equipment

    a. syringe
    b. needle
    c. alcohol and cotton ball
    d. sterilization equipment
    e. appropriate insulin
    f. orange or injectable doll or ball

Explain each of the objects to the child
Demonstrate sterilization of syringe

    a. separate syringe and needle
    b. sterilize in a pan of boiling water
    c. remove plunger of syringe by lifting near end
    d. remove barrel of syringe and place plunger inside
    e. remove needle by hub and attach to syringe
    f. cleanse rubber stopper of bottle with alcohol sponge
    g. draw up correct amount of insulin

Place syringe in appropriate spot to maintain sterility
Cleanse area with cotton ball saturated with alcohol
Insert needle into orange, doll or ball
Pull back on plunger
Inject insulin into orange, doll or ball
Remove needle and cleanse area with alcohol sponge
Rinse syringe and return to appropriate storage place
Discard cotton ball
Free discussion

usually given in combination with an intermediate-acting insulin, such as NPH. The usual schedule is to give the child two injections each day. The morning dose is usually two-thirds of the daily requirement, while the other one-third is given before dinner in the evening.

The child and parents must remember that a syringe calibrated with the appropriate markings must be used with their particular insulin prescription. Most often, U100 insulin is used, although both U40 and U80 are available. An inaccurate dose will result from mixing the wrong insulin with the wrong scale. The bottles are clearly marked and the differences in labels are shown to the child and parents.

Insulin must be stored out of direct sunlight and can be maintained at room temperature. The vials which are not being used on a daily basis are refrigerated.

In helping the parents to determine whether to use disposable syringes, the cost factor is of utmost importance. The parents may feel the cost is minimal compared to the convenience obtained. Some parents decide to use the glass syringe, but get a couple of disposable ones to have on hand for travel or in case the glass syringe breaks. Regardless of which type is chosen, more than one syringe is bought so that there is always one available. Some children use an insulin pump, but these are still relatively expensive and are being used only selectively (Fig. 9-4).

The insulin pump is an electromechanical devise designed to mimic the release of insulin by the pancreas. Unlike the pancreas, however, which secretes variable

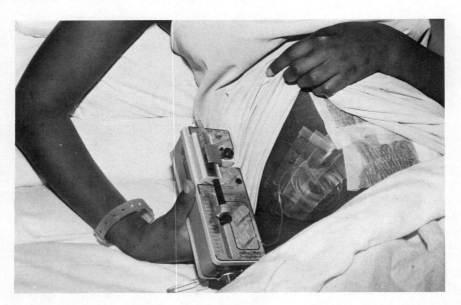

Figure 9-4. This adolescent exhibits her insulin pump. Newer pumps are smaller, weigh less, have more advanced pre-programming capabilities and alarm systems. *(Photo by H. Riggs)*

amounts of insulin in response to a constantly changing blood glucose level, the portable insulin pumps currently in use deliver fixed small amounts of insulin continuously, with the capability of delivering larger doses prior to meals (Fredholm, 1981, p. 2024).

Both the child and parents need opportunities to ask questions and to express concerns about giving injections. Periodically, insulin is discussed so that there are opportunities for the child and parents to get answers to their questions. A possible new problem can be lipodystrophy. Lipodystrophy is often the result of inadequate rotation of injection sites. The atrophy of the subcutaneous fat can be decreased by using a one-half to five-eighths inch needle that penetrates the skin and goes no further (Guthrie, 1977). When lipodystrophy occurs, the family and child need assistance to assess the rotation schedule that is being used and to plan a new rotation schedule, if indicated.

Dietary Management

A condition such as type I diabetes that requires continual monitoring of dietary intake can easily become boring or frustrating to the entire family. When any member of the family constellation requires special attention to dietary intake, there is the possibility of improving the nutrition of the entire family; there is also the potential of disrupting the family patterns for buying, preparing, and serving meals.

There are several principles that guide the dietary management of these children:

1. The diet must be adequate to meet the child's nutritional requirements for growth and development. As the child is not fully grown, these requirements are changing frequently.
2. Cultural and racial food preferences of the family must be taken into consideration.
3. The ability of the family to afford the foods that are suggested is of utmost importance.
4. The diet must be acceptable to the entire family.
5. The diet is planned to achieve good metabolic control by minimizing hyperglycemia and hypoglycemia, obesity, and hyperlipidemia.
6. Foods that are liked by the child are included in the diet, while foods that are disliked are minimized.
7. Meals and snacks are planned to conveniently fit in the child's day and are consistent with the family's pattern for eating.
8. Special attention is needed when the child is under stress, has increased activity, or has an infection.

During the initial diagnostic period, the family is introduced to the dietary restrictions necessary to control the disease (Fig. 9-5). At this time, the family and child learn that diabetes is a disease that is controlled but not cured. During the long-term management of the condition, this fact becomes very obvious to the

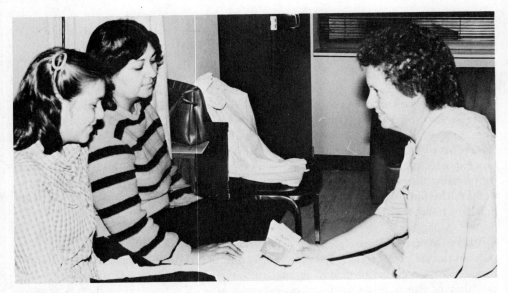

Figure 9-5.   The nurse provides nutrition counseling for the school-age child with diabetes and her mother. *(Photo by D. Haskin)*

child and family, for when dietary control is not adequate, the child is vulnerable to hypoglycemia or hyperglycemia. During the early management of the disease, it is stressed that proper dietary management is actually a strict adherence to a nutritionally sound dietary intake. The diet is therefore appropriate for all members of the family, with slight variations for age. There are different protocols for the dietary management of these children, ranging from a "free diet" to selecting from exchange lists to weighing the food. However, all of the protocols are based on the principles provided above.

Data does not show that strict adherence to dietary management of the disease results in a better long-term prognosis for the child. However, dietary control can decrease the number of hospitalizations that interfere with the child's ordinary daily activities. The current focus on changing the dietary intake of all Americans to improve health is reflected in the dietary management of these children. For example, at one children's center, the American Heart Association diet of 55 percent total calories from carbohydrates, 30 percent from fat, and 15 percent from protein is followed. The carbohydrate calories are derived from a 70 percent starch and a 30 percent mixture of lactose, sucrose, and fructose. The ratio of polyunsaturated to saturated fats is also adjusted to the recommended 1.2/1 ratio, while cholesterol is restricted to 250 mg/day (Drash, 1978). The family is alerted to the fact that this arrangement of nutritional intake is being readily selected by many persons in order to improve or maintain physical well-being. In addition, the family and child are assured that the child's appetite will guide the dietary management. Therefore, if the child is hungry and is not gaining excessive weight, the dietary intake can be increased. The way the child feels influences the arrangement of the food intake; the child is always made to feel as comfortable as possible by decreasing the fluctuations in the blood glucose levels. Despite adequate control, the late vascular complications of the disease can still occur, so emphasis is placed on the ongoing need to decrease hyperglycemia by controlling diet and administering insulin at an adequate rate throughout the child's life.

The nutrition management is usually directed by a dietician or nutritionist. The family and child are usually given dietary lists that provide them with knowledge of the calories, carbohydrates, proteins, and fats in each food group. A child of school age is capable of learning exchange patterns. These children can therefore choose school snacks and lunches on the basis of their exchange system knowledge. Periodically, the child's dietary pattern is discussed so that it is certain that this part of the child's management is understood.

The school nurse and teachers need to know the child has diabetes. They should know that the child may need supplements during school hours. The child should carry hard candy or some other source of glucose for periods when he or she feels weak. Also, if a snack is necessary during school time, it can be planned so that the child does not appear to be getting special privileges.

An important consideration when one is planning the child's dietary intake is the amount of activity the child will be engaged in. In keeping the emphasis on a "normal life," adjustments will have to be made for increases in activity. On a day when the child has gym, nutritional intake is adjusted. The lunch may be changed slightly to include additional protein. This protein is valuable, as it maintains the blood sugar level more adequately than do carbohydrates.

Another important aspect of the diet is to be certain that the child eats at regularly scheduled intervals. Children tend to eat sporadically unless supervised. They are too busy playing to come in to eat, or the TV show is at an intense point and cannot be left. Depending on the lifestyle of the family, the regulation of time for the child to receive food may be a big hurdle to overcome. In some families, meals are seldom, if ever, prepared, with the children assuming the responsibility for getting food when hungry. Under these conditions, the food restrictions and requirements will have to be discussed thoroughly and often with the parents and child. Trying to teach the mother who does not have an appreciation for the value of good nutrition to prepare nutritious meals is a challenge. In addition, she may feel these meals are a financial burden. In many families, meal times are flexible. They are planned around busy people's variable daily schedules. This system of meal planning is likely to cause difficulty for the child with diabetes. The child may become weak or listless while waiting for meals; the physiologic response may cause him or her to be irritable. To prevent this happening, the child may have to be fed before the rest of the family.

EXERCISE

The inclusion of exercise in the treatment protocol is based on the notion that the child who is well controlled can benefit from exercise as it:

1. Decreases insulin requirements.
2. Decreases peak glucose levels following meals.

3. Reduces ketonemia.
4. Helps to control or prevent obesity.
5. Improves cardiovascular stability.
6. Reduces hyperlipidemia.
7. Improves self-image and esteem.

The child who is not controlled can be adversely affected by exercise so a prime consideration in suggesting an exercise program is to be certain that the child's diabetes is controlled prior to starting the exercise program.

Exercise is planned so that the child can complete the program on a consistent and continuous basis. The exercise program should be able to be done by the child alone or at most with one other person. In this way, it will be easier to achieve the exercise protocol. The child does not have to like doing the exercise, but it will be more acceptable if the child enjoys exercising. If the whole family engages in exercise together, the child is facilitated in achieving the goal.

A detailed exercise plan is negotiated with the child and given to the family. This exercise protocol is monitored closely to be certain that the child is giving attention to this important component of his or her care.

Identity as a Diabetic

The child is helped to develop an identity as a diabetic with specific needs. The achievement of this goal evolves over time. A diabetic identity facilitates the child's awareness that certain things are essential to his or her well-being, such as a nutritious diet, insulin injections, control of glucose metabolism, and closer medical supervision. The child is helped to understand the relationship between diet, exercise, and insulin requirements and how these are altered by certain life experiences, such as infections, stress, and growth. As the child internalizes the diabetic identity, the implications for his or her lifestyle are discussed. Caution is used during this internalization of a diabetic identity so that the child does not equate the identity with a perceived identity of himself or herself as being defective. The child is encouraged to engage in decision making so that he or she is involved in the resolution of conflicts that emerge as a result of being a diabetic.

Teaching About the Disease

Thus far the teaching has been based on the tasks necessary to have the disease kept under control. This is only the beginning in helping the child and parents to understand the disease. A simple explanation of the "three P's," such as the one that follows, is essential:

1. Polyuria: increased amount of urine due to the sugar accumulation in the blood and ultimate excretion by the kidneys.
2. Polydipsia: increased thirst caused by the excretion of large amounts of fluid with the sugar.
3. Polyphagia: increased appetite due to the body's inability to utilize starch and sugars adequately.

The parents and child also need to know the signs and symptoms of impending danger, such as light-headedness, sweating, restlessness, or rapidly beating heart, which are the results of too much insulin. Sugar should be taken immediately. Conversely, the child may have to actually experience some of these conditions before he or she really understands the states that are being described. The child is able to get to the "sugar" without too much disruption in the ordinary schedule during periods of hypoglycemia. This will decrease the chances of the child's using imaginary excuses to get special attention. An illustration would be as follows. The school-age child is frequently pressured by ordinary school routines. He or she is not allowed to escape from this pressure, but rather is encouraged to work under it and to cope with the situation. The child with diabetes could easily decide that he or she is having an insulin reaction and leave the room to get a sugar supply. It is better to have the sugar in the desk or in his or her pocket and have him or her get it without leaving the room. Then the child is not tempted to try to use the disease as an escape valve when the going gets rough.

The Somogyi effect is also explained. In this effect, the child becomes hypoglycemic in the early morning hours. The family is cautioned to check for excessive perspiration during sleep by checking the bed linen for dampness. The child may complain of nightmares, morning headache, or interference with sensorium, such as grogginess or fogginess and irritability. Frequently, the treatment for this condition is to decrease or redistribute the child's insulin.

Skin Care and Foot Care

Cleanliness is an important part of skin care. This is especially important, as any child is prone to receive many cuts and scrapes which easily become infected if they are not kept meticulously clean. The healing process is longer in diabetes, and prevention is the best way to counteract this delay.

Foot care is also very important. Few people actually cut their toenails correctly. The child is shown how to cut the toenails straight across and not rounded, as is frequently the practice. Correct footwear is also imperative. If the child's shoes are too tight, the feet easily become prone to ingrown toenails and secondary infections. Well-fitting shoes will also cut down the number of callouses the child develops. If the child develops foot problems, he or she should get early medical attention before the condition has a chance to advance. Bathing of the feet with proper drying and an application of talcum powder is encouraged. The area between the toes is given special attention. If the skin is dry, it may be necessary to apply a soothing lotion. After daily bathing, a clean pair of well-fitting white cotton socks are worn. Because the blood supply to the feet is frequently diminished in diabetes, the child may feel more comfortable in a heavier sock than his or her peers wear. He or she may also need a slipper sock or loose woolen socks to wear to bed.

Additional Preparation for Life

The child with diabetes needs a consistent plan for living comfortably with the disease. The plan includes the normal things that children enjoy doing. The child is encouraged to go to summer camp. If he or she is not accepted at a regular camp, there are specific camps for children with diabetes. The child may benefit from having contact with another child who has the disease. He or she is encouraged to call this acquaintance when he or she needs answers to specific questions about coping with the disease. It is best to have as the reference a person who had the disease during childhood so that he or she knows what the child is going through. It is also important for the child to feel free to contact the people in charge of his or her medical supervision. The child is the best judge of how he or she feels and can explain it best to the professional personnel. A simple phone call may be all that is needed, and the child may be able to avoid missing school an entire day to go to the physician's office or clinic. The use of groups to help talk about feelings is also common. Children of similar ages can discuss the problems they face in coping with diabetes. In addition, the children can decrease the loneliness or isolation that result from having a long-term illness. These groups can be led by a variety of health care providers. Often there are two leaders, one representing psychology or psychiatry, the other representing medicine, social work, or nursing.

The child should also be given the opportunity to wear an identification bracelet or necklace describing his or her physical condition. He or she is also offered a card to be placed in a wallet. These ideas are not always received kindly by the child. He or she does not like to be different and frequently interprets these measures as overt examples of how he or she is different. The ideas are introduced by a person who is willing to spend time talking over the reasons for having such identification. The child can then make his or her own decision as to whether or not they are essential.

Infectious Processes

Children frequently develop infections that they do not call to the attention of their parents. Anything that does not incapacitate them is frequently ignored. A throat infection, in its early stages, is not evident to the parent. Unless the child makes the illness known, the parent considers the child well. In combating the infectious process, the body may develop a slight temperature elevation. This, too, can go unnoticed by the parent. This elevation influences the body's metabolism. When the metabolic rate is changed, the insulin requirements are also affected. The child needs additional insulin if he or she is to satisfactorily combat the infection. The child's cooperation in reporting early signs of sickness is imperative. The parent then must seek medical advice regarding an alteration in insulin requirements, dietary changes, or changes in activity. The parents are cautioned against altering insulin dosage on their own unless this is part of the management they have been taught.

In addition to early recognition of infection, parents are cautioned about having the child unduly exposed to other children with infectious diseases. They are also encouraged to have the child's immunizations kept up to date. Periodic review of the child's immunization status is important as information in relation to current immunization protection emerges. It is also necessary to have the child with diabetes receive whatever new immunizations are developed. The child may offer some resistance to receiving additional injections, but objections are overruled because of the benefits derived. If the child is exposed to another child with a severe infectious process, it is also important to talk this over with the child's physician to see if prophylactic therapy is indicated.

During an infectious process, urine testing is especially important. During times of infection the urine must be monitored very closely. In addition to testing for sugar, acetone levels are checked. The degree in normal variations is what is significant. Physicians differ as to what the best maintenance is for the child. If the physician prefers the child to have +1 sugar in the urine, then the deviation from +1 is what is significant. If the child has been maintained on negative urine values, then a deviation of +2 is more significant to this child. All children are maintained without acetone secretion, so any acetone is significant. A physician is called if acetone is present. One of the best suggestions to the parents regarding infection is, "When in doubt, call."

Eye Care

Another important consideration in treating the child with diabetes is the care of the eyes. It is well known that in older individuals there is a proneness to blindness. There is reason to believe that there is a greater than normal possibility that type I diabetics will have changes in vision. However, the onset of changes in vision is not well documented, and neither is the relationship between the severity of the disease and the severity of the changes in the eye. The changes in vision may be of a temporary or a permanent nature. The important aspect for the nurse to remember is that vision changes can be in direct relation to fluctuations in the blood sugar; therefore, a child who is out of control may have blurring of vision which is only temporary in nature. The parent and child are both aware of the necessity of having yearly ophthalmologic examinations. Included in the eye assessment can be retinal photography.

Other Complications of Diabetes

The degree to which the parents are introduced to the possibilities of complications is extremely individualized. The introduction is done according to the developmental stage of the child and the parents' ability to cope with new information. For instance, it is well known that the child with diabetes may develop arteriosclerosis. A simplified explanation is given—one that the parent can utilize effectively. The parents and the child may be informed of the potential for vascular disease to occur at the time that stress electrocardiography is scheduled, or they may be told about potential kidney problems when an Addis count and creatinine clearance, excretion of protein, and lyosomal enzyme tests are scheduled. In addition, the potential for neurologic sequelae can be explained when nerve conduction studies are scheduled. As the results of the various tests are received, the family and child can be appraised of the child's condition. At this time, the relationship between the child's metabolic status and the side-effects of the disease can be explained.

According to Engel (1962, p. 241), "patients certainly, regardless of their level of education and sophistication, prefer to blame their illness on something they caught or ate or that happened to them, and consequently to think of disease as something apart from themselves." An example would be insufficient insulin as the cause of (rather than the mechanism involved in) diabetes.

Considerations for Age

The toddler or preschooler with diabetes begins the medical regimen by having the parents take total responsibility for his or her care. This necessitates the parents being fully aware of their responsibilities for the child, and it requires that the health care providers spend a great deal of time in preparing the parents. As the child grows older, he or she assumes increasing responsibility for his or her care. The parents' role is then decreased, in that their responsibility is changed to supervision of the child in his or her self-management.

As the child grows older, the parent is helped to relinquish control to make the child feel total responsibility for his or her own personal management. This is frequently very difficult when the parent has assumed all of the care for several years. However, it is very important to have the child feel as normal as possible, and normality requires that he or she begin to establish his or her own identity and responsibility for himself or herself. The diabetic regimen becomes part of the child's daily routine and does not require a great deal of additional time. The child is given credit for assuming increased responsibility for management of his or her health care.

The school-age child's successful adjustment to the disease is reflected in adequate school progress. This is reflected in the child's attendance record and the child's scholastic achievements. The child is also involved in all areas of the school program, including gym and swimming. The child's successful interactions with peers and involvement in extracurricular activities can be assessed through self-reports and school reports. The health care providers, the family, the child, and school personnel collaborate to make the child's readjustment to school effective.

When the child nears adolescence, it is hoped that he or she will be mature enough to assume major responsibility for care. The adolescent needs additional information about the disease over and above what was given in earlier stages. The adolescent who reads that most diabetics have early vascular changes may decide to give up as he or she witnesses changes in the course of the illness. The adolescent will need time to explore feelings about the disease and the implications of sequelae for his or her well-being. The adolescent cannot be protected from learning that the life expectancy of a person with type I diabetes is decreased. However, the adolescent is appraised of the advances that have been made in the control of the disease so that hope is maintained despite the morbidity of the disease.

The adolescent with diabetes has a special need to discuss the implications of the use of drugs and alcohol and the special considerations regarding human sexuality. A group session is an excellent way to discuss these concerns. The adolescent is often concerned about slow maturation and appearance of secondary sex characteristics. Sharing this concern with others leads the adolescent to understand that this is common and that better control of the disease through insulin change and nutrition management will lead to changes in development which lead to successful achievement of this developmental milestone. The female adolescent is informed that menses can be delayed slightly.

The late adolescent period is when the adolescent is achieving the goal of independence, with a selection of a vocation and possible marriage partner. The adolescent often requires counseling to know how to share his or her disease with a potential partner. While type I diabetes does not result in sterility, there are some special concerns when a female has diabetes and desires to have children. Sharing this information with a potential partner can be very threatening, and the adolescent needs assistance in achieving this goal.

The adolescent who is rejected by a potential partner may blame the disease for the rejection. The adolescent is painfully aware that differences exist between his or her peers and himself or herself. Counseling helps the adolescent to realize that all adolescents witness rejection. However, at a time when the adolescent craves acceptance by the opposite sex, the realistic appraisal of rejection is very difficult. The adolescent is aided in successful achievement of vocational and marriage goals when counseling is reality-based and the counselor is truthful and empathetic.

Even though the parent has been told why the child cannot be treated with oral agents, the adolescent will need his or her own explanation. As he or she grows to adulthood, this will be even more significant, as he or she may talk to co-workers and find someone who developed diabetes later in life and is being treated solely with oral agents.

Education of Parents or Significant Others

Benoliel (1975) expresses the opinion that the role of the parents is substantially altered when they are given the added responsibility for carrying out the medical regime. They are now expected to socialize the child and to be surrogates to the physician. Their normal socialization process has to be transformed to include the behaviors necessary for maintaining control of the disease. This change in socialization procedure may be difficult to achieve, especially if the parents do not fully understand their responsibility to the medical regime.

Parent education is a most significant segment of the overall management of care of the child with a disability. It is particularly relevant to parents of children with diabetes in view of the hereditary aspects of the illness. Parent education can be achieved in many ways. One is the large lecture approach. In this method, an expert is usually available to give a prepared speech describing the disease process. In addition, he or she may cover aspects of child care, implications of the disease for the family, information regarding services offered in the community, and perhaps a brief explanation of some of the current research in the field. From this lecture, parents utilize the process of *selective perception*. They filter out those aspects which are easy to accept, digest, and use and apply in their own situation. This educational approach is a good stepping stone to other processes which involve greater participation of the parents. Lectures can also be supplemented by written information on the topic. Again, this written material lends itself to selective perception. The parents can easily ignore the pamphlet completely or skim it and find areas which enhance or support their knowledge of the topic. They are still able to avoid areas which may be particularly uncomfortable for them.

The smaller group meeting lends itself to another type of parent education. In this approach, the parents are afforded the security of a group to help them express their hostility, fears, fantasies, inadequacies, and expectations regarding the disabled child and his or her management. The group provides a curtain of protection not generally found in the one-to-one relationship of parent and health care provider. This protection plays an especially significant role, as the parents frequently fear alienating the professional workers who they inwardly feel they need for the care of their child. The small group eventually helps the parents to look at themselves and to see the relationship of their own behavior to the behavior of their disabled child. The group can also be valuable in exposing the parents to new ways of handling the child and can provide them with very concrete suggestions for day-to-day living. In addition, the parents have a healthy avenue for release of their feelings. They may feel freer to express their hostility about the cost of insulin to parents who also share the burden than to outsiders or even relatives who may see insulin as a life-saving factor and therefore feel the parents should be very thankful for its existence rather than complaining about its cost. The other parents, with similar concerns, are often able to pick up on the clues and expand the topic to get to some of the deeper concerns.

The need for parent education is readily accepted, but the avenue for providing this education is not firmly established. Experimentation and research with different techniques and procedures continue in many areas and will eventually lead to a more scientific basis for determining individual needs. In the interim, many different approaches are being taken to meet the needs of parents and children.

Monitoring the Disease Process
Over Time

Monitoring of the disease process can be a difficult task. There are a variety of ways to monitor the disease and newer methods are being introduced periodically. There are advantages and disadvantages to most of the methods and the physician will determine which methods are used at a particular time.

The semiquantitative urine sugar using 2-Drop Clinitest, previously described, is the most popular way to monitor the disease process of children under 10 years of age. For older children with controlled diabetes the strip methods are frequently used, for example: the Diastix, Keto-Diastix, Clinistex, Test-tape, or Chemstrip G.K. The Diastix has the closest similarity in color to the Clinitest tablet method and is sometimes chosen for that reason. However, any of the types can be used effectively when the child's disease is not out of control. When control is not maintained, the Clinitest method is used until control is regained.

There are limitations to the strip method of monitoring the disease. This method only measures concentrations of sugar up to 2 percent while excretions of sugar in the range of 10 to 12 percent are not uncommon.

The urine sugars are dependent on the glucose threshold of the kidney. The normal glucose threshold is approximately 160 mg/dl while glucose thresholds of children with diabetes are quite variable with ranges of 130 to 190 mg/dl. In addition, the glucose threshold of children with diabetes is relatively stable for the first 5 to 10 years after the onset of the disease but there is a gradual increase in the glucose threshold over time with higher glucose values being associated with negative urine sugar testing. This knowledge makes it evident that during the long-term management of the child's disease, semiquantitative urine testing can become inadequate for monitoring the child's physiologic responses to the disease.

Home blood glucose monitoring (HBGM) is becoming a common part of the management for these children. It is possible to use this technique in combination with urine testing or as the only method for monitoring the disease. The initial cost of the equipment is often offset by insurance coverage. The Autolet with the associated stylets provide the child with an easy way to obtain the blood sample for analysis. The blood sample is placed on a glucose-oxidase-impregnated strip which is read visually or by a meter such as the Glucometer, Dextrometer or Statek. Generally, two blood samples are obtained each day. The child is taught to read the test and directions are given to change insulin dosages on the basis of the results. The management routine tries to gain control of the disease as indicated by a morning glucose level of 80 to 120 mg/dl and an afternoon value between 120 and 150 mg/dl.

Another monitoring technique is the glycosolated hemoglobin (Hemoglobin A_1). This is done periodically in association with other monitoring techniques. The level of glycosolated hemoglobin represents the mean blood glucose concentration that was achieved during the preceding 8 to 12 week period. The normal values range between 5 and 7 percent and the goal of therapy is to maintain the child with diabetes at a level less than 10 percent. This objective data is shared with the child and family to help them understand how adequately the child's disease is being controlled.

Another important part of the monitoring of the disease is how well the child feels. Children can be well controlled, by virtue of the results of each of these techniques, and still not feel well. It is imperative to teach the child and family to discuss with the health team how the child is feeling so that attention is focused on this important area. Adjustments can be made in the management of the disease to help the child to feel better.

Monitoring of the disease is a particularly important part of the child's management over time as many life stresses and developmental needs can interefere with the successful control of the disease. Techniques for monitoring the disease are becoming more refined and it is possible to understand the disease through these techniques. It is important, however, not to lose sight of the uniqueness of each child while focusing on the advances in therapy.

Group Meetings

The organization of groups of children with similar disabilities and groups of parents of children with similar disabilities has received attention. The question of whether a group will be beneficial to a particular family is not an easy one to answer. The first consideration is given to the leadership of the group. Intelligent leadership is of top priority. One parent may benefit from a group led by another parent, while another one might be more comfortable if a professional person is leading the group.

The goals of the group are explored before suggesting that a child or parent attend the meeting. If the goal of the parent group is to raise money to support research, some parents may not be interested. If the goal of the group is to share common problems relating to rearing the child with a disability, the parent may be more interested.

Shostrom (1969) discusses groups in relation to sensitivity training. Some of his remarks are extremely applicable because the focus of many groups designed for children with disabilities, or their parents, is really on the way the individual feels about the disease and the ways of coping with it. The group frequently makes the individual focus on very "touchy" points. In this respect, some groups can be destructive rather than constructive for some individuals. The points that seem relevant to this discussion are the size of the group, the leadership, timing of joining a group, and avoidance of a group composed of close associates.

Size of Group.   To be fruitful, a group of less than six persons is not suggested. It is believed that a larger group is needed to work effectively with problems. A group of more than 16 is considered too unwieldy for a leader to handle, even with assistance. Therefore, the parent or child can use the size as a determinant in whether or not to join a particular group.

Leadership.   Shostrom (1969) makes reference to a study by Margaret Rioch that found that "natural leaders," without benefit of group work, can be as effective as highly trained workers. This point merely relates back to my comments about leadership and discourages health care providers from "downgrading" a group simply because it does not have professional leadership.

Timing of Joining a Group.   In relation to timing, Shostrom suggested that one should never join a group as a "fling, binge, or surrender to the unplanned." He suggests that a crisis (such as a disability) deserves more consideration and planning and that a decision to join a group should get the same consideration.

Avoidance of Close Associates.   Due to the nature of the group interaction, it is suggested that a person not join a group composed of close social or professional acquaintances. The nature of the discussions may be embarrassing under these conditions. Shostrom suggests that emphasis be placed on the confidentiality of the interactions in the group to guarantee the participants a measure of privacy.

Groups can be a most rewarding experience if utilized effectively. The parents or child decide if the group meets their particular needs.

Timing plays an important role in the adjustment of parents or children to a group. They may not be ready for a group at the onset of the disability but may be ready for it after a period of adjustment. For instance, school-age children may not benefit from hearing about another child's difficulties in getting regulated on insulin during the adolescent growth spurt if they are just learning to give themselves injections. The other child's difficulties may be more anxiety-producing to them than beneficial, but they may benefit greatly by meeting with other adolescents with similar problems when they reach adolescence.

In the same vein, parents who are overwhelmed with the problems of adjusting to a new disability may find other parents' problems more than they can handle. As time goes on, they may receive satisfaction and consolation by knowing that other parents have had difficulties similar to their own and have been able to "get over the hurdle."

The personalities of the parents and child may also influence their interest or lack of interest in joining a group. Some people do not enjoy being a part of a group, whereas others flourish with this type of activity.

As health care providers, we share with the parents and child the groups that are available and their functions. The decision to join or not to join the group is made by the individuals involved.

Regardless of the type of intervention utilized, whether it be group or some other process, the aim is to help the family and child gain a conscious appreciation of the crisis situation in order to solve problems creatively. This attempt at grasping the situation helps these people to achieve mastery of the difficult situation that resulted in the "crisis-like" situation. By learning to cope with the cause, the child or parents may be able to prevent further crises from developing.

REFERENCES

Benoliel, J.Q. Childhood diabetes. In A.L. Strauss, (Ed.), *Chronic illness and the quality of life.* St. Louis: Mosby, 1975.

Drash, A.L. Managing the child with diabetes mellitus. *Postgraduate Medicine* 63:85, 1978.

Engel, G.L. *Psychological development in health and disease.* Philadelphia: Saunders, 1962.

Fredholm, N.Z. The insulin pump: New method of insulin delivery. *American Journal of Nursing* 81:2024, 1981.

Gorwitz, K., Howen, G.G., Thompson, T., et al. Prevalence of diabetes in Michigan school-age children. *Diabetes* 25:122, 1976.

Guthrie, D.W. Children with diabetes. *Nursing* 7:48, 1977.

Hughes, J. Psychodynamic aspects of chronic disease and childhood diabetic management. Report of the Fifty-first Ross Conference on Pediatric Research, Columbus, Ohio, 1967.

Maluccio, A.N. A task-based approach to family therapy. In C. Getty & W. Humphreys (Eds.), *Understanding the family.* New York: Appleton—Century—Crofts, 1981.

Marshall, R.N. Juvenile diabetes mellitus. *American Family Physician* 25:193, 1982.

Nelson, W.E. *Textbook of pediatrics* (7th ed.). Philadelphia: Saunders, 1960.

Pharma-tips. Tile and Till. Indianapolis, Indiana: Eli Lilly 68:18, 1971.

Shostrom, E.L. Group therapy: Let the buyer beware. *Psychology Today* 3:37, 1969.

Travis, L.B. *An instructional aid on juvenile diabetes mellitus* (6th ed.). Galveston, Texas: Squibb and Sons, 1980.

Weil, W.B. Diabetes mellitus in children. In H.L. Barnett (Ed.), *Pediatrics* (16th ed.). New York: Appleton—Century—Crofts, 1977.

BIBLIOGRAPHY

Banion, C.R. The child with diabetes. *Comprehensive Pediatric Nursing* 3:21:1978.

Bennett, D.L., & Ward, M.S. Diabetes mellitus in adolescents: A comprehensive approach to outpatient care. *Southern Medical Journal* 70:705, 1977.

Berger, M., & Vranic, M. Exercise and diabetes mellitus. *Diabetes* 28:147, 1979.

Bircak, J., Mechelkova, D., Silesova, J., et al. Muscular and metabolic changes in child diabetes. *Pediatrics* 32:213, 1977.

Bruhn, J. Psychosocial influences in diabetes mellitus. *Postgraduate Medicine* 56:113, 1974.

Crosby, E.F. Childhood diabetes: The emotional adjustment of parents and child. *Canadian Nurse* 73:20, 1977.

Drash, A.L. The control of diabetes mellitus: Is it achievable? Is it desirable? *Journal of Pediatrics* 88:1074, 1976.

Drash, A.L. Managing the child with diabetes mellitus. *Postgraduate Medicine* 63:85, 1978.

Fenske, M. The endocrine system. In G.N. Scipien, M.W. Barnard, M.A. Chard, et al. (Eds.), *Comprehensive pediatric nusring*. New York: McGraw—Hill, 1975.

Fitchett, K. Juvenile diabetes. In S.M. Steele (Ed.), *Child health and the family*. New York: Masson, 1981.

Fonville, A.M. Teaching patients to rotate injection sites. *American Journal of Nursing* 78:880, 1978.

Friedland, J.M. Learning behaviors of a preadolescent with diabetes. *American Journal of Nursing* 76:59, 1976.

Gallagher, J.R. *Medical care of the adolescent* (2nd ed.). New York: Appleton—Century—Crofts, 1966.

Gellis, S.S. Infants of diabetic mothers. In W.E. Nelson (Ed.), *Textbook of pediatrics* (7th ed.). Philadelphia: Saunders, 1960.

Guthrie, D.W. Children with diabetes. *Nursing 77* 7:48, 1977.

Guthrie, D.W. Exercise, diets and insulin for child with diabetes. *Nursing* 7:48, 1977.

Guthrie, D.W., & Guthrie, R.A. Diabetic children: Special needs, diet, drugs and difficulties. *Nursing* 3:10, 1973.

Guthrie, D.W., & Guthrie, R.A. DKA: Breaking a vicious cycle. *Nursing* 78:60, 1978.

Hames, C., & McFarlane, J. Children with diabetes learning self-care in camp. *American Journal of Nursing* 73:1362, 1973.

Hauser, S.T., & Pollets, D. Psychological aspects of diabetes mellitus: A critical review. *Diabetes Care* 2:227, 1979.

Hayter, J. Five points in diabetic care. *American Journal of Nursing* 76:594, 1976.

Isenburg, P.L., & Barnett, D.M. Psychological problems in diabetes mellitus. *Medical Clinics of North America* 49:1125, 1965.

Jackson, R.L. Management of the young diabetic patient. Report of the Fifty-first Ross Conference on Pediatric Research, Columbus, Ohio, 1965.

Jelnick, L.S. The special needs of the adolescent with chronic illness. *American Journal of Maternal—Child Nursing* 2:57, 1977.

Kohler, E. Diabetic day. *Clinical Pediatrics* 17:24, 1978.

Koski, M.L., Ahlas, A., & Kumento, A. A psychosomatic follow-up study of childhood diabetics. *Acta Paedopsychiatrica* 42:12, 1976.

Malone, J. I., Van Cader, T.C., Edwards, W.C. Diabetic vascular changes in children. *Diabetes* 26:673, 1977.

McFarlane, J., & Homes, C.C. Children with diabetes learning self-care in camp. *American Journal of Nursing* 73:1362, 1973.

Moore, M.L. Diabetes in children. *American Journal of Nursing* 67:104, 1967.

Ory, M.G., & Kronenfeld, J.J. Living with juvenile diabetes mellitus. *Pediatric Nursing* 6:47, 1980.

Paz-Guevara, A.T., Hsu, T.H., & White, P. Juvenile diabetes mellitus after 40 years. *Diabetes* 24:559, 1975.

Pond, H. Parental attitudes toward children with chronic medical disorder: Special references to diabetes mellitus. *Diabetes Care* 2:425, 1979.

Schulman, D. Tips for improving urine testing techniques. *Nursing* 6:23, 1976.

Sultz, H.A., et al. Is mumps virus an etiologic factor in juvenile diabetes? *Journal of Pediatrics* 86:654, 1975.

Sussman, K.E. (Ed.). *Juvenile-type diabetes and its complications.* Springfield, Ill.: Thomas, 1971.

Tarnow, J.D., & Tomlinson, N. Juvenile diabetes: Impact on the child and family. *Psychosomatics* 19:487, 1978.

Tietz, W., & Vidmer, J.T. The impact of coping styles on the control of juvenile diabetes. *Psychiatric Medicine* 3:67, 1972.

Tomm, K.M., McArthur, R.G., & Leakey, M.D. Psychologic management of children with diabetes mellitus. *Clinical Pediatrics* 16:1151, 1977.

Wishner, W.J., & O'Brien, W.D. Diabetes and the family. *Medical Clinics of North America* 62:849, 1978.

10

Health Promotion of the Child with Physical Disabilities

Shirley Steele

Improved health care management of childbearing women permits earlier detection of problems. The high-risk pregnancy is monitored by a variety of means, such as sonograms, oxytocin challenge tests (OCT), amniocentesis, and urinary excretion tests for estriol determination. This intensive surveillance of a pregnancy may result in the parents developing fears that the child will not be "normal." The parents may develop realistic fears concerned with whether the pregnancy is of too great a risk to the woman or fetus to warrant its continuation. Each test that is done may be anxiety-provoking, and the anxiety may be heightened or lessened by the test results. A test result that signals fetal distress may cause the woman to begin grieving for the "normal" child she hoped and planned for. A woman whose pregnancy is progressing normally may have a sonogram late in the pregnancy to determine fetal size or position and learn that she has a placenta previa or other problem that is asymptomatic but can be diagnosed by the sonogram. This discovery helps with the monitoring and management of the pregnancy, but it can cause the parents to feel disbelief or dismay.

Whether the pregnancy was considered of high risk from conception or evolved as high-risk during the process, many of the treatments are the same. There need to be changes in the woman's lifestyle that help to promote the best possible outcome from the pregnancy. She may need to make alterations in the amount of activity she can have, alter her dietary patterns, make changes in employment or recreational activities, make revised arrangements for other children, alter her relationship with her sexual partner, or make arrangements for the possibility of additional financial considerations. The way the woman is able to cope with these changes in her lifestyle is assessed by the nurse so that she or he can help to support the woman through the immediate crisis and help to enable her to manage the potential crises that may occur, such as a premature delivery, a surgical procedure, or an infant born with a disability or an inability to survive.

PREMATURE LABOR

When labor begins prematurely, the family is not fully prepared for the activity. Depending on the length of gestation, the early delivery predisposes the infant to potential hazards. The health care providers and family are faced with the situational crisis which surrounds the birth of an infant before the expected date of arrival. Aguilera and Messick (1978, p. 75) state:

> Research have identified four phases or tasks the mother must work through if she is to come out of the experience in a healthy way.
>
> 1. The mother must realize that she may lose the infant. This anticipatory grief involves a gradual withdrawal from the relationship already established with the child, during the pregnancy.
> 2. She must acknowledge failure in her maternal function to deliver a full-term healthy infant.
> 3. After separation from the infant due to a prolonged hospital stay she must resume her relationship in preparation for the infant's homecoming.
> 4. She must prepare herself for the job of caring for the infant through an understanding of the infant's special needs and growth patterns.

Mothers who are more distressed when the infant is in danger are actually dealing with the stress in an effective manner. The mothers who are less concerned are actually the ones who are closer to a crisis situation.

According to Aguilera and Messick, a crisis is defined as the point at which a person cannot solve a problem using established coping mechanisms. As a result, anxiety is heightened and tension is aroused. The person finds himself or herself mentally upset and unable to solve problems. Crisis intervention is essential to help the person to return to normal equilibrium. Crisis intervention is viewed as short-term, inexpensive, and focused directly on the problem that precipitates the crisis.

The stress or crisis of prematurity is a major problem for the mother to resolve. If the stress situation is exaggerated by the child being disabled, it poses a potentially greater crisis. An attempt is made to establish support systems for the family members so that they can cope with these two situational crises that are potentially devastating to the family. In addition to the effects on the mother, there is evolving evidence that fathers are indirectly affected by these situations, as there is a higher incidence of divorce in families with disabled children. It is important to facilitate the early mother–child and father–child bonding by allowing interaction as early and as frequently as possible.

According to Ross (1964, p. 56):

> It is the mother who "produces" the infant, it is she who "gives" it birth. If the "product" turns out to be defective (a term used here to include all defects in the

child, whether physical or intellectual), the mother perceives this as a defect in
something she has produced.

The mother who delivers in the hospital may have her feelings of defeat
reinforced by the hospital staff. The maternity unit is considered to be a "happy"
unit. Fortunately, most of the events taking place there result in a new life and a
fulfillment of a goal for the child's parents. The child with a defect is not an
ordinary part of the unit. The staff frequently withdraws and does not give the
mother the support she needs to cope with the birth of a child with a defect.
According to Ross (1964, p. 56):

> The mother is thrust into the stark reality very soon after the birth. The father,
> because of his less active role in the birth and immediate postdelivery period,
> can deny the situation longer than the mother. The father also is able to fall back
> on the defensive fantasy that the child is not really his own.

The nursing personnel in the delivery room have a vital role to play in
helping the parents to begin the coping process. The nurse is careful of her or his
facial expressions. Even the forehead above the surgical mask can give nonverbal
clues that something is wrong. Withholding the infant from the mother's sight is
another way of saying that the child is "less than expected." If the mother has
actively participated in the labor and delivery process, she will be eager to view
the child immediately after birth. It is only fair to prepare her for the child with the
defect and to introduce her to her child. The silence which frequently prevails
during this crisis period in the delivery room is most anxiety-producing for the
mother. She may very well imagine a child more severely disabled than her infant
actually is. This needless anxiety may influence the future mother—child
relationship. In addition, it may lead to the mother's mistrusting the medical and
nursing personnel, in whom she will need to have confidence during the
long-term care of the child.

After the announcement of the birth of an infant with a disability has been
made to the parents, many different defense mechanisms may be utilized by the
parents. Some of these defense mechanisms are described by Ross (1964) and are
summarized briefly here. She may choose to repress the incident, trying to keep
the disabled child out of her conscious awareness. She may utilize projection,
trying to treat the child as though the source of the infant was outside herself. She
may utilize sublimation, whereby she represses the impulse until it can be
changed from a socially objectionable to a socially valued outlet. She may use
intellectualization, whereby she controls affects and impulses through thinking
about them instead of experiencing them. Another possibility is displacement,
which can involve aggressive impulses against herself. Another mechanism is
controlling; this allows her to interfere with suggestions or attempts of others, or
allows her to comply without thinking. Denial is a very commonly utilized
mechanism; it allows the mother to keep threatening perceptions from coming to
the surface. Withdrawal is a mechanism which may occur as a temporary and
immediate reponse to a threat and usually lasts only until she is able to bring
another defense mechanism into play.

An understanding of the possible mechanisms the mother uses contributes to the nursing management. The mechanism of withdrawal is frequently utilized immediately after delivery. It can be expressed by a desire to sleep. This can be very beneficial for the mother, as she needs rest following the labor and delivery. She also needs sleep to aid in developing strength to deal with the stress produced by delivering an infant with a disability.

Defense mechanisms help the parents during crisis periods. The assistance the parents receive can turn these defense mechanisms into useful strategies for coping with the unique problems. The use of denial, for instance, is not abnormal at first. However, its persistence can be abnormal. How, then, can the nurse help the mother to relinquish the use of denial? One way is to show the infant to the mother early. The infant is shown to the mother while the nurse is available to answer questions. The mother is encouraged to explore the child slowly and carefully. The nurse observes the mother closely to interpret her tolerance level. If it is evident the mother cannot benefit from further time with the infant and nurse, then the session is terminated. A new time is set up for the mother to see the infant again. Viewing the child in the nursery can help to prepare the mother for the next visit. Rooming-in is not discouraged unless the infant is severely disabled and needs vigilant observation. The less severely disabled infant may benefit by being close to the mother so that when she feels the urge to see and handle the infant, she can do so. The policies governing many maternity areas sometimes interfere with the optimum times for mother–infant or father–infant interactions to take place. Rooming-in can circumvent this problem. The concept of family-centered maternity care can facilitate the successful integration of the disabled child into the family unit.

Following the birth of an infant, the mother undergoes a period of time when she relates to the infant in terms of who he or she looks like. This is a short period of time that aids in the mother's task of establishing maternal identity. It is hypothesized that mothers of infants with defects can be hampered in their process of establishing maternal identity. It is felt that these mothers have a decreased ability to cope with an infant if there is any kind of stress during the pregnancy or during the child's early life. A child with a defect is frequently a product of a stressful pregnancy and is an additional source of stress at birth. Mothers have reported shock, anxiety, and hostility towards their children with defects. These reactions interfere with the mother's ability to establish bonding with the infant.

The more natural the periods of time the mother and infant spend together, the easier the process of adjustment is for both of them. Special care necessary for the infant is introduced slowly. The mother cannot be expected to assume responsibility for these procedures until she has an appropriate orientation demonstration and practice. When the mother is able to assume the responsibility for these procedures, her denial of the infant's condition is usually lessened or alleviated.

Ross (1964) states that "religious attitudes" may offer rationalizations whereby the child with a disability comes to be viewed as a special sign of grace, for only the most worthy of mothers would be "entrusted" with the care of a disabled child. This is but one variable that can influence the mother's reaction to her infant. The verbal responses of the mother may give clues to her real feelings regarding the infant. However, her verbal responses may be conditioned by her background or her family rather than by her true feelings.

Another conditioned response might be in relation to old wives' tales, such as, "I expected the child to be affected because I was scared during a thunderstorm." This comment not only indicates an attempt to find a reason for the disability, it represents a conditioned response that is not based on fact. The mother's true feelings are not unleashed in the statements. A nurse's response might be, "It is difficult to understand the reasons for an infant being born with a disability. It is also natural to be disappointed." This is probably not the appropriate time to deal with misconceptions about the old wives' tales. This can be handled during later interactions.

The impact of this birth is extremely personal and individualized and no set plan of care will meet the mother's needs. The nurse needs to be alert for clues and to act appropriately. For instance, the mother may ask the nurse if she has ever seen another infant with this defect. The nurse needs to show her or his concern for the infant and then to answer the question. An example would be, "I know you are concerned about your infant's cleft lip and I can certainly appreciate your concern. I have seen many other infants with similar problems." Statements of this nature can help the mother to learn that she is not the only person to witness this problem.

The mother and father begin a mourning process for the normal child who was expected. This mourning process progresses from the initial phase of numbness and disbelief, to the dawning awareness of the disappointment and feeling of loss with the accompanying affective and physical symptoms, to an intense re-experiencing of the memories and expectations, which gradually reduce the hypercathexis for the idealized child. This mourning process is a very important part of the postdelivery period. Mourning is a strenuous process and it leaves very little energy for the person to deal with other activities of daily life. The timing of this is crucial, as it happens right after the stress situation of birth. The imposition of too many crisis situations at the same time makes it extremely difficult for the person to regain equilibrium. During mourning, the mother is extremely vulnerable. Less is needed to upset her than would ordinarily be the case. Her ways of handling past stress situations play a big part in her adjustment to this crisis situation.

The mother needs time to work through her own feelings. Frequently, a medical social worker can be instrumental in helping her with this process. Caplan (1959) states that it is a very difficult thing for a family, particularly for a mother, to deal with a child who has a congenital anomaly or a birth injury. If she is left on her own, she is very likely to develop a disturbed relationship with the child and so compound the difficulties of rearing.a child with a disability.

Specific care of the infant is demonstrated prior to discharge, and the mother returns the demonstration before discharge from the hospital. The nurse discusses adaptations needed in the home and the family's plans for completing arrangements. If the family is interested, a referral to a community health nurse is made.

DISCHARGE

Mother and Infant

Early discharge of maternity patients results in a short period of time being available for the mother to adapt to her situation prior to discharge. Early discharge can be beneficial in reuniting her with her normal home situation. However, it also means that responsibility for tasks associated with the family are prematurely added to her schedule while she is still involved in grief work.

As time passes, the mother is usually in a better position to begin to manage the problems that result from the child's disability. The information given the mother during her confinement will need to be discussed to make certain that she has retained the information for use. It is natural that she will be able to ask more questions as she begins the actual care of the child.

The mother may need encouragement to bathe and hold the child. Her normal maternal instincts to care for the child may be overshadowed by her fear of the defect. If the defect necessitates a change in bathing techniques, a community health nurse can demonstrate the altered bathing procedure. An example of this might be a child discharged with an untreated meningomyelocele. With her other children, the mother has used a small plastic bath tub. With her disabled child, she is hesitant to use this method, so she does not bathe the infant. A community health nurse can demonstrate proper handling of the child and bathing with a sponge or washcloth. During the bathing demonstration, the nurse emphasizes the need to prevent pressure on the sac. The mother is taught to place a protective shield below the meningomyelocele. A small piece of plastic or saran wrap can serve this purpose (Fig. 10-1). The nurse tells the mother to observe for drainage and to report it to her physician. She or he demonstrates the proper positioning after the bath, placing the infant on the abdomen rather than on the back. If the lesion is very large, the sac may need support with sandbags on each side of the infant. The infant's head is turned to the side and the usual precautions are taken to avoid suffocation. Positioning is especially important as the infant may have a decrease in motor control, being unable to move the head without assistance. Care of the child with a myelomeningocele is covered in greater detail in the chapter.

The reactions of others to the infant influence the mother's reactions. It is very difficult to form positive feelings when everyone else seems repelled by the situation. The nurse is in a perfect position to demonstrate a positive response to the infant. To be most effective, the nurse needs to work through her or his own feelings regarding the defect. The nurse views the infant alone before viewing the infant with the mother present, if this is possible. Then she or he has an opportunity to "see beyond the defect" to view the infant as an individual. Focusing on the child as a person first and on the disability later is an important part of learning how to cope with disabilities.

A situation involving the birth of a child with a cleft lip provides an example with which to illustrate an appropriate positive response by the nurse. When an infant is born, the cleft becomes a barrier to the normal tendency for the mother to kiss and hug the child. The nurse can demonstrate acceptance by warmly hugging the child. This close interaction, accompanied by endearing words, can

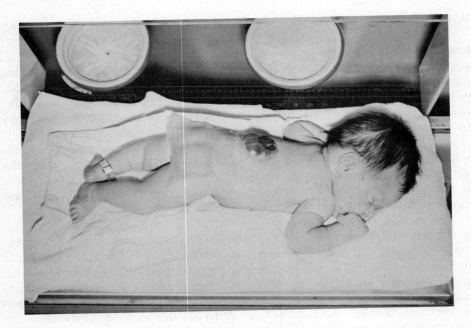

Figure 10-1. Protective shield placed below the meningomyelocele of an infant.

be very reassuring to the mother. After cuddling the child and smiling warmly, the nurse can place the infant in the mother's arms. A statement such as, "You must be eager to know what the doctors can offer your baby" will be useful in determining the mother's readiness for information and need for support.

It is important to realize that the extent of the defect has little bearing on persons' responses. Even a very small defect, such as an extra digit, can cause some people concern. The nurse attempts to predetermine the amount of concern the family has for the defect. The impact of any defect, no matter how small or large, can be determined only by direct association with the parents. Each parent will have a individualized reaction to the disability that influences the nursing management.

The Mother without the Infant

The early discharge of the mother results in a separation of mother and infant. The infant may not be ready for discharge because of the disability. The parents are encouraged to visit the infant regularly.

The nurse is able to evaluate how the mother is coping with the separation during regular visits. She or he is able to assess how the mother is readjusting to her family. The period prior to the infant's discharge can be effectively utilized to provide the mother with opportunities to grieve for the normal child she expected and to derive satisfaction from the child she delivered.

The nurse refers to the child by name to emphasize to the mother that she has another child. Discussions with the parents about the infant and the problems connected with the disability help to bring the infant into the mainstream of the family. If the infant is not included in the conversation with the parents by telephone or during visitation, separation provides the parents with an opportunity to deny the existence of the problem and perhaps even the existence of the infant.

Separation can be effectively utilized to give the mother an opportunity to recover from the crisis created by the birth prior to assuming responsibility for the infant's care. However, the separation period is enriched by regular visits to the hospital to see the child. The parents are given the opportunity to touch, hold, and feed the infant as the infant's condition permits. In this way, they begin to know the child while someone else is assuming the primary responsibility for the child's care.

The mother discharged without her only child may feel a real emptiness when she returns home. She expects a reward for her labor and delivery. Going home without her infant does not fulfill her expectations. She may long for her infant just to talk to. Her days may be filled with loneliness. The mother who has young children may find her days less empty during these trying hours. However, the other children are too busy with their own lives, and regaining their mother's attention, to be concerned with their mother's sadness. The mother's vulnerability increases when she does not have someone to share feelings with and to talk to about the infant.

It is very important for the mother to receive progress reports from the hospital. These reports can be given by the physician, the nurse, or the clergy. All are in a position to offer the mother information from their own special vantage point. The physician is responsible for keeping her up-to-date in relation to the medical plans and the infant's prognosis. The nurse keeps her informed of the infant's eating, weight gain, sleeping, and any developmental milestones achieved. Mothers appreciate knowing that their infant yawns when finished eating, or sucks on his or her fist, or has one lock of hair that curls. These are the very personal things which help the mother identify with the infant as a person. The clergy provides another dimension. A clergy has an "extended power" which gives solace to a person who "believes." When he or she calls and says, "I saw Danny today," he or she provides a source of "higher" quality. The visit and call are an important part of the mother's routine while waiting for the infant to be discharged. If possible, a time is arranged with the mother by each of the health care providers so that she does not get needlessly apprehensive when the telephone rings. It is human nature to expect the calls from the hospital to be "bad news." If she becomes anxious by the ring, she may not be able to benefit from the messages planned to reduce her anxiety. The mother also needs to be aware that she can call the nursery to find out about her infant. This spontaneous call may help to relieve some anxiety as it builds up.

When it is evident that the infant is nearing the time for discharge, the mother is asked to spend extended periods of time at the hospital assuming total care for the child. In this way, she can get support and help if it is needed before assuming full responsibility for the child's care.

Chronic Sorrow

Olshansky (1962) points out that the ability of parents to handle the problems of the disabled child will tend to vary with the passing of time. The parents' ability to cope coincides with significant milestones in the child's development. For example, the child born with cerebral palsy may be a great shock to the parents. The initial shock is cushioned when the child survives the initial critical period after delivery. The child learns to suck after practice and patience and begins to gain weight. The parents receive satisfaction from their child's physical progress. They begin to question whether the original diagnosis of cerebral palsy is legitimate. When the child does not sit up at 6 months, they relate this to the rough start. When the child still does not sit up at 9 months, they become aware that he or she is much slower than other children. When the child is not able to sit at 12 months, their disapppointment is evident. They are reminded of the diagnosis and they are made painfully aware of their child's problem. At this point in time, the parents are less likely to function as effectively as when a crisis is not present. At the next major developmental milestone, they may again be reminded of the diagnosis. This continues throughout the child's life cycle. Some of the milestones may be more "pain-producing" than others. These might be the milestones of going to regular school, or late adolescense, when the child should be planning marriage. This phenomenom is called chronic sorrow.

Parent Education

The parents are considered as integral and vital members of the health care team. The parents need to know exactly what they are expected to do for the child. Health care providers must teach the parents how to manage their child in the home throughout the period when the child needs additional health care services.

The young child spends the majority of his or her time at home. The child with a severe anomaly spends an even greater amount of time in the home. To guarantee maximum function for the child, the home must provide a milieu beneficial to learning and growth. Most of the responsibility for this nurturance resides with the parents or other caregivers. Therefore, the parents need to be aware of ways to stimulate their disabled child's development.

Infant stimulation programs are available in some communities to encourage development of children with disabilities. Early stimulation programs focus on strengthening the mothering or parenting role. The curriculum includes developmental assessment, feeding techniques and behavior, nutritional guidance, techniques for developing sensory and motor skills, and behavior-shaping techniques. The early institution of programs is an attempt to capitalize on the most significant period of growth (Godfrey, 1975). A benefit of these programs is that the child is not developing poor habits that are difficult to break by the time he or she reaches the age to enter school, and medical care can be sought to correct or treat disabilities at an early age.

Children with severe anomalies need periodic re-evaluation so that the parents have an up-to-date report of assets. The parents also need help to know when to expect the child to achieve additional skills. For example, a child with cerebral palsy may have a gross motor deficiency. The mother learns to expect the child to be slower than her other children. She continues to feed the child without re-evaluating to see if the child is maturing enough to begin the developmental task of self-feeding. During the occupational therapy or nursing re-evaluation, the child is fitted with a feeding device, the child is placed in a comfortable chair with a feeding tray, and a bib is applied. The child is given puréed food and encouraged in self-feeding. The child's efforts are rewarded and encouraged by praise. He or she is allowed to continue feeding himself or herself until he or she seems to be tiring or becomes frustrated with the task. This demonstration helps the parents to include self-feeding in the daily routine.

After the re-evaluation of the child, the parent is given specific realistic goals to achieve before the next clinic visit. In the interim, the mother is encouraged to telephone when she has a question.

GRIEF RESPONSES TO LONG-TERM ILLNESS AND DISABILITY

Children with long-term illness are constantly reminded and serve as reminders to others that their health status deviates from wellness. The realization that all is not well can cause grief, bereavement, and mourning. In contrast to the grief reactions caused by death, which are eventually resolved, the reactions to long-term illness persist for extended periods of time and may never be resolved. In actuality, the parents of a child born with a disability can engage in chronic sorrow that simulates the grief response surrounding death. The child who has a long-term illness is aware that his or her parents' grief response cannot be resolved, as the illness cannot be reversed.

Kübler-Ross (1969) identifies five phases of grief associated with the dying process: denial and isolation, anger, bargaining, depression, and acceptance. It is usually assumed that these same responses occur commonly with any significant loss. The degree of the grief response and the length of time it lasts can vary significantly. A major difference between the loss by death and the loss by disability is that the client is actually present to mourn his or her own loss.

Grieving that takes place before a loss takes place is termed *anticipatory grief.* This reaction is seen in hospital units when a child becomes so incapacitated that the caretakers are unable to receive gratification from interacting with their own child. The caretakers, in their anticipation of the death, interact with other children on the unit. The same reaction occurs when separations less final than death occur. For example, when an adolescent is preparing to leave home for college, a parent can go through a grief reaction, actually mourning the anticipated loss of the adolescent from the home.

The loss of a part of a body or the significance of long-term illness or disability can result in periods of mourning. The mourning period is influenced by the meaning of the loss to the child, the impact the loss has on the child's lifestyle, and the responses of significant others to the loss. There is a wide variation in the way that children respond when an insult affects their personal being. Careful observation and assessment are warranted to draw inferences about the impact of the insult on a particular child.

The meaning of the grief responses to illness or disability can only be understood if the child's total environment is taken into consideration. The degree of permanence associated with the loss influences the grief response. Initially, the child usually feels that it is possible to recover completely from the insult and that life will return to "normal" within a short period of time. At the same time, however, the child questions his or her self-worth and the worth of himself or herself to others on the basis of current reality. While the child clings to the desire to be free of the pain of change necessitated by the disability or illness, anger arises when the return to "normal" fades from reality. Anger can interfere with interpersonal relationships with persons that can be most helpful in providing the child the assurance needed to get through the grieving process. The same responses can be taking place in the minds of the caretakers, making it difficult to help families to be supportive of one another. Therefore, the disability can not only interfere with the child's ability to interact effectively with others, it can interfere with the ability of others to engage in effective interpersonal relationships with the child.

The behaviors expressed by the child and caretakers are dynamic and vary according to the point on the grief continuum that each reaches. Werner-Beland (1980) cautions that through the expression of grief behaviors, the child is seeking reassurance that he or she did not do anything wrong that resulted in the insult, that he or she is still acceptable to others, and that no additional harm will result in either the physical or psychologic domains.

There is still a great deal to learn about the grief, mourning, and bereavement that take place when long-term illness or disability occurs. For example, why are some children who have severe disabilities able to achieve adequately in the community while others are not? Why does the grief of a child with a "minor illness" sometimes exceed the grief of a child with a "major illness?" The important factor to keep in mind is that reactions to illness and disability are individualized, and therefore phases of grieving are a framework that helps in understanding but that does not result in a prescription for care. Management is based on the responses of the child during the period following the insult and is adjusted according to the ongoing changes in the child's behavior. In addition, the family system is considered, as the loss belongs to each member of the family and roles are adjusted within the family on the basis of the loss.

Fostering Growth and Development

The infant, toddler, and preschool years are often spent in the home. However, some disabled children have the advantage of attending educational programs that supplement the care given in the home. As most of the care and nurturing takes place at home, the family environment is particularly important to the child's welfare.

When a child has a disability, the expectations of the family for the child are often lowered. This can result in the child actually achieving at a lower level. While the family should not set unrealistically high expectations for the child, too-low expectations are equally detrimental to the child's progress.

During the preschool years, the child is achieving several major psychosocial stages. According to Erikson (1963), the infant acquires a sense of trust while overcoming a sense of mistrust, the toddler acquires a sense of autonomy while combating a sense of shame and doubt, and the preschooler is acquiring a sense of initiative while overcoming a sense of guilt. During each of these stages, the disabled child is more vulnerable to negative responses due to the effects of the disability on the child and family. Recognizing that the disabled infant can develop mistrust more readily than an able-bodied infant, that a disabled toddler can have shame and doubt, and that the disabled preschooler can have a sense of guilt leads to the realization that counseling and parent effectiveness training are essential components of the health care management for these families.

As the child reaches the school-age years, the influence of persons outside the child's family increases. Starting school can be the first time that the disabled child is separated from the family for extended periods of time. It is in school that other persons assess the child's growth and development and draw assumptions about the child's needs. It is at this time that the child's perception of himself or herself becomes more apparent to others.

Self-perception

Some of the usual parameters used to assess a child's perception of self are not as useful when evaluating a child with a disability. Factors that are usually evaluated to assess a child's perception of self include:

1. Posture.
2. Quality of voice.
3. The role assumed in free play activities.
4. Conversation and speech content.
5. Quality and content of drawings.
6. Quality and content of storytelling.

These areas need to be assessed carefully, as a child with a disability can have a posture deficit that interferes with the child's assumption of an appropriate posture. In this instance, the poor posture is not necessarily a reflection of the child's perception of himself or herself. Another example is when a child with cerebral palsy has a voice of poor quality due to muscle involvement rather than due to a decreased perception of himself or herself.

Even though the six factors listed above can be influenced by organic components, it is well to keep them in mind when assessing the child's perception of himself or herself as they have a bearing on the way the child perceives himself or herself.

The projective technique of storytelling also aids in assessing how the child perceives himself or herself and his or her environment. Using a relatively ambiguous picture, the child is asked to tell a story that will be influenced by the child's knowledge, values, attitudes, and feelings. A child without physical or mental limitations uses his or her imagination and projects a story that is representative of his or her experiences and self-concept. A child with a disability can have limited experiences and can tell a story that is less descriptive than an able-bodied child will give. However, storytelling can give clues to the loneliness and feelings of rejection that the child harbours due to negative stimuli that he or she receives.

The child's perception of his or her physical development plays an important role in the way he or she views himself or herself. Frequently, the physical development of the child with a long-term illness is hindered, causing the child concern, frustration, and/or disappointment. Common variances in physical development include short stature, asymmetry, slow development, and distorted muscular development. While these interferences are real, it is essential to understand the child's perceptions of the differences, as it is the perceptual accuracy or inaccuracy that determines appropriate intervention measures. For example, if the child states that he or she is ugly because one ear is lower than the other (perceptual accuracy), the nurse can acknowledge that it is true that one ear is lower than the other and then call attention to a positive physical feature, such as beautiful blue eyes or attractive hair. In this way, the nurse is able to influence the child's overall perception of himself or herself by giving the child positive affirmation for positive attributes while acknowledging the reality voiced by the child. When a child states that he or she is stupid because another child called him or her stupid (perceptual inaccuracy), the nurse can state that he or she does not agree with this assessment and give the child examples of his or her attributes that discredit the peer assessment. For example, the nurse can cite an accomplishment of the child that is age-appropriate to emphasize the child's cognitive skills that negate stupidity. In addition, the nurse encourages the child to demonstrate age-appropriate skills to peers and then praises the child for accomplishments so that his or her peers are made aware of the child's abilities. Children with long-term illness are more susceptible to negative criticism than able-bodied children, so it is essential to find ways to provide them with affirmation that positively influences their perception of themselves.

The child's perception of his or her cognitive abilities influences whether or not he or she believes that it is possible to be a competent human being. The child develops self-confidence by mastering increasingly complex skills. If the child witnesses failures while attempting developmental tasks, negative perceptions of himself or herself can emerge. When a child has a developmental disability, he or she is often painfully aware of weaknesses. It is essential to provide the child with opportunities to exhibit mastery and to emphasize these achievements so that the child's perception of himself or herself can include a sense of competency.

Other Persons' Perceptions of the Disabled

Richardson (1969) found that when a visible impairment is present, there is a tendency for social interactions to be strained. He studied the preferences of children and found that given a choice, the children preferred:

1. A normal child.
2. A child with crutches and a leg brace.
3. A child in a wheelchair.

4. A child with a left arm amputated.
5. A child with a facial disfigurement.
6. An obese child.

This order of preference prevailed with uniformity among various age and ethnic groups of children. Furthermore, Richardson found that children's negative attitudes about visible impairments increased with age. This factor is especially significant, as it is verified that the physical impairment can continue to be a social barrier beyond the child's early socialization period.

Affirmation Techniques

Affirmation techniques for children with visible disabilities are not very different from affirmation techniques for able-bodied children. However, it may be necessary to make these techniques more noticeable to help to counterbalance negative stimuli that are more prevalent in the disabled child's experiences. Suggested affirmation techniques include the following:

1. Focus on the child's assets and teach the child to recognize these assets.
2. Establish an environment where the child is genuinely respected and his or her activities are vital rather than merely being time-consuming or "busy-work."
3. Give praise to the child in front of others so that attention is called to the child's accomplishments.
4. When discipline or corrective action is necessary, implement it in privacy rather than in front of others.
5. Encourage the child to develop a close relationship with another child who is able to show him or her interest and concern.
6. Have the child display accomplishments where others can see and appreciate them.
7. Praise the child for small but significant progress in any domain—e.g., intellectual or social skills or mobility.
8. Give praise freely for small, significant accomplishments; do not wait for major accomplishments to occur before giving praise.

PUBLIC LAW 94-142

Undoubtedly, one of the most compelling laws was passed in 1975. It is known as the Education of All Handicapped Children Act and is commonly referred to as Public Law 94-142. Promoters of the law rejoice over the message the law supplies, while opponents to the law continue to deny the message of the law while proposing reasons that the law is unrealistic.

PL 94-142 requires that handicapped children be educated with nonhandicapped children to the greatest extent possible. The law directs society to educate these children in the least restrictive environment (LRE) and have individualized educational programs (IEP) for each child.

An IEP is a written plan for each handicapped child that includes:

1. A statement of present level of performance.
2. Short-term educational objectives.
3. Yearly goals.
4. Specific special education and related services.
5. The date special services will start and the duration of these services.
6. The extent of participation in regular classroom activities.
7. Objective criteria for evaluating the success of the program.

The IEP can be assessed to determine if each child is receiving adequate services on an ongoing basis.

The LRE guidelines include very few specific criteria. However, it is generally assumed that the criteria suggest the following:

1. There should be nonhandicapped children in the same setting.
2. Nonhandicapped and handicapped children should have experiences together, and the extent of this interaction should be documented.
3. The physical facilities should be adaptable to meet the needs of the handicapped children.
4. Parents, children, and selected advocates have the right to question any educational recommendations that lead to special class placement of handicapped children.

The law and legal actions arising from it clearly indicate that school districts must assess their practices and, if necessary, bring them into alignment with the intent of the law. As a result of the language of the law, many persons openly discuss the pros and cons of "mainstreaming."

Mainstreaming

Society has a long history of separating persons who do not fit the "norm" of the mainstream of society. Therefore, it is not surprising that implementation of PL 94-142 has not been met with universal enthusiasm.

Architectural barriers and expensive buildings that preceded passage of the law make the enactment of the law difficult or expensive. School districts invested large sums of money to erect schools that segregated the able-bodied and learning-able children from the disabled and mentally disadvantaged children. Teachers were prepared in "special or exceptional education" to teach these children by special means and with special equipment and curriculums. Vast resources accumulated for educating these children away from other children. Often this model of education did not adequately prepare the child with a disability to function at his or her maximum level in society.

The mandate to change this model of education raised many unresolved questions and issues which persist to the present day. Some of the questions and issues are as follows:

1. How can a small school district afford to provide very specialized services needed to educate multiply handicapped children, such as occupational, physical, and speech therapies?
2. How can parents who cling to the notion that a specialized school is better than mainstreaming their child in a regular school be satisfied with the new model?
3. How can attitudes of peers, teachers, school nurses, and principals be changed to accept these children into regular classrooms?
4. What effects will the integration of children with special needs have on the quality of education that the other children receive?
5. The burden of proof is on school officials to justify removal of any handicapped child from regular classrooms and campuses. Will this result in legal cases when parents feel their children are not receiving the services consistent with the full intent of the law?
6. How can school administrators deal with community attitudes that prevent them from dismantling separate and segregated programs that exist in their schools?
7. Are there sufficient personnel resources to help the disabled child who does not adapt readily to a new, less protective school environment?
8. If the disabled children progress less slowly in a regular school environment, can adjustments be made in the school placement to accommodate the child's needs?
9. Should school districts be required to bear the total expense of removing architectural barriers that interfere with the education of handicapped children?
10. Without clear and unambiguous data to support the notion that children should be mainstreamed, does the law move school personnel more quickly than is justified?
11. Are some handicapped children going to be disadvantaged by being in a regular classroom when conditions are not fully conducive to meeting their needs?

It is obvious from this list of questions that mainstreaming is a subject that raises lively debate. The possibility that PL 94-142 will solve all of the educational problems of handicapped children is slim. Yet few persons can deny that the intent of the law is sound. The time is long overdue for society to be responsive to the special needs of children with special problems. Society is clearly more humane when opportunities are provided for all children to participate equally in its offerings. Disabled children are worthy of the same consideration and opportunities as children without handicaps. However, it will take a great deal of education to change the attitudes and feelings of members of society who doubt the value of children who do not fit their model of the norm. Laws are powerful motivators, but laws alone cannot change attitudes that are deeply ingrained in traditions that are counter to the law.

Adapted Physical Education (PL 94-142)

The law focuses on physical education as a component of the curriculum. It mandates that physical education be provided for all handicapped children. The law implies that despite their handicaps, these children are essentially well and have the same needs for exercise, play, and psychomotor development as their nonhandicapped peers.

The law requires that physical education be adapted to meet the needs of the handicapped child regardless of the degree of handicap that is present. Physical education is identified as a *primary service* of education, which makes it distinctly different from such services such as physical and occupational therapy, which are *related services* (Duke and Sherrill, 1980).

Adapted physical education is the science of analyzing movement, identifying deficiencies within the psychomotor domain, and providing remediation that focuses on the identified deficiencies. Consistent with the requirements of the IEP, yearly goals are established for psychomotor achievement, with identified objectives, beginning date, duration of services, and the integration that is taking place with able-bodied students clearly stated.

Adapted physical education can be offered in a variety of formats, such as:

1. Regular physical education class.
2. Regular class with modifications.
3. Part-time participation in a special program.
4. Total participation in a special program.
5. Individual instruction.

The rationale for the particular placement is noted in the IEP, and the decision for the selection of the particular format is clearly identified.

The adapted physical education program is influenced by a variety of factors, including:

1. Effects of medication on activity.
2. Effects of medication on behavior.
3. Current physical well-being.
4. Limitations posed by the health problem.

In order for safety to be considered, it is important to have arrangements for first aid and guidelines for emerging medical services available. The health care providers are an essential component of the adapted physical education program, as they provide guidance to the program to help in its safe implementation.

Physical Activities

The child with a physical disability may have a great deal or a minimal amount of interference with body function. In either case, the physical activity that the child engages in will have to be realistically assessed and adjusted to meet his or her needs. Often, the more severely involved child has increased amounts of leisure time, as the child is excluded from many activities of daily living that fill in the able-bodied child's day. The creative use of leisure time becomes imperative for the child who has an increased amount of time to spend on leisure. Usually, leisure time is filled in with recreational activities. Recreational activities are usually geared to the able-bodied child, so considerable attention is focused on how to adapt recreational activities to make them meaningful for the disabled child.

The role of recreation in the life of the disabled child can not be underestimated. At times, the primary way that these children have to participate in social interactions outside of the family is through recreation. Attempts are made to integrate the disabled child into activities that involve able-bodied children, as well. Otherwise the disabled child can be segregated into a system that only includes other disabled children. Many sports activities can be successfully adapted to meet the recreational needs of disabled children regardless of the severity of their disability and its resultant handicap.

The use of sports to augment the physical therapy of disabled children is essential. Sports activities help to improve muscle function. The child is encouraged to try to use motions that contribute to his or her therapy routines. During sports activity, the child can gain self-confidence and be motivated to surpass goals that are established in therapy. Successful attainment of goals is achieved during sports, as attention is removed from the disability and focused on the spirit of the games, which makes achievement fun for the child. Consistent participation in sports can lead to an increase in the child's physical tolerance, which ultimately can contribute to greater participation in the prescribed therapy program. For example, a group of disabled children, mostly children with various types of cerebral palsy, were involved in an exercise program for 1 hour 3 days a week. Prior to and following the activity, the children's respiratory function was monitored.The children showed an increase in respiratory function after 4 weeks of activity.

Exercise can also provide the disabled child with a sense of freedom. Children with muscle problems feel improved when participating in water play in a pool. The water helps to buoy the child up and results in a relaxed feeling that is not witnessed at other times. In addition, the joy that emanates from these children during recreation is hard to ignore. The child's life is enriched through participation in a variety of athletic activities.

The exercises or recreation that are chosen for the disabled child are based on:

1. The child's preferences.
2. The child's potential to have some success at the activity.
3. Assurance of safety by reducing risk factors.
4. Utilizing the child's assets effectively.
5. Minimizing the child's deficits.
6. Providing a source of enjoyment or fulfillment.

7. Whether the disability is stable, will be improved, or will be increased with time.
8. The child's motivation.
9. Willingness to be flexible, as the child's endurance may be diminished at times.
10. Cost of the activity, including special equipment for adapting to the children's special needs.
11. Integrating the activity with the child's environment.

The exercise program for the disabled child involves the same three parts as for able-bodied persons: the warm-up, the endurance phase, and the cooling-off period. The warm-up phase is approximately 5 minutes of rhythmic, slow stretching of the trunk and extremity muscles, if this is possible. A gentle moving of the head, alternate walking–jogging, and arm circles are examples of warm-up activities. The endurance phase is approximately 30 minutes in length. Activities during this period are vigorous enough to cause deep breathing but do not cause oxygen deprivation. The cooling-off period allows the body to return to normal function gradually. It lasts about 5 minutes and includes gross body movements that use range of motion of the joints (Cantu, 1980).

Resources

To be successful, the recreation plan for the disabled child must be consistent or compatible with the family's lifestyle. It is possible for the child to be able to do more than the family is able to facilitate effectively. In these instances, creative ideas can lead to the successful inclusion of the child in additional activities that are supervised by persons outside the family unit. For example, the child may be able to participate in the Special Olympics if an interested adult can act as the child's sponsor when the family cannot assume this responsibility. Contacting local resources to see what accommodations can be made is an essential part of planning for the child's exercise and ongoing recreational activities. Sporadic occasions, such as the Olympics, camping, and field trips, should not be missed because adults did not make arrangements for the child to be involved in these important activities. Children with specific disabilities can be aided by an ongoing communication with national organizations that are geared to their problem (see list in Appendix C).

Even more valuable to the disabled child and his or her family are the resources in their own community. A variety of resources are listed in the *Leisure Time Activities* manual (Department of Health and Human Services, 1980):

1. YMCA, YWCA.
2. Senior citizen centers.
3. Scout troops.
4. Colleges or universities.
5. Women's centers.
6. Church groups.
7. Ethnic clubs.

8. Dance studios.
9. Movement centers.
10. 4-H clubs.
11. Gardening clubs.
12. Libraries.
13. Drama workshops.
14. Camera clubs.
15. Little Leagues.

While any of these organizations can potentially accommodate children with disabilities, it is essential to investigate their willingness to do so before referring a disabled child to them. The more awareness that the community has of the needs of disabled children, the more likely it is to incorporate these children into its activities. Community awareness is a goal that is part of the successful integration of disabled children into the community.

Physical fitness does not have to depend on group activities, however. The child with a disability can participate in a wide variety of outdoor activities that can be facilitated by the family, such as (Department of Health and Human Services, 1980):

1. Boating.
2. Campfires.
3. Camping.
4. Canoeing.
5. Climbing.
6. Fishing.
7. Horseback riding.
8. Hiking and nature walks.
9. Outdoor cooking.
10. Skateboarding.
11. Skating.
12. Skiing.
13. Sledding.
14. Snowshoeing.
15. Tobogganing.
16. Woodcraft.

Caution should be exercised when planning experiences for the disabled child, as some of these activities involve risk of injury and precautions need to be taken to minimize this risk. Even able-bodied children are prone to injury during some of these activities, but this does not preclude their participation in the activities. The same premise prevails for the disabled child, but more caution is taken to make sure that adaptations are made to decrease the potential for injury to occur. Thinking through potential risks before the child engages in the activity and providing proper instruction in the skill tend to decrease injuries. In addition, the child may need assistance for longer periods of time than an able-bodied child until the skill is mastered.

New Activities

Introducing new activities can be facilitated by giving consideration to the following:

1. Progress slowly, offering familiar activities first. Use repetition, because reinforcement of learning is needed.
2. Introduce a new part of the activity at the beginning of the session before fatigue is present.
3. Be kind, firm, and patient. Use a positive approach.
4. Give clear, concise directions.
5. Show respect for the child by calling him or her by name.
6. Encourage active participation in the entire session.
7. Demonstrate activities thoroughly.
8. Participate in the activities when it is appropriate to do so.
9. Show enthusiasm for the activity.
10. While demonstrating activities, note when the skills will be useful at other times.
11. Consider the individual ability and attention span of each child.
12. Set realistic goals and offer praise for accomplishments.
13. Provide choices of activities.
14. Do not keep children waiting for long periods before the activities begin.
15. Keep activities interesting by introducing variations in the same theme.
16. Build in friendly competition at periodic intervals.
17. Keep a record of the child's accomplishments that can be shared with others.

Evaluating Ongoing Activities

The child with a disability can become bored with activities and be unable to express the boredom. Questions that can be used to determine if the activity is appropriate for the child include:

1. Does the child seem to be enjoying the activity?
2. Is the child experiencing anything "new" as part of the activity?
3. Is the activity especially designed to meet the specific needs of the child?
4. Are there any challenging aspects to the activity?
5. Is there a need for additional assistance to help the child achieve at a higher level?
6. Can the activity be adapted to allow the child more freedom of movement?
7. Are additional supplies needed?
8. Does the activity increase the child's social interaction skills?
9. Does the child lose interest in the activity prematurely?

10. Does it take an unusual amount of adult intervention to maintain the child's interest?

The value of activities for assisting in growth potential is well known. Making the activities challenging, stimulating, and fun is part of the nursing management of care for these children.

BIOFEEDBACK

Biofeedback is gaining increasing acceptance as an adjunct to therapies that are used in the management of clients who require muscle re-education to help alleviate their symptoms. Biofeedback is used to help the client become aware of the amount of muscular tension that is present in a particular muscle in his or her body. Biofeedback can indicate to the child when small changes in the tension levels of muscles take place.

Biofeedback is instituted when the environment is conducive. The treatment is most beneficial when the room is quiet and free of distractions and the client is sitting in a semireclining position. With sensors (electrodes) attached to a control panel and placed on the child's muscles, the child is guided to raise or lower the tension that exists in a particular muscle. Therefore, biofeedback can sometimes be useful in helping the child with a flaccid muscle to improve its function or in helping a child with a spastic muscle to inhibit some of the spastic activity. Successful use of the biofeedback is dependent on several factors, but an important factor is the degree of physiologic damage that is present in the muscle. For example, biofeedback has been used to treat torticollis (re-educating two muscle sites simultaneously, focusing on the weak and the strong muscles involved in the disorder, Clinical EMG Handbook, 1978). However, biofeedback might be useless when a child has severe flaccidity of muscles of the legs associated with myelomeningocele.

The child and caretakers are advised that the equipment does not produce the changes in the muscle tension; it only provides a way to visually or auditorily indicate the amount of muscular tension that is present. Therefore, a therapeutic plan is established to help the child to assume responsibility for the desired changes in the muscle through individualized management plans. For example, the child who needs to reduce muscle tension can be taught relaxation exercises to help to achieve this goal. The sensors provide feedback to the child as to whether or not the goal is being adequately achieved.

Obviously, biofeedback is not the method of choice for changing the muscle tension that is present in all conditions that cause childhood long-term illness. It is, however, a technique that is proving beneficial in the treatment protocols of many children. Therefore, it should be considered as a potential therapy when the equipment is available, when therapists are trained in the technique, and when families are eager to be involved in the process. Biofeedback principles have been used in the management of hypertension, stress reduction, reduction of pain, and postural defects.

HUMAN SEXUALITY

The human sexuality needs of children with long-term illness or disability are often ignored to a greater extent than the human sexuality needs of their able-bodied counterparts. The family life education that these children receive to prepare them to live successfully within the community is often inadequate.

Gender Identity Formation

Gender identity begins at birth when the infant is identified by the external genitalia as being either a male or a female. When the genitalia are not clearly male or female in appearance, ambiguity occurs. If the external genitalia are developed adequately, the infant is usually ascribed a name consistent with the gender. Occasionally, traditional male or female names are given to infants whose sex is the opposite of that usually associated with the names, but this is not the usual cultural practice. The infant is handled in a manner consistent with his or her particular gender, and all types of customs are started that imprint the specific gender on the infant. Although pink and blue are not the only colors of infant clothes, the clothes are still frillier for females and more tailored for males. So gender identity is part of the early socialization process of the child.

Money and Ehrhardt (1972) note that during the preschool years, it is important for males and females to know that being either male or female is important and to be proud of this sexual identity. As the preschool child is socialized, awareness of maleness or femaleness is emphasized and an attempt is made to help the preschooler feel proud of being either male or female. Throughout childhood, the child's identity is developed and the differences in gender become clearly established (Figs. 10-2 and 10-3).

The gender identity of children with disabilities is not always clearly established during the socialization process. Due to the disability, the child can receive mixed signals about identity, and the child's socialization process does not always emphasize the human sexuality aspects included in the socialization of able-bodied children. In fact, as adolescence approaches, adults seem to underplay the human sexuality needs of these children and seem to discourage the child from expressing his or her sexuality. Consequently, sexual identity confusion is often found in children with disabilities (Fig. 10-4).

Self-image (Self-concept)

The person's self-image consists of self-esteem, self-identity, and body image. The body image is the child's unique way of perceiving his or her physical self. Body image includes the child's perception of function, appearance, sensation, and mobility. Self-concept also includes the child's social self: moods, beliefs, values, goals, other's opinions, and personal feelings about the self. Therefore, the child's self-image is integrally connected with sexual well-being.

The child develops an image of himself or herself over time. Environmental factors influence the way the child's image of himself or herself evolves. Positive reinforcements from the environment lead to a positive self-image, while consistent negative reinforcements can cause the child to question himself or herself.

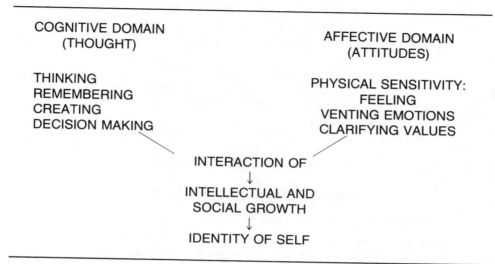

COGNITIVE DOMAIN
(THOUGHT)

AFFECTIVE DOMAIN
(ATTITUDES)

THINKING
REMEMBERING
CREATING
DECISION MAKING

PHYSICAL SENSITIVITY:
FEELING
VENTING EMOTIONS
CLARIFYING VALUES

INTERACTION OF
↓
INTELLECTUAL AND
SOCIAL GROWTH
↓
IDENTITY OF SELF

Figure 10-2.   Throughout the socialization process, the child's cognitive and affective behaviors are developing and lead to a clear identity of self.

The younger the child, the less ability he or she has to question the cues that he or she receives from others about his or her value as a person. The child's limited cognitive abilities interfere with his or her ability to test out the accuracy of others' opinions of his or her attributes. For example, if an adult tells a child that he or she is stupid, the child frequently takes this assessment at face value. The child is unable to assess whether or not he or she is stupid, so he or she adopts

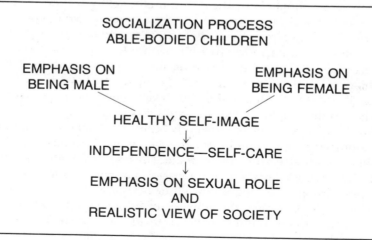

SOCIALIZATION PROCESS
ABLE-BODIED CHILDREN

EMPHASIS ON
BEING MALE

EMPHASIS ON
BEING FEMALE

HEALTHY SELF-IMAGE
↓
INDEPENDENCE—SELF-CARE
↓
EMPHASIS ON SEXUAL ROLE
AND
REALISTIC VIEW OF SOCIETY

Figure 10-3.   Socialization process of able-bodied children, leading to a healthy self-image and the expression of a sexual role.

SOCIALIZATION PROCESS
DISABLED CHILDREN
↓
DEPENDENT PERSON
LACKING SELF-CARE ABILITIES
DIMINISHED SELF-IMAGE
↓
DECREASED EMPHASIS ON SEXUAL ROLE (OR ASEXUAL)
AND
UNREALISTIC VIEW OF SOCIETY
AND
SEXUAL IDENTITY CONFUSION

Figure 10-4. Socialization process of disabled children, leading to a diminished self-image and a decreased expression of the sexual role.

the opinion of another. Therefore, messages that are given to young children need to be accurate and to focus on the child's attributes so that he or she is able to develop a positive self-concept.

A child who has a noticeable disability can receive negative reinforcement that raises doubts and uneasiness about his or her value. In addition, the child only has to look in the mirror to see that his or her body is different, and often there are unattractive aspects. For example, a child with cerebral palsy can view an image that has twisted muscles, drooling of saliva, and awkward body movements, all of which make it difficult for the child to give positive reinforcement to himself or herself. Some children have insults to their body image that make them have doubts about their continuing ability to have self-worth. For example, a female child who has surgery for a brain tumor followed by steroid therapy and chemotherapy can look in the mirror and see an image that is more male than female in appearance. In addition, adults who do not know the child often refer to the child as being the wrong sex, which confuses the child further. This ambiguity interferes with the child's ability to have a sense of sexual well-being. The strengthening of the child's self-concept is essential to counterbalance the negative feedback that the child receives.

As the child increases in age, the body begins to change and the child's body image is adjusted to incorporate the change. As adolescence approaches, the changes in the body structure are dramatic. The adolescent attempts to adapt to these physical changes, engages in increased introspection, and uses feedback from the peer group to compare himself or herself with culturally determined norms. The transitions that the adolescent is going through can result in uncertainty and turmoil, and the body image adjustment can be delayed by the adolescent's uncomfortableness with his or her changing body. The adolescent seems to have intense concern about the physical appearance of the body and whether or not it is normal.

The child with a disability already knows that the physical appearance of his or her body is different from the "norm," so the adolescent period can raise the adolescent's level of concern about the "strangeness" of his or her body. It is rare for the physically disabled adolescent to receive positive feedback from peers about the appearance of his or her body. At best, other adolescents with able bodies tend to ignore the disabled appearance of the disabled adolescent; at worst, they tend to ridicule or make fun of it.

The adolescent is eager to know if his or her emerging body is sexually adequate. Atypical sexual development is poorly tolerated. The atypical development can be a difference in stature or configurational or anatomic differences, such as enlarged breasts in males or delayed breast development in females. Any changes or deviations from the "norm" can result in a loss or lowering of self-esteem.

Disturbances in body image can be reflected in an increased concern or overconcern with appearance and body function or by exhibition of behaviors such as anxiety or depression. These behaviors are an expression of the way that the adolescent is attempting to cope with conscious and subconscious feelings about himself or herself.

The child with a disability is more vulnerable at this period because of the increased importance of the body to effective social interactions. Even long-term disabilities are re-evaluated by the adolescent, and the problem takes on a new significance. The obviously incongruous sexual development has particularly deleterious effects on the adolescent's emotional development. Examples of incongruous sexual development include gynecomastia and pseudohermaphroditism. Essentially, adolescents feel that being different is actually being inferior.

Adolescence is a time when fantasies and experiments with intimate relationships take place. These fantasies and experimentation evolve from a lifetime of experiences that contribute to the way the adolescent expresses his or her maleness or femaleness. Caretakers have influenced the adolescent's feelings about sexual adequacy throughout the early years. An adolescent who is reared with positive adult interactions throughout childhood is likely to enter new heterosexual experiences with less anxiety and trepidation than an adolescent who has sensed the caretaker's ambiguity about his or her appearance and sexual identity.

The peer group of adolescents can be extremely negative towards adolescents with disabilities. The unkind reactions often expressed by peers is probably a reflection of the able-bodied adolescent's uneasiness with himself or herself combined with his or her own fear of being different. Interacting with adolescents with disabilities raises uneasy feelings that the adolescent is incapable of handling effectively. Adolescents discriminate against persons with handicaps, give them lower status in the group, and frequently ostrasize them. The handicapped adolescent receives less attention from the opposite sex and is often treated with open contempt and hostility. Consequently, able-bodied adolescents take advantage of the differences of their peers to gain advantage in the group and to gain advantages with members of the opposite sex. When the feedback from the peer group is negative, the disabled adolescent begins to accept the values of the group and places disvalue on himself or herself.

The social setting in which the adolescent with a disability is reared and interacts with others is a powerful force in determining whether or not the adolescent has opportunities to engage in positive heterosexual relationships.

Body Image Boundaries. A variety of circumstances contribute to the child's development of a sense of body image boundaries. The infant has little awareness of his or her body boundaries and how the body is part of the environment. As the child matures, awareness of the boundaries of the self develops and the child tests out his or her relationship to the environment. The young child has difficulty sharing things in the environment, as he or she does not have a good idea of the boundaries. The toddler is often heard saying, "No, mine!" or "Mine!" because there is no clear distinction between the self and things beyond the self.

Some children are overwhelmed by environmental stimuli, while the same stimuli may be handled effectively by other children. The young child responds to the feelings that these stimuli generate and he or she does not stop to analyze feelings before expressing them. Consequently, temper tantrums or screaming can be the result of an adult's request for a child to do something that is not conducive to his or her understanding of the self and its boundaries. An example of this is when a preschool child with cerebral palsy who is confined to a wheelchair is prematurely asked to place weight on his or her legs, which are outside of the internalized body boundaries. Some children who do not see their legs from a sitting position do not have a body image that includes the legs. When the child is asked to stand on his or her legs, fear arises, as the child does not feel that he or she is able to stand. As a result of knowing only a few ways to respond, screaming is a common outcome of this situation. The child's body boundaries need to be expanded to include the legs before the child can risk trying to stand. When the child's body image boundaries include the legs, the feelings of fear are decreased and more positive behaviors are expressed.

The body image and boundaries are changing fequently on the basis of responses the child receives from others in the environment. However, unexpected change in the boundaries of the body is not easily assimilated. The child who has a traumatic amputation of a lower extremity can have "phantom limb pain" or may stand up without remembering that the extremity is missing because the body boundary changes are not internalized as yet. Internalization of changed body boundaries is achieved by various children at different rates. Effective management of the child's care is based on an understanding that the child needs time to make changes in body image boundaries before therapy can be instituted. In the case of a child with an amputation, ambulation with crutches helps the child to perceive the changed physical status of the body, and viewing the results of the loss of an extremity in the mirror helps to make the child's body image realistic. Time, counseling, and support will help the child to match his or her body image boundaries with the actual physical self.

Body image boundaries are significant when sharing human sexual responses. Being clear about boundaries facilitates a positive interaction, while ambiguous boundaries are likely to produce negative interactions. For example, when the child knows his or her boundaries, it is easier to have a positive physical contact, such as hugging or kissing a loved one, as the child moves himself or herself through the environment and makes a tender contact with another person. A child who does not know boundaries engages in crude physical interactions that result in less positive interactions for both the child and the significant other. Early physical interactions provide the child with feedback that influences future behaviors. If the child gains confidence through early physical interactions, he or she is encouraged to continue to develop more sophisticated interactions with increasing age. Eventually, sharing of oneself with another involves consent to invade one another's boundaries. Comfort with invasion of boundaries is facilitated by being clear about boundaries and being willing to respect each other's right to maintain the boundaries when necessary. Sharing invasion of the boundaries can give each participant a feeling of gratification when respect and tenderness are maintained.

Sexuality Development in the Disabled

Different types of sexuality can be expressed: heterosexual, homosexual, and bisexual. The values of health care providers can influence their ability to be helpful to or supportive of persons who select a particular sexual lifestyle. The health care provider also needs to explore values that influence the attitudes and beliefs connected with the expression of human sexuality by the disabled person.

Sexuality is often equated with the genital organs instead of being equated with the totality of expression of femaleness or maleness. Sexual intercourse can be procreative or recreational in nature. Traditionally, the procreative nature of sexual experiences is stressed more than the recreational nature of sexual experiences. Many myths exist about the human sexuality needs and concerns of children, adolescents, and adults. In order to discuss human sexuality of the disabled, it is necessary to understand that sensuality and sexuality are aspects of the human experience and that sexuality can be expressed with or without sexual intercourse. Human sexuality is important to the human experience even when reproduction is not a wanted or potential outcome.

The young child with a disability begins to understand human sexuality at an early age if adults take advantage of situations to expose the child to concepts that influence his or her behaviors. The young, able-bodied child is exposed to many opportunities to try out social skills. The disabled child is provided fewer of these opportunities. Therefore, attention is placed on engaging the disabled child in interactions with able-bodied children in order to try out social skills and to observe skills that are successful in engaging others in positive social interactions. Every attempt is made to decrease the social isolation of the disabled child during the formative years.

The young child needs to learn the correct names of body parts and their location. All of the body organs are treated with equal respect to cut down on the possibility of a view that some organs are lacking merit. The child who develops a respect for all the body parts is expected to gain interest in maintaining the body at a maximum level of functioning. The child is taught how body parts are treated within a social frame of reference—e.g., genitals are covered and arms are exposed. During the time that young children are developing an awareness of the social context of the body, discipline for violating social norms is confined to a discussion of why certain behaviors are expected. Punishment for breaking social norms is withheld.

The child with a disability can express displeasure with particular parts of the body, especially the disabled part. For example, the child with paralyzed lower extremities might say, "I hate my skinny legs." The nurse might respond, "It is OK that you feel that way about your legs. You may not like your legs, but did you notice what pretty hair you have? All of us have some parts of our bodies that we like less than other parts. What part of your body do you like?"

The appearance of the child is enhanced by focusing special attention on grooming. The child is encouraged to assume increasing responsibility for his or her appearance. Affirmation is given for an attractive appearance by focusing on particular aspects, such as an attractive dress or neatly combed hair. In addition, the child is encouraged to look in the mirror to assess his or her own appearance so as to gain awareness of when changes in appearance contribute to an attractive appearance.

The child is introduced to aids that assist in enhancing his or her appearance. For example, Velcro strips on clothing may help to make clothing fit more adequately, or an attractive covering may contribute to the appearance of a neck brace or a wheelchair. These items can be used to stress the child's femaleness or maleness.

The young disabled child is introduced to roles of family members and the importance of both males and females in the family. The child is introduced to the notion that each member of the family contributes to the family in particular ways but that it is not essential to ascribe traditional roles to persons on the basis of sex. If the child needs special consideration because of disabilities, this is put into the context of how each person within the family is treated as an individual whom all other family members respect and of how family members help each other to achieve the highest level of functioning that is possible. The disabled child benefits in the same way that an able-bodied child does by learning the identified male or female role. Gender identity is enhanced by experiences that allow the child to try out complimentary role functions. Therefore, the female child is engaged in activities with the father and the male child is engaged in activities with the mother.

During the school-age years, the child models behaviors and imprints further the masculine or feminine role. The child with a disability needs to develop habits that are consistent with the role. In addition, health care providers are expected to treat the child with respect and not to expose the child to unnecessary scrutiny or observations that suggest to the child that he or she is unusually different from other children. When the child is examined, privacy is maintained and the child's permission is sought before undressing or examining is begun. In this way, the disabled child develops in the same way as his or her peers.

During this period, the disabled child is introduced to books about sexuality.

Discussion groups help the child to express feelings and to learn what feelings are valued by others. Expression of feelings is an important part of human sexuality.

During the adolescent years, increasing emphasis is placed on gaining independence. This independence includes attention to both emotional and economic parameters. With independence, the disabled adolescent needs to develop a sense of responsibility for his or her actions. As self-identity develops, the adolescent needs to be engaged in social relationships that result in both positive and negative interactions. Through these experiences, the adolescent is helped to deal with rejections and to put rejections in proper perspective. The adolescent with a disability may witness more rejections than able-bodied adolescents, but preparation for the rejection can help to decrease the after-effects of rejection. Role-playing potential incidents can assist in achieving this goal. The adolescent can benefit by discussing human sexuality concerns with other disabled persons. In this way, the adolescent can express frustrations and disappointments and learn that others have experienced similar circumstances. The adolescent needs to know that there is no "sexual norm." Each person exhibits his or her own unique sexuality.

The adolescent also needs to have discussions about myths and misconceptions about the human sexuality potential of disabled individuals. The adolescent is made aware that it is normal to have sexual feelings and to want to express these feelings in interactions with others. The adolescent is also informed of the possibilities that others will be unrealistic about his or her sexual potential. Misconceptions range from the disabled person being asexual to the notion that disabled persons are "oversexual."

The life of a disabled adolescent can be filled with loneliness if he or she is not able or capable of interacting with others outside the family. Opportunities need to be provided for adolescents to interact with both able-bodied and other disabled individuals. When a trusting relationship is established, sessions are planned to discuss concerns about specific sex-related activities. In these sessions, the adolescent develops values and an ethical system that guides future sexual activities. The goal of these sessions is to engage the adolescent in activities that decrease loneliness and increase his or her ability to be comfortable in sexual encounters.

The appearance of the adolescent continues to be of major concern. The adolescents are taught how to control things that influence how they impress others, such as changes in the skin, oral hygiene, control of odors with deodorants, and manners. Reinforcement for expected behaviors, use of mirrors and photographs, and videotaping can all help to increase the adolescent's awareness of how he or she looks. Group sessions on grooming can help adolescents to help one another to improve and to take responsibility for their appearance.

Parents and other individuals in the community influence the human sexuality outcomes for the disabled individual. There are many attitudes, such as overprotection and disapproval, that interfere with the disabled person's ability to have a successful sexual life. The outdated notion that disabled individuals are not entitled to participate in sexual experiences interferes with successful adjustment of disabled persons. Other adults need to support the disabled adolescent in social interactions and to limit their resistance to these interactions. Society needs to increase its sensitivity to the needs of the disabled so that architectural barriers and negative attitudes can be decreased to allow social interactions to take place more freely. Most important, a change in orientation towards the human sexuality needs of disabled persons needs to be made so that respect of this part of their lives is guaranteed. The parents can often benefit from participating in a parents' group. In these groups, the parents are encouraged to share their feelings about the adolescent and any concerns related to the expression of sexuality. Oftentimes, the parents express a fear that if their adolescent engages in social interactions, he or she will be hurt. While this is a natural concern, the parents are helped to understand that pain is part of human interactions and that the adolescent will have difficulty gaining self-identity and independence if roles are not tried out.

The disabled older adolescent may need help in exploring ways to increase opportunities for satisfactorily expressing his or her sexuality. Suggestions that can be beneficial include the following:

1. Masturbation, with or without the use of fantasy, if acceptable to the adolescent, can lead to orgasm.
2. The adolescent can explore areas of sensual response through tactile stimulation of the entire body.
3. The adolescent can use a mirror to explore areas of the body that cannot be seen readily.
4. The adolescent can use relaxation techniques to decrease anxiety associated with human sexuality.
5. The adolescent can use massage as part of sexual expression.
6. The adolescent can use vibrators, if acceptable.
7. The adolescent can use pictures, if acceptable, for sexual arousal.
8. Group discussions of sexual concerns may be helpful.
9. Increased communication between partners can be encouraged.
10. Exploration of each other's body can be encouraged.
11. Muscle exercises may be helpful to increase muscle tension.
12. Use of pictures and explanation of the anatomy and physiology of males and females can be helpful.
13. Values clarification exercises about human sexuality can be used to bring about more positive attitudes.
14. Warm baths, showers, and soft music can be used to increase sexual arousal.
15. The adolescent can identify likes and dislikes related to sexuality.
16. Breathing exercises may help to increase relaxation.
17. The breath can be held to increase arousal.

The sexual expression of persons with disabilities can be interrupted by a variety of problems. An honest explanation of the problems that emerge is an essential part of the rehabilitation needs of these individuals.

Possible interference with human sexual experiences can result from appearance, lack of control of bodily function, involuntary movements, and dependency due to the handicaps. Effects of appearance can be overcome if the American overdependence on beauty is decreased and the person is able to project a warm and loving personality despite physical disabilities. However, differences in appearance are exaggerated by appliances that help the disabled person to have more mobility, such as prostheses, leg braces, wheelchairs, and crutches. While these advances offer the disabled person more opportunities for social interactions, they tend to accentuate the differences in the appearances of disabled and able-bodied persons. Lack of control problems are more difficult to compensate for, as incontinency is not associated with acceptable adult behavior. When a body functions in infantile ways, the body image is often impaired and it is difficult for the person to obtain or maintain a positive sense of self concerning sexuality needs and potential. Other problems that can be faced by a person with a disability include lack of partners, decreased self-esteem, changed self-image, altered sensations associated with sexual experiences, fear of failure, unwillingness to experiment, changes in interest in sexual intercourse, and depression. An important point to keep in mind is that sexuality is unique to each person. Therefore, there is some danger in discussing problems of a sexual experience without knowing the person. However, it is possible to consider circumstances that may influence the sexual functioning of persons with particular disabilities in order to be able to help the person make choices about sexuality. Specific problems that are commonly associated with particular disabilities follow.

Spinal Cord Injuries

A female who has a spinal cord injury, still maintains the fertility associated with able-bodied females. Fertility can be a very serious consideration, as the disabled person has special problems in using contraceptives and in reproduction. For the woman to make sound judgments, she needs to know the types of contraceptives that are available, their convenience of use, the special side-effects caused in their use by the disability, the side-effects for able-bodied females, and the advantages of each type of contraception.

One of the major considerations when selecting a contraceptive is the ability to use the contraceptive effectively, either alone or with assistance. Another consideration is the female's ability to recognize untoward effects of using the contraceptive. Another concern has to do with the family planning goals of the woman or couple. Special problems that are often encountered are as follows:

1. Because the woman is more prone to thrombophlebitis due to immobility, there are increased risks when the "pill" is selected.
2. Early signs of thrombophlebitis may not be heeded due to loss of sensation.
3. Intrauterine devices (IUDs) can be risky when there is decreased uterine sensation, as the pain or cramping that are early signs of problems may be ignored.
4. Assistance may be needed in checking for the IUD strings to determine changes in placement.

5. Diaphragms and jellies cause some unique problems with placement and application—assistance may be needed.
6. When recurrent bladder infections occur, diaphragms may be counterindicated.
7. Dislocation of diaphragms can occur with weak pelvic muscles and when the Credé maneuver is used.
8. Jellies and foams can be useful in association with condoms—assistance with application may be needed.
9. Tubal ligation can be effective when reproduction activity is completed (Thornton, 1981).

Positioning for comfort and effective intercourse can be determined by experimentation. As bowel and bladder incontinence is of concern, attention to the associated bodily functions is indicated. If a Foley catheter is in place, it can remain in place if the woman feels comfortable. If not, the Credé maneuver or intermittent catheterization can be done prior to intercourse to decrease incontinence. Likewise, a bowel program should include attention to decreasing bowel evacuations during intercourse. When an attendant is needed to assist with bodily functions, preplanning is essential. The assistance of an outsider, such as an attendant, as part of the sexual experience must be acceptable to both partners.

The sexual experiences of a person with a spinal cord injury can be improved by exploration and experimentation. At a time when the person feels confident about trying, opportunities to explore sexual activities of many types can be suggested for consideration. Included are exploration of erogenous zones, use of vibrators, oral—genital sex, cuddling, massage, and masturbation. Many of these suggestions require that the person develop a new orientation and perhaps a change in values. Therefore, counseling is essential to help the person to be able to consider the utility or merit of the activities.

Other concerns that can emerge are painful intercourse (which can sometimes be resolved by lubricating the vagina with water-soluble lubricant, such as KY jelly) and pregnancy (which can cause increased susceptibility to thrombophlebitis, bladder infections, and, sometimes, spontaneous unassisted delivery due to lack of sensation or inability to detect clues that labor is progressing, such as chills, sweating, or pressure).

Communication is used to decrease the surprises connected with the sexual experience. For example, before undressing, the person with a disability can explain the constraints that will influence the experience, such as the presence of a Foley catheter. The preparation for a sexual encounter also includes an explanation of the assistance needed to engage in the activity, such as assistance in undressing. The partners can assist one another in playing down the inconveniences associated with the disability.

Communication is an essential component of the human sexual experience. The person with diminished sensation needs to clarify and direct so that each partner receives gratification from the experience. As new areas of sensation are discovered, this information is shared so that similar experiences are included in future sexual encounters. Communication requires a giving and receiving of feedback that allows each partner to be aware of when actions result in a positive experience. Satisfying another results in an increase in self-esteem. Attention paid to responses results in sexual satisfaction even when severe interference with bodily function is present.

The male with a spinal cord injury may not have the ability to have an erection or to insert the penis into the vagina. In this instance, the female needs to take the incentive to "stuff" the penis. In some instances, penile prosthetics are available to assist in this function. Sexual satisfaction and gratification can increase the male's sexual capacity.

Another way to increase sexual satisfaction for some disabled persons is to engage in active fantasy during the sexual experience. Fantasy is often used to increase sexual pleasure by both able-bodied and disabled persons.

Ostomies

Alterescu (1981) identifies three categories of concerns that affect the sexual parameters of the lives of persons with ostomies: mechanical, physiologic, and psychologic. One of the major problems is the ostomy bag, which can interfere with the mechanical aspects of the sexual act or the psychologic reactions of either partner. Changes in position can limit the problems associated with wearing a pouch on the abdomen, but it is more difficult to decrease or eliminate psychologic responses. As the pouch contains human excreta, it often causes a sense of revulsion that is difficult to overcome. In addition, the pouch can be responsible for odors that are difficult to eliminate. Offensive odors can interfere with either partner's ability to find enjoyment in the sexual encounter. In addition, psychologic responses such as depression, fear, and grief can interfere with sexual interest or ability. Physiologic disabilities such as nerve damage and/or scarring can interfere with sexual adequacy. Males who have S2 to S4 parasympathetic nerve damage may be unable to achieve or maintain an erection, while ejaculation may be impossible when L1 to L3 sympathetic nerve damage exists. Scarring of the perineum of a female can interfere with satisfaction from the sexual act due to painful sensations.

Human sexuality counseling for these persons is based on their own desires and the specific problems that are identified. Sensitive listening will help to identify interventions that are warranted to help the client or partner be as fully engaged as possible in sexual responses that will enhance his or her life. The initial responses of either partner can change as time elapses. Therefore, counseling is geared to the expressed needs of the client and partner.

Cerebral Palsy

The involuntary muscle activity of persons with cerebral palsy can interfere with the usual positioning for sexual intercourse. Exploration of comfortable positions can facilitate a successful encounter. A discussion of the involuntary movements and potential outcomes can decrease the partner's surprise if movements are not smooth and soothing. Discussing limitations with a partner before engaging in an intensive experience can result in a more successful and gratifying experience.

Some persons with cerebral palsy may have limitations in speech. This further
interferes with their ability to have a successful sexual encounter.

The female in a wheelchair may have the same predisposition to thrombophlebitis that was discussed in the section on spinal cord injury. Therefore,
"the pill" is often discouraged as a contraceptive choice in these clients.

Hand dexterity can be lacking in clients with cerebral palsy. This can
interfere with the client's ability to use certain types of contraceptives. An
able-bodied person may be needed to assist with the proper placement of these
contraceptives; if the partner is not capable, a third person may be necessary to
fulfill this function. Third persons' influences on sexuality experiences are
individualized, and increased communication between the partners is required
for a successful sexual relationship.

Sensory Impairment

Communication facilitates a satisfactory human interaction. When there is a
visual or hearing impairment, communication can be impaired. When sight is
absent, the visual stimulation that enhances the sexual experience is hampered.
However, the other senses are capable of compensating for the visual sense if
environmental conditions support the sexual interaction. For example, it is not
easy to start communication with another individual when sight is impaired, as
the exact location of the other person may not be known; nor is it possible to
know discriminating factors about the person, such as age, height, and weight.
Even after a conversation is started, the blind person is disadvantaged by not
being able to detect nonverbal clues to another person's interest in pursuing a
romantic encounter, such as flirting, eye movements, and pleasurable responses
to advances. Therefore, the blind person is more dependent on verbal feedback to
know whether or not to advance a relationship.

The hearing-impaired or deaf person can have difficulty engaging in social
interactions, as usual activities, such as telephoning, can be impossible. In
face-to-face encounters, the hearing-impaired person can watch the nonverbal
responses to communication but may have difficulty interpreting verbal clues.
For example, it is necessary to address the hearing-impaired person so that lip
reading is possible. Distinctive movements of the mouth facilitate better communication. In addition, if both partners can use signing, it aids in the expression
of human sexuality.

In an intimate relationship, the hearing-impaired person does not have the
advantage of hearing when advances are pleasurable, so the partner needs to
show satisfaction through facial expressions and bodily movements that signal
satisfaction.

MANAGEMENT OF SPECIFIC DISABILITIES

Asthma allergy is one of the most common chronic diseases of childhood. It is the
fifth most common reason that children are taken to a physician. Approximately
1,500,000 children have this disease. It is the disease that is responsible for the

greatest number of days of absence from school. Asthmatic children are often susceptible to infections. Absence from school may occur in the first or second week of the new term due to sudden exposure to the nose and throat infections of classmates. Since asthma is a long-term problem, early diagnosis and effective ongoing management are important in avoiding complications.

Harvey (1982) hypothesizes that the child who has asthma has an overabundance of antibodies to certain substances. He suggests that the situation causes a heightened antibody response whenever the child inhales an allergen or antigen. The union of the antigen and the antibody leads to a reaction that releases chemicals from the mast cells, such as histamine, serotonin, bradykinin, and SRS-A. The chemicals cause the symptoms of the allergy. The allergic reaction that takes place in the nose is termed allergic rhinitis or hay fever; in the lungs, it is asthma; in the eyes, it is allergic conjunctivitis; and on the skin, it is eczema or hives. (Harvey, 1982). This hypothesis is not accepted by all experts. Another hypothesis is that the child with allergies actually has a decreased number of antibodies and a consequently decreased resistance to substances that cause allergic responses.

Two basic factors are involved when a child has an asthmatic attack: the child has a constitutional predisposition to form antibodies and the offending substance must be present.

Asthma may be due to intrinsic or extrinsic causes. The substances that cause asthma are broadly classified into two groups: ingestants and inhalants. Ingestants are the most common cause of asthma in younger children. Some of the common offenders include wheat, chocolate, milk, eggs, and citrus fruits. Inhalants are classified as indoor or outdoor. Common outside offenders are grass, trees, and weeds. Tree and grass pollens are more common causes during the springtime, while weeds are more commonly the cause in the fall. Common inside offenders are house dust, wool, feathers, molds, and animal dander. Drugs are also implicated as substances that can cause an allergic response ranging from hives to asthma.

In addition, the environment can contribute to asthma. Cold air can precipitate an attack and changes in atmospheric pressure, dampness, wind, and low humidity are associated with attacks. Severe environmental pollution, such as smog is also problematic for children who have a predisposition to asthma. Other factors that can precipitate asthma are hair sprays, perfume, tobacco smoke, and chemical vapors.

Asthma can begin at any age. However, the infant who wheezes is often allergic to food, while the child 1 to 5 years of age is often allergic to household substances and the child over 5 is often allergic to outside substances. Some children outgrow their allergies, but more often children's allergies increase as they are exposed to additional allergens. Older children are often allergic to a combination of indoor and outdoor substances.

Asthma is more common in males prior to puberty and more common in females after puberty. This is probably the result of symptoms decreasing in males rather than of the problem increasing in females.

Emotional factors can precipitate an asthma attack. However, the child must have a predisposition to asthma before emotional factors can contribute to an attack. When the attack is accompanied by shouting, crying, or rapid breathing, a physiologic attack that results may be triggered by emotions. For example, spasm of the bronchial tubes can be produced by rapid breathing (Fig. 10-5).

Asthma usually starts as an isolated episode of wheezing. The wheezing is usually mild and does not last long. Initial attacks of asthma are often precipitated by respiratory infections. As the allergic responses continue, the attacks are more frequent and can be prolonged. The normal bronchiole is constricted during an attack, causing interference with air passage during the bronchospasm (Fig. 10-6).

In the acute asthmatic attack, the severity of symptoms depends on the inflammatory reaction of the mucosa, the amount of bronchospasm, and the degree of airway obstruction and distention of the alveoli. As the attacks become more frequent, they may not be associated with infection, but there may be clear runny secretions from the nose prior to onset. The discharge is probably due to a nasal allergy. This is usually followed by a dry, hacking, nonproductive cough, and wheezing follows the cough.

When proper allergic management is provided, the effects are often reversible. In long-term cases, response to medication may be poor due to changes that have taken place in the bronchi and alveoli, resulting in lowered vital capacity and deformity of the chest cavity.

The mortality rate for asthma has shown an upward trend from 1963 on. It is hypothesized that the increased mortality rates are associated with the increased use of pressurized aerosol medications that dilate the bronchial tree. Cortisone has also been implicated (Harvey, 1982).

Assessment

The allergy history is the initial step in the diagnosis of asthma. The mother is asked a series of questions in an effort to implicate substances that precipitate the asthma. Questions that identify symptoms, seasonal occurrence, precipitating factors, and family history are asked. At times, the family has a good sense of what is contributing to the child's problem, while at other times the history provides few insights into the problem.

If a child is having an asthma attack, he or she probably will appear short of breath. As the child attempts to take deeper breaths, the expiratory phase of respiration is prolonged and wheezing occurs. The child's skin may be pale and a flush can appear on the face. When severe respiratory interference takes place, the lips are a deep, dark red color and cyanosis can occur if respiration is not improved. During acute attacks, the child is often anxious, and this is reflected in his or her facial expression. Some children sit upright with hunched over shoulders when an attack occurs. If the child attempts to talk, the phrases are short and panting can take place between words.

When the chest is examined, breath sounds are coarse and loud. Rhonchi are coarse, and wheezing is heard. When the attack is severe, breath sounds and rales are often audible without instrumentation. Shallow or irregular respirations are common.

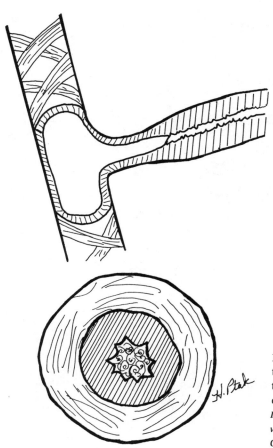

Figure 10-5. (Top) Longitudinal section of bronchiolar obstruction. (Bottom) Enlarged cross-section of obstructed bronchiole. *(From O'Hara, M. In S.M. Steele (Ed.), Nursing care of the child with long-term illness. New York: Appleton — Century — Crofts, 1977.)*

Children who have frequent and chronic asthma can develop a fixed thoracic cavity referred to as a barrel chest. These children use their accessory muscles to support respiration.

Often the child is not having an attack when brought for an evaluation and may seem not to have any problems. In these instances, the mother and child are asked to describe an attack so that the description can be included in the record.

Management

There are two modes of therapy for children with asthma. One mode is designed to prevent the attacks and the other mode is to treat an attack after its onset. Attention to the environment is essential. As the child spends approximately 50 percent of his or her day in the bedroom, it is targeted as a place that needs to be allergy-free (Fig. 10-7).

For infants, elimination diets are common, although there is considerable difference of opinion among physicians as to which foods tend to cause allergic reactions; milk, wheat, eggs, and citrus juices are usually among those listed to be

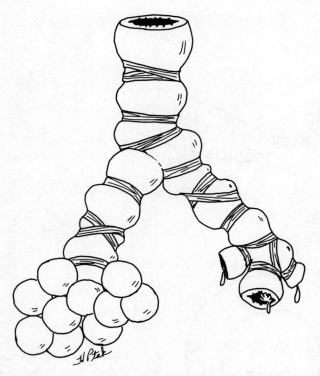

Figure 10-6. Normal bronchiole and constriction of air passages during bronchospasm. *(From O'Hara, M. In S.M. Steele (Ed.), Nursing care of the child with long-term illness. New York: Appleton—Century—Crofts, 1977.)*

eliminated. Peanut butter is often also listed as an offender in preschool or school-age children.

When foods are being eliminated, a hypoallergenic diet is usually instituted. Milk is usually replaced in the diet by a soybean preparation. Rice, oats, or barley cereal is also used in the diet. Meat (such as lamb) is added later. The restricted diet is usually supplemented with synthetic vitamins. After a week on a regimen, one new food may be added at a time and the infant is observed for any reaction. Later, when foods are reintroduced, the physician may add milk, wheat, and eggs. A written diet, clearly stated (including foods to avoid), is given to the mother. Reading of labels for content is stressed. The mother is provided directions on keeping a log of the foods that are eaten by the child. She also records any responses to the foods, such as an increase in a skin rash or wheezing. Upon return visits to the office or clinic, the nurse reviews logs recorded by the mother and uses the opportunity for teaching and counseling.

For older children, a menu may be offered in which some of the foods causing allergic reactions are omitted. If improvement is noted, foods that were omitted are reintroduced over a 2 week period. If symptoms return, then the offending food is identified. Clinical trials and accurate recording of offending

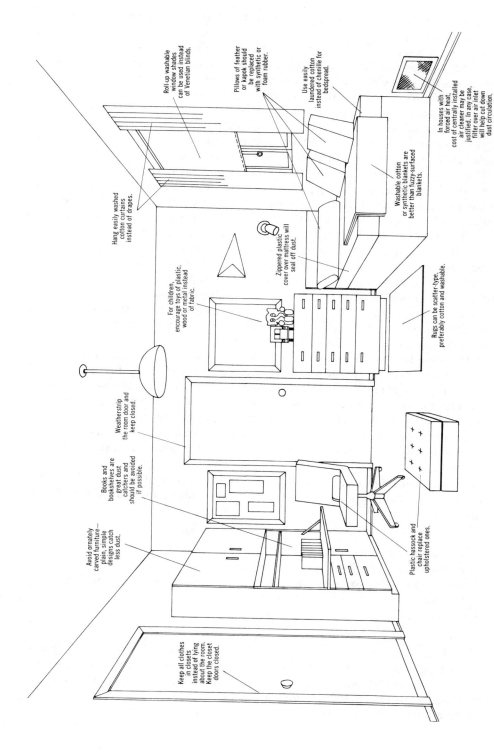

Roll-up washable window shades can be used instead of Venetian blinds.

Pillows of feather or kapok should be replaced with synthetic or foam rubber.

Use easily laundered cotton instead of chenille for bedspread.

In houses with forced air heat, cost of centrally installed air cleaner may be justified. In any case, filter over air inlet will help cut down dust circulation.

Hang easily washed cotton curtains instead of drapes.

Washable cotton or synthetic blankets are better than fuzzy-surfaced blankets.

Zippered plastic cover over mattress will seal off dust.

For children, encourage toys of plastic, wood or metal instead of fabric.

Rugs can be scatter-type, preferably cotton and washable.

Weatherstrip the room door and keep closed.

Books and bookshelves are great dust catchers and should be avoided if possible.

Avoid ornately carved furniture—plain, simple designs catch less dust.

Plastic hassock and chair replace upholstered ones.

Keep all clothes in closets instead of lying about the room. Keep the closet doors closed.

Figure 10-7. How to "desensitize" a room. *(Courtesy of A.H. Robbins Co., Richmond, Va.)*

substances helps in interpreting the results of dietary management of the problem (O'Hara, 1977).

It is often necessary to do skin testing to determine which antigens are responsible for the child's problem. After the antigens are identified, hyposensitization is started by giving the child a series of injections. The injections contain an abstract of the offending substances. Hyposensitization is begun by giving the child a very weak dose of the antigen and slowly increasing the dosage. The process usually takes several months to complete. The hyposensitization is not always successful, but when used in combination with avoidance of known substances, it can contribute to a decrease in the number of asthma attacks that the child has to endure. Hyposensitization is not effective for food allergies.

An important part of the management of children with asthma is the use of breathing exercises and chest hygiene. Breathing exercises teach children how to get air in and out of the lungs with the least expenditure of energy. This method helps the child to avoid anxiety when an attack is felt. Exercises are also prescribed to increase physical fitness. For example, stretch exercises can increase the flexibility of the ribs, and sit-ups can strengthen the muscles of the abdomen, aiding expiration. Chest hygiene includes percussion, vibration, deep breathing, and coughing, which help to clear the child's bronchial tree of mucus.

Medications play an important role in relief of asthmatic symptoms. Two major drug groups are used in the treatment: bronchodilators and beta-2 sympathetic agonists. The bronchodilator cromolyn sodium by Spinhaler is fast-acting and effective. Beta-1 agonists, such as Alupent, Proventil, and Berotic, are effective as aerosols. During acute phases of asthma, several other substances are used to relieve inflammation and bronchospasm, such as adrenalin, ephedrine, aminophylline, and, in extreme situations, corticosteroids. Aerosols of Isuprel and Bronkosol-2 are commonly used. Expectorants, antibiotics, and sedatives are sometimes indicated. Self-prescribed medication is discouraged. Most intractibility is caused by medications and not by psychologic or environmental factors.

The child with asthma is usually seen in an outpatient setting. When the child comes to the clinic in the midst of an asthmatic attack, the nurse determines:

1. The time of onset.
2. Factors that contributed to the present attack.
3. Medications that are presently being taken—the dose and schedule.
4. Measures taken to control the current attack.
5. Health status during the prior week.

The child is started on room-temperature oral fluids. When possible, fluids that are enjoyed by the child are given, such as Hawaiian Punch or Kool-aid. Water can be alternated with these fluids. Large amounts of fluid help to liquefy secretions and keep the child's mind occupied.

Medications are prescribed to try to control the attack. At times, it is necessary to give medications parenterally. Supportive measures during therapy include:

1. Keeping the environment calm.
2. Diversional activities that do not involve activity, such as reading and listening to music.
3. Protection from environmental hazards, such as cigarette smoke and drafts.
4. Having the child sit upright with an overbed table to rest the arms at chest-high level.
5. Positive feedback for taking adequate amounts of oral fluids.
6. Adult interactions to give the child support and encouragement.
7. Providing opportunities for the child to express concerns (Steele, 1981).

When it is impossible to resolve the asthma attack in the outpatient setting, it is necessary to admit the child to the hospital. In the hospital, the child can receive continuing medication therapy, oxygen or mist therapy, chest hygiene, and emotional support.

After the acute phase of the illness is resolved, the child is discharged and attempts are made to return the child to normal activities.

Education

A major part of the long-term management of children with asthma is education to prepare the child to have as normal an existence as possible. The school-age child is encouraged to attend school and to participate in all activities. As active interactions such as physical education can precipitate an asthmatic attack, some precautions are necessary.

With the advent of cromolyn sodium, activities which were once thought to be out of the question can now be open to these children. Cromolyn sodium— Aarane or Intal—can be used to prevent attacks rather than to treat them. It is not a bronchodilator or a bronchial mucus liquifier. It is thought to prevent attacks by interfering with the release of histamine and a slow reacting substance of an aphlyaxis (SRS-A) during an antigen–antibody reaction. This drug permits the child to exercise and to participate in normal activities with peers without difficulty. It can be used prior to anticipated emotional stress (such as participation in a school play or examination and exposure to Christmas trees, dust, or pets) and while on vacation. Each capsule contains a powder, which is inhaled. A special container (Spinhaler) pierces the capsule so that the powder is spun out. The child must tip the inhaler upwards, breathe very deeply, and hold his or her breath before exhaling. Inhalation of one capsule is usually recommended 1 hour prior to exposure and then every 3 to 4 hours, up to four times a day, during the period of exposure (O'Hara, 1977).

Swimming is considered to be the best sport for children with asthma. Precautions may be indicated to protect the child from unnecessary exposure to antigens—e.g., avoidance of tall grass on the playground or avoidance of mats in the gym that may have molds on them. Generally, the child is encouraged to actively participate in physical education. It may be necessary to teach school personnel about the reasons that the child should not be excluded from these activities.

The child also needs to have information about his or her disease and measures that can be used to manage it effectively. A helpful book for both child and parents is *Teaching My Parents About Asthma* (Parcel et al., 1976). In this resource the child can learn self-help activities for proper management and control of the problem. The provision of information can contribute indirectly to improved school attendance. Therefore, every opportunity is taken to improve the child's knowledge base.

Freudenberg et al. (1980) provide guidelines to help parents decide whether or not to send the child to school. The child should attend school under the following conditions:

1. Stuffy nose but no wheezing.
2. Mild wheezing that clears after giving medications.
3. Good exercise tolerance (ability to participate in usual daily activities).

The guidelines for keeping the child out of school are as follows:

1. Evidence of infection: red throat, sore throat, or swollen glands.
2. Fever over 100°F orally or 101°F rectally: skin hot and flushed.
3. Wheezing that continues to increase 1 hour after medication is taken.
4. Too weak or tired to take part in routine daily activities.
5. Breathing pattern that is irregular, labored, or rapid: respiratory rate over 25/minute while at rest.

As being unable to breathe is a frightening experience, both the child and the parents need to be able to respond appropriately during respiratory distress. They are taught cardiopulmonary resuscitation (CPR) methods. In addition, the parents and child are appraised of correct responses to take in an emergency— e.g., they are given the telephone number of the local mobile emergency medical system or the hospital emergency room.

At times, the parent–child relationship contributes to the precipitation of asthmatic attacks. When counseling is not successful in relieving the sources of disagreement, it may be necessary to treat the child away from home. Two possibilities are summer camp and residential placement. Summer camp is effective even when there is no interference with the parent–child relationship. Residential care is a more drastic step that is taken only when more conservative approaches fail. In the residential center, counseling is a major component of care.

CYSTIC FIBROSIS

Cystic fibrosis is an inherited disease of children in which there is dysfunction of all or most of the exocrine glands. The incidence is thought to be 1 in every 500. Approximately 1 in every 25 Caucasians carries the autosomal recessive gene for this disease. Each parent must carry a recessive gene for the disease that the child inherits if the disease is to be present. If the child only inherits one gene, he or she is a carrier. There is a one in four chance of a child inheriting the condition when both parents have the gene. This condition can range from a very mild form of the disease, with good nutrition and no respiratory involvement, to the severe form, with extensive pulmonary obstruction and marked malnutrition that imposes very limited activity. Cystic fibrosis is the most common cause of chronic lung disease in Caucasian children. Dramatic changes have taken place that allow for greater life expectancies for these children. For example, life expectancy in 1950 was 4 years, while in 1976 it was 17 years for females and 21 years for males.

Clinical manifestations of the disease are due to involvement of three areas: the pancreas and other abdominal organs, the lungs, and the exocrine sweat glands. Secretions from the exocrine glands are thick and tenacious. These thick, abnormal secretions block the ducts of the exocrine glands, causing infection, atrophy, and atresia. The abnormal secretions also cause obstruction of organ passages, resulting in chronic pulmonary disease, pancreatic insufficiency, and intestinal obstruction (Figs. 10-8 and 10-9). The vicious cycle of cystic fibrosis can be treated with proper management (Fig. 10-10).

Diagnosis is made from the family history, enzyme studies, pulmonary function tests, and a sweat test. When meconium ileus occurs in the newborn, surgery is usually required to relieve the intestinal obstruction. The lumen of the small intestine is plugged with putty-like meconium near the ileocecal valve, which is inspissated. Abdominal distention and vomiting occur.

A sweat test is done to determine the sweat chloride level. When the child does not have cystic fibrosis, the sweat level is below 40 mEq/liter. A sweat test of 50 mEq/liter or above is suggestive of cystic fibrosis.

Pulmonary function tests are performed to establish the child's pulmonary status. The pulmonary function tests identify the child's forced vital capacity, forced expiratory volume, and peak expiratory flow rate. The child is encouraged to take an active interest in the pulmonary function tests and the results. If the child is advised of the test results, he or she can be encouraged to work to improve the test results. The desire to improve pulmonary function is based on the knowledge that the most common cause of death is lung damage, which results in an oxygen intake insufficient to support life.

The long-term management of these children can be carried out in either an outpatient or an inpatient setting. Due to the severity of this disease, hospitalization can be a common occurrence for these children.

Chest Hygiene

Nebulization therapy is utilized to moisten and thin respiratory mucous secretions and to disperse the appropriate agent, such as bronchodilators, antibiotics, or mucolytic agents, onto the mucous membranes of the tracheobronchial tree. The aim of nebulization therapy is the provision of particles of water or of water-containing medication for deposition in the repiratory tract at the site of the disease process. The size of the particles deposited is determined by the nebulizer used as well as by the solution and the humidity of the air used for nebulization (O'Hara, 1977). Aerosol treatment is often used prior to percussion

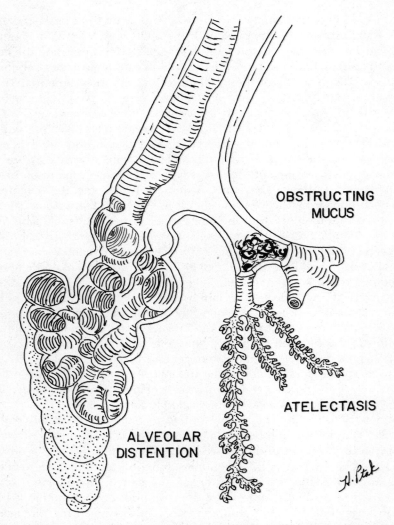

OBSTRUCTING
MUCUS

ATELECTASIS

ALVEOLAR
DISTENTION

Figure 10-8. Schematic representation showing pathology resulting from accumulation and obstruction. *(From O'Hara, M. In S.M. Steele (Ed.), Nursing care of the child with long-term illness. New York: Appleton—Century—Crofts, 1977.)*

and vibration. A mask or mouthpiece can deliver the aerosolized solution, which is expected to liquify secretions and enlarge the bronchial tubes (Harvey, 1982).

A major part of the management of these children pertains to proper care of the chest. The parents and child are aware of the need to complete chest hygiene techniques routinely to help to keep the chest from accumulating secretions. Postural drainage, percussion, and vibration are done daily (Figs. 10-11 and 10-12). Percussion is a vigorous procedure. Although percussion sounds like pounding, it should not be painful. Percussion is done by cupping the hands with the thumbs and fingers closed. The wrists are rhythmically flexed and entended

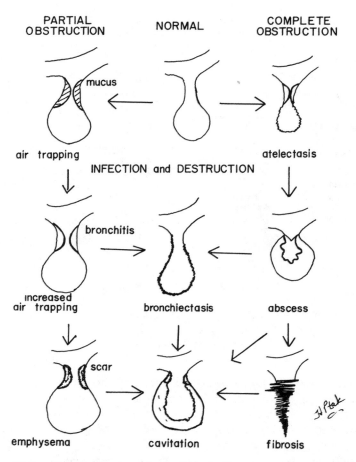

Figure 10-9. Pathologic physiology of cystic fibrosis. *(From O'Hara, M. In S.M. Steele (Ed.), Nursing care of the child with long-term illness. New York: Appleton— Century—Crofts, 1977.)*

during percussion. Vibration follows percussion. The function of vibration is to increase the velocity and turbulence of exhaled air, which results in increased movement of secretions. Vibration is performed by placing flattened hands and a stiffened wrist over the drainage area. The hands are gently shaken back and forth while the child exhales after a deep breath (Harper, 1981). In addition, play can be used to assist with chest hygiene. The child can be taught to hang head-down from a jungle gym or to stand on his or her head or do other calisthenics. The ongoing need for this therapy can become very frustrating and monotonous, leading to noncompliance. Even though the child and family can see the benefits of the treatments, compliance can be difficult to maintain.

Breathing exercises are taught to children by age 3. The child can blow up balloons or blow soap bubbles to increase lung volume. The breathing exercises

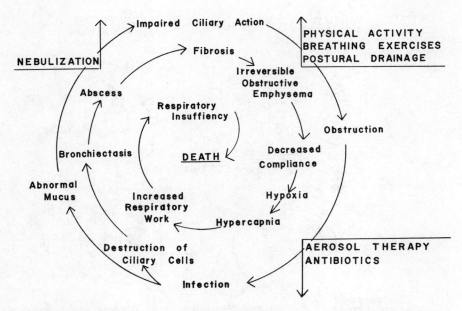

Figure 10-10. The vicious cycle of cystic fibrosis and complicating infections can be broken by effective therapy. *(From O'Hara, M. In S.M. Steele (Ed.), Nursing care of the child with long-term illness. New York: Appleton—Century—Crofts, 1977.)*

taught to older children focus on increasing function in particular areas of the lungs. Exercises are also taught to correct postural deficits.

A major concern of the child is the persistent, hacking cough. The cough can be embarrassing to the child and can cause the child to be ridiculed or avoided by peers. As the cough is a major way to free and remove secretions, it is essential that the child not try to suppress it. Other children need assurance that the cough is not contagious. Teachers must be aware that although the cough is distracting, the child should not be discouraged from coughing, as this would be detrimental to his or her health.

Pancreatic Control

The loss of pancreatic function requires dietary and drug management. Due to obstruction of the ducts, enzymes are not available, so that ingested food cannot be digested adequately. The problems result in very large, frequent, foul-smelling stools. The child's diet is kept low in fat, and, due to difficulty absorbing fat-soluable vitamins, water-soluble vitamin supplements are given. Pancreatic enzymes are given with meals. Extremely large numbers of tablets are needed to achieve control. The child may have a voracious appetite but still appear malnourished. The child may have a protruding abdomen due to large quantities of stool and gaseous distention.

Education

The educational program focuses on personal hygiene. The increased sodium chloride in the sweat makes skin care an area of concern. In addition, in warm

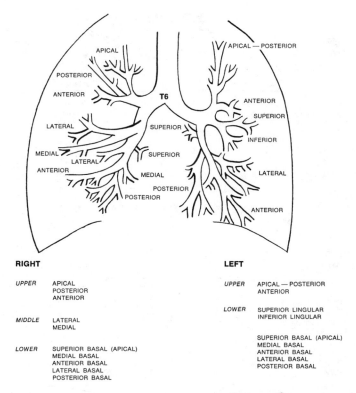

APICAL
POSTERIOR
ANTERIOR
LATERAL
MEDIAL
ANTERIOR
LATERAL
T6
SUPERIOR
SUPERIOR
MEDIAL
POSTERIOR
POSTERIOR
APICAL — POSTERIOR
ANTERIOR
SUPERIOR
INFERIOR
LATERAL
ANTERIOR

RIGHT		LEFT	
UPPER	APICAL POSTERIOR ANTERIOR	*UPPER*	APICAL — POSTERIOR ANTERIOR
		LOWER	SUPERIOR LINGULAR INFERIOR LINGULAR
MIDDLE	LATERAL MEDIAL		
			SUPERIOR BASAL (APICAL) MEDIAL BASAL
LOWER	SUPERIOR BASAL (APICAL) MEDIAL BASAL ANTERIOR BASAL LATERAL BASAL POSTERIOR BASAL		ANTERIOR BASAL LATERAL BASAL POSTERIOR BASAL

Figure 10-11. Segments of the bronchial tree. *(Courtesy of the Children's Orthopedic Hospital and Medical Center, Seattle, Wash.)*

weather it is necessary for the child to ingest increased amounts of salt to compensate for losses.

Discoloration of the teeth can occur as a side-effect of taking tetracycline. While the discoloration cannot be removed, good oral hygiene is essential so that further damage to the teeth does not occur.

The child needs to avoid infectious processes. It is often difficult to keep the child away from other children with infections that can be harmful to the child with cystic fibrosis. Antibiotics are used freely with these children. Early medical attention is needed for infection.

The child and family are encouraged to take advantage of materials supplied by the Cystic Fibrosis Foundation. Other educational aids are often supplied by specialty clinics that serve these families.

Genetic counseling may be sought. A referral may be necessary to receive this important service.

The financial strain caused by the disease can be of concern to the child and family. As the child gets older, he or she may withhold information about impending illness to protect the family from further financial strain. Both the child and the family are counseled on the importance of early medical intervention at the first sign of infection.

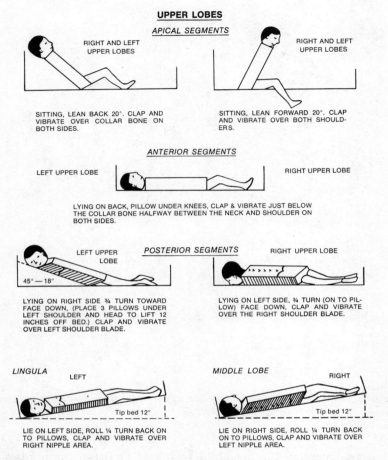

Figure 10-12. Instruction sheets provide aid in teaching parents procedures to be done at home. *("Upper lobes" courtesy of the Children's Orthopedic Hospital and Medical Center, Seattle, Wash.; "Lower Lobes" adapted from design and material by Eloise Draper, LPT—available from the Pediatric Department of the University of Louisville Medical School. Louisville, Ky.)*

The disease can also cause unrest in the family, as the parents often feel unable to leave the child with a baby sitter and they feel constrained by the chest hygiene requirements and often delay vacations or outings because of them.

Normalization of the activities of the child with severe cystic fibrosis is difficult but is still a goal. The constant attention to the child's special daily needs makes it difficult to treat this child like other children in the family. The constant realization that complications can occur and that life expectancy is decreased add to this difficulty. The child's emotional adjustment to the illness is better, however, when he or she does not feel different from his or her peers.

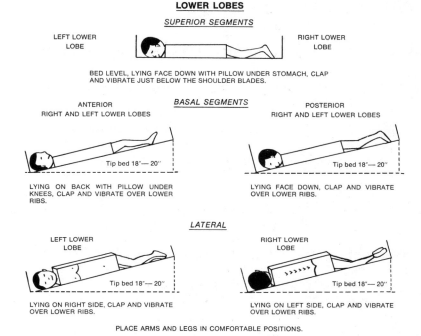

LOWER LOBES

SUPERIOR SEGMENTS

LEFT LOWER LOBE

RIGHT LOWER LOBE

BED LEVEL, LYING FACE DOWN WITH PILLOW UNDER STOMACH, CLAP AND VIBRATE JUST BELOW THE SHOULDER BLADES.

BASAL SEGMENTS

ANTERIOR
RIGHT AND LEFT LOWER LOBES

POSTERIOR
RIGHT AND LEFT LOWER LOBES

Tip bed 18"— 20"

Tip bed 18"— 20"

LYING ON BACK WITH PILLOW UNDER KNEES, CLAP AND VIBRATE OVER LOWER RIBS.

LYING FACE DOWN, CLAP AND VIBRATE OVER LOWER RIBS.

LATERAL

LEFT LOWER LOBE

RIGHT LOWER LOBE

Tip bed 18"— 20"

Tip bed 18"— 20"

LYING ON RIGHT SIDE, CLAP AND VIBRATE OVER LOWER RIBS.

LYING ON LEFT SIDE, CLAP AND VIBRATE OVER LOWER RIBS.

PLACE ARMS AND LEGS IN COMFORTABLE POSITIONS.

PROCEDURE FOR POSTURAL DRAINAGE

1. CLAP ABOUT A MINUTE IN EACH POSITION
2. VIBRATE DURING 5 EXHALATIONS; REST ON INHALATIONS
3. COUGH
4. REPEAT PROCEDURE IF SO ADVISED BY DOCTOR
5. DO 3 TIMES A DAY (UNLESS OTHERWISE ORDERED BY DOCTOR)
   A. MORNING — BEFORE BREAKFAST — DO UPPER, RIGHT, MIDDLE, AND LEFT LINGULA LOBES.
   B. MID-DAY — BEFORE LUNCH OR AFTER SCHOOL — DO RIGHT MIDDLE, LEFT LINGULA, AND LOWER LOBES.
   C. EVENING — BEFORE DINNER OR BEFORE BED — DO UPPER AND LOWER LOBES.

Figure 10-12. (cont.). Instruction sheets provide aid in teaching parents procedures to be done at home. *(Adapted from design and material by Eloise Draper, LPT.; available from Pediatric Department of University of Louisville Medical School, Louisville, Ky.)*

MENINGOMYELOCELE AND HYDROCEPHALUS

Meningomyelocele is an outpouching of the spinal cord through an opening at the back of the vertebral column where bone formation is lacking. Meningocele is a less severe deformity, with the outpouching consisting of the coverings of the spinal cord while the cord itself is not in the sac. Spina bifida occulta is a lesser condition, with no pouching of the meninges and spinal cord but insufficient formation of the vertebra.

The most common location for the defects is the lumbar or lumbosacral area of the spine. Occasionally a lesion is located in the cervical area. Lesions located higher on the vertebral column result in more severe disabilities. The most commonly occurring type of this disability is the most severe form: meningomyelocele.

The etiology of meningomyelocele is not completely understood. However, two hypothese are presented:

1. Failure of the neural tube to close during normal embryonic development.
2. Rupture of the tube after its closure.

The rupture hypothesis is more ascribed to at the present time. Dorsal fusion of the tube begins at the center at approximately the 21st day in utero and proceeds in cephalic and caudad directions simultaneously. By the 25th day, the cephalic pole is fused, and by the 29th day, the caudad pole is fused. Although not thoroughly accepted, morphology has shown changes that are consistent with rupture after closure, giving support to this notion (Bunch, 1978). The effect dietary intake during pregnancy may eventually play an important role in the prevention of this condition. Improved intakes of vitamins and possibly minerals in the diets of women who are pregnant have been associated with a decrease in the incidence of the condition.

Several musculoskeletal deformities are associated with meningomyelocele that may be present at birth or occur later in particular children. Clubfoot deformities are common at birth. Dislocated hips can be present at birth or occur later. Contractures are common at any time, and scoliosis is more common later. All of these conditions complicate the child's care, as casting and surgery carry increased risks with children with this condition.

In cases in which meningomyeloceles occur at or above the eighth thoracic vertebrae, trunk and lower extremity paralysis is present. Lesions occurring at the third or fourth lumbar level result in lower extremity paralysis, but the hip, thigh, and trunk muscles are not involved.

Prenatal screening for neural defects is possible. Two tests that screen for alpha-fetoprotein are the blood serum test and amniocentesis. The blood test is taken during the 14th to 16th weeks of pregnancy, while an amniocentesis is recommended at about the 16th week of pregnancy. The alpha-fetoprotein is elevated when a neural tube defect is present in the fetus.

Immediately after delivery, the child is kept warm, as the interference with the neural system interferes with the infant's temperature regulation ability. Frequently, an isolette is utilized. The infant is placed on his or her abdomen with his or her face to the side. A plastic strip is usually applied below the meningomyelocele over the rectal area (Fig. 10-1). The mildest form of adhesive is used to keep it in place. Disposable plastic urine collectors with their mild self-adherent can be easily applied. Saran Wrap, which has a tendency to adhere to skin surfaces, can be tried. The shield helps to protect the lesion without the necessity of covering the area with dressings. The lesion itself usually is treated by exposure to air.

The infant frequently has associated bony abnormalities. Commonly occurring bony deformities are dislocation of the hip, severely turned-in feet or rocker-bottom flatfoot, scoliosis, kyphosis, and lordosis (Bleck, 1982). Positioning is imperative to prevent the infant from developing contractures or from aggravating bony deformities. A physical therapist and a physiatrist usually evaluate the child to determine the child's muscle potential. Prevention of infection and rupture of the sac is essential. The sac is observed for drainage of spinal fluid. When drainage occurs, a light-weight moist saline dressing is sometimes prescribed. Early surgical correction is often undertaken to prevent more serious muscle involvement and neural deterioration. The surgical correction of the lesion is frequently preceded by a shunting procedure for the hydrocephalus. The shunt is done to control the increased cerebrospinal fluid pressure that may result from repairing the sac.

HYDROCEPHALUS

Hydrocephalus is caused by an excessive accumulation of cerebrospinal fluid (CSF), usually due to interference in the circulation or absorption of CSF. The accumulation of fluid results in enlargement of the ventricles. Hydrocephalus can be communicating or noncommunicating. The CSF in the communicating type flows freely throughout the system, but it does not reach its main absorption site in the arachnoid villa. The CSF in noncommunicating hydrocephalus does not flow freely due to obstruction that prevents the fluid from reaching the subarachnoid spaces. The usual flow of CSF is described in Figure 10-13.

The accumulation of CSF results in an enlargement of the child's head. Therefore, if hydrocephalus is diagnosed, shunting procedures are indicated to control head enlargement.

Diagnosis of hydrocephalus can include a variety of assessments. Measurement of the circumference of the head and correlations with norms for head size are done. Transillumination of the skull, using a flashlight with a rubber adapter, is also done to see if the light results in localized glowing. Radiography of the skull can be used to determine the thickness of the skull bones, separation of the sutures, and widening of the fontanelles when computerized axial tomography (CAT) is not available. CAT is used to visualize the brain. It provides a picture of the variations of tissue density, the ventricular system, and the presence of densities, such as a tumor or cyst. A variety of other diagnostic procedures can be used, such as pneumoencephalography, ventriculography, and ventricular taps.

Shunting Procedures

There are several types of shunting procedures. Two of the most common types are the ventriculoarterial and ventriculoperitoneal. Shunts are accomplished by inserting plastic tubing into the ventricle and connecting it to the extracranial site. A one-way valve is used to open at a specific pressure and close when the pressure is below the specified level. The positioning of the infant postoperatively is determined by the type of shunting procedure, the meningomyelocele, and the postoperative evaluation of the fontanelles. Usually the child is placed on the

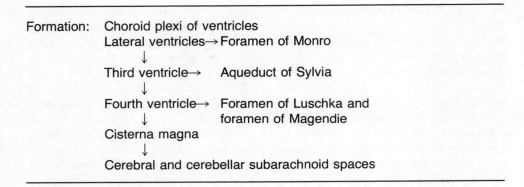

Formation: Choroid plexi of ventricles
           Lateral ventricles→Foramen of Monro
                 ↓
           Third ventricle→   Aqueduct of Sylvia
                 ↓
           Fourth ventricle→   Foramen of Luschka and
                 ↓   foramen of Magendie
           Cisterna magna
                 ↓
           Cerebral and cerebellar subarachnoid spaces

Figure 10-13.   Flow of cerebral spinal fluid.

unoperated side to prevent pressure on the shunt valve from occurring. Amador (1969, p. 1220) explains, "Valve systems are usually inserted and they are pumped frequently postoperatively to remove small pieces of matter which may find their way into the tubing and valve systems." Hospitals vary in their practice as to whether nurses and parents are taught to pump the system. In any event, the nurse evaluates the child to help determine if there is an obstruction in the system. The fontanelle becomes full or tense when there is an interference with the flow of cerebrospinal fluid. The child becomes listless, may fail to feed or may begin vomiting, and is irritable and fretful. He or she does not respond to voice or touch as quickly when there is an obstruction. Early recognition of increased intracranial pressure allows the physician to investigate the obstruction and to make a revision, if necessary. Another problem associated with shunts is infection. Signs of infection include changes in the vital signs and the symptoms associated with increased intracranial pressure. Over a long period, the shunt will need revisions due to the growth of the child, and the child may dislodge the tubing from its site as he or she grows. To date, no tubing has been found that can successfully "lengthen" with the child.

Management of Meningomyelocele
Following the shunting procedure, the meningomyelocele is usually corrected, although some physicians prefer to close the meningomyelocele first and to insert the shunt later. After closure of the sac, the positioning of the infant depends on all the contributing factors. A general principle is to keep the infant off the operative sites. Changing of position is especially important to prevent respiratory complications. The infant is usually fed in the crib or isolette until healing begins to take place. Burping must be done cautiously, depending on the location of the meningomyelocele lesion and surgical incisions.

As soon as the infant's condition is stabilized, the mother begins to hold and feed the child. She is taught the signs to note in relation to the shunting procedure. She is given explicit directions for bathing the infant, with special emphasis on the operative sites. She is given directions for passive exercises to the lower extremities, if indicated. The parents need to become aware of the necessity and value of close medical follow-up for their child. The parents are aware of the complications that might result from the decrease in circulation to the lower extremities and are taught about such preventive measures as keeping the infant dressed warmly and preventing pressure. Decubitus can develop from bedclothes which are tucked in too tightly. The infant's limited ability to turn himself or herself is explained so that the parents will turn the child periodically.

Elimination

The child's urinary system also needs close supervision. The paralysis caused by the neural damage frequently results in urinary dribbling. Some children can learn to empty their bladders by crying, turning, laughing, or sneezing. This is called a Valsalva maneuver (Bleck, 1982). The object is to drain the bladder regularly to prevent stagnation of urine and subsequent infection. Another method used to achieve this goal is the Credé maneuver. Credé is the application of pressure over the bladder area. It is easily accomplished by exerting gentle pressure with the palms of the hands. The mother is taught to express the urine manually at definite intervals. When the child gets older, he or she is taught to do the Credé maneuver. The process can be facilitated by using toys to help the child put pressure on the bladder. Such toys as balloons, horns, bugles, and plastic bubbles can all be utilized when the child is sitting on the potty chair or toilet. The older child, who has outgrown these toys, can be taught to pucker up his or her cheeks with air and then blow slowly through closed lips. Additional pressure can be created by placing the hand over the lips and causing more resistance. It is necessary to check with the physician to get approval to teach the Credé maneuver as it is sometimes contraindicated. Even when it is utilized, the infant is usually wet more frequently than the child who does not have a disability. The skin of the child is prone to breakdown, as it has poorer nourishment and less adequate temperature control. Frequent diaper changing and cleansing of the area is necessary. If a rash begins, exposure to the air is tried. It is sometimes necessary to apply an ointment, such as A & D or Desitin, to help alleviate the rash. If skin breakdown occurs, the mother is cautioned to call the physician for directions.

Kidney involvement usually increases with time. It is one of the most challenging aspects of the long-term management. The child is prone to frequent urinary infections, which are difficult to control with medications due to resistance. The child who dribbles all the time is usually diapered to keep her* outer clothing dry. This diapering provides an excellent medium for bacteria to multiply in when it is wet for long periods. The diaper is usually covered with a plastic panty that further adds to the warmth, and the warmth contributes further to the bacteria formation. When the child is old enough to enter school, it

---

*Here I use the pronouns "her" and "she" because the urinary problem is more difficult to control in females. In males, there are urinary appliances which are fairly successful. However, males should also be given time to go to the bathroom. They must empty the appliance and wash and dry the penis to protect it from excoriation due to continual contact with the urine.

is important to plan times for him or her to go to the bathroom to change the diapering. If there is a space available, diapering can be brought to school once a week and stored. If there is no space available, the child brings adequate daily supplies. Storing the supplies in a child's lunch box or small doll suitcase lessens the child's resistance to taking them. A definite time is established for the child to go to the bathroom, as the child cannot feel wetness, and frequently the odor of urine is more noticeable to others than to the child.

Depending on the severity of the accompanying handicaps and the facilities available, the child may need help to complete personal care. Handrails help a great deal, especially if one is placed near the toilet and another near the sink. It is also convenient to have a table available near the sink so that supplies can be placed conveniently on it.

The child's skill in learning self-help skills in urine and stool control can be delayed. In a study by Sousa et al. (1976), it was found that toileting skills were delayed more than any other self-help skills that the child needs to learn. This study found that bowel control was not established until 17 years of age (Bleck, 1982).

The ileal conduit is a procedure that has declined in use in recent years. If the child has a urinary diversion and is wearing a prosthetic device, it is important that specific times to use the bathroom are established. The urinary appliances also have a tendency to develop odors. These can be fairly well controlled by washing the appliance frequently, airing it on a routine basis, using deodorant or vinegar in the wash water, using deodorant tablets in the pouch, and keeping the child's skin clean and dry. The child needs at least two appliances so that they can be alternated and aired adequately.

Several different varieties of appliances are used. One utilizes a leg bag for collecting the urine; another has a pouch. The one with the leg bag is made of a soft rubber and is easy to keep clean. The advantage of the appliance is that it creates less pressure on the stoma. Occasionally, pressure from an appliance can cause the stoma to herniate. The disadvantage of this appliance is that the leg bag shows with females, and this can be embarrassing. The bag fits under the trousers of the male, so it is not as much of a problem (Figs. 10-14 and 10-15). The appliance with the pouch has the advantage of being easily concealed under clothing, but it is more difficult to keep odor-free if it is not cleansed frequently and adequately (Figs. 10-16 and 10-17).

Both types of appliances are connected to a urinary collection bottle at night. This facilitates better drainage. It also allows the child to move around freely without putting pressure on a bag of urine.

The skin surface near the appliance is washed with soap and water and dried thoroughly. There is a tendency for skin irritation to develop. This may be due to the skin reacting to the cement used to apply the device or due to urine leakage. At times the skin problem becomes severe and the appliance has to be left off so that the skin can be exposed to air and light.

Intermittent self-catheterization is increasing in use with these children. The procedure calls for clean catheters rather than sterile ones. Children over the age of 5 years are candidates for this self-care technique for controlling urinary

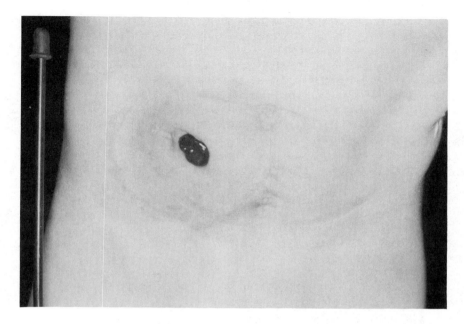

Figure 10-14. A healed stoma. The skin area around the stoma demands excellent care.

incontinence. It is easier for male children to learn this technique, as the urinary meatus is easily visualized. A hand mirror used to see the meatus and diagrams are useful to help orient the child. The amount of time that it takes for the child to be self-sufficient in this procedure varies. The parents and nurse are supportive of the child's efforts and offer praise for accomplishments. In the event that the child is not successful at a particular age, he or she is advised that he or she may be able to try to achieve continence with this method at a later date.

The bowel incontinence associated with myelomeningocele is more easily regulated than the urinary incontinence. A convenient time for utilizing the toilet is determined. In large families, this can be a problem. The child frequently needs extra time to complete evacuation. Suppositories are helpful in getting the pattern established. A Ducolax suppository is inserted prior to a meal and then the child is placed on a potty chair or toilet after the meal. After a while, the child usually evacuates without the suppository. The success of the bowel training may also be directly related to the dietary and fluid intake of the child. The mother and child are both aware that any significant changes in dietary intake may interfere with evacuation and cause incontinence during the day. If stools are constipated, stool softeners such as Colace or Doxinate are often prescribed to prevent impaction, which often requires digital removal and enemas. The bowel evacuation may be more successful if it is scheduled for the evening. The morning hours may be too hectic in the household. Occasionally, suppositories, an adequate diet, and good timing are not sufficient for evacuating the bowel. It may

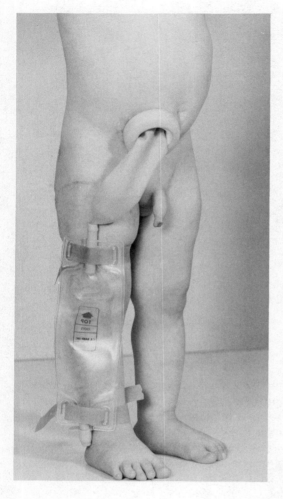

Figure 10-15. Ileal appliance with a leg bag for urine collection.

be necessary to resort to enemas. The least amount of solution of a commercially prepared enema, such as Fleet's, is utilized to stimulate the movement. The pattern of establishing a time that is consistent from day to day cuts down on the incontinence and the embarrassment that it causes.

Bracing

The bracing of the child also contributes to the nursing responsibilities. Bleck (1982) states that the level of paralysis influences the child's ability to walk. The following guidelines help to determine if the child can walk:

1. Above the 12th thoracic level: no practical walking.
2. From 12th thoracic to 4th lumbar: partial household ambulation with braces and crutches.
3. From 4th lumbar to 2nd sacral: community ambulation.

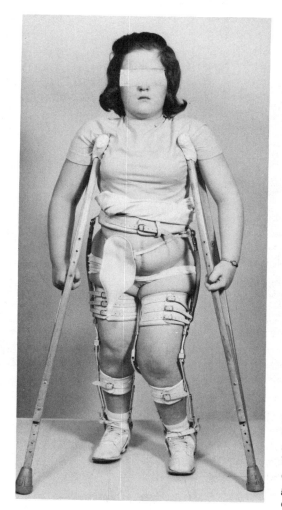

Figure 10-16. Mary is 13 years old. She has a repaired myelomeningocele, arrested hydrocephalus, repaired bilateral dislocated hips, and ileo conduit. She is an outstanding student and gets around well with the use of crutches and long braces.

Prior to the time that the child is ready to ambulate, special braces are available to help the child to enjoy his or her environment. Special self-standing braces are provided at approximately 11 to 15 months of age. Such a brace is called the orthopodium or A-frame brace. The parapodium, with hip and knee joints, is used when the child is expected to achieve sit–stand mobility. Parapodium use begins in 15 minute intervals. Use the parapodium several times a day during the first week to help the child adapt to it. Slowly increase the length of time it is used until it is tolerated for extended periods of time. Check the skin after using. Reddened areas that do not disappear within 30 minutes of the removal of the parapodium are reason for concern. The brace needs to be checked for proper fit or it is likely to cause skin breakdown.

After the child is comfortable in the brace, he or she can learn to roll and sit using the brace. The child needs to learn to fall safely in the brace. When the child

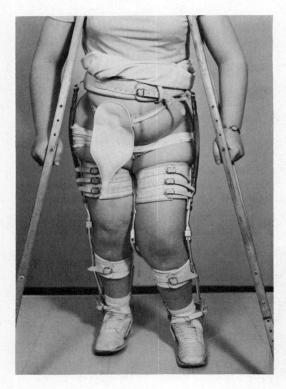

Figure 10-17. Here Mary illustrates the wearing of her urinary drainage appliance. The waist belt can be removed and washed or replaced. The bag is washed and dried and deodorant tablets are inserted. Note she does not wear a leg bag and this appliance will be completely covered by her dress.

is ready to learn to walk, the braces must fit properly if the child is to utilize them effectively. In addition, the joints must move freely. Dust collects in the joints and must be removed. Oiling is also necessary. The leather parts should not be cracked. The leather can be preserved by the use of saddle soap. The braces are checked frequently, especially during growth spurts (Fig. 10-18).

The child's lower extremities do not grow as consistently as the trunk; however, he or she may gain weight and the braces may be too tight. The child is encouraged to use the braces consistently. It is often easier to push a child around in a wheelchair, but this does not help in future adjustment to life. The emphasis is on making the child as self-sufficient as possible, and bracing can increase the child's ability to ambulate if there is sufficient motor function. The child is also taught to check the legs and feet for pressure areas using a hand mirror. This is done on a daily basis, as decubitus forms quickly.

Skin Care

As the paralysis of the lower part of the body is a major consideration, skin care of this area is of major concern. The parents and child are taught to check the skin areas frequently, especially where skin surfaces come in contact with each other or with appliances. In addition, attention must be focused on protecting the areas from extremes of hot and cold. The skin can be protected from burns by checking

Figure 10-18. Braces must be checked frequently. The leather, buckles, straps, and hinges are all in excellent condition at this time. *(Photo by H. Riggs)*

the temperature of the bath water before the child is submerged. The child can use additional clothing when outside temperatures are below freezing, and areas that have concentrated heat (such as radiators or ovens) are avoided. Prevention is the best treatment, as healing is difficult to achieve when paralysis is present.

Fractures

The child is prone to fractures due to osteoporosis. As there is no pain associated with lower torso or extremity fractures due to the paralysis, the parents and child are taught to check for signs of swelling, redness, warmth, and fever if trauma occurs. Again, healing is a problem, so prevention is essential. When a fracture occurs, however, the parents should not be made to feel that they are the cause of the fracture. They are told that the child's bones are brittle and that spontaneous fractures can happen even with the most diligent handling.

Nutrition

The monitoring of the child's nutrition is of special concern, as these children have a tendency towards obesity due to their inactivity. Modifications in the diet are based on the height and weight assessments of the child.

Counseling

The nurse plays an important role in counseling the parents and the child. The parents usually have many questions relating to growth, education, employment, finances, and so forth. Frequently, the parents know the answers to many of their questions, but they need an opportunity just to talk with someone.

In a study by Curtis et al. (1972), 100 clients over the age of 12 years were studied and the following data emerged:

1. Eighty percent of the clients were able to walk.
2. Twenty-eight percent of the clients used crutches or braces.
3. Twenty percent of the clients used a wheelchair.
4. Sixty-five percent of the clients had good bowel control.
5. Thirty-five percent of the clients had good urinary control.

6. Clients with ileal conduits were the best controlled and most satisfied.
7. Thirty-eight percent of the clients had arrested hydrocephalus.
8. Approximately half of the clients had ventriculoatrial shunts.
9. Eighty-nine percent of the clients had an IQ of 80 or above.
10. Seventy-nine percent had graduated from high school.
11. Twenty-seven percent were in college or college graduates.
12. Fifty-eight percent of those who reached adulthood were employed.
13. Of 28 males, 4 were married and of 41 females, 17 were married.
14. "Normal" sex activity was claimed by 43 percent of the males and 24 percent of the females.

In another study, Shurtleff et al. (1975) focused on the sexual activity of 50 long-term survivors with myelomeningocele and found the following:

1. Thirty-five percent were too handicapped to engage in sexual activity.
2. Of the remaining 65 percent, 30 percent (15) were virginal.
3. The remaining 35 percent (18) reported coitus.

Both males and females described varying degrees of satisfaction from genital stimulation and intercourse. Only one of the five sexually active males was able to achieve an erection; one of the impotent males had three children. There were 17 children born to parents with meningomyeloceles, and they were all able-bodied.

The children may need additional assistance in dealing with their questions. Their limited understanding prevents them from gaining satisfaction from many of the answers given them. They find it very difficult to live in a world where their peers are so different from themselves. The child needs to learn to appreciate assets and to focus less on his or her deficits. The child may fantasize that his or her body is not disabled. The use of fantasy can help the child to cope. As the child's cognition increases, the child will be better able to understand limitations and to use techniques to adapt to the environment.

The intellectual ability of these children is usually normal or slightly below normal. However, these children are often delayed in social skills. In a study by Sousa et al. (1976), it was found that adolescents had less proficiency in age-appropriate social skills than children of younger years. The researchers concluded that social interaction skills were the only skills that did not progress with age (Bleck, 1982). The educational and vocational potential of these children is influenced by their ability to socialize, so these skills need consistent attention for the child to reach his or her maximum level of attainment.

DEFORMITIES OF EXTREMITIES

A number of anomalies can occur in the extremities. They may be obvious anomalies, such as a missing extremity or extremities, or less noticeable conditions, such as a dislocated hip. The duration of care is frequently dependent upon the time lapse between discovery and therapy. For instance, a dislocated hip discovered in the nursery and treated immediately usually requires only short-term therapy for correction. If the condition is not detected until the child is walking, the medical therapy usually spans a long period of time.

Amputations

Amputations are congenital or acquired. Congenital amputations are present at birth. Acquired amputations are usually the result of trauma or surgery. The most common causes of traumatic amputations are automobile and other vehicular accidents. Surgically induced amputations are common in the treatment of malignant bone tumors.

The upper extremity can be amputated at many levels. The classification of upper extremity amputations is related to the level of the amputation. The following terms are used to describe upper extremity amputations, beginning at the shoulder: shoulder disarticulation (S/D), short above-elbow (A/E), standard above-elbow (A/E), elbow disarticulation (E/D), very short below-elbow (B/E), short below-elbow (B/E), medium below-elbow (B/E), long below-elbow (B/E), wrist disarticulation (W/D). The location of the amputation influences the functional ability that is associated with the amputation.

The functional ability of the child is significantly better when the amputation is unilateral. Bilateral upper extremity amputations result in decreased functional ability, as the child is unable to complete learning of fine motor skills.

The prosthesis contains the following components that are assembled to try to duplicate the function of the natural arm and hand:

1. Suspension, a method to hold the prosthesis on the child's body.
2. A socket to interface with the skin.
3. Mechanical joints to replace the lost joints.
4. A terminal device, such as a hook, to serve some of the functions of a hand.
5. A source of power to preposition the terminal device and to activate it.

The hook is a far more functional terminal device than artificial hands. The child usually wants an artificial hand to alternate with the hook for more formal occasions.

If a prosthesis is required, it is usually fitted before the child is 8 to 10 months of age. The fitting is scheduled when the child is able to achieve sitting balance. The prosthesis will probably need to be replaced every 15 to 18 months due to growth requirements and use.

The child with a missing extremity requires long-term care to guarantee that the prosthesis is functioning effectively. The skin areas are monitored closely to prevent breakdown due to the added stress produced by the prosthesis.

The infant born with a missing or severely deformed upper extremity is missing one of his or her sources of gratification. The newborn clenches and sucks on his or her fists. It may be useful to supply a pacifier to the infant to help compensate for the missing fist. As the normal infant grows, he or she is ambidexterous. The infant with the missing hand is forced into a preference early unless a prosthesis is fitted to aid the child. The infant is able to use the prosthesis to help in playing with toys and later in learning to crawl and sit. The prosthesis helps to stabilize the body and provides the weight lost by the missing extremity. The prosthesis becomes imperative when the child's neurologic system begins to mature. He or she is capable of doing all types of two-handed activities and needs the prosthesis to complete tasks. The early prosthesis has an uncomplicated design. As the child grows, a prosthesis that can bend, grasp, lift, pull, and so forth is needed to replace the first simple design. The early prosthesis demands much less care than the more complicated type. The infant and child prostheses are worn over a tee shirt to protect the child's skin from excoriation. The straps are kept clean and in good repair. Attention must also be given to the rubber bands, the joints, and the cables. All parts are kept in excellent condition in order to provide maximum function.

In addition to checking the prosthesis for functional ability, the nurse needs to encourage the child to use the prosthesis consistently. The more uniformly the child uses the prosthesis, the more secure the prosthesis feels. The child who is permitted to go without the prosthesis for indefinite periods develops one-handed skills and may resist using the prosthesis. As he or she develops, the one-handedness may become a disadvantage that cannot easily be corrected. The child is likely to complain about the weight of the prosthesis. The prosthesis weighs more than a natural arm, but the child is assured that after wearing the prosthesis for several weeks, the heaviness will not be as noticeable.

There is shrinkage of the remaining arm after wearing a prosthesis for a period of time. Adjustments in the prosthesis are required after this shrinkage takes place so that the prosthesis fits properly. The parents and child are told about the shrinkage in advance, so they are prepared for this situation. Shrinkage results from the reduced use of the residual muscles, bandaging, elastic "stump shrinkers," and pressure from the prosthesis. Shrinkage is one of the long-term problems associated with amputated extremities.

Lower extremity classifications beginning at the hip follow: hip disarticulation (H/D), very short above-knee (A/K), short above-knee (A/K), medium above-knee (A/K), long above-knee (A/K), very long above-knee (A/K), knee disarticulation (K-D), short below-knee (B/K), standard below-knee (B/K), long below-knee (B/K), and Syme's amputation. Amputation of a lower extremity interferes with ambulation. At times, transfer skills are also impaired. Transfer skills are more difficult when a bilateral amputation is present.

Bilateral amputations usually require that the child use two canes as well as the prosthesis to achieve satisfactory ambulation. A high energy expenditure is associated with this type of ambulation, influencing both the child's pulmonary and his or her cardiovascular function.

The components of a lower extremity prosthesis include adequate suspension, socket, joint replacement, and ankle—foot assembly.

The child who requires a lower extremity prosthesis is fitted at 10 to 15 months of age. The prosthesis is indicated when the child begins to pull up in an attempt to stand. As the child is growing, the prosthesis will probably need replacement about once a year.

Lower-extremity prostheses are usually more readily accepted than upper extremity prostheses. This is due to the almost impossible task of getting around on one leg. The length of the affected extremity may influence this. One child with an almost perfectly formed leg refused to wear the prosthesis that provided him with a foot because the prosthesis slowed down his gait. He preferred to play sports without the prosthesis and consequently frequently injured the tissue at the end of the amputated extremity.

Injury to the tissue of the remaining extremity is a critical problem. When it occurs, the prosthesis is left off during the healing process. This can inconvenience the child. It is wise to have a pair of crutches available in case this happens. Then the child will not miss school during this time. Care of the tissues is best provided by the use of a soap such as Dial. The area is rinsed thoroughly and dried. In the hot weather, powder may reduce itching. A stump sock made of virgin wool is placed next to the skin. The sock should fit smoothly and is washed daily. The prosthesis fits over the sock. There is a tendency for the remaining part of the extremity to shrink with time. The child should not attempt to remedy this by adding extra socks or stuffing cotton or the like in the prosthesis. The prosthetist is consulted for all repairs or revisions to the prosthesis. Home repairs can result in expensive errors.

Other problems that are complications of amputations include edema, contractures, infections, pain, and bone overgrowth. Edema can be caused by constriction of the remaining extremity. Evaluation of the cardiovascular system is warranted to determine if there is a circulatory problem. Edema can also be caused by shrinkage, which results in trauma to the end of the extremity due to improper weight-bearing. Edema can result in ulceration if it is not controlled.

Contractures are the result of decreased range of motion or are secondary to scarring of the skin across the joint.

Infection can occur as a result of ulcerations or lack of cleanliness. Therefore, cleanliness and early treatment of breakdown of skin areas is essential.

Pain can be associated with neuroma. Periodic rubbing, tapping, and massage can reduce the sensitivity of a neuroma. Early pain associated with amputations is called "phantom limb" pain.

Bone overgrowth can occur because the bone grows faster than the skin of the remaining extremity. This can result in the bone end coming through the skin. Surgery may be necessary to correct this problem.

The school nurse plays a key role in introducing other children to the prosthesis or in helping the child to tell the other children about it. The child may be asked to demonstrate how to use the prosthesis. The children need to be cautioned about pushing or shoving the affected child. They should understand that the child may need more time to master certain sports. They need to know that at times the child with a lower prosthesis uses crutches instead of the prosthesis. This introduction helps to erase the unknown element and helps the children to appreciate the disability and what it means to their classmate.

The nurse talks with the teachers to help them understand the implications of the prosthesis. One important factor is that the child may tire more easily due to the added energy needed to use the prosthesis. The child may need a short rest period after gym, before beginning other school activities. The teachers should try to treat the child as "normally" as possible but not completely dismiss the possibility of fatigue. Gym is encouraged, as well as swimming. Unless a special lightweight prosthesis is available for swimming, the regular prothesis is removed and the child is taught to swim with one lower extremity. An upper-extremity prosthesis may have to be removed during contact sports to protect the other children from accidental injury.

Much of the adjustment the child has in later life is dependent on early experiences. Therefore, it is worth the extra effort during early years to have the child adjust to the prosthesis. Even with patience, it is not unusual for the adolescent to rebel against the prosthesis and the reasons for the anomaly. If he or she has been given honest answers all along, the adolescent period is easier. He or she may become quite hostile to the health care providers who are responsible for managing the long-term care. Hostility toward the parents is also common. Venting feelings may be all that is necessary to make the adolescent feel better. He or she may need a period to talk over problems with others with similar anomalies. The adolescent may need counseling when he or she realizes that it is more difficult to achieve some of the developmental milestones, such as dating or getting a job. With professional counseling, the adolescent is usually able to make an adequate adjustment to the disability.

In addition to the ways already spelled out, nurses can be helpful to children with a prosthesis in the following ways:

1. The mother may need help in adjusting clothing to compensate for the prosthesis. Instead of disappointing the child because a garment does not fit, snaps or a zipper may be inserted in the side to accommodate the prosthesis. The use of Velcro strips on clothing can also be suggested.
2. When the child is hospitalized, the nurse should be sure the child wears the prosthesis whenever his or her condition warrants it. Failure to encourage the child to wear it may further his or her dislike for the prosthesis. He or she may get the idea that the nurses, too, think it is useless.
3. During hospitalization, make a place available for the child to wash his or her stump socks and to hang them up to dry. If the child is able to assume this chore, he or she is encouraged to do so. If not, the nurse or parents assume this function for the child. The socks should not be sent to the laundry, as the harsh detergent is detrimental to them.
4. The school nurse checks the gait of the child with a lower-extremity prosthesis. She or her may be the first one to detect an ill-fitting prosthesis or an irritation to the tissue. Children frequently try to hide these facts so they do not have to go to the physician.

The majority of cases of missing extremities are amenable to the use of prosthetic appliances. However, there are anomalies of the extremities that cannot be improved by prostheses. Some children are born with severely deformed hands. For various reasons, the hand may not be amputated to permit a prosthesis to be fitted properly. It may be necessary to devise appropriate utensils to teach the child to feed himself or herself (Fig. 10-19). An occupational therapist is usually available to do the initial training. The nurse then visits the home to see that the adaptations are being effectively utilized. Encouragement needs to be given to let the child feed himself or herself. The mother must realize that this may be a long and tedious process, but the end results are worth the additional effort, as the child feels gratification from independence that results from self-feeding.

Other adaptations that may help the child to achieve successful self-feeding are a deep dish with sides and a suction cup on the bottom of the dish. This helps the child by keeping the food on the plate and the plate on the table. A back edge attached to the plate can aid in getting the food on the spoon. The suction cup on the bottom keeps the dish from moving out of the child's reach (Fig. 10-19). The use of a "cobbler-type bib" decreases the chances of soiling clothes. When the child is ready to drink from a cup, a training cup with a cover and spout is useful. The wide cup without the handle adjusts to the deformity of the hand. The child can grasp the cup on each side and raise it to his or her mouth. If the cup drops, it will not spill, because the cover is on securely.

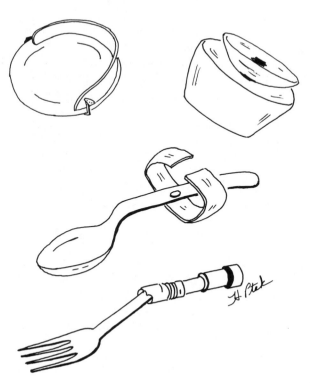

Figure 10-19.   Utensils adapted for use with children who have deficits in hand function.

When the deformity does not lend itself to prosthesis application or an appliance, the child is taught to eat by holding the utensil in his or her toes. This method is taught because it makes the child more self-sufficient, even though the technique may seem socially unacceptable to some persons.

CEREBRAL PALSY

Cerebral palsy involves abnormal movements and posture that result from an irrepairable insult to the brain. The results of the insult are not progressive, but deficits become more evident as the child develops and tries to keep up with the requirements and tasks associated with his or her particular age.

There are many things that seem to influence the lack of neurologic intactness resulting in cerebral palsy. A conservative estimate of the number of children who have this condition in the United States is 4.5 cases per 1000 population (Easton and Halpern, 1981).

Due to brain damage, the child with cerebral palsy is unable to inhibit and control reflexes. Therefore, the reflexes are uninhibited and exaggerated. Due to this, the child is impaired in the voluntary control of motions. Involuntary control of motions is more difficult when the child is excited, so lack of control is exaggerated during these periods.

The etiology of cerebral palsy cannot always be determined. However, prenatal viral, bacterial, and protozoal infections are suspect, with rubella, toxoplasmosis, and syphilis being positively identified with the condition. In the prenatal period, toxic conditions of the mother, such as taking noxious drugs, toxemia, and eclampsia, are causative. Maternal anemia, anoxia, and hypotension are also associated with cerebral palsy.

During the delivery, the most common causes of cerebral palsy are anoxia and hemorrhage. The infant who is born prematurely has a higher risk of developing the condition; this is sometimes attributed to trauma, but trauma does not have to occur.

Postnatally, meningitis, encephalitis, brain trauma, and anoxia can all result in cerebral palsy. Vascular problems, such as hemorrhage, emboli, and thrombosis, can also be causative.

Cerebral palsy can be classified in the following topographic way:

1. Monoplegia: one extremity involved.
2. Diplegia: lower extremity involvement; sometimes mild involvement of upper extremities, as well.
3. Paraplegia: lower extremity involvement.
4. Hemiplegia: the upper and lower extremity on the same side are involved.
5. Quadriplegia: all four extremities are involved.

The symptomatology or physiologic classification includes spasticity, athetosis, dystonia, rigidity, ataxia, tremor, mixed, and undetermined. The most commonly occurring symptoms are spasticity, ataxia, and athetosis. In addition, there can be associated behavior manifestations, such as hyperkinesis, distractibility, and short attention span. Occasionally, perseveration is a behavioral response. In this instance, the child is unable to discontinue one activity in order to respond to another. The child seems to be stuck at one stage and cannot disengage.

Associated physical deficits found in children with cerebral palsy include visual and auditory deficits, which are also due to the brain damage. Other problems that may be present and that influence the rehabilitation program include contractures, dental problems, scoliosis, and seizures. In addition, problems such as dietary problems, bowel and bladder incontinence, mental retardation, communication disorders, and respiratory infections may compound the management.

These children have problems with body image and self-concept that are common to persons with disabilities. Special attention is focused on these needs as well as on the specific deficits that are identified.

Activities of Daily Living

Children with mild to moderate involvement can become independent as concerns dressing skills. When the child shows signs of interest and maturity, removal of garments can be taught and practiced. After undressing is achieved, the child can try putting on garments. Loose-fitting clothing with Velcro strips can aid in this process. Zippering and buttoning skills that require fine motor coordination are practiced on a toy until they are mastered (Fig. 10-20). Contractures of the hip, shoulder, and knee can lessen the child's ability to learn dressing skills. Despite these problems, the goal is to have the child master the ability to dress independently.

Teaching of personal hygiene skills is started at an early age. Children with hemiplegia are usually successful at mastering these skills. Children with more extensive involvement may need adaptive devices, such as handrails or a seat across the bath tub, to be independent.

It may be difficult to achieve independent implementation of perineal hygiene, especially when the child has poor sitting balance or when contractures of the hip, shoulder, or elbow are present. A sponge on a long handle may be useful for increasing independence in this task.

Self-feeding and Nutrition

The early problems in feeding the child with cerebral palsy can influence the mother–infant relationship. Very often, these infants have poor sucking reflexes, have difficulty swallowing, tend to drool feedings, and are easily fatigued by attempting to feed. These behaviors interfere with the infant's ability to get adequate nourishment and satisfaction and comfort from feeding. The mother who attempts to feed the infant can get very frustrated when the child cannot consume adequate amounts in a reasonable amount of time. In addition, the irritability resulting from inadequate satisfaction of hunger can give signals to the mother that she is not a "good mother." A vicious cycle of relative dissatisfaction

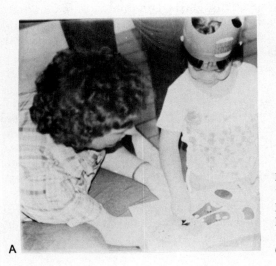

Figure 10-20. **A.** The nurse assists the child in dressing skill mastery by practicing on toys designed for this purpose. *(Photo by M. McGinnis)* **B.** The child's motor development of the hand. *(By H. Ptak)*

REACH, GRASP, RELEASE

THUMB AND FINGER GRASP

FINGER USE

B

occurs as the mother tries to feed the infant, the infant stops feeding prematurely and starts to cry soon after the feeding from hunger, and the mother tries again to feed the child and is unsuccessful once more. Neither the mother nor the infant can derive satisfaction or trust from an interaction of this nature. Therefore, the mother needs assistance with feeding techniques and she also needs support so that she does not interpret the infant's lack of ability as being due to poor mothering skills.

Early feeding episodes can influence the child's ability to master self-feeding in later years. The occupational therapist is usually the team member who takes major responsibility for this part of the child's rehabilitation program. The nurse collaborates with the occupational therapist and the family on the practical application of feeding techniques in the home environment (see Appendices A and B).

The most common nutrition- or feeding-related problems of children with developmental disabilities include:

1. Excessive weight gain or inability to gain weight.
2. Growth retardation.
3. Excessive appetite or anorexia.
4. Delayed self-feeding.
5. Drug—nutrient interactions.
6. Neurologic dysfunction that interferes with feeding.
7. Refusal to try new foods.
8. Dislike for foods of different textures.
9. Disruptive behaviors at mealtime.
10. Inability or lack of willingness to self-feed.
11. Excessive intake of carbohydrates.

The list clearly documents that nutritional problems are commonly associated with the management of children with developmental disabilities.

Most mildly and moderately afflicted children can learn to self-feed. The motor development of the child's hand influences his or her ability to participate in the various activities of daily living (Fig. 10-20). It is sometimes necessary to adapt the dishes and utensils to meet the child's needs (Fig. 10-19). Severely involved children may benefit from using a mechanical feeder. This device gives the child the feeling of independence even when more physical involvement in the feeding process is impossible to achieve.

Mobility

Many children with cerebral palsy are unable to achieve ambulation without assistive devices. A variety of resources can be prescribed to aid the child such as a cane, a broad-base cane, crutches, and a walker (Fig. 10-21). In addition, some children are aided by either short or long leg braces (see the preceding section on meningomyelocele). Many of the children will be fitted with wheelchairs to increase their mobility. Motorized wheelchairs are available when the child has

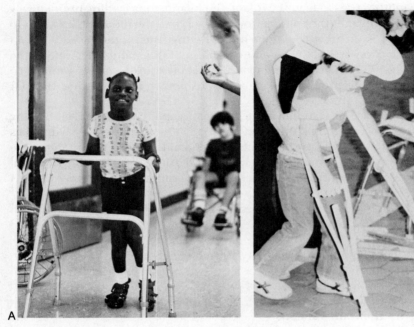

A   B

Figure 10-21.   **A.** A walker and a wheelchair are both means to get the child
to explore the environment. *(Photo by N. Patrick)* **B.** Learning crutchwalking to
facilitate ambulation. *(Photo by M. McGinnis)*

insufficient control to use the upper extremities to propel a wheelchair effectively.

The physical therapist is usually responsible for directing the management
of the child's motor functions, especially motor functions resulting from lower-
extremity capabilities. The physiatrist and orthopedic specialist are also interested in this part of the child's management. The nurse collaborates with these
team members to facilitate the practical application of these skills in the home
environment.

Communication

A major problem for many of these children is interference with communication
skills. A lap board with communication symbols can be placed across the
wheelchair to help the child to communicate. This method has increased the
child's ability to relate to others, but it is a crude method of communication that
only partially compensates for deficits in verbal communication. Speech therapy
can focus on acquisition, retention, interpretation, and application of information. The degree of impairment influences the child's ability to be successful in
any of these areas. Both verbal and nonverbal means of communicating are used.
Computer technology is contributing to the verbal potential for some of these
persons who have intellectual capabilities but who have impaired communication skills.

Socialization

The child with minimal involvement is socialized in much the same way as an able-bodied child. However, a child who is more involved has more difficulty being socialized, as there are deficits in many spheres of development. Early case finding is important so that the parents receive assistance with parenting skills that foster the child's development and so that the interdisciplinary team skills can be utilized to bring the child to his or her maximum level of functioning.

In terms of priorities, socialization skills ultimately may surpass all the other skills that the child needs to master (Fig. 10-22). Being able to interact with other persons in an acceptable manner influences the child's eventual vocational potential. As these children are reaching adulthood in increasing numbers, it is essential to socialize them in a way that is consistent with a maximum degree of independence. The varieties of living arrangements that exist for clients who are mentally retarded are similar to those for clients with moderate to severe cerebral palsy (see Chapter 11).

Surgical Interventions

The child with cerebral palsy is frequently familiar with the hospital, as surgical procedures are often done in an attempt to increase the child's motor function. Heel cord lengthenings, lengthening of various muscles and tendons, release of contractures, and correction of deformities of various areas are common occurrences throughout the lives of these children. The degree of improvement in motor function due to these various procedures is not well documented, nor is the impact of the improvement in the quality of life clearly substantiated. The preparation of these children for surgical intervention and the postoperative management of these children are areas in which nurses can have a significant role in improving the quality of life of these children.

SENSORY DEFICITS

Two sensory deficits that are often associated with other disabilities are hearing and vision deficits. These losses can also occur without association with other

Figure 10-22. A child who cannot stand is able to play ball lying on a scooter board. *(Photo by H. Riggs)*

disabilities, however. Early detection of these losses is essential so that the child's learning and development are not hampered severely by the deficits. Screening for hearing and vision problems is usually a part of a comprehensive screening program. Screening is the process of sifting through a population of children (ages birth through 21) to identify:

- Psychologic problems.
- Communicative problems.
- Social functioning level.
- Physical functioning level.
- Developmental concerns.
- Educational functioning.

The assessment process provides data (1) to determine the child's present level of functioning, (2) to determine the child's needs, and (3) to make appropriate referrals to address these needs.

Hearing Screening

Hearing screening is done in a location where the ambient noise level is low. Screening is more satisfactory when it is done in an area that does not have noise from mechanical equipment, such as heating units or air conditioners. The screening place is also kept apart from such areas as cafeterias, gyms, music and art rooms, shop areas, and rest rooms. Keeping the environmental noise levels down helps to protect the test stimulus so that the child is able to concentrate on the test frequencies and intensities. Sound-isolated rooms are recommended for optimum hearing screening, when possible.

A program that encourages hearing conservation is carried out in public schools. The school nurse is often given the responsiblity to plan and conduct the screening program, using technically competent persons to assist with the testing. When a child fails a screening test, it is repeated. If the child fails the second test, referral is instituted. There are a variety of protocols available to guide the screening procedure, and the agency guidelines are used to establish the screening program. In addition to the selected protocol, Roeser and Northern (1981) propose the following:

1. Avoid letting the child observe the dials by setting the child at an oblique angle so that the tester and audiometer are out of the child's peripheral vision.
2. Avoid giving the child visual clues by using facial expressions or eye or head movements that influence the child's response.
3. Avoid faulty placement of the headphones, as proper placement of the external auditory canal is necessary for proper testing.
4. Avoid giving instructions that are not understood adequately by the child.
5. Limit noise in the testing area.
6. Avoid long testing periods, as the test can usually be completed in 3 to 5 minutes.

7. Avoid inadequate administration of the test tone, which can result in inaccurate responses when the tone is presented less or more than 1 to 2 seconds.

The National Conference on Identification Audiometry makes the following recommendations for conducting hearing screening:

1. Test in acoustically treated test rooms.
2. Frequencies for identification audiometry of school-age children are 500, 1000, 2000, 4000, and 6000 cps.
3. Frequencies 500, 1000, 2000, and 6000 cps are screened at 10 dB, and 20 dB are used for the frequency 4000 cycles.
4. Failure criteria: failure to respond at 10 dB at 1000, 2000 or 6000 cps or at the 20 dB level at 4000 cycles.
5. The same failure criteria are used for both the screen and the pure-tone threshold test.

These guidelines are similar to the recommendations made by the Committee on Audiometric Evaluation of the American Speech and Hearing Association, with the following differences:

1. There is no recommendation that the hearing screening be conducted in an acoustically treated test room.
2. The frequencies of 500 and 6000 cps are excluded.
3. Rescreening of failures is mandatory (Wilson and Walton, 1982).

After the screening procedure identifies a failure, the child is referred for additional evaluation. A battery of tests, including tympanometry, intra-aural reflex testing, and eustachian tube testing, is frequently done. The tympanometry provides information about the air pressure of the middle ear, the parameters of stiffness or flaccidity of the eardrum, the integrity and mobility of the eardrum and ossicular chain, and the resonant point of the middle ear system. Intra-aural reflex testing gives information about the mobility and integrity of the ossicular chain and the sensorineural system, and eustachian tube testing provides data about the patency and function of the eustachian tube (Feldman, 1982).

Classification of Hearing Losses

Two common classifications of hearing loss are used. "Hard of hearing" denotes a hearing impairment, whether permanent or fluctuating, that adversely affects a child's educational performance but that is not included under the definition of "deaf." The second category is "deaf." This indicates hearing impairment so severe that a child experiences difficulty in processing linguistic information through hearing, with or without amplification. Educational performance is adversely affected.

Other significant terms related to hearing are:

• Genetic hearing loss: inherited loss of hearing through autosomal dominant, autosomal recessive sex- or X-linked, and chromosomal abnormalities.

- Acquired hearing loss: loss of hearing during the prenatal or perinatal periods or later in life due to viral infections, toxicity from drugs, toxic chemical exposure, decreased intrauterine oxygen supply, maternal illnesses, injury to the ears, or treatment for other serious illnesses.
- Selective hearing loss: normal hearing for some frequencies and a substantial loss for other frequencies.

Management

As a result of hearing loss, a child may need:

1. Special academic help.
2. Special consideration of social−emotional needs.
3. Special attention to learning style.
4. Attention to home−environmental requirements.

The goal of management is to maximize the child's use of his or her residual hearing and to find ways to compensate for losses. Total communication protocols are commonly used; they include:

1. Use of sign language (Ameslan).
2. Finger spelling.
3. Speech.
4. Lip reading (speech reading).
5. Gestures.

The child who has a severe hearing loss from birth is slow to master speech and language skills, while the child who acquires a hearing loss may not have problems in these areas. Hearing-impaired children who are fitted with hearing aids have less difficulty learning language skills. However, their speech is still of lower quality than the speech of able-bodied children.

To facilitate the child's ability to lip read, the family is encouraged to face the child when speaking and to make clear lip movements when speaking. In addition, the child's hands can be placed on the face of the speaker to "feel" movements of speech.

The child will need consistent encouragement and guidance during childhood to develop age-appropriate skills. As the child does not appear "disabled," he or she is not usually protected from potential harm. For example, the deaf child cannot hear a siren that warns others about potential danger. In addition, the child cannot hear the ordinary noise of cars and can run into the street without thinking. The parents cannot "warn" the child by verbal commands of impending danger. Therefore, the family must patiently prepare the child to live safely in the environment.

As the child's world expands, he or she learns that other persons are not eager to interact with persons who cannot hear well. It is common for people to withdraw from those who cannot hear accurately and to cause social isolation of the severely hearing impaired.

Societal education is essential to improve the quality of life for these children. Common characteristics of successfully integrated students in the classroom include:

1. Good use of residual hearing.
2. Amplification in adequate working condition.
3. Full-time hearing aid use.
4. Academic skills, social interactions, and behavior skills consistent with those of peers.

Vision Screening

The Snellen and Schering charts are the most common ways to conduct vision screening. In a well-lighted room, the child stands 20 feet from the chart and occludes one eye and then the other. The childs reads the letter or pictures or points in the direction of the symbols, depending on which version of the chart is used.

Vision screening can detect ptosis, strabismus, amblyopia, eye infections, and visual acuity problems (Fig. 10-23). Vision is a major determinant of whether or not the child is able to learn. Therefore, early screening, referral, and treatment of problems is essential, as visual problems can interfere with the child's ability to succeed in achieving developmental tasks. In addition, problems that are not isolated and treated effectively can lead to permanently impaired vision.

Criteria for referring preschool children include:

1. Three-year-old with 20/50 vision or less.
2. Four-year-old with 20/40 vision or less.
3. One-line differences between two eyes.
4. Children with strabismus.

Criteria for referring school-age children include:

1. Through third grade, 20/40 vision or less.
2. Fourth grade and above, 20/30 vision or less.
3. One-line differences between two eyes.

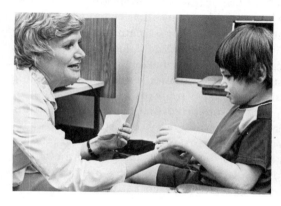

Figure 10-23. The nurse prepares the child for vision testing. Here she prepares the child to cover her eye. Children with disabilities need practice with the testing situation prior to doing the vision screening.

Children meeting any of these criteria are rescreened prior to referral. In addition, observations of the child that may indicate vision problems are considered, such as squinting, rubbing eyes, excessive blinking, straining to see, tilting the head to one side, holding a book close to the eyes, or getting close to objects or persons to see details. Common complaints of children that are sometimes associated with vision impairment include dizziness, headaches, itchy eyes, and blurriness of vision (Holland, 1982).

There are two common classifications of vision loss. Blindness refers to an anatomic and functional disturbance of the sense of vision. There is total loss of light perception. Visual impairment is any interference with the expected norms of vision, such as central vision function, peripheral visual function, binocular visual function, and color perception. The deviation can be partial or total, temporary, reversible, progressive, or permanent (Hoover and Bledsoe, 1981). In essence, severe visual impairment is a loss of such magnitude that it is necessary to use special aids and other senses to master tasks that are ordinarily achieved through use of vision.

Severe visual impairment in childhood can be the result of prenatal factors. Hoover and Bledsoe (1981) state that prenatal factors are responsible for 10 percent of visual problems. Friedreich's ataxia and retinitis pigmentosa are examples of conditions that contribute to this morbidity statistic. Prenatal influences were responsible for approximately 65 percent of severe vision problems in children under 5 years of age in 1962. Retrolental fibroplasia (RLF) was responsible for approximately 15 percent of severe vision problems. Other major contributors in the under-5 age group were neoplasms, infections, and injuries. In the under-19 age group, there are approximately 70,000 visually impaired children. In addition to these severely affected children, there are estimates of 7,500,000 school children with some type of vision defects (Whaley and Wong, 1979).

Prevention

A major thrust in the area of sensory loss is prevention. As prenatal factors play an important part in the morbidity rates, prenatal care is advocated. Prenatal care results in a reduction in the number of premature and low-birth infants, who are more vulnerable to vision deficits. In addition, the close monitoring of oxygen therapy for immature neonates is warranted to protect their vision.

Vision screening in the early years can lead to early treatment or correction of a variety of eye problems that can decrease vision if left unattended. In addition, the parents and child are counseled about behaviors that are consistent with the promotion of good vision, such as proper lighting while reading, reading in areas that do not cause unnecessary strain on the eyes, using eyeglasses or contact lenses, when prescribed, keeping a proper distance from television, using a light during television viewing after daylight, avoidance of eye-straining work for excessive periods of time, proper rest and nutrition, and yearly eye examinations.

Parents of young children are advised of the tentative dangers to the child's vision due to use of certain toys. Toys that have pop-out pieces are particularly dangerous to preschool children because these children get very close to toys and a "jump out" or "pop out" part can hit the child in the eye, causing serious injury. In addition, older children are counseled that flying objects can cause serious damage. Examples of these are arrows shot from bows, darts shot from guns or aimed at dart boards, beebees from guns, and so forth. Trauma to eyes can also occur during contact sports and childhood "rough house" games. Calling these situations to the parents' and later to the child's attention can decrease the incidence of trauma.

Management

Eyeglasses or contact lenses can often improve visual impairments. However, the child who is blind cannot be helped by an appliance. The management of these children includes attention to every aspect of living, as it is very difficullt to learn about the environment without the use of the visual sense.

Use of touch is a valuable way for the child to learn about his or her environment (Fig. 10-24). A braille system can help the child to read through touch. Talking records, a white cane for walking, and a seeing eye dog can be beneficial in the educational process of these children.

The child's environment needs to be learned and maintained in a stable state so that the child can get around without serious injuries occurring. The family's cooperation in verbally explaining the environment is essential to the child's ability to be independent.

The child will need to be exposed to experiences that other children take for granted. As the child cannot see what is happening, he or she is hesitant to

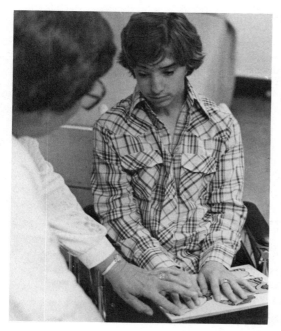

Figure 10-24. This adolescent who acquired blindness in an automobile accident learns to use the tactile sense. *(Photo by N. Patrick)*

engage in new or nonfamiliar activities. However, these actvities are essential to the growth and development of the child. As the child experiences swinging, jumping, running, and so forth, some of the fear of motor activities is decreased. However, this does not happen quickly or spontaneously, so the parents are advised to keep orienting the child through verbal cues and guided assistance. The safety of the child is also at stake, so the family needs to be astute to the child's whereabouts and activities.

The parents learn that the child's auditory and tactile senses develop to compensate for the child's loss of vision. The child explores the face and shape of others through touch to learn what they "look like." This behavior is encouraged, and the child is asked to describe what he or she "sees." In this way, the seeing person can correct misconceptions of the child and confirm correct impressions. For a child who has never seen, some concepts are impossible to learn through touch alone. For example, the child is not able to discriminate variances in skin color that contribute to his or her understanding of race. The child's auditory sense is heightened. Many sounds that are discounted by persons who see are troublesome to someone who cannot see. For this reason, sounds are explained so that the child learns to discriminate between sounds that are signals of danger and ones that are benign.

The family is encouraged to enroll the child in an educational program at an early age. These programs can help the family with the child's educational program. Some of these programs also teach the child activities of daily living that the child is slow to master. Teaching strategies that are appropriate for children with slow development are also used with blind children. It takes a great deal of patience to teach the child without vision to master his or her environment.

SCOLIOSIS

There are two common types of structural scoliosis: idiopathic and neuromuscular. The neuromuscular type is usually caused by a paralytic condition, such as cerebral palsy or myelomeningocele.

Scoliosis is a potentially progressive condition that affects children during their active growth phase of development. All children who have remaining epiphysial growth are considered to have a potentially progressive scoliosis. This usually includes males to age 17 years and females to age 15 years. Spinal curvatures progress in a lateral direction; vertebral body rotation is related to convexity and concavity of the curvature. The scoliosis is the result of vertebral body changes that cause pressure on the intervertebral disks. Since rotation of the thoracic spine is associated with lateral curving, there are also changes in the ribs, causing structural deformities.

The classification of scoliosis relates to the anatomic site in the vertebral column where the curvature is located: cervical curve, C1 to C6; thoracic curve, T2 to T12; cervicothoracic, between C7 and T1; lumbar, L1 to L4; thoracolumbar, T12 or L1; and lumbosacral, L5 or below (Cailliet, 1975).

There are three reasons why early diagnosis and treatment of scoliosis is warranted: (1) appearance, (2) relief or prevention of pain, and (3) prevention of cardiopulmonary complications. The diagnosis is confirmed by x-ray and the Cobb method of measurement of the degree of curvature.

Management

The goal of management is to have the child reach maturity with a straight, balanced, and stable spine. Treatment can be nonoperable or operable.

Exercises are usually prescribed in association with other therapy. The value of exercises is probably gained as a result of improved posture, increased flexibility, and improvement in muscle and ligament tone. The exercises decrease effects of bracing: muscle atrophy stiffness and restricted respiration from thoracic pad pressure (Watts, 1979). Exercise also contributes to the child's overall feeling of well-being and can contribute to an increase in self-esteem.

The Milwaukee brace is the most commonly used bracing appliance. It is prescibed for children with a 20° to 45° curvature. The brace consists of a molded pelvic portion of plastic, front and back metal uprights, and a ring around the neck. Corrective forces are applied by the pressure pads affixed to the uprights. The brace is worn 22 to 23 hours each day until the child reaches skeletal maturity (Bleck, 1982). Nighttime bracing is sometimes continued until early adulthood. Another less bulky brace is the Boston bucket. A variety of other braces are also used. Choice of a brace is partially determined by the response of the child and parents. Acceptance of the brace will increase the child's compliance with treatment.

Casting (plaster jackets) for scoliosis treatment is rarely selected today for nonsurgical treatment, as braces are more acceptable and do not require the 24 hour therapy casts require. Casting still accompanies some surgical corrections.

Traction is also used in some treatment protocols. Examples are Halo-pelvic and cephalopelvic traction. Traction is usually used prior to casting or surgery.

Another technique that is being used selectively for correction of idiopathic scoliosis is the use of electrospinal instrumentation (Bobechko et al., 1979). This method is considered to be as effective as the Milwaukee brace for some children. The main advantage is that it is not bulky like the Milwaukee brace, so it decreases the obvious difference in physical appearance that is present when the child wears a brace.

The treatment is conducted at nighttime, so the child's therapy is not obvious to peers. The child has a surgically implanted receiver, and a transmitter—antenna component is used. Stimulation of muscles is produced in an attempt to alter the direction of growth of the spine. The child can be taught to do the treatment himself or herself.

Surgery is usually recommended when the curvature is 50° or more. Depending on the type of surgery selected, the child may or may not be placed in a body cast for an extended time period. Surgical procedures that are commonly used are the Harrington rod, Dwyer instrumentation, and the Luque rod procedures. These procedures fuse the spine, achieving this goal in approximately a year. In these procedures, rods are placed along the child's spine, and screws, staples, cables, or wiring are used. The choice of procedure is influenced by the type and severity of the condition, other conditions, the age of the child, and physician preference.

The child's skin integrity is checked when bracing or casts are used in management. Braces or casts that are too tight can cause ulceration or constriction of circulation. It is necessary to trim casts that cause these changes or to remove or adjust the brace to restore skin integrity. The child is advised to wear a white cotton T-shirt under the brace to protect the skin. Underpanties are worn over the brace to prevent wrinkling, which contributes to skin breakdown. As casts and braces are worn for extended periods of time (several months or years), the child's compliance with suggested techniques for preserving skin integrity can help to limit secondary decubitus.

A major benefit of the Milwaukee brace is that it can be removed for bathing and swimming on a daily basis. These possibilities contribute to the child's physical and emotional well-being. Casts cannot be removed to promote these activities, and this has contributed to the decline in the use of casts.

The long-term use of appliances can make the child feel alienated or different from his or her peers. As the time when treatment is instituted is usually the same time that physical appearance is of major concern to the child, every attempt is made to focus on ways for the child to look attractive. The Milwaukee brace cannot be concealed from peers, but wearing an attractive scarf over the neck ring can contribute to a more aesthetic appearance. In addition, more loosely fitted clothing can help to disguise the plastic mold and uprights. Newer braces are less obvious and can be concealed more easily than the Milwaukee brace. Therefore, children often prefer the smaller brace. Long-term brace wearing can contribute to bodily changes that can be of concern to the child, such as changes in the color of the skin where pressure is applied, delayed breast development in females, fat accumulation in the thighs, changes in the shape of the thorax, and scarring from pressure sores. These complications can further contribute to the child's negative feelings about bracing. Close monitoring of the child can decrease the occurrence of complications.

Education

The child who develops scoliosis is often concerned about the progressive nature of the disease. Unfortunately, it is not always possible to assure the child that progression will not occur. The child is appraised of developments and is shown x-rays and curvature measurements so that he or she can understand why certain decisions about therapy need to be made. The child may be discouraged by the long-term need for bracing and casting, but surgery is even more threatening. It is often difficult for the child of this age to accept the notion that after long-term immobilization, the problem will not automatically resolve. The child will need ongoing counseling so that concerns are expressed and the child feels a part of the decisions that are made.

A major concern is body image integrity. The young child who has to integrate braces or casts into his or her body image and then has to change his or her image when their use is discontinued, needs opportunities to talk about himself or herself, to see pictures of himself or herself, and to see signs of changes that are being accomplished by treatment. The child's clear understanding of his or her body image is dependent on the health care providers' willingness to be concerned with the child's emotional well-being while trying to correct the physical deformity.

Prior to surgical intervention, the child is prepared for the surgical procedure and the postoperative management. When continued immobilization is used, the child is prepared for this eventuality. It is helpful to have the child discuss the impending surgery and its anticipated results to assess the child's understanding of the treatment. It is also possible to have the child draw a picture of his or her back problem prior to surgery and to draw the back with anticipated changes. The pictures can give clues about the child's level of understanding of the problem and surgery. Children who do not seem to realize that the surgery can correct the curved spine can be shown pictures of other children before and after surgery. In this way they can learn the anticipated long-term outcomes, and they can be helped to understand that outcomes of this significance take extended periods of time to achieve.

Group meetings of children with long-term bracing or casting can help the children to be supportive of one another. In these rap sessions, the children can share ways to make living with appliances more tolerable and can encourage one another during stressful periods. If a group cannot be assembled, establishing a telephone network can serve a similar purpose. Children of similar ages can be supportive of each other, while the older children can encourage the younger ones with their therapy.

Parent support groups can also be of value as the parents try to encourage the child to comply with therapy and withstand ongoing long-term management.

CONGENITAL HEART DISEASE

The initial reaction of parents to a diagnosis of congenital heart disease may be one of fear and anxiety. These reactions do not necessarily diminish with time, because the thought that the defect is still there is always in the parents' minds. Fear and anxiety may very well increase as the child shows signs of illness. Such signs may be the appearance of cyanosis, becoming easily fatigued, inability of the child to breastfeed or consume adequate amounts of formula, periods of dyspnea, or overt fainting spells. These symptoms are periodic reminders to the parent that there is something wrong with the infant's or child's heart even though the defect is invisible.

Some interesting facts about the emotional implications of congenital heart disease in children influence the management of children with heart disease. A key point is that mothers seem to live in constant fear that the children will die. This idea is supported by the slow and poor physical development of the child, the frequency of illness, and the somewhat undesirable personality of the child. The child is frequently negative, whiny, and irritable. Despite this undesirable behavior, the mothers feel unable to discipline the child because of the fear of aggravating the cardiac condition. It is imperative to help the parent, particularly the mother, to understand her responsibility to her child. The mother needs an explanation of the disease in simple terminology. She also needs assurance that sudden death is not usually a threat.

The mother is encouraged to treat the child as normally as possible. She is encouraged to set limits for the child consistent with the limits set for other children of similar developmental age. Many parents admit that it is very difficult to treat the child like their other children, and they feel the need to give the child special considerations which may not be consistent with goals for achieving independence.

Assessment

The infant with a congenital heart defect is more prone to cyanosis of the extremities. Newly born infants have a normal tendency towards cyanosis, as the blood does not circulate freely to the extremities. This immature pattern of circulation is complicated by a cardiac defect. The color of the extremities of a newborn without a cardiac anomaly will usually improve by adding warmth via blankets or clothing. When there is a lack of oxygenation due to cardiac involvement, the extremities remain blue-tinged despite the application of warmth. The infant's color is also assessed around the oral mucosa. The cyanosis tends to worsen when the child cries. Older children may also have overt signs of poor oxygenation of their tissues, and there may be clubbing of the fingers or toes.

The child with congenital heart disease is frequently a smaller child than his or her able-bodied peers; this may be secondary to the pathologic condition. In addition, the child who is not stimulated to be active and to have the same routines and exercises as the able-bodied child is less likely to mature physically. This lack of encouragement may influence the child's total development. The restrictions that the parent puts on the child may influence self-image. Green and Levitt (1962) studied constriction of self-image in children with cardiac problems. They found that the self-portraits of children with cardiac conditions show that these children have a "smaller" self-concept than able-bodied children have. That is, when an able-bodied child draws herself or himself in relation to a peer, he or she always pictures himself or herself as the larger, whereas the child with a cardiac condition draws himself or herself the same height as his or her peer. The effects of social and perceptual experiences are also thought to influence body image. The small size of drawings may be the result of feelings of needing continual help and being dependent on parents. The drawings are often interpreted as the child viewing himself or herself as small and insignificant as an individual.

The respiratory rate and pattern are indicators of the amount of oxygenation and cardiac output available to the infant or child. The newborn has shallow, rapid respirations. This irregular pattern is exaggerated when a child has a cardiac defect. The most dramatic reponse to the diminished oxygenation is the retracting chest. The retractions are often accompanied by grunting sounds and obvious laboring of respirations when there is a severe defect. This interference with respirations is exaggerated when attempts are made to feed the infant.

Blood Pressure

The blood pressure of children is being assessed more conscientiously to see if there is a correlation between elevated blood pressures in children and hypertension in adults. In a study by Lauer et al. (1975) on school-age children, virtually no hypertension was found in children ages 6 to 9 years of age. However, in the 14- to 18-year-olds, 8.9 percent had systolic hypertension, and 12.2 percent had elevated diastolic readings. Hypertension was seen in both the systolic and diastolic recordings in 4.4 percent of the adolescents. The criteria used to determine hypertension were a systolic pressure of 140 mmHg or above, or a diastolic pressure of 90 mmHg or above. In addition to the children diagnosed as hypertensive, 16.7 percent were considered to have elevated blood pressure readings. The children with cardiac defects were in a higher risk group than the able-bodied children screened in the Lauer study. Therefore, the blood pressure recordings are more significant for the former children.

The size of the cuff is very important. The cuff should not be less than half the length of the upper portion of the child's arm or more than two-thirds of its length. In the newborn, the flush method is used. Children with cardiac defects often have blood pressures taken on all four extremities. Each recording is clearly marked as to the extremity used.

Pulse

The pulse rate can be taken radially or apically. The apical pulse is often the method of choice with children with cardiac problems. To evaluate the child's circulatory status, it is not unusual to have recordings also taken of the temporal, carotid, pedal, popliteal, and femoral pulses. It is important to note the quality of the pulse as well as the rate. The pulse is counted for a full minute, as these children frequently have irregular rhythms, and counting for a full minute thus gives a more accurate assessment.

Feeding

The infant with moderate to severe cardiac anomalies often has difficulty feeding. Signs exhibited during feeding include: (1) poor sucking, (2) frequent regurgitation, (3) difficulty swallowing, (4) prolonged feeding times, and (5) irritability following feedings. The symptoms are more pronounced when the infant has a complicated cardiac problem.

The nurse helps the parent to learn to feed the child in a way that causes the least amount of fatigue. When the infant is bottle fed, this can be done by making sure that the nipple holes are adequate, that the infant is held in a semiupright position, that the formula has the greatest amount of carbohydrate content in the least amount of fluid, that the child is bubbled frequently and gently, that frequent rest periods are provided, that frequent small feedings are given, and that the mother is provided adequate time to adjust to feeding the infant while there is professional help available. It is impossible to set up a time table suggesting when the mother will be able to assume the total responsibility for the feeding of the infant. Early initiation in a positive manner is essential as a beginning. Frequent problems with feeding delay the mother's ability to assume the feeding role independently. She needs reassurance that she is progressing adequately, and she is given explanations of why the problems in feeding occur.

In preparation for discharge, the parents are advised that it may take a while for the infant to adjust to being home. They should gauge the infant's feedings by his or her response to them. The infant may prefer a schedule of 2 ounce feedings every 3 hours rather than four hourly feedings. Feedings should be completed within 40 minutes so that the infant can rest between feedings. The parents are advised that it is not uncommon for an infant with a congenital heart problem to vomit a feeding. However, vomiting three consecutive feedings is reason to call the physician.

The preschooler with a congenital heart disease may need help from his or her mother to supplement feedings, because he or she tires easily and may not receive an adequate nutritional intake. The mother provides the child with an opportunity to feed himself or herself, but she must be aware of her responsibility to lend a hand, when necessary. The child with a congenital heart disease still needs to establish the same autonomy any other child has, and his or her own self-limitations are the best guide in judging how much independence is possible. Helping the child when he or she is tired gives him or her a sense of trust in adults. This sense of trust is of utmost benefit when the child is subjected to periods of hospitalization, especially if the child is faced with surgical correction. If the child has had positive experiences with adults when helping has become necessary, he or she trusts them when other stressful situations arise.

The parents can be taught to assess the child's respiratory status during feeding periods. They can gauge the child's tolerance on the basis of the changes they observe. If the respirations become increased or more irregular, they know the self-feeding should be stopped to allow the child to rest. In the same way, cyanosis can be used to determine the child's tolerance for feedings.

Crying

The parents are often concerned that crying will adversely affect the child's heart condition. Because they fear what will happen if the infant continues to cry, they often hold the infant for extended periods of time. The parents need to learn the difference between a cry that warrants attention and one that will stop shortly without attention.

Medications

Teaching the parents to give the infant medications is an essential part of the discharge planning. Drugs commonly administered to these infants include digoxin (Lanoxin) and a diuretic such as furosimede (Lasix).

The parents are advised that digoxin must be administered in the dose that is ordered. The digoxin is given with a dropper, placing it halfway back in the child's mouth. The child's head and shoulders are elevated to facilitate swallowing. The parents are advised not to repeat the dosage when some of the drug is spit out or vomited. If problems persist with giving the correct dosage, the physician should be notified. The physician is also notified when two consecutive doses of digoxin are missed.

When a dose of digoxin is forgotten, the parents are advised to give the next regularly scheduled dosage at the usual time. They should not try to make up for the forgotten dose. The digoxin is usually scheduled to be given one hour before or two hours after a feeding. This is done to facilitate absorption of the medication.

Specific directions are given for each prescribed drug, and the parents demonstrate competency in giving the drugs before the infant is discharged.

The parents are advised to store the digoxin and other drugs in a locked cabinet or similar safe place. They are cautioned that drugs are safe in prescribed doses but can be lethal if taken accidentally. If accidental poisoning does occur, emergency care is sought immediately.

A calendar which clearly notes the child's medication schedule is developed so that the parents are reminded when to give the prescribed medications. They are cautioned not to change doses or add over-the-counter drugs to the child's protocol without seeking advice from the physician.

Other Parameters

The assessment process also focuses on common problems of the child with a congenital heart deficit, such as poor or inconsistent weight gain, fatigue with or without exercise, difficulty sleeping in a flat position, frequent upper respiratory conditions, anoxic episodes, fainting, increased perspiration, dyspnea, squatting posture, clubbing of fingers or toes, increased irritability, and delay in achieving developmental milestones. During the interview and physical examination, it is possible to assess the absence or extent of these findings and to obtain the parents' perception of the degree of disability caused by each. In addition, it is necessary to determine whether the parents feel that the symptom is improving or getting worse with increasing age.

Diagnostic Procedures and Preparation of the Child

A great number of diagnostic procedures can be used to establish the diagnosis of heart disease and the child's readiness for surgery. Two of the more common ones are nonintrusive electrocardiography and intrusive cardiac catheterization.

Electrocardiogram (EKG). The EKG records the activity of the heart. The electrical impulses of the heart result in contractions and relaxation of the heart. The EKG shows the cardiac cycle of the child. In a normal rhythm, the contraction of the atria is the first wave, the P-wave. The contraction of the ventricles are related to the Q-, R-, S-, and T-waves. The tracing is obtained by having the child lie in a supine position in bed or on the table in the treatment room. The child is prepared by explaining the reason for the recording. For example: "John, the doctor wants a drawing of your heart action. This does not hurt and will not take long. We have a special machine to do this drawing. It looks like a brown box, but when the cover is open you will see it is a very special box. It is equipped to draw lines. You might think it is scribbling or you might think it looks like the 'Etch-a-Sketch game.' [If you have an Etch-a-Sketch game, this can be used to demonstrate what you mean to the child.] Special paper comes through the machine and it will be used to make a very long line picture. To get this picture, we must place special pieces of metal on your body. [Show the child an electrode.] Before this is done, a special liquid, which comes from a tube and may feel cool, is put on several parts of you—like your arm. The liquid and the metal will be removed after the heart drawing is finished. You can help by lying still while the EKG is done. Do you have any questions?"

After the procedure is completed, the electrode compound is removed and the child can resume usual activity. More sophisticated recordings, such as an echocardiogram, vector cardiogram, and a phonocardiogram, may also be done. These cardiograms give more specific data regarding the defect. The phonocardiogram gives a more accurate understanding of the heart sounds than the stethoscope can give. The vector cardiogram gives an idea of the heart's three-dimensional anatomy. The echocardiogram utilizes ultrasound to record the echo of each portion of the heart. Coats (1976, p. 264) states, "By tracking the same structure throughout several cardiac cycles, its motion as well as its configuration can be visualized."

Cardiac Catheterization. Cardiac catheterization provides a much clearer picture of the specific defect than electrocardiography. This clearer picture is not obtained without an increased risk. The procedure is considered a surgical procedure requiring parental consent. A radiopaque catheter is inserted into the cardiac chambers and vessels. The catheter can trace anatomic defects, measure pressure in the chambers, and sample the oxygen content of the blood. It is possible to establish a more definitive diagnosis with this technique. It may be done in a special cardiac catheterization laboratory or in the operating room.

The parents must have a clear understanding of the procedure and be given sufficient time to ask questions. The thought of anything entering their child's heart can be especially threatening to them. There is evidence that cardiac catheterization is an anxiety-provoking experience for the parents. Their fear can be easily transmitted to the child.

The explanation given the child depends on age and level of understanding. The toddler or preschooler needs to know that he or she will not be able to eat or drink the morning of the procedure. He or she will also be medicated, as it is necessary for the child to be as relaxed as possible for the procedure. The school-age child and adolescent may enjoy seeing a diagram of the heart and the pathway of the catheter. The child also needs reassurance that the procedure will not cause undue pain or discomfort. The chief discomfort the child experiences is the local pain created by doing the cut-down. Common sites for the cut-down are the groin in younger children and the arm in older children.

The major aspects of the preoperative preparation of the child for cardiac catheterization include:

1. Scheduled time and day of the procedure.
2. Approximate length of time needed to complete the procedure.

3. Preoperative medications and anticipated reactions.
4. Requirements to omit food and fluids.
5. Apparel that will be worn, such as a johnny coat.
6. The way the child will be transported and whether or not a parent can accompany the child.
7. The place where parents can wait during the procedure and who will keep them appraised of developments.
8. Appearance of room where catheterization is done—a visit to the setting or pictures can be used.
9. Responsibility of the child during the procedure, such as lying still or listening to stories.
10. Area where the child will be after catheterization is completed—again, a visit, picture, or description is given.
11. Limitations or restrictions after the procedure is completed—lying flat, ability to drink, etc.

The nurse or technician accompanying the child during the procedure wears a lead apron as protection from the x-ray being used to follow the direction of the catheter. The nurse stays at the head of the table and attempts to provide diversional activities during the catheterization. The time needed to complete the procedure varies, but the nurse is prepared to entertain the child for as long as 3 hours. In the early periods, when the child is not yet bored, storytelling or reading books is effective. Later, the child may get tired of lying supine and more creative things, such as magic tricks, can be tried. During the procedure, the child needs assurance that things are progressing satisfactorily. If possible, he or she should be told approximately how much longer it will take.

If the child is of school age or an adolescent, he or she may enjoy learning the names of the various pieces of equipment in the laboratory, such as the fluoroscope, the electrocardiogram, the pressure recorders, the oscilloscopic apparatus, and blood analyzing equipment. It must also be understood that this equipment can be extremely frightening, as its size is overwhelming and the space provided is usually minimal, making the room appear cluttered and frightening. The use of pictures, mobiles, brightly colored walls, and friendly personnel helps to lessen the negative impact of such an area.

After the catheterization is completed, the cut-down is removed and a dressing is applied to the area. The child is usually kept flat in bed for several hours. The child's vital signs continue to need monitoring for the next 24 hours. A drop in vital signs or bleeding at the site of the cut-down may indicate internal bleeding, necessitating prompt attention from the physician. This is not common, but it is entirely possible that, despite the most careful maneuvering, the catheter can rupture the vessel or cause phlebitis. The risks involved in left-heart catheterization are higher than those in right-heart catheterization because of the increased difficulty in reaching the left side. It must also be remembered that the more serious and complicated heart conditions carry a higher risk, as the physicians cannot always predict the defects prior to catheterization. These defects may allow the catheter to pass in other areas than expected. In addition, younger children run a higher risk due to the smaller size of the heart, which causes more difficalty in passing the catheter and in visualizing the parts. Children included in these categories need more constant observation.

The insertion site dressing is observed for drainage. If bleeding is present, pressure is applied and the extremity is elevated. Bleeding is reported promptly to the physician and charted.

Fluids by mouth are started immediately. If tolerated, solid foods are given at the next meal time. Usually the child can tolerate ordinary feedings within 24 hours.

The parents and child (if he or she is old enough) deserve an explanation of the findings as soon as possible after completion of the catheterization.

Preparation for Anesthesia. In many agencies, the physician from the department of anesthesia assumes the role for preparing the child for anesthesia. In agencies where this is not done, the nurse can incorporate this into the preoperative plan. Models of the operating room and pictures are good visual aids for helping parents and children understand the complicated surgical unit. Using small items for demonstration purposes is also included in the preoperative preparation. The mask that is put over the child's face is an example of this. The mode by which the child gets to the operating room, the clothes that the people in the operating room are wearing, a description of odors common in the operating unit, and a statement that the child is not awake during the operation are all included in the discussion. An attempt is made not to tell the child that he or she will be asleep but rather to tell him or her that it is a special type of sleep that is induced by medication, so that the child will not fear going to sleep after the surgical procedure. The child is also told that a doctor watches closely during the entire time he or she is in this special sleep and takes responsibility for awakening him or her from the special sleep at the end of surgery. The child is told exactly when he or she will be separated from the parents. For instance, if the child can be accompanied to the operating room by the parents, he or she should know this. If the policies of the hospital do not permit parents to accompany the child, then the child and parents should know this. The child should know by what means he or she will be taken to the operating room and who will take him

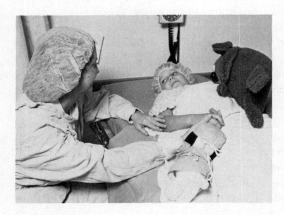

Figure 10-25. The child brings her favorite toy to the preoperative waiting room and the nurse uses a toy dressed in operating room garb to talk to the child.

or her there. For instance, the child needs to know if he or she is to go on an adult-type stretcher or if a small carriage will be used. He or she should know if a person dressed in a green outfit will come to the room or if a nurse that he or she is familiar with will take him or her. The child can choose one or more toys to take to the operating room (Fig. 10-25). A notation is made on the Kardex regarding the child's choice so that the toy or toys are included in the preoperative check list. This is all based on the idea that the more the child knows, the less fear of the unknown there will be and the less possibility for misunderstanding.

CARDIAC SURGERY

Despite the daily anxieties created by having a child with congenital heart disease, the parents are not always willing or ready to accept cardiac surgery as therapy. It is the responsibility of the physician and also of some of the other members of the health care team (such as the social worker, nurse, or clergy) to help the parents to understand the rationale for surgery and to help them to make intelligent decisions regarding it. The parents frequently find it difficult to make the decision for the young child, as he or she is too small to help in the decision. The older child can be included in the discussion, and his or her reactions can be evaluated as part of the decision-making process.

Surgical correction of cardiac defects has been developed within the last 40 years. The major advances in cardiac surgery were fostered by the advances made in cardiopulmonary bypass techniques. Within the past 20 years, open heart surgery has become possible due to the pump oxygenator. Because of the recency of surgical procedures, the parents may have little or no experience with heart defect correction, making it more difficult for them to make an informed choice.

Many factors can influence the parents' decision regarding surgery. When the newborn is severely handicapped and gasping for breath, the parents may be eager to have surgery as they see it as an only chance for the infant to survive. With a toddler or preschooler who is severely incapacitated by the heart defect, the parents may view the surgery as another stressful situation to which they would rather not subject the child. This reaction is especially common when the child is hospitalized frequently and reacts poorly to hospitalization.

When the child's physical appearance mimics the severity of the defect, the rationale for surgery is more evident. However, when the child looks and acts "normal," it is more difficult to understand the necessity for the surgery.

Another factor that may influence the parent's attitude toward surgery is the medical information they receive regarding the defect. Due to the difficulty in making definite diagnoses in infants, the parents are often given conflicting or false information. If they are told the child will "grow out of it," they may reject the surgery on this basis. The parents may also doubt the competence of the medical personnel who have not been able to give an exact explanation of what is wrong with the child's heart or to provide an accurate assessment of the child's prognosis.

Another realistic factor in the decision-making process is the financial strain the surgery might cause. A social worker or financial counselor can be helpful in discussing this concern with the parents, as many surgical procedures are quite expensive. The family finances can be strained further if the surgery cannot be performed locally. Many times, these children are referred to specialty hospitals for the surgical procedure.

Traveling long distances may make the decision difficult, especially if this means separating the mother and child from the rest of the family for a long period of time.

The risk which surrounds the surgical procedure and the projected life expectancy can also be relevant factors in the decision. The reactions of relatives and friends as well as the parents' experience with other families who have had similar surgery can also influence the parents' decision to have or not have the surgery done.

Varieties of Congenital Heart Defects

There are a variety of congenital heart defects that are amenable to palliative or corrective surgical procedures. Some of these are patent ductus arteriosus (PDA), atrial defect, ventricular defect, coarctation of the aorta, pulmonary stenosis, tetralogy of Fallot, and transposition of the great arteries.

Preparation for Surgical Intervention

The age of the child is one of the primary factors in the preparation for cardiac surgery. It is most appropriate to identify the child's ability to understand the preoperative preparation and to adjust it accordingly. The child is made aware of the environment(s) in which he or she will be before the operation, after the operation, and during convalescence. Depending on the clinical facilities, there may be one or several places. The preparation of the child is best done in small sessions and when the child is fairly well rested. It is good to plan sessions after the rest period that normally takes place on the hospital unit. The preparation gives the child an opportunity to ask questions, to act out fears, and to digest new information. In keeping with normal developmental factors, the teaching includes the use of toys or books appropriate to the age of the child. The child is exposed to the same types of things that he or she will be exposed to postoperatively. The child is introduced to tourniquets, to syringes, to blood pressure cuffs, to oxygen equipment, to suction equipment, to blow bottles, and to the intensive care unit if it is to be utilized. The child may have previous experience with some of these things, but including them gives the child an opportunity to express how he or she feels about them.

For instance, it would be quite rare for a child with a congenital heart disease not to have had his or her blood pressure taken. But this does not mean that a blood pressure cuff is omitted from preoperative teaching. A good way of seeing how the child feels about the blood pressure cuff is to have him or her apply it to a doll and to see how he or she explains to the doll what he or she is going to do or how it is going to feel. This interaction gives valuable clues regarding how to introduce blood pressure taking to the child postoperatively. Each of the other items are introduced to the child in the same manner. In addition, puppets can be used in preoperative preparation. It is sometimes easier for the child to express how he or she feels through a puppet than it is to express how he or she feels to a professional person, eye to eye. With a puppet, the child finds it perfectly legitimate to explain that he or she does not like being stuck with needles or that he or she does not want to have surgery done or to share fears of separation. Giving the child an opportunity to express these things makes it easier to provide anticipatory guidance. It also helps to identify ways that the child will be able to express anxiety postoperatively. For instance, if he or she used the puppet effectively preoperatively, then why not use the puppets postoperatively, as well? If the child was unable to utilize the puppets for self-expression preoperatively, then postoperatively they will probably not be useful. The nurse records in the nursing notes the reaction of the child to the preoperative teaching so that the people caring for him or her immediately postoperatively have the advantage of this information.

The child is taught how to deep-breathe and to turn postoperatively. If the child is taught deep breathing by blowing plastic bubbles, then this method should be available postoperatively to achieve the same purpose. If the child is taught deep breathing by blowing up balloons, a good supply of balloons should be available postoperatively for this procedure. If the blow bottles are utilized with a particular color water in them preoperatively, the same color water is used postoperatively. The preoperative preparation and the postoperative care are structured the same way so that the child is able to practice what he or she was taught.

The child who is to be cared for in an intensive care unit is oriented to that unit preoperatively. The child benefits from being introduced to nurses and being called by name by them. This helps the child to realize that the nurses know him or her and that he or she will not get lost by being moved to another area in the hospital. This is especially important for the younger child who fears separation and abandonment. The school-age child also benefits from this, because he or she appreciates people knowing who he or she is and respecting him or her as a person.

Sleep

Another valuable preoperative evaluation is of the child's sleep patterns. The nurse keeps a record of the child's sleep patterns during the day as well as at night (Table 10-1).

A preoperative sleep pattern gives clues as to how the child ordinarily sleeps. It helps in postoperative positioning for comfort. The comfort measures can also be altered by specific positioning that is required due to the surgery.

The sleep pattern also shows how long the child ordinarily sleeps during a certain period. Nursing care is planned so it does not interrupt unnecessarily these normal sleep patterns.

One of the major nursing objectives is to provide the child with adequate rest despite the many procedures that are necessary following cardiac surgery. This is achieved by planning treatments and medications to meet the child's individual

TABLE 10-1.
Sleep Pattern of Child (John, Age 8, 12/8/82)

Time	Example	Medications
7:00 A.M.	Sleeping, left side, soundly	None
7:15 A.M.	Beginning to awaken	
7:20 A.M.	Fully awake and alert	
2:00 P.M.	Took 15 min to fall asleep Brown teddy bear	Digitalis—10:00 A.M. Phenobarbital $\frac{1}{4}$ gm—10:00 A.M. and 2:00 P.M.
3:00 P.M.	Awake and alert	
9:00 P.M.	To bed at 8:00 P.M.—tossed, restless—asleep on left side Two stuffed toys Prayers at bedtime	Phenobarbital $\frac{1}{2}$ gm—8:00 P.M.
11:00 P.M.	Very restless—awake	None

needs. This necessitates good organization so that the child is only disturbed from sleep when it is essential to do so. In this way, the child can complete a sleep cycle and be more rested.

Elimination

Preoperatively, the child is usually up and around. After the initial urine specimen is collected, elimination is not monitored unless the child is on intake and output. The child is free to go to the bathroom. Prior to surgery the child is given practice in using the bedpan. It is helpful to have the child use it a couple times to familiarize him or her with how it feels and the adjustments needed to void or defecate using the bedpan and/or urinal.

It is also important to record the words used by the child to describe the need to eliminate. If new words are taught, they are frequently forgotten during periods of acute stress, and the child reverts to familiar words. A Foley catheter is frequently used postoperatively, and it is explained to the child during the preoperative preparation.

Constipation is guarded against both pre- and postoperatively, as it is not good for the child to strain to defecate. If fluids and diet are not regulated to overcome this problem, then the physician can order a stool softener, such as Colace.

The Intensive Care Unit

After the surgical procedure is completed, the physician completes the child's chart before he or she leaves the operating room (Fig. 10-26). Frequently the child will be taken care of in an intensive care unit.

The intensive care unit has both positive and negative aspects in caring for the child undergoing cardiac surgery. Some of the positive aspects are that the nurses are usually more knowledgeable about the equipment and acute care

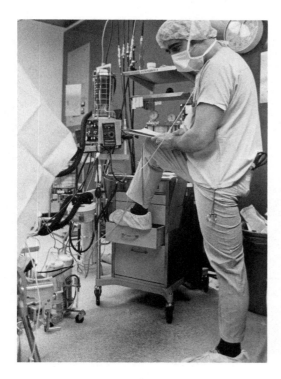

Figure 10-26. The child's chart is completed before the child leaves the operating room.

aspects of the postoperative period. The equipment is readily available for any emergency (Fig. 10-27). Medical personnel usually respond more quickly to a call from this area. The unit usually is in closer proximity to the operating room, so when any emergency arises the child can be returned quickly to the surgical area. The negative aspects are usually concerned with the fact that the nurses frequently are so overly involved in the physical care of the child that they relegate to lesser importance the emotional aspects of the child's care. Another negative aspect is that the child is in an area where all of the children are acutely ill, and when he or she is awake, the seriousness of the condition of the other children is repeatedly exposed. The child seldom has the advantage of seeing some children up and running around or hearing the cheerful laughter of children at play. He or she is frequently in an environment that is more cluttered and frightening than the rooms on the convalescent floors. The environment can be adjusted to be more childlike. For the child in an oxygen tent this can be easily achieved by hanging mobiles inside the tent, by placing toys in the tent (ones that are appropriate, such as rubber or wooden ones), by adding musical toys to the tent to cut down on the noise of the motors the child is exposed to, and by making the child's visual field more colorful and less distorted (Figs. 10-28 and 10-29). The child who is immobilized should have some type of toy or book within his or her visual field so that it is not necessary to turn around to find it. When the child wakes up, he or she sees color or animals or things that are ordinarily in a child's world.

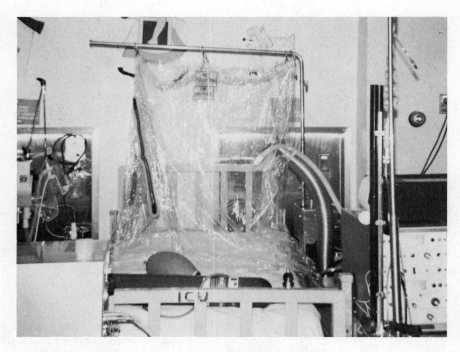

Figure 10-27.   An intensive care unit ready for a child returning from cardiac surgery. Emergency equipment is readily available.

The nurse is an important member of the postoperative managament team. The nurse spends the most time with the child (Fig. 10-30). In addition, the nursing team members collaborate with one another to provide the most efficient and effective care for the child (Fig. 10-31).

The parents are given an opportunity to be introduced to the intensive care unit, if they so desire, prior to surgery. Some parents have stated that the visit to the intensive care unit has produced so much anxiety preoperatively that they felt less able to cope with their child's anxieties than if they had not visited it. Other parents have felt that it is a very important part of helping them to be more relaxed and to be able to cope postoperatively. If they are not taken to the unit, they are told where it is and the easiest way to get there. A small model of the unit can be used to orient the child and the parent. The use of the model makes it possible to orient the family members without having them see the other postoperative children. They are also made aware of restricted or different visiting hours, if they exist.

The first time the parents see their child after surgery is a tense moment for them. It is essential for the health care providers to give their support and to be available for them to ask questions.

Parents are relieved to see that their child is receiving expert care. A viewing window is sometimes more satisfactory than entering the intensive care unit

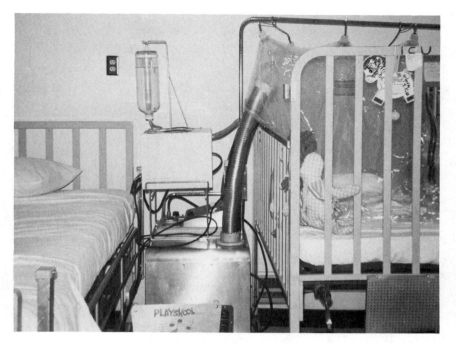

Figure 10-28. Intensive care unit combining children's world and medical world.

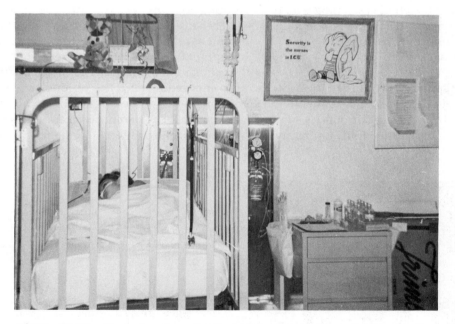

Figure 10-29. Try to imagine what the child across the room thinks when he or she wakes up and sees this acutely ill child. Note the attempts to brighten up the environment.

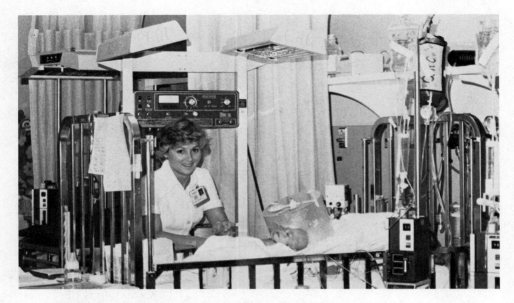

Figure 10-30.   The child is returned to the pediatric intensive care unit for postoperative care.

when the child is sleeping (Fig. 10-32). A nurse, viewing with the parent, can point out particular aspects about the child and his or her care. For instance, the parents may be so distracted by the equipment that is being used that they may benefit initially by an explanation of the equipment rather than an explanation of the child's progress. It takes time and courage for the parents to look past the equipment and to the child. After the parents understand the various pieces of equipment and their function, they are prepared to visit with the child when he or she is awake. The child is soothed and comforted by parents who are able to be available to the child during periods of pain and discomfort.

Figure 10-31.   Nurses collaborating on the child's progress and management in the pediatric intensive care unit.

Figure 10-32. A mother and father view their acutely ill child through the intensive care unit window. The nurse is available to answer questions and give support.

Postoperative Care

In the postoperative period, it is important to capitalize on the preoperative preparation of the child. For instance, as soon as he or she returns to the intensive care unit or area for immediate postoperative care, introductions are made in the following manner: "Johnny, this is the intensive care unit you visited yesterday. I am your nurse, Miss Jones. Remember, I called you Johnny yesterday and said, 'See you tomorrow'? You are going into the oxygen tent that you saw yesterday. This oxygen tent may feel a little cool and may feel a little damp. This is to be expected. If you are cool, let me know so I can cover you, and I will wipe you off if you have moisture dripping on you. You now have the chest tubes you saw on the doll, Johnny; they are on your left side. Don't touch them. Soon I will ask you to breathe nice and deep. I will give you a balloon to blow, like you did yesterday. It will not be as easy to blow today as it was yesterday, but each day it will get easier."

In this way the child is reintroduced to the environment and to what has gone on prior to surgery. Consistent use of this technique assists the child in his or her recovery and aids the nurse in gaining the child's cooperation. The child is consistently reminded that while he or she has pain now, each day it will improve. He or she needs more assurance that things will get better. The child is usually more interested in himself or herself and the immediate environment than in the future, and therefore, he or she needs more reassurance that the pain is transient in nature. The child also wants immediate gratification of needs, and he or she should know how to get gratification. If he or she must call for the nurse, then he or she should know how to do this. If a nurse will be in constant attendance, then the child needs to know this.

During the immediate postoperative period, the child derives satisfaction from having physical needs met adequately. However, as he or she begins to progress in the convalescent period, more and more attention is given to emotional needs. The child who has undergone cardiac surgery frequently is exposed to a large number of people delivering care immediately postoperatively. Due to this, he or she is not always aware of who is directly responsible when he or she wants something. The nurse can play a key role in this by always identifying when she or he is responsible for care and who is responsible when she or he is not available. In addition to meeting the emotional needs of the child, the nurse is responsible for many of the other procedures that are done to and for the child during the immediate postoperative period.

Chest Tubes and Suction

In a three bottle suction drainage system, the first bottle collects drainage from the chest cavity and is connected by a short tube to the water-seal bottle, which is connected to the suction control bottle. The suction control bottle has three tubes. One tube is open to the atmosphere at one end and immersed in water to 15 to 20 cm at the other end. This tube is the section control tube. The second tube attaches to a suction source. The third tube connects the suction bottle to the rest of the system (Fig. 10-33).

Connection of the suction source results in the creation of subatmospheric pressure. Air is pulled into the suction tubes by two sources—air from the chest cavity is pulled through the water-seal bottle and air is drawn in from the atmosphere into the suction control tube.

When the system is draining adequately, the following are observed:

1. Bubbling in suction control bottle.
2. The water in the water-seal bottle fluctuates.
3. Occasional bubbling in the water-seal bottle with expiration; however, continuous bubbling is suggestive of an air leak and must be corrected (Harper, 1981).

The chest tubes are checked to make sure there is no kinking. The bandage around the tube is free of drainage, and if drainage appears, it is encircled and watched for any increase. A Kelly clamp is available for each tube that is in place. In case of emergency, the clamp is placed as close to the chest wall as possible.

The tubes are securely anchored to the bed to help prevent undue tension

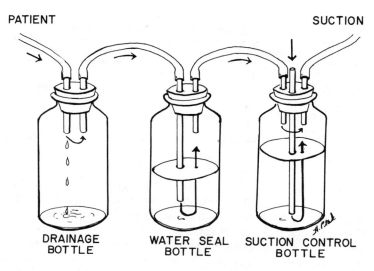

Figure 10-33. Three-bottle system for closed chest drainage.

on them. This can be achieved by placing adhesive tape around the tubes without constricting them and then using a safety pin to pin the adhesive to the sheet.

The tubes also need special attention when the child is turned. Care is taken not to have the child's weight resting on the tubes. The tubes must also be checked after turning to maintain adequate draining.

The nurse must also know who is responsible for emptying and measuring the chest drainage. The procedure may vary from one institution to another. Some measure drainage every eight hours and others measure it daily. The amount, color, and consistency of chest drainage are recorded.

Vital Signs

Preoperatively, the vital signs are recorded by both physicians and nurses. Each has an opportunity to cross-check their results with the other. In addition, vital signs are often obtained under differing sets of conditions. These results are carefully recorded so that they are available postoperatively for comparison (Table 10-2).

The variations in rates with activity can be used as gauges in planning postoperative activity. The use of varying areas for counting the pulse rate can also be useful postoperatively. If preoperatively all the pulse rates were taken on the left radial pulse, and postoperatively the child has a cut-down or intravenous infusion in that area, then the child's routine has to be disrupted. It is better to teach the child that pulses may be obtained radially, apically, femorally, carotidly, or on the feet (dorsalis pedis). Explain to the child that any of these areas may be used postoperatively to obtain the pulse. Letting the child count his or her own pulse or the nurse's pulse is also helpful in gaining cooperation.

Pulse rates vary from one cardiac condition to another and from a child of

TABLE 10-2
Vital Signs and Activity (John, Age 8)

Time	Activity	Pulse Area	BP	R
8:00 A.M.	Just awakened	100, Radial (lt)	100/62	16
11:00 A.M.	Active play	110, Radial (lt)	104/64	20
		122, Carotid (rt)		
12:30 P.M.	Following self-feeding	110, Radial (rt)	104/64	24

one age to a child of another age. This creates problems in knowing what is "normal" for a certain child. The child's rate may also change due to the nature of the surgery. For instance, a child with coarctation of the aorta may lack pedal pulses. Postoperatively, this rate is established by improvement in blood flow.

The blood pressure is another valuable monitor. If possible, the child's pressure is always taken with the same cuff. This is usually fairly easy to accomplish in a small, well-equipped intensive care unit. The cuff is applied snugly and anchored securely before being inflated. This can be achieved if the child is prepared adequately. The child needs to know that the cuff will feel tight on his or her arm when it is inflated. The child may enjoy holding the dial so that you can read it. This makes him or her feel a responsibility for helping with his or her own care. The acutely ill child may not be able to participate but may benefit from having a toy to hold during the procedure. If it is necessary to recheck the reading, be sure to tell the child that the cuff is being inflated again. Frequent rechecking may cause the child anxiety, so optimal conditions are achieved prior to beginning. Optimal conditions include proper positioning of the child and the cuff, removal of clothing between the cuff and the arm, as little noise as possible, and turning off any motors that may safely be eliminated during the short period of time needed to complete the reading.

The respiratory rate is more variable than the pulse rate or the blood pressure during the immediate postoperative period. The respiratory rate can be significantly decreased during sleep or due to postoperative medication. The respiratory rate can be significantly increased by apprehension. It can be quite irregular when the trachea needs suctioning. Sternal retractions can develop when there is respiratory distress. Some of the variations have little significance, while some of them are indicators of postoperative distress. The nurse monitors the respirations and takes action to change situations that adversely affect the respiration rate. For example, suctioning may clear the passageway and reestablish a normal respiratory rate. A rapid, shallow rate may indicate more serious difficulty and, coupled with other unfavorable vital signs, such as a decrease in blood pressure, may require immediate medical intervention.

The child frequently returns from the operating room with an endotracheal tube. The endotracheal tube provides an open airway. The tubes come in a variety of sizes: tubes 3.0 mm to 4.50 mm in diameter are used for infants and young children. Tubes 7.0 mm in diameter are used for older children.

The endotracheal tube allows for deep tracheobronchial suctioning, when indicated. The suction tube is inserted through the tube to maintain airway patency. If the child does not have adequate respiratory ventilation, he or she is placed on a ventilator. The child is removed from the ventilator as soon as adequate respiratory function is established. The endotracheal tube is removed when the child is fully conscious and ventilator assistance is no longer necessary.

Other Recordings

The central venous pressure (CVP) is also monitored closely. This is done to be sure that the child is not receiving too much intravenous fluid or losing too much blood. The CVP is a recording of the amount of pressure in the right atrium. It is the reading used to evaluate the balance between the blood being pumped into the systemic circulation and the venous return to the heart. The CVP falls slightly with inspiration and it rises slightly with expiration. The readings should remain fairly stable if the child is progressing satisfactorily.

The child's condition may be followed by continuous cardiac monitoring. The monitoring system is capable of printing out EKGs, playing back sections of the recording, producing an alarm for other than heart rate changes, and signaling problems with the monitoring equipment. Continuous monitoring is usually achieved with two leads and one ground. The right electrode is placed below the child's right sternum, the left electrode is placed at the level of the child's lowest palpable rib, and the ground is placed at the same level as the left electrode but on the child's right side. Monitoring is usually continued until the child's condition stabilizes.

The child's intake and output are recorded every 4 hours until his or her condition is stable. Urinary specific gravity recordings are frequently ordered during the early postoperative period.

Maintaining Fluid and Electrolyte Balance

The child usually returns from the operating room with parenteral fluids running. The physician's order sheet is consulted for the proper amount and drops to be administered. The IV is counted and regulated to be sure that the flow has not been disturbed during transportation. Depending on the postoperative course, oral intake is usually begun soon. This intake is divided to allow for evening and night personnel to offer the child fluids. Spacing of the allowed oral intake decreases the child's possibility of extreme thirst.

The child will probably have an in-dwelling catheter immediately postoperatively. This necessitates additional care of the perineal area. The measuring of urinary output may be on an hourly basis during the immediate postoperative period. As the child progresses, it may be measured every 8 hours. When a catheter is not in place, the child is placed on a bedpan or offered a urinal on a routine basis to encourage voiding.

Figure 10-34 is a comparison of the adult and infant extracellular water turnover for a day. This will help to emphasize the extreme importance of keeping accurate account of all the fluid entering or leaving the child's body.

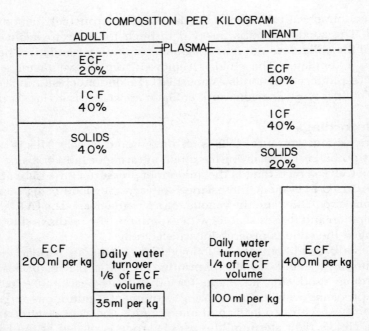

Figure 10-34. Body water partition and comparison of daily water turnover to the extracellular fluid volume in the newborn and the adult. *(Courtesy of Statland, H. Fluid and electrolytes in practice. Philadelphia: Saunders, 1963)*

Normal individuals of all ages require 100 to 150 ml of maintenance water per 100 calories metabolized. Since the infant and child have higher metabolic rates per kilogram than does the adult, the younger client needs more water per unit of weight (Statland, 1963; Table 10-3).

In addition, the nurse is aware of the ordinary maintenance requirements of fluid. According to Statland, the amount of water given approximates the fluid expended for ordinary physiologic activity. Studies in both infants and adults

TABLE 10-3.
Approximate Energy Expenditure During Parenteral Fluid Therapy

Age	Weight (kg)	Calories Expended		Maintenance Water
		Total (per 24 hr)	Per kg (per 24 hr)	Per 100 cal (ml)
4 Months	5	500	100	100
2 Years	15	1250	83	100
10 Years	30	1700	57	100
Adult	60	2300	38	100

Adapted from Statland, H. *Fluid and electrolytes in practice.* Philadelphia: Saunders, 1963.

indicate that these losses are roughly proportional to energy expenditure (Table 10-4). The intake also includes fluid to replace losses during the operative and postoperative periods.

The nurse determines losses which are not easily measured—the loss by perspiration, drainage, or bed-wetting. The wet sheet may be a poor way to estimate loss, as fluid quickly spreads in sheets and gives a false impression of a large loss. However, it is important to include this information in the nurse's notes—for example: "Sheet changed—moderate amount serosanguineous drainage in area of chest bandage. Drainage appeared between 8:00 and 10:00 A.M."

In addition, the nurse needs to observe the child for perspiration. It is not enough to assume that if the johnny shirt is dry, then he or she is not perspiring. The perspiration may show on the forehead or the palms of the hands. A flushing of the child's face is also significant, as it may be a clue to additional water losses.

Oxygen Therapy

The child usually receives oxygen immediately postoperatively. This can be achieved by using an isolette, a hood, a nasal cannula, or an oxygen tent.

The administration of oxygen by isolette provides a fairly constant oxygen supply unless the top of the isolette is opened. Most nursing care can be effectively administered through the portholes. If the top is opened, the infant may become hypoxic. If so, the isolette is closed and a high concentration of oxygen is delivered to resaturate the isolette. The liter flow of oxygen is prescribed by the physician. The 40 percent concentration may be used for a very small infant; however, it is not nearly so important to keep this concentration for older children who are not as prone to visual damage from oxygen flow.

The oxygen tent does not guarantee as good a supply of oxygen. A wider area is involved, the lightweight plastic canopy is less effective than the harder plastic of the isolette or hood, and there is more possibility for oxygen to escape because the tent is only tucked under the mattress or bed linens.

According to Crocker (1970), continuous ultrasonic nebulization is never

TABLE 10-4.
Usual Expenditures of Water Per 100 Calories Metabolized

Expenditure	Water (ml)
Insensible perspiration	45
Lungs	15
Skin	30
Sweat (sensible perspiration)	20
Stool	5
Urine	30—80
Total	100—150

Adapted from Darrow and Pratt; from Statland, H. *Fluid and electrolytes in practice.* Philadelphia: Saunders, 1963.

used in infants and probably is not used in older children either, as it may supply as much as 6 ml/minute of fluid to the child and, particularly in intubated infants, water intoxication may occur. It is possible to supply the infant or child with the total daily water requirement by ultrasonic nebulization.

The nurse observes the child for signs of cyanosis. Cyanosis usually appears first in the child's fingernails. For this reason, any nail polish is removed prior to surgery and left off during the child's postoperative period. Other areas to observe are the child's lips and the area around the oral orifice. Cyanosis may be an expected symptom due to the child's cardiac condition, and it may not disappear as a result of a palliative cardiac procedure.

Adequate suctioning is also necessary to provide an adequate oxygen supply. The nasal passage is kept clean and mucus is suctioned from the trachea. Sterile technique is adhered to during suctioning to cut down on the possibility of infection. Deeper suctioning may be necessary to maintain an adequate airway.

Crocker (1970) recommends that assisted ventilation be performed prior to suctioning episodes when a tracheostomy is in place. This ventilation is done with a suitable bag or adaptor for 3 to 5 minutes prior to suctioning in order to prevent the rapid aspiration of oxygen from the airway, with resultant hypoxia.

Coughing, Turning, Deep Breathing
Coughing, deep breathing, and turning the child every 1 to 2 hours aids in the maintenance of oxygenation. As the child's condition improves, the frequency of these procedures can be changed to every 4 hours.

Cardiopulmonary Resuscitation (CPR)
The nurse is available to complete emergency procedures when necessary. One method that can be life-saving is CPR. The ABCs of cardiopulmonary resuscitation are Airway, Breathing, and Circulation. The signs of cardiac arrest are the absence of a heartbeat and absence of a carotid pulse. The signs of respiratory arrest are apnea and cyanosis. The goal of CPR is to counter these symptoms by ventilating the lungs and compressing the heart by manual pressure. The airway must be clear of vomitus, mucus, or obstructions. The child's head and neck are hyperextended to open the airway. The child's jaw is pulled forward and up to prevent the tongue from falling backward and obstructing the passage. The child's nose is closed off and mouth to mouth resuscitation is begun. In smaller children the mouth and nose may be covered by the nurse's mouth, the object being to assure a tight seal. The nurse repeats the mouth to mouth every 5 seconds. To compress the heart, the nurse uses the heel of her or his hand. She or he puts pressure over the chest wall at a rate of 80 to 100 compressions per minute. This is continued until rhythmic heartbeat and pulse return.

Reorientation to Time and Place
The intensive care unit is equipped with clocks and calendars to help reorient the child to time and place. The younger child enjoys having a children's clock. The type wound up by pulling chains can be fun. The older child benefits by having an ordinary clock. The clock should be close by the bedside so that the child can

refer to it easily. For older children, the calendars can be of the conventional type, with scenes depicting areas of the child's interest. For the younger child, a calendar can be made and large numbers used. The numbers can be added daily so that he or she knows the last one up is the day's date. In addition, cloud, rain, sun, or snow pictures can be added so the child knows the weather. This is especially important if the child cannot see out of the window. Changes of the weather can be made during the day if changes occur outside. This is helpful, too, if the parents are unable to get to the hospital because of inclement weather—the child will have already been oriented to that possibility.

Assessments

The child's body is assessed for warmth. Is it only warm to touch on the trunk despite a slight postoperative temperature elevation? What is needed to warm the child's cold extremities? Is a pair of cotton socks or mitts adequate? Does he or she need three cotton blankets inside the tent to rest comfortably? Or does he or she toss and turn and try curling up to get warm despite the use of three blankets?

Is the child's pain being managed effectively? In relation to medication for pain, does the child rest quietly after absorption or does he or she still have the look of anxiety in his or her eyes? Does he or she seem to need medication to achieve needed rest? Does he or she seem to need medication after visits from the physician, parents, or laboratory technician? Does the child cough better if he or she receives medication prior to coughing? Does any one procedure, such as suctioning, trigger a need for medication?

Is the child able to get adequate periods of rest? Are persons interrupting the child's sleep unnecessarily? Can night–day conditions be simulated to help the child sleep more adequately? Is sleep interrupted by pain?

Are the child's emotional needs being met? How often is the family visiting? Do family members call to ask about the child's condition when they do not visit? Are ways to include the parents in the child's management being devised and implemented?

How is the family coping with the crisis? Do either of the parents seem unduly stressed? Have the parents been provided opportunities to talk with any health care team members to whom they wish to speak? Do the parents ask questions and do they seem satisfied with the answers that they receive?

Convalescence and Discharge

The convalescent period depends on the surgery and its follow-up supervision. The degree of activity is prescribed by the physician. The parents and child are fully informed of the activity allowed as well as any restrictions. They are advised of the need for medical supervision and are given their follow-up appointments. They also need to know any adverse signs that necessitate immediate medical care.

The child who experiences a significant improvement in physical condition due to surgical repair may have a difficult time adjusting to his or her new status. The child and parent may need time to accept the fact that the child is capable of more vigorous physical activity now that the surgery is completed. The child needs time to adjust to the extended privileges of independence with peers. He or she may also have difficulty adjusting to the more strenuous educational goals that are now possible.

If the surgery has been less successful, the parents and child have to learn to cope with the permanence of the condition and to readjust their goals in relation to the limitations that are still imposed by the cardiac condition.

CHRONIC RENAL FAILURE

Chronic renal failure occurs as a result of disease or injury. When the kidney fails, one or all of its functions fail. At this point, treatment of the child with hemodialysis or peritoneal dialysis is essential if life is to be maintained. Kidney failure can be caused by glomerular disease, congenital anomalies of kidney development, vascular nephropathies, malignancy, hereditary nephropathies, hereditary cystic diseases, and interstitial disease. The estimate of chronic renal disease in children is 2.5 cases per million from birth to 16 years of age or 5 cases per million population from birth to 21 years of age. In 1975, there were 1372 transplants done for children under 16 years of age (Topor, 1981).

Peritoneal Dialysis

Peritoneal dialysis is a procedure that is used when there is severe kidney damage or impending renal failure. In this procedure, dialysis is performed by using the peritoneum as the dialyzing membrane.

The child and family are prepared for peritoneal dialysis via simple truthful explanations and diagrams. Prior to the procedure, the child empties his or her bladder. The abdomen is shaved, scrubbed with an antiseptic solution, and covered with a sterile drape. Prior to the stab wound, a local anesthetic is given. A stylet is passed through the incision and a catheter is inserted and sutured in place. The child's weight is obtained and then the peritoneal dialysis is started.

During the dialysis, the child's weight is obtained approximately half-way through the procedure and at the completion of the dialysis. Vital signs are taken every 4 hours. The peritoneal fluid is cultured before and after dialysis, and dressings are changed at the end of the procedure, leaving a dry, sterile dressing in place.

While the procedure seems relatively simple, it is not without dangers. It has made dialysis available to more persons than was possible when only the artificial kidney (hemodialysis) was available.

According to Boen (1964, pp. 69–71), the following are some of the major advantages of peritoneal dialysis when compared with the artificial kidney:

1. Simpler equipment makes it available in nearly every hospital.
2. Abrupt changes in blood volume can be avoided.
3. There is ample opportunity to change the composition of the irrigating fluid. It is therefore possible to avoid an insufficient or excessive correction of disturbances in electrolyte or water balance.

4. It can be used after surgery or with patients with bleeding tendency.
5. When increased protein breakdown is evident, peritoneal dialysis can be used longer.

The major disadvantages to peritoneal dialysis cited by Boen (1964, pp. 69–71) include the following:

1. Water is removed more slowly by this procedure.
2. Infection is a possibility.
3. The intestine can be perforated during introduction of a trocar.
4. A loss of about 40 gm of protein may occur.
5. Abdominal pain and discomfort may occur.
6. It can't be used where abdominal injury is present or with severe peritonitis.
7. Sterile irrigation fluids are necessary with peritoneal dialysis, but not with the artificial kidney.

Before the dialysis is started, abdominal fluid is aspirated for culture. A warmed, commercially prepared dialysis fluid is hung on an intravenous pole, and the solution flows through the tubing into the child's peritoneal cavity.

The fluid takes approximately 10 to 15 minutes to fill the cavity. The fluid remains in the cavity 20 to 30 minutes before it is drained off. Draining of the fluid into a drainage bottle takes 15 to 20 minutes (Fig. 10-35). Peritoneal dialysis usually is continued for 36 to 48 hours.

During the procedure, the child can have respiratory distress due to the pressure of the solution on the diaphragm. The child is helped to relax so that this increase in fluid does not cause undue abdominal discomfort. Preparation for the "full feeling" helps the child understand what is happening and lessens fears.

Infection is a potential side-effect of this procedure. This danger can be minimized by keeping the dressing and area around the catheter as clean and dry as possible. Periodic cleansing with antiseptic solution and application of sterile dressings under aseptic technique lessen the possibility of infection. When new solutions are added, they must be added under aseptic conditions, and any medications (such as heparin and antibiotics) are added with care. The child is kept away from other children and adults with infections, as his or her resistance to infection is decreased. If members of the health care team or family are not feeling well, they should not visit the child.

The loss of protein is especially significant, as it adds to the malnutrition and wasting prevalent in these children. It is important to have the child eat nutritious meals, as the child's anorexia improves due to removal of waste products that were toxic. Following dialysis, the child may have a heightened interest in food.

Nursing responsibilities also include warming the solution before hanging a new bottle. A solution at body temperature is less likely to cause discomfort than a cold solution. The nurse also keeps an accurate intake and output record (Table 10-5). If the child retains the fluid, he or she may be turned carefully to aid the gravity drainage (the child is usually in a supine position with his or her head elevated approximately 45° during the dialysis). The tubing must also be kept free

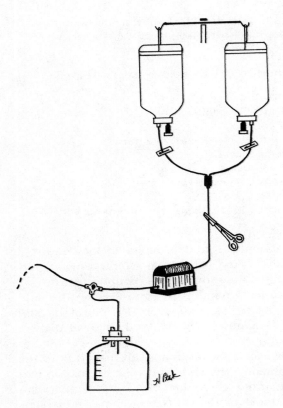

Figure 10-35. A. Equipment for peritoneal dialysis.

of kinks to provide adequate drainage, and it must be observed for small clots or waste material that may interfere with flow. If flow cannot be re-established by "milking the tube gently," the physician is notified. Heparin is sometimes ordered to decrease the clot formation, or the physician may need to move the catheter to a better position.

Coughing and deep breathing are encouraged to decrease the possibility of pneumonia developing. There are several signs that signal distress. Increased respirations may indicate that too much fluid is being administered. Occasionally, a child complains of shoulder pain, which is probably due to the same cause. Abdominal pain may be a sign of peritonitis or infection. Diarrhea is a common side-effect of dialysis. A deterioration in the child's mental state may be related to the electrolyte exchange. All of these signs are reported to the physician and recorded accurately.

Recently, continuous ambulatory peritoneal dialysis (CAPD), commonly referred to as portable dialysis, became possible for selected child clients. The portable dialysis requires tubing, a fluid bag, and gravity, making it an easy way to receive therapy. The children have increased freedom, as the therapy can be conducted in their home environments. This method of therapy may increase in popularity in the next few years, as it definitely can be a less expensive and more natural way for the child to be managed.

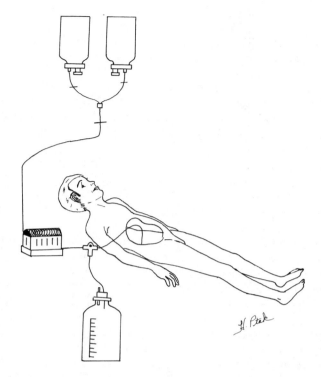

Figure 10-35. B. Schematic drawing illustrating intermittent peritoneal dialysis in use.

TABLE 10-5.
Record of Peritoneal Dialysis Therapy (John J., Age 12, 8/31/82)

Strength of Solution
Bottle 1 (as ordered)
Bottle 2 (as ordered)

Medications
Added Heparin 0.5 cc

Solution In
Start 12:00
End 12:20
Volume 300

Solution Out
Start 1:20
End 1:40
Volume 275

Differential (Drainage Balance, + or −)
+ 25

Hemodialysis

The purpose of the artificial kidney is to circulate the child's blood through a semipermeable membrane of cellophane in order to allow water, salts, urea, creatinine, and other substances of smaller molecular weight to diffuse through it while preventing larger substances, such as blood cells, bacteria, viruses, and blood proteins, from passing through. The process simulates the filtering action of the walls of the glomerular capillaries. The child's blood is pumped through a tube of cellophane surrounded by a dialipsate that resembles the normal salt concentration of human plasma. Blood impurities and constituents diffuse through the cellophane into the surrounding solution, which is then discarded. The blood, after passing through the cellophane tube, is returned to the child (Parrish, 1981). In order to achieve this goal, either an arteriovenous fistula or an arteriovenus shunt is used. The fistula is constructed by connecting an artery of the forearm to a vein in the same area. If a shunt is used, a plastic catheter is placed temporarily in the artery and the artery and vein are brought together. The kidney machine is connected to the in-dwelling catheter.

The hemodialysis may be viewed by the parents as the "cure" for their child's disease. However, the child is frequently in the advanced stages of disease before the treatment is chosen, and a "cure" is highly unlikely. Raimbault and deRecherches (1973) suggest that the young child is unable to integrate the idea that the artificial kidney is essential to his or her life. Due to this inability, he or she needs an adult at his or her side during treatments to lessen fears of abandonment and alienation. These authors suggest that older children display their inability to assimilate the value of the treatments through outbursts of aggression, anger, and negativism. They also may act indifferently toward people with whom they must interact. The child is searching for someone to help integrate a "nonsymbolizable situation" through these covert responses (Raimbault and deRecherches, 1973, p. 69).

The standard dialysis fluid is an aqueous solution containing blood cations: sodium, potassium, calcium, magnesium, and anions (chloride and acetate). Fairly standard orders are used in pediatric hemodialysis. They are:

1. Hematocrit before each dialysis.
2. Weekly blood urea nitrogen, creatinine, sodium, and potassium.
3. Biweekly carbon dioxide, calcium, and phosphorus.
4. Monthly hepatitis-associated antigen test, antibody screening, protein electrophoresis, alkaline phosphatase, serum glutamic–oxaloacetic transaminase.
5. Quarterly magnesium.
6. Semiannual x-ray bone age (wrist and hand).
7. Monthly height (Steele, 1981).

When peritoneal dialysis is used with children with chronic renal failure who have diabetes, "a dialysate with a glucose concentration of 2.5 percent and heparin 200 units are used. The blood sugar is checked at the onset of each dialysis run, and 10 units regular insulin are given for each 100 mg/dl over 300 mg/dl" (McCarthy, 1981, p. 2033).

Arteriovenous shunts for the dialysis involve placement of a Teflon cannula in an artery and adjacent vein. The child's dialysate, dialyzer, and medication orders are prescribed by the physician. The following orders are observed:

1. Weight, temperature, and respirations before, half-way through, and at completion of dialysis.
2. BP and pulse before dialysis and every 15 minutes until stabilized and then every 30 minutes.
3. Heparin loading dose, 50 units/kg, then as necessary hourly to maintain clotting time between 20 and 30 minutes.
4. Regional heparinization within 14 days of an operative procedure.
5. Blood flow at initiation of dialysis and midway through.
6. Dialysis shunt care with hydrogen peroxide and antiseptic before and after dialysis; fistula care with antiseptic.
7. During symptomatic hypotensive episodes, discontinue negative pressure and place the child in the Trendelenburg position. If the child does not respond, administer 0.9 percent saline or protein solution through the dialysis line.
8. Culture and obtain a Gram's stain of the shunt site that is erythematous or warm or has purulent discharge; blood culture if the child is febrile.
9. Administer Benadryl 1.25 mg/kg orally for itching.
10. Administer Tylenol 120 mg orally if the child is younger than 6 years of age or 240 mg if he or she is older than 7 years, for headache that is not associated with fever.
11. Notify the physician if seizures occur, if the child has an elevated temperature or chills, if child is hyperkalemic (greater than 6—change the child to a concentrate without potassium), and if the hematocrit is below 18 before dialysis.
12. Administer 0.9 percent saline slowly for muscle cramping (Steele, 1981).

Hemodialysis is usually continued for a period of 4 to 6 hours. This can seem like eternity to a child who does not like to sit still for long periods of time. Diversional activities are planned to help the child tolerate the procedure. The adolescent often enjoys talking on the telephone during these periods. The treatments can be more palatable when the parents are present during the procedure. They can eat their meals with the child to make the day seem more natural despite the crowded, technical appearance of the dialysis unit.

Between the dialyses, the child is allowed free activity. If he or she is of school age, appropriate lessons are provided. As the dialysis is usually done only three times a week, it may be possible for the child to go out on pass or to return home between treatments.

There are usually ongoing dietary restrictions. These restrictions can include decreased sodium, potassium, and phosphorus. Oftentimes fluids are restricted, as well. The dietitian consults with the child and family to make the meals as attractive as possible, as the child is often anorexic.

The noise level in the dialysis unit has been defined as a stressor by adults on hemodialysis (Baldree et al., 1982). It is hypothesized that similar stress may be felt by children who have renal failure and are treated with dialysis. Maintaining control of noise levels and playing quiet music can be helpful during treatments.

The physiological stressors that are most troublesome to adult clients on hemodialysis include muscle cramps and fatigue. These are hypothesized to be of similar concern to children on hemodialysis. Management measures to decrease fatigue are checking for and treating anemia and promotion of sleep that is adequate for the child's age.

Baldree et al. (1982) found that the most commonly used coping behaviors of adults on hemodialysis were maintaining control over the situation and hoping that things would get better. Children probably use these behaviors, as well. Over time, it becomes increasingly difficult to use coping behaviors to effectively contend with hemodialysis treatments.

The cost of dialysis is presently offset by Medicare coverage. However, there is growing concern about the high cost of these treatments, and the prediction is that coverage will decrease significantly in the near future. This may place added financial stress on the family. The family is encouraged to discuss any financial concern so that assistance is provided when it is available to offset some of the expenses that are incurred.

KIDNEY TRANSPLANTATION

The use of transplanted kidneys is increasing in the child population. This is usually reserved for clients with irreversible renal damage. Successful transplants were first done between identical twins and are now successful between less closely related individuals because of tissue cross-matching and the use of immunosuppressive drugs.

Obtaining satisfactory kidneys for transplantation is not a simple process. The tissue match and blood type must be compatible. A living donor has to undergo major surgery without being promised any definite results for the recipient. A kidney from a cadaver must be selected very carefully to be sure it is healthy, and kidneys can only be obtained after the person is officially pronounced dead, a time which is increasingly difficult to judge due to modern technology used to prolong life. Obtaining kidneys raises many ethical questions that make it more difficult to provide the organ necessary to try to prolong another's life. While the child is waiting for a compatible kidney, he or she is maintaining on intermittent peritoneal dialysis or hemodialysis. The child's tissue and blood types are entered into a regional computer system that matches available kidneys with waiting persons.

When a living donor is found, the child and donor are admitted to the hospital for more extensive blood work and kidney function tests. If the donor is found compatible, both the donor and the child are scheduled for major surgery. The child is started on drug therapy approximately 1 week before surgery. The donor may then be discharged until the day before surgery. If the child is severely debilitated, transfusions may be indicated preoperatively. On the day of surgery, each client has a surgical team responsible for his or her care. The donor kidney is removed and refrigerated (cooling to 4°C is achieved by immersing the kidney in cold saline solution for 5 minutes or by direct perfusion of the kidney with a special solution cooled to 4°C). The cooling process prepares the kidney for prolonged ischemia without causing functional defects. The recipient is prepared to receive the donor kidney. The usual site for the kidney is the right iliac fossa (Fig. 10-36). The kidney is turned over so that its posterior side is anterior to make it easier to anastomose the renal vein to the external iliac vein and the renal artery to the hypogastric artery. The ureter is anastomosed to the recipient's ureter at the kidney pelvis or directly into his or her bladder.

In some instances, the kidneys (bilateral nephrectomies) are removed approximately a month prior to surgery and the child is maintained on dialysis. This gives the child an opportunity to recover from major surgery before being subjected to the transplant.

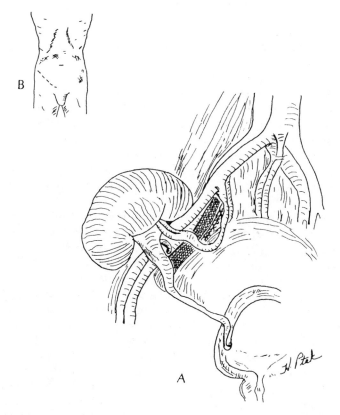

Figure 10-36. A. Kidney transplant. The new kidney is placed in the recipient's iliac fossa on the side opposite the side from which it was taken. **B.** Incision site.

In other instances, the surgeons prefer to remove the recipient's diseased kidney(s) and/or spleen at the time of transplantation. Mention is also being made of correction of urinary tract defects in combination with transplants. An example of such a repair would be a YV plasty.

The spleen is considered to play a role in the rejection process, but many surgeons now believe its removal does not significantly reduce the possibility of rejection, so they are not routinely removing the organ. The removal of the kidney(s) is based on the theory that the diseased kidney(s) can play a major role in postoperative infection.

It is also important to keep in mind that as the recipient surgical team members are preparing the child to receive the kidney, they may decide that the child's possibilities of accepting the donor kidney are too slim and that the surgery will not proceed. In this case, the donor surgical team is notified not to proceed with removal of the kidney. A reason for cancellation of the surgery is severe cardiac failure in the child. Frequent communication takes place between the two surgical teams during the procedure to make sure that both clients have the best possible care and consideration.

Postoperative Care

Immediately postoperatively, the kidney usually excretes adequate to large amounts of urine. This can make the family extremely optimistic, even if they have been told this is the expected outcome. The urine excretion has its darker side also; it is a hazard because with the excretion come resultant fluid and electrolyte changes. These changes pose a threat to the child's life and are monitored carefully. Vital signs are taken every 15 minutes during this early stage; the temperature is taken at least hourly. The child usually has a nasogastric tube that is connected to gentle intermittent suction. If a catheter or catheters are in place, they are connected to drainage. Urine is checked frequently for specific gravity, sugar, acetone, protein, and color. The physician usually leaves specific directions for calling him or her regarding the results. For instance, if the urine has +2 acetone, the physician is notified. In addition, there are specific orders regarding regulation of intravenous fluids. They are given in accordance with the previous hour's urine output. In addition, intravenous flow is regulated to take into consideration nasogastric drainage, usually every 4 hours. Weights are also taken and may influence the parenteral fluid requirements.

After the period of diuresis, the child's urine output stabilizes, followed by a period of adequate renal function. This quiescent period is sometimes followed by a period termed "rejection crisis." This attempt at rejection is signaled by scanty output, proteinuria, elevated temperature, weight gain, hypertension, or uremia. Immunosuppressive drugs are given to counteract the rejection; commonly used agents are Imuran, prednisone, actinomycin C, and antilymphocytic globulin (ALG) (Table 10-6). Peritoneal dialysis may be instituted if anuria persists or if the electrolyte imbalance is severe. The large doses of steroids may cause gastric irritation (ulcers), and an antacid may be given to counteract this response. Stools may be tested for guiac as a precautionary measure.

As soon as the nasogastric tube is taken out (usually on the first postopera-

TABLE 10-6.
Immunosuppressive Medications

Name	Side-Effects
Imuran (azathioprine)	Bone marrow depession (leukopenia)
Prednisone	Rapid withdrawal may cause severe rejection in addition to adrenal insufficiency
	Transient retention of salt and water
	Increased blood pressure
	May raise BUN
	Euphoria or emotional instability
	Increased appetite
	Diabetes mellitus
	Cushnoid conditions:
	Purplish or reddish striae of skin
	Development of supraclavicular fat pads
	Abnormal growth of hair
	Rounded contour of face
	Delayed healing
	Masking effect on infections
Actinomysin C	Irritations of mucus membranes
ALG (anti-lymphocytic globulin)	Severe pain, fever, edema, and swelling at injection site
	Chest pain
	Muscle cramping
	Shortness of breath
	Flushing or cyanosis
	Nausea and vomiting

Adapted from Bois, M.S., Barfield, N.B., Taylor, C.E., et al. Nursing care of patients having kidney transplants. *American Journal of Nursing* 68:1245, 1968.

tive day), if bowel sounds are present, the child is started on oral fluids. If these are tolerated, he or she is progressed to a soft diet. Any diet restrictions are based on symptoms, but generally the diet is fairly free to encourage the child to eat and begin to rehabilitate.

During the time the child is hospitalized, his or her decreased ability to counteract infection due to drugs used to delay rejection is considered. The parents are made aware that they will need to take precautions to guard against infection when the child is discharged. Besides infection and rejection, other complications of transplantation include hemorrhage and leakage of urine.

The child continues taking medications after discharge, so the parents must have explicit directions regarding them. Refer to Table 10-6 for side-effects of particular drugs—these should be included in the parent teaching. In addition, the parents should be aware of signs and symptoms that necessitate medical intervention (Table 10-7). Late rejection crisis usually occurs between the 3rd and 26th months after surgery. This wide variation in time makes it difficult to prepare the family for the situation.

After discharge, the child is followed very closely on an outpatient basis. The parents must understand the value and rationale for this continued close supervision. In addition, they must be helped to begin to let the child develop independence so that his or her additional years are well spent.

While many cases have successful outcomes, it must be kept in mind that death is a real threat postoperatively. The techniques used for transplanation of kidneys have improved, but success cannot be guaranteed. However, the chance that a child facing imminent death might survive almost seems to make any risk worth taking. But in order for the child's life to be prolonged, it may be necessary for another healthy person to risk donating his or her healthy kidney on the basis of his or her present excellent health, even though today's good health does not guarantee tomorrow's good health. If a parent donates a kidney to his or her child, is it unreasonable for him or her to feel he or she has made a real sacrifice

TABLE 10-7.
Signs and Symptoms Heralding Complications in Kidney Transplant Patients

Signs and Symptoms	Causes
Skin infections ("herpes")	Lower resistance of the body
Dysuria, frequency or burning on urination	Urinary tract infection
Hematuria	Urinary tract infection or homograft rejection
Oliguria or anuria	Inadequate fluid intake or homograft rejection (urinary tract obstruction)
Pain in the kidney site or any abdominal pain	Homograft reejection or gastrointestinal complications
Lethargy	Homograft medication side-effects, rejection, or electrolyte imbalance
Elevated temperature	Homograft rejection or infection
Joint pain	Medication side-effects (steroids)
Rapid increase in weight	Excessive fluid or food intake, or decreased renal function
Nausea or vomiting	Infections, gastrointestinal complications
Vertigo, postural hypotension	Antihypertensive medications or electrolyte imbalance
Headache	Hypertension, medication side-effects, excessive sodium in diet, central nervous system infections
Chest pains and respiratory difficulty	Pulmonary embolism, pneumonia, atelectasis, or cardiac complications
Change in bowel habits and in color or consistency of stools	Hepatitis, ulcers, hemorrhoids, fecal impaction, or bowel obstruction
Visual disturbances (blurring, dizziness)	Medication side-effects (antihypertensives, steroids), glaucoma, cataract

From Bois, M.S., Barfield, N.B., Taylor, C.E., et al. Nursing care of patients having kidney transplants. *American Journal of Nursing* 68:1243, 1968.

and expect a return for this sacrifice? If a relative donates a kidney, is it unusual for the parents to feel they owe the person something? These are questions that make the psychologic implications of kidney transplants almost as great as the surgical ones.

A posttransplant side-effect in children is growth retardation. The slow growth is thought to be the result of several factors: (1) persistence of metabolic acidosis, (2) bone age and the degree of bone disease, (3) steroid therapy, and (4) persistence of hypophosphatemia (Toper, 1981). Children under 7 years of age at the time of transplantation have a tendency to experience growth acceleration and eventual attainment of normal height, while children over 7 years of age at the time of transplantation do not witness this growth acceleration.

Females who are amenorrheic during dialysis usually resume menstruation within a year following transplantation. Puberty and normal sexual development are outcomes of the return to normal renal function following transplantation. Despite these outcomes, many adolescents' body images and self-esteem are diminished. The lowered self-esteem is probably the result of the multiple insults that occurred prior to transplant, invasion of privacy, surgical trauma and scars, effects of steroid therapy, and frequent illnesses and hospitalizations, which confirm his or her difference from others.

REFERENCES

Aguilera, D.C. & Messick, J.M. *Crisis intervention.* 3rd ed. St. Louis: Mosby, 1978.

Alterescu, V. Sexual functioning following creation of an abdominal stoma. In D.G. Bullard, & S.E. Knight (Eds.), *Sexual and physical disability.* St. Louis: Mosby, 1981.

Amador, L.V. Congenital anomalies. In O. Swenson (ed.), *Pediatric surgery* (3rd ed.). New York: Appleton—Century—Crofts, 1969.

Baldree, K.S., Murphy, S.P., & Powers, M.J. Stress identification and coping patterns in patients on hemodialysis. *Nursing Research* 31:107, 1982.

Bleck, E.E. Myelomeningocele, meningocele, and spina bifida. In E.E. Bleck & D.A. Nagel (Eds.), *Physically handicapped children.* New York: Grune and Stratton, 1982.

Bobechko, W.P., Herbert, M.A., & Friedman, H.G. Electrospinal instrumentation for scoliosis: Current status. *Orthopedic Clinics of North America* 10:927, 1979.

Boen, S.T. *Peritoneal dialysis in clinical medicine.* Spingfield, Ill.: Thomas, 1964.

Bois, M.S., Barfield, N.B., Taylor, C.E., et al. Nursing care of patients having kidney transplants. *American Journal of Nursing* 68:1245, 1968.

Bunch, W.H. Myelomeningocele. In W.W. Lovell & R.B. Winter (eds.), *Pediatric orthopaedics.* Philadelphia: Lippincott, 1978.

Cailliet, R. *Scoliosis.* Philadelphia: Davis, 1975.

Cantu, R.C. *Toward fitness: Guided exercise for those with health problems.* New York: Human Sciences Press, 1980.

Caplan, G. *Mental health and consultation.* Washington, D.C.: U.S. Dept. of Health, Education and Welfare, 1959.

Coats, K. Techniques in cardiac diagnosis. *Nursing Clinics of North America* 11:259, 1976.

Crocker, D. The critically ill child: Management of tracheostomy. *Pediatrics* 46:286, 1970.

Curtis, B.H., Butler, J.E., & Emerson, C.C. Follow-up study of 100 patients over age 12 with myelomeningocele. In *American Academy of Orthopaedic Surgeons Symposium on Myelomeningocele.* St. Louis: Mosby, 1972.

Department of Health and Human Services. *Leisure time activities: A resource manual for developmentally disabled individuals and their advocates.* DHHS Pub. No. (OHDS) 80-29006. Washington, D.C.: DHHS, 1980.

Derhoff, E. & Feldman, S.A. Behavior perspectives in children with chronic disabilities: A pediatric viewpoint. *Journal of Developmental and Behavioral Pediatrics* 9:97, 1981.

Duke, K.W., & Sherrill, C. Adapted physical education: Perspective on systematic implementation. *Journal of School Health* 50:270, 1980.

Easton, J.K.M., & Halpern, D. Cerebral palsy. In W.C. Stolov & M.R. Clowers (Eds.), *Handbook of severe disability.* Washington, D.C.: U.S. Department of Education Rehabilitation Services Administration, 1981.

Erikson, E.H. *Childhood and society* (2nd ed.). New York: Norton, 1963.

Feldman, A.S. Diagnostic application and interpretation of tympanometry and the acoustic reflex. In J.B. Chaiklin, I.M. Ventry, & R.F. Dixon (Eds.), *Hearing measurement* (2nd ed). Reading , Mass.: Addison–Wesley, 1982.

Freudenberg, N., Feldman, N., Clark, N.M., et al. The impact of bronchial asthma on school attendance and performance. *Journal of School Health* 50:522, 1980.

Godfrey, A.B. Sensory-motor stimulation for slow-to-develop children. *American Journal of Nursing* 75:56, 1975.

Green, J., & Levitt, E.E. Constriction of body image in children with congenital heart disease. *Pediatrics* 29:438, 1962.

Harper, R.W. Chest therapy. In *A Guide to respiratory care.* Philadelphia: Lippincott, 1981.

Harper, R.W. Management of chest tubes. In *A guide to respiratory care.* Philadelphia: Lippincott, 1981.

Harvey, B.H. Asthma. In E.E. Bleck & D.A. Nagel (Eds.), *Physically handicapped children* (2nd ed.). New York: Grune & Stratton, 1982.

Harvey, B.H. Cystic fibrosis. In E.E. Bleck & D.A. Nagel (Eds.), *Physically handicapped children* (2nd ed.), New York: Grune & Stratton, 1982.

Holland, S.H. 20/20 vision screening. *Pediatric Nursing* 8:81, 1982.

Hoover, R.E., & Bledsoe, C.W. Blindness and visual impairments. In W.C. Stolov & M.R. Clowers (Eds.), *Handbook of severe disability.* Washington, D.C.: U.S. Department of Education Rehabilitation Services Administration, 1981.

Kübler-Ross, E. *On death and dying.* New York: Macmillan, 1969.

Lauer, R.M., Connor, W.E., Leaverton, P.E., et al. Coronary heart disease risk factors in school children: The Muscatine Study. *Journal of Pediatrics* 86:697, 1975.

McCarthy, J.A. Diabetic nephropathy. *American Journal of Nursing* 81:2030, 1981.

Money, J.W., & Ehrhardt, A.A. *Man and woman, boy and girl: Differentiation and dimorphism of gender identity from conception to maturity.* Baltimore: John Hopkins University Press, 1972.

O'Hara, M.N. Nursing care of the child with respiratory problems. In S.M. Steele (Ed.), *Nursing care of the child with long-term illness.* New York: Appleton–Century–Crofts, 1977.

Olshansky, S. Chronic sorrow: A response to having a mentally defective child. *Social Casework* 43:30, 1962.

Parcel, G.S., Tiernan, K., Nader, P.R., et al. *Teaching my parents about asthma.* Galveston, Texas: Department of Pediatrics, The University of Texas Medical Branch, 1976.

Parrish, A.E. End-stage renal disease. In W.C. Stolov & M.R. Clowers (Eds), *Handbook of severe disability.* Washington, D.C.: U.S. Department of Education Rehabilitation Service Administration, 1981.

Raimbault, G., & de Recherches, M. Psychological problems in the chronic nephropathies of childhood. In E.J. Anthony & C. Koupernik (Eds.), *The child in his family.* New York: Wiley, 1973.

Richardson, S.A. The effect of physical disability on the socialization of a child. In D.A. Goslin (Ed.), *Handbook of socialization theory and research.* Chicago: Rand McNally, 1969.

Roeser, R.J. & Northern J.L. Screening for hearing loss and middle ear disorders. In R.J. Roeser & M.R. Downs (Eds.), *Auditory disorders in school children.* New York: Thieme Stratton, 1981.

Ross, A.O. *The exceptional child in the family.* New York: Grune & Stratton, 1964.

Shurtleff, D.B, Hayden, P.W., Chapman, W.B., et al. Myelodysplasia. *Western Journal of Medicine* 122:199, 1975.

Sousa, J.C., Gordon, L.H. & Shurtleff, D.B. Assessing the development of daily living skills in patients with spina bifida. In G. Stark (ed.), *Studies in hydrocephalus in spina bifida. Developmental Medicine and Child Neurology* 18 (Suppl. 37):134, 1976.

Statland, H. *Fluid and electrolytes in practice.* Philadelphia: Saunders, 1963.

Steele, S. *Child health and the family: Nursing concepts and management.* New York: Masson, 1981.

Thornton, C.E. Sex education for disabled children and adolescents. In D.G. Bullard & S.E. Knight (Eds.), *Sexuality and physical disability.* St. Louis: Mosby, 1981.

Topor, M. Chronic renal disease in children. *Nursing Clinics of North America* 16:587, 1981.

Watts, H.G. Bracing in spinal deformities. *Orthopedic Clinics of North America* 10:769, 1979.

Werner-Beland, J.A. Theoretical concepts of grieving. In J.A. Werner-Beland (Ed.), *Grief responses to long-term illness and disability.* Reston, Va.: Reston, 1980.

Werner-Beland, J.A. Physical disability and grief resolution. In J.A. Werner-Beland (Ed.), *Grief responses to long-term illness and disability.* Reston, Va.: Reston, 1980.

Whaley, L.F., & Wong, D.L. The child with sensory or communication disorder. In *Nursing care of infants and children.* St. Louis: Mosby, 1979.

Wilson, W.R., & Walton, W.K. Identification audiometry accuracy: Evaluation of a recommended program for school-age children. In J.B. Chaiklin, I.M. Ventry, & R.F. Dixon (Eds.), *Hearing measurement* (2nd ed.). Reading, Mass: Addison—Wesley, 1982.

BIBLIOGRAPHY

Adams, G. The sexual history is an intergral part of the patient history. *American Journal of Maternal—Child Nursing* 1:170, 1976.

Allen, B.L., & Ferguson, R.L. The operative treatment of myelomeningocele spinal deformity—1979. *Orthopedic Clinics of North America* 10:845, 1979.

Amundsen, M.J. Nurses as group leaders of behavior management classes for parents. *Nursing Clinics of North America* 10:319, 1975.

Anderson, B. The patient with scoliosis: Carole, a girl treated with bracing. *American Journal of Nursing* 79:1592, 1979.

Anfenson, M. The school-age child with cystic fibrosis. *Journal of School Health* 50:26, 1980.

Anger, D. The psychologic stress of chronic renal failure and long-term hemodialysis. *Nursing Clinics of North America* 10:449, 1975.

Arneson, S.W., & Triplett, J.L. How children cope with disfiguring changes in their appearance. *American Journal of Maternal—Child Nursing* 3:336, 1978.

Arnheim, D., & Sinclair, W. *The clumsy child.* St. Louis: Mosby, 1975.

Avey, M. Primary care for handicapped children. *American Journal of Nursing* 73:658, 1973.

Avner, E., Harmon, W., Ingelfinger, J., et al. Mortality of chronic hemodialysis comparable to that of renal transplantation in pediatric end stage renal disease. *Proceedings of the Clinical Dialysis and Transplant Forum,* 1980.

Barnard, K.E., & Erickson, M.L. *Teaching children with developmental problems,* (2nd ed.). St. Louis: Mosby, 1976.

Bean, M.R., & Bell, B.J. Nursing intervention in the care of the physically handicapped child. *Nursing Clinics of North America* 10:361, 1975.

Blakeslee, B. (Ed.). *The limb deficient child.* Berkeley, Calif.: University of California Press, 1963.

Blas, P., & Finch, S.M. Sexuality and the handicapped. In J.A. Downey & N.L. Low (Eds.), *The child with disabling illness: Principles of rehabilitation.* Philadelphia: Saunders, 1974.

Bower, F. (Ed.), *Distortions in body image in illness and disability.* New York: John Wiley, 1977.

Boyle, I.R., di Sant'Agnese, P.A., Sack, S.A., et al. Emotional adjustment of adolescents and young adults with cystic fibrosis. *Journal of Pediatrics* 88:318, 1976.

Bradford, D.S. Anterior spinal surgery in management of scoliosis. *Orthopedic Clinics of North America* 10:801, 1979.

Brooks, H.L., Bunnell, W.P., & Mitchell, P.L. You can help children with scolisos. *Patient Care* 15:111, 1981.

Bullard, D.G., & Knight, S.E. *Sexuality and physical disability.* St. Louis: Mosby, 1981.

Bullingnon, B., & Sexton, D. Families of multi-handicapped children in residential institutes. *Children Today* 5:13, 1976.

Butt, K., et al. Transplantation in children. *Dialysis and Transplantation* 5:59, 1976.

Caine, D. Psychological considerations affecting rehabilitation after amputation. *Medical Journal of Australia* 2:818, 1973.

Cecarelli, C.M. Hemodialytic therapy for the patient with chronic renal failure. *Nursing Clinics of North America* 16:531, 1981.

Chambers, J.K. Assessing the dialysis patient at home. *American Journal of Nursing* 81:750, 1981.

Cianci, J., & Lamb, J. Matching organ donors and recipients. *American Journal of Nursing* 81:544, 1981.

Cle, T.M. Sexuality and physical disabilities. *Archives of Sexual Behavior* 4:389, 1975.

Cloutier, J. & Measel, C.P. Home care for the infant with congenital heart disease. *American Journal of Nursing* 82:100, 1982.

Cole, R.B., *Essentials of respiratory disease.* Philadelphia: Lippincott, 1976.

Comarr, A.E., & Gunderson, B.B. Sexual function in traumatic paraplegia and quadriplegia. *American Journal of Nursing* 75:250, 1975.

Comfort, A. (Ed.). *Sexual consequences of disability.* Philadelphia: George F. Stickley, 1978.

Connors, M. Ostomy care: A personal approach. *American Journal of Nursing* 74:1422, 1974.

Crigler, L. Sexual concerns of the spinal cord injured. *Nursing Clinics of North America* 9:703, 1974.

Cropp, G.J. Exercise-induced asthma. *Pediatric Clinics of North America* 22:63, 1975.

Cummings, S.T. The impact of the child's deficiency on the father: A study of fathers of mentally retarded and of chronically ill children. *American Journal of Orthopsychiatry* 46:246, 1976.

Davis, F.D. Current strategies in the procurement of cadaveric kidneys for transplantation. *Nursing Clinics of North America* 16:565, 1981.

Davis, G.T., & Hill, P.M. Cerebral palsy. *Nursing Clinics of North America* 15:35, 1980.

Davis, R.E. Family of physically disabled child reactions and reasoning. *New York State Journal of Medicine* 75:1039, 1975.

Debuskey, M. (Ed.). *The chronically ill child and his family.* Springfield, Ill.: Thomas, 1970.

deToledo, C.H. The patient with scoliosis: The defect, classification and detection. *American Journal of Nursing* 9:588, 1979.

Donaldson, J. Changing attitudes toward handicapped persons: A review and analysis of research. *Exceptional Children* 46:504, 1980.

Drotar, D., Doershuk, C.F., Stern, R.C., et al. Psychosocial functioning of children with cystic fibrosis. *Pediatrics* 67:338, 1981.

Duke, K.W., & Sherrill, C. Adapted physical education: Perspective on systematic implementation. *Journal of School Health* 50:270, 1980.

Dunlap, K.H., Stoneman, Z., & Cantrell, M.L. Social interaction of exceptional and other children in a mainstreamed preschool classroom. *Exceptional Children* 47:132, 1980.

Facteau, L.M. Self-care concepts and the care of the hospitalized child. *Nursing Clinics of North America* 15:145, 1980.

Ferguson, J. Late psychologic effects of a serious illness in childhood. *Nursing Clinics of North America* 11:73, 1976.

Fine, R.N., Malekzadeh, M.H., Pennisi, J., et al. Long-term results of renal transplantation in children. *Pediatrics* 61:641, 1978.

Finnie, N. *Handling the young cerebral palsied child at home.* New York: Dutton, 1975.

Fitting, M.D., Salisbury, S., Davies, N.H., et al. Self-concept and sexuality of spinal cord injured women. *Archives of Sexual Behavior* 7:143, 1978.

Flechsig, L. Living with cerebral palsy. *American Journal of Nursing* 78:1212, 1978.

Floor, L., & Rosen, M. New criteria of adjustment for the cerebral palsied. *Rehabilitation Literature* 37:268, 1976.

Fox, G.L. The family's influence on adolescent sexual behavior. *Children Today* 8:21, 1979.

Frauman, A.C. Sexuality in adolescents with chronic illness. *American Journal of Maternal–Child Nursing* 4:371, 1979.

Friedberg, D.Z., & Litwin, S.B. The medical and surgical management of patients with congenital heart disase. *Clinical Pediatrics* 15:324, 1976.

Friedman, L.W. Amputation. In W.C. Stolov, and M.R. Clowers (Eds.) *Handbook of severe disability.* Washington, D.C.: U.S. Department of Education Rehabilitation Services Administration, 1981.

Friedrich, W.N. Ameliorating the psychological impact of chronic physical disease on the child and family. *Journal of Pediatric Psychology* 2:26, 1979.

Gayton, W.F., Friedman, S.B., Tavormina, J.F., et al. Children with cystic fibrosis: Psychological test findings of patients, siblings and parents. *Pediatrics* 59: 888, 1977.

Gayton, W.F., & Friedman, S.B. Psychosocial aspects of cystic fibrosis: A review of the literature. *American Journal of Disease of Children* 126: 856, 1973.

Gearheart, B.R., & Weishabn, M.W. *The handicapped child in the regular classroom.* St. Louis: Mosby, 1976.

Geddes, D. *Physical activities for individuals with handicapping conditions.* St. Louis: Mosby, 1974.

Geiger, R., & Knight, S. Sexuality of people with cerebral palsy. *Medical Aspects of Human Sexuality* 9: 70, 1975.

Geist, R.A. Onset of chronic illness in children and adolescents: Psychotherapeutic and consultative intervention. *American Journal of Orthopsychiatry* 49:4, 1979.

Ghory, J.E. Exercise, the school and the allergic child. *Pediatrics* 56:948, 1975.

Girdany, B.R. Vesicoureteral reflex and renal scarring. *Journal of Pediatrics* 86:998, 1975.

Gordon, S., & Snyder, C.W. Family life education for the handicapped. *Journal of School Health* 50:272, 1980.

Gottlief, J., & Gottlief, B. Seterotypic attitudes and behavioral intentions toward handicapped children. *American Journal of Mental Deficiency* 82:65, 1977.

Grief, E., & Matarazzo, R.G. *Behavioral approaches to rehabilitation: Coping with change.* New York: Springer, 1982.

Gudersmith, S. Mother's reports of early experiences of infants with congenital heart disease. *Maternal—Child Nursing Journal* 4:155, 1975.

Gump, P.A., & Mei, Y.H. Active games for physically handicapped children. In E.M. Avedon, & B. Sutton-Smith (Eds.), *The study of games.* New York: John Wiley, 1971.

Gunn-Brooks, J., & Matthews, W.S. *He and she: How children develop their sex-role identity.* Englewood Cliffs, N.J.: Prentice-Hall, 1979.

Gutch, C.F., & Stoner, M.H. *Review of hemodialysis for nurses and dialysis personnel.* St. Louis: Mosby, 1971.

Haddock, N. Blood pressure monitoring in neonates. *American Journal of Maternal—Child Nursing* 5:131, 1980.

Hale, G. *The source book for the disabled.* New York: Paddington, 1979.

Hall, P., Lindseth, R., Campbell, R., et al. Scoliosis and hydrocephalus in myelocele patients. *Journal of Neurosurgery* 174, 1979.

Handlers, A., & Austin, K. Improving attitudes of high school students toward their handicapped peers. *Exceptional Children* 47:228, 1980.

Hanigan, K.F. Teaching intermittent self-catheterization to young children with myelodysplasia. *Developmental Medicine and Child Neurology* 21:365, 1979.

Hanson, E.I. Effects of grief associated with chronic illness and disability of sexuality. In J.A. Werner-Beland, (Ed.), *Grief responses to long-term illness and disability.* Reston, Va.: Reston, 1980.

Hardy, W.G. National Conference on Identification Audiometry Committee: Identification audiometry. *Journal of Speech and Hearing Disorders* [Monograph Suppl] 9:26, 1981.

Hedahl, K.J. Helping children establish positive attitudes towards disabled persons. *Pediatric Nursing* 7:11, 1981.

Hogan, R. *Human sexuality: A nursing perspective*. New York: Appleton—Century—Crofts, 1980.

Hooper, G. Getting it straight. *Nursing Mirror*, 151:16, 1980.

Hopkins, J., & Armstrong, S. Psychotherapy for adolescent dialysis patients. *Dialysis and Transplantation* 5:54, 1976.

Hussey, C.G. Surviving a handicap in everyday life: How to help. *American Journal of Maternal—Child Nursing* 4:46, 1979.

Hymovich, D.P. Assessment of the chronically ill child and family. In D. Hymovich & M. Bernard (Eds.), *Family health care*. New York: McGraw—Hill, 1979, vol. 1.

Ingelfinger, J., Grupe, W.E., & Levy, R.H. Growth acceleration following renal transplanation in children. *Kidney International* 14:793, 1978.

Isaacs, J., & McElroy, M.R. Psychosocial aspects of chronic illness in children. *Journal of School Health* 50:318, 1980.

Jackson, P.L. Chronic grief. *American Journal of Nursing* 74:1288, 1974.

Jackson, P.L. Digoxin therapy at home: Keeping the child safe. *American Journal of Maternal—Child Nursing* 4:105, 1979.

Johnson, W. *Sex education and counseling of special groups: The mentally and physically handicapped, ill and elderly* (2nd ed.). Springfield, Ill.: Charles C. Thomas, 1981.

Jones, E. The role of nurses in caring for handicapped children. *Journal of School Health* 49:147, 1979.

Jones, T.W., Sowell, V.W., Jones, J.K., et al. Changing children's perceptions of handicapped people. *Exceptional Children* 47:365, 1981.

Kelly, C.M. Empathetic listening. In J. Stewart (Ed.), *Bridges not walls* (2nd ed.). Reading, Mass.: Addison—Wesley, 1977.

Kennaird, D.L. Oxygen consumption and evaporation water loss in infants with congenital heart disease. *Archives of Disease in Childhood* 51:34, 1976.

Kiechl, F., Pollack, J., Cooper, D., et al. The comparative efficacy of theophylline and Cromolyn in suppressing exercise-induced bronchospasm. *Journal of Allergy and Clinical Immunology* 57:250, 1976.

Kikuchi, J. A preadolescent boy's adaptation to the traumatic loss of both hands. *Maternal—Child Nursing Journal* 1:19, 1972.

Knowles, R.D. Positive self-talk. *American Journal of Nursing* 81:535, 1981.

Kweskin, S. Send a chronically ill child to camp? *Patient Care* 11:98, 1979.

Larter, N. Cystic fibrosis. *American Journal of Nursing* 81:527, 1981.

Lawson, B.A. Chronic illness in the school-aged child: Effects on the total family. *American Journal of Maternal—Child Nursing* 2:49, 1977.

Lederberg, A. The language environment of children with language delays. *Journal of Pediatric Psychology* 5:141, 1980.

Levine, D.B. Pulmonary function in scoliosis. *Orthopedic Clinics of North America* 10:761, 1979.

Lewy, P.R., & Belman, A.B. Familial occurrence of nonobstructive, noninfectious, vesicoureteral reflex with renal scarring. *Journal of Pediatrics* 86:851, 1975.

Lord, L. Guest editorial: New directions in work with children with communication disorders. *Journal of Pediatric Psychology* 5:121, 1980.

MacElman, R.M. Society vs the wheelchair. *Pediatrics* 63:576, 1979.

Mandleco, B.H. Monitoring children's reactions when they are hospialized for percutane-ous renal biopsy. *American Journal of Maternal—Child Nursing* 1:288, 1976.

Mathews, E.S., & Ransohoff, J. Hydrocephalus. In J.L. Barnett (Ed.), *Pediatrics* (16th ed.). New York: Appleton—Century—Crofts, 1977.

Mattson, A. Long-term physical illness in childhood: A challenge to psychological adaptation. *Pediatrics* 50:80, 1972.

Mauer, S.M., & Lynch, R.E. Hemodialysis techniques for infants and children. *Pediatric Clinics of North America* 23:843, 1976.

McCain, G.C. Parent created tape readings for hospitalized children. *Children's Health Care* 10:104, 1982.

McCling, M. The legal rights of handicapped school children. *Educational Horizons* 54:25, 1975.

McCloskey, J.C. How to make the most of body image theory in nursing practice. *Nursing* 6:68, 1976.

McCollum, A.T. *Coping with prolonged health impairments in your child.* Boston: Little, Brown, 1975.

McCollum, AT., & Gibson, L.E. Family adaptation to the child with cystic fibrosis. *Journal of Pediatrics* 77:571, 1970.

McCrory, W.W., Shibuya, M., Yano, K., et al. Recent trends in the mortality rate from renal disease in children and young adults in New York City. *Journal of Pediatrics* 87:928, 1975.

McElroy, D.B. Hydrocephalus in children. *Nursing Clinics of North America* 15:23, 1980.

McNat, W.L. The sexual needs of the handicapped. *Journal of School Health* 48:301, 1978.

Micheli, L.J., Magin, M.A., & Ronvales, R. The patient with scoliosis: Surgical management and nursing care. *American Journal of Nursing* 9:1592, 1979.

Minde, K.K., Hackett, J.D., Killou, D., et al. How they grow up: 41 physically handicapped children and their families. *American Journal of Psychiatry* 128:1554, 1972.

Mitchell, J.C., Frohnert, P.P., Kurtz, S.B., et al. Chronic peritoneal dialysis in juvenile-onset diabetes mellitus. *Mayo Clinic Proceedings* 53:775, 1978.

Money, J.W. *Sex errors of the body: Dilemmas, education, counseling.* Baltimore: Johns Hopkins Press, 1968.

Mooney, T.O., Cole, T.M., & Chilgren, R.A. *Sexual options for paraplegics and quadriplegics.* Boston: Little, Brown, 1975.

Morley, W.P. Asthma and exercise: A review. *American Corrective Therapy Journal* 31:95, 1977.

Morrison, E.S., & Prico, M.U. *Values in sexuality.* New York: Hart, 1974.

Myers, G.J., Cerone, S.B., & Olson, R.L. (Eds.). *A guide for helping children with spina bifida.* Springfield, Ill.: Charles C. Thomas, 1981.

Nathan, S.W. Body image of scoliotic female adolescent before and after surgery. *Maternal—Child Nursing Journal* 6:139, 1977.

New, C. Coping with newly diagnosed blindness. *American Journal of Nursing* 75:2161, 1975.

Odiorne, J., & Tenerowicz, C. Adolescent sexuality. In J. Howe (Ed.), *Nursing care of adolescents.* New York: McGraw—Hill, 1980.

Orenstein, D.M., Franklin, B.A., Doershuk, C.F., et al. Exercise conditioning and cardiopul-monary fitness in cystic fibrosis. *Chest* 80:392, 1981.

Osaka, K., Tanimura, T., Hirayama, A., et al. Myelomeningocele before birth. *Journal of Neurosurgery* 49:711, 1978.

Owen, S.L. The three R's and HBP: A unique approach to school health and high blood pressure education. *Image* 8:13, 1976.

Palfrey, J., Mervis, R.C., Butler, J.A. New directions in the evaluation and education of handicapped children. *New England Journal of Medicine* 298:819, 1978.

Passo, S. Malformations of the neural tube. *Nursing Clinics of North America* 15:5, 1980.

Passo, S. Positioning infants with myelomeningocele. *American Journal of Nursing* 74:1658, 1974.

Patterson, C.J., & Massad, C.M. Facilitating referential communication among children: The listener as teacher. *Journal of Experimental Child Psychology* 29:357, 1980.

Patterson, G.R. *Living with children.* Champaign, Ill.: Research Press, 1980.

Patullo, A.W. The socio-sexual development of the handicapped child. *Nursing Clinics of North America* 10:361, 1975.

Penticuff, J. Development of the concept of self: Implications for the teacher's role in promotion of mental health. *Educational Horizons* 55:15, 1976.

Press, J.B., & Pinkerton, P. *Chronic childhood disorder: Promoting patterns of adjustment.* London: Henry Kimpton, 1975.

Posy, R.A. Creative nursing of babies with heart disease. *Nursing* 4:40, 1974.

Powers, A.M. Renal transplantation: The patient's choice. *Nursing Clinics of North America* 16:551, 1981.

Rapp, D. *Allergies and your child.* New York: Holt, 1972.

Reiss, J.A., & Menashe, V.D. Genetic counseling and congenital heart disease. *Journal of Pediatrics* 80:655, 1972.

Richardson, G.E. Educational imagery: A missing link in decision making. *Journal of School Health* 51:560, 1981.

Ritchie, J. Children's adjustive and affective responses in the process of reformulating a body image following limb amputation. *Maternal–Child Nursing Journal* 6:25, 1977.

Ritchie, J. Nursing the child undergoing limb amputation. *American Journal of Maternal–Child Nursing* 5:114, 1980.

Robinault, I.P. *Sex, society and the disabled.* New York: Harper and Row, 1978.

Rodger, B. Comprehensive care for the child with chronic disability. *American Journal of Nursing* 79:1106, 1979.

Rose, M.H. Coping behavior of physically handicapped children. *Nursing Clinics of North America* 10:329, 1975.

Rose, T.L. The education of all handicapped children act (PL 94-142): New responsibilities and opportunities for the school nurse. *Journal of School Health* 50:30, 1980.

Rowe, A. *Food allergy: Its manifestations and control and the elimination diets.* Springfield, Ill.: Thomas, 1972.

Sappon-Shewin, M. Another look at mainstreaming: Exceptionality, normality, and the nature of the difference. *Phi Delta Kappan* 60:119, 1978.

Sato-Viacrucis, K. Preschool vision screening: A new method fills a need. *Journal of School Health* 46:480, 1976.

Scherr, M.S., Crawford, P.L., Sergent, C.B., et al. Effects of biofeedback techniques on chronic asthma in a summer camp environment. *Annals of Allergy* 35:291, 1975.

Schneider, M.R., Melton, B.H., & Reisch, J.S. Effects of progressive exercise program on absenteeism among school children with asthma. *Journal of School Health* 50:92, 1980.

Schulman, K. Meningomyelocele. In H.L. Barnett (Ed.), *Pediatrics* (16th ed.). New York: Appleton—Century—Crofts, 1977.

Schwachman, H., Khaw, K.T., & Kowalski, S.M. The management of cystic fibrosis. *Clinical Pediatrics* 14:1115, 1975.

Shor, V.Z. Congenital cardiac defects: Assessment and case finding. *American Journal of Nursing* 78:256, 1978.

Simkins, R. Asthma: Reactive airways disease. *American Journal of Nursing* 81:522, 1981.

Smith, E.D. Perceptions of sexuality. In S. Steele (Ed.), *Child health and the family: Nursing concepts and management.* New York: Masson, 1981.

Stearns, S.E. Understanding the psychological adjustment of physically handicapped children in the classroom. *Children Today* 10:12, 1981.

Stone, B., Beekman, C., Hall, V., et al. The effects of an exercise program on change in curve in adolescents with minimal idiopathic scoliosis. *Physical Therapy* 59:759, 1979.

Symonds, M.E., & Wickware, L. Sex education of children with disabilities. In A. Comfort (Ed.)., *Sexual consequences of disability.* Philadelphia: George F. Stickley, 1978.

Tallal, P. Language disabilities in children: A perceptual or linguistic deficit? *Journal of Pediatric Psychology* 5:127, 1980.

Tishler, C.L. The psychological aspects of genetic counseling. *American Journal of Nursing* 81:733, 1981.

Travis, G. *Chronic illness in children: Its impact on child and family.* Stanford, Calif.: Stanford University Press, 1976.

Tropauer, A., Franz, A., & Dilgard, V. Psychological aspects of the care of children with cystic fibrosis. *American Journal of Diseases of Children* 119:424, 1970.

Tudor, M. Nursing interventions with developmentally disabled children. *American Journal of Maternal—Child Nursing* 3:25, 1978.

Van Vechten, D., Satterwhite, B., & Pless, I.B. Health education literature for parents of physically handicapped children. *American Journal of Diseases of Children* 131:311, 1977.

Vining, E.P.G., Accardo, P.J., Rubenstein, J.E., et al. Cerebral palsy: A pediatric developmentalist's overview. *American Journal of Diseases of Children* 130:643, 1976.

Vipperman, J.F., & Rager, P.M. Childhood coping: How nurses can help. *Pediatric Nursing* 6:11, 1980.

Vlasak, J.W. Mainstreaming handicapped children: The underlying legal concept. *Journal of School Health* 50:285, 1980.

Vodola, T.M. *Diagnostic—prescriptive motor ability and physical fitness tasks and activities for the normal and atypical individual.* Neptune City, N.J.: VEE, 1978.

Waechter, E.H. Developmental consequences of congenital abnormalities. *Nursing Forum* 14:108, 1977.

Waechter, E.H. Developmental correlates of physical disability. *Nursing Forum* 9:90, 1970.

Walters, J. Coping with a leg amputation. *American Journal of Nursing* 81:1349, 1981.

Westervelt, V.D., & Turnbull, A.P. Children's attitudes toward physically handicapped peers and intervention approaches for attitude change. *Physical Therapy* 60:896, 1980.

Wolf, S.I. Exercise, the asthmatic child and PL 94-142. *Pediatric Nursing* 6:21, 1980.

Wooldridge, C.P., & Russell, G. Head position training with the cerebral palsied child: An application of biofeedback techniques. *Archives of Physical Medicine and Rehabilitation* 57:407, 1976.

Yamamoto, K. *The child and his image.* Boston: Houghton Mifflin, 1972.

Yaros, P.S., & Howe, J. Responses to illness and disability. In J. Howe (Ed.), *Nursing care of adolescents.* New York: McGraw—Hill, 1980.

Young, R.K. Chronic sorrow: Parents' response to the birth of a child with a defect. *American Journal of Maternal—Child Nursing* 2:38, 1977.

Zuzich, A.M. Grief in parents of a child with a birth handicap. In J.A. Werner-Beland, (Ed.), *Grief responses to long-term illness and disability.* Reston, Va.: Reston, 1980.

11

Health Promotion of the Child With A Learning Problem: Mental Retardation

Peggy Drapo

Nursing involvement in the field of mental retardation did not start with the recent trends brought about by normalization concepts, deinstitutionalization, and legislative efforts such as the Education of all Handicapped Children Act of 1975 (PL 94-142). Nurses have been working with people who are mentally retarded since the early history of nursing (Bullough and Bullough, 1969). What these trends do mean to nurses, however, is that mental retardation can no longer be just a specialty area in an institution or agency serving the retarded. The trend of normalization is to bring persons who are retarded into the mainstream of society. Nurses must be prepared to meet the normal health needs of those individuals as well as the needs that are unique to their related disabilities.

In the past, nursing care of people who were retarded was custodial in nature, but this is not the care that nurses are being challenged to provide today. What makes the challenge so stimulating is the spectrum of needs in all spheres of daily living that these clients present to us. Their health needs call for a great deal of education and expertise on the part of the nurse.

Retardation is not easy to define, since it is not a clear-cut condition. It is not just the result of a disease, although it can be. There are over 350 known causes (Menolascino, 1977). Before exploring some causes, it is helpful to discuss the definition and some related terms.

Mental Retardation. According to the American Association of Mental Deficiency, mental retardation refers to "a significantly subaverage general intellectual functioning existing concurrently with deficits in adaptive behavior, and is manifested during the developmental period" (Grossman, 1977).

Subaverage General Intellectual Functioning. This refers to the measure of scores on intelligence tests which have been standardized. The tests are administered to measure vocabulary, comprehension, visual functioning, memory, reasoning, and judgment. Mental retardation begins at two standard deviations below the mean score of 100.

Standard Deviation. This is an index or measure of variability or range of distribution of scores. This measure depicts how much people in a group are alike or unalike. For all practical purposes, the range covers six standard deviations—three are above the mean and three are below. For the normal range, approximately two-thirds (or 68.3 percent) of the scores are within one standard deviation above and below the mean.

Standardized Tests. These tests are designed to measure a sample of individual performance and are given under formal conditions with definite rules. The test results are interpreted in relationship to predetermined normative information (in areas mentioned in the definition of subaverage general intellectual functioning). Scores from these tests are converted to standard scores and IQ scores from which the standard score mean of 100 has been derived for persons within given age groups. The standard deviation is set at 15 points for the Stanford-Binet and 14 for the Wechsler (Table 11-1).

Normal Distribution. This is a score distribution that in graphic forms resembles a bell-shaped curve (Fig. 11-1). Scores are distributed around the mean, and there is approximately the same number of scores above the mean as there is below it. Fewer scores will be found farther from the mean (Table 11-2).

Table 11-2 indicates that 47 percent, approximately one-half of "all" persons, have IQs within 20 points of 90 through 109; an IQ of 140 or above would be considered extremely high, since fewer than 1 percent (0.6) of the total population reach this level, and fewer than 1 percent have IQs below 60. In the cumulative

TABLE 11-1.
Test Scores that Reflect Mild, Moderate, Severe, or Profound Retardation*

Degree of Retardation	Stanford-Binet	Wechsler
Mild	52–67	55–69
Moderate	36–51	40–54
Severe	20–35	25–39
Profound	Below 20	Below 25

*Intelligence scores that fall between the mentally retarded and normal are 68 to 83 for Stanford-Binet and 70 to 84 for Wechsler. An old term used for these scores is "borderline." You may still see this used in the literature, but it is not really a good term.

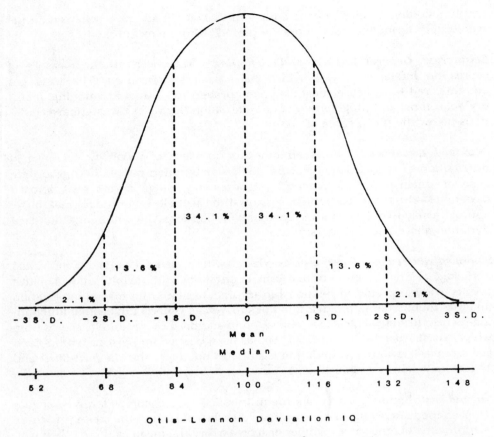

Figure 11-1. Bell-shaped curve.

percentages given, it is noted that 3.1 percent have IQs below 70, usually considered the mentally retarded category. This column may be used to indicate the percentile rank (PR) of certain IQs. Thus an IQ of 119 has a PR of 89, since 89.4 percent of the IQs are 119 or below. An IQ of 79 has a PR of 10.6 or 11.

Adaptive Behavior.   This term applies to one's ability to get along in the environment. Adaptability relates to maturation, social skills, and learning. Maturation refers to motor, socialization, and communication skills and skills of daily living. Social adjustment refers to relationships, meeting society's expectations, and the ability to be socially and economically independent.

Developmental Period.   The figures in the literature vary according to which theory you are reading about, but generally speaking, ages from conception to 16 or 18 years of age are included in the developmental period.

TABLE 11-2.
Normal Distribution of IQs with a Mean of 100 and a Standard Deviation of 16

Range	Percent of Persons	Cumulative Percent
140 and above	0.6	100.6
130–139	2.5	99.4
120–129	7.5	96.9
110–119	16.0	89.4
100–109	23.4 } 46.8	73.4
90–99	23.4	50.0
80–89	16.0	26.6
70–79	7.5	10.6
60–69	2.5	3.1
Below 60	0.6	0.6
Total	100.0	

From Mitchell, B.C. *Test Service Notebook 13: A Glossary of Measurement Terms.* New York: Harcourt Brace Jovanovich.

The Client.   For the purposes of this chapter, nursing will deal with the individual in a nurse–client relationship in the community. When speaking of the individual in the hospital, we will refer to a nurse–patient situation.

The definition of mental retardation by the AAMD is less negative than some definitions in its implication, because it does not spell out the disabilities and is widely accepted among professionals; however, it has a fault. The mentally retarded have potential for growth, given opportunities for learning and social experiences, which the definition does not stress (Menolascino, 1977). Diagnosis of mental retardation must be made by many members of the health and educational team after a battery of examinations and tests. The diagnosis should not be made lightly.

Important in the diagnosis is a medical history. Causes of mental retardation may be found in prenatal, perinatal, or postnatal factors, so the medical history is very important. It should bring out information regarding past abortions, premature deliveries, any complications of deliveries, toxemia, developmental defects or genetic problems, and any stillbirths or deaths of infants in the family.

Besides the family medical history, a complete biopsychosocial assessment is done. This includes a complete neurologic exam and a psychiatric assessment. When risk factors are found, long-term follow-up for developmental lags is indicated. These tests involve professionals from many disciplines.

Incidence of Mental Retardation.   It has been estimated by the President's Committee on Mental Retardation that 3 percent of the people in the United States are retarded. That means that over 6,500,000 persons have this diagnosis. Mental retardation is often associated with other disabilities. In 1970, the U.S. Office of Education stated that the number of handicapped individuals was

7,083,000 within the age span of birth to 19 years in this country. Patterson (1978) states that 25,000,000 persons would be served if nursing services were provided to those individuals and their family members.

IMPLICATIONS FOR NURSING

Where, then, does the role for nurses begin in mental retardation? Deciding which nursing specialty has the most contact or responsibility to the client is like trying to find which came first, the chicken or the egg. All nurses have a part in this field. Perhaps a logical place to start is the school nurse and community health nursing, where aspects of preventive nursing can begin as health teaching, assessment, screening, and referral services.

Sometimes communication between the school and the physician is a problem, and often the physician relies on parents to provide information to the school regarding the child's health problems (Katcher, 1974). Likewise, school professionals sometimes call parents to discuss the child's problems and expect them to notify the physician. Included in the child's health care team are the therapist, the classroom teacher, the family, the nurse, administrators, the guidance counselor, the psychologist and psychiatrist, the physician, the dentist, and the social worker (Drapo, 1981). Each member brings a specialized body of knowledge to the team, and one does not function as well without the others. Katcher (1974) suggests that when the school has a problem, it would be very helpful to spell out exactly what the problem is. He states that school nurses too often just give short phrases, such as "check heart murmur" or "check eye chart." Perhaps the reason is that the teachers or school nurses are ill at ease in dealing with children with mental or physical disabilities or because they are reluctant to suggest medical problems to the physician. But school teachers and school nurses do indeed know what behaviors or health state the "normal" child is supposed to exhibit, and when the child deviates from that "norm," those deviations are described to the physician in a professional manner.

ASSESSMENT

The nursing role, in this case, is to listen to the teacher describe observations of the child's behavior or physical problem. She or he then schedules the child for a complete *nursing assessment*, which involves not only physical data but psychologic and sociologic data as well. This may mean a home visit is necessary (see appendices E, F, and G). When the data are gathered and problem lists are compiled, a plan is formulated that includes the parent's and the teacher's input. If the problem the teacher has described to the school nurse has not been resolved, then referral is made. With the data compiled in such a manner, documentation of the findings needs to be pointed out to the physician or other referral source. Most physicians welcome this type of information prior to their examination of the child, and it should in no way intimidate the nurse to give an account of nursing assessment and interventions. Even if the physician finds nothing abnormal with the child, the teacher and the school nurse know that they have been practicing good preventive health care in the best interest of the child and family.

Included in the *health history* which the nurse takes from the parents, is a complete description of the child's complaints or behaviors at home. This history is enhanced by a questionnaire relating to more common physical problems, such as allergies, appetite, bowel problems, urination, recent infections, and upper respiratory problems. The questionnaire might also include other less common problems, such as enuresis, skin lesions, bruising, or joint pains. Usual childhood illnesses are also covered.

Past medical history is discussed in relation to surgical procedures and medications. The child's habits are also important, involving speech, emotions, nervous tics, and educational and developmental histories. The age at which the child progressed to each developmental milestone, such as walking, talking, toilet training, feeding and dressing himself or herself, is extremely important. The mother's prenatal and perinatal information is also needed. Likewise, the *newborn health record* is summarized, if possible (Katcher, 1974).

Most retardation is diagnosed in the school-age child, and this is because mild retardation is the most common level of mental retardation—89 percent or 5,500,000 persons (Capute, 1979). These children usually are not detected until they are unable to compete with children their own age. There are recognizable symptoms that nurses can use in assessment.

The *personal/social developmental* symptoms of mental retardation include immature social behavior, whereby the child may prefer to play with children who are younger than himself or herself. Social judgment may be poor and the child may not say or do appropriate things for that age level. The child may try to get attention by "acting out," or the child may withdraw from other children. Since the child is experiencing difficulty on tests and competing in school work because he or she is not able to learn as quickly, he or she may become afraid to try. The natural curiosity that children have may be diminished in these children because of that fear to try. Children who do not try and are therefore not able to practice do not develop competencies which are needed to develop a good *self-concept*. They cry often and become frustrated easily. Frustration coupled with a poor self-concept leads to anxiety.

Other areas of assessment are to be found in *cognitive development*. Children with learning problems are unable to transfer learning from one situation to another. For instance, the children may learn that the sky is blue but be unable to recognize that birds are blue, an easter egg is blue, or that an automobile color is blue. In tasks that require problem solving, the child constantly requires help to think through to a solution. The child is unable to think in the abstract. Heaven, death, and God are abstract concepts. Size is abstract. A child who is retarded cannot tell what a big object is or a small object is without actually being able to compare them by seeing them. The child cannot learn in an unstructured setting. He or she is not able to make generalizations about what is going on around him or her and apply it to learning. Other things that affect cognitive abilities are short attention span, inability to remember well, and problems in understanding new ideas.

The child who is retarded may also be deficient in *language skills.* He or she may communicate so poorly that he or she cannot be understood, and he or she may not be able to remember a sequence of verbal commands or instructions.

Motor development may also be deficient as concerns body control. The child may be awkward and clumsy and therefore trip and fall a great deal. When performing activities requiring motor skills, his or her attention may be drawn to other things or he or she may not be able to follow directions related to motor activities. The child often does not try new activities but persists in doing the same thing over and over. Children who are retarded are not as active as other children and often sit in a corner by themselves. Sometimes they have self-stimulatory behaviors, such as rocking back and forth, head banging, or stereo-typed finger or hand movements.

Other problems the nurse carefully assesses are in the *sensory motor* area. Often children who are retarded also have visual and hearing problems. The nurse may notice that the child cannot tell the difference between two objects, such as a real orange and a wax one or a picture of an orange. The child may not be able to see the difference between two different coins or may not be able to track a moving object. He or she may not be able to tell the difference between sounds, such as a bell ringing or a horn blowing. Of more concern is that the child cannot tell where the sound is coming from. This can be dangerous for the child in relation to personal safety in the community.

Children who have severe mental disabilities are usually more easily recognized. Some symptoms of problems that are more severe are poor swallowing or sucking, hypotonia, poor feeding skills, an energy level that is diminished or extremely heightened, dull facies, convulsive disorders, and physical anomalies related to chromosomal disorders.

It is of vital importance for the nurse to assess the environment in which the child who is retarded must live and learn (see Appendix G). These areas of assessment in the home are:

- Equipment: such as beds, chairs, toilets, clothes closets, and sinks: are they the correct height for the child to reach? Is he or she protected from harm?
- Learning materials: does the child have toys that are appropriate? Are they stimulating? Does he or she have a place where it is possible to play freely? Is there a storage area to keep materials in and are there shelves for toys that are easily reached?
- Significant others: does the child have a supportive person in the environment who can help him or her to achieve? Is the child encouraged to make choices and to learn independence? Does he or she have limits set? Does he or she have someone who can teach skills for daily activities?
- Play equipment: does the child have a safe outdoor area with several sensory motor experiences available? Is the play equipment suitable for his or her age and ability?

PLANNING

Planning for the person who is retarded is as individualized as possible. A person who is retarded is first a person and second a member of a group or a patient in the hospital. Prevention of illness may be the nursing goal, just as restoration of function and health is the nursing goal in the hospital (see Appendix J). Wherever the nurse–client situation is, the care plan contains this information:

- Background information: information gathered from the nursing assessment, health history, family history, and medical records.
- Client needs: records are not always available to the nurse with this information, so much is dependent on the assessment. Included in the assessment are abilities in language and sensory areas, both expressive and receptive; behavioral and social development; and intellect, which includes the ability to understand health teaching. Both the client's strong points and areas of need are outlined.
- Client–nursing goals: this area may be planned with the parent, another health team colleague, the client, or the teacher. The goal might be for the client to learn to identify foods in the basic four food groups so that he or she can plan and shop for meals which are nutritious. Perhaps the goal will be to teach the client not to fear the IPPB machine which helps him or her to cough following surgery. In any case, planning around the motor skills, self-help skills, language and communication skills, cognitive skills, and social skills is important for the successful attainment of any goals.
- Stepping stones: the day to shop for meals is not the day to begin teaching about nutrition. The day of surgery is not the best day to begin teaching a client about postoperative care (providing the surgery is elective). Persons who are retarded learn slowly and with much reinforcement. A series of activities at the appropriate level of cognitive and motor functioning is begun as early as possible. One series of lessons is built upon another. The same lesson can be planned around different activities. Use of pictures and stories can be utilized, followed by puppets discussing the same information. Use of equipment that lets the client participate in the learning is another method. For instance, boxes of food and canned goods can be set up for the client to choose certain foods as he or she would in a store; or the IPPB machine can be brought in to look at and to discuss with the client or his or her parents. These activities are stepping stones in achieving the goal.
- Nursing referrals: very often, in working with clients who are retarded the nurse, based on the assessment, may plan for referrals to other professionals. For example, the agency nurse may refer a situation to a social worker or a counselor. The client may need medical services or therapy. The hospital nurse may refer him or her to the Public Health Department or the Department of Human Resources. When the services become a part of the plan, the nurse should be sure to write

dates, times, telephone numbers, names, and the rationale for the referral. Also included in this referral is information about where the client will meet with the therapist or specialist, who will accompany him or her and how feedback is received from that meeting.

- Evaluation: decide before beginning to teach how to evaluate the outcomes and leave the room to record this on the care plan.

Care plans used in the hospital with a parent's or guardian's consent can be copied and sent back to the school nurse or to the physician's office. Care plans may help in any future hospitalizations and serve as a teaching tool for other health care providers. They open a line of communication between nurses in various health agencies. Nursing care plans serve to document individual care given to meet the health needs of persons who are retarded. Other nursing activities related to hospital routine may be added. Care plans help other health care providers to see the nurse as a part of the client's education and health team. The school nurse ideally sends information about the child to the hospital nurse prior to admission. This trading of information helps to make sure that the child's health needs are met adequately.

IMPLEMENTING THE PLAN

Children who are retarded need *structured environments*. They can learn and behave better when they know exactly what is expected of them. *Organization* is important because it provides an order to their day and reinforces the previous day's learning. Clients who are retarded need to be separated from too much stimulation and interruption. They need a place in a school room, at home, or elsewhere that is their own.

When health teaching is done, the materials used to teach are simple and all of them are kept at the child's eye level. Assessment of the physical problems that often accompany mental retardation gives clues to the positioning that is needed to provide the correct visual level.

Children who have learning difficulties need freedom to examine the world they live in. Children with a history of failure often think they cannot succeed at activities other children engage in. But success comes from doing. Completing a given task or having a "hands on" experience is very important to gaining competence.

Children know when people are sincere and want them to succeed. They respond to touch, eye contact, and praise (Fig. 11-2). If is often very difficult for a nurse to watch a child struggle to complete a task, but finishing the task for him or her is not the answer. Remember the stepping stones. Simple instructions and having a task divided into small segments encourages learning. If, for instance, the goal is to teach the child to brush his or her teeth, the child should be taught to brush with water before learning to squeeze toothpaste onto the brush. Following that, the child learns to rinse the brush and his or her mouth with water.

Figure 11.2. Texas Woman's University nursing students teach client at ARC the importance of exercise. Clients also learn to assist each other. *(Photo by Texas Woman's University Media Center)*

Children learn from watching a demonstration of a skill if it is done slowly over and over again. It may be necessary to guide the child's hands through the skill first (Figs. 11-3, 11-4, and 11-5). Children respond to praise and to positive rewards. This may encourage them to try harder. Try several forms of rewarding, both physical (such as a pat on the head or a hug) and material (these rewards are chosen with care—candy rewards are not often a good idea).

All children learn through the use of the senses of touch, hearing, and sight. They need to be taught the task or concept in several ways and then need the opportunity to practice. If a child cannot see the storybook, he or she should be able to feel it. Providing learning materials to teach health care demands creativity on the part of the nurse.

The nurse's role in society is also to teach other people the effects that handicapping conditions have on the body and to make the public aware of the humanness of everyone. Nonhandicapped peers need to gain a sense of awareness of the problem of the handicapped. This is an ongoing task of the nurse and fits under the title of advocacy. The success of normalization begins with working with those with whom the child who is mentally handicapped has contact. It begins with children in the schoolroom and extends to a community where group homes will open. Lobbying for legislation, lecturing on ethical issues, and holding fund raisers for activity centers will all help in the normalization process. Awareness can be taught in the classroom by discussing frankly what disabilities mean and then by teaching all of the similarities the children share. Perhaps the child with retardation has a particular skill and this can be discussed; in addition a sharing time can be utilized to discuss everyone's hobbies and skills.

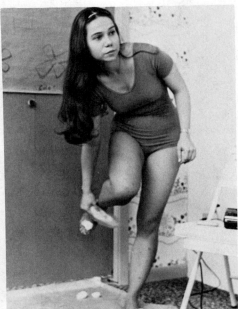

Figure 11-3. Texas Woman's University nursing student presenting a grooming class shower demonstration to ARC clients at their activity center in Denton, Texas. *(Photo by Texas Woman's University Media Center)*

Figure 11-4. Texas Woman's University nursing student teaching grooming class in hand care to ARC client. *(Photo by Texas Woman's University Media Center)*

Figure 11-5. ARC clients participating in grooming classes taught by two Texas Woman's University nursing students. *(Photo by Texas Woman's University Media Center)*

WORKING WITH PARENTS

Chinn et al. (1979) discussed phases that families of retarded children often move through before they are able to accept the child. *Denial* is one of the most difficult problems the nurse faces in dealing with the family. The birth of a child with a disability poses a definite problem to the family ego. Because of that denial, it is often impossible to begin effective teaching with the parents immediately. By refusing to admit the problem exists, the parents hope it will go away. By giving the parents information about normal child development and asking them to visit a classroom or center where other children who have the same problem are located, the nurse helps the parents make comparisons. The parents may become *angry* and accuse the nurse of singling out their child to find fault with. These feelings are a natural reaction and are not meant personally for the nurse. Letting the family know that health care providers respect their opinions and feelings reduces the anger they feel.

Another difficult adjustment the parents must make concerns *projection of blame*. It may be that one parent is blaming the other or blaming in-laws. The parents may think that their child's problem is the fault of the physician who delivered the child, or the school, or the teacher. Parents are *fearful* for their child's future, and the futures of unborn children, or for the grandchildren they will have. They feel *guilty* for having brought the child into the world and therefore they may feel that every suggestion that is made to them is made because they are inadequate parents.

It is particularly frustrating when the family goes from one physician to another and one agency to another looking for cures. They are particularly susceptible to quacks who promise a cure or a treatment by some unorthodox procedure. *Withdrawal* and *depression* are sometimes the outcome when the parent is finally able to admit that the diagnosis is correct. These feelings may become pathologic if the family cannot resolve them. The nurse supports the child and parents as much as possible while the parents attempt to deal with these feelings.

The desired outcome of *acceptance* of the child's diagnosis is not easy to attain. Understanding what behaviors constitute acceptance is a help to the nurse. Even parents of nonhandicapped children often have trouble accepting their children. Accepting a child simply means that the parent has a willingness to help a child learn something he or she is not able to do, helping him or her become independent by giving him or her tasks to do and choices to make. It means giving children encouragement to practice and the right to fail without being ashamed. Love and acceptance go hand in hand in convincing the child that when he or she fails it is possible to try again.

Other conditions may present temporary barriers to the nurse in working with children who are retarded. Sometimes the parents' culture is unfamiliar to the nurse (Brownlee, 1978). If they speak a language other than the nurse's native language, then an interpreter must be found. The nurse needs to find out who it is in the family who makes decisions. How does that culture view mental retardation? How does it view health care and health care facilities?

Some families have many problems to deal with that are not related to their handicapped child, such as poverty, illness, or legal difficulty. The nurse needs to become a health care advocate for the whole family. Open lines of communication aid in ensuring that the child receives the best care the nurse is capable of providing.

Nurses, no matter where they practice, need to keep a file of referral sources for families. Some of the agencies that may be of assistance to parents are as follows:

The Association of Retarded Citizens has a membership made up of parents and other family members, interested professionals, and community friends of the retarded. Every state and almost every city in the country has a chapter. If your city does not, write for information to the:

National Association for Retarded Citizens
P.O. Box 6109
2709 Avenue E East
Arlington, Texas 76011

The Local School District assists in finding services for the child. The child from 0 to 3 years of age must be served if he or she is deaf or blind. Most schools have preschool programs for children from 3 years of age and up who are handicapped. As a nurse, be involved in Child Find, as mandated by Public Law 94-142, which states that all handicapped children must be located who are not receiving a free appropriate education. They must be programmed for an education in the least restrictive environment possible.

Universities that have a health science program or special education department may have programs funded by grants to serve the young child. For instance, Texas Woman's University in Denton, Texas has a program, Child Success Through Parent Training, which is funded through the U.S. Department of Special Education Programs. This program assists the family who has a handicapped child from 0 to 3 years of age by providing parents with professional help and resources. Other universities may have similar grants or programs.

Many hospitals in large cities have *birth defect centers* which give help and assistance to families with children who are mentally retarded and/or physically disabled.

Genetic counseling is offered in most states through the state health departments or the departments of mental health—mental retardation. Some are affiliated with universities and colleges of medicine. These agencies involved with genetic counseling are usually in contact with a state or regional Genetic Diseases Control Network provided by the Department of Health. By contacting a local health department, you may get the name of many agencies that offer help with specific genetic problems.

Infant stimulation programs also exist throughout most states. Many are run through the auspices of state schools for the mentally retarded and some are run through hospital's birth defects centers. These programs have evolved during the last few years to serve the needs of children 0 to 3 years of age who are developmentally delayed and may be at risk for mental retardation. Early intervention can accelerate a child's development and prevent other problems from occurring.

The United Cerebral Palsy Association may provide services for the child, since it works with children with delays resulting from many causes. The United Cerebral Palsy of Western New York, located in Buffalo, New York, has a very complete program that covers infants, toddlers, young adults, parent education, home-school programs, a foster grandparent program, preschool classes for children 3 years of age and over, developmental progress classes, consultations, college and university affiliations, home services, a diagnostic treatment facility for health services, an adult day treatment program, residential facilities, social recreation, and public education. The residential facilities also provide for respite care. Similar programs are available in other locations.

PREPARING FOR THE FUTURE

Parents who have kept their children at home often worry about the day when they will be too old to care for them. Parents formerly had only two alternatives: institutionalization in large facilities located miles from their home or keeping the children at home. When they grew too old to care for their retarded child, parents knew that their other children would be faced with the problem of caring for a brother or sister in their homes. This posed a difficulty for most young adults who had families of their own. During the late 1950s, Bank and Mikkelson (1969) described normalization to the world, and Nirje (1969) began the thinking that clients who were mentally retarded did not have to live in institutions. He felt that community living was an alternative for them. Wolfensberger (1972) defined deviancy as being different from other people in a nonpositive way. He felt that any person in society deemed unlike his or her peers because of behavior or appearance was socially segregated. Isolation, labeling, and institutionalization were outcomes (Bank and Mikkelson, 1969; Nirje, 1969; Wolfensberger, 1972).

Nirje (1969) suggested that normalization allows the person to be treated as a human being, with a day like those of others, a routine, learning experiences, and choices. If one looks at the individual in an institution and compares the lifestyle of society in general to the lifestyle of that person, normalization falls far behind.

Many institutions of a few years ago were large, rambling buildings with neutral-color paint and brick in every room. The floors were marble or tiled. There were rows and rows of beds, with everyone's bedspread (if they had a bedspread) the same color. Clothing was bought in size lots and placed in a common closet. Attendants chose the size of clothes to give to people. Nothing was personalized. No one could keep possessions, since there was no privacy, and if one was not fortunate enough to have a family to visit on occasion, he or she had no significant person to love or receive love from. There were no curtains, no bathroom doors, and no place to spend time alone (within a positive context). The food on Monday tasted like the food on Friday and every day in between. Persons who were severely retarded sat in corners of rooms and stimulated themselves in any way they could simply because there was nothing else to do. The moderately retarded and the mildly retarded were mixed together, sometimes with the severely retarded. Soon everyone seemed the same. In 1966, Blatt and Kaplan photographed pictures of clients in the huge wards of institutions, males and females dressed like social outcasts roaming about in a restricted environment. They did not have good dental care or personal grooming. The pictures were shocking. Arguments have gone on for years about where the mentally retarded should live. Because of ignorance on the part of the general public about the plight of the retarded, these arguments still continue. Clients did have a roof over their heads, clean clothes, and food, which is more than some severely deprived children had. But the pictures told another side of the story, and quality of life became an issue.

Even though normalization concepts have been around since the 1950s and 1960s, there are still institutions with people in them who should not be there. There are many institutionalized persons who could be living in the community. Why is that?

No institution can open its doors and place the persons who are retarded into communities without adequate preparation. The clients need to be educated about life. Life is not simple in our society. One cannot hug a stranger walking down the street or in a supermarket even though this behavior may be ignored or overlooked at the institution. One cannot masturbate openly or drool down the front of one's clothes if living in the community is a goal. Restraint and the delay of gratification are hard lessons for persons who are retarded to learn. The community is not always a safe place to live and classes must be offered for the client to learn about such things as pedestrian safety. And then, community living demands learning about money management, sex education, nutrition, grooming and hygiene, and how to tell time. One must learn a skill and be able to hold a job. Normalization is hard work and takes commitment from the clients and from the community members who share neighborhoods with them and pay taxes to support their programs. Commitment from the client, his or her family, and the staff of institutions are necessary if community living is to become a reality for more of these clients. Commitment is often thwarted by the fact that there is never enough money and never enough staff members to do all that is necessary in order to achieve the goal. Though it is possible to become impatient with the bureaucracy, the reason normalization has been slow in coming about can be appreciated. Programs had to be set up in colleges and universities to prepare professionals in education and the health fields to work with mentally retarded. Advocates had to promote legislation and public awareness to support the trend.

Just when everything seemed to be going well, inflation, budget cuts, and politics have threatened the gains made over the last 30 years. Institutions of the past were the places they were because of lack of funding and because concepts about the personhood of the retarded had not been understood by professionals or the general public. Today institutions are changing. The developmental needs of the client are being met rather than just needs based solely on custodial care (Schulman, 1980). Dormitories are being furnished with more appropriate home-like furniture, area rugs cover the tiled floors, pictures and hanging baskets of plants detract from the plainness of walls (Fig. 11-6).

Volunteers are encouraged to be friends to clients and to serve in many different ways. They bring the community to the institution when the client cannot be in the community. The education and sharing is a two-way street. When an institution becomes a community project, there is little opportunity for the abuses of the past to occur. In return, the institution gains some valuable advocates for its programs.

Many people contribute to normalization even in an institution. The Foster

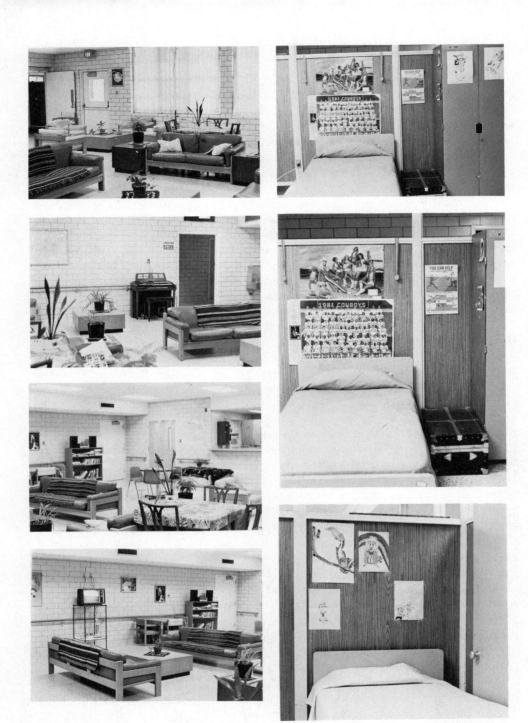

Figure 11-6. Young adults' men's dorm—day room, Denton State School, Denton, Texas. Note the home-like appearance that is provided for these clients which includes the individualization of personal space. *(Photo by Texas Woman's University Media Center)*

Grandparents Program was a big step in the right direction, and the involvement of organizations in the communtiy who take persons who are retarded to functions in the community or provide financial means for them to do so is another.

Institutions provide services to the community by providing use of their resources (Schulman, 1980). Outreach teams and other professionals of the institutions serve as consultants to parents and others in the community. State schools can be a source of education for the student in fields of education and health services. They are excellent places to educate student nurses who are learning concepts of neurologic nursing, mental retardation, and genetics (Drapo, 1981).

The current trend is to deinstitutionalize individuals by placing them in small group homes in the community. There are some who will remain in this situation as it provides the least restrictive environment for them, and there are others who, given appropriate training, will be able to advance to halfway houses and even to independent living (Figs. 11-7 and 11-8).

In group homes, the stress on health care is on prevention (Figs. 11-9 and 11-10). A thorough understanding of the client's physical and mental condition is necessary. If the group home offers a residential nonambulatory situation, it is important to have a registered nurse on the staff. If the home is ambulatory, the nurse may oversee the health care of several group homes.

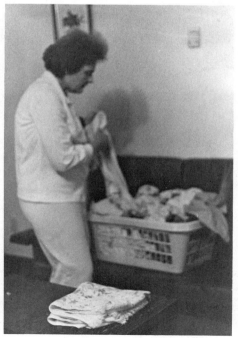

Figure 11-7. These clients are learning skills needed to be successful in independent living. (Photo by Texas Woman's University Media Center)

Figure 11-8. Independent living offers clients the opportunity for more privacy and responsibility. *(Photo by Texas Woman's University Media Center)*

Figure 11-9. Sandy Oaks Group Home kitchen (Big Sky Joint Venture, Abilene Home Office). *(Photo by Texas Woman's University Media Center)*

Figure 11-10. This Sandy Oaks Group Home client shows off his room, which he shares with two other men. *(Photo by Texas Woman's University Media Center)*

Nurses can provide: physical assessments; referrals to community medical care or other services; maintenance of health records; the enaction of or teaching of others to follow physician's medical orders; health education, sex education, and staff education about client's health issues; health consultation for the staff; work on public awareness; instructing parents about the client's health care; and teaching clients those procedures related to their specific disability that are necessary to become or remain independent.

The reason that many independent living facilities do not employ a nurse in more than a consulting position is because some administrators do not understand the extended role of the nurse in today's health care system. Nurses can, in fact, save employers a great deal more than they cost. The child health nurse who has a philosophy about the importance of preventive health care as a promotion for normalization is worth his or her weight in gold to a sponsoring agency for group homes. The nurse whose office is a health center rather than a school infirmary is a resource person sought after by parents, staff members, and administration (see Appendices H and I).

SUMMARY

Mental retardation is most frequently diagnosed in the school-age child, since mild retardation is the most frequent level of retardation. The school nurse is likely to be the one to initiate referrals to specialists of the health team based on his or her own assessment and in collaboration with the educational team. The diagnosis comes as a result of a complete study over a period of time, involving many health and educational assessments. Care of the child and the family thereafter becomes an ongoing function of the nurse.

Mental retardation has many causes. The nurse should be involved with the community in efforts to prevent its occurrence whenever possible. This effort should be shared by all nurses, but in particular by the community health nurse. Genetics nurses are also involved at this level. Their role is invaluable in both clinical care and education. Case finding is a special role of community health, genetic, and school nurses.

Child health nurses are involved with health promotion related to childhood accidents and disease. The nurse is involved in health teaching to prevent problems that are leading causes of mental retardation. Nurses who specialize in prenatal and perinatal care of the infant and families are very important team members as regards both prevention and early case finding.

Regardless of the cause of mental retardation, when it occurs within a family, it is often a major trauma. Constructive use of the nursing process in any of the roles of nurses becomes even more demanding in mainstreaming handicapped school children and the deinstitutionalization of persons who are retarded and/or physically disabled.

The nursing process often crosses other specialty areas in function, and nurses are cognizant of a broad spectrum of skills that are needed to provide clients with appropriate services. Nursing intervention in psychosocial problems is as necessary to the well-being of the whole personhood of the client and his or her family as is care of biologic problems. The client who is retarded is not unlike others in developmental and psychosocial needs; all require assistance in movement through these areas in the course of a normal life span. Each person moves at his or her own rate. Nurses can be facilitators of the process.

REFERENCES

Bank, M., & Mikkelson, N.E. A metropolitan area in Denmark: Copenhagen. In *Changing patterns in residential services for the mentally retarded.* Washington, D.C.: President's Committee on Mental Retardation, 1969.

Blatt, B., & Kaplan, F. *Christmas in purgatory.* Boston: Allyn and Bacon, 1966.

Brownlee, A.T. *Community, culture, and care.* Saint Louis: Mosby, 1978.

Bullough, V., & Bullough, B. *The emergence of modern nursing* (2nd ed.). New York: MacMillan, 1969.

Capute, A.J. Mental retardation. In R. Hoslam & P.J. Valletutti (Eds.), *Medical problems in the classroom.* Baltimore: University Park Press, 1979.

Chinn, P., Drew, C., & Logan, D. *Mental Retardation: A life cycle approach.* Saint Louis: Mosby, 1979.

Drapo, P.J. The nurse as a caregiver in the mainstreaming of children and adults with handicaps. In C. Hernandez-Logan (Ed.), *Caregiving: a multidisciplinary approach.* Palo Alto, Calif.: Rand E. Research Associates, 1981.

Grossman, H.L. (Ed.) *Manual on terminology and classification in mental retardation.* Washington, D.C.: American Association on Mental Deficiency, 1977, p. 11.

Katcher, A.L. The neurologically based pediatrician and deviant development. In R. Hyatt & N. Rolnick (Eds.), *Teaching the mentally handicapped child.* New York: Behavioral Publications, 1974.

Menolascino, F.J. *Challenges in mental retardation.* New York: Human Sciences Press, 1977.

Nirje, B. The normalization principle and its human management implication. In *Changing patterns in residential services for the mentally retarded.* Washington, D.C.: President's Committee on Mental Retardation, 1969.

Patterson, N.J. Nursing education in mental retardation: Status and needs. In J. Curry & K. Peppe (Eds.), *Mental retardation.* Saint Louis: Mosby, 1978.

Schulman, E. *Focus on the retarded adult.* St. Louis: Mosby, 1980.

Urban, H., Schassor, L., Rogers, C., & Kirkpatrick, N. *Meeting the nutritional needs of the multiply handicapped.* Buffalo: United Cerebral Palsy Association of Western New York, 1981.

Wolfensberger, W. *The principle of normalization in human services.* Toronto: National Institute on Mental Retardation, 1972.

BIBLIOGRAPHY

Alexander, M.M., & Brown, M.S. *Pediatric physical diagnosis for nurses.* New York: McGraw–Hill, 1974.

Baker, B.Y., Brightman, A.J., & Hinshaw, S.P. *Toward independent living.* Champaign, Illinois: Research Press, 1980.

Conference report. Placing the mentally retarded: Where shall they live? *Hospital and Community Psychiatry* 29:596, 1978.

Dowler, C. Prenatal care. In J. Curry & K. Peppe (Eds.), *Mental Retardation.* Saint Louis: Mosby, 1978.

Evans, J. *When you care for handicapped children: Texas Department of Human Resources guide for working with young handicapped children.* Austin: Special Projects Division, Southwest Educational Development Laboratory, 1979.

Ferhalt, J. *Clinical assessment of children.* Philadelphia: Lippincott, 1980.

Hyatt, R., & Rolnick, N. *Teaching the mentally handicapped.* New York: Behavioral Publications, 1974.

Milunsky, A. *The prevention of genetic disease and mental retardation.* Philadelphia: Saunders, 1975.

Petrillo, M., & Sanger, S. *Emotional care of hospitalized children* (2nd ed.). Philadelphia: Lippincott, 1980.

Philip, A. *Neonatology.* Flushing, N.Y.: Medical Examination, 1977.

Whaley, L. Genetic counseling. In J. Curry & K. Peppe (Eds.). *Mental retardation.* Saint Louis: Mosby, 1978.

12

Health Promotion of the Child with a Life-threatening Illness

Shirley Steele

The nurse caring for the child with a life-threatening illness needs to be ready to cope with many situations. She or he may be the person settling the ward after the death of a child. She or he may be called upon to give support to the grieving family. She or he may find herself or himself giving support to other staff members or students who are feeling stressed by the illness.

To be able to meet these challenges effectively, the nurse should know the normal grieving process, be aware of the many ways that adults view death, know at what ages children understand death, and have constructive means to cope with this knowledge.

The adult (and also the child) undergoes a predictable sequence of events when going through the grieving process. According to Engel (1962), the first stage is shock and disbelief, followed by a stage of awareness, then a restitution state, and finally resolution of the loss. However, the parents of a child who dies may never resolve the loss. It is now evident that many parents actually grieve for the child throughout their lives.

Reactions to Life-threatening Illness and Death

The child with a life-threatening illness frequently evokes an immediate feeling of sympathy from the adults in the environment. After the initial reaction, the adult gradually rearranges feelings in accordance with other significant factors learned about the child. Feelings of sympathy may change to impatience if the child's behavior is disruptive, or sympathy may change to overprotection if the child is afraid and insecure, and so forth.

It is important to consider the conditions under which the adult is functioning in order to appreciate his or her reaction. The parent who has recently undergone other stressful situations may feel that he or she is being treated unfairly. He or she may become quite upset and shout obscenities at the physician giving the information. He or she may also be very hostile toward the nurse, who seems to support the physician's opinion. The parent who has recently gone through a grieving process may have that experience immediately revived and begin crying hysterically.

Age is a major factor in influencing reactions to a life-threatening illness. When the child is a newborn, people frequently remark it is not so bad because the parents did not have a chance to know the child. This is certainly far from the case, because the parents have been planning for the child since they knew of the child's conception. The mother is especially vulnerable, as she has been uniquely involved with the developing infant since conception. An infant born with a life-threatening illness puts the mother under a great deal of stress.

A life-threatening illness interferes with the rapid development of an infant. The illness can interfere with the excitement that accompanies early develop-ment. Just as the infant is gaining socialization skills, the illness can cause regression, resulting in disappointment of significant others. A serious illness in a previously healthy child is considered a great loss. During the time when childhood is often fairly carefree, the child is stressed by having to cope with illness that does not often affect an individual of his or her age. The child's independence diminishes, and adults must assume increasing responsibility for the child due to the catastrophic illness.

The adolescent who has entered college seems to have everything to live for. The shortening of his or her life is considered a tragedy. On the other hand, death of the adolescent who has "copped out" or is addicted to drugs is frequently written off as "no loss" when death occurs.

The nature of the disease entity or other precursor of death is a factor that influences reactions. Adults often find it more acceptable for a child with a disability to die than they do for an able-bodied child to die. There are also diseases which have particularly tragic connotations. One of these diseases is cancer. Many people still view it as a brutal disease and sometimes contagious or a cause for disgrace. People also think of cancer as a disease of "old age" and find it particularly difficult to accept in children.

Environmental conditions play a part in the way persons respond to life-threatening illnesses. Why is it that when a child of a prominent family is fatally ill, there is often more concern than when a child from a deprived family is fatally ill? There seems to be some misconception that children from "better" homes have more reason to be spared serious or fatal illness. This may be partially based on the fact that these parents usually provide consistent medical supervision to their children, and therefore the children should not be suscepti-ble to life-threatening illness. It may also be partially based on the fact that the nurse is more closely associated with other professional people, and he or she therefore wants to believe that such a fate cannot happen to professional people because that would include him or her in the potential parent category for having current or future children with premature susceptibility to death. On a busy, understaffed unit, a child with a fatal illness may be resented because he or she demands so much additional and emotion-laden care that it is difficult to respond positively to the child and family. A terminally ill child may dampen the cheerful attiude of a small pediatric unit that prides itself on keeping the children happy and minimizing the effects of hospitalization. In a well-equipped intensive care unit, the child with a terminal illness may be taken as so much a part of the expected routine that the nurses become too impersonal and neglect emotional needs, which are heightened due to fears of death as well as the effects of separation from his or her usual environment.

A person from a culture that permits its people to "act out" their grief is frequenïly less likely to be tolerated by health care providers than people from cultures which are "stoic" and "quiet" about their grief. Therefore, children from families of these less tolerated cultures may be treated differently in the health care facility.

Particular seasons may influence people's reactions to life-threatening illnesses. People seem to react more intensively when a child is very sick around a special holiday, such as Christmas. If death occurs, the neighbors and friends are especially sympathetic: "What a shame to spoil their Christmas. Every Christmas they will remember this." Holidays also increase stress within families, so a life-threatening illness is tolerated less adequately.

People frequently tend to feel that the family that has only one child suffers a greater loss than families with more children, or that the loss of a male child is more difficult than the loss of a female child, or that loss of a child with a superior intelligence is a greater tragedy than loss of a child of lesser intellectual ability. Some feel that it is easier for a woman of childbearing years to have a child die than for a woman who has completed her childbearing cycle, perhaps believing a future child can take the place of the child who is dying or dies.

Availability of loved ones to be with the dying child is another factor that influences the reactions to life-threatening illness. If a significant other is separated by a great geographic space and cannot be with the child, everyone feels quite sympathetic. If this person is on the way home, everyone seems to "hold their breath," hoping that arrival will take place before the child's condition worsens or before death actually takes place.

This list of reactions could be continued *ad infinitum*, as the eminent loss of a child is usually viewed as a tragedy in American society. The list given is incomplete, but it reflects the wide diversity of reaction responses that can occur and helps to put the upcoming discussion into perspective.

The student of nursing who cares for the child frequently has responses to life-threatening illness in children similar to those of the parents of the child. As the female student is frequently of child-bearing age, she can feel a real closeness to the situation. At first learning the diagnosis, the student may experience the same type of disbelief and denial that the parents have. The student is in a period when having children can be foremost in his or her mind. The student's own close association makes it difficult to handle the situation from a professional vantage point rather than from the viewpoint of an involved parent. If the students have children of their own, they frequently see the client as if he or she were their own child. Students may shy away from caring for the child because they are not able to cure the child. Students frequently wish or request not to be assigned a child with a life-threatening illness. They fear they will be incapable of handling the situation and unable to talk to the parents without showing overt affective responses, such as tears, facial expressions of hopelessness, anxiety, and so forth. Students seem to be especially fearful that the child will die while they are caring for him or her and that they will not be able to function effectively during this stressful period.

The student frequently uses his or her own faith as a means of coping with the situation. He or she is influenced by recent experiences with other clients with life-threatening illness or clients who have died. In addition, the student may have recently witnessed death in his or her personal life, which can influence responses to the child. Recent bereavement can make it too painful to face another life-threatening situation.

A common mistake in caring for the child with a life-threatening illness is to expect the child to act as if he or she is terminally ill. Children usually do not want to be sick, and they attempt to camouflage their illness. The adults in their lives need to keep this in mind. Children feel more relaxed when they are treated with normalcy. When coping with a serious illness, the child with a medical condition, such as leukemia, is greatly concerned by the new situation. It is difficult enough for the child to cope with the introduction of a large number of medications, painful diagnostic procedures, or radiation therapy without additional changes in the environment and the way the adults in his or her life respond to him or her.

The parents of the child with a life-threatening illness usually play a big role in the hospitalization. Their role needs to be supported by making the hospital environment comfortable and humane. They must be helped to feel a part of the health care team so that they feel a sense of belonging and control. The other relatives and siblings should not be excluded from the management of the child's care. The child benefits during extended hospitalizations from visits from relatives, siblings, friends, and pets. Too often, when a child dies the other children only remember the "well" sibling who went to the hospital, as they saw very little of the child as he or she progressed through the illness. The hospitalized child also feels very isolated by the hospitalization periods. He or she is not used to the individual attention of the parents and has learned to share them with other siblings. If the hospital does not permit children to visit, then each time the child is discharged from the hospital the parents and children must make a readjustment to the usual family routine, and this is often quite difficult. The other relatives are also included as much as possible in the child's management decisions. They often put pressure on the parents to change decisions which have been realistically made in the hospital. Many a well-meaning grandparent has forced the family to seek another medical decision in a far-off place that has publicized a "cure" or new method of care. This medical shopping can be expensive and disruptive to the child and the family as a whole. The shopping can, however, have the positive effect of relieving some of the family's guilt feelings as they gain satisfaction from "knowing they have done all they can."

The diagnosis of a life-threatening illness is certain to have a disrupting effect on the family. The goal of intervention is clearly to help preserve the stability of the family unit.

Of particular significance to nursing personnel is the searching for any and all information on the disease that parents undertake. They seem to have to know all the current facts about the disease and its prognosis. This information needs to be discussed and validated so that the parents have the best information that is available to guide their decisions and actions. Parents should be given avenues for using their energies effectively, and while the child is hospitalized, this may be accomplished by establishing a care plan that allows the parents to be with their child and to be involved in the child's management to the desired degree.

It is important during the early stages of the illness to help the parents to learn to cope with the diagnosis. At this stage, the child is usually not incapacitated, and the parent is certainly able to provide a great deal of his or her care. Parents must not be abruptly separated from the child. Helping them to feel they are an integral part of the care is an excellent way to help them to cope with the situation. As the illness progresses, they will be helped to assist with the care whenever they feel capable of contributing. They are introduced gradually to the progressive deterioration in the child's condition and see first-hand the added responsibilities this deterioration produces. The parents become increasingly willing to let the nurse take over as the child becomes increasingly difficult to manage.

Mothers do not give up hope until their child is actually moribund. This is especially important to keep in mind when giving care to the child. Because the parents have a great deal of hope until very late in the child's illness, they will not understand a nurse's early pessimism. They do not want to realize that nurses who have experience with life-threatening illness have more evidence to support an attitude of pessimism when certain illnesses are present. The parents' attitude is based solely on their involvement with and their hope for their child, and they want health care providers to respond in the same way, preserving hope.

It is important for the nurse to understand that what we consider to be an appropriately realistic attitude for the parents is not one that necessarily involves acceptance of the fatal prognosis. A realistic attitude may only be an acknowledgement that the child is seriously ill. As the illness progresses, the parents become painfully aware of the irreversibility of the situation and their hope for recovery diminishes. It is not necessary to insist that the parents relinquish all hope for research that will find a cure for the disease before their child's death. The parents cannot help but have some appreciation of their child's serious illness as the medical intervention is instigated and implemented.

Reactions to children with life-threatening illness are varied and intense. As such, observations will help to determine appropriate intervention.

LEUKEMIA

Acute leukemia of childhood is a primary malignant illness that involves the bone marrow. It is characterized by abnormal proliferation and lack of cell differentiation. The illness is associated with a suppression of normal hematopoiesis that leads to infection, pallor, and bleeding. Infiltration of the leukemia cells into the normal extramedullary tissue can lead to hepatosplenomegaly and lymphadenopathy (Nesbit and Kersey, 1976).

A diagnosis of leukemia is established by morphologic examination of the peripheral blood and bone marrow. The specific diagnosis is based on the type of cell that is involved. The four main types of childhood leukemia are lymphocytic, myelobastic, monocytic, and undifferentiated. Although leukemia can be acute (or subacute) or chronic, most leukemia of childhood is of the acute variety, involving immature cell formation. Acute lymphocytic leukemia (ALL) is the most common type of leukemia of childhood.

Morphologic classification of leukemia is difficult to establish. Therefore, leukemias are also classified by functional characteristics. Two subpopulations of normal human lymphocytes are characterized by different cell surface markers: thymus-derived lymphocytic (T-cells) and thymus-independent lymphocytic (B-cells). This classification contributes to the treatment protocols established for treating leukemia.

Some form of cancer affects 7500 chilldren younger than 15 years of age in the United States each year. Cancer is a leading cause of death in the school-age population; it is second only to accidents (Young and Nuller, 1975).

The advances in the treatment of childhood cancer have turned many cancers from rapidly fatal diseases to long-term illnesses of childhood. Childhood cancer is considered a long-term illness with an uncertain outcome. Some childhood cancers have excellent prognoses, and at some treatment centers 50 percent of first-time cancers lead to 5-year survival rates. However, the predictability of cancer prognosis is erratic, and the threat of death is a continual partner in the ongoing management of these children.

Generally, the younger the child is at the onset of the cancer, the greater is the risk of a poorer prognosis. However, there are even exceptions to this hypothesis.

The long-term nature of many of the childhood cancers has many physiologic, psychologic, social, and cultural implications. While the management of each child and family is unique, the goal of the management of all the children is to foster growth and development of the child in all spheres. During the course of the therapy, the family members undergo extreme periods of stress that they feel they cannot control. Therefore, the family's response to the child can interfere with the promotion of adequate development if ways are not provided to overcome and mediate the stress.

Diagnosis

One of the most stressful periods in the management of childhood cancer is when the diagnosis is made. This diagnosis profoundly influences the lives of every member of the family and eventually influences the lives of persons outside the family as well.

At the time of the diagnosis, the parents can feel completely out of control. The reactions to the diagnosis are almost universally strong, with feelings of anger, disbelief, guilt, and grief emerging as typical responses to the frustration of not being able to help their child.

The initial response to the diagnosis is often followed by several days of feelings that vary from hostility to depression. The parents often blame themselves for the child's illness and search for a cause, often hoping to find a reason that can be reversed. The early feelings of parents rarely are forgotten, and many feel that the parents will carry these feelings in their unconscious throughout life.

The diagnosis of childhood cancer is often feared as a "death sentence." Despite statistics to the contrary, parents feel the threat of death as a major part of their lives. The threat of death leads to feelings of helplessness, confusion, panic, and disorganization that can be difficult to overcome.

As the reactions of parents are commonplace, they are viewed as being natural sequelae to having to live with a diagnosis of childhood cancer. These reactions, then, serve as coping mechanisms that are unique for these families.

While the prognosis is usually uncertain, the courses of therapy are more certain. Parents are often provided an opportunity to discuss the advantages and disadvantages of the various protocols for therapy, but their emotional status may poorly equip them to participate in the decision-making process. They will be expected, however, to decide where the treatment will be given, as treatment is usually started immediately. The family usually has the option to receive care by their usual primary physician or to be transferred to a cancer specialty center. Even the decision of where to receive care can be difficult to make in the limited time available to them.

The shock that accompanies the diagnosis leads to selective hearing and poor retention of information. Therefore, the parents are given the information they require as often as necessary to help them to gain an awareness of the illness, treatment, and day-to-day management of the child. It is not unusual for parents to deny that they were given information at an earlier time. Consistent, honest, and timely discussions will help to alleviate the parents' concern that they are not being given the information they desire. Opportunities are provided for them to read information, ask questions, and discuss any area that is of concern so that open channels of communication are established.

The parents need to feel that they are helping the child to cope with the long-term illness. When they feel secure that no one is treating them unfairly, they are more capable of helping the child.

Laboratory Verification of Leukemia

Early symptoms of leukemia, such as pallor, fatigue, elevated body temperature, and easy bruising, are indicators for a complete blood count (CBC). The hemoglobin is checked to determine the degree of anemia that is present, and the white cell count (WBC) and differential provide data for assessing whether an infective or a malignant process is involved. A positive diagnosis is associated with an extremely high WBC and a malignancy in one of the white cell types. Another laboratory finding consistent with leukemia is the number of lymphablasts (blasts) and immature lymphocytes that are present, as these are not normally present. Platelets are usually decreased, as well (Karni, 1976).

The bone marrow test is the test that is performed to confirm the presence or absence of leukemia, as most blood cell formation (except for lymphocytes) takes place in the bone marrow. The bone marrow can provide information about the number, types, and degree of maturity of the cells that are produced. Figure 12-1 is a schematic diagram showing a theory of the way blood cell production is carried out in the child's body. The lymphocytes are produced by the spleen or lymph nodes. In leukemia, however, the lymphoblasts are thought to infiltrate the bone marrow and to establish centers for the production of lymphocytic cells. Therefore, the bone marrow test is able to provide information useful in diagnosing and monitoring the leukemia processes.

Lumbar punctures are done to analyze the cerebrospinal fluid (CSF) for leukemia cells. Leukemia cells are able to infiltrate the CSF and cause symptoms of headache, dizziness, and nausea. The laboratory analysis of the CSF includes gross appearance, presence of red and/or white blood cells, total proteins, glucose, and presence or absence of infectious agents, such as bacteria, a virus, or a fungus. Ordinarily, the CSF is colorless and cell-free; infiltration of the CSF by leukemia cells results in a turbid or cloudy appearance, inclusion of cells, an elevated total protein, and changes in the glucose level. Microbial agents may or may not be present.

A multimodal treatment approach is often instituted with many children being treated in cancer specialty units of large medical centers. Although this is not the only way that treatment can be offered, it is one that is often selected, as these centers have access to the most advanced drugs and research findings to guide management.

Drug Therapy

Seven major classes of drugs used in childhood cancer are hormonal agents (steroids), enzymes, alkaloids, purine antagonists, alkylating agents, folic acid antagonists, and antibiotics. As these drugs are intended to interfere with the proliferation of cells in the child's bone marrow, they tend to decrease the child's immune responses. The depression of the bone marrow results in a leukopenic response. In addition, these drugs can also destroy lymphoid and phagocytic cells, and so further decrease the immunologic activity of the body. Finally, the chemotherapeutic agents tend to alter the child's ability to produce antibodies. These anticipated side-effects of therapy leave the child particularly vulnerable to infections.

The child health nurse often needs special skills to administer these medications. Depending on the age of the child, even oral medications can be refused. Creativity (as in making a game of the task) is often wise. Bringing the familiar, such as a favorite television character, into the picture helps to make the unknown medication more acceptable. The added threat of injections increases the demands on the nurse. The best approach is to restrain the child as needed for protection, be truthful that the injection will hurt, and then give the injection quickly and skillfully. Always allow ample time following the administration to comfort the child. Most often, the medications are given intravenously. The in-dwelling needle is observed closely, as is the surrounding tissue for signs of infiltration. Many of the drugs can cause painful areas if infiltration takes place. The physician is notified of suspected difficulties with the intravenous so that

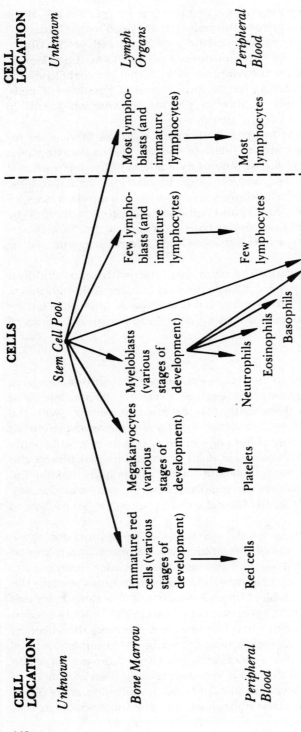

CELL LOCATION

Unknown

Bone Marrow

Peripheral Blood

CELLS

Stem Cell Pool

Immature red cells (various stages of development)

Megakaryocytes (various stages of development)

Myeloblasts (various stages of development)

Few lymphoblasts (and immature lymphocytes)

Most lymphoblasts (and immature lymphocytes)

Red cells

Platelets

Neutrophils
Eosinophils
Basophils
Monocytes

Few lymphocytes

Most lymphocytes

CELL LOCATION

Unknown

Lymph Organs

Peripheral Blood

Figure 12-1. Schematic diagram illustrating one theory of the normal production of blood cells (red cells, white cells, and platelets). In normal production, cells originate from a "stem cell pool" of unknown location. These stem cells seed the bone marrow and lymph organs. Red cells, platelets, and most white cells (neutrophils, eosinophils, basophils, monocytes, and a few lymphocytes) originate in the bone marrow. When these cells mature, they migrate into the peripheral blood. Most lymphocytes are formed in the lymph organs (spleen and lymph nodes) and then migrate into the peripheral blood. Researchers believe that monocytes may originate from both the stem cell pool and myelocytic precursers. *(From Karni, K.R. In I.M. Martinson (Ed.), Home care for the dying child. New York: Appleton–Century–Crofts, 1976)*

appropriate action can be taken. Oftentimes, it is necessary to restart the intravenous in another site and to treat the tender areas with soaks. Intrathecal medication is also used. Reactions to the medications are charted, and these responses are communicated to the physician. Side-effects are common. Prolonged nausea and vomiting may necessitate cessation of a particular drug based on the physician's and nurses' assessment of the child.

During the long-term management, the child will receive a variety of different drugs. The protocols are based on a variety of factors, such as age, response to previous drugs, length of remission, existence of infection, and results of laboratory tests. Each time a new protocol is introduced, the parents are given an explanation of the therapy and its anticipated results. The parents can become discouraged or encouraged by the response of the child to therapy. They will need assistance to support their child through another round of toxic therapy. At times, the treatment seems worse than the disease, and it is easy for the parents to lose interest and faith in the therapy.

Most cancer drugs have limitations. They are known to be toxic, damaging normal cells and tissues as well as leukemia cells and tissues. In addition, most of the drugs cannot continue to be effective for extended periods of time. The child's body becomes ineffective and lacks the resistance that is necessary for the drugs to continue to be effective. This option leads to relapse and a change in drug therapy. The physician must prescribe drugs that will be effective while not being so toxic that they will not be tolerated by the child.

The initial treatment of the leukemia is called the induction phase. In this phase, the goal is to induce a complete disappearance of signs, symptoms, and pathologic evidence of the disease. When this is achieved, the child is in complete remission. Complete remission is evidence by a hemoglobin level of approximately 11 gm/100 ml, a neutrophil reading of less than 1500, absence of blast cells, and a platelet count of $100,000/mm^3$. In addition, the physical signs of leukemia have cleared, such as pallor, bruises, and tiredness. The bone marrow shows lymphocytic blasts, 0 to 5 percent; lymphocytes and blast cells, 0 to 40 percent; or monolymphocytic blasts, 0 to 5 percent (Nesbitt and Kersey, 1976). Generally, a combination of drugs is administered to achieve remission during the induction phase. An example is a combination of prednisone, vincristine and L-asparaginase.

In the maintenance phase, attempts are made to keep the child in remission as long as possible and with the least degree of toxicity. Drugs which are commonly used are methotrexate, L-mercaptopurine, and cyclophosphamide; however, protocols can vary from one institution to another and change in response to newer drugs and evidence of success. The length of time that long survivors are maintained on drugs is also an evolving decision.

Drugs are also used in conjunction with symptoms such as infections and bleeding. The drug management is therefore an important part of the long-term management of children with leukemia.

Irradiation

Irradiation for treating childhood cancer is usually done in conjunction with chemotherapy. Irradiation needs to be assessed thoroughly, as it is known to cause secondary malignancy and interference with the child's future growth. The adverse side-effects of irradiation have led to lower doses being administered to children. For example, radiotherapy to the head is thought to cause difficulties in learning and alopecia; the loss of hair can be reversed, but the learning deficits are probably not reversible, causing long-term problems for the child. Side-effects of radiotherapy include nausea and vomiting, which is often excessive and requires drug therapy to control. Antiemetics, such as compazine and Tigan, are often given as suppositories or by injection to relieve these symptoms. Anorexia is also a side-effect. As cranial radiation causes alopecia, it is important to prepare the child and family for this outcome and to make preparations for how the child will manage the loss, such as having a wig made from his or her own hair, purchasing a wig, wearing head gear of many types, or having a head bald.

While radiotherapy has many side-effects, it is successfully used to help control the leukemia at various points in the long-term management of the child.

Assessing the Family's Coping Skills

The nurse or social worker usually assesses the family's coping skills soon after the diagnosis is made. Factors that influence the family's ability to cope include:

1. Numbers and ages of persons in the family.
2. Structure of the family (i.e., single or double parents, etc.).
3. Lifestyle of family.
4. Experience with illness, especially catastrophic or chronic illness.
5. Financial situation, including health and hospitalization insurance.
6. Employment status (i.e., both parents employed, client employed?).
7. Support system (i.e., extended family or friends).
8. Primary health care pattern (e.g., family physician?).
9. Strategies used by the family to cope during other stressful situations (i.e., church influence, assistance of friends, maladaptive examples).
10. Tolerance for separation of family members (i.e., potential influence of hospitalization on the family).
11. Transportation possibilities (i.e., ability to get to the hospital or other health care facility with ease).
12. Other stressful life events that may be taking place in the family concurrently (i.e., pregnancy, loss of a job, etc.).

FAMILY MANAGEMENT

During the long-term management of the cancer, attempts are made to facilitate communication among family members. It is often difficult to achieve this goal, especially when faulty communication patterns existed prior to the illness. In addition, communication is complicated during the highly stressful periods that are common with childhood cancer.

Each family member is encouraged to share his or her feelings about the illness with other members of the family. The feelings that emerge are not always ones that are empathetic to the ill child and his or her illness and treatment. Long-term illness that is life-threatening arouses a whole array of emotional responses, some of which seem more appropriate than others. No matter how appropriate the feelings may seem, they need to be expressed and shared so that other members of the family know how to deal with them.

The siblings of the child with cancer are particularly vulnerable to emotional sequelae as they can feel that their own needs are being poorly met by the parents, who are emotionally involved with the ill child. The siblings often feel abandoned by the parents and left out of the decisions that affect the family. Improved communication among family members can help the siblings feel more secure during this stressful long-term illness. In addition, it is imperative that the parents find time to share themselves with the well children even during periods of highest stress. This consideration for the feelings of the siblings helps the siblings to feel some satisfaction during difficult times.

Stressful Periods

Besides the time of diagnosis, other periods of high stress are major treatment periods, such as changes in drug therapy; surgery; periods requiring hospitalization; periods of relapse or side-effects; termination of treatment; serious infections or uncertainty of prognosis; impending death; and the death and bereavement period. During all of these periods, the parents will need more concern for their personal needs and more opportunities to interact with health care providers. If the crisis is too severe, the parents may need the help of a counselor, such as a psychologist, psychiatric clinical nurse specialist, or psychiatrist to provide additional support and counseling.

Finances

A major area of concern to parents is their ability to cope with the financial strain caused by the illness. Despite health insurance, the family often has ongoing expenses that contribute to their feelings of stress caused by financial matters. In a study by Cairns et al. (1981), the nonmedical costs of the illness were examined. The parents were asked to keep a weekly log of nonmedical expenses related to their child's illness. The median weekly total was $39.90. The largest categories of expenses were related to transportation, food, and miscellaneous items that included telephone calls to relatives to inform them of the child's condition and gifts for the client or siblings left at home. The families also estimated the loss of salary caused by the illness. Approximately half of the study population said there were losses in this category, and the median loss was estimated at $68.94 per week. Combining this with the out-of-pocket expenses, the financial drain on the family was $88.20 per week. This cost was compared to the family's salaries, and it was estimated to be 26.2 percent. It is easy to see why these families complain about financial problems even when they have adequate hospitalization coverage.

The Child's Response to Illness

The child with leukemia is faced with a life that is filled with surprises, painful procedures, toxic treatments, and ongoing medical management. The child becomes the key figure in a life drama that is often stressful, confusing, changeable, and unpredictable. The child is clearly part of a crisis situation with an outcome that can be skewed.

There is no predictable pattern to the way the child responds in this drama of life, but there are some scenes that are common under these conditions.

1. The child's response will be influenced by the responses of the parents, other significant adults, peers, and siblings.
2. The child's response will be influenced by the degree of "loss of control" the child senses during the long-term management.
3. The child often is scared and has a feeling of helplessness.
4. The child's limited past experience interferes with his or her ability to perceive the illness and its treatment realistically.
5. The young child can use active fantasy that can make the situation much worse than it actually is.
6. The child can grieve for the "normal" self that is lost with illness.
7. There is a change in the child's body image due to the illness and the side-effects of treatment.
8. Active participation in the illllness treatment can lead to regaining a sense of mastery that is often stifled by illness.
9. The child often experiences intense emotional conflicts and is appropriately fearful during stressful periods.
10. The child can feel stripped of dignity, especially during periods of hospitalization.
11. It is possible for the child to believe that the hospital is not a friendly place to be.
12. The child can regress in developmental level due to the illness and its management and a feeling of being out of control.
13. It is natural to develop feelings of being an outcast or of being different and out of place.
14. The child can feel sorry for himself or herself and ashamed of his or her body's appearance.
15. Preoccupation with the illness.
16. Symbolic attachment to family members can result.
17. If support is not appropriate, the child can be resentful, act up, and refuse treatment.
18. Sleep and behavior disorders can result.

CHILD MANAGEMENT

Successful management of the child with leukemia is based on an appreciation of the illness and the child's unique response to it. The goal of management is to help the child to function at a developmental level that is consistent with his or her age. In order for this to occur, the child's environment is monitored closely.

The child's coping mechanisms will influence his or her ability to function effectively in the area of cognitive, psychologic, and emotional domains despite interference with the physiologic domain.

Maintaining Self-esteem

The child is actively involved in the treatment of the illness by giving accurate and sensitive explanations that are age-appropriate. Whenever appropriate, demonstrations precede procedures to orient the child to the reality of the situation. When painful procedures are planned, the child is prepared for the pain and given ways to manage the pain. The child is allowed to play with instruments that cause pain and to act out procedures in play situations. Through play and involvement, the child feels that he or she has some autonomous function and can use self-control.

It is important to help the child to maintain or improve his or her sense of self. Body awareness activities are planned so that the child is able to feel satisfied with his or her revised body and body image. Opportunities are provided for the child to discuss concerns and to ventilate discontent with his or her changed body so that he or she can deal effectively with the prolonged illness.

Make-believe and fantasy are used by the child to cope with the illness. Opportunities to use fantasy to effectively deal with the periodic stressful episodes in the illness are helpful for some children. The ability to use fantasy as a coping mechanism is individualized, and some children are unable to benefit from this strategy. When fantasy is possible, it is useful to have the fantasy include opportunities for mastery, growth, or to make a change in the meaning of the situation the child faces. For example, the child can master swimming the English Channel, or the child can gain 10 years of age, or a repugnant smell can be transformed to the smell of a favorite food during fantasy.

School

The child of school age can benefit from being returned to school. School can help the child to realize that it is possible to live normally with a life-threatening illness. However, a return to school is not without problems. The child is dramatically different in appearance after treatment for cancer is instituted. In addition, the child can lack the energy required to engage in all the school activities that are expected of his or her age-consistent peers. Despite problems in readjustment to school, the child can be helped to develop and mature more realistically during the school experience.

School phobia is thought to be a response to long-term cancer therapy (Lansky et al., 1975). However, Deasey-Spinetta's research (1981) did not verify this. She found that the children willingly attend school even though absences are common due to illness and clinic and hospital visits. The study showed that these children have concentration problems, difficulty completing school assignments, a higher rate of learning disabilities, and low energy levels. The children also have socialization differences from their peers: they are less likely to reach out to others, to initiate activities, to try new things, and to freely express positive or negative feelings.

In order to successfully reintegrate the child into the school setting, the child, parents, teachers, principals, and school children need to be aware of the child's potential and limitations. While the school personnel are given accurate and adequate information to understand the child' illness prior to his or her return, the child can also help them to understand his or her condition after returning. It is not possible to spare the child the possibility of uncomfortable experiences, but it is possible to prepare the child to cope with this potential by playing out situations that might happen.

Deasey-Spinetta (1981) stresses that the school's function in the child's management is to facilitate learning. The teacher and school cannot be expected to act as an extension of the medical facility. Therefore, the medical management of the child's illness is not the responsibility of the school personnel. However, school personnel need medical knowledge so that they can adjust the learning plan to successfully accommodate the change in the child's learning status. For example, the inclusion of certain drugs in the child's protocol can result in hair loss. The loss of hair has implications for the child's ability to socialize in school. The teacher needs to know why the child is wearing a particular head gear and needs to prepare the other children to expect the child's changed appearance. Developments of this nature are transmitted to school personnel at appropriate intervals in the child's therapy. Long-term effects of drug and radiation therapy influence the child's intellectual ability. Particular areas of concern in regard to learning are being identified, such as a predisposition to difficulty in achieving mathematic concepts, memory loss, and loss of emotional control.

The child is managed most appropriately in school by skirting the problem areas and helping the child to grow through the use of areas that are intact. The child can benefit from resource rooms that provide remediation in weak areas, increased attention to socialization skills, and consistent teaching. When the child is unable to attend school, tutoring is essential to try to keep the child from falling too far behind in school work.

Other problems that may need to be addressed are fears that the condition is contagious, inability of the child to cope with harassment from peers, embarrassment caused by becoming ill in school and losing control of some bodily functions, and so forth. The school personnel need to be sensitive to the child's needs and to provide support during unforeseen experiences.

Nutrition

The child who feels ill has a decreased appetite and often is intolerant of food. In addition, the child's emotional responses to illness influence the child's desire and ability to tolerate nourishment. The child with cancer is prone to extended periods of poor nourishment because the illness and its treatment adversely affect the child's desire to eat. During periods of chemotherapy, the toxic effects of the drugs can result in vomiting and other gastrointestinal symptoms that contribute to a decreased nutritional status. In addition, lesions of the mouth can contribute to anorexia, and lesions of the gastrointestinal tract can interfere with getting adequate nutrition. Radiation can also result in a decreased interest in food due to gastrointestinal side-effects. Irradiation of some areas of the body causes additional symptoms that decrease appetite—e.g., head and neck irradiation results in dryness of the mouth or loss of taste, and irradiation of the abdomen results in formation of fibrous tissue that can result in obstruction of the gastrointestinal tract.

Some surgical procedures influence nutritional intake temporarily. Surgery of the gastrointestinal tract can influence the child's appetite and eating patterns for fairly long periods. Postoperatively, the child can have nausea, cramps, sweating, or faintness due to malabsorption of essential nutrients.

Management of Nutrition Problems. The child with mouth lesions is given bland foods or liquids that are high in calories, such as milkshakes or eggnogs. Sipping liquids through a straw is sometimes tolerated better than drinking from a glass or cup. The child provides clues about the foods that are desired and tolerated when lesions are present.

During periods of mild nausea, the child may tolerate small frequent sips of clear soup, Koolaid, jello water, and carbonated drinks such as cola or ginger ale. The child may enjoy having these liquids frozen into attractively shaped ice cubes, which can be sucked. The child can also suck lollipops or pieces of hard candy when liquids are not appealing. As the nausea subsides, dry toast, white rice, soda crackers, or other favorite dry crackers can be given. The child's dietary intake is increased by giving the child small, attractive portions of foods that the child selects. If the child is so disinterested in food that he or she will not give any indications of what food would seem good, he or she is offered cubed chicken, scrambled eggs, creamed soups, cooked cereals, puddings, or ice cream. Alternating the offerings can make the child more interested in trying a particular food. Keeping portions very small helps the child to look at the food without getting overwhelmed by the task.

The appetite of the child varies throughout the treatment of cancer. While at most times the appetite is decreased during treatment, prednisone can increase the child's appetite. In addition, the child may eat during periods of increased emotional well-being and refuse food during periods of depression. These fluctuations in eating can make it frustrating to try to provide the child with adequate fluids and nutritional intake. Trying to decrease the stress associated with feeding can contribute to more satisfactory outcomes. However, the ill child can easily learn that control of nutrition intake is one area that he or she can influence. Refusing to eat is a method of control that can frustrate caregivers. When refusal of fluids and nutrients is severe, parenteral fluids are given to counteract dehydration. At times, tube feedings are given for extended periods. Occasionally, the child is discharged with tube feedings being required.

Interest in providing the child with adequate nutrition during stressful periods can cause parent–child conflict. Every attempt is made not to let this happen. Parents are encouraged not to bribe the child to eat and not to ridicule the child when food is refused. Praising the child when fluids and food are accepted can lead to a more positive outcome.

During periods of extreme gastrointestinal upset, the child can develop long-term aversion to food. The sight and smells of food can become negative clues to the child. Offering foods that have mild odors and that look attractive can diminish this outcome.

When the child is in remission, nutritional needs can contribute to repairing the body and increasing the child's strength. Avoiding junk foods during remission is suggested so that during periods of remission the child's nutritional status is improved and the child becomes better prepared to tolerate future periods of relapse, new malignancies, recurrences, and treatments.

HOSPITALIZATIONS

The intermittent admission to the hospital of the child with leukemia is a necessary but dreaded experience. Hospitalization usually means that the leukemia is not well-controlled or that secondary problems are present. With the long-term survival now possible, secondary and tertiary lesions are occurring.

Hospitalization usually brings painful procedures to the heightened awareness of the child. Although the child has periodic bone marrow aspirations and lumbar puncture procedures on an outpatient basis, hospitalization is synonymous with increases in painful procedures and fear of the unknown. Common problems encountered in the hospital management of these children include:

1. Fluctuations in weight.
2. Ways to help the child cope with the loss of hair.
3. Emotional lability, ranging from laughing to crying.
4. Gastrointestinal side-effects of medications.
5. Combating infections of many varieties.
6. Controlling bleeding—internal and external.
7. Central nervous system involvement, ranging from dizziness to seizures.
8. Loss of memory.
9. Increased stress and anxiety.
10. Peripheral neuropathies, ranging from weakness to paralysis.
11. Hearing or vision losses.
12. Brain damage or hydrocephalus.
13. Behavior problems.
14. Socialization problems.
15. Family relationship problems.
16. Mourning or grief process.
17. Coping with fear of death.
18. Coma.
19. Oxygen therapy.

Separation

One of the major concerns of the child with cancer is the fear of separation or abandonment. Hospitalization brings these concerns into the child's consciousness. Hospitalization is usually required for periods when complex care is needed, when pain control measures are increased, or when the family is no longer able to handle the child's management at home. In order to decrease the effects of separation, family members are encouraged to come and go as they desire and to spend extended periods of time at the hospital.

Isolation is only used when the probability of infection is so great that the effects of separation caused by isolation are of less importance. The young child is poorly equipped to understand the positive effects of isolation.

Painful Experiences

The child is faced almost daily with painful experiences. The experiences can be both emotional and physical in nature. Knowing that painful experiences are part of the hospital experience increases the child's vulnerability and makes him or her less able to cope with impending situations.

Preparation for experiences helps the child to gain control and to be able to trust the health care providers who produce the pain. Playing out painful or frightening experiences after they are completed serves as a catharsis and helps the child tolerate hospitalization. Sensitivity to the child's needs and feelings makes it possible for the child to endure procedures in one hospitalization that few normal children will experience in a lifetime.

Painful experiences can be lessened by touch during the procedure. For example, the mother or nurse can hold the child's hand during a bone marrow aspiration or can stroke the child's forehead during an intravenous infusion of medication. Touch reduces the isolation felt by the child and increases the bond between the adult and child.

The child often likes to choose the adults whom he or she wants present during painful experiences. The child is soothed by the presence of a loved one and feels more secure when these persons share in the painful experience.

The child often tolerates painful experiences better when a relative calm surrounds the experience. When disorganization surrounds these experiences, the child's level of anxiety is increased and the ability to cooperate is decreased. Therefore, it is important to have the child sense that adults in the environment are in control of the situation and competent to assume the responsibility for completing procedures efficiently and effectively.

Hypnosis is being successfully used to decrease the negative effects of experiences faced by the child with cancer (Hartman, 1981). For susceptible children, hypnosis can be used to reduce unpleasant memories of painful procedures, and hypnotherapy can contribute to the control of side-effects of the chemotherapy. Imagery is also being used to help the children contend with their illness. Imagery such as "shooting at bad cells" helps the child to feel some control and decreases the child's anxiety about having a life-threatening illness. Relaxation measures of any type can help the child to disengage from the discomfort of procedures.

Unfortunately, there are times when painful experiences are exaggerated by factors beyond control, such as inability to get an intravenous started on the first try, difficulties in completing bone marrow aspirations, pain intensified by treating an infected area, and so forth. Because of these inevitable circumstances, the child can lose faith in the ability of health care providers to be helpful and in parents to protect him or her from unnecessary harm. In addition, the child's frustration can be elevated when adults seem to place blame on him or her with statements like, "If you wiggle I will not be able to get this intravenous started."

Truth-telling

The child benefits from age-appropriate discussions about his or her illness and the course of the illness. Hospitalization makes the child aware of the seriousness of the illness. Truthful explanations about treatment and outcomes help the child to understand why hospitalization is necessary and why certain procedures are being done. The children often ask questions that are difficult to answer. When answers are unknown, this is shared with the child, when answers are known, the child benefits from this knowledge. When a child asks a painful question, such as, "Am I going to die?" it is often difficult for adults to respond effectively. Children sense when adults are covering up information that is known, and this leads to mistrust, which poorly equips the child to contend with long-term illness.

Privacy

The provision of privacy in the hospital is seldom assured. The child and family live in a room where people seldom knock before entering, move personal items without permission, and enforce regulations about dress, sleep, eating, and so forth that are inconsistent with their normal routines. In addition, intrusion on the child's body is done with little preparation or respect and privacy is violated completely. Every child needs periods of privacy to meditate and contemplate. The hospital setting is ill-prepared to meet this need. The adolescent client is especially vulnerable when privacy is lacking. The adolescent can become very frustrated with these conditions and display asocial behavior as a result of persistent violations of privacy.

Infection

Infection is the major cause of death in children with cancer. Factors contributing to infection are as follows:

1. Malnutrition.
2. Long periods of hospitalization.
3. Interruptions in cutaneous surfaces.
4. Use of in-dwelling catheters.
5. Local reactions to radiation treatments.
6. Decreased WBC counts (immunosuppression).
7. Stress.
8. Primary illness.

One of the most critical infections in a child who is immunosuppressed involves *Pneumocystis carinii*—an opportunistic condition characterized by an insidious onset of dry, nonproductive cough while the child is free of rales or other signs of consolidation. To assess for this condition, the nurse looks for redness or pain in an area not previously affected, malaise or a decrease in the level of alertness, or temperature greater than 38.6°C.

Fevers of unknown origin are common in immunosuppressed children. Temperatures of 38.6°C not resulting from blood transfusions, positive blood cultures, and known pathogenic reactions are presumed to be bacterial in nature and are treated with broad-spectrum antibiotics.

Many of the infections that occur with cancer are bacterial in nature. Causative agents include *Escherichia coli (E-coli)*, *Pseudomonas*, and *Klebsiella*. The Gram-negative infection caused by *Serratia marcescens* seems to be increasing in incidence. Blood cultures are obtained and antibiotics are prescribed for children with granulocytopenia to combat the organism. A combination of antibiotics is usually selected—for example, aminoglycoside (Gentamycin) and cephalosporin (Cephalothin). Carbenicillin is added when the child is profoundly granulocytopenic or when the child is at high risk for infection by *Pseudomonas* organisms (Culbert and van Eys, 1977).

If the child has an adequate granulocytic count, antibiotic therapy may be delayed until the reports on cultures and antibiotic sensitivities are ready. When these reports are available, the child is started on therapy for the specific causative agent.

Viral infections that are common in children with cancer are those caused by herpes and cytomegalovirus. Live virus vaccines, such as poliomyelitis and measles vaccines, are avoided. Ara C therapy is used for varicella and herpes simplex infections in some instances.

Fungal infections (such as thrush) and vaginal infections are common. The *Candida albicans* organism is usually responsible. Other fungal infections include aspergillosis, coccidioidomycosis, cryptococcosis, and histoplasmosis.

Protozoal infections, such as *Pneumocystis carinii* pneumonia affect approximately 6 percent of children in cancer remission. These infections are suspected when children have signs of pulmonary disease.

There are many measures that can be used to try to decrease the numbers of infections that children with immunosuppression get. These measures include:

1. Avoidance of other children and adults with known infection.
2. Meticulous hand washing before treating or touching the child.
3. Consistent oral hygiene, using warm saline for mild mouth lesions, diluted Cepacol for rinses, and dilute lidocaine viscous solution for pain relief.
4. High oral fluid intake to decrease the status of the urine in the bladder.
5. Chest hygiene or intermittent positive pressure (IPPB) when pulmonary signs are present.
6. Preparation of skin surfaces with povidone—iodine solution prior to all skin punctures.
7. Cleansing of perineal—perianal areas with warm water and applying povidone—iodine solution when problem areas arise.

8. Avoiding use of rectal thermometers and suppositories as routine measures.
9. Observing in-dwelling intravenous catheters and changing sites as indicated; intravenous tubings and solutions should be changed every 48 hours.
10. Sterile Foley catheter irrigations twice daily.
11. Observing skin integrity, including mucus membranes, daily.
12. Responding to the child's cues about painful areas even when there is no apparent lesion.

The control of infection is a major goal of the care of children with leukemia. The nurse is responsible for conducting ongoing assessments of the child and for teaching the parents to conduct these assessments while the child is at home.

Bleeding

Bleeding is another common problem associated with the decreased numbers of platelets common in children with leukemia. Platelet transfusions have decreased the incidence of death caused by bleeding. However, it is still a major problem, especially in association with infection. Common types of bleeding are epistaxis and gingival bleeding. Cleansing the child's mouth and using soft toothbrushes or sponge sticks are indicated. When bleeding continues, salt pork packs or dry tea bags are sometimes used (Stagner and Wood, 1976).

The platelet counts are often used to determine the amount of activity the child can engage in. For example, a platelet count below $50,000/mm^3$ poorly prepares the body to clot blood, so contact sports are restricted when counts of this kind are present. The child is given the platelet counts and is advised when to return to unrestricted activity. The child can also observe his or her own body for bruises and learn that these bruises occur more frequently when platelets are low.

Visual signs of frank bleeding, such as oozing from sites, epistaxis, and blood in stools or vomitus are all upsetting happenings. The child and parents need increased support during these times. Bleeding can result in anemia or in increasing the anemia associated with drug therapy. The management of bleeding includes controlling the source, transfusions as indicated, increased periods of rest, controlling associated infection, and monitoring the child's activity so that it does not contribute to the bleeding.

OUTPATIENT MANAGEMENT

The long-term care of the child with leukemia takes place in the child's home. Therefore, it is essential that the family knows how to manage the child safely in the home and that the family has a definite plan for follow-up care. The child needs frequent medical care, so it is necessary for the child to have a primary physician to assume this role, and the child probably will return to the specialty clinic for periodic assessments, as well. This follow-up care is coordinated so that interference with attendance at school is minimized.

Family members are shown how to assess the child for infection and bleeding while the child is hospitalized. They are taught how to assess the laboratory findings to know when the child is more prone to infection and bleeding. They are also aware of measures to take when early signs are present and know to call the physician whenever they are in doubt of their own ability to assess a particular situation.

The family also accompanies the child for outpatient evaluations that include procedures like bone marrow aspirations, lumbar punctures, and transfusions. The family is told how to prepare the child for these experiences so that the child is less fearful of the follow-up visits. The family is aware that after a visit to the outpatient clinic or office, the child's behavior may regress, with periods of whining, clinging, or withdrawal as common symptoms.

It is important to remember that children with long-term illnesses learn to integrate their specialty clinic into their normal lifestyle. For the school-age child, social groups then include the family, community, peers, school, and clinic. The way he or she perceives the clinic is largely dependent on interpersonal relationships. This places a great responsibility on the nurse in the clinic to become acquainted with the children and to assume a major role in making the clinic experience as positive as possible. In addition to personal identity, the nurse should be sure that privacy is guaranteed each child, that he or she is accompanied for painful procedures, that he or she is prepared for all clinic procedures, and that his or her next clinic appointment is scheduled to least interfere with his or her personal plans. With pediatric care rapidly moving to the outpatient departments, which are physically not ready to accept the large influx of clients, good interpersonal relationships can be a great compensation. Other nursing contributions to personalizing the outpatient care of children with a life-threatening condition might include the following techniques. The regularly scheduled visits to the clinic are known in advance. All professional personnel review the past records prior to visiting the child for his or her clinic examination. Children are approached in the waiting area and addressed by name. Facts which are easily compiled, such as birthdate or upcoming special events, can further add to the individualizing of care. A comment such as, "Birthday wishes are in store for you this week!" can be helpful. A supply of children's birthday cards can be kept on hand to be signed by the child's physician and nurse. Other similar occasions can be acknowledged in the same manner. Children enjoy surprises, and small, inexpensive gifts can be wrapped and put into a grab bag. This will further suggest to the child's significant others the professional personnel's interest in children. To any particular child it will signify a direct interest in him or her.

The waiting area is well-equipped with toys and activities to make the waiting period seem shorter. A donated supply of magazines can be useful for the parents. Films, filmstrips, posters, and pamphlets can also be utilized in the waiting area. Some of this material can be geared to the children, while others may appeal to the parents and the children can utilize the time playing in another area.

The waiting area should have comfortable seats for both the children and the parents. It should have a crib or play pen available for infants who could not be left at home. The waiting area should also be equipped with machines offering nutritious food items, such as fruit juice, milk, and crackers. Coffee is also considered a friendly offering, and, if possible, it should be available for the adults.

It also helps to have the waiting area clean and aesthetically appealing. This will diminish the complaints of attending an outpatient service.

Some communities have living accommodations for families who need to stay close by the specialty hospital but do not require inpatient management. The Ronald McDonald houses are an example of this type of outpatient living arrangement.

The financial strain caused by the long-term management of these children can be lessened when accommodations of this nature are available.

Outpatient Nursing Intake Interviews

The nurse in the outpatient department conducts an interview with the parent and child on each visit. It is important to know how the child is adjusting or coping between visits. The nurse is able to elicit this information by offering the child and parent an acceptable situation in which to verbalize. The parent is taught to keep accurate records between visits, and records are shared at this time. The records should indicate the medications the child has received between visits, with emphasis placed on identifying medications that were not given or tolerated. In addition, the record contains estimates of vomiting or diarrhea to determine the hydration status of the child. If the child has an elevated temperature, it should also appear on the record. New areas of hemorrhage or infection are recorded. The interview provides for privacy and is carried out in a relaxed manner. If the interview seems hurried, appropriate information may be withheld or assessed inaccurately. It is important to know how much of a strain this long-term illness is having on the family. If it is reasonable, the whole family should come for visits rather than just the client and parent. This can serve several purposes. One, the other children learn to appreciate some of the stress placed on their affected sibling. They also can see that the child is receiving excellent care and that everything possible is being done to prolong his or her life. Another important point is that the other children frequently suffer when there is a child in the family who needs a great deal of attention. Counseling may be indicated for the other children to help them understand what is taking place with their brother or sister. They may also need explanations for their parents' behavior. If possible, the interview should precede the physical examination so that the information gathered can be shared with the physician and other team members.

The following are examples of forms which can be utilized for outpatient nursing intake interviews. The first one is suggested when one is interviewing the parent and child together on the initial visit. The second one is useful for follow-up visits. The third is for interviewing school-age and adolescent children without their parents. The fourth form is suggested for planning effective nursing care during the visit and also for determining needs for referral to other agencies. As the majority of these children return frequently to the clinic, a Kardex is

FORM 1.

```
┌──────────────────────────────────────────────────────────────────┐
│                     UNIVERSITY HOSPITAL                            │
│                           U.S.A.                                   │
│  INITIAL NURSING INTAKE INTERVIEW (OUTPATIENT)                     │
│  Name _____ Age _____ Date _____       │
│      I.   Reason for appointment                                   │
│     II.   Previous appointment or hospital admissions              │
│               (date, reason, action taken)                         │
│    III.   Family constellation                                     │
│     IV.   Habits:                                                  │
│               Eating (describe amount, how often, types of food,   │
│                  likes, and dislikes)                              │
│               Elimination                                          │
│               Sleeping                                             │
│               Language development                                 │
│               Play—peer groups                                     │
│      V.   Allergies                                                │
│     VI.   Activities of daily living                               │
│               Independent                                          │
│               Dependent                                            │
│               School                                               │
│               Social interests                                     │
│    VII.   Special needs, fears, problems                           │
└──────────────────────────────────────────────────────────────────┘
```

especially useful in compiling information. The simple guideline in utilizing these tools is to give as comprehensive a picture of this child and his family as possible.

Outpatient Examination

When the child's turn comes to go to the examining room, the nurse should greet the child and parents. The child is encouraged to help in his or her preparation. He or she is encouraged to guess his or her weight, to take his or her own oral temperature, and to undress and get into the proper garb. The client is provided privacy during this procedure.

Questions that the child can adequately answer are asked of him or her directly. An attempt is made to have the child feel he or she is an integral part of the visit, not just an appendage. The child and parents are introduced to the physician, if they have not previously met him or her. They are also introduced to students of any profession who may be present during the examination.

In a busy clinic, the nurse is able to teach the parent what signs to observe while the child is receiving a transfusion, to be able to organize the work load to permit visitation with the child who is spending a period of time in the OPD, and to offer support and a listening ear to the child and his or her significant others. If any procedures or treatments are done in a different area, the nurse gives the

FORM 2.

UNIVERSITY HOSPITAL
U.S.A.

FOLLOW-UP NURSING ASSESSMENT BASED ON PARENT RECORD—KEEPING AND INTERVIEW

Name _____ Age _____ Date _____

   I. Reason for appointment
       (routinely scheduled or requested)

  II. Hospital admissions or emergency treatment since last visit
       (date, place, reason, actions taken)

 III. Social behavior since last visit
       (include school attendance, interactions with parents, siblings, peers)

  IV. Medication regime
       (include reactions to drugs, omissions, etc)

   V. Vital signs
       (include elevated temperatures and weight assessment)

  VI. Blood tests
       (include any results from blood work completed at other places and
       today's results)

 VII. Changes in activity since last visit
       (disabilities, regression in development)

VIII. Physiologic assessment
       (estimates of vomiting, diarrhea, new bruises, petechiae, mouth
       lesions, etc)

  IX. Changes in family status

FORM 3.

UNIVERSITY HOSPITAL
U.S.A.

NURSING INTERVIEW OF CHILD (OUT-PATIENT)

Name _____ Age _____ Date _____

   I. Reason for appointment

  II. Preparation for visit

 III. Habits:
       Eating
       Elimination
       Sleeping
       Play—peer groups

  IV. Activities of daily living
       Independent
       Dependent
       School
       Social interests
       Relationships with siblings

FORM 4.

```
+----------------------------------------------------------------+
|                    UNIVERSITY HOSPITAL                         |
|                          U.S.A.                                |
|            OUT-PATIENT NURSING INTERVENTION                    |
|                                                                |
| Name _____ Age _____ Date _____ |
|                                                                |
|   I.   In relation to child (incorporating principles of       |
|        normal and development)                                 |
|   II.  In relation to family                                   |
|   III. Community resources available to meet nursing objectives|
|   IV.  Follow-up plan of care                                  |
+----------------------------------------------------------------+
```

parents and child adequate directions to the area. This will help to decrease the amount of anxious activity spent in finding unfamiliar areas.

The visit to the clinic is completed when the family has an updated data base about the child's condition and management, and when a follow-up visit is scheduled.

HOME CARE

As home care programs have expanded, the care of the child with a life-threatening illness has not created any great problems. Depending on the particular home care program, the child has received in the home the services of laboratory technicians, oxygen therapists, and medical and nursing personnel, and physical and occupational therapists and pastoral care. The parents who have participated in the program seem to receive satisfaction from keeping their ill child at home as long as possible. The added security of knowing they can telephone a professional person any time during the day or night lessens their anxieties. The child benefits greatly by not being separated from his or her home and family for long periods. With this added comprehensive home care, it becomes evident that the community health nurses in any area may be seeing a great many more clients with a fatal prognosis than they have in the past. Children may go to the hospital only for surgery or complicated therapies and immediately return home for their continuing care. This procedure necessitates better and faster communication between the hospital and home. An effective home care plan is based on the ability of the parent or family to assume a great deal of responsibility for the child's care. Parent education is essential prior to placing the child on home care services. Some parents even learn to administer intravenous medications. An in-depth explanation of the treatment program is provided so that the parents are able to cooperate fully. The parents' intellectual and emotional capabilities are assessed to determine when and how they will be started on the parent education program.

A particular model of home care when the child is nearing death is hospice care. Hospice care continues after the death of the child to help the family during the bereavement period.

REFERENCES

Cairns, N.U., Clark, G.M., Black, J., & Lansky, S.B. Childhood cancer: Nonmedical costs of the illness. In J.J. Spinetta & P. Deasy-Spinetta (Eds.), *Living with childhood cancer*. St. Louis: Mosby, 1981.

Cantu, R.C. *Toward fitness*. New York: Human Sciences Press, 1980.

Culbert, S.J., & Van Eys, J. Principles of total care: Physiologic approach. In W. W. Sutow, D. Fernbach, & T. Nietti (Eds.), *Pediatric clinical oncology* (2nd ed.). St. Louis: Mosby, 1977.

Deasey-Spinetta, P. The school and the child with cancer. In J.J. Spinetta & P. Deasey-Spinetta (Eds.), *Living with childhood cancer*. St. Louis: Mosby, 1981.

Engel, G.L. *Psychological development in health and disease*. Philadelphia: W.B. Saunders, 1962.

Hartman, G.A. Hypnosis as an adjuvant in the treatment of childhood cancer. In J.J. Spinetta & P. Deasey-Spinetta (Eds.), *Living with childhood cancer*. St. Louis: Mosby, 1981.

Karni, K.R. The view from the laboratory. In I.M. Martinson (Ed.), *Home care for the dying child*. New York: Appleton—Century—Crofts, 1976.

Lansky, S.B. Lowman, J.T., Vats, T.S., & Gyulay, J.E. School phobia in children with malignant neoplasma. *American Journal of Disease of Childhood* 129:42, 1975.

Nesbitt, M., & Kersey, J. Acute leukemia of childhood. In I.M. Martinson (Ed.), *Home care for the dying child*. New York: Appleton— Century—Crofts, 1976.

Stagner, S.A., & Wood, A., The child with cancer on immunosuppressive therapy. *Nursing Clinics of North America* 11:21, 1976.

Young, T.L., Jr., & Nuller, R.W., Incidence of malignant tumors in U.S. children. *Journal of Pediatrics* 86:254, 1975.

BIBLIOGRAPHY

Bivalec, L.M., Berman, J. Care by parent: A new trend. *Nursing Clinics of North America* 11:109, 1976.

Bowlby, J. Grief and mourning in infancy and early childhood. *Psychoanalytric Study of the Child* 15:9, 1960.

Brown, H.C. The child with acute lymphocytic leukemia. *American Journal of Maternal—Child Nursing* 3:290, 1978.

Clapp, M.J. Psychosocial reactions of children with cancer: A program for rehabilitation. *Nursing Clinics of North America* 11:73, 1976.

Crosby, M.H. Control systems and children with lymphoblastic leukemia. *Nursing Clinics of North America* 6:407, 1971.

Cyphert, E.R. Back to school for the child with cancer. *Journal of School Health* 43:215, 1973.

Donaldson, M.H. The multidisciplinary team approach to the care of children with cancer. *Cancer Review* 1:2, 1977.

Easson, W.M. *The dying child*. Springfield, Ill.: Thomas, 1970.

Edmonston, W.E. *Hypnosis and relaxation: Modern verification of an old equation*. New York: Wiley, 1981.

Eiser, C., Intellectual abilities among survivors of childhood leukemia as a function of CNS irradiation. *Archives of Disease in Childhood* 53:391, 1978.

Evans, A., Practical care for the family of a child with cancer. *Cancer* 35:871, 1975.

Ferguson, J.H., Late psychological effects of a serious illness in childhood. *Nursing Clinics of North America* 11:83, 1976.

Fley, G., & McCarthy, A.M.: The child with leukemia: The disease and its treatment. *American Journal of Nursing* 76:1108, 1976.

Foley, G., & McCarthy, A. The child with leukemia: In a special hematology clinic. *American Journal of Nursing* 76:1115, 1976.

Fond, K.I. Dealing with death and dying through family-centered care. *American Journal of Nursing* 7:53, 1972.

Futterman, E., & Hoffman, I. *Crises and adaptation in families of fatally ill children: The child in his family.* New York: Wiley, 1973.

Futterman, E., & Hoffman, I. Transient school phobia in a leukemic child. *Journal of the American Academy of Child Psychiatry* 9:477, 1970.

Gartner, C.R. Growing up dying: The child, the parents and the nurse. In R.G. Caughill (Ed.), *The dying patient.* Boston: Little, Brown, 1976.

Greene, P. The child with leukemia in the classroom. *American Journal of Nursing* 75:86, 1975.

Greene, T. Current therapy for acute leukemia in childhood. *Nursing Clinics of North America* 11:3, 1976.

Green-Epner, C.S. The dying child. In R.E. Caughill (Ed.), *The dying patient.* Boston: Little, Brown, 1976.

Gyuley, J. Care of the dying child. *Nursing Clinics of North America* 11:95, 1976.

Gyuley, J. *The dying child.* New York: McGraw–Hill, 1978.

Kagen-Goodheart, L. Reentry: Living with childhood cancer. *American Journal of Orthopsychiatry* 47:651, 1977.

Kirten, C., & Liverman, M. Special educational needs of the child with cancer. *Journal of School Health* 47:170, 1977.

Klopovich, P. Immuno-suppression in the child who has cancer. *American Journal of Maternal–Child Nursing* 4:288, 1979.

Koocher, G.P. Talking with children about death. *American Journal of Orthopsychiatry* 44:404, 1974.

Lacasse, C.M. A dying adolescent. *American Journal of Nursing* 75:433, 1975.

Lansky, S.B., Lowman, J.T., Vats, T., et al. School phobia in children with malignant neoplasm. *American Journal of Diseases of Childhood* 129:42, 1975.

Leventhal, B., & Hersh, S. Modern treatment of childhood leukemia: The patient and his family. *Nursing Digest* 3:12, 1975.

Manchester, P.O., Ferrero, C., & Myers, M.M. The child with cancer: A plan of care. *Pediatric Nursing* 4:72, 1978.

Mann, S. Coping with a child's fatal illness. *Nursing Clinics of North America* 9:81, March 1974.

Martinson, I.M. *Home care for the dying child.* New York: Appleton–Century–Crofts, 1976.

Morrow, M. Nursing management of the adolescent: The effect of cancer chemotherapy on psychosocial development. *Nursing Clinics of North America* 13:319, 1978.

Myers, M.H., Heise, B.S., Li., F.P., et al. Trends in cancer survival among U.S. white children, 1955–1971. *Journal of Pediatrics* 87:815, 1975.

Nirenberg, A. The day hospital: Ambulatory care for the adolescent with cancer. *American Journal of Nursing* 79:500, 1979.

Pearse, M. The child with cancer: Impact on the family. *Journal of School Health* 47:174, 1977.

Potter, S. Critical infection in the pediatric oncologic patient. *Nursing Clinics of North America* 16:699, 1981.

Powell, K. Host defense mechanisms: The immune compromised host. *Pediatric Nursing* 4:13, 1978.

Sachs, M.B. Helping the child with cancer go back to school. *Journal of School Health* 50:328, 1980.

Sherman, M. *Feeding the sick child*. DHEW Pub. No. (NIH) 78-795. Washington, D.C.: Department of Health, Education, and Welfare, no date.

Spinetta, J.J. The dying child's awareness of death: A review. In S. Chess & A. Thomas (Eds.), *Annual progress in child psychiatry and child development*. New York: Brunner/Mazel, 1975.

Spinetta, J.J., Rigler, D., & Karon, M. Anxiety in the dying child. *Pediatrics* 52:841, 1973.

Spinetta, J.J., Maloney, L.J. Death anxiety in the outpatient leukemic child. *Pediatrics* 56:1034, 1975.

Stagner, S.A., & Wood, A. The child with cancer on immunosuppressive therapy. *Nursing Clinics of North America* 11:21, 1976.

van Eys, J. The outlook for the child with cancer. *Journal of School Health* 47:165, 1977.

van Eys, J. (Ed.). *The truly cured child*. Baltimore: University Park Press, 1977.

Voors, B.B. *Pneumocystis carinii* in the immunosupressed child. *Cancer Nursing* 2:4, 1979.

Wollnick, L. Management of the child with cancer on an outpatient basis. *Nursing Clinics of North America* 2:35, 1976.

Wood, A. *Drugs vs cancer*. DHEW Pub. No. (NIH) 78-786. Washington, D.C.: U.S. Department of Health, Education, and Welfare, 1977.

Wood, A. The pediatric nurse practitioner in a pediatric cancer clinic. *Pediatric Nursing* 4:47, 1978.

Appendices

Nutrition History (Birth through Infancy)

Name: Age:

1. Is _____ breastfed? _____
   If yes, does _____ also receive milk or formula?
   If yes, what kind? _____ How often? _____ What amount? _____
2. Is _____ formula fed?
   If yes, what kind? _____ How often? _____ What amount? _____
   Describe how you make the formula.
   Does the formula contain iron? _____
   Does _____ take any liquids besides the formula? _____
   If yes, what kind? _____
   Do you add anything to the formula? _____
3. How many times a day does _____ eat, including formula or breastfeeding?
4. Does _____ take a bottle to bed for naps or nighttime?
   If yes, what is in the bottle? _____
5. What solid foods does _____ eat each day? _____
6. Describe a typical day's feeding for _____.
7. Have you discovered any things that _____ likes or dislikes? _____
8. Do you think _____ has an allergy to any foods? _____
9. Does _____ seem satisfied after eating? _____
10. Do you give _____ any vitamins? _____

APPENDIX B

Nutrition History (Toddler through Adolescence)

Name: Age:

1. Describe what _____ ate at his or her last meal.
2. How many times does _____ eat a day?
3. What times are these meals eaten?
4. Where are meals eaten?
5. Give me an example of the foods eaten at
   Breakfast
   Lunch
   Dinner
   Snacks
6. How much time does it take _____ to eat?
7. Do you feed him or her any of the meal?
   If yes, describe any self-feeding that is done.
8. What do you do when _____ does not finish a meal?
9. Where does _____ eat his or her meals?
10. What are _____ favorite foods?
11. What foods does _____ dislike?
12. What does _____ like to drink?
13. How much liquid does _____ drink at meals? Per day?
    If age-appropriate, is any of this taken by bottle?
    Is a bottle taken to bed?
14. Does _____ have any allergies to food?
15. How often do you introduce new foods to _____?
    At what time in the meal are they introduced?
16. Do you feel you have any problems with getting _____ to eat adequately?
17. Do you give _____ any vitamins or iron? How much?

Examination First Hours

WEEKS GESTATION

PHYSICAL FINDINGS		Findings by gestational age (weeks 20–48)
Vernix		Appears (20–21) · Covers body, thick layer (~24–33) · On back, scalp, in creases (38–39) · Scant, in creases (40–41) · No vernix (42+)
Breast tissue and areola		Areola and nipple barely visible, no palpable breast tissue (24–33) · Areola raised (34) · 1–2 mm nodule (36–38) · 3–5 mm (38) · 5–6 mm (39) · 7–10 mm (40–41) · ?12 mm (44–45)
Ear	Form	Flat, shapeless (20–31) · Beginning incurving superior (33) · Incurving upper 2/3 pinnae (36) · Well-defined incurving to lobe (38–42)
	Cartilage	Pinna soft, stays folded (23–30) · Cartilage scant, returns slowly from folding (33–34) · Thin cartilage, springs back from folding (36–38) · Pinna firm, remains erect from head (42)
Sole creases		Smooth soles without creases (22–31) · 1–2 anterior creases (33) · 2–3 anterior creases (35) · Creases anterior 2/3 sole (36) · Creases involving heel (38) · Deeper creases over entire sole (42) · Creases over entire sole (45)
Skin	Thickness & appearance	Thin, translucent skin, plethoric, venules over abdomen, edema (20–29) · Smooth, thicker, no edema (33–34) · Pink (36) · Few vessels (38) · Some desquamation, pale pink (40) · Thick, pale, desquamation over entire body (42–46)
	Nail plates	Appear (20) · Nails to finger tips (33) · Nails extend well beyond finger tips (44–45)
Hair		Appears on head (20) · Eye brows and lashes (25–27) · Fine, woolly, bunches out from head (29–34) · Silky, single strands, lays flat (37–39) · ?Receding hairline or loss of baby hair, short, fine underneath (42–44)
Lanugo		Appears (20) · Covers entire body (24) · Vanishes from face (35) · Present on shoulders (38) · No lanugo (42)
Genitalia	Testes	Testes palpable in inguinal canal (30) · In upper scrotum (38) · In lower scrotum (42)
	Scrotum	Few rugae (28–31) · Rugae, anterior portion (37) · Rugae, anterior (40) · Rugae cover (40) · Pendulous (42)
	Labia & clitoris	Prominent clitoris, labia majora small, widely separated (31–34) · Prominent clitoris, labia majora larger, nearly cover clitoris (36) · Labia minora and clitoris covered (42)
Skull firmness		Bones are soft (20–27) · Soft to 1" from anterior fontanelle (29) · Spongy at edges of fontanelle, center firm (36) · Bones hard, sutures easily displaced (38–39) · Bones hard, cannot be displaced (42)
Posture	Resting	  Hypotonic, lateral decubitus (22–25) · Hypotonic (27–28) · Beginning flexion, thigh 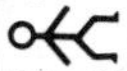 (30) · Stronger hip flexion  (32) · Frog-like (34) · Flexion, all limbs  (36) · Hypertonic (38–39) · Very hypertonic (42–44)  
	Recoil – leg	No recoil (20–21) · Partial recoil (33) · Begin flexion, no recoil (34–35) · Prompt recoil (38)
	Arm	No recoil (20–26) · Prompt recoil, may be inhibited (37–38) · Prompt recoil after 30" inhibition (42)

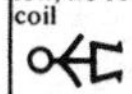

Weeks scale: 20 21 22 23 24 25 26 27 28 29 30 31 32 33 34 35 36 37 38 39 40 41 42 43 44 45 46 47 48

Figure B-1. Clinical estimation of gestational age. An approximation based on published data. *(Reproduced with permission, from Kempe C.H., Silver H.K., O'Brien D. (Eds.). Current pediatric diagnosis & treatment (5th ed.). Los Altos, Calif.: Lange Medical, 1978)*

465

Confirmatory Neurologic Examination To Be Done After 24 Hours

Weeks Gestation: 20 21 22 23 24 25 26 27 28 29 30 31 32 33 34 35 36 37 38 39 40 41 42 43 44 45 46 47 48

Tone

Physical Findings	Entries (by gestational week)
Heel to ear	No resistance; Some resistance; Impossible
Scarf sign	No resistance; Elbow passes midline; Elbow at midline; Elbow does not reach midline
Neck flexors (head lag)	Absent; Head in plane of body; Holds head; Turns head from side to side
Neck extensors	Head begins to right itself from flexed position; Good righting cannot hold it; Holds head few seconds; Keeps head in line with trunk > 40° (A pre-term who has reached 40 weeks still has a 40° angle)
Body extensors	Straightening of legs; Straightening of trunk; Straightening of head and trunk together
Vertical positions	Arms hold baby, legs extended?; Legs flexed, good support with arms
Horizontal positions	Hypotonic, arms and legs straight; When held under arms, body slips through hands; Arms and legs flexed; Head and back even, flexed extremities; Head above back

Flexion angles

Physical Findings	Entries (by gestational week)
Popliteal	No resistance; 150°; 110°; 100°; 90°; 80°
Ankle	45°; 20°; 0°
Wrist (square window)	90°; 60°; 45°; 30°; 0°

Reflexes

Physical Findings	Entries (by gestational week)
Sucking	Weak, not synchronized with swallowing; Stronger, synchronized; Perfect; Perfect, hand to mouth; Perfect
Rooting	Long latency period slow, imperfect; Hand to mouth; Brisk, complete, durable; Complete
Grasp	Finger grasp is good, strength is poor; Stronger; Can lift baby off bed, involves arms; Hands open
Moro	Barely apparent; Weak, not elicited every time; Complete with arm extension, open fingers, cry; Stronger; Arm adduction added; ?Begins to lose Moro
Crossed extension	Flexion and extension in a random, purposeless pattern; Extension, no adduction; Still incomplete; Extension, adduction, fanning of toes; Complete
Automatic walk	Minimal; Begins tiptoeing, good support on sole; Fast tiptoeing; Heel-toe progression, whole sole of foot; A pre-term who has reached 40 weeks walks on toes; ?Begins to lose automatic walk
Pupillary reflex	Absent; Appears
Glabellar tap	Absent; Appears
Tonic neck reflex	Absent; Appears
Neck-righting	Absent; Appears; Present after 37 weeks

Figure B-2. Confirmatory neurologic examination to be done after 24 hours. (Reproduced with permission, from Kempe C.H., Silver H.K., O'Brien D. (Eds.). Current pediatric diagnosis & treatment (5th ed.). Los Altos, Calif.: Lange Medical, 1978)

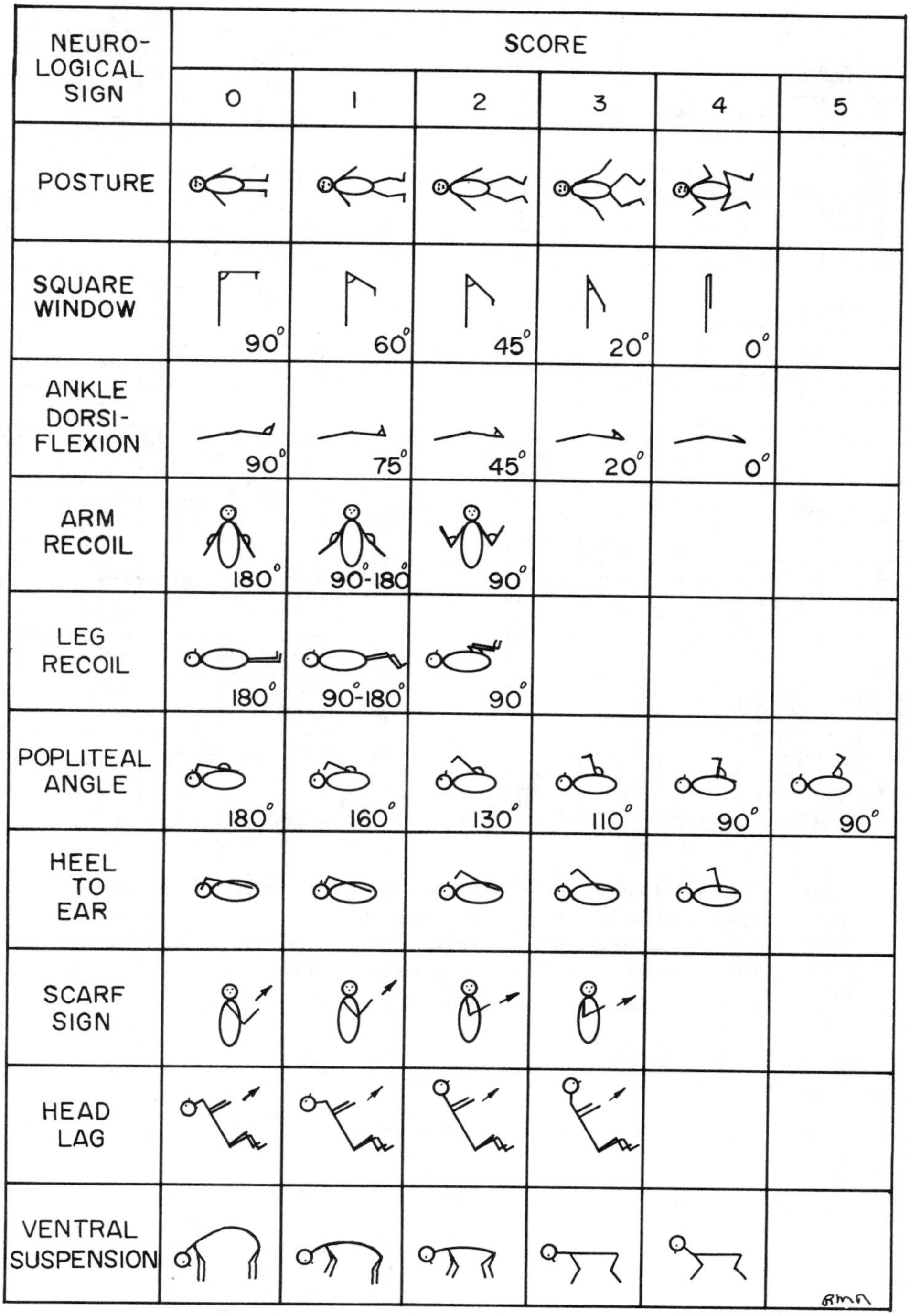

Figure B-3. Clinical assessment of gestational age in the newborn infant.
(Reproduced with permission, from Lilly, M.S., Dubonitz, V., Goldberg, C. Clinical assessment of the newborn infant, Journal of Pediatrics 77:1–10, July, 1970)

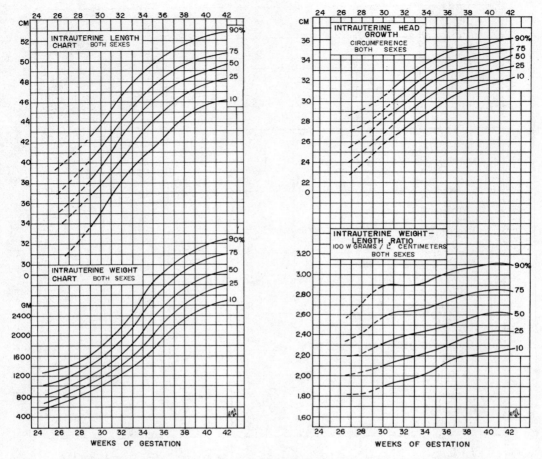

Figure B-4. Percentiles of intrauterine growth in weight, length, head circumference, and weight-length ratio. *(Reproduced with permission from Lubchenco, L.O., Hanson, C., Boyd, E. Intrauterine growth in length and head circumference as estimated from live births at gestational ages from 26 to 42 weeks. Pediatrics 37:403−8, 1966)*

APPENDIX C

National Organizations for the Disabled

1. The American Blind Bowling Association
    150 N. Bellaire Ave.
    Louisville, Ky. 40206

2. Blind Outdoor Leisure Development
    533 E. Main St.
    Aspen, Colo. 81611

3. American Athletic Association for the Deaf
    3916 Lantern Drive
    Silver Spring, Md. 20902

4. United States Deaf Skiers Association
    159 Davis Ave.
    Hackensack, N.J. 07601

5. National Foundation for Happy Horsemanship for the Handicapped
    Box 462
    Malvern, Pa. 19355

6. National Handicapped Sports and Recreation Association
    4105 E. Florida Ave., Third Floor
    Denver, Colo. 80222

7. National Wheelchair Basketball Association
    110 Seaton Bldg.
    University of Kentucky
    Lexington, Ky. 40506

8. Special Olympics
    Suite 203
    1701 K St., N.W.
    Washington, D.C. 20006

9. American Coalition of Citizens with Disabilities
    1346 Connecticut Ave., N.W.
    Washington, D.C. 20036

10. Joseph P. Kennedy Jr. Foundation
    1701 K St., N.W.
    Washington, D.C. 20006

TABLE B-1.
Scoring System for External Physical Characteristics

External Sign	Score*				
	0	1	<2>	<3>	<4>
Edema	Obvious edema of hands and feet pitting over tibia	No obvious edema of hands and feet; pitting over tibia	No edema		
Skin texture	Very thin, gelatinous	Thin and smooth	Smooth; medium thickness; rash or superficial peeling	Slight thickening, superficial cracking and peeling, especially of hands and feet	Thick and parchment-like; superficial or deep cracking
Skin color	Dark red	Uniformly pink	Pale pink; variable over body	Pale; only pink over ears, lips, palms, or soles	
Skin opacity (trunk)	Numerous veins and venules clearly seen, especially over abdomen	Veins and tributaries seen	A few large vessels clearly seen over abdomen	A few large vessels seen indistinctly over abdomen	No blood vessels seen
Lanugo (over back)	No lanugo	Abundant; long and thick over whole back	Hair thinning, especially over lower back	Small amount of lanugo and bald areas	At least 1/2 of back devoid of lanugo

Plantar creases	No skin creases	Faint red marks over anterior half of sole	Definite red marks over > anterior ½; indentations over > anterior ⅓	Indentations over > anterior ⅓	Definite deep indentations over > anterior ⅓
Nipple formation	Nipple barely visible; no areola	Nipple well-defined; areola smooth and flat, diameter < 0.75 cm	Areola stippled, edge not raised, diameter < 0.75 cm	Areola stippled, edge raised, diameter > 0.75 cm	
Breast size	No breast tissue palpable	Breast tissue on one or both sides, < 0.75 cm	Breast tissue both sides; one or both 0.5–1.0 cm	Breast tissue both side; one or both > 1 cm	
Ear form	Pinna flat and shapeless, little or no incurving of edge	Incurving of part of edge of pinna	Partial incurving whole of upper pinna	Well defined incurving whole of upper pinna	
Ear firmness	Pinna soft, easily folded; no recoil	Pinna soft, easily folded; slow recoil	Cartilage to edge of pinna, but soft in places, ready recoil	Pinna firm cartilage to edge; instant recoil	
Genitals: Male	Neither testis in scrotum	At least one testis high in scrotum	At least one testis right down		
Genitals: Female	Labia majora widely separated labia minora	Labia majora almost cover labia minora	Labia majora completely cover labia minora		

*If score differs on two sides, take the mean.

Adapted from Farr, V., Mitchell, R., Neligan, G., et al. *Developmental Medicine and Child Neurology* 8:507, 1966.

TABLE B-2.
Clinical Criteria for Gestational Assessment

	Gestational Age		
	0–36 Weeks	*37–38 Weeks*	*39 Weeks+*
Sole Creases	Anterior transverse crease only	Occasional creases anterior two-thirds	Sole covered with creases
Breast nodule diameter	2 mm	4 mm	7 mm
Scalp hair	Fine and fuzzy	Fine and fuzzy	Coarse and silky
Earlobe	Pliable, no cartilage	Some cartilage	Stiffened by thick cartilage
Testes and scrotum	Testes in lower canal, scrotum small, few rugae	Intermediate	Testes pendulous, scrotum full, extensive rugae

From Usher, R., McLean, F., & Scott, K. Clinical significance of gestational age and an objective method for its assessment. *Pediatric Clinics of North America* Vol. 13:835, Philadelphia: W.B. Saunders Co., 1966.

TABLE B-3.
Sample Items from the Teaching and Feeding Scales*

	Feeding Scales	Teaching Scales
Sensitivity to Cues	Parent comments verbally on child's hunger cues before beginning feeding. Parent positions infant so that eye-to-eye contact is possible. Parent does not offer food when the child looks away, looks down, turns away, or turns around.	Parent gets child's attention before beginning the task. Parent positions child so that child can reach and manipulate materials. Parent changes position of child and/or materials after unsuccessful attempt by the child to do the task.
Response to Distress	Parent stops or starts feeding in response to the child's distress. Parent changes voice volume to softer or higher pitch in response to child's distress.	Parent makes soothing nonverbal response to child's distress. Parent changes voice volume to softer or higher in response to child's distress.
Social-Emotional Growth Fostering	Parent is in *en face* position for more than half of the feeding. Parent praises child or some quality of the child's	Parent laughs or smiles at the child during the teaching. Parent makes constructive or encouraging statement to the child during teaching.

(continued)

TABLE B-3. (*Continued*)

	Feeding Scales	Teaching Scales
	behavior during the feeding. Parent uses gentle forms of touch during the feeding.	Parent does not make negative or uncomplimentary remarks about the child.
Cognitive Growth Fostering	Parent talks to the child using at least two words at least three times during the feeding. Parent encourages and/or allows the child to explore the breast, bottle, food, cup, bowl, or the parent during feeding.	Parent describes perceptual qualities of the task materials to the child. Parent uses explanatory verbal style more than imperative style in teaching child. Parent responds to child's vocalizations with verbal response.
Clarity of Child's Cues	Child signals readiness to eat. Child has periods of alertness during the feeding. Child makes contact with parent's face or eyes at least once during feeding.	Child widens eyes and/or shows postural attention to task situation. Child vocalizes while looking at task materials. Child grimaces or frowns during the teaching episode.
Responsiveness to Parent	Child responds to games, social play, or social cues of parent during feeding. Child vocalizes or smiles within 5 seconds of parent's vocalization. Child shows a change in level of motor activity within 5 seconds of being handled or repositioned by parent.	Child looks at the parent's face or eyes when parent attempts to establish eye-to-eye contact. Child smiles at parent within 5 seconds after parent's verbalization. Child gazes at parent's face or task materials after parent has shown verbal or nonverbal alerting behavior.

*The full scales, along with scoring manuals, are available at cost on request from the first author. A continuing education training course is offered in conjunction with the University of Washington School of Nursing and Child Development and Mental Retardation Center and is necessary to achieve observer reliability. Contact Georgina Sumner, Director NCAT, Mail Stop WJ-10, University of Washington, Seattle, Washington 98195 for further information about the training.

APPENDIX D

High-risk Factors Associated with Mental Retardation

1. Maternal history (prior pregnancies).
   a. Repeated abortions (two or more).
   b. Premature deliveries.
   c. Pregnancy complications.
      (1) Fetus.
         (a) Placental abnormalities.
         (b) Anoxia.
      (2) Mother.
         (a) Toxemia.
         (b) Drug, alcohol history.
   d. Prior history of child.
      (1) Congenital defects.
      (2) Developmental lags or defects.
      (3) Genetic defects.
   e. Multiparity.
2. Prenatal.
   a. Age of mother.
      (1) Below 16.
      (2) Over 30.
   b. Premature bleeding.
   c. Premature ruptured membranes.
   d. RH incompatability.
   e. Hydraminos.
   f. Maternal infection or disease.
   g. Low income.
   h. No prenatal care.
3. Perinatal.
   a. Toxemia.
   b. Abnormal presentation.
   c. Fetal distress.
   d. Prematurity.
   e. Prolonged labor.
   f. Low Apgar score.
   g. High birthweight.
   h. Congenital defects (hydrocephalus, etc.).

4. Postnatal.
   a. Low birthweight.
   b. Respiratory distress.
   c. Kernicterus.
   d. Brain injuries.
   e. Poisoning.
   f. Hormonal deficiencies.
   g. Metabolic disorders.
   h. Sociocultural problems.
5. Genetic.
   a. Single-gene disorders.
      (1) Autosomal.
      (2) X-linked.
         (a) Recessive.
         (b) Dominant.
   b. Chromosomal aberrations.
      (1) Autosomal.
      (2) Sex chromsomes.
         (a) Nondisjunction.
         (b) Translocation.
         (c) Deletions.

APPENDIX E

Physical Assessment

Name:_____   Family information:
Birthday: _____   Name of parents of guardian:

_____

Address: _____
Telephone number: _____

	Abnormal Finding (check with red ink)	Genetic Checklist
Past medical history and family pedigree Include mother's prenatal and perinatal information, if possible Childhood diseases Allergies		Observe for genetic or familial health problems
General survey Mental status Body development Nutritional state Sex and race Age Appearance Speech		Note if patient seems within normal limits of growth Is the body weight within normal limits?
Vital signs		Coarctation of aorta (take pressure in both arms and legs)
Head and neck Skull		Note size: Microcephaly Hydrocephaly Note shape: Oxycephaly Scaphocephaly Trigonocephaly Sutures regularly closed by 9−19 months

(continued)

	Abnormal Finding	Genetic Checklist
Hair		Note hair patterns, hirsutism, whorls, hair line (scalp)
Skin		Note "punched out" skin lesions, (facial) depigmentation, café-au-lait, other discoloration, moles or other lesions; note skin turgor
Neck		Check for shortness, thickness or webbing, reflexes, limitation of movement.
Trachea		
Clavicles		
Face		Note
		Spacing of features
		Hypertelorism
		Hypotelorism
Eyes		Micro-ophthalmia
Visual acuity		Protruding suborbital ridge
Fundoscopic: O.D., O.S.		Ptosis of lid
Vessels		Shape of eye
Background		Slant of eyes
Macula		Epicanthal folds
		Eye lashes—growth
		Eye brows—growth
		Color of iris
		Lens
		Any extraocular motions
		Tearing or blinking
Nose and sinuses		Note symmetry of nares, describe shape
External		
Bone and cartilage		
Frontal and maxillary sinuses		
Internal		
Nares		
Turbinates		
Mucosa		
Exudate		

	Abnormal Finding	Genetic Checklist
Mouth and throat Lips Buccal mucosa Tongue Teeth Gingival mucosa Tonsils Uvula Palate		Check for dry or cracked areas on lips, clefts, suture lines indicating closure of cleft Check palate slope, size of jaw, shape and placement of teeth, growth and color of gums, shape and size of tongue Notice if there is a configuration in the tongue Is the frenula at midline? Is the uvula at midline?
Ears Describe external appearance Canal Tympanic membrane Result of Weber Rinne Audiometric screening (should begin at 3 years)		Check for unusual folds, ironed out ear, prominent ear, lack of ear lobulus, ear tags or pits, low-set ear, or rotation of ear

Tip of pinna should cross line from corner to eye

Measure verticle line up from lobe to cross horizontal line

(continued)

	Abnormal Finding	Genetic Checklist
Ears *(contd.)*		Abnormal: low-set and more than 10° angle
Chest AP diameter Auscultation Palpation Skin		Notice irregularities, such as unusual protrusion or funnel chest, pigeon breast or barrel chest, extra nipples, moles, pigmented or depigmented areas; notice hairy areas
Abdomen Auscultation Palpation **Kidney** **Liver** **Spleen** **Lymphatic System** **Heart:** auscultation **Peripheral pulses** **Genitalia** (per agreement of agency) **Musculoskeletal** Posture Gait **Spine**		Note girth, color, skin lesions, lumps, or bulges Describe umbilicus Abnormal growth for age Describe secondary sexual characteristics Check muscle strength and tone Check for symmetry of size, carrying angle of arms, clinodactyly, polydactyly, syndactyly, length of toes and fingers; describe fingernails, shape of hands and feet Dermatoglyphic findings
Neurologic Motor Cerebral Cerebellar Fine Gross		Problems with gait or coordination?

	Abnormal Finding	Genetic Checklist
Romberg **Sensory** (explain how tested) I II III* IV* V VI* VII VIII IX X XI XII		Sensory equilibrium Any complaints of difficulty with smells? (I) Any visual aura described? (II) Any problem with ability to see colors? Nystagmus* (III, IV, VI) Drooping of lids* Unequal pupils* Diminished sensations of face and jaw, forehead, closure of jaw (V) Movement of facial muscles (VII) Any hearing loss (VIII) Phonation, position of uvula, swallowing, gag reflex (IX) Movement of head, shrugging of shoulders (XI) Protrusion of tongue (XII)

Signed: _____

Date: _____

---

*Test Together.

APPENDIX F

Skills Assessment

- Communication.
    Ability to write or print.
    Ability to read (describe level).
    Expressive (describe).
    Receptive (describe).
- Ambulation.
    Describe method.
    Describe gait (if applicable).
    Describe adaptive devices, if any.
- Fine and gross motor activity.
    Describe ability with fine.
    Describe ability with gross.
- Behavior and social adjustment.
    Ability to delay gratification.
    Manners.
    Self-image.
    Friendships.
    Temperament.
    Grooming.
    Hygiene.
    Understanding of sexual role (appropriate for age level).
- Competencies (sports, hobbies, talent).

APPENDIX G

Environmental Assessment

Family members (significant others)
Size of home
Child's room
Effective stimulation
  Inside home (toys, books, music)
  Outside of home (family yard): play
  equipment and exercise or
  relaxation
Social (opportunities to meet and
  interact with others)
Peers (persons of same age group)
Clubs, organizations or classes
  (hobbies or skills)

Religious training
Pets
Vacations
Special outings

Volunteers

Employment

Opportunities to make choices
Opportunities to learn ADL skills

APPENDIX H

Role of the Nurse in a Group Home Complex

1. Assessment.
   a. Physical assessment.
   b. Skill assessment.
   c. Environmental assessment.
   d. Psychologic assessment.
2. Based on these assessments, the nurse will:
   a. Make referrals.
   b. Order needed equipment.
   c. Confer with other members of the health team.
   d. Write individual nursing care plans with ongoing progress notes.
   e. Confer with parents.
   f. Provide information to community agencies, such as job sites and hospitals, that are involved with the client.
   g. Educate the client in areas in which the assessment reveals he or she has need, or toward goals agreed upon with the health team. This may include:
      (1) Sex education.
      (2) Drug education (illicit drugs).
      (3) Self-examination of breast.
      (4) Nutrition education.
      (5) Weight reduction or weight gain.
      (6) Self-medication (legal and prescribed drugs).
      (7) Child care.
      (8) Prenatal teaching.
      (9) Postnatal education.
      (10) Skin inspection and skin care.
      (11) Grooming and hygiene.
      (12) Dental hygiene.
      (13) Safety.
   h. Maintain health records. This will include:
      (1) Sending a report to be filled out by the person to whom a referral is made and seeing that these reports are shown to the medical director prior to placing in the client chart. The best method we found is using a three-ring notebook with areas divided off. Filing is simplified. The health record should be kept in the nursing office. The client's work and behavioral record may be kept elsewhere, but all health records should be treated with confidentiality. The records should be made available to all professionals working with the client. One runs into legal and ethical problems, however, if counselors, work supervisors, and teachers are allowed to copy medical records and send them to everyone who requests them. A nursing summary of the client's diagnosis and health problems

may be placed in the client's work folder elsewhere if another unit needs background medical information.

(2) Following up on problems by reviewing all of the charts at least monthly.

(3) Charting every nursing interaction and the outcome on behalf of the client.

(4) Recording up-to-date medication information on charts.

(5) Scheduling the client for a medical examination at least once a year and following up on medical orders. The medical examination should be preceded by the nursing assessment and any problem areas should be brought to the physician's attention.

3. The nurse must be proficient in carrying out emergency care for clients in such areas as:

   a. Cardiopulmonary resuscitation (CPR).
   b. Burns.
   c. Evaluation of various cardiac conditions of clients in the group home.
      (1) Signs and symptoms.
      (2) Procedures for treatment of the emergency.
   d. Choking.
   e. Diabetes (coma and insulin reactions).
   f. Fainting.
   g. Falls and fractures, head injuries.
   h. Hemorrhage.
   i. Seizures.

4. Management of psychiatric problems.

5. Nursing procedures.

   a. Nursing procedures related to bedside care in areas of:
      (1) Hygiene and grooming.
      (2) Dietary procedure, including syringe or tube feeding.
      (3) Vital signs.
      (4) Medication administration.
      (5) Dressings.
      (6) Enemas.
      (7) Charting routine.
      (8) Care of the dead.
      (9) Infection control techniques.
         (a) Sterile technique procedures.
         (b) Clean technique procedure.
         (c) Nursing care of clients with head lice, scabies.
         (d) Nursing care of clients with communicable diseases.
         (e) Isolation and reverse isolation techniques.

   b. The nurse must also be adept at nursing procedures which are often regular and routine in a rehabilitation setting.
      (1) Bowel and bladder programs to prevent incontinency.
         (a) Intermittent catheterization (clean).
         (b) Credé.

        (c) Bowel training.

        (d) Catheterization (sterile).

    (2) Exercise programs.

    (3) Skin care.

    (4) Transferring—bed and wheelchair.

    (5) Oxygen therapy.

    (6) Positioning.

    (7) Colostomy care.

    (8) Gavage—lavage.

    (9) Suctioning procedures.

    (10) Tracheostomy care.

    (11) Venipuncture for blood tests and IV therapy.

6. The nurse will need to be able to handle the health problems of individuals related to developmental needs that children and adults face in any setting.

7. Besides a health record for clients, the nurse keeps a clinic log of all activities that are involved in presentations of health education programs, community education, writing, meetings, home visits, consultations, and attendance at continuing education programs, etc.

8. The agency nurse keeps a storeroom of visual aids that are located through such organizations as the National Dairy Council or the U.S. Department of Agriculture. A reading file of health information about specific physical and mental problems of the clients within the center is also an important contribution to the health team.

9. Grant writing is a skill that is becoming more and more important. Grants may be obtained for such purposes as providing funds for health teaching booklets and assisting in research.

10. The role of the nurse can be flexible as energy and imagination or as structured as agency policy. By working in a professional manner with other members of the health team, the nurse should be able to keep her role from conflict with any other role. Nursing, though it may cross over into other disciplines, should be complementary to these disciplines. Each specialty looks at the needs of the client within its own educational framework. Putting everyone's ideas together makes the plan a whole.

APPENDIX I

Nursing Care Health Plan

Agency: ARC—Denton Activity Center
Client's name: Mary Jones
1800 Bluedon St.
Denton, Texas 76201
Phone: None
Family: Mr. and Mrs. Andrew Jones
(Same address)
Nurse evaluator: Peggy Drapo, R.N.

Phone: 382—7425
Birthday: 3—10—60
Admission to program:
12—17—81

See nursing health assessment in client's chart. Nursing assessment revealed problem areas for client's general health. Following a meeting with client, ARC—Denton Director, and program counselor, this plan was decided upon.

Description of Client's Level of Function:

A. *Abilities in area being considered:*

Mary is able to perform skills in the kitchen, such as washing dishes and cleaning the refrigerator and stove; she understands kitchen safety related to the stove, sharp instruments, and household cleaners; she can set the table and demonstrates knowledge of safe food handling (i.e., refrigeration, storage, and cleanliness).

B. *Areas needing improvement:*

Mary does not have an understanding of nutrition. She does not bring a lunch to school that is healthful. She eats "junk" food from the vending machine in the store next door to the ARC building. She cannot identify foods in the basic four food groups. She is never given the opportunity to plan a meal, select foods, or prepare meals. She has worked in her family kitchen setting the table and cleaning up after a meal.

Mary has several cavities in her teeth and her oral hygiene is poor. Her parents inform us that they live on a limited retirement fund and are not able to pay for dental work.

Referrals:

1—15—82   Referred by Ruth Tompkins, ARC—Denton Director, to Texas Rehabilitation Counselor for evaluation prior to appointment for vocational evaluation. Medical and psychologic evaluation will be done.

2—12—82   Referred by nurse to Texas Woman's University Dental Hygienist for evaluation.

Reports:

3—1—82 **Psychologic**   Dr. Angela Burke, Director, North Texas State University Psychology Clinic, 788—2631 reports that

Mary is functioning in reading skills at a second to third grade level. She believes that Mary will be able to read simple menus if they are printed and will be able to read labels on foodstuffs in the markets. Her vision is not impaired. See medical file for complete report. IQ range moderate on WAIS-R.

3−4−82 **Vocational**

Dr. Clinton Wainwright, Director, North Texas State University Rehabilitation Studies, 788−2488. Becky Mulroy Senior Evaluator. Vocational evaluation to be completed in the near future.

3−15−82 **Dental**

Texas Woman's University Dental Hygiene Program. Sherry Peel, Clinic Receptionist. Clinical Instructor, Marilyn Henderson. Senior dental hygiene student, Patty Miller.

    Screening 2−23−82—Patty Miller.
    Prophylaxis treatment 3−2−82—Patty Miller.
    X-ray 3−9−82—Patty Miller.

Several suspicious areas found. Communication to parents with information regarding Baylor College of Dentistry as a resource for family.

Other Health Services Utilized:

Agency or department: Speech Therapy
Goal: To improve communication skill

Agency Information:

3−15−82

Marie Newell, 387−6169, will schedule with Speech Language Therapist. Therapy will begin 3−22−82, weekly, on Tuesday−Thursday for 50 minutes per session, MCL Building 806, Texas Woman's University.

Client−ARC Goals for Nursing Intervention:

3−4−82 **Cognitive skill**

A. *Nutrition knowledge:* To learn basic 4 food groups.

    1. In a small group, Mary will listen to a discussion about the foods found in the four basic food groups.

    2. Mary will attend a movie depicting where foods found in the four basic food groups are obtained and how they are shipped to market.

    3. Mary will play a color-coded food group game to learn to identify various foods within the groups.

3−18−82 **Cognitive and motor skills**

B. *Selection of food:* Develop skills in selecting nutritious foods.

    1. Mary will plan menu, write a shopping list.

2. She will demonstrate ability to read package and can labels.
3. On the completion of the above, she will shop for food in a simulated situation in our center.
4. Mary will shop for food in a real situation.

3–24–82 **Motor skills**   C. *Preparation of food:* Develop skill in preparing a meal.
1. Premeasures food—demonstration by nurse.
2. Premeasures food—demonstration by client to nurse.
3. Mixes ingredients according to recipe.
4. Prepares meal items in a step formation according to cooking times required. A question and answer format will be used to teach.
5. Times food by demonstration and return demonstration.

4–2–82 **Social skills**   D. *Entertains friend at meal—develops social skills.*
1. Serves meal using safety and hygiene.
2. Entertains friend using good table manners and conversation skills.
Evaluation (for notes):

Nutrition knowledge
Selection of food
Preparation of food
Entertaining

Related Plans:
Arrange for budgeting of money with counselor.
Arrange for someone to shop with client.
Help client make arrangements with counselor to invite a friend for dinner party.

APPENDIX J

Nursing Care Plan (In-hospital Stay)

Name: Bill Johnson, Jr. **Address:** 111 Wheat Street, Denton, Texas
Phone: 222—0000
Birthday: 4—28—70 **Parents:** Mr. and Mrs. William Johnson, Sr.
Date: 2—15—82 **Admission time:** 8:00 A.M.
Religion: Catholic
Allergies: Milk
Medications: No medication
Other pertinent information: Patient has Down's syndrome.
Reason for hospitalization: Repair of inguinal hernia
Care plan completed by: Peggy Drapo, R.N.

Patient Strengths and Needs:

A. *Strengths:* Twelve-year-old boy with *ability to speak* well enough to be understood by hospital personnel. Can *sight read* some printed words. Understands *simple concepts. ADL skills* are good. *Hygiene* is good.

B. *Areas of need:* Patient is *shy* and demands that mother stay with him day and night. Is fearful of strangers and especially of those in hospital uniforms. He *gets lost* easily, according to his mother, and it has been requested that he not leave the room unaccompanied by an adult. He is scheduled to have surgery 2—17—82. Needs *preop teaching* and some activity to help *occupy his time* during hospital stay.

Nursing Referrals:

2—15—82, 9:30 A.M.	Notify volunteer services to send the "play lady" with selection of materials.
11:30 A.M.	Volunteer services supplied patient with

    1. Cut and paste material.
    2. Art book and colored pencils.
    3. Two books and pictures.
Will return in 2 days to renew supplies.

Notified:

2—15—82	X-ray—chest.
2—16—82	Lab for blood work, urinalysis.
2—15—82	Dr. Anderson—surgeon.
2—15—82	Dr. Jason Andrews—anesthesiologist.
2—15—82	Hospital chaplain.
2—17—82	Respiratory therapy, IPPB treatments postop.

Nursing Goals:

Preop teaching: To reduce fear and ensure better cooperation for preop and postop procedures.

2—15—82 afternoon	1. Bedside teaching—Bill will listen to nurse discuss "breathing machine" for IPPB treatments following surgery, preop hypo, hospital hat for surgery.

2—16—82 morning	2. Nurse will read *Jimmy Goes to Surgery*, a hospital publication, and discuss the pictures with Bill. The book will be left with the mother, who will read it again to Bill later.
2—16—82 evening	3. "Pedi Bear," a puppet will demonstrate how to use the IPPB machine.
2—16—82 P.M.	4. Nurse will teach about preop injection.
2—16—82 P.M.	5. Patient will give "Pedi Bear" an injection.
2—17—82	6. Nurse will review teaching with patient prior to preop hypo.

Evaluation:

P.O. day
3—19—82.

Bill experienced some dismay at the preop hypo but was fairly cooperative and quieted easily. He helped apply the Band-Aid. Following surgery, he needed some encouragement to use the IPPB treatment the first time, but following that he cooperated fully. The play materials supplied by volunteer services were utilized daily and were a great help in occupying his time. Bill displayed little fear of the hospital personnel following the preop teaching session. He was discharged P.O. day 4 to his home in satisfactory condition.

Index

Italic *f* refers to figure.
Italic *t* refers to table.

INDEX

DATE DUE

Demco, Inc. 38-293